D0934436

Forgotten Valor

General O. B. Willcox

Eng.d by A.H.Ritchie.

Forgotten VALOR

The Memoirs, Journals,

& Civil War Letters of

Orlando B. Willcox

EDITED BY ROBERT GARTH SCOTT

The Kent State University Press, Kent, Ohio, & London

© 1999 by The Kent State University Press,
Kent, Ohio 44242
Library of Congress Catalog Card Number 99–21762
ISBN 0–87338–628–0
Manufactured in the United States of America

05 04 03 02 01 00   5 4 3 2

Frontispiece: Brig. Gen. Orlando B. Willcox. *Special
Collections Division, U.S. Military Academy (USMA)
Library (West Point, New York).*

Library of Congress Cataloging-in-Publication Data
Willcox, Orlando B.
Forgotten valor : the memoirs, journals, and Civil War
letters of Orlando B. Willcox / edited by Robert
Garth Scott.
p.   cm.
Includes bibliographical references and index.
ISBN 0-87338-628-0 (alk. paper) ∞
1. Willcox, Orlando B.   2. Generals—United States
Biography.   3. United States—History—Civil War,
1861–1865 Personal narratives.   4. United States.
Army biography.   5. United States—History—Civil
War, 1861–1865—Campaigns.   I. Scott, Robert
Garth, 1957– .
II. Title.
E467.1.W715A4   1999
973.7'3'092—dc21   99-21762
[B]

British Library Cataloging-in-Publication data are available.

'Tis not for fame—I've had my little day—
I write to clear my head & warm my heart.
What though my forehead touch among the clouds,
My feet take hold on Earth, my star is set;
Enthusiasms tempered to sobriety.
—O. B. WILLCOX

CONTENTS

§ ILLUSTRATIONS

§ MAPS

§ PREFACE

That this book has come about at all is nothing short of a miracle, and the circumstances surrounding the discovery of the Orlando B. Willcox papers—the largest collection of Civil War papers to surface in half a century—make a story in themselves.

The journey that ultimately led me to the collection began, oddly enough, with an officer whom Willcox probably heard of but never really knew, a major in the 20th Massachusetts Volunteer Infantry named Henry Livermore Abbott. Always in the thickest of the fighting, Henry Abbott had, by virtue of his own bravery and leadership ability, established himself as something of a legend in the Army of the Potomac. Gen. John Sedgwick thought him the "bright, particular star" of the army, and Gen. George G. Meade himself had earmarked Abbott for greater things. A minié ball on the second day of the Battle of the Wilderness ended any chance Henry had for greater glory: like that of his older brother, Edward ("Ned") before him (killed at Cedar Mountain) and so many other young officers, Henry's light was snuffed out before it had fairly begun to shine.

During research on my previous book, *Fallen Leaves: The Civil War Letters of Major Henry Livermore Abbott*, I had made numerous attempts to track down any surviving Abbott descendants, hoping they might have further information on the book's subject. Though neither Henry nor his brother Edward ever married or had children, they did have numerous brothers and sisters, and I was convinced that the chances were good that at least one of them had surviving descendants.

Nevertheless, no lead I had yielded success. Although the Abbotts were one of the first families of the Bay State, the numerous Massachusetts-based genealogical societies were able to provide only the most meager information, and my own attempts to trace the line by searching census and other public records were fruitless. And so the effort was abandoned; *Fallen Leaves* went to press, and following its publication in the fall of 1991, I moved on to other things.

By the summer of 1993, with the Abbott book well behind me, I was immersed in writing a biography of Maj. Gen. Francis Channing Barlow, a noted division commander in the Army of the Potomac. It was then that I received a most unexpected, though highly welcome phone call—a call I shall never forget. It was mid-afternoon on a typically bright June day, and I was, just then, in the middle of painting our living room. When the phone rang my initial reaction was one of annoyance; I was convinced it was merely another solicitor, as had already been the case two or three times that day. (My wife had been after me for some time to get an unlisted number, but for some reason I had never bothered; now I was beginning to see the advantages.) Setting the paint roller down, I wiped off my hands and picked up the receiver.

It was a friendly voice, a refined voice, a woman's voice:

"Hello, Mr. Scott?" the voice asked, hesitatingly.

"Yes?"

"Is this the same Robert *Garth* Scott that edited *Fallen Leaves?*"

Oh lord, I thought, it's another buff who wants to tell me about some ancestor who fought under so and so and was wounded at such and such a place and they even have his enlistment papers and isn't that just wonderful! . . . But, if they had bothered to read my book. . . .

"Yes it is," I replied in my best "kind of you to call" voice.

"Well, my name is Elizabeth Abbott de Mowbray, and I am Henry Livermore Abbott's great niece. . . . I hope I haven't caught you at a bad time."

I sat down.

"Hello? Mr. Scott?"

"Yes. . . . How did you find me? That is, how did you get my number?"

"The phone book."

"Oh."

"Yes, I took a chance that you might be listed, and the inside back flap of *Fallen Leaves* mentioned that you lived in Grand Blanc, Michigan, and so it was just a matter of a little detective work, you see. I hope you don't mind."

"Mind? No, no, not at all! In fact, I was hoping that somehow, some way, something like this might happen."

We talked for over an hour. I explained to her my unsuccessful efforts at tracking down Abbott descendants, thanking her profusely for calling. As it turned out, her father, a graduate of the Naval Academy with a distinguished war record in his own right, was Henry Livermore Abbott II (named for his uncle), the son of Henry's younger brother, Grafton St. Loe Abbott, who had married a daughter of Charles Francis Adams, Jr. Mrs. de Mowbray lived in London, but she had returned to her hometown of Washington, D.C., for a brief visit and to arrange for the sale of the house of her parents, both of whom were now deceased. She had learned of my book through a friend, who had spotted the review on the front page of the *New York Times Book Review*, and thought it an opportune time to contact me.

"The main reason I was calling," she explained, "was that I have some of Great-Uncle Henry's personal effects—his watch, sash, prayerbook, and a scrapbook kept by his mother. Oh! I think there are some photographs as well. Would you be interested in seeing them? I will be here in Washington for several more weeks and would certainly welcome a visit from you."

This was just what I was hoping to hear. In my several years of research and editing, this young officer from Massachusetts had edged his way into my life, and it was difficult, even with the book behind me, to let him go. To see something that belonged to him and to hear family stories about him was more than I had hoped for. Also, it just so happened that my wife Karen and I were planning a visit east anyway—a combined vacation for us and our two daughters, and a research trip for me; a stop to visit Mrs. de Mowbray in Washington would fit in well with our itinerary.

We set up a date for the visit, and our conversation concluded with an interesting side remark by Mrs. de Mowbray:

"By the way," she said, "my great-grandfather on my mother's side was Gen. Orlando Willcox. I have some of his papers as well. Perhaps, while you're here, you would like to take a look at them."

The remark caught my attention. I was, of course, somewhat familiar with Willcox—that is, I knew that he had led a division in the Ninth Corps, as my first book, *Into the Wilderness with the Army of the Potomac*, had outlined the movements of his command in that pivotal battle. Of the man himself, however, I must confess I knew very little—I was even unaware that he was a native of my home state of Michigan!

But I was beginning to feel guilty for running up Mrs. de Mowbray's phone bill. Her remark about General Willcox's papers had been made so matter-of-factly that I dismissed it as unimportant—probably his commission papers or service record, I thought. Anyway, it was the Abbott items that I was most interested in—that I could not stop thinking about.

"Of course, I'd love to see his papers," I replied, "and I look forward to meeting you."

I hung up the phone, still unable to fathom the implications of it all, and a bit flushed with excitement. One thing was for certain: I was finished painting for the day.

Thursday, July 8, 1993, was one of those sweltering days typical of summertime Washington, the air so thick and muggy that you practically need gills to breathe. Thankfully, the roomy new conversion van we had recently purchased had air conditioning, so that the ride up from Fredericksburg, Virginia (where we had spent the previous two days), was at least tolerable, even in heavy traffic. (There is simply no escape from Washington traffic, but at least we could escape the heat.)

When we pulled into the driveway of the large, white, federal-style home, Mrs. de Mowbray quickly appeared at the door to greet us. We were soon seated in the living room, enjoying glasses of lemonade, exchanging introductions, and discussing the details of our trip. The interior of the house was much more homey than one would suppose from the imposing exterior. The living room was warmly furnished and comfortable, a sharp contrast of colonial and modern America. Mrs. de Mowbray's son, Stuart, age six, was deeply engaged in watching the *Adventures of Dark Wing Duck* on the television, while his great-great-great-grandfather, congressman Edward St. Loe Livermore, glared down from above the mantel, in seeming disapproval of young Stuart's selection of program.

Following the necessary small talk, my two daughters were left to entertain Stuart, and my wife and I were ushered up half a flight of stairs into the study. This room, with its distinctly masculine flavor and nautical motif, had obviously been the domain of Mrs. de Mowbray's father, Capt. Henry L. Abbott, USN. Here we were left to browse the bookcases, while Elizabeth (as Mrs. de Mowbray now insisted we call her) disappeared to get some things.

The library holdings were chiefly, though not exclusively, books on American history, many of them by and about Adamses—some in fact (as was obvious from the bookplates and inscriptions) had belonged to Adamses themselves, or to the Abbotts. It was then that I began to feel somewhat intimidated by the lineage of our gracious hostess, for her family is the essence of what might be called the American aristocracy. It is a family whose history is in fact the history of our country—a family, as I later learned, that often holds its reunions at the White House.

Elizabeth soon returned bearing the artifacts I had come to see: Henry's silver baptismal cup; his watch—a gift from a fellow officer of his regiment; his prayerbook, with an inscription by his mother; his scarlet sash, and that of his brother Ned; and a photograph of a portrait of Henry, owned by Elizabeth's sister, painted on his last visit home in early 1864.

And then there was the scrapbook, with a letter from Henry to his parents, thanking them for the ring containing a lock of Ned's hair; the clipped newspaper articles telling of Henry's own death in the Wilderness; the letters of condolence from his division commander, Gen. John Gibbon, and from Col. Theodore Lyman of Meade's staff; and a similar letter from another fellow officer of the 20th, young Oliver Wendell Holmes, Jr. There was also a postwar letter to Henry's father from a Harvard classmate, one Lane Brandon of Mississippi, who had remained close to Henry despite the war, in spite of the fact that Brandon served as an officer in the 21st Mississippi—a Confederate regiment—and even though he and Henry had come face to face one cold December day in the furious fighting in the streets of Fredericksburg.

We read these things aloud, Elizabeth, Karen, and I, sitting in that Washington study, removed by more than a century and a quarter from the events of those terrible days. Our eyes were filled with tears, nonetheless, as we were moved and drawn closer by those things that had been preserved in the scrapbook kept by Elizabeth's great-grandmother, a woman who had lost two sons in battle. We read those things, and suddenly it seemed as if they had not occurred so long ago after all.

It was now clear to me that there should be a new edition of *Fallen Leaves*, in which I would incorporate much of the new material from the scrapbook, as well as some other letters of Henry's that I had managed to acquire since the first edition was published. So, with Elizabeth's permission, I took the scrapbook to a nearby office supply store to have it photocopied. By the time I returned it was well past lunchtime—as Stuart and the girls reminded us—and so we reconvened at a local hamburger establishment. There we further discussed the Abbott items, and there Elizabeth told us some of the family stories surrounding Henry and his older brother, Ned.

Then, as we sipped our sodas, the talk turned to Elizabeth's other noted relative, General Willcox.

"As I mentioned in our telephone conversation," she said, "I have some of the general's papers at home, if you would care to see them."

Now that I had seen the Abbott material and photocopied the items that I felt were most important, the chief reason for my visit was completed, and I was now only too willing to see what she had relating to General Willcox.

"I'd very much like to see his papers," I assured her. "That is, if it's not too much trouble."

"Well, there are several boxes packed away in the attic, but I'm sure we can drag them out without too much trouble."

"Several *boxes?*" I asked, unsure if I heard her correctly. "General Willcox's papers are in several *boxes?*"

"Oh yes," Elizabeth responded. "I'm afraid the general was something of a pack rat. He saved everything. It's all quite disordered, and I'm not quite certain what's in there, but I'm sure you would find it interesting."

I still could not quite comprehend just what, exactly, she might be talking about when she referred to "some of the general's papers," but my interest was piqued, to say the least.

Back at the house, we were led up the stairs, past the study, and up a second flight to a third-floor attic room, the kind with a low, sloping ceiling. Opening a closet, Elizabeth dragged out an old wooden steamer trunk with decaying leather straps, as well as several other boxes. She opened the trunk lid, and my jaw fell to the floor.

"Some of the general's papers" turned out to be the understatement of the century. The trunk was literally stuffed to the lid with papers, documents, of every kind. I sat down and began a cursory examination of the contents. There were bundles of telegraphic dispatches, envelopes of hand-written field dispatches marked *South Mountain, Antietam, Fredericksburg,* and the like (most of them, as I suspected even then, never published in the *Official Records*). There were stacks of official after-action reports and of correspondence with scores of other notable Civil War personages. Much of it was, as Elizabeth had said, "disorganized." A loose, crumpled piece of paper turned out to be a letter from Gen. Ambrose Burnside. Three other letters, lying loose in the trunk, were from Elmer Ellsworth, the first Union martyr of the war.

I opened another box: it contained General Willcox's personal wartime correspondence, carefully preserved in initialed, leather-bound folders. Another folder contained much of his early postwar correspondence, letters from generals McClellan, Hancock, Sheridan, Meade, Hooker, McDowell, Stoneman, Humphreys, Tidball . . . the list goes on and on. There were over a dozen handwritten letters from Sherman alone. And there were letters from former Confederates as well, including generals James Longstreet, Henry Heth, and William Mahone.

I opened yet another box and saw there the most historically lucrative find of them all—the general's memoirs.

This was the kind of moment that most historians can only dream about; I could hardly believe it was happening to *me*. Who among us has not often wondered what undiscovered treasures other people have tucked away in their attics? This time I was able to find out.

I was not quite sure what to say, and for a time I said nothing at all. I sat there, mouth agape, staring at my wife. When at last I had collected myself, I asked Elizabeth if she knew how significant this collection was. She knew the papers were important, she said, but was not quite sure what to do with them. She would soon be returning to England, and the papers would have to go into storage somewhere.

"Would you be interested in doing something with them, Robert?"

That was a question I was not at all prepared to answer.

"What, exactly, do you mean by the phrase 'doing something with them'?"

"I realize it is a lot to ask," she said, "but would you be interested in taking them and keeping them for a time? Perhaps you could do something to organize them . . . that is, until we can arrange for a more permanent disposition for them."

Further discussion revealed that Elizabeth's cousin, the general's great-grandson Bill Willcox, a Washington-based attorney, had one day intended to organize and perhaps edit the papers himself, but he had recently been married, and it might be years before he could take on such a project.

This was, unquestionably, the opportunity of a lifetime. But there were a number of factors that caused me to hesitate to accept the project. First, there was the tremendous responsibility of the task; there was a fortune in autographed, historically significant material in those boxes, and I was quite uneasy about being entrusted with their safekeeping. Secondly, there was the matter of Elizabeth's family. If there were relatives who might object to a total stranger taking off with the general's papers, that would certainly be understandable and I was not about to argue with them. Lastly, I was in the middle of writing the biography of General Barlow—the book was half finished. Was I willing to set that project aside for the several years it would obviously take to complete the Willcox assignment, whatever that might entail?

Elizabeth placed a phone call to her cousin, Bill, and explained her proposal. I spoke with him as well. Yes, he had once hoped to edit grandad's papers, but if I was willing to accept the assignment, well, then, I had the family's blessing. He had read *Fallen Leaves* and was much pleased with my work; furthermore, he expressed himself as convinced that I could be trusted, and that if anything could be done with the general's papers, I was probably the one to do it.

That conversation certainly removed any doubt in my mind about accepting the job. I had by this time more or less convinced myself that the Barlow project could wait, but that General Willcox could not. The ring of opportunity had presented itself—it was up to me to grab it. And so, after talking the matter over with my wife, I agreed to take the papers home and see what I could do with them.

The question now was how to get them home—a thought that had hardly occurred to me until that moment. There was more than enough cubic footage in our new van, but it had three rows of seats and was full of luggage besides. Did we have room for the trunk and boxes? Karen and I went outside to examine the situation and found that by rearranging some of the suitcases we could unfold the back bench seat, on which the trunk and boxes would fit nicely. Then it was a matter of getting the trunk and three heavy boxes out of the attic, down two long flights of stairs, out of the house, and up into the van—and all in ninety-plus-degree heat. The steamer trunk was by far the worst; it might as well have been filled with sand, rather than old papers. Yet somehow Karen and I managed it, pushing and pulling, step by step, panting, puffing, and perspiring every step of the way.

By the time we had the van loaded, it was nearly five o'clock. We were tired, the kids were hungry, and I am sure that Elizabeth and Stuart were ready to call it a day. And so we bid our good-byes and headed out on the long road home. A journey that was to last the next six years had begun.

We spent the night in a historic old inn atop a hill overlooking the Potomac at Harpers Ferry. It was an especially uneasy night for me. I slept little, ruminating on the great responsibility that I had been entrusted with, and on the work that lay ahead. I was also more than a little anxious to have a good look at the items in those boxes, for it was clear to me that no one, not even the family, was fully aware of what was contained in the collection.

We rose early the next day and ate a light breakfast, in preparation for the long drive back to Michigan. In light of recent events, though, none of us could resist a quick tour of the nearby Antietam battlefield before we actually began our homeward trek. I had never visited Antietam before, although I had passed very near it while on my way to visit other, equally historic Civil War sites. Driving from Harpers Ferry through Shepherdstown, West Virginia, we crossed the Potomac near the old ford where Lee's army had waded across on its way to the battlefield. On the bluff overlooking the Potomac to the left of the road I pointed out the elegant old mansion "Ferry Hill Place," the boyhood home of Henry Kyd Douglas of Stonewall

Jackson's staff, whose memoir, *I Rode with Stonewall*, is one of the classics of Civil War literature. Continuing our drive over the hilly countryside, we enjoyed the pleasant scenery of the rolling, rocky landscape so prominent in that part of Maryland as we drove on into the historic town of Sharpsburg.

Passing through town, we followed the green "Antietam Battlefield & Visitors' Center" signs and were quite surprised to come upon the battlefield so suddenly: row after row of cannons and caissons, the snakey zigzag of rail fences over rolling ground dotted here and there with the historic farms bearing the familiar names of Miller and Poffenberger, all exactly as I had pictured, from my reading.

It was still early morning when we arrived; the visitors' center was not yet open, and the park was deserted. The mist still lay white and heavy on the ground, curling around the artillery pieces and creeping through fence rails, just as the smoke of battle must have on that day in 1862. In the midst of it all, nestled along the fringe of the West Woods, was the white square-block building of the Dunker Church—the meeting house of the hardworking, peace-loving German Baptist Brethren (known as the "Dunkers" because of their baptismal ceremonies)—that so ironically found itself situated in the epicenter of the bloodiest single day's battle in American history. There it sat, its freshly whitewashed walls, once so profusely pockmarked by shell bursts and minié balls, now silent and stoic, oblivious to our presence. I pulled the van off to the side of the road and stopped for a moment to consider that building, wondering what secrets it held, what it *really* had witnessed on that September day in 1862. Driving off at last, I was left with the distinct feeling of being out of place, out of time, not quite sure which was the anachronism: the church or me.

I must admit that pressed for time as we were, our tour of the northern section of the battlefield was somewhat hasty, though nonetheless impressive. The Miller farm, the Cornfield, the East Woods, were all as I had pictured them, often appearing much as they had during the battle. There are no disconcerting views of hovering steel towers or fast-food franchises to spoil the scenery as there are at a host of other major battle sites; while the Antietam battlefield has its problems with encroachment, it nevertheless remains in a remarkable state of preservation, due in a large measure to the fact that it is located somewhat off the beaten path.

Finishing our tour of the northern and central sectors (including a stop at the Bloody Lane, where I climbed the old stone observation tower for a breathtaking view), we wended our way to the southern part of the field, which we were most anxious to see. It was an eerie feeling, indeed, driving over that field, reading the markers signifying the various positions of

OBW's trunk and some of his papers.

"Willcox's Division, Ninth Corps," aware that all that remained of the general himself was in the back of our van. What a moving sight it was when we rounded a bend and the historic stone span of the Rohrbach Bridge (forever after known as Burnside's Bridge) first came into view. There the Ninth Corps had endeavored to carry the bridge by assault but paid dearly for the privilege; a lone brigade of Georgians, posted in the woods on the hillside opposite, overlooking the bridge, tore the Union ranks apart with showers of musketry. And there too Willcox and his division eventually crossed the Antietam and fought their way up the grassy heights, nearly reaching Sharpsburg itself.

We drove straight home after that, some five hundred miles, finally pulling into our driveway sometime around 11:00 P.M. We unpacked the van, carefully unloaded the boxes, and at last I had my first opportunity to examine the contents of the collection. I spent the entire night sifting through the contents, amazed at my further discoveries: the general's dispatch books containing copies of orders sent, and numerous journals, with entries covering nearly every significant phase of Willcox's life; his days as a cadet at West Point, his service in the Mexican War, duty on the plains, and even his time as a prisoner in the Civil War. One journal had even been written while he was still in prison, outlining his then-recent experiences at first Bull Run, where he was wounded and captured. There were original wartime sketches, too (published here for the first time), drawn by a private in Willcox's division, and volumes of poetry, written by Willcox at various stages of his life.

Then there were the scrapbooks, carefully compiled by Willcox himself, mainly containing newspaper articles outlining his military career, death notices of old friends, and a host of other mementoes, such as pressed leaves from numerous battlefields and headquarters encampments, an evergreen "sprig from Bolivar Heights plucked near the Battery at that point, while the first firing was going on." When dawn came I had barely made a dent in the collection, and I went to bed still uncertain about what my role was going to be with the collection, beyond getting it into some kind of order.

"A CERTAIN, QUIET DIGNITY"

Within a week of returning home from the East, I was beginning to remove much of the collection from the trunk and cardboard boxes, transferring the contents to more durable plastic containers.

Most of the collection was, and is, in remarkable physical condition. The bulk of the material predating 1900 is intact—much of it, especially the Civil War material, looking as if it could have been written yesterday. This is primarily due, of course, to the quality of the paper on which the letters, diaries, dispatches, etc., were written. That paper, which has a low acid content, has held up well over the years.

Documents postdating 1900, however, are for the most part, in a rapidly deteriorating condition. The paper on which Willcox wrote most of his memoirs, for instance, is yellowed and brittle, and even with the most careful handling it tends to crumble at the edges. The documents written or printed on this type of paper, however, make up but a small percentage of the entire collection, which may be estimated conservatively at more than three thousand documents in all.

Having somewhat familiarized myself with the material, I sat down to the real work at hand: transcribing the memoirs, journals, and letters, which span nearly an entire lifetime. I was not long into this work before I realized that it contained the makings of a book, as Willcox himself had intended all along. At that point of my work, however, I was not certain what type of book it was going to be. A traditional biography seemed perhaps the most likely; certainly a biography of General Willcox seemed warranted, given the tremendous role he had had in the war. As I read his journals, memoirs, and letters, however, it became apparent that there was too much valuable firsthand information to waste on a traditional biography. Why, I asked myself, should someone else tell Willcox's story when he has told it so well himself?

There is an immediacy in first-person accounts that a third-person biography can never have, and it is as apparent in Willcox's memoirs as in any other primary account of the war. Reading it one gets the sense of being transported back to another age: it *is* 1844, and we *are* with Willcox at old West Point, nervously awaiting examination before the board of visitors. We are with him again on the "trackless sea of grass," where "cool breezes whistle loud" as we ride pell-mell amongst a herd of a thousand thundering buffalo.[1] We are there too in the maddening summer of 1861, lying wounded and captured on the field at Bull Run; and again that autumn, sitting in a jail cell in Charleston, South Carolina, with the prospect of the hangman's noose bleakly before us. It is a journey well worth taking, and in making it one can hardly fail to marvel at the miracle of the written word, whereby memories can be passed on to distant generations.

Willcox spent much of his later years striving to finish his autobiography, but ill health and the plagues of old age at last forced him to halt work on the project. Yet he had made good progress. While the memoirs themselves are not as complete as we could wish or as Willcox preferred, with the inclusion of his journals and letters they certainly paint a full enough portrait of his life to warrant publication.

Willcox wrote his biography in largely chronological order, beginning with his birth and childhood, and ending with the close of the Civil War. Whether he intended to continue the book into the postwar years is questionable, as I have found no notes or outline chapters relating to that period. Though he had a long military career after the Civil War, serving at various outposts in Virginia, New York, Arizona, and finally securing the plum assignment of commander of the Old Soldiers Home in Washington, D.C. (these later events being described in a concluding chapter), the primary focus of this book is from the period of his birth through the Civil War.

1. From the poem "The Pleasures of Retirement," by OBW, 3d canto, beginning with the 45th stanza. The work remains unpublished.

While Willcox wrote the nucleus of his autobiography between 1885 and 1905, it may be said, in an altogether different sense, that he at least began planning the book while in his teens, for that is when he began making entries into his many journals. Throughout his military career, from West Point to Mexico, on the rolling western plains, and in the malarial swamps of Florida, Willcox remained devoted to his journals, for he loved to write. That period saw him publish two novels and one short story, as well as a fair number of poems, some of which were published in the Boston papers while Willcox was stationed at that historic city. Indeed, it was the writer's, not the warrior's, life that Orlando secretly longed for: "Oh a diamond pointed pen/And a seat in a rich boudoir!" he wrote. "Me thinks I could fling pearls & rubies every time, like bubbles from a gold mounted meerschaum pipe."[2]

These journals, scrapbooks, letters, together with the massive amount of official material (reports, dispatches, etc.) he had preserved over the years, served General Willcox well when he sat down to write his memoirs. It is apparent that he not only consulted them as reference material but quite often quoted directly from them as well. Moreover, all these sources served to refresh his memory concerning events, long since past, that he might otherwise have forgotten, or remembered differently, as is often the case with memoirs.

All of this material I had at my disposal, not to mention notes the general had made for eventual use in his work, including his correspondence with many Civil War notables relating to specific battles in which they were engaged. All of it proved invaluable.

Numerous problems arose, however, as with any edited work. Chief among them was that General Willcox had sometimes drafted more than one version of a chapter. There are, for instance, two accounts relating to the capture of the town of Alexandria, each containing valuable historical information unique to that account. Moreover, Willcox had recorded his observations relating to the death of Elmer Ellsworth at Alexandria in a separate notebook, which he included in neither of the two above-mentioned drafts but which he may well have intended to use in a final chapter.

Another case concerns his chapter on the Battle of Bull Run. There is among the Willcox papers a notebook, which he kept while in prison. In that notebook, following the heading "Strictly Private, & written for

---

2. From OBW's journal, entitled *Quotations, Diaries, Interpolations, Thoughts &C, Heterogeneous & Desultory*, 1849 to 1894, entry of Dec. 3, 1857. There are many lapses in this journal, with no entries during the Civil War.

my family" is a detailed account of the battle and his subsequent wounding, capture, and early prison experiences. It is a historically significant document, because it was written shortly after the battle and during his incarceration, though he did not continue the account past the time spent in the Charleston city jail. The chapter Willcox wrote specifically for his memoirs concerning his experiences at Bull Run and in prison was written long after the fact and is not as detailed as the earlier account, though his prison experiences are more complete in this chapter than in the former version. How does an editor deal with this predicament? Clearly it would not be practical to publish more than one version of the same account. But how could I concentrate on just one draft and completely ignore pertinent information in another? These were questions I pondered for some time.

The answer, of course, was to piece the various versions together, using the most complete account as a base and inserting important information from other accounts to form a complete, finished chapter. But was such a practice acceptable? Indeed it was, for that is exactly the practice that C. Vann Woodward employed in his Pulitzer Prize–winning work *Mary Chesnut's Civil War* (New Haven: Yale University Press, 1981). Because Mary Chesnut had left several versions of her now famous diary, Dr. Woodward was faced with much the same problem as myself. He overcame it by using the 1880s diary as a base and adding material from the other versions to "complement and supplement" the 1880s text, using angle brackets < > to indicate where material had been inserted.

It is precisely that policy that I have adopted in editing the Willcox memoirs. Material inserted into the base chapter (first source) from a second one is enclosed within single angle brackets < >; an excerpt included from a third source is identified by double angle brackets « », and so on; notations are given to identify from where the passages were taken. In this manner the integrity of the original source is maintained. It must be noted, however, that this practice has been employed only in his memoirs; the journals and letters remain substantially in their original form.

At times, Willcox himself incorporated excerpts from his journals into his memoirs, chiefly in chapter 9, relating to the Seminole War. This practice I have continued throughout the book, separating such entries from the actual memoir by the heading "Journal Entries," followed by the appropriate date. In this way the memoir has been significantly enhanced, again without damaging the integrity of the original. This practice is particularly valuable in some of the later chapters, which are not as complete as the earlier ones; in fact, Willcox himself may have employed it, had he lived to see the work finished.

Although the general probably did not intend to publish his letters, I have done so here, as they provide valuable insight often not found in the memoirs or journals. I have also taken the liberty of including letters from other individuals either written to General Willcox or that relate specifically to him. There are, for example, the letters written to Marie Willcox by the general's aides. (Willcox usually wrote his wife almost daily, but there were times, such as after the Battle of the Crater, when he was simply too exhausted. At such times his aides often volunteered to write home for him.) There are also significant letters to Willcox from his friend Ambrose Burnside.

With the major editorial decisions out of the way, I had only to deal with the usual problems one faces when editing such a work, primarily relating to the spelling, capitalization, and punctuation peculiarities of the author. Willcox, for instance, habitually capitalized the words "Mother" and "Father" in his letters and journals. The original has been maintained. He also usually capitalized "Army" even in a general reference; when applicable, however, the lowercase "army" has been substituted. In his early journals he also often failed to capitalize the first word of a new sentence; such mistakes have been corrected.

Like most people of his day, Willcox's orthography was a cross between common usage and his own peculiar style. He often used z where he should use s, and vice versa. He wrote "leizure" in place of "leisure," for example, and "surprize" for "surprise." He also wrote "stopt" for "stopped," "stept" for "stepped," "brot" for "brought," and "tho" for "though." These spelling peculiarities have been retained, as they give us a flavor of his writing style. Following a popular style of the nineteenth century, Willcox often used the British spelling for words, writing "honour" for "honor," and "colour" for "color." As his choice between the British and American spelling of these words was somewhat erratic, the standard American spelling is retained for all. In the early journals, Willcox often used "shew" for "show" (a practice common in the eighteenth and early nineteenth centuries). This spelling disappears in his later writings; the more modern "show" has been imposed throughout. Also, at times Willcox made two words out of one: "some times" for "sometimes," "grave yard" for "graveyard." He hyphenated "to-day" for "today." In each of these cases the original form has been maintained.

Punctuation posed another problem, particularly in his journals and letters. Run-on sentences have been broken up with semicolons where the author improperly used commas. Where the author ended a question with a period rather than a question mark, the proper punctuation has been inserted.

Willcox also used abbreviations at times, particularly in his letters and journals: he frequently wrote "rec^d" for "received," and "yr." for "your," for example. These words have been spelled out. Abbreviations indicating rank, such as "gen'l" for "general" or "capt." for "captain," have been retained when preceding a name but spelled out if used separately. Obvious abbreviations have otherwise been maintained in the letters and journals but spelled out in the memoirs, as the latter represents a more formal text.

Following a popular practice of his day, Willcox sometimes used an initial to indicate a name, such as "L" for "Lovell," or "B" for "Burnside." The original is maintained when the reference is obvious; otherwise the name has been spelled out. Although Willcox rarely misspelled names of individuals, he habitually misspelled the last name of Gen. Samuel P. Heintzelman as "Heinztleman." That error has been corrected.

Upon occasion in writing his memoirs Willcox would change the narrative's point of view from first person to third person and back again. Personal memoirs in the third person were not uncommon in the nineteenth century, but it could become confusing if the usage was not consistent. In the few such cases in his writing I have put the narrative into the first person. I have also broken up lengthy paragraphs into shorter ones.

Willcox was often careless when quoting from reports, orders, and other works in his memoirs; what appears in his original manuscript is close to the original source but nevertheless inaccurate. Where it was clearly the author's intention to quote directly rather than paraphrase, I have referred to the original material and made the quotations accurate.

The book's layout has posed some problems. I have in some instances changed the name of chapter headings if the name originally used seemed inappropriate. This includes the title of the book. General Willcox originally intended it to be "Shoepacs to Spurs: My Sixty Years of Service." I have changed the title, as no one today would know what "shoepacs" were—in fact, few people save Willcox himself seemed to know what shoepacs were even in the nineteenth century. (They were wooden shoes worn by the *habitants*, settlers of early Detroit.)

I have used the following editorial symbols throughout the journals, letters, and reports:

. . . Ellipsis points indicate a deletion made by the editor.
[ ] Brackets have been used to enclose comments made by the editor.
All parentheses ( ) are those of the author.
‹ › Angle brackets indicate material inserted from a separate source, written by the author but not included in the original chapter.

It has been my intention to interfere as little as possible in the telling of the story and to let General Willcox speak for himself. Editor's introductions were necessary for a number of the chapters, but I have otherwise kept my editorial comments in the main text to a minimum, reserving the greater part of my interventions for the footnotes. Orlando Bolivar Willcox is the true author of this book; while I, as editor, may have changed *how* he said some things, I have in no way altered *what* he said.

In the six years I have spent editing this work, poring over the personal papers of Orlando Willcox and reading the deepest, most intimate thoughts of his memoirs, I have come to know him even better, perhaps, than did many of his closest acquaintances. He has become a part of my life, a part of our family, as had Henry Abbott before him. Sifting through his personal papers I have felt his presence as though he had been looking over my shoulder. In a sense we became partners in a book that has been a long time in the making. I feel particularly fortunate to have had a hand in helping him complete the work. I can only hope that he would be pleased with the result. It is a difficult thing for one who has not been in a similar situation to understand. Yet it is my earnest hope that those who read this work will develop the same sort of affection and admiration for this much-neglected soldier as I have.

If I have done my job adequately, they can hardly fail to do so, for Orlando Bolivar Willcox has left us a remarkable story. The most respected military man from his state at the outbreak of the rebellion, he rose to become one of the most prominent division commanders of the war. Yet apart from the most basic details of his service, the man himself has remained something of a mystery for over a century. But now, through his memoirs, journals and letters, Brevet Maj. Gen. Orlando Bolivar Willcox has at last stepped from the shadows of obscurity into the light of recognition. In the process he has revealed himself to us more intimately, perhaps, than any other division commander of the Civil War. He has shared with us his deepest thoughts and emotions, and the most unforgettable memories (both pleasant and horrific) of his extraordinary life.

Near the end of his life, General Willcox wrote a friend: "I hope to preserve in my memoirs a certain quiet dignity at least."[3] That he has done, for such was his nature. Orlando Bolivar Willcox was a quiet, dignified man with a defined sense of what it meant to be devoted to one's family, country, and God, a man whose inner strength and moral fortitude allowed him to retain those values even in the midst of the chaos of a hostile world.

3. OBW to Frank Hosford, June 18, 1903, from OBW's copy in the Willcox papers.

§ ACKNOWLEDGMENTS

THAT THIS book has come to pass after lying dormant for generations is primarily due to the foresight of the Willcox family, not only in having preserved the documents, but in having kept the collection intact. That I have been able to have a hand in producing this book is the result of the Willcox family's profound trust and confidence in one whom they barely knew. That trust allowed me to work with the general's papers in the comfort of my own home—an ideal situation that would make many historians envious—greatly facilitating the enormous task that had been delegated to me. To Elizabeth Abbott de Mowbray, who first contacted me about the papers; to Bill Willcox, who carefully read page proofs, making many helpful suggestions; and to the rest of the Willcox family, I owe my deepest thanks. I hope this book will serve to repay them for their patience with me during the six years it took to see this work to completion.

I would also like to thank my wife, Karen, and my daughters, Kristen and Rachel, for their unwavering support and patience, and for putting up with my clutter and the long hours I spent tying up the computer.

Although the basis of this book was provided by General Willcox himself, it was nonetheless necessary, as with any other historical work, to tap the resources and information from numerous libraries and institutions. Because Orlando Willcox was, by happy coincidence, a Michigan native, I was fortunate to have been able to do a great deal of research at the nearby Flint Public Library. That library's excellent collection of books on early Detroit allowed me to identify many of the obscure individuals mentioned by OBW in his early journals and memoirs of his youth. The Flint library also has a complete collection of the *The War of the Rebellion: The Official Records of the Union and Confederate Armies*, which, of course, is an invaluable tool to any Civil War researcher. The library staff was also very cooperative in acquiring many other books relating to OBW (including his novels) through the interlibrary loan system.

As always, Michael J. Winey, curator of the United States Army Military History Institute, and his assistant, Randy Hackenberg, were extremely cooperative in providing photos from their massive collection. Alan Aimone, of the West Point Library, was also of service in acquiring photos from the collection of the U.S. Military Academy. And David L. Poremba, of the Burton Historical Society of the Detroit Public Library, aided me by providing rare images from that collection. The Chicago Historical Society and the Anne S. K. Brown Collection of the John Hay Library, Brown University, also provided photos.

The production of maps is an important step in the publication of any work on the Civil War, and the cartographers who specialize in this field are a rare breed. I was fortunate enough to find Bill Nelson, of William L. Nelson Cartography and Graphics, in Accomac, Virginia. His work in transcribing my scribblings into the excellent finished maps was nothing short of miraculous. Thanks, Bill, for your skill and your patience in putting up with my endless revisions. I should state, however, that any errors that may have slipped through in the published maps are my responsibility, and are in no way the fault of Mr. Nelson.

Thanks, also, to my father-in-law, Ron Carlson, who read an early draft of the manuscript and offered some valuable suggestions.

Finally, I must express my gratitude to the wonderful and friendly people at The Kent State University Press. First, to the director, Dr. John T. Hubbell and senior editor, Dr. Julia Morton, for seeing something of value in my book and in agreeing to publish it. Also, managing editor Joanna Hildebrand Craig and assistant editor Erin Holman, who were invaluable in recommending changes regarding style and format. And a special thanks to Pelham Boyer, who, as a line editor and Civil War specialist, offered good advice and caught many mistakes that escaped me, including a few errors in my transcription of Willcox's writings. Then, too, are the many people behind the scenes at Kent State who assisted in the design and publishing of this book; you may be unknown to me, but your work is much appreciated. To all of the above named people and institutions (and no doubt to many others whom I have shamelessly forgotten) I am forever indebted.

INTRODUCTION

A Voice from the Past

MORE THAN six score and ten years have now passed since we emerged from the crucible that was our Civil War. The guns that once roared on a hundred fields have long since fallen silent; the faded banners, torn and tattered, stand as mute sentinels in state capitols and museums across the country. And the men—the soldiers, blue and gray, who passed through the maelstrom of battle—they are but a memory, the last veteran of the last column of the last review having disappeared over the distant horizon some forty-odd years ago.

And yet we remember them, because, in a very real sense, they are still with us. We still see their faces in thousands of photographs; we hear their voices in hundreds of thousands of memoirs, diaries and letters. This book is a chance for one such voice to speak again.

Brevet Maj. Gen. Orlando Bolivar Willcox never lived to see his memoirs published, and for ninety years after his death those memoirs, along with the rest of his papers, lay virtually untouched and forgotten, tucked carefully away in a trunk in a Washington, D.C., attic. Yet from the time he made his first journal entry in the autumn of 1840 until the effects of old age forced him to halt work on his memoirs shortly after the turn of the century, Orlando Bolivar Willcox strove to record the story of his life.

And what a life it was. Born in what was then the "frontier military town" of Detroit, Michigan, in 1823, "O. B." (or Bolivar, as he was generally called by his friends) was, as he later described himself, "a youth, all gentleness and joy . . . a yearning, bright, religious boy" who immersed himself in litera-ture, particularly history, and who by nature would have preferred a career behind the pulpit or a writer's desk to one in the camp and field.[1]

Yet it was a military career that he opted for, a course dictated to him more by circumstance than desire. And while he did make a mark for him-self both as a poet and a novelist, as a soldier he would gain greater fame.

Orlando Willcox came of age during the turbulent antebellum era, when the slave issue was paramount and the winds of civil war were just beginning to stir. Beginning with the oath he took as a plebe on the plain at West Point in the summer of 1843, Willcox's military career would span five decades. Whether it was following "Old Fuss and Feathers," Gen. Winfield Scott, on the road to Mexico City, or chasing Indians and buffalo on the plains, fighting boredom and Seminoles in the malaria-infested swamps of Florida, or escorting an escaped slave named Anthony Burns through the mob-filled streets of Boston, Orlando Willcox would witness and indeed participate in some of the most important events in American history. But it was the trau-matic events of 1861–1865 that would propel him into the national limelight as one of the prominent figures in the war for the Union, and in the long shadow cast by those four years every other achievement of his life fell into comparative insignificance.

In the autumn of 1857 he retired from the service to practice law and raise a family in his native Detroit, but O. B. quickly became discouraged with the "dull cold pall" of civilian life, much preferring the hardships and camaraderie of the army. "O! what a very proper set they are at home!" he declared. "The fact is I am not a proper man. I never dare hope to be. It makes me feel at times as if I were in a straight jacket, to look on the very faces of the polite lunatics."[2] And so, when the thunderbolt of war finally struck in Charleston Harbor (as many knew it would) and an imperiled country and an overwhelming sense of duty called him to once again buckle on his sword, Orlando Willcox welcomed the chance to escape from what he considered the absurdities of civilian life.

As one of the most highly respected military men in his state, Willcox helped to organize the 1st Michigan Volunteer Infantry, was appointed colonel of that regiment, and took it to Washington soon after President Abraham Lincoln's initial call for troops.

1. From OBW, "The Pleasures of Retirement."
2. From OBW's *Journal, Quotations, Diaries, Interpolations, Thoughts &c, Heterogenous and Desultory* entry of Dec. 3, 1857 (hereafter referred to as OBW's *Second Journal*). See chapter 9, p. 236.

On the morning of May 24, 1861, he became one of the first Federal officers to cross the Potomac when he led his own regiment and the 11th New York Fire Zouaves, under Col. E. Elmer Ellsworth, over the Long Bridge into Virginia and captured the historic town of Alexandria. During that event Ellsworth, a close friend of the Lincoln family, became the first martyr of the Union when he was shotgunned while descending the stairs of the Marshall House after tearing down a Confederate banner that had been flying from the roof within sight of the capital.

At the Battle of Bull Run, Willcox, now commanding a brigade in Brig. Gen. Samuel P. Heintzelman's division, led an attack against the Rebel position on Henry Hill, where he was wounded in the arm and captured (though the initial newspaper reports were that he had been killed, much to his family's distress). For his heroic actions at Bull Run Willcox would in 1895 be awarded the Congressional Medal of Honor.

While a prisoner of war, Willcox and several other Union officers were scheduled to be executed as a reprisal, because a like number of Confederate privateers had been captured by the Union navy and sentenced to be hanged as pirates. For a time, it seemed as if the civil strife might degenerate into the sort of bloodbath that often characterizes such conflicts. In the end, however, the matter terminated peacefully, with the Lincoln administration commuting the sentence of the privateers and agreeing to treat them as legitimate prisoners of war; nonetheless, it had been a trying ordeal for Willcox and his family, and for everyone else involved.

After being exchanged on August 16, 1862, Willcox was released from prison and feted as a hero in Washington. There, he was treated to a dinner with President Lincoln, who handed him a commission as brigadier general. Returning briefly to Detroit, the new brigadier was given a triumphal welcome. According to the *New York Herald*, which offered the best account of the August 27 celebration, "The banks, public buildings and prominent stores and houses are gayly decorated with the 'Red, White and Blue,' and at the point where the procession is to enter Woodward avenue there are evergreen trees planted across the street, making a sort of triumphal arch." Governor Austin Blair, Senator Zachariah Chandler, the Honorable Lewis Cass, and other notables were on hand to greet the general upon his arrival.

In a speech on the Campus Martius, Willcox made clear his views on prosecuting the war:

I have nothing to say in reference to the policy of the question of slavery; but I say this: Here is a monster that lies curled up in our midst, and that threatens, with its scaly coils, to crush out freedom, and its name is slavery. [Cheers.] I, a democrat, who have been always a democrat, who am a democrat this moment, who am opposed to interfering with the rights of the States—I say that the political government now seeking to fasten itself on the South is nothing more nor less than a monster, with slavery at the bottom—and the scum of creation—Southern chivalry—at the top of it. [Laughter and applause.] It is my firm belief that we, democrats and abolitionists, can now shake hands. [Laughter.] There is no more need of talking about measures to put out slavery, or measures to protect the domestic institutions of the South; for this war, with its thunder and its mighty revolutions, is of itself crushing out slavery, and you need not say any more about it. [Cheers.] Mr. Davis and his compeers do not wish you to do anything more than to raise the banner of emancipation, because they know that the people of the South would be more roused by an anti-slavery war than by any other. I therefore am opposed to raising an anti-slavery flag, or making anti-slavery proclamations. The President is right on that, and I stand by him in it. [Applause—in which even Senator Chandler joins.][3]

It is interesting to note that Willcox, who had been embittered against the Southern people during his trying thirteen months in Confederate prisons and spoke of Southern chivalry as "the scum of creation," nevertheless remained friends with many of the Confederate officers who had been his classmates at West Point. With Confederate Gen. Henry Heth in particular Willcox maintained a close relationship for the remainder of his life, notwithstanding the war that pitted them directly against each other on the field of battle. In their old age they often sat together and discussed those long-ago days, the war in which they had both served, and the battles where they had faced each other from opposite sides of the field.

For those old comrades, blue and gray, who had perished in the struggle, Willcox could only mourn. To his dying day he believed that men from his division had killed his old friend and classmate Confederate general A. P. Hill in the final assault on Petersburg. "Would I could grasp the noble fellow by the hand this day," he lamented, some thirty years later. They had been as brothers once, and nothing—neither war nor death—could ever change that.

Rejoining the Army of the Potomac in early September 1862, Willcox was given command of the First Division, Ninth Corps. He led it with particular distinction at the Battle of South Mountain (Fox's Gap) on September 14, 1862, where his troops engaged the Confederates in a bloody, hand-

3. Quoted in the *New York Herald*, Aug. 30, 1862.

to-hand melee. Three days later the division crossed a certain stone bridge over Antietam Creek (known ever after as "Burnside's Bridge") and, sweeping up the grassy slope before the town of Sharpsburg, entered what remains the bloodiest single day in American history. Willcox was, as usual, in the thickest of the fight, having two horses shot from under him. Pushing his division to the top of the heights in the waning hours of the battle, the general saw what appeared to be "a clear front and signs of confusion at Sharpsburg." A crushing blow against the wavering Confederate lines before him appeared within his grasp. Yet Willcox's battle ardor was quickly snuffed out: he receieved orders to withdraw.

The general's wife, Marie, wrote of that critical moment at Antietam (no doubt reflecting the thoughts of her husband) after touring the field with him some weeks later. The enemy, she wrote, "were fairly beaten, and running! panic-stricken, his [Willcox's] men having gained all the important positions and the crest of the hill when . . . he was ordered to retire, which order he received three times before he obeyed it. It would have turned a doubtful fight into a glorious victory, and probably would have bagged a large number of the rebels. Such a chance only occurs once in a life time. If you would only see the ground you would understand the whole thing perfectly."[4] The observation raises another of the what-if scenarios that have cropped up since the battle ended. *What if* Willcox had been allowed to push on into Sharpsburg? Would A. P. Hill's reinforcements have been checked? Could Lee's entire army have been driven into the Potomac? One thing is certain: Lee's army had never been so close to total defeat as it had been at Antietam, and it would not face such a danger again until the closing days at Appomattox.

During the Fredericksburg campaign, Willcox assumed command of the Ninth Corps, directing it in the disastrous assault against the heavily defended Confederate position atop Marye's Heights, west of town, on December 13, 1862. As a corps commander and a close friend of commanding general Ambrose Burnside, Willcox had occupied a chair in the high-level councils of war that planned the battle; nevertheless, he had never been very sanguine of the result so long as the Confederates remained entrenched on the heights. "I can truly say the failure of our bold, impracticable attempt upon the enemy's fortified lines was not unexpected," he confessed to his wife after the debacle. "We dared the lion in his very den, & skulking behind his lair he held us at bay."[5]

4. Marie Willcox to her mother, Oct. 8, 1862.
5. OBW to his wife, Dec. 16, 1862.

When the Ninth Corps was transferred to Lexington, Kentucky, in April 1863, Willcox went with it, commanding both the corps and the District of Central Kentucky. Willcox's command of the corps was temporary, however; he was soon superseded by Maj. Gen. John G. Parke. Parke and the Ninth Corps were transferred to Vicksburg, Mississippi, in June, and Willcox was sent to Indianapolis, Indiana, where he assumed command of the Department of Indiana and Michigan. The general's chief mission there was to enforce conscription and, in a more delicate matter, to relieve tensions between Indiana governor Oliver Morton and the War Department. It was all a bit overwhelming for the new brigadier, and he later confessed that he felt as though he had been caught up in "a war of giants."

To make matters worse, Willcox soon learned that the fabled Confederate raider John Hunt Morgan had cut loose with his mounted guerrilla force on what was to be his great raid through Kentucky, Indiana, and Ohio. Working desperately, Willcox dispatched troops to intercept the Rebel horsemen. He did not capture Morgan and his men as was hoped, but Willcox was nevertheless successful in impeding their progress, limiting their depredations in the Hoosier state, and forcing them into Ohio, where most of the band were finally trapped and apprehended.

In September 1863, Willcox was sent to Camp Nelson, Kentucky, the jumping-off point for a campaign into east Tennessee. The chief goal of the campaign (long favored by Lincoln) was to liberate this region of loyal Unionists from the grip of the Confederacy. It would also enable Union forces to protect Cumberland Gap and later to harass Gen. James Longstreet's forces, then besieging Knoxville.

In March 1864, Willcox returned east, again commanding a division in the newly reorganized Ninth Corps, now led by his old friend Burnside and operating in conjunction with the Army of the Potomac. Willcox took part in all the major battles of Grant's campaign of 1864, from the Wilderness to Cold Harbor, most notably at the Ny River, near Spotsylvania Court House on May 9.

Willcox further distinguished himself in many of the battles that occurred during the siege of Petersburg, including the initial assaults on June 17–18, 1864, and at the disappointing Battle of the Crater on July 30. In the action on the Weldon Railroad, August 19, Willcox and his division effectively saved the day.

On March 25, 1865, when Robert E. Lee made his last desperate attempt to break the siege by assaulting the Federal lines at Fort Stedman with three Confederate divisions, it was Willcox's division that received the assault.

Though a portion of his line was broken, Willcox's men launched a desperate counterattack on the front and flanks of the assaulting column and stopped the Rebel forces in their tracks, effectively plugging the break in the line. Yet as this book will reveal, neither Willcox nor his division has received the credit for their role in blunting the Rebel attack. Their work has to a great degree been overshadowed by the actions of Gen. John F. Hartranft and his division on that day—chiefly due to the self-promoting efforts of Hartranft himself. Yet according to Willcox and many other prominent officers involved (including John Tidball, who commanded the Ninth Corps artillery at Fort Stedman), the bulk of Hartranft's division did not arrive on the scene until the breach had been plugged and the Confederates driven back into Fort Stedman itself.

When President Lincoln, who had been visiting Grant's headquarters at nearby City Point, viewed the sight of the assault later that day, he happened to come upon General Hartranft, who proceeded to brief the president on the attack and the repulse of the Confederates at Fort Stedman. Impressed by Hartranft's version of the Stedman affair, President Lincoln named him a major general on the spot, forgetting General Willcox (who was still overseeing affairs on his front and thus unable to greet the president) altogether.[6]

This is not, however, to detract from the contribution that Hartranft and his troops made to the battle; their counterattack at Fort Stedman was, in a broad sense, the last shovel-full of dirt on the grave of the Army of Northern Virginia. It is, however, my hope (as it would have been the hope of General Willcox and the men who served under him) that this book will ensure that credit is finally given to the general and the troops who received and repulsed Lee's last-gasp effort to break the siege that was slowly strangling his army.

Eight days after the Confederate attack on Fort Stedman, Willcox's division brought an end to the ten long months in the trenches when in the last attack of the siege it snapped the Confederate line and became the first Union force to enter the city of Petersburg.

By anyone's estimate, Orlando Bolivar Willcox was one of the central actors in the Civil War and one of the finest division commanders ever to serve in the Army of the Potomac. Yet today we hardly know him—not because his life was without significance, for significant it most certainly was, but rather because his journals, letters, and memoirs, the literary remains of

6. For more on Fort Stedman, see chapter 24.

his life, have been locked in a trunk, virtually untouched, since his death some ninety years ago. Except for an article he wrote for the *Century Magazine* series "Battles and Leaders of the Civil War," and a few other obscure writings (chiefly in newspapers), Orlando Willcox's voice has hardly been heard.

This book, then, is his chance to speak again, to tell the story he longed to tell.

Dedication by Gen. Orlando B. Willcox

WHO CAN sufficiently estimate the influence of a wise mother? My mother's presence on earth always seemed a link between me and Heaven, and to her I owe much of what little success I have had in a checkered career. In my absences from home I seldom wrote her of my troubles, but I have never had a heavy affliction without her seeming to know and feel it. Sometimes it came to her in dreams, and who can tell how much her prayers have effected in such cases?

Often times, when no other hope has cheered me up, the feeling that her loving spirit was watching and praying over me lifted up my heart. Besides, to no other could I go or write for advice on any subject whatever with better profit. Such a strong mind, so sagacious, so courageous and yet so judicious and worldly-wise. I think that her most prominent traits were energy of character and goodness of heart. The two words that she never seemed to admit in her dictionary were selfishness and impropriety.

But unlike women generally of such masculine natures, her heart always melted at the slightest calamity happening to her friends or neighbors. I have often seen her weeping over a newspaper paragraph, and yet, plunged as we were in debt at times, with a young family to support and educate, in the darkest hours, not a tear would show itself on her resolute face. Kindness to others was the first moral precept of her life and example. Never unkind to a servant, never turned a beggar away empty, always sympathetic and wisely advising her afflicted friend and neighbor of high or low degree, she was something of a moral power in the community beyond her social rank.*

To these words, written in the hey day of my manhood before she died, but at a time of her dangerous illness, I could only add that her loss to me would be more than a bereavement of her presence, it would be the loss of a check on my impulsive nature, and the wisest of counsellors in every coming emergency—of which, indeed, there were many to come, as you shall see.

---

* As paraphrased by O. B. Willcox from his *Second Journal* entry for May 1851, pp. 69–71.

ONE

The Boyhood of "Captain Potato"

I AM the son of Charles and Almira Willcox. My birthplace was Detroit, then the capital of the almost wholly unsettled and far-reaching territory of Michigan. I was born the 16th of April, 1823. At that time Detroit was a frontier military town not yet greatly altered from the ancient French place, which had long been a remote outpost of Bourbon authority in the New World. The old French population was still dominant in numbers, and many persons who had participated in the thrilling historical events of the latter half of the eighteenth century were living in the American city, and in its suburbs across the river, which latter still acknowledged the sovereignty of George III.

Many witnesses of the great siege of Detroit by the ablest of Indian generals, veterans of the Revolution, and survivors of the sad days of the war of 1812 walked the streets of the little city, and nearly all of them became known to me. Thus my boyhood was passed in an atmosphere of historical reminiscence, and among surroundings that naturally suggested military life. . . .

The conditions and surroundings of my boyhood and youth were such as might well have turned my attention to a military career. But there were circumstances in the lives of several of my forbears that may also have influenced me in that direction, as 'tis often said that we derive all our mental as well as physical traits from one or more of our ancestors.

My first American ancestor on the paternal side was William Willcoxson, son of John, of Middlesex, England. A tradesman in London, William crossed the ocean in 1634 and settled at Hartford, Connecticut, with his wife, two daughters and eight sons. The oldest son, Joseph, grew up at Hartford and became one of the town, or colonial, council. Another descendant—John, from whom I am derived—settled at Killingsworth, which lies in New Haven County. The others scattered themselves abroad, [being of a more] enterprising spirit. Among them were the first settlers at Willcox Landing, James River, Virginia, and Edward, who went to Rhode Island and became a partner in business with Roger Williams.[1]

My great-grandfather, John, of Killingsworth, contracted a run-away match with Grace North, of the Guilford North family in the old country. With the daughter he sailed away and joined his brethren in Connecticut. On the decease of Lord North in 1792, one of my grandfather's brothers embarked for London to claim his share of the North family estate. A letter was received from the young man on his arrival in England. And, that being the last ever heard of him, it has always been supposed that he was secretly made way with—a tradition that has no sufficient evidence, and we remain proud of the North connection!

John Willcox, another son of John and Grace North Willcox, was my grandfather. He had a military turn, and served with several regiments during the Revolution of '76, turning out first, at the age of 19, with a company that volunteered and marched into Massachusetts on the scare at Lexington and Concord. Although he served afterwards in several regiments with Washington's army during the Seven Years War of independence, I cannot find his name among the commissioned officers—from which fact I opine that he never rose to distinction. And although the heraldry books trace the Willcoxson names back to the early wars in France, and even to the Crusades, I cannot locate my military heritage with any other than the John Willcox, of Killingsworth, aforesaid. While making this acknowledgment, I have to smile at the credulity of so many of my countrymen who make boast of their ancient, and even royal pedigrees—derived from the Heraldry shops of London at a trifling cost.

Another link in the family chain of which we may well be proud is the name of Capt. Joseph Willcox, of Killingsworth, an officer on the staff of General George Washington, and who, like his chief, was one of the original members of the Society of the Cincinnati.

1. Roger Williams (1603?–1683), founder of the colony of Rhode Island and the town of Providence (1636).

That there is a military strain in the Willcox race may be inferred from the fact that so many bearing the family name, in its different spellings, have taken part in our wars. Three score participated in the Revolution, and three score and eight served during the Rebellion.

To go west was an early impulse in old New England, and thus it happened that both my father [Charles Willcox] and mother had settled in western New York, before the War of 1812. My father early left the old homestead to better his fortunes. He first spent several years with his favorite brother, Edward, at Danbury, Connecticut. Danbury was, at the time, head center of the hat trade with which business my father became sufficiently acquainted, that with his credit in Connecticut, he was able to start "on his own hook." From Danbury he moved to western New York, and there he met and courted my mother, and they were married at Nunda [February 6], 1815.[2]

My mother's maiden name was Almira Rood. The Roods were of good, old, and what would now be called "strenuous" Connecticut stock, and tillers of the soil. Her grandparents were among the early settlers in the wilds of Litchfield County, Connecticut, where they were slave owners to some extent down to the latter part of the eighteenth century. Her grand uncle, John Griswold, married Bathsheba North, from whom was born the some time celebrated Indian fighter, Captain John Griswold. And here we light upon a military strain running through both of [my] ancestral houses. . . .

One of the descendants of this famous old fighter, John Griswold, graduated from the celebrated law school at Litchfield in 1775, was elected captain of a company in the Revolution, and joined the army. Offered the position of aide on Washington's staff, he declined in deference to the wishes of his regimental commander. After the war, he became judge of the Court of Common Pleas, was several times a state senator, and in the war of 1812 he was nominated by President Madison as secretary of state for the North West Territory under the unfortunate Hull[3]—doubly unfortunate, for with

2. Willcox's parents married at Nunda, New York, February 6, 1815. He gives a different date for their marriage in his memoirs. The date here is from the Willcox family genealogical chart.

3. William Hull (1753–1824). Born in Derby, Connecticut, Hull entered the Revolutionary army as a captain but was rapidly promoted and became inspector of the army under Baron von Steuben, participated in numerous battles, and was thanked by General Washington for his services at Morrisiana. In 1805 Hull was appointed the first governor of the Michigan Territory, holding that position until superseded by Gen. Lewis Cass in 1813. During the War of 1812, Hull surrendered Detroit without firing a shot, for which he was court-martialed in Albany, New York, in 1814, found guilty of cowardice, and sentenced to be shot. The sentence was remitted by President Madison, however, and Hull fought for the remainder of his life to clear his name.

such a judicious and brave man as Judge Griswold by his side, who knows but what Hull's rash fall might have been averted!

My mother's parents removed to Onondaga County, New York, and took up lands, about the beginning of the last century. In 1807 my mother was married to her first husband, John Powers. She often described him to me as a bright young gentleman of good parts and fond of music and dancing— a trait inherited by my half-sister, Mary Taylor. John Powers gave his life to his country in the War of 1812. He joined the army as lieutenant and became a captain. He fought on the Niagara frontier, where he was wounded and captured by the British and sent down to the horrible prison hulks at Quebec, where he died of his wounds or was starved to death. The "deep damnation of his taking off" [was to leave] my mother a [young] widow . . . with an infant at the breast as the only substantial reminder of her husband, and a shadow of the last war with Britain.

Being a woman of spirit, and unwilling to depend on her brothers for support, my widowed mother began her new life by teaching school. This she continued to do until her marriage with my father in 1815, at Nunda. As there was no town in that section of sufficient growth or prospects for a successful business, the newly married couple "pulled up stakes" and moved to Detroit, which town, besides being already quite a thriving business place, was a favorite residence for officers of the War of 1812, and their families. It was, moreover, the seat of government for the whole Northwest, and a depot for the long-established fur trade. Here my father found his opportunity, and connecting the manufacture of hats and caps with furs, both at Detroit and outlying posts on the St. Clair River and at Mackinaw, he soon built up a thriving business.

He must have stood well in the community, for during the time of my childhood he was a vestryman of old St. Paul's Church, and one of the town trustees. As I remember him, he was a man of mild aspect and quiet manners, yet a rigid Episcopalian, which was perhaps the only inheritance he had derived from the North family of England. But his better inheritance was the love of literature, to which his well-remembered mahogany book case and writing desk testified. Reading, writing, and hunting were his chief diversions from business cares. But while literary taste descended more or less to all of us, an unfortunate hunting expedition threw us into deep mourning. His death came by a malarial fever after duck shooting on the little river Ecorse, a few miles below Spring Wells. This event happened in 1827, when I was only four-and-a-half years old.

The death of my father wrought an abrupt change in our circumstances, from ease, affluence and happiness, to comparative poverty. For it soon became known that his large business had been wrecked, unwittingly to himself, by a rascally partner in charge of the posts at St. Clair and Mackinaw; and it took all there was of the establishment at Detroit and our comfortable homestead on Jefferson Avenue to pay the debts. I do not know whatever became of the old partner, but I am glad to acknowledge that his own family were the first to share our grief.

Fortunately, my mother was not one of the sort that sit down helpless in misfortune's chair. With her accustomed energy she was soon up and doing, bought a lot on credit from an old friend, Mr. Joseph Campau,[4] richest of the old *habitants*,[5] well up town, and she managed, by hook or crook, to build a good two story house, quite equal to the majority of houses in the neighborhood.

I need not develop the family history further than to say that of the six brothers and sisters, three were old enough to assist their mother in keeping our heads above water. My oldest brother, Charles, was sent to father's friends in New Haven to be educated. My immediate senior brother, Eben North, obtained some employment, but more scholarly in his tastes he afterwards studied law under Chancellor Elon Farnsworth,[6] and ultimately became a lawyer of good repute. Charles learned the printer's trade, was taken into Sheldon McKnight's[7] *Detroit Free Press* in the early days of that famous journal, and became its foreman. The girls were already sufficiently educated to lend an industrious hand as music school teachers. . . .

4. Note by OBW: "Joseph Campau (1769–1863) a grandson of Marquis Jacques Campau, who settled Detroit with Cadillac in 1701. A patriarch among merchants, a public spirited and generous man, and leader of the French people of the old Northwest. His large family of descendants is still active in the affairs of Detroit. I was acquainted with several of his sons, and one nephew, Alexander Campau, who is still living, is one of my few surviving boyhood friends. Daniel J. Campau, a grandson of Joseph, has long been prominent in National affairs—a member of the Democratic national committee since 1892, and former chairman of the National campaign committee."

5. The *habitants* were the early French settlers of Detroit who farmed and trapped along the river and some distance inland.

6. Elon Farnsworth (1799–1877). A native of Woodstock, Vermont, Farnsworth moved in 1822 to Detroit, where he made a reputation as an effective lawyer. Upon the organization of the Territory of Michigan into a state, Farnsworth was named chancellor, holding that office from July 1836 until March 1842, the courts of chancery then being distinct from the law courts of the territory. He was the Democratic nominee for governor of the state in 1839, and regent of the University of Michigan for many years. Farnsworth also helped to found St. Paul's Episcopal Church in Detroit. He and his wife, Hannah Blake Farnsworth, had two daughters, Marie and Caroline ("Caro"), Marie becoming the first wife of OBW in 1852.

7. Sheldon McKnight (1810–1860) was editor and founder of the Detroit *Free Press* from 1830 to 1836, postmaster of Detroit from 1836 to 1841, and state representative from Wayne County, 1857 to 1858.

On the whole we were a happy family, and on good terms with our neighbors, irrespective of religious bigotry, so intolerant in those days. For I may add that the head of the house did not share her late husband's exclusive notions of Church borders, and was on good terms with all denominations, although herself a Presbyterian. Many of her friends were French Catholics, and one of our most frequent visitors was the jolly French priest, Father Richard,[8] famous in northwestern history. He came often to hobnob with my mother, who was always sociable, and enjoyed laughter and lively conversation with men of parts. Moreover, she despised those denominational antipathies that so often prevent good fellowship in the social circle. As there were as many French Catholics as American Protestants in our community, life would have been unbearable with religious intolerance. And why should Christians so far forget the teachings of Christ as to burn each other, either at the stake, after the fashion of our forefathers—or in any other form?

Life on the Frontier in those days is so fully described in an old and now forgotten book of my own, under the name of Walter March: viz., *Shoepac Recollections, and the French Side of the Story of Detroit*,[9] . . . that I need no longer dwell on the circumference. Furthermore, as some learned pundit writes the best part of biography is auto-biography, I will proceed with number one, and his youthful fortunes and misfortunes.

My first experience on the benches occurred in a little frame school house on the Common, and not far from Fort Nonsense—a circular parapet and old relic of Indian troubles. The school was little more than an infant

8. Note by OBW: "The Very Reverend Gabriel Richard was one of the famous and beloved priests of the old Northwest. He was a descendant of Bishop Bosquet, and a member of the order of St. Sulspice. He came to Detroit as Vicar-General of the Northwest and as pastor of old Ste. Anne's in 1798. He devoted himself with great love and zeal to the intellectual and temporal as well as spiritual welfare of the people of that ancient parish, and was also prominent in all public matters. He brought the first printing press into Michigan territory and printed the first newspaper on it. He enlivened his paper with humorous articles and caricatures. In an early scarcity of money he introduced, perhaps invented, the first "shinplasters" with success. He was elected as delegate to congress in the year of my birth (the only Catholic priest who ever sat in the national legislature) and devoted his entire salary to paying a debt on his church. After thirty-four years of the truest of Christian service he died of cholera, a martyr to his devotion to his people, in the great epidemic of 1832. He was mourned as deeply as he had been beloved by all, and his name is still one to conjure with for good in the now great city in which he passed away."

9. *Shoepac Recollections: or Way Side Glimpses of American Life*, OBW's first novel, published under the pseudonym of "Walter March" (New York: Bunce and Brothers, 1856). It is a historical novel set in old Detroit. The book's characters are based on people OBW knew in his boyhood (the actual identities of the characters were plain to residents of the city), and its main character, Walter March, is based on OBW himself.

Almira Willcox, mother of OBW.
OBW Collection.

Jefferson Avenue, Detroit, ca.
1850. *Burton Historical Collection,
Detroit Public Library.*

school, and was taught by Perley Ann Meade, who was a sister of deacon David Meade of our church. She married afterwards Mr. Charles Crocker, the Nevada miner and railway millionaire of San Francisco. She was an excellent teacher, and the best lesson she taught me was descriptive of the period, in the shape of a good thrashing, which stings to this day.

Rising in growth and years, my next school was in the same neighborhood, taught by a Mr. Burrows, another of the female sort, against whom the older boys revolted, pummeled, and finally drove out of town. Our third was the professional school master Crane, who had "black eyes and fierce whiskers, one black and the other red, except when dyed." Mr. Crane began his rule by thrashing the six tallest and best connected boys of this aristocratic little city. But he gave interesting lectures on mathematics, chemistry, and magnetism, and took the town by storm. Peace to his ashes.

From that haughty spirit in the flesh I gained my first ideas of mathematics. My next and last school at Detroit was a branch, in fact the beginning of the University of Michigan, taught by the Rev. Chauncey M. Fitch. His assistants were Scotch and Irish gentlemen, Messrs. Harvey and Grey. From these good men I learned a little Latin and declamation. And this ended my course on the school benches. My most valuable instruction, excepting that at West Point, has come from book reading, yet which, as you shall soon discover, was quite desultory.

In the first place, as soon as I was old enough to find employment, I was obliged to help [in] turning the family grind stone, beginning at a small pittance. This I was able to do at first out of school hours, but as I rose to hard clerical work, which became more engrossing, I had to quit school, at least in the winter time—as was the case for two winters. Later on I was given a place in the senate chamber of the Territorial Legislature, as page. This gave me more time for reading, and I may add, for writing, as I had to prepare the legislative manual for the second session.[10]

Sooth to say, all my leisure was not so usefully employed, for I had some wild oats to sow. I had formed companionships with the wild blades at school, among whom I soon became a most mischievous leader—known officially as "Captain Potato" in our secret society of night rowdies. Among my jolly companions were several fellows afterwards known to climb bigger ladders, youngsters who became officers in the army and navy, prominent

10. Note by OBW: "I am proud to state that my colleague as page in the Territorial Senate was Henry B. Clitz, afterward a graduate of West Point [1845], and a gallant officer in the Rebellion; and that the page in the House was Horace S. Roberts, afterward a brave captain in my 1st Michigan Volunteers, who was its second colonel, and afterward died gloriously on the bloody field of Second Bull Run."

lawyers, and members of Congress. Most prominent of these was Anson Burlingame,[11] now chiefly known as the first foreign minister received in the Court of China. He was a handsome fellow in his youth, tall and straight as an Indian. In fact, he had Indian blood in his veins that glowed in his dark eyes and lent music to his voice. . . .

Burlingame was, I think, the son of a farmer. He received his school and college education by the help of the Davenport family of Detroit, graduated at Harvard College, married and settled at Boston, by which city he was elected to Congress. That which gave him greatest notoriety was his speech in the House, denouncing Preston C. Brooks of South Carolina for assaulting Charles Sumner in the Senate Chamber. Mr. Potter, who was a member from Pennsylvania, acting in behalf of Brooks, challenged Burlingame to mortal combat, which the latter accepted; and having choice of weapons, place, and time, he chose rifles, and named Niagara Falls, for which place he started with his seconds and gun next morning. But his doughty opponent failed to appear. I believe his excuse was that the rifle was not a weapon known in such use by gentlemen. Perhaps the real reason was the report that Burlingame could hit a squirrel at forty yards.

My friend [Burlingame] remained in Congress until 1861, when he was appointed Minister to Austria, where he was not received, on account of his sympathy with Kossuth.[12] But Burlingame was no fire-eater, and at school he was so quiet and peaceful that he became rather a moderator of mischief in our nightly sallies to make night hideous. In this respect his coolness on one occasion served us well.

This was at the time narrated by Walter March,[13] when a row occurred at Singing School. One of the leaders of the Potato Band, John Walker, who

---

11. Anson Burlingame (1820–1870). Born in New Berlin, New York, in 1820, Burlingame moved to Detroit in 1833. Graduating from the Detroit branch of the University of Michigan and in 1846 from the Harvard Law School, he entered Massachusetts politics, serving in the state senate from 1853 to 1854. In 1854 he was elected to the U.S. Congress, serving there until 1861. Although first elected to Congress on the Know Nothing ticket, he later became a Republican, becoming one of the founders of that party in Massachusetts. His speech on June 21, 1856, castigating Representative Preston Brooks for his attack on Sen. Charles Sumner prompted Brooks to challenge Burlingame to a duel (the duel never took place). Appointed minister to Vienna by President Lincoln in 1860, Burlingame spent the remainder of his life in diplomatic service, most notably in China. He died in St. Petersburg, Russia, on February 23, 1870.

12. Lajos Kossuth (1802–1894), Hungarian patriot and foremost leader of the revolution of 1848–1849, he dedicated himself to freeing his country from the Austrian regime. The revolution was eventually suppressed by Austria, with the assistance of Russia.

13. The episode was described by Willcox, under his pseudonym "Walter March," in *Shoepac Recollections*.

afterwards became a navy officer, threatened to strike down a deacon of the church who held the door, our way out having been blocked to prevent our escape from the constable who had been sent for to arrest us. Anson, although actually present, had not participated in the disturbance, and now he laid his hand on John and said, "It won't do John, we are all too well known." It is needless to add that we were arraigned before the court next day, and that the Potato Band was no longer a thorn in the side of the obnoxious singing masters, and ceased to "make Rome howl" at night.[14]

This chanced all the better for me, and for my book reading, which I now began to pursue assiduously, particularly in novels and plays. I presume you have never heard the names of the most famous novels of that day—*Alonzo and Melissa*, and *The Three Spaniards*, and *The Castle of Udolpho*.[15] But by good fortune my taste became turned to better ways. There were two English boys in my neighborhood, named Brutus and Romulus Kennedy, who had a taste for good reading, and there was a learned barber named William Clay who was a bibliophile in his way. And between the attractive home of the Kennedys (Mrs. Kennedy being famous for her cakes and buns) and the barber's book shelves, I soon learned to appreciate not only Sinbad the Sailor and the Travels of Capt. Gulliver, but *Pilgrims Progress* and other old English books (I have several of the latter in my library still—Camden's *Britannia*, the *Canterbury Tales* and Burgoyne's Plays),[16] for the little old man

14. Another member of the Potato Band (also known as "Rowdy Club No. 1") was Friend Palmer, of Detroit. Palmer, though not directly involved in the incident, was nevertheless a witness. He recalled that when Willcox and his two companions were arraigned before the recorder's court, the boys "pleaded guilty, and the recorder, in view of their youth, let them off with a scathing lecture, that, I will venture to say, no member of the club present, and indeed no one of the large audience in attendance, ever forgot.... One of them, the captain of the club, [Willcox] was moved to tears when the recorder alluded to his widowed mother, the other two received the lecture with apparently stolid indifference. The recorder was Asher B. Bates, and when the three got clear of the court room, they vowed vengeance then and there, and if a fitting opportunity ever presented itself, they would take it out on his hide. But as time went on and the sober second thought asserted itself, they came to see that he was right and their animosity gradually died out." General Friend Palmer, *Early Days in Detroit* (Detroit: Hunt & June, 1906), pp. 724–25.

15. See Daniel Jackson, *Alonzo and Melissa, or The Unfeeling Father. A Tale Founded on Fact* (New York: Leavitt & Allen, 1855); George Walker, *The Three Spaniards: A Romance*, 3 vols. (London: Sampson and Low, 1800); Ann Ward Radcliffe, *The Castle of Udolpho, an Operatic Drama* (London: 1808). This work was based on Radcliffe's previous novel, *The Mysteries of Udolpho*, 1794.

16. John Bunyan, *The Pilgrim's Progress*, 1678; William Camden, *Britannia*, (R. Newbery, 1586); Geoffrey Chaucer, *Canterbury Tales*, 1400; John Burgoyne (1722–1792), English general and dramatist, chiefly known for his controversial role in the American Revolution. His most successful play was *The Heiress*, 1786.

did not thrive by the edge of his razor alone, nor did he scorn to turn an honest penny at a book trade.

Nor must I forget another old friend, one James Baker, a Scotchman, with whom I spent many pleasant hours over Burns and Goldsmith,[17] and from these poets I contracted a passion for scribbling verse which I long continued to enjoy and occasionally to print, under anonymous names.[18] This drew me apart from my fellows. Day after day I wandered in "God's first temple," the woods. But it was not always thus wise that my nights and spare days were spent. At the fire-side of our French acquaintances in town, or on the neighboring farms, I loved to sit, night after night, and listen to their stories of the early settlers, the pioneers, priests, voyageurs, and soldiers, and their struggles, so long cut off, if not forgotten by the civilized world. I was entranced with their account of the mysterious agencies of the wilderness by which their forefathers had been environed. . . .

Returning to my boyhood's evolution and mental growth, I must say that no sooner were the sources of chance reading exhausted, than good fortune, or more literally, the pastor of our church, dear old Dr. Duffield,[19] threw open to me his extensive library. He had an extensive range of books, from gay to grave, from Walter Scott to [Edward] Gibbon. Concerning the latter, he said he could trust me to read it, warning me, of course, concerning the author's skeptical unfairness towards that Church which has changed Europe from barbarism to civilization.

I never can sufficiently acknowledge the good dominie's help at, perhaps, the turning points of my up-making. Fortunately, by his advice, the greatest part of my spare time was soon directed to history. A boy of seventeen who can enjoy Gibbon's *Decline and Fall of the Roman Empire* will find most

17. Robert Burns (1759–1796), the prolific but short-lived Scottish poet, who penned such beloved poems as "The Cotter's Saturday Night," "Tam O'Shanter," and "To a Mouse," the cantata "The Jolly Beggars," and over two hundred songs, including "Auld Lang Syne" and "Comin' Thro' the Rye"; Oliver Goldsmith (1730–1774), Anglo-Irish journalist, essayist, novelist, dramatist, and poet. His chief works were his novel *The Vicar of Wakefield* (1766), the plays *The Good-Natur'd Man* (1768) and *She Stoops to Conquer* (1773), and his poems "The Traveller" (1764) and "Deserted Village" (1770).

18. OBW wrote volumes of poetry. Some of his works appeared (chiefly under the pseudonyms "Italice" in the *Oswego Times* and "Jonathan Punch" in the *Boston Post*) between 1852 and 1856.

19. Note by OBW: "Rev. George Duffield (1795–1868) a famous Presbyterian divine, who preached at Detroit for thirty years. Father of Rev. George Duffield, Jr., Gen. W. W. Duffield, D. Bethune Duffield, Gen. Henry M. Duffield, and Mrs. Isabella Graham Duffield Stewart, who all achieved prominence."

other histories light reading.[20] Moreover, one who is employed in a store or office before breakfast, and has either [to] go to school or to return and stand behind a counter all day, and yet go on with his books at night, must have some strong desire for the history of his native place and country.

That there was such a town as Chicago I had first heard in 1832, when the bustle through our household at Detroit testified preparations for a long journey. My eldest sister, Mrs. Charles [Mary] Taylor, was to accompany her husband, and my little sister [Julia] was to go with them "through the woods" to a new home, and the matter was much discussed in our neighborhood. It was said that most of the roads were frightful, villages, taverns, and even farmhouses few and far between, and no stage coaches. Consequently, the party must needs take their own conveyance, a covered wagon, with trunks, bedding and cooking utensils, and be otherwise provided to "camp out." The latter feature particularly struck my own fancy, and I recklessly offered to take little Julia's place, but the elder sister wanted her for company, and the child knew so little of the hardships in store that she clapped her hands for joy—and went.

It was in the month of May 1832 that they left our home in Detroit to seek a new home still further west. The Black Hawk War stared them in the face. Much of the route was to be by way of Indian trails, few regular roadways being yet laid out, much less improved. All their stores, including Mr. Taylor's shot-gun and some bedding, was packed in the covered wagon, and as the country between Detroit and Ypsilanti was swampy, they covered but ten or twelve miles the first day, and slept at "Coon" TenEyck's tavern at Dearborn. . . .

My own first long journey from my birthplace and boyhood home was around Lakes Huron and Michigan to what is now the mighty city of Chicago. This took place nearly seventy years ago. I went to visit my sisters. I was at the time eleven years old. The journey was a tedious one, and vastly different from one by the many swift steamers and swifter railroad trains that now leave Detroit for Chicago daily.

It was in the early spring of 1834 that I left Detroit for Chicago in a sailing vessel. Our schooner lay ice-bound at Mackinaw for a week. But one of my Detroit school boy friends, Garland Whistler, afterwards known in the army as "Beau" Whistler, invited me to the old fort, the oldest and long

20. Edward Gibbon, *Decline and Fall of the Roman Empire*, 6 vols., London: 1776–1788. OBW had misidentified the author as William Gibbon, and the first word of the title as "Rise" rather than "Decline."

Mary Powers Taylor,
half-sister of OBW.
OBW Collection.

one of the best on the lake, where his father, Major Whistler, was in command.[21] The major was a veteran of the War of 1812. Together we explored the island, climbed the Arch Rock, 150 feet high, Pyramid Rock, 285 feet high, and Lover's Leap, 145 feet, and visited all the natural curiosities of the magic island. We ran races and shot bows and arrows with the Indian boys. Quite a band of Potowatomis, with three squaws and children, had canoes drawn up on the beach, with . . . embroidered moccasins and buckskin hunting shirts and leggings for sale. . . .

On arriving at the destined "port," the schooner dropped anchor a mile or so from the sand bar, which choked the mouth of the Chicago River, and we rowed ashore in the dinghy. There were no signs of a harbor but a dredge boat at the bar and the beginnings of a lighthouse on the north side. We landed on the south side, opposite the cemetery, where skeleton feet of the victims of the late cholera season stared us in the face, so to speak, the foot boards of the coffins having been washed away, a gruesome sight that made me shudder.

21. Garland Whistler was the son of Maj. (later Col.) William Whistler, 4th U.S. Infantry.

But at the landing I found my sister Mary and her good husband, waiting to embrace me. It was a curious medley of log houses, wooden shanties and clapboard structures, and a few good shops and dwellings, scattered along the river on the south side, that we had to drive through for a mile. I noticed but one brick building in the business part of the town, and perhaps a dozen shops, the most conspicuous of which was John Hogan's store, well up the river, Kinzie & Whistler's tall store, and the Wolf's Head Tavern at the point. But stretching out indefinitely into the prairie were to be seen considerable numbers of "prairie schooners," and a goodly lot of emigrants. I do not remember other houses of size except those mentioned, and a Mr. LaFramboise's farm house, standing not far out and surrounded by truck gardens. There was also a Methodist meeting-house in evidence at the point. The twin branches of the Chicago River were spanned by two shaky bridges, connecting the point with both the south and north sides. The north side was nearly a wilderness, inhabited only by a Mr. and Mrs. John [H.] Kinzie,[22] and one French family, and the "woods" boasted of the only school house in town. But little heeding or caring for the town, I was chiefly anxious to meet my little sister, Julia Trumbull Willcox, who ran out to greet me at Wolf Point.

I was put to school in a log house, which stood in the north side woods in "Kinzie's Addition," and my school fellows were mostly garrison boys and half breeds. I forget the actual name of our teacher. I think it was Baldwin, but he was an awkward, long-legged pedagogue, familiarly known as "Dominie Sampson." He was very kind-hearted, and by no means up to the tricks of "we uns," as the Kentucky boys would say. . . .

The prices of town lots went up with a bound, from "forty dollar wagon" valuation, to fabulous demands. The dredging of the river from the disappearing sand bar to Wolf Point being completed, a tall schooner sailed in, or rather, was drawn up to the Point by drag ropes, which were manned by the frantic citizens themselves, amid hurrahs and bell ringings and waving of handkerchiefs. Our schoolmaster, Dominie Sampson, catching sight of the vessel from the windows of the log school house, exclaimed, "there she goes boys, school's dismissed!" and set his long legs in motion for the shore, at the head of us all, hatless, with his long hair streaming behind like a storm flag. Although I little comprehended at the time the importance of the occasion to the future of Chicago, the whole affair left a stronger impression on my boyish memory than any other happening in the new city. . . .

22. John H. Kinzie was the son of John Kinzie, Sr. (1763–1828), who had first settled in Chicago in 1804.

From my relatives during my residence at Chicago, I learned much of the trying history of the little place from the time of their arrival there in 1832, two years before my own. I have also had access to journals of this period kept both by Mr. and Mrs. Taylor, and from these several sources I have prepared the following account of the earliest days of Chicago.

Scarcely had they gone to rest on the night of their arrival than they were aroused by Chicago's only landlord, Mr. J. B. Beaubien, with the news that "Black Hawk was coming!" and were told to hurry up and accompany the Beaubien family to the fort. The confusion itself was frightful, weeping women separated from their husbands who were arming themselves for defense, children screaming as they were snatched from bed and hurriedly dressed by their mothers, dogs yelping, and boys shouting "to arms" as they ran from house to house towards the fort.

At the barracks, pandemonium reigned supreme as the women and children were huddled together, thirty to forty in a room. Fortunately, an old friend, Col. J. V. D. Owen, the Indian agent, called, and with little Julia in his arms, he escorted them to the shelter of his own quarters. Furthermore, the colonel was confident that the whole thing was a senseless scare, otherwise he should have been notified by his own Indians. Nevertheless, what with the shock already experienced and the bedlam still going on, all sleep was out of the question for the rest of the night.

On June 3, 1832, Mr. Taylor started out to prospect the town, which, with its meager population, looked, from a business point-of-view, like a bubble in the air, buoyed up chiefly by great expectations. These were based on the actual needs of the state of Illinois for a harbor on Lake Michigan, towards which active steps had already been taken in Congress, in connection with certain railway projects. These, together with the marvelous fertility of the back country, and finally the ultimate realization of LaSalle's[23] dream of the connection of the Chicago River with the Mississippi.

Meantime, there was not even a lighthouse, nor any other sign of a harbor, except the little river that crept sluggishly between rushes and sedgy banks to an impassable bar on the lake. There were few shops and no warehouses in sight, no rialto, nor any main street, and but two or three stores of any size, the one tavern and no lodging houses. In fact, there was no apparent chance for a business opening, unless it might be for a more commodious hotel to meet and accommodate travelers, prospectors and country people with their teams. The best of the shops and houses were of clapboards and logs. But the people seemed to be wide awake with the energy

23. Rene Robert Cavelier, Sieur de LaSalle (1643–1687).

still characteristic of that stimulating atmosphere. Several vessels already lay off the bar, laden with merchandise and lumber, and lime was being unloaded from a scow or two on shore.

Fort Dearborn, near the river's mouth, with its white walls and black-muzzled guns, seemed to give a picturesque assurance of safety, and the whistle of the plow boy on the prairie was heard beyond the Indian wigwams, a mile or so out from the junction of the two branches of the little river. The fort was commanded by Capt. and Bvt. Maj. De Lafayette Wilcox, a distant relative, not wanting in courtesy and hospitality, which was quite a refreshing circumstance to the new comers.

As for hotels, the Beaubien House stood some way below the fort on the lake shore, and out of touch; but at Wolf Point, there was a little group of log houses, at James Kinzie's store on the point, with a tavern stand. The latter was adorned by a swinging sign of a wolf's head, which had given that section the name of Wolf Point, and towards that point the little town straggled up along the south side of the river. The north side was called the "John Kinzie Addition." It was pretty much woodland, scarcely connected with the town proper. But for those who may be curious to get at the beginning of things, I may add that the first house in Chicago, a log cabin, was built on the north side of the river, opposite the fort, by a San Domingo negro named "Ausable" [Jean Baptiste Point duSable], who sold it to a French fur trader, Li Mai, who in turn sold the hut to John Kinzie [Sr.], and Mr. Kinzie's daughter (afterwards Mrs. Gen. David Hunter,[24] of the army) was the first child born at Chicago. In the opinion of the knowing ones, the drift of the town was towards Wolf Point; and [as] Mr. Kinzie was willing to yield the tavern stand to a new comer, and as no adequate business opening appeared in sight, Mr. Taylor took over the stand on one year's lease. The tavern consisted of a small frame two story building with verandah and several log attachments, store house, kitchen and barn. The Kinzie store goods lay mostly in produce for country teams and Indian supplies. There was a Potowatomi village near, and bucks and squaws were always in sight. But these did no ways alarm the Taylor family, as they were more or less familiar with the tribe, and knew some of their chiefs, as we shall have occasion to see.

But to show how little demand there was as yet for town lots, I may mention that in looking for a permanent location, Mr. Taylor was offered two

24. David Hunter (graduated 24th, United States Military Academy, 1822), then a lieutenant of the 5th U.S. Infantry, stationed at Fort Dearborn, married Maria H. Kinzie, who had been born at Chicago in 1807. However, it was Maria's elder sister, Ellen Marion Kinzie, who was given the distinction of being the first white child born in Chicago (a claim that has since been disputed by historians).

town lots for a forty dollar wagon. But "Rome was not built in a day," and strange to say the "rush" came with the [Black Hawk] war, which now had begun to loom up over in Wisconsin.

A great event was at hand, viz., the presidential election of 1832. "I was in the timber," says Mr. Taylor in his journal, "getting out the frame for a new house." [Mr. Taylor continued:]

Election day had entirely escaped my mind, and on returning I found voting going on at my tavern. The judges were all opposed to me in politics; most of them were not voters. They had polled votes all on their own side. Some of the voters claimed to be Jackson men, and wanted to change their votes. I told the judges they had got the start of me, and it would be but fair play to rub out all and begin anew. They finally agreed to this, and I sent my train out and brought in all the voters that could be found. We carried the day by three, if I recollect rightly. Both sides were liberal. It was agreed that no one should be challenged. We allowed Indians to vote in case they had lived up to the citizens' standard of civilization. And so ended the first presidential election in Chicago.

Shortly afterwards, Judge Young and District Attorney Ford, afterwards governor, held U.S. District Court in the dining room of my house, at the fall term of '32, Richard J. Hamilton being clerk. The only lawyer in court was a Mr. Hancock.

Meantime the Sacs and Foxes in Wisconsin were growing turbulent. Outrages and depredations had been committed as usual by the settlers, and being unredressed by the government, these were met first by Black Hawk and Keokuk with strenuous and manly remonstrances. Then a flag of truce or peace talk had been fired upon, probably by unresponsible parties. The warwhoop was sounded, a party of local volunteers was defeated, and a body of Wisconsin militia took the field under Col. Silliman. Of course every rumor coming from such a distance before the days of telegraph was magnified as it travelled, and hence followed the first scare in our neighborhood, which already has been described. But something more serious was now looked for. The report came that Col. Silliman had been defeated, a vague alarm prevailed throughout the Northwest, and the arrival of General [Winfield] Scott's army was anxiously looked for at Chicago.

When the news of Silliman's defeat became known, the terror of it quickly spread through the settlements from Rock River to the lakes, and with it soon came word that the Indians were actually advancing on our town. At this, settlers from [the] back country pulled up stakes and flocked to the fort with all their families. Most of our own citizens did the same. The best that Major Wilcox could offer for his own kins people was to put them in a room with thirty other women and children.

New rumors coming kept up the alarm next day, but Mrs. Taylor, returning home with Julia, determined to take the chances rather than spend another night at the fort, even against the advice of two friendly Potowatomi chiefs, Billy Caldwell and Robinson. Seeing that they could not persuade her to leave home, they told her that she was a "brave," and that they would keep close to her. Accordingly, they brought over at nightfall, Wabuncia, a highly respected Indian chief who was well known to all the tribes, with his squaw and two other old bucks, to spend the night—saying that Wabuncia told the Sacs that "if either Black Hawk or Keokuk dared to molest Wabuncia's friend, the whole Potowatomi nation would rise against them." Of course they received a hearty welcome and a little fire water at the hand of the inmates of Wolf Tavern. The squaw and another Indian were given room in the hall, and Wabuncia and the other bucks squatted down on the porch. Here I may as well give Mr. Taylor's account of this night:

My wife and her little sister Julia and a hired man constituted our family. In the evening my brother Anson came and later on came Gillis—a rough customer nicknamed "Hardcase"—who had been driven out of the fort for drunkenness. This "recruit" I took into service for the war, on condition that he was to stand guard all night and that I should issue to him one quart of whiskey during the twenty-four hours. And so there were four of us, with two guns, an axe and a pitchfork. My wife was prepared for the worst with a sharp poniard or stiletto. I blockaded the doors, posted the sentinels and placed myself at a window, axe in hand, determined to defend my castle to the last.

Every hour I went the rounds to see the watchmen at their stations and to issue to Gillis his ration of whiskey—he muttered, "the hours seem devilish long." We were kept in a state of siege during two or three days and nights, during which we were joined by a brace of refugees with rifles.

But everything remained quiet except that on one night we heard a shot from our outpost on the prairie. "Hardcase" Gillis came in, puffing and blowing and reported that he had shot a redskin scout, adding that "no Indians couldn't fool me by grunting like a hog; they tried to fool me before when I was on a scout." Of course he wanted a gill of whiskey extra in reward for a dead Indian. And then he went on to state that while he was lying in the grass watching out, he heard something advancing towards him with mighty great caution: that he held fire until he could see his eyes, when he let off old "Sukey"—as he called his rifle—and that if we would go out thar with him, he would show us a dead Indian, sure as you're born.

It was agreed that a patrol should go with Gillis and myself to the spot. Meantime, the little garrison reserve were all on the alert. We advanced with due caution in dead silence. The dead "grunter" . . . proved to be a genuine porker, much to the merriment of all the party except Hardcase, who hung down his head with some discomfiture. Nevertheless, he soon recovered his wits, saying, "Wal, boys, I reckon I'll stand treat and I'll sit up with the corpse 'til mornin' agin the Injuns and wolves."

In June, generals Scott and [William] Worth arrived with troops on board the *William Penn*. Seventeen of the list had died of cholera on the way up, and fifty-two were stricken after landing. Two other boats with troops on board failed to arrive in time—possibly on account of the terrible disease. Detroit was suffering badly from the contagion. One could hear on the streets the shrieks of the dying, which I remember too well. The arrival of Scott with even so small a division of the army and more expected, put an end to all fears for the capture of the place, but the dreadful scourge they had introduced was perhaps more fatal than an attack by the savages might have been.

I may as well add here that another division of the regulars under Major Zachary Taylor had started from below for the Fox River country, and were soon to be heard from by runners. The Sacs (pronounced commonly "Saucks"), under Black Hawk, were numerous and brave enough to defy the volunteers in the absence of our little scattered army of regulars. The Foxes, who were supposed to be their allies, were but the remnants of the tribe that had besieged Detroit in older times. Their chief was old Keokuk, who, however, was not sporting for another fight. Black Hawk himself was not unfriendly to the Americans. Major Taylor had known him since 1822, and vouched for his good behavior up to the time when, after the removal of his tribe to the west of the Mississippi, where they were unfurnished with means and implements, and had come back to the Rock River annually to do their planting and raise their crops, and until the late quarrels with the settlers. It was the old story of bad faith, false promises, and no protection on the part of the government against encroachments of the pale faces.

General Scott's advance pacified the town, meantime, and as it turned out that the hostiles had not come within eighty miles of Chicago, our refugees, with their families, bedding, cattle and wagons, began to return homeward, fleeing from a still worse enemy, the cholera, which the troops had brought with them.

General Scott soon gained communication with, and possibly directed, Major Taylor. But the latter was the real hero of the campaign. His defeat and capture of Black Hawk at the battle of Ash Creek put an end to the war, and Black Hawk was brought in and taken round the country on what looked like an exhibition show. It was said that Eleazer Williams, of the Green Bay Mission (who afterwards claimed to be Louis XVII, the lost Dauphin of France), commanded Taylor's Indian scouts. He had distinguished himself in the War of 1812 as a scout for Macomb at the campaign of Plattsburg. . . . The question of his royal descent is one much discussed in these far later days of "Lazarre" stories and plays.

Mr. Taylor writes that early in the state of siege, Col. Bailey came down to command the volunteers, as the refugees began to call themselves, and one night the colonel saw fit to order an alarm in order to test the courage and alacrity of those who were gathered around the fort, without giving those at the tavern, now called Fort Wabuncia, any notice. "Next night, we returned the compliment in kind," says Mr. Taylor:

At midnight we began with war whoops and discharges of our firearms, followed this up with more Indian shouts and dances, and set a hay stack on fire. Then all was still. Of course there was a panic below among the people inside and outside of the fort, the troops drawn out and posted for defense. At day light the matter was inquired into by Maj. Wilcox, and a number of us were arrested and brought before him. But on account of the disorder prevailing, James Kinzie and myself were discharged from custody, and the others turned loose later on. Colonel Bailey was present at the court of inquiry, and looked rather sheep-faced. But Major Wilcox soon saw the humor of it.

During the war scare, the Indians were not the only source of anxiety. As many as fifty-seven refugees swooped down upon the house, hungry, thirsty and dirty, most of whom were clamorous for bed and board. They broke into the pantry and ransacked the kitchen and bed rooms. Few had brought with them bedding or other provisions, and they preyed upon our meagre little establishment like wolves, until the scare let up and rations were issued at the fort, upon requisitions of the governor of Illinois. As long as our means lasted, they were freely divided with these suffering families, but if one may judge of their sense of gratitude from the remarks of one querulous old woman, it was cheap at any price. "I hope

Black Hawk will catch Mrs. Taylor first one; she pretending to be such a boone (sic) and too proud to come and live at the fort like the rest of us." The old lady's indignation perhaps grew out of the circumstance that she had been refused quarters at the Wolf's nest, but simply for want of room.

"But what associations, to be sure, cluster round that log tavern," says Mrs. Taylor. "In that little house a Sunday School grew up, consisting of children of Julia's age, who gathered round our hymn book, and there in 1833 we first partook of communion and organized a church—the First Presbyterian—in the room where General Scott had taken his hasty plate of soup, prepared by my own hands, on his first landing, bringing with him so much joy and relief."

"How many hearts were made glad," continues Mrs. Taylor, "when it was heard that we were to be supplied with a permanent Minister of the Gospel, and we saw the little vessel dancing on the foam of Lake Michigan, which heralded the arrival of the Reverend Jeremiah Porter from Sault Ste. Marie. A place of worship was extemporized for the new pastor by Major [John] Fowle of the garrison, at a carpenter's shop, and his first sermon was from the words of the carpenter's son at Nazareth, 'Herein is my Father glorified that ye bear much fruit, so shall ye be my disciples.'"

By this time the prairie had become dotted with farm houses, and trains of covered wagons stretched on out of sight. Earliest of the settlers on the west, excepting James Kinzie, were the LaFramboise family, who were my relatives' [the Taylors's] only near neighbors for some time . . . until a bridge was built connecting them with the little business world on the south side, soon after the war when people began to flock in. But this was not until after the war, which first attracted public notice to our possibilities. The bridge just mentioned was a rickety affair, built by Anson Taylor, the roadway consisting of log puncheon, fastened to the stretchers by oak pins. It was quite a time before Mr. Taylor could secure lumber and mechanics for his own house. The nearest sawmill was at DuPage, but Mr. Taylor hired a few choppers, went into the woods himself and got out sufficient timber for the frame, which had time enough to spare for seasoning before the clapboards and shingles could be obtained. . . .

By the time I arrived in Chicago, in place of the memorable old log tavern there stood a three story frame building, a sky scraper for those times, Kinzie and Forsythe's store. The Wolf's Head, described in my sister's diary, and that swung its sign through the troubled seasons of war and cholera, had disappeared and become a legend. The "Anson Taylor bridge" had been destroyed by a sudden spring flood, and a new one supplied the missing link, where now many iron trestle bridges carry passengers over the Chicago where I shot muskrats.

JOURNAL ENTRIES, 1836–1841[25]

In the spring of 1836 I found a weak resolution to serve my God. I went to a meeting, headed by a Mr. Parker, and before the little part of the world there assembled around my purpose, I went boldly up to the front of the room, and raising my arm with all the pride that infested my weakness, I said aloud, "I am an Orphan, but will receive Christ for my father," and burst into womanish tears. God had melted my heart, but had not poured over the flowing mass the oil of his Grace and Heavenly strength. Consequently, I slowly backslided into "the world," and the effervescence soon died away.

Aside from the weakness of the stand I had taken, there were other causes to produce its downfall. I was proud, and never raised my humble prayer to God for *His* aid, but went on careless and heedless, and forgot in a short time the road I had undertaken to travel on. . . .

In the ensuing summer, my love for God was entirely swallowed up in the love of a mortal object. I flirted, made love, ridiculed religion, wrote sonnets, lost my peace of mind, took long evening walks, threw up my books and common sense, neglected business, looked grave at times, drank at the sweet fountain until I swelled up, went into the country to cool down, came back again, kissed Cupid, caught the fever & ague, was taken sick (and on my back two weeks), got well, came out, and found my faith flown away.

Thus ended the dream; but the reality came afterwards. The object of [my] sweet hopes had been sent abroad to school to break up the affair (for it had taken the wings of spreading scandal, and flown over the city), but she had promised to write me, and thus keep on our intercourse. In the full faith of this, I soon sent her a long, sweet, pithy, lover-like letter, but received in return a . . . confused little bit of a mass of nothing at all.

This species of cooing I had never been acquainted with, and forthwith the letter was consigned to the flame, and a strange coincidence is that the

25. The following entries are taken from OBW's earliest journal, titled simply *A Journal from April 16, 1823 to Oct. 2, 1840—and from That Time to* [title left unfinished]. The journal actually contains entries from the early 1840s (earlier entries obviously having been torn out) until 1850, with primary focus on OBW's years as a cadet at West Point. Referred to hereafter as OBW *West Point Journal.*

letter which ended this nice affair found its *grave* in the same place where my public resolutions to serve a greater than its author, found its *birth;* and one ended in flames, the other in "smoke." Thus I was left with love for neither; therefore it is but natural for me to say that Satan immediately found in me a willing votary.

During the winter I made it my business to *disturb singing schools,* and but one affair of that kind shall here find narration. A company of about twenty [the notorious Potato Band] went scattering along into a certain singing school, with the determination of raising a rumpus. A young man and myself were dressed in female apparel, and walked up to one of the front seats on the ladies' side of the house, and excited no little attention by our constant conversation, which was carried on with no want of dignity of speech or action. At the intervention where many began to gather around us, and we judged it no longer safe to remain, we started for the door, and when half way there, I raised a whistle to my mouth, and the shrill tones it sounded forth gave rise to a shout from my companions in glory that shook the church to its very foundation stones; and, while the conductors of the school were recovering from the surprise, astonishment, and confusion into which the affair had thrown them, we all made our escape in safety.

Other things of a similar nature occurred that winter which never have come to light, and upon which my mouth remains mute, and my pen chokes the tattling ink. Suffice to say, at one of them, in a singing school, I was arrested, tried at the mayor's court (March 11, '38), found guilty, and fined one dollar, together with the payment of the costs of the court. Of the justice, or the injustice of the verdict, I will not speak. But its effects upon me were good. I never regret that it happened. It awoke me from the torpor of apathy, under which I had long slumbered—leant me one chapter of human life—timely pointed me to the gates of woe—wound me against my course of conduct—showed me that I must begin to choose my path of life—spread myself before me, with all my defects—pointed to the fields of philosophy and at once let down the bars of indifference that I might walk therein.

Into those fields I stepped at once. I culled the sweetest flowers, drunk at the purest fountains, listened to the warbling of the most mellifluous birds, basked in the unclouded sun, rolled in the honey of disdain for custom and the world, walked in the smoothest paths and bathed in the cleanest waters; and at the end of a year found myself, alas, again at the bars of indifference, from which I first had started.

"Ah me," I cried, "whither shall I go. If I go back from whence I have just come, I shall find myself at the end of another year in the same spot where

I now stand, and though I may pass many hours of sweet bliss, I shall gain nothing at the end. But when the archer of the dead is ready to hurl his dart at me, I shall then be here, and he will slay without mercy the virtues of fruitless philosophy, and carry me to the regions of the damned." An evangelist then came to me and pointed up a long, "straight and narrow way," and said, "that leads to the realms of bliss beyond the grave. Come away from the bars of indifference, and walk ye in it."

I fain would have followed his directions, but a "still small voice" cried within me, "selfish mortal! think that the Lord of those realms will receive you after you find there is no *other* way, and make him your *last* resort? no! he will stamp the seal of condemnation upon your selfishness, and cry out, "why came ye not unto me at first? Depart ye cussed, into the regions ye fain would have dwelt in, prepared for Devils and such as ye."

I threw myself upon the ground, and tossed myself in agony, but growing cooler, I arose and turned again towards the bars of indifference. The evangelist again came unto me and said, "why goest thou not up, what is there to impede thy progress?"

"Selfishness," I groaned, "base, damning selfishness."

"Bend thy knees," he replied, "and ask the intercession of the great Redeemer; tell him your woes, and you will soon be healed; ask of him, for he saith, 'seek and ye shall find,' and he will open up the way."

I did. I prayed, I besought, I entreated till I sweat with agony, but not till I scalded myself with tears did he come down to answer my petition. But oh, then such sweet joy I found in him, that made me look back with disgust and abhorrence upon the fields I had just left, and gird up my waist to commence the straight and narrow path.

And so I went "on my way rejoicing." Yes, what I have expressed in figures is all true, and on the first day of November, 1840, I united myself to Christ's visible church (under Mr. Geo. Duffield), and hope, and believe my name is registered on the bright pages of His invisible Church above; and after all, there is more true, and substantial *philosophy* in religion than in all the systems laid down by those that have been called the most profound philosophers of the human heart. . . .

1841

March 22d

This day Mrs. Hutchins, the wife of my employer, went "the way of all the earth.". . .

23d

I was impressed with a remark of the sexton to-day, who, while plough-ing his way through the mud to the graveyard, to oblige me with the choice of a lot, said on my apologising for the trouble I was causing him, "that is not a trouble which comes within the sphere of my duty."

24th

While the funeral train was wending its way to the grave yard, I could not but liken the one who drove the first train to the head man of the nation: for we followed him through his various course in such a manner, as that when he drove through ditches, we followed, and when he drove on the dry ground we did likewise; consequently he was responsible for the whole procession.

Now the President has just as much means of doing good or harm in his country as had the sexton in the funeral train. He is the great sexton of the political, and moral procession, always in motion in this republic. If he leads to prosperity over a smooth road, he is a good "sexton." If he leads over a broken, rugged, or miry way, to adversity and ruin, he is not fit for his charge; and in both cases he is liable not only for himself, but for the whole State. . . .

[April] 5th

I have this day chosen for my motto, "Always be moderate," and I think I can find no better garment to wrap around the "Bundle of Life."

April 10th
God will sustain us.

Last evening I went to a prayer meeting of the young men, held after the stores were closed. All were expected to make a prayer, and being aware of this I felt very anxious about the one I should make. I did not feel myself capable of praying before others, in an edifying manner, and therefore was afraid to make the attempt.

While the others were praying, I endeavored to think of what I should say, and how I should say it; and my heart almost sunk within me when I discovered to myself that even this was sinful. Then I almost made up my mind to decline when called upon for my prayer. But when my turn came, I could not well decline, but with a voice faint and choked with despondency and agitation, I raised my supplication to little above a whisper and pro-ceeded. But before I had prayed a minute, I felt strengthened, and the wants and wishes of the little band of petitioners soon came into my mind, and were disburdened in a solemn, warm, humble, and affectionate manner. I know my prayer was interesting; and grateful for my unexpected success, I arose from my knees, feeling that none other than God had sustained me.

WHAT A CHANGE!

I knew a major in the army when quite a child, who often was at our house, and sometimes took notice of me. I knew a proud ex-major when I first came into this store, that used to come in, ranting and swearing, to buy brandy! He knew me, but did not deign to recognize me. I was a poor clerk in a store! That accounted for it.

I knew a man whom sickness had brought low, and had awakened to a sense of his unworthiness before God. He recovered. One day he came into the store—a Christian—he took me by the hand, and calling me by the name by which he often had called me in my childhood, he enquired of my health. What a change indeed! While a man of the world, proud, profane, and haughty; when a man of Christ, meek, condescending, considerate and kind! That man is Major Forsyth. . . .[26]

May 5th

This day I have witnessed a scene more sickening to my soul than any I had ever witnessed before. Being on one of the back streets of the city, I chanced to see two ladies of my acquaintance, bearing some dishes in their hands, enter a wretched looking house. I supposed at once that they were on some visit of charity, and, imagining that they might need some assistance, I followed them into the place.

Upon getting into the room, I started back at the discovery of a corpse. The room was destitute of the meanest furniture (aside from a bed stead, and an empty cupboard) and 7 or 8 children, begrimed with dirt, and clothed in rags, were crawling around the floor.

Upon the bed stead lay a dying woman, groaning in pain, and at her side stood an aged nurse and the two ladies, endeavoring to comfort the dying one's last moments by the words of hope and consolation. In the upper room of the house lay another woman, probably in her dying agonies. The family had but just buried one of their number, who had sickened and died in the space of a very short time.

26. Maj. Robert A. Forsyth, a former paymaster in the U.S. Army, served for a time on the staff of Gov. Lewis Cass and was a longtime resident of Detroit. Forsyth, who was "widely known" in Detroit and "universally popular," was fond of horses; in winter he could often be seen racing his sleigh on the Detroit River, or up and down Jefferson Ave. One of his competitors was a young captain stationed in Detroit following the Mexican War—Ulysses S. Grant.

The inmates of this house were colored people, who had just come into the city; and apparently they had come to meet death half way in [their] journey; but they were meeting the "Grim Tyrant" with the hope of religion sitting upon their brows. I could not but feel differently towards them than if they had been white people. Pain and misery seemed more lenient towards them than towards the whites, as if they commiserated the misfortune of their color.

I have a very strange disposition, and it seems sometimes, as though I was not at all fitted to *enjoy* this life, but rather a life to come. And then again I think I never can become fitted for the Abode of the Blessed, as I am so inconsistent in my conduct, and so wickedly rash in most of my actions. And I do not know what I should do, were I left alone to work my own way, by *my* good deeds, to the Kingdom of God, as I certainly could never pursue even an equal amount of meritorious conduct to balance the evil to which my heart is prone.

How dear then ought Christ be to me; for it is through him alone that I shall reach (if I ever do) the Kingdom of God. Oh tell me not that there was no need of an atonement; without it who would have a hope of Heaven? But with it, who, that takes advantage of its means, has not the hope of eternal life?

I feel the value of this thing the more I reflect upon it. I never could reach Heaven through my own merit. Why suppose I make the will of God; what saves me from his wrath? My own good deeds, that were before, or afterwards committed? God tells me not so. But, He says, thou shalt not sin against my holy laws. Here is the command; now when I break it, am I not exposed to its penalties? How then shall I escape; by what I have done which is not against his will? He says thou shalt love thy neighbor as thyself, and suppose I do so; but at the same time, refuse to love God, which He commands me to do also. Shall the *obedience* to one law afford excuse for the *disobedience* of another? If so, then the *disobedience* of the one law takes away all the merit of *obedience* to the other, for it is a "poor rule that will not work both ways." But through the merit of the atonement, Christ steps in, and by pardoning the *disobedience*, makes the *obedience* acceptable unto God, and in consequence of *that*, my soul is saved.

But where is that love which is so justly due Christ from me? I can talk of it, and write about [it], but is it in my heart? Oh no. I fear there is more love for Christ on my pen, and at the end of my tongue, than in the bottom of my heart. I am one of those beings who can only feel when they talk, and are talked to, and only think when they write. Oh I wish that the love of Christ was the predominant feeling of my heart; then I could think of it, and feel it at all times.

By-the-way: I am not much of a thinker. To be sure, I catch up an idea, sometimes, and hold it [in] my mind a few moments, but I do not look beyond the surface, to see of what it is composed; but rather, hold it as a child holds a toy in his hand, for a moment looks at it, and then throws it away. Sometimes I may *catch* myself in deep reflection, but no sooner do I find that I am truly there, than I turn my thoughts to thinking over whatever I may have been reflecting about, without pursuing the subject itself any farther. I drop it not because of a wish to do so, but because I am unable to reconnect the chain of my ideas; at least until I become unaware of what I am thinking, and then, perchance, my mind runs from a sort of *void* into the contemplation of the subject.

It *is* possible for a man to become unaware of what he is thinking. For when a man is taken up with a subject, he is so lost to everything else, that the subject will exercise all the powers of his mind. For as a man cannot entertain two ideas in his mind at the same time, so he cannot think of one subject, and think at the same time that he is reflecting upon that subject; for when he turns his mind from the subject to his thoughts of the subject, he surely thinks of his own thoughts, and not of the subject itself. . . .

But this difficulty only impedes my meditations while I am not committing them to paper. When I write down my ideas, I am led on by one idea to another thro' the whole subject, in a sort of connection, and I can bear the interruptions which are occasioned by writing, the occasional abstraction of my mind from my subject, because I always have something before me, which comes from that which I have just written, or from a sort of knowledge—no matter how imperfect—of the principal parts of my subject. In this way I go on and write, either until my subject is exhausted, or my knowledge of it put to use, or until I become fatigued. . . .

June 23, 1841

This day I commenced to ask a blessing at the table of my mother's family. The thing was suggested to me by one of the boarders yesterday, and it was most joyfully acceded to on my part. It was very affecting to all, and my mother and sister were obliged to leave the room, so overcome were they with their feelings, and so fast flowed the tears from their eyes. It must have been very affecting indeed.

Woman is like the wasp, which is the most restless, graceful, and in its sting the most painful of the insect tribes. . . .

I can conceive of nothing in nature that has such a thrilling influence over me as *woman*. It seems, sometimes, when I am about to approach her, as if my whole soul and mind were bound together and struggling to burst from me; now I feel a pressure at my brain, and now at my heart; and when I enter into conversation with her, it seems as though all but a little mental strength had left me, and as if that little was in the utmost confusion. My tongue becomes clogged; my ideas are all absorbed in one great feeling, either to please her, or in the contemplation of some vague, uncouth, uncomprehensible idea concerning myself, and I can feel the blushes stealing even through my brain!

Detroit, July 10, 1841

I, O. B. Willcox, do hereby declare my fixed resolution never to partake of more sweet meats than is reasonable, as the same has been the means and perhaps I may say the only means of all my ill health for a year or two past.

O. B. Willcox

What an infinite idea a foolish man has of himself! I sometimes think that were *I* placed in certain situations, I could surpass all the greatest men of the world, in the glory and grandeur of my actions! I scarcely ever read the life of an Alexander or a Solon without being inflated with the idea of my ability to soar far far beyond them! But, perhaps, just there, a little, though perhaps uncontrolable failing will bring itself into my mind, and all my vanity is dashed into fleeting vapour, which soon flies away; and then, again, I remember of having read that the greatest men thought themselves the meanest, and from the sense of my own emptyness arises the thought that I certainly must be something, or I would not thus think so meanly of myself at times! Thus I reason myself into these foolish ideas of my ability; thus are they dashed to vapours; and thus do I console myself.

There is nothing in nature so inconsistent as man, and the best way for an individual to cure himself of inconsistency is to arm himself with a perfect knowledge of himself, and to have a complete control over all his actions. The latter he can acquire by the assistance of God in a short time; but as the form requires a whole life, I propose to myself the following question:

How may a man obtain a knowledge of himself in the earliest and most perfect manner?

Ans[wer]: 1st By comparing himself with others.
          2d By carefully observing all his actions, and the motives from which they proceed.

3d Trouble will show a man what he is if he will choose to look at himself. In order to detect the different colors of light, it is necessary to darken the rooms. So the false glare of prosperity may prevent our finding ourselves out, but the shades of adversity enable us to distinguish the different parts of which our characters are composed.

4th Religion is the best touchstone of all.

There is a pleasure arising from an intercourse with the learned great that far surpasses all other social enjoyment, to the mind of one the least fond of literature. Communion with the opposite sex, I will allow, is productive of much happiness, but it is transient; and but too soon it fixes upon the mind a feeling too romantic for the business of life in any occupation, except indeed that of a poet. . . .

Though the communion of the opposite sex has a great effect in cheering our spirits, and even sometimes *electrifying* our very soul, yet it is but a flash and in a moment all is gone. But in an intercourse with men of literary parts whom we respect, in consequence of the light that is thrown upon our minds thereby, our soul is lifted up more and more under its serene and pleasing influence, and . . . it changes the whole manner of our mind for the better, and for the happier. This change is permanent in most cases. So place me in whatever circumstances you may, but only give me the enjoyment of intercourse with the literary part of the community, and be I brute or savage, and that very intercourse makes me a man.

West Point: "No Gate of Heaven"

[Shortly after reaching his eighteenth birthday, Orlando Willcox, like so many other young men his age, was faced with the prospect of planning for a future career. Though, as he later wrote, "My first desire in life was to be a preacher," he also began to think in terms of a military career.[1] The latter choice no doubt had its origins in the associations Willcox had had with the veterans of the Revolution and the War of 1812, though the reality of the prospect grew when he learned that he might be able to land an appointment to the United States Military Academy at West Point.

Faced now with a difficult choice that would determine the course of the rest of his life, Willcox "sought the advice of the old pastor of our church— Mr. Duffield—as to whether I should become a minister or a soldier, and after hearing me through, he advised me to become a soldier."

Realizing that Willcox's long-held ambition to become a minister had a firmer foundation in pleasing his mother than in serving the church, the kindly old cleric, displaying a high degree of common sense, advised the boy to become a soldier. "There would appear in this advice something inconsistent with religion," Willcox later wrote, "but it is not so." Reverend Duffield pointed out that "West Point would afford me a good education, without expense to my mother; and as an officer has many opportunities of doing good, both my education and position would enable me to be a useful Christian."

1. See chapter 6, page 173, for OBW's full entry concerning his discussion with Rev. Duffield.

And so it was that, on January 19, 1843, Willcox arrived in the muddy little town that was the nation's capital, seeking an appointment to West Point. After ten long days on the road he was "tired, sleepy & essentially knocked up," but full of bright hopes for the future.[2] The next day—defying all convention in such matters—he would set out to secure his appointment: he would go to see the president. The appointment would come (after a good deal of logrolling on his part), but Willcox would find West Point more of a stumbling block to his good intentions than a young man his age could withstand.]

MY FIRST visit to Washington was made more than sixty years ago, and resulted in a very important change in the course of my life. It was undertaken by me for the purpose of securing an appointment as a cadet at West Point. In this I was successful, under difficult conditions, and the final result has been that Washington has been my place of residence at different times, and under varying circumstances for many years.

The trouble I experienced was through the breach between President [John] Tyler and the Whigs in Congress. My mother and myself had received assurances from the recently elected Senator from Michigan, William Woodbridge.[3] His family were among our warmest friends and neighbors in Detroit. The other Senator was Augustus S. Porter,[4] while the state's only member of the lower house was Jacob M. Howard[5] (afterwards U.S. senator), a lawyer of ability and a quasi friend of our family. Mrs. Senator Woodbridge was a daughter of John Trumbull, the once eminent author of *M'Fingal*.[6] My sister Julia was named after this lady, Julia Ann Trumbull.

The winter of 1842–3 had set in severely when Senator Woodbridge wrote us a letter at Detroit saying that the Michigan delegation in Congress had broken off from President Tyler and that if I wanted an appointment to West Point, as he knew I did, I had best come on to Washington at once, as

2. OBW *West Point Journal*, entry for Jan. 19, 1843.

3. William Woodbridge (1780–1861), secretary and acting governor of the Territory of Michigan, 1814–1828; Territorial delegate to Congress, 1819–1820; delegate to the Michigan constitutional convention, 1835; U.S. senator (Whig), 1838–1839, 1841–1847; governor, 1840–1841.

4. Augustus S. Porter (1798–1872), U.S. senator from Michigan (Whig), 1839–1845.

5. Jacob M. Howard (1805–1871). Born in Shaftsbury, Vermont, Howard moved to Detroit in 1832, where he undertook the practice of law. Active in Whig politics, he served in the state legislature in 1838 and in the U.S. Congress from 1841 to 1843. Joining the Republican Party at its inception, Howard was elected to the U.S. Senate in 1862, serving the Radical Republican cause until his death in 1871. He was one of the few people whom OBW held in open contempt.

6. John Trumbull, *M'Fingal: An Epic Poem in Four Cantos* (M. Carey, 1791).

the delegation had no influence with the President. I started at once, in the warmest wraps I could get, for Cumberland, Maryland—then the nearest railway town. I was bundled off in a stage coach by way of Toledo. My ticket secured me a back seat, but, giving way to one new passenger after another, I was transferred to the middle, then to the front, and finally to a seat with the driver outside, who was civil enough to say "you never can kill a boy."

This last outrage occurred in the woods crossing the Allegheny mountains where the cold wind blew big guns. But notwithstanding this rough experience, I arrived safely at my destination and secured a comfortable room at Willard's, the principal hotel of the city. It was a squatty building of two or three stories. My little chamber was on the second floor and there I was foolish enough to deposit all the money I had brought along, some one hundred dollars, and during one of my log-rolling expeditions at the Capitol or White House, "every room on the floor was pilfered"—or so said the clerk on my return. On rushing up to my room with Bull Run racing speed, in a panic as you may imagine, I became equally astonished and delighted to find my trunk intact and the money safe. Of course, like a good boy, I fell on my knees and thanked my Heavenly Father.

Washington was then a place of even more magnificent distances than it is now, particularly as the chief conveyance from end to end was Shank's Mare, with an occasional omnibus lift over the cobblestone pavements of Pennsylvania Avenue between the White House and the Capitol. I remember but one house on the south side and that was Hancock's oyster shop, and this I recall chiefly because I there enjoyed the delicious bivalve fresh from its native salty rocks. It stood near the present site of the City Post Office and still does the same business.

On the opposite side of the avenue stretched along a number of shops, offices, etc.—the business part of the town. Among the offices, that of the *Globe*, the Democratic organ, edited by the venerable but not over good-looking head of the Blair family,[7] easily caricatured, and that of the *National*

7. Francis P. Blair, Sr. (1791–1876), editor of the Washington *Globe*, a Democratic newspaper, from 1830 to 1854. Born in Virginia and raised in Kentucky, Blair had owned slaves himself but was nonetheless committed to maintaining the Union. A personal friend and political advisor of Andrew Jackson, he opposed South Carolina during the nullification crisis of 1832. When the Republican Party was formed, however, Blair joined it, and at the Chicago convention of 1860 he supported Lincoln for the presidential nomination. Exercising his tremendous political influence, Blair continued to advise Lincoln throughout the war, supporting both the Emancipation Proclamation and colonization efforts. His son, Montgomery Blair, served in Lincoln's cabinet as postmaster general. Francis P. Blair, Jr., served as a senator from Missouri and brigadier general.

Intelligencer, Gales and Seaton,[8] editors and proprietors. Both papers were of national and international interest. The *Evening Star* came next, some ten years later, at first printed on the single side of an eight-by-ten-inch sheet.

While on the subject of structures of that day I may as well say that there were a few decent buildings at the west of the city, particularly on G Street south—among them the Octagon, into which President and brave Dolley Madison had moved after the sack of the White House in 1812. This house still stands in equally as good—perhaps in better—shape, and is occupied by the Architect's Club. There were some others on that side of the avenue, while some, perhaps many, others stood on H Street northwest, and were occupied by officers and clerks of the War and Navy Departments, with their charming families.

Further down stood the Treasury and Patent Office buildings with dwelling houses, principally north of Pennsylvania Avenue. The property on the avenue, south, from the Treasury to the Capitol, which space speculators of early days expected would form the heart of the rising city, was pretty much vacant. But there were numerous and fairly good dwellings all round Capitol Hill—mostly, but with some notable exceptions, boarding houses, and here most of the senators, members and clerks of the two houses lodged. The Kirkwood, on the site of the present Raleigh, was the nearest hotel.

But to business. Of course my first duty and pleasure was "to see the Governor," as we still called Senator Woodbridge, and from him to learn the ropes. He advised me to see the President the first thing, urging me at the same time to "make friends" with the negro messenger who dominated the hall and doors of the President's reception room.

I introduced myself early to this so-called "public functionary," and told him of my travels in the stage coach, etc., and what I had come for.

"Gor Almighty!" he exclaimed, "you come alone all the way from Michigan to see the President! Boy, you see the men (he did not say "gentlemen") sitting around dar. They are senators and members [of Congress], but they can wait. Some of 'em will never see him. You shall see Massa Tyler fust of all."

This was my first successful *coup-de-main*. But what was to follow? On being ushered into the great presence with more or less trepidation, I found President Tyler to be a tall, slender gentleman, with pleasant blue eyes and light hair, a prominent nose, denoting decision, if not obstinacy of char-

8. Joseph Gales (1786–1860) and William W. Seaton (1785–1866) were editors of the *National Intelligencer* for forty-eight years. The *Intelligencer,* one of the premier Washington papers, became a daily in 1813, supporting the Whig party.

acter, as I have since thought, and bland, kindly Virginia manners, such as those of the Masons and other Virginia families we had known at home.

After hearing my little story and stating the main object of my visit, the President smiled at my allusion to the status of the Michigan delegation. But he took my hand and said: "My young friend, I will do the best I can for you." My heart leaped into my mouth so I could scarcely speak, as I withdrew from the august presence, shook hands with my kind darkey stage manager—as you may call him—and skipped down stairs "Boston times," thinking the game as good as won.

On the same day I took some letters from my lucky trunk and called on Mrs. General Alexander Macomb,[9] wife of the Commanding General of the army, with a letter from one of my mother's Detroit friends, either Mrs. Major Biddle, or Mrs. Major Whiting of the army—I forgot which lady.

The Macomb mansion was one of the few pretentious houses in the western part of the city. It stood on the corner of what are now Seventeenth and I streets. It was afterwards occupied as my own headquarters towards the close of the Confederate war, and subsequently known as the University Club.

The Macombs, by the way, were an old Detroit family and Mrs. Macomb had known my mother and all about us. She treated me quite civilly and at once put me on a new trail. It seems that the father of her niece, Miss Eliza Wilson, was chief clerk in the office of the Chief of Engineers, General Totten,[10] who had charge of the whole West Point Academy business. Through that office all the cadet appointments were issued.

Miss Eliza being now at home with her aunt, I was duly introduced to the charming girl. She gave me a note to her father, whom I promptly called upon at his office next morning, finding him also very civil and courteous, and inclined to "aid me all he could in my quest," giving me the *modus operandi*, in other words, "the ropes," for securing appointments to the Academy, the main strand of which was that the M. C. from every district made the

9. Gen. Alexander Macomb (1782–1841). A native of Detroit, Macomb entered the army as a cornet of cavalry in 1799. Earning rapid promotion, Macomb served as colonel of the 3d Artillery during the War of 1812, seeing action at Niagara and Fort George. Promoted to brigadier general in 1814, he defeated British forces at Plattsburg, New York, in September 1814, driving them back to Canada and earning promotion to major general. In 1828 Macomb was made general in chief of the army. His last service was in the Seminole campaign of 1835. He died in Washington, D.C., on June 25, 1841.

10. Joseph G. Totten (1788–1864) (3d, USMA 1805), was at the time a colonel and the chief engineer of the army. He had served on the Niagara frontier during the War of 1812, and as Gen. Winfield Scott's chief engineer during the Mexican War. During the Civil War he supervised the construction of the Washington defenses.

"nomination," which of itself would secure the appointment, leaving little or no action on the part of the President himself except in the appointments "at large," or under some rare and peculiar circumstance. Mr. Wilson added: "Perhaps General Totten may be able to give you some good advice how to proceed," and thereupon he took me in and introduced me to the General himself, whom I found very courteous, kind and well disposed. He confirmed Mr. Wilson's information, adding "the sooner you see Mr. Howard, the better. There may be other applicants," and this he said significantly.

The General and the whole Totten family proved life-long friends. . . . The General's office was in the old War department. This and the Navy Department were about where the handsome marble buildings now stand, just west of the White House. But the former were rather squatty buildings of brick and stucco, something like our old South Barracks at West Point.

As soon as possible after my interview with General Totten, I started downtown to report proceedings to "the Governor." . . . Not finding him at home, I climbed the hill to the Senate chamber and finding from the door-keeper that he was not present, but probably on duty in some committee room, I went to the gallery to survey, as I often afterward did, the august Senate of that historic period.

I still hear several of the Senators in my mind's eye. Many were most striking figures. On the extreme left stood Senator John C. Calhoun,[11] speaking in an animated manner. His was a rather short and slim figure, crowned by long, disheveled hair—like most Southern men of the day— beneath which his dark eyes fairly burned with excitement. His gestures were not ungraceful, and his voice, although somewhat shrill, was softened by southern intonation.

I think he was followed first by Henry Clay,[12] who rose from his seat not far from the Clerk's desk. He was a taller man than Calhoun and not quite so thin, with blue eyes, long, lanky hair and a silver-tongued oratory. . . .

11. Sen. John C. Calhoun (1782–1850), vice president under John Quincy Adams and again under Andrew Jackson. In 1832 he became the first vice president to resign from office when, as leader of the nullification controversy, he became alienated from President Jackson. As U.S. senator from South Carolina, Calhoun became the leader of the "fire-eaters" and the states rights movement. One of the great orators of his day, Calhoun, along with Daniel Webster and Henry Clay, was part of the "Great Triumvirate" of the Senate.

12. Henry Clay (1777–1852), of Kentucky had served in the U.S. House of Representatives intermittently from 1811 to 1825. He and John C. Calhoun persuaded the south of the necessity to declare war on Great Britain in 1812, and he later served as one of the commissioners at the Treaty of Ghent in 1814, ending the war. Elected to the Senate in 1831, he served there until 1842 and again from 1849 until his death. Though defeated numerous times in his bid for the presidency, Clay was a powerful figure in Congress, where his efforts at mediation earned him the nickname the "Great Compromiser."

Speaking of orators, is it not queer that none of our greatest orators have ever achieved the Presidency, not even Daniel Webster,[13] the Hercules of them all? "The God-like Daniel" was not a Senator at the time of my first visit, being then Secretary of State. But I was reminded of him by the violent speech uttered by Mr. McDuffie,[14] Calhoun's colleague, sitting by that great man's side. I never before or since have heard such a torrent of invective. . . .

Perhaps the most impressive-looking man in the Senate chamber at the time was Thomas H. Benton,[15] a man of great height and corresponding amplitude, sitting on the left of the Clerk's desk. When he rose to speak, it was on some question concerning the acquisition and settlement of the Oregon territory. He looked like "some tall cliff that lifts its awful form, swells from the gale and midway leaves the storm," as the poet alone could express it. But he spoke in the minor key, perhaps you might say in a rumbling tone. From the tenor of the debate I fancy that the question of bringing into the Union new and free territory from the West had already aroused the South.

On my visit to the lower House I had the pleasure of listening to both Caleb Cushing and ex-President John Quincy Adams.[16] Cushing was attacking Tyler, but the venerable Quincy Adams was up on another subject— the right of petition. Both were Whig champions. Cushing's oratory fell far below that of either Clay or Calhoun. It was perhaps on a level with that of our late lamented President McKinley, or on second thought nearer to Joe Cannon's.[17]

13. Daniel Webster (1782–1852) served as secretary of state under presidents William Henry Harrison and John Tyler, 1841–1845, and again under Millard Fillmore, 1850. It was as the Whig senator from Massachusetts, however, that Webster achieved his greatest renown as the preeminent champion of the Union.

14. George McDuffie (1790–1851), Democratic representative and senator from South Carolina. Served as governor of South Carolina, 1834–1836, and U.S. representative, 1821–1834; elected to the Senate to fill the vacancy created by the resignation of W. C. Preston; reelected to the Senate 1842–1846.

15. Thomas Hart Benton (1782–1858). Powerful Democratic senator from Missouri from 1821 to 1851 and U.S. representative from 1853 to 1855. His daughter Jesse became the wife of John C. Frémont.

16. Caleb Cushing (1800–1879) was then Whig representative from Massachusetts, though he became a Democrat in 1843, the year President Tyler appointed him U.S. commissioner to China. He served as a general during the Mexican War.

John Quincy Adams (1767–1848). The sixth U.S. president, 1825–1829, served eight terms in the House of Representatives, 1831–1848, being the only former president to serve in Congress.

17. Joseph Gurney Cannon (1836–1926). As U.S. representative from Illinois, Cannon served twenty-three terms in Congress. He was Speaker of the House from 1903 to 1911 and

The speech of the "Old Man Eloquent" Adams, who was standing, or rather walking, up and down the middle aisle, flourishing his arms, and gushing forth in torrents of invectives, [struck] me as a small but violent edition of the remarks of the junior Senator from South Carolina.

If it be thought strange that I, a boy of nineteen, should have taken so much interest in and cherished so long the incidents of those Congressional proceedings, I may add that from my school boy days I had been fond of declamations, and from service as page in the first State Legislature of Michigan I already knew something of legislative proceedings. I regret that I cannot recall more of the politics of that day—I hate politics—but now all I remember is that they were awfully "mixed."

One reason, and perhaps the chief reason, for the exciting debate over Oregon and the expansion of those days was the recent visit of Dr. [Marcus] Whitman[18] to Washington. Whitman was an enterprising missionary who had pushed on beyond Vancouver, and established a flourishing missionary colony among the Cayuses at Walla Walla. His object now was to warn the government authorities that the English were pushing into Oregon, and unless opposed in time, that they would soon occupy its broad rivers and beautiful valleys in a climate as delightful as the Garden of Eden. . . .

But let me return to the personal part of my story. I found our Representative member from Michigan, Mr. Howard, on whom now all my chances depended, anything but gushing in his welcome, particularly after I had explained the object of my visit. "Oh!, yes, Willcox," he said, "I'll do all I can but I don't see why I must do it all," whereupon he sat down and wrote a formal letter to the President, or Chief of Engineers, for which I thanked him with a boy's fervor. Without stopping to look at the letter, I trotted off to General Totten's office and handed him the document. After reading it over the good General exclaimed: "Why sir, this is not a nomination—but I'll fix it," whereupon he endorsed it as follows: "I desire the within to be considered as a formal nomination of young Willcox for the cadetship."

---

was serving in that capacity at the time OBW penned this memoir. Cannon's domineering role as Speaker led Congress to pass a resolution in 1910 limiting the powers of his office.

18. Dr. Marcus Whitman (1802–1847) was indeed one of the most influential of the early missionaries to the American West, taking both the Christian faith and medicine to the Indians. Whitman, through his writing, called attention to the fertility and resources of the Oregon Territory, and he accompanied the first train of emigrants to cross the continent. Whitman, however, met a tragic end when an outbreak of measles proved fatal to numerous Cayuse Indians in the fall of 1847. When Whitman's medicine proved ineffectual, the Cayuse suspected him of poisoning them. Whitman, his wife, and fourteen others of his party were massacred on November 29, 1847. Whitman College (at Walla Walla) and Whitman County were later named in his honor.

After two more visits to our Representative, I had the good fortune to have things put in proper form and, the main purpose of my first campaign in Washington being accomplished, I bade farewell to Senator Woodbridge and the distinguished Chief of Engineers and prepared to start for home.

I cannot refrain from the surmise that Mr. Howard's reluctance to my appointment may have been, and probably was, due to the fact that a son of Harry Cole, of Detroit, was likewise a candidate. I surmise this from the reason that young Porter Cole was actually appointed a year afterwards.

During my stay here at that time, I became well acquainted with Matthew Saint Clair Clarke, Clerk of the House. He held the office several years and I became also well acquainted in the course of time with his family. His son, Johnny, was afterwards appointed cadet at West Point and was consigned to my friendly care. But he was too fond of play, and failed. Mr. Clarke's oldest daughter married our beloved and distinguished assistant in drawing, Dick Smith.[19] With another daughter, Miss Annie, I fell violently in love. (Of course) she married a better man, General Franklin of the Engineers.[20] None of the family are living. The Franklins both died at Hartford. Alas, almost all of my old contemporaries have passed to the "other side."

It is unnecessary for me to recount my enjoyment of my first trip through the Hudson Highlands, nor the pleasure I felt at my actual landing at West Point [June 12, 1843], the first step in a military career. My transports were suddenly interrupted by an orderly who abruptly demanded our names and took us in convoy, like prisoners, to the library building, passing by the way the old antediluvian North and South Barracks and some spruce cadets who eyed us queerly, as if we had come to the feast in strange garments, but who made no audible comments. But we were hailed from the Barracks by others, in a jocular way, as plebes "just come down" as it were on a raft or something primitive, at which our orderly snickered, but we could not see where the joke came in, as we were decently dressed, to say the least. The appearance of an officer put an end to our first taste of "devilling."

The soldier guided us into an office, where a most courteous, old and now well-remembered clerk, with an Irish accent, Mr. O'Maher (Tim), received our names and residences and entered them in a descriptive book. Then the soldier said "about face," and marched us up to the commandant, a tall,

19. Lt. Richard S. Smith (30th, USMA 1834), drawing instructor at West Point.

20. Annie Clarke, to whom OBW refers as "A.L.C." in his journals; William B. Franklin (1st, USMA 1843), would become a prominent figure in the Army of the Potomac during the Civil War, rising from brigade command to command of Burnside's Left Grand Division at Fredericksburg. He died at Hartford, Connecticut, on March 8, 1903.

West Point on the Hudson as it appeared when OBW first arrived. *USMA Library*.

impulsive captain, who brusquely said: "South Barracks, Company D," and thus labelled and consigned, we entered our quarters. It was a seven-by-nine room with two little iron bed steads, wash stands and chairs, and lockers for our under-clothing and future uniforms. As for our present "cits clothes," they were destined to be soon returned to civil life, on the backs of fellows who had failed in their examinations, and the furlough men.

This disposition of our surplus belongings gained us the good will and friendly advice of the fellows, which enabled us to settle down with some tranquility to learn the ropes. Towards evening a drum was beaten and echoed by the call of a cadet non-commissioned officer, standing in front of our quarters: "New cadets! turn out for parade." New cadets! Ah, then, we were not mere "things," as one of the wicked imps called us on the way across the plain.

"Fall-in, two ranks" was the next order, and we were marched out on the plain, led by a corporal with stripes on his arms, assisted by two other corporals on our "flanks." The business of the latter gentlemen seemed to be to make things lively by frequent commands falling on wounded ears, quickening awkward feet. "Close up there! Keep step! Hep, hep, hep!" But in a few minutes things came easier, and we were drawn up in line at parade rest and had the exquisite pleasure of seeing our first dress parade, hearing a fine band on the lovely plain, and listening to the echoes of the sunset gun rolling up from Fort Put[nam] to Cro'Nest and "over the hills and far away."[21]

Marching to supper at the mess hall followed, and then a half hour of release from quarters, which gave me an opportunity to see my old school fellows, James Snelling[22] and Henry B. Clitz. They seemed more amused than surprised by the account of our reception, and gave greetings and advice in exchange for news from home. Thus came the evening of my first day at the military academy. I felt taken down several inches from the giddy finale when I left home.

At call to quarters we went at our arithmetic, geography, etc., for examination purposes until tattoo and taps, when lights were out and we jumped into bed. Then came a rap on the door by a cadet officer, looking in to see if all were present and accounted for. We dropped asleep, uncertain whether we were to be dragged out of bed, or hung at the windows.

First call for reveille next morning afforded us barely time to slip on our clothes, tumble out for roll call and begin the second day. I need not follow the routine further, but I often wonder what became of Joe, shoe-black. He never forgot to give the plebe his first touch of tactics. I noticed that he did not blacken the rear end of my shoes and I told him so. "A soldier never looks at his heels," he said. That was the first and last liberty any of the "bums," as the common soldiers are called, ever took with the cadets. On the contrary, once fairly known as cadets in uniform, we were treated with marked civility by officers and men. Reciprocally, the first lesson one learns at West Point is that you must be a gentleman.

After study and recitation hours, the "plebes" were drilled by themselves and not assigned to companies until going into camp—by which time it became known who had passed examinations; the rest were "found" and

21. OBW later remembered the evening parade at the academy, in unpublished revisions of his semiautobiographical short story "West Point: A Tale":

Who that ever witnessed the lovely scene can ever forget it: the precise yet quite nimble march of those boys in white pants, the notes of the band floating over the plain, the setting sun, the evening gun reverberating among the hills that once looked down on Washington with their steadfast gaze and divine faith. As the last [sounds] die away with the vesper cannon, the line breaks, the companies wheel off, the band strikes up anew, and with a quick, light-hearted step, the young soldiers march back. It is one of the prettiest movements known, that wheeling into an apparent maze and quickly unfolding into order and vanishing like [visions] of the northern lights in the heavens.

22. James G. Snelling (24th, USMA 1845), died at Cincinnati, Ohio, in 1855.

sent to their homes.[23] One of these gentry is reported to have said to his mother: "Behold your son who was lost and am found"—now an old gag.

By this time also the "plebes" of the preceding year became third classmen. Some of them were our corporals, and felt their chevrons as they should. The third classmen did what devilling the situation demanded to make the "plebes" know their places. "Here, 'plebe,' bring me a pail of water and be quick about it," was one of my first orders in camp. Except a little shaking out of bed of nights, I was not further molested. My first tent-mate was Dan Beltzhoover,[24] who consoled himself with his violin and played it well for his years. Many a night I was awakened by delicious strains of his music, softened to escape the ear of the sentinel, a needless precaution for sentinel and guard alike were only too glad to hear it.

Before marching into camp, one of our recreations had been to visit the riding hall and watch the graduating classmen riding, jumping and cutting Turk's head. Among them all, I best remember "Sam Grant," the roughest of the rough riders and most expert of Turk's head cutters, afterwards one of my truest friends, the great general and President, Ulysses. It is with pleasure that I note in the newspapers, as I write these lines, that his grandson, Ulysses S. Grant III, made a fine record at the academy, and is said to be at the front in his class.[25]

Turk, a bay, and Valentine, a sorrel, were the two favorite horses at old West Point, but only for the best and strongest riders. Old Val was a bouncer, much like a bucking Mexican horse, except [for] his huge size. I never cared to back him but once, and went up so high that I was glad to turn him over to Burnside, Griffin, or A. P. Hill,[26] the latter the crack rider of my class and a Confederate general in embryo.

23. Being "found" meant to be "found deficient" at examinations or, more simply, to flunk out of the academy.

24. Daniel M. Beltzhoover (12th, USMA 1847).

25. Ulysses S. Grant (21st, USMA 1843), future Union army commander and eighteenth U.S. president; U. S. Grant III (1881–1968) was still a West Point cadet when OBW penned this memoir. He graduated in 1903 and retired as a major general (temporary).

26. Ambrose E. Burnside (18th, USMA 1847). After serving in Mexico and the southwest, Burnside resigned his commission to manufacture a breech-loading rifle bearing his name. During the Civil War he rose from colonel of the 1st Rhode Island Volunteer Infantry to command the Ninth Corps and eventually the Army of the Potomac at the Battle of Fredericksburg. Burnside was one of OBW's closest friends. After the war he served three terms as governor of Rhode Island, and later as U.S. senator, until his death on Sept. 13, 1881.

Charles Griffin (23d, USMA 1847), commanded Battery D, 5th U.S. Artillery, at First Bull Run but eventually rose to command a division during the Civil War. He died at Galveston, Texas, Sept. 15, 1867, in a yellow fever epidemic.

A. P. Hill (15th, USMA 1847). The only member of the Class of 1847 to see real fighting during the Mexican War, Hill began the Civil War as colonel of the 13th Virginia Infantry but

Speaking of classmates, I may as well mention a few of them here. The best scholar was John C. Symmes, son of the famous astronomer of "Symmes' Hole" memory. . . . Symmes, Jr., . . . my classmate, seemed to be a matter-of-fact cadet. He excelled at everything, by dint of hammering. He became first captain of the corps and graduated in the ordnance—only to spend the most of his life on flying machines.[27]

[Ambrose E.] Burnside was the idol of the class, our leader in everything but studies. Benny Havens[28] worshipped him next to Andrew Jackson. Burnside was tall, commanding, and manly, so mature-looking that it was whispered that he had taken his son's warrant and come in his place. But the joke fell flat. He was the soul of "fun, frolic and friendship," a model soldier in appearance, and so frank and manly that everybody trusted him. Even the authorities felt the spell—a charm which enabled him to pull through divers scrapes himself, and his classmates, at a pinch. Unfortunate at Fredericksburg, partly from want of hearty cooperation on the part of certain of his subordinates and blamed as he was by a Court of Inquiry convened at Petersburg over the Mine affair, his career from Roanoke Island through the Civil War was patriotic and heroic, noble and generous to a fault. His magnanimity was shown when he consented, against his wish and judgment, to relieve McClellan in command of the Army of the Potomac, as we shall see further on.

Next to Burnside in class estimation stood my particular friend and associate for life, Julian McAllister,[29] a large, robust, society man. He was the son of Judge McAllister of Savannah, and his mother was of Huguenot descent—both distinguished and charming persons. Julian was our authority on all questions of manners and etiquette and one of the few cadets

---

achieved prominence as a division and corps commander in the Army of Northern Virginia. He was killed in front of Petersburg, Virginia, on April 2, 1865, just one week before the end of the war.

27. The "Symmes's Hole" theory, put forth by the elder Symmes in 1819, was based on his belief that "the Earth is hollow and habitable within, containing a number of solid concentric sphere, one within the other, and that it is open at the Poles 12 or 16 degrees! I pledge my life in support of this truth, and am ready to explore the hollow, if the world will support and aid me in the undertaking." OBW further described his classmate, Symmes, Jr., as being "eccentric and rather unsocial, but that his head was well balanced may be testified by the fact that he became first captain of the Corps. No doubt he would have become distinguished equally with other of our classmates who rose to high rank in the war of Secession, had he not chosen the Ordnance Department & finally become disabled by disease and exposure in the line of duty and so returned from active service." OBW, "Detroit Memoir, 1823 to ——", Willcox Papers.

28. Benny Havens owned a popular eating and drinking establishment near the Academy, frequented by many a cadet seeking unauthorized diversions.

29. Julian McAllister (4th, USMA 1847).

Cadets at West Point in the mid-1840s. *USMA Library.*

who voluntarily attended chapel. There might have been more, but for our compulsory attendance which after all did more good than harm.

Our chaplain was the Rev. Mr. Parks,[30] an enthusiastic preacher of High Church principles, to the horror of many Christians and the conversion of some skeptics. It was said that he made more Roman Catholic than Protestant converts. General [William S.] Rosecrans and Father Deshon, the Paulist of New York, became the most eminent of those whose footsteps were believed to have been turned to Rome.[31] Some complimentary allusion

30. Rev. Mr. Martin P. Parks, West Point chaplain and professor of ethics.

31. William S. Rosecrans (5th, USMA 1842) earned notoriety during the Civil War as commander of the Army of the Cumberland at the Battle of Stone's River (December 31, 1862–January 2, 1863) and at the Battle of Chickamauga (September 19–20, 1863). After the war he served as U.S. minister to Mexico (1868) and was elected to Congress from California (1880). He died at Redondo, California, on March 11, 1898.

George Deshon (2d, USMA 1843). A roommate of U.S. Grant, Deshon adopted the Catholic faith after being influenced by William S. Rosecrans. One of the founders of the Missionary

to the Pope once slipped from our chaplain's lips in a fervid discourse, whereupon there was a little tempest in a tea-pot among the straight-laced, and some of the "mutual friends" carried the news to the chaplain as a warning, which he took thuswise, exclaiming in his next: "Pope! Pope! You'd all be Popes if you could." However, I must say that he knew just how far to go without losing his place.

There were more than an average number of men in my class who subsequently became more or less prominent generals. Besides Burnside, there were A. P. Hill, [Henry] Heth, [Charles] Griffin, [Romeyn] Ayres, [John] Gibbon and [James] Fry, all of whom were fair scholars, but not "dry bones."[32]

The most popular, if not most prominent, cadet in the corps during my four years at West Point was George B. McClellan.[33] He stood next to the head and was first captain in his class. His was one of the most faultless personalities I ever have known. He was full of life and enthusiasm, had charming address and manners, was void of pretension, and a steadfast friend. I loved him like a brother. He was a leader and organizer, natural born.

"Stonewall" Jackson, now the most celebrated, was perhaps the least promising member of the same class.[34] He looked like a country clodhopper

Society of St. Paul the Apostle (the Paulists), he helped plan and build St. Paul's Cathedral in New York City.

32. Henry Heth (38th, USMA 1847—last in the class) became a prominent division commander in the Army of Northern Virginia. His troops opened the Battle of Gettysburg on July 1, 1863. Prominent in the fighting in the Wilderness, at Spotsylvania, and at Petersburg, Heth faced Willcox on the field of battle on several occasions. He died in the District of Columbia on September 27, 1899.

Romeyn B. Ayres (22d, USMA 1847). Ayres led Battery E, 3d U.S. Artillery, at First Bull Run and later commanded a brigade and then a division in the Fifth Corps, Army of the Potomac. He died at Fort Hamilton, New York, on December 4, 1888.

John Gibbon (20th, USMA 1847), born in Philadelphia but raised in North Carolina. Three of Gibbon's brothers went south when the war began. Gibbon earned distinction as the original commander of the Iron Brigade during the Civil War and later as a division commander in the First and Second corps, Army of the Potomac. By January 1865 he was commanding the Twenty-fourth Corps, and he served as one of the commissioners to receive Lee's surrender. After the war, Gibbon fought Indians in the west. He died in Baltimore, on February 6, 1896.

James B. Fry (14th, USMA 1847) served as assistant adjutant general to Irvin McDowell during the First Bull Run campaign.

33. George B. McClellan (2d, USMA 1846), future commander of the Army of the Potomac, Democratic presidential candidate (1864), and governor of New Jersey. McClellan died at Orange, New Jersey, October 29, 1885.

34. T. J. Jackson (17th, USMA 1846) achieved everlasting fame as "Stonewall" Jackson, with his renowned campaigns in the Shenandoah Valley in early 1862 and as a division and corps commander in the Army of Northern Virginia. OBW would face Jackson's brigade at First Bull Run. Jackson was mortally wounded by his own men on May 2, 1863, during his successful flank attack against the Union forces at Chancellorsville. He died eight days later.

at first coming. He was very reserved and probably had little or no school education—which is only one kind of education for the whirlpool of American life. From low down, by dint of the most laborious and persistent "boning," he gradually worked his way up into the Artillery numbers. I saw him one night after taps when lights were out, lying flat on his stomach on the floor, studying his book by the dim light of the coal fire grate. It is the man who rises that succeeds. The fellows who came to West Point best equipped from college for a walk over, even if they graduated ahead, have seldom achieved greatness. The head men in studies and merit marks, which latter [have counted toward class] standing for some time before, during and after my time, became good engineers or ordnance officers, but seldom reached the highest commands. In fact the only exception I remember was Robert E. Lee.[35]

The mention of the above fact need be no encouragement to the "lazy bones," or the careless—for it is the men who work the hardest and do the most that reach the top, and the laggards are left behind, of course. To be sure, Time and Chance happen to all things, but the "chance," my children, must be diligently improved.

On the whole, ours was not a studious class. One might call it the Runt class. Henry Heth and John De Russy,[36] two of our brightest men, ran for foot [of the class]. Though, like Burnside, Heth spent his Saturday evenings with Benny Havens and was a gay reveller, like his old chum, he settled down after graduation to steady work in his profession. He wrote a new book of infantry tactics, while Burnside invented a new gun. At the outbreak of the Civil War, Heth went out with Virginia, his native state, and became one of Lee's most trusted officers. On the occasion of his funeral in 1899, his remains lay in state at Richmond and were buried with public honors. I never knew a warmer friend, or a better or more gentle and patient man, husband and father.

Another of my intimates was A. P. Hill, like Harry Heth, a Virginian and equally popular. Hill was the beau ideal of a cavalier, lithe and active, with fine manners, a good swordsman, an accomplished rider, altogether a dashing fellow, and something more—a steady student. He graduated in the artillery. His slender figure he retained to the last. Alas that so fine a career

---

35. R. E. Lee (2d, USMA 1829) first earned acclaim as an engineer officer on Winfield Scott's staff during the Mexican War. Lee declined command of the Union army at the outset of the Civil War to serve his native state of Virginia, but he would achieve lasting fame as commander of the Army of Northern Virginia. After the war Lee served as president of Washington (later Washinton and Lee) College in Lexington, Virginia, dying there on Oct. 12, 1870.

36. John De Russy (36th, USMA 1847), died at Fort Monroe, 1850.

should terminate in battle on a retreat before the enemy he had faced so long and well. He was killed at the fall of Petersburg, commanding the rear guard on its evacuation. My own division entered the city first and set out in pursuit. Hill was killed in the last brush by one of my own men.[37] You can imagine how the catastrophe dampened the elevation I felt over the final success of my gallant division after the longest siege of the war. Would I could grasp the noble fellow by the hand this day. A handsome monument has been erected at Richmond to his memory. Peace to his ashes.

Nicknames abounded in the class. Symmes was "old Swipes." Two of our handsome fellows were "Lucy" Long and "Agnes" Gibson. Then there were "Legs" Patten, and "Guts" (pronounced "Juts") Seward, son of the great Secretary; "Beau" Neill, a Philadelphia exquisite; "Pompey" Gibbon, "Dandy" Woods—anything but a dandy;[38] "Dr." Ayres, a striking caricature of a country doctor; "Evangelist" Willcox, otherwise "Coxey." Full names were seldom heard. Burnside was "Burn," and his chum, Henry Heth, was "Harry." The use of sobriquets were, however, confined to intimates. But McClellan was generally then, as in the Civil War, called "Little Mac."

How quick the boys are to note peculiarities. One of the best drill instructors was called "Leather Head," from his floundering attempts at speech-making, to which he was rather prone.[39] Superintendent Major Delafield[40] was always "Old Dell," and the teachers, as is generally the case at college-schools, were all dubbed something kind or ridiculous. The most beloved of our favorites was Professor Kendrick,[41] universally known as "Old Dad," from his fatherly manner and kindness in the section room,

37. A. P. Hill was actually killed by Corp. John W. Mauch, 138th Pennsylvania, which belonged to the 3d Division, Sixth Corps. Willcox, however, always believed that one of his own men had killed his friend Hill.

38. The classmates previously unidentified in this work were as follows: Richard H. Long (19th, USMA 1847), died at Fort Gibson, Indian Territory, 1849; Horatio G. Gibson (17th, USMA 1847); George Patten (10th, USMA 1847); and Augustus H. Seward (34th, USMA 1847).

Thomas H. Neill (27th, USMA 1847) began the Civil War as colonel of the 23d Pennsylvania, leading the regiment during the Peninsula Campaign. He led a brigade of the Sixth Corps at Chancellorsville, Rappahannock Station, and in the Wilderness, and a division at Spotsylvania and Cold Harbor. Neill later served on the staff of Maj. Gen. Phil Sheridan during the Shenandoah Valley campaign of 1864. After the war he remained in the army, serving as commandant of cadets at West Point and as colonel of the 8th Cavalry. He died at Philadelphia, Mar. 12, 1885. Joseph J. Woods (3d, USMA 1847).

39. "Leather head" was J. Addison Thomas, commandant of cadets—also called "Ethical Tom" by the cadets. His motto was "Keep up the strut!"

40. West Point superintendent Richard Delafield, also known as "Dicky the Punster."

41. Henry L. Kendrick (16th, USMA 1835), assistant professor of chemistry, mineralogy, and geology. At Puebla, during the Mexican War, he ordered his battery to "fire at the crisis."

where he always helped the fellows out of difficulties and never allowed one to miss a question. Withal he was a man of infinite humor, quite a *belle esprit* and a favorite with men and women alike.

That he was also a soldier of nerve, the following anecdote will show. He had a crippled left hand. It is known that had he immediately sought the hospital on receiving the injury, his hand might have been saved from disfigurement and paralysis. The professor was conducting an experiment in chemistry in the presence of one of his cadet sections. There was an explosion and the old soldier's hand and arm were cruelly lacerated. He evidently thought he had a lesson in self-control as well as in chemistry to teach. He ordered back, on the pain of disobedience, the cadets who sprang to his assistance; then, turning to another retort, suffering tortures though he was, he completed the experiment. Then he dismissed the section and walked to the hospital to find that his delay had cost him the use of his hand.

Each class in the corps was arranged in sections of about equal numbers, sufficient to hear the members of each section recite within the hour's time presented for each head. Each section came under one or another of the full professors; the assistants were lieutenants of the army, on temporary detail.

The professors, with the Superintendent and Commandant of Cadets, formed the Academic Board. In determining the standing of each cadet at the semi-annual examinations, conduct or demerit marks counted.[42] The most severe and sarcastic professor in my time was Prof. Mahan . . . professor of Engineering and Grand Tactics; next to him came Prof. Bartlett, "old Bart," in Philosophy, more amiable but nervous to a degree; Prof. Weir, the gentlest of men and mildest of teachers and his efficient and popular assistant, Lieutenant Smith, presided over drawing and painting.[43]

There were few enough of "Old Dad's'" style of teaching in my day at the Academy. He taught; the other instructors, for the most part, silently listened to your lesson or demonstration and marked you accordingly. This also seemed to be the Harvard style, from Senator Hoar's account.[44] Prof.

42. An accumulation of two hundred demerits in any one year would cause a cadet's dismissal from the Academy. The most accrued by OBW was 120, during his fourth (senior) year.

43. Dennis Hart Mahan, professor of civil and military engineering and the art of war, left a lasting impression upon many of his students; William H. C. Bartlett, professor of natural and experimental philosophy (physics); Robert W. Weir, drawing instructor, who "disciplined their hands to draw what their eyes could see."

44. George F. Hoar (1826–1904), Whig abolitionist from Massachusetts, backed the Free Soil movement in 1848, joining the Republican Party soon after its inception. He served in the U.S. House of Representatives (1869–1877) and in the Senate from 1877 until his death.

Church,[45] however, a splendid mathematician, and the cleverest demonstrator of the Academic Board, was a notable exception to this vicious rule. And dear old Claude Berard, our French professor, was another. It hurt his feelings to have a pupil miss. As for the other teachers in French—the less said the better.

Our fencing master, de J,[46] was a "daisy." Old "Show me de Point," was his sobriquet. The dullest idiot could not fail to learn something of the sword master. After the Mexican War he became professor of Spanish. That we had also a dancing master goes without saying, for every gentleman in those days was expected to know how to dance.

Our recreations in winter were few, except the bread and potato gathering called "hash" after taps, a forbidden fare and relished all the more. Thanksgiving day we had turkey for dinner, and Christmas and New Year's were calling days and feast days at the mess hall. These were about the only recreations that broke the monotonous grind of the long, cold winter. The present era of athletics run had not yet dawned. In summer we had flirtation on the cliff walks, hops, camp-songs and a ball. Mrs. General Winfield Scott was the patroness of my class. She wrote for us in the year we graduated the well known song, "Changing the Grey for the Blue." That and "Benny Havens," long may they live to cheer the class and other gatherings—whether in the regions of Alaska or China or the Phillipines, as of old on the plains of Mexico and in the Florida swamps.

The first encampment was more endurable than we had feared as plebes. The winter studies and the first semi-annual examination gave a raking over and weeding out of the class, and brought a sorrow to those who were "found," and warning to those who were left. Some able men and some gay birds fell by the remorseless report, "Found Deficient." But we all turned out and gave them three hearty cheers as they started off in the stage for the railway station and the wide, wide world.

We entered upon the following summer encampment in the highest spirits. No longer plebes, our turn came at "devilling" the new-comers and playing corporal. I speak as we felt then, but not as I feel now. However, I am glad to say that no cruelties were practiced by my class and that I became disgusted with the customary performance.

45. Albert Ensign Church, professor of mathematics, became a dear friend of OBW. His teaching methods lacked enthusiasm, however.
46. Fencing master Patrice de Janon.

Not until the second summer were we fully admitted to the social privileges of old cadets, even at the games, but, particularly at the hotel and the hop room, where we had to meet visitors of more or less rank and distinction from New York, Washington and abroad. This gave us more knowledge of the world and of society, so useful to all and particularly necessary to polish the manners of the "country jakes" and budding officers. . . . I could mention other cadets from the rural districts who rubbed up well at the Academy and who afterwards filled high places. But I presume the same may be said of every college and nearly every class.

War prevailed between the third and fourth classes until after we returned to barracks, and never quite died out. But to the second class, the graduates of 1845, we became warmly attached. It was the most gentlemanly class I ever knew, particularly the Southern fellows, Bee, Ward, etc.,[47] and such men from the North as Henry B. Clitz.

It was Bee and Burnside, old friends, who opened the first battle of Bull Run, on the right, with their opposing brigades, and both sides mourned the fate of Bee, no one more so than the writer. He always stands out in my memory as the beau-ideal of a gentleman. At the close of the second term, 1845, came furlough and home for two months, stopping long enough in New York City to see the world, i.e.: Castle Garden, the Bowery Theatres and Barnum's museum, where the elder Booth[48] and the Giant Lady respectively shown. At that time Cedar street seemed to divide uptown from downtown, on Broadway, which seemed to come to a halt at Union Square. But Madison Avenue and Fifth Avenue had begun to loom up in aristocratic pretension.

On going home I visited my sister [Julia], Mrs. David A. McNair, at Kalamazoo, since one of the finest towns in the state [of Michigan], but then little more than a village. Happening to appear in my cadet uniform on the street, a hue and cry was raised by the boys at such a phenomenal appearance, forcing me to take ignominiously to my heels.

I can only recall one more incident of a primitive nature in that part of the wild west. A revival meeting was going on, and the new converts on one occasion became so excited, shouting, singing and crying, that one of the sisters, a fat lady of middle life, finally threw herself on the floor and rolled, roared, and kicked up her heels and screamed "Hallelujah!" until one of the brethren put a stop to the performance, I forget how. The presiding elder

47. Barnard E. Bee (33d, USMA 1845) led a Confederate brigade at Bull Run until his death, July 21, 1861; James N. Ward (28th, USMA 1845) died at St. Anthony, Minnesota, in 1858.

48. Junius Brutus Booth (1796–1852), a noted actor and the father of Edwin and the infamous John Wilkes Booth.

was a noted circuit rider who seemed to set the house ablaze with his fiery eloquence and unrestrained ground and lofty tumbling on the pulpit stage. I had attended a number of revival meetings before, but this one capped the climax. At a subsequent time in the anti-slavery period of the history of the country, I saw, or rather heard, of more of the power of a religious orator to rouse the feeling of a whole congregation to a state of frenzy, which defied all restraint of law and order. But I submit that the most contemptible exhibition is when the preacher talks war from the sacred pulpit, and mingles politics and religion with tactics, most ignorant of what he is most assured.

Returning from furlough after meeting most of my classmates at New York, the old place looked like another "home in the Highlands," instead of the frowning giant's castle it seemed to look on my first knock at the gate as a "plebe." Everybody greeted us warmly. Even Old Tom [J. Addison Thomas], our impulsive commandant, unbent at parade and stumbled into a speech, from which he extricated himself by the usual "eh, eh! Companies, right wheel." But he never made mistakes in his drill. Of course furlough had unbent if not loosened our gait and habits somewhat, but a few reports for carelessness in ranks or "not keeping step," soon corrected all that, and we settled down to the hardest part of the whole four years, the second class course—physics and the application of the higher mathematics. In the next and last year's course we extend more fully into military subjects proper, such as tactics, strategy and engineering. Speaking of the latter, the idea has occurred to me of late that now that we have entered into our new career as a first class power, it might be well for the academies and colleges, whenever civil engineering is taught, to connect with the course some practical military engineering—especially since this country always must, or thinks it must, rely upon our citizen soldiery for its armies of the future. I might go even a little further, but this is not the place for such details.

In regular order after returning from furlough, the corporals became sergeants, Symmes, Burnside and McAllister at the top and I found myself quartermaster sergeant under Quartermaster Dabney H. Maury,[49]

49. Dabney H. Maury (37th, USMA 1846) had graduated from the University of Virginia and was studying law prior to entering West Point. Following service in the Mexican War he returned to the Military Academy, where he taught geography, history, and ethics. Beginning the Civil War as a captain of cavalry in the Confederate service, Maury later became chief of staff to Maj. Gen. Earl Van Dorn, serving with distinction at the Battle of Pea Ridge, Arkansas. He fought well at Iuka and Corinth, Mississippi, and was later appointed commander of the Department of the Gulf, a position he held until the end of the war. One of the founders of the Southern Historical Society, Maury died at his son's home in Peoria, Illinois, on January 11, 1900.

an intimate friend, afterwards a Confederate general of prominence and never "reconstructed."

The year passed by without any notable event affecting the class and we entered the last year's course full of high hopes, destined to a rude shock during the summer encampment. One of the graduates had run down to New York and reappeared in complete uniform as an officer of the army. The lieutenant "gave a treat" to his old friends in my class—some eight or ten fellows—at his old room in North Barracks. Champagne was drank quite freely, I must confess and the officer of the day got wind of the spree. The result was that with some half a dozen others I found myself in arrest and confined to camp. What made the matter worse was that the class had taken a pledge against intoxicating liquors during the remainder of our term. This pledge was given to save a classmate from expulsion, but it embraced a saving clause, viz: that the signers were not bound to refuse the invitation of an officer. Now as ill luck would have it, our friend's commission took effect on the day after the North Barracks affair, although his appointment had been announced together with his assignment to a regiment, in orders published by the War Department and he was received and treated as an officer.

We were kept quite a while in suspense and arrest before a court martial was ordered. The delay was presumably due to the question arising under the pledge. But the authorities finally ordered a court and we were all convicted on grounds that I thought then, and think now, unjust if not contemptible. My own case seemed aggravated because I was one of the committee that had negotiated the pledge; I say aggravated, not from any knowledge of my own of the sentiment of the court, but from the review of the case by the Secretary of War, published in the orders which stigmatized my "argument" on the technicality in question as the "use of logic in a question of honor." This was the unkindest cut of all. I did not mind being reduced to the ranks—as we all were—and a long confinement to limits—so much as the blow at my honor, particularly as I believed, from some pressure that had been brought to bear to induce me to plead guilty as charged, and from the long delay in ordering the court, that the authorities had grave doubts concerning the pledge in question.

I do not feel at liberty to publish the name of the lady who pleaded most strongly.[50] Suffice to say she was one of my most intimate circle of friends and that her father was chief of a military corps in Washington.

50. This was Annie L. Clarke.

Mr. President and Gentlemen of the Court Martial

Not having explained the ground of my defence in questioning the witnesses, I beg leave to lay them before you now.

I am charged first with a violation of the 113 paragraph [of Academy Regulations]. The fact of its being customary for cadets to drink with officers without its being considered a violation of this paragraph has been, I think, satisfactorily established.

I drank with Lieut. Adams,[51] two days after he had been relieved from duty of every species; after he had abandoned permanently the cadet's uniform, finished the whole academic & military course & received his diploma. I will admit that technically speaking he was not *then* an officer, because it was then a few days before the 1st July; but this technicality, I humbly consider, is one of mere convenience in fixing a nominal expiration of cadetship which otherwise would fluctuate between the 13th & 30th of June. But, as has been proved, all graduates are treated as officers of the army both by cadets and officers of the Academy.

To show the light in which graduates are *really* considered, I will mention the fact of Lieut. Dutton's[52] having *married* on the 27th June last. This is an act considered by the Regulations as equivalent to *resignation*, but no notice was taken of it.

When such a mode of treatment becomes as customary as it is proved to have become, might it not fairly be regarded by the cadets as good grounds for the opinion and practice which prevails of accepting civilities at the hands of graduates, as well as before as after the 1st July, without it being considered a violation [of the] 113th paragraph? And it is upon the ground that such opinion and practice were prevalent at the time, that I rest my defence. In drinking with Lieut. Adams I did not stop to consider the propriety of a universal custom of cadets, but knowing it to exist, I followed it in company with other cadets who would have considered it a violation of honor to drink with an unauthorised person, and who drank in good faith with Lieut. Adams as an officer of the army.

I am charged, 2d, with "conduct prejudicial to good order and military discipline."

51. John Adams (25th, USMA 1846) eventually became a Confederate general, killed at the Battle of Franklin, November 30, 1864.
52. William Dutton (15th, USMA 1846) died in New York City in 1862.

The 1st specification, intoxication, I must admit, to this extent, viz., that I was somewhat under the influence of strong drink during a very short period of time. The time must have been short, as it is proved that altho' I drank at about noon, yet in the course of the afternoon, when my tentmate saw me, he did not observe any evidence whatever of my having been under such influence. This shows, likewise, that the degree of intoxication must have been very slight. Cadet [Lewis C.] Hunt testifies, that when he saw me just previous to my going to sleep, I was in my right mind and gave no evidence in my conversation of the presence of liquor. As I was not on military duty on that day, and as it is proved that I behaved in no boisterous or disorderly manner, I beg the court to consider how far my guilt of this specification sustains the ch[ar]ge.

The 2d specification contains, by implication, the breach of a pledge; not in the act or manner of drinking, but in the effects, viz., intoxication. In order that these effects should constitute a violation of the pledge, there should be, either the *intention* to get intoxicated, or timely *foreknowledge* that such would be the result of drinking. Neither of these is shown by the testimony, but a state of things quite the reverse. The intention of my drinking is proved to have been nothing but a mark of civility towards a very great friend, who, I beg leave to state, expected to join a regiment marching against the enemy, and whom it would have been ungenerous to refuse to take a "cup of kindness" at parting.

So much for the intention. It was not proved that I drank more than once, nor then all that was poured into the glass, and it was the opinion of the witness that I did not drink enough to intoxicate under ordinary circumstances. Thus it appears that my intoxication was not only unintentional, but unexpected, and could not have been by me foreseen. It was likewise proved, as I have before shown, that it was neither violent nor of long duration. The whole force of the evidence on these points goes to show, that, a small quantity of liquor operating, just before dinner time, upon an empty and unaccustomed stomach, produced such a degree of intoxication, that on falling asleep in the middle of a summer's day, I slept so soundly, that when disturbed only sufficiently to awaken a person under ordinary circumstances, I did not awaken. *This* the evidence shows, and nothing more, except perhaps, that in a very short time I recovered from it entirely. Now can this accident, this misfortune be construed into a solemn violation of the pledge?

The 3d specification is, entering camp in the dress of a civilian on the night of 10th July. From the fact that no charge of unauthorized absence is preferred, and from the proof given that *in accordance with "good order and military discipline"* I went to the guard tent, and was passed into camp by the officer of the guard, I leave you to consider whether the specification, even *if true*, helps to sustain the charge. But my whole dress was in uniform, except a loose sack coat, thrown on at the house of the officer whose family I was visiting; and there was so little attempt at disguise that a new cadet sentinel, born into the Corps scarcely a month before, recognized me, and that in the night, and without my going very near him.[53]

I have thus endeavored to show, Mr. President and Gentlemen, 1st, that in drinking on 20th June, I drank in good faith with Lt. Adams as an officer of the army, and in accordance with the prevailing custom and civilities of the post; and that therefore I was not consciously guilty of the violation of the spirit of the 113th paragraph Academy Regulations.

2d, that my conduct while under the influence of liquor was not at all improper.

3d, that my intoxication was accidental, and therefore no violation of my pledge to the [superintendent].

And 4th, that in entering camp on the night of the 10th July, there was no attempt at disguise.

Having done this, gentlemen, I shall leave my case in your hands with confidence, for I know you will consider, that you have in keeping, not only the humble fortunes of a cadet who is almost ready to graduate, but likewise the reputation of your younger brother. How dear to any man must be his reputation! In my case, a character pronounced by my commanding officer, "perfectly unexceptionable", and by the chaplain, even "one of the most exemplary in the corps of cadets." And yet, by what a slender thread it hangs! The error or the accident of a moment! Owing to the stubborn letter of the military law, you may not be able to exonerate me from all blame, but I pray you, yield to the mild dictates of Charity, which rejoices in the *unlettered truth*, and save my reputation at least from dishonor.

Respectfully submitted,
O. B. Willcox

Since I have had some experience both as a Judge Advocate on occasion and as a lawyer, I have often asked myself why was not the lieutenant himself brought to trial wither as a cadet or an officer?

However, youth is elastic in normal conditions, and although the official consequences of the trial lasted longer, yet as we all believed that the best

53. The U.S. Military Academy "Register of Merit" for this period indicates that OBW received eight demerits on July 10, 1846, for having "passed over a sentinel post into camp between tattoo & rev[eille]."

sentiment at the Academy, certainly that of the officers and professors' families, was on our side, we settled down to our winter studies nearly as light hearted as ever. I say "nearly," for in midwinter a little event occurred which raised a ripple of uncertainty in certain quarters as to whether I had really recovered [from] the shock.

Being assigned to declaim at the Dyalectic Society before a crowded house, I selected the passionate declamation of a woman in a madhouse, "I am not mad!" Dressed in a long grey overcoat, with a bit of powder on my face, it seems I played the part to such a height of frenzy that some of the good people, not cadets, spoke out: "Poor fellow, his mind is affected after all, and no wonder!" Truly I had not anticipated such a draw on the sympathy of spectators, much less was I entitled to it. The whole affair was forgotten in a week, when the next "Dy" took place; except that now and then some classmate in later years has recalled the incident, among the reminiscences of "Benny Havens, O." Really the Mexican War swallowed up all the incidents of that winter and we were impatient enough to change the grey for the blue and have a hand in the scrimmage, which nobody thought would last even as long as it did.

We graduated at the end of June, 1847, after ordering our uniforms to New York and listening to no end of grave advice from the dons on duty, patriotism, high honor and valor, winding up with care of person in the field, and left for our homes more impatient than ever for assignments to regiments and corps.[54] Then came those most precious of all moments, farewells at home. And in a few weeks a dozen of us were on our way to Mexico for the war.

JOURNAL ENTRIES AND LETTERS, 1843–1847

West Point Academy
June 12, 1843
Left Detroit June 6th, passed on to New York City on the evening of the 10th, spent sabbath, and came here to day about 10½ o'clock. Gave name to orderly on dock and was obliged to rap out myself forthwith. Passed through half a dozen ordeals and was sent to quarters. Had a sensation of loneliness and felt like a stranger. Dinner at noon, got stared out of countenance by every rascally cadet about premises. After dinner found a few friends, began to feel a little more Richards-himself-ish. Afternoon drilled

54. OBW graduated 8th out of 38 graduates in the Class of 1847.

1½ hours, straightened and bent &c, most fatigued to death. Called upon Cadet Augur,[55] and offered a mattress by him, and let me ever remember his kindness. . . .

Order of duty, 1st day. Report, give my name, residence, parents' name, age, description of clothes in possession &c, make deposit. Sent to captain cadets, assigned quarters, sent to sutler, receive room fixtures and other necessaries, and go back to quarters. Suck thumbs till dinner time, then march to mess. Afternoon, go to recitation room, return to study till 4½ o'clock, march out to drill till six, parade 6½, supper at 7 o'clock. After supper, ½ hour leizure, beat to quarters, study hours till 9½, and tattoo, go to bed, lights extinguished by taps 10 o'clock. Rise next morning reveille five o'clock. Roll call, get room in order, out again at six, drill till 7½. Breakfast. Study till 12, writing lessons till 1, dinner, etc.—Go to adjutant's office, give calling & pecuniary situation of parents, &c. Go to tailor's, get measured. Thus the curtain riseth—

One evening, one of my room-mates having tooth ache, desired me to find him a pipe to smoke some pepper. It being study hours, I could not visit any of the rooms, and going to the guard, I asked them for a pipe. The captain stept up imperiously and asked me if I knew I was acting improperly, and seemed inclined to run upon me. I replied that I had asked him civilly, and he might answer as he pleased. At this he ordered me to my room under arrest! I quietly returned; soon after [the] corporal [of the] guard came in, stated that all was joke, and that the captain had himself gone to fetch the pipe, which proved true, and so no bones were broken.

June 22d

Examined by surgeons, stript first, all but shirt, and then putting on pants, stript shirt, rather embarrassing. 32 inches round breast.

June 24

Cadets went into camp to day, turned out before breakfast in the morning, to help them pitch the tents, poor Plebes obliged to do all the work.

---

55. Christopher C. Augur (16th, USMA 1843). A native of New York, Augur was raised in Michigan, from which state he received his appointment to West Point. He commanded a division under Maj. Gen. Nathaniel P. Banks in Virginia and Missouri. Wounded at Cedar Mountain on August 9, 1862, he later served in the Mississippi River campaigns of 1862–1863, leading the left wing of Banks's force in the siege and capture of Port Hudson. He commanded the Department of Washington, D.C., from October 23, 1863, until the end of the war. He died at Washington on January 16, 1898.

Afternoon. Cadets turning out to escort Gen'l Scott[56] to the boat; a few of us went down to the river, to get a sight. Went out upon a narrow ridge of rocks, and were there but a few moments when we saw a large sail boat, manned by two men, capsize. The men clung to the boat, and seeing a boat push off to their aid, we kept our place on shore, watching the poor fellows endeavor to keep up.

While thus engaged, a corporal and file of men came up to us and asked if we knew we were off limits; [we] replied "did not." [We were] ordered to fall in between the men, & marched towards camp. Our way was rugged and steep, and we obeyed the men with such alacrity, and walked forward so promptly that we made the poor devils sweat and puff & blow, with heat and fatigue. Arriving at camp, [we were] placed in "guard tent" for a few moments, and discharged, laughing heartily at the expense of the "escort"—

June 26th

Examined by Academic board. I was merely asked to perform an operation in addition of vulgar fractions, asked a few questions in numbers, read a few lines, wrote a sentence, and dismissed, feeling that there had been more cry than wool.

The old cadets take every method to plague the new ones: in the night the guard will come to a tent, order a man out, accuse him of making a noise, & perhaps not waiting for him to put on his clothes, hurry him off to the guard tent.

On Sunday, June 25, new cadets marched to the chapel, where we received a wholesome lesson of kind advice from the parson. He advised us 1st, not to make any more acquaintances than possible; 2d, begin right on the start, and then easy to keep right; be careful of associates, be contented, live in hope, obey orders, endure what cannot be amended, trust in God to protect and direct us; and finally requested us to give him our names to abstain from intoxicating drinks while at West Point.—Except when on furlough, leave of absence, or visiting families on the Point, many acceded and among them myself. Thus I fulfilled a promise made to my mother just before I left home.

This place is no "gate of Heaven," but rather a gate of Hell. If the history of every cadet were known, how many who came here Christians would be found to have gone away Devilsmen[?] Already, though I came here but

56. Winfield Scott was then a major general.

scarce two months since, do I find my heart fearfully gone astray. Those habits of prayer which were once my delight seem to have been broken up, and I find it irksome to maintain that close walk with God which vital piety imperatively demands.

Among my numerous failings, pride stands itself a host, and almost preeminent. To this source I can trace a thousand sins every day. . . . It is necessary for my success in this institution, I plainly discover, to maintain the strictest watch over my smallest actions. If I would invoke Divine assistance, I must observe all the regulations strictly. It is best to keep myself to myself, and never forget myself, and thus may I find myself at the end of the term a credit to myself. But if I do otherwise I may lose myself, and my fall could be attributed to no one but myself.

Sept. 3d, 1843

What a strange mess of inconsistent, incongruous things is the heart of man! What a picture of folly, what an offensive mire of impurities, what a tale of weaknesses, & broken resolutions, forgotten and neglected! It sets itself upon one train of action with zeal, soon forgets that it has left others full as important; it comes to a sudden stand in the pursuit of a good work, and shoots off upon some tom fool errand in the dark. . . .

I almost think I have been laboring under a species of insanity for the past week. I am cursed with a suspicion of men, and that of the meanest sort. Not that they are immoral, cheats, liars &c, but that they do not look upon me as I deserve & love me as they love each other. I have been brooding over imaginary slights, and anticipations of bad treatment in my future academic course from my fellow cadets, to an extent that is really dangerous to the equilibrium of sanity. I can attribute this to what seems to me to be the true cause, and I begin to feel it my duty to break away from the rule of such monsters.

I have very sociable feelings (if not manners) and have made the good will of my fellows an idol! and I think God has been punishing me for my weakness and wickedness. It is my duty to look to Him for happiness and not to my fellow man. This world is cold, selfish, sordid, inconsiderate and regardless of feeling. I know this from what I have seen, heard, experienced; and being a part of the mass, I know it *from what I am.* This world taken in mass cannot make a man happy; it does not satisfy the longings of the soul, its excitment & pleasures do not fill up the measure of our cup. A man may enjoy wealth, and what it brings to him may satisfy at times his desires; but I speak of men in their conduct to each other. A man cannot live contented and be happy in nothing but the treatment of his fellow men. I must look no longer there for happiness, but to God I may look with confidence.

But this is not the only respect in which my heart has gone astray. I have been looking down with contempt upon those whom I considered below me, heedless that I was below others and subject to the same lash. I was awakened however by a circumstance where I was the sufferer. It is easy to form resolutions, much easier than to keep them, but trusting in Him who is my shield against every danger, I humbly, fearfully, yet sincerely subscribe to the following Resolutions—

1st That I will treat every fellow being as a gentleman and a Christian should do.

2d That I will do my utmost to become more humble & meek, & practice self denial when it is required either for my growth in grace or for my advancement in my studies.

3d That I will have but three objects in view from this time until I graduate. First of all to lead a holy life; second to stand as high in my class as possible; third to mind my own business and let other people's alone.

4th I will abstain from the use of tobacco from this day until I go on furlough.

5th That I will comply with all the regulations of the Institution.

6th That I will employ all my time to the best advantage.

7th That I will eat, drink and sleep as little as is consistent with health.

8th That I will be systematic and regular in all things, especially my studies.

I am now beginning a new course of life. I am separated from home and friends, have a name to carve out for myself, a soul entrusted entirely to my own care. My character is not yet formed, my principles not so firmly fixt as that they cannot be moved. I must then be watchful. I must form good habits. I must keep good resolutions and eschew evil ones. I must remember that I am responsible for my advantages and that it is my solemn duty to fit myself for usefulness in the world. It is no small matter that I am now contemplating my profession for life is being fixt, it will be an honorable one, and yet alas it will be beset with snares, it may be the means of making my name a blessing or of ruining my soul.

Oh thou who has brot me here, who hast watched over my mother, and over me, keep my heart in the right way; strengthen my understanding, and give me strength to resist the influence of evil example, of all wicked passions, and of all things that might draw me from the straight and narrow way. . . .

If a man would recount daily to himself his privileges, advantages, and blessings, he would be nearly always happy.

Sept. 1st, 1843

Our section (fourth class) were arranged alphabetically last night. I was placed within one of the foot of the last (5th) section, both in mathematicks & French, which will compose our 1st year's course.

Sept. 17th transferred to the 2d section in French, & to 3d in math—

Sept. 25 transferred to the 2d section in math.

Sept. 26th commenced this day Gibbon's *Rome*.

Sept. 30 transferred to the 1st section math—

West Point

Sept. 7th, 1843

Dear Eb,[57]

I'm over head and ears in debt in the way of letters and I write this to you more as a receipt than as payment. We marched out of camp on the 30th and if I felt a little more sentimental I would give you a description, but *boning* dry mathematics, and the sounds of the French alphabet, has, like autumn winds, blown away the flower of my fancy and left but the stalk. I go to work at my studies in an easy way, not being obliged to study very hard in Algebra, as I am somewhat familiar with the first of it; but they do things up brown here, and no half way work about it.

Our class was arranged alphabetically and that placed me within four or five of the very foot. This is a disadvantage because there are many above me who may do no better and yet maintain their places, and it will be uphill work for me to rise. But rise I will. Transfers will be made in about two weeks, and then this child will leave *the immortal* (as the *last* section is called).

I hope and believe the return of the furlough men was a rich scene, they all stopt in New York until the very day they were obliged to be here, and then all (or nearly) came in the same boat. They all felt fine, and shouted, and were embraced by their fellow cadets with a soldier's welcome. A few hours and all was changed. They had to take off their fine clothes, get their long hair clipt, and so commence the duties of a soldier. There was many a

57. Eben N. Willcox, brother of OBW, attorney and founder of the street railway system in Detroit, having secured the original franchise from the Common Council in 1862. He married Louise Cole, daughter of Henry S. Cole, of Detroit. "He will be remembered," said a close friend, "for his promising opening youth, his brilliant career at the bar, and his stirring speeches in the cause of the Union at the outbreak of the civil war." He was also a noted breeder of thoroughbred horses.

long face in camp next day. I can imagine how they felt, and how I shall feel when (if nothing happens) I return from furlough.

You want to know all about my pecuniary affairs. The tale is simple, and may soon be told. I had to purchase many little things to commence with; but the principal items of any amount were a dress coat, and six pr's summer pants, about $22. My expenses from the time of arrival till examination amounted to about $12.00, and board, and sundries too numerous to mention since that, all together amount to about $25. *more than my pay*, which commenced 30th June. Board costs about $9. a month, and washing $2.00. We have also to pay the Band, Barber, Porters &c (each one of us his share) and we have raised subscriptions to send home cadets that were rejected.

Instead of turning my citizen clothes over to the quartermaster, I let a man who went home have a part of them, and from him I received a mattress, and sundry small articles worth about $15.00 (so much, as good as saved). I shall have to get another coat and a pr. winter pants soon, but I hope to get out of debt by or before January, since on the 1st of this month I was in debt only about $25.

But there is nothing to fear on the score of money matters; would to Heaven you were as free from that "casking care" as I am. And as I think I can save $75 or so in two years (perhaps I can save more than that, but a man must not be niggardly here) I have the consolation of feeling that I *may* then deny myself the pleasure of a visit home, and send the money to Mother. But I hope the necessity will not exist, but *if it does* I can show a specimen of the Willcox smack, and glory in the action.

What did old Zeke have to say about West Point? Port' Cole and I tried to show him round, and he seemed to be pleased. Tell him I should be glad to hear from him. I like him much. One reason is because he likes you and admires you. The fact is that every breeze that comes up from the West bears something in your praise. Continue to be a man, and to be more and more worthy of praise. Religion would do more than anything else for you, and by my love, and for the sake of your good I beseech you possess yourself of it, put it not off till after your admission to the bar.

Your advice concerning the loafers and gentlemen here is very good! but the lines are not drawn exactly as you think. It is rather between "clever fellows," and "mean" men. The hard cases mostly belong to the first class, and many clever, steady, good fellows are classed with the latter.

To give you a specimen, two men that stand at the foot of the third class, and whose morals are about as low, are "fine fellows," "gentlemen," &c, while the *head man* of the same class, and a true specimen of a gentleman, is *cut* and called a loafer. But for all [that] it will be *policy* for me to associate with the "loafers," as much as possible. I care but little about associating with the men generally of the corps, a few chosen spirits have ever gathered the fruits of my friendship. . . .

I have received a letter from Mr. Duffield. I shall strive to make Mrs. Woodbridge *"respect"* as well as "love" me, to whom and family the very best compliments. . . . Love to Mother, Julia & Rachael. . . . Now rooming with Hunt,[58] glorious. Keep me advised of the drift of family affairs. Send me more papers. Study hour's commenced. Time's up.

Yours in haste,
Orlando

West Point
Oct. 28th, 1843

My mind has been for a few weeks past in a most singular state. It seems on looking back upon it as tho' I had been wandering around some vast plain, not knowing where to tarry & rest, nor inclined to sit down at any one of the cool streams which were running on every side. New objects seemed continually to be coming into sight, new roads tempting me to follow, wild flowers and strange springing up around me and filling the air with delicious fragrance.

What is this *Prairie?* It is a new field of thought, a new *pasture* for the mind. I discover a new world! rising like a thick mist from the murky pursuits of the crowd, and gathering itself upon the mountains of reason & religion; the sun pours down his bright beams, and oh the bright hues of the mental vision! Me thinks I see a new object of life, or rather new reasons for the attainment of that desirable end of man's being, which, while all think they know, none strive to attain with half the zeal manifested in eating a *dispeptic* dinner.

But yet these things are but shadows before me for I cannot discern their form or composition. They seem mongrels of philosophy & piety. They invite me to follow, while yet they lead the way over such dangerous chasms & precipices that it is evident I cannot. Yet the road beyond seems smoother, and I feel strongly inclined to make the attempt. I look down upon the busy world below & find it following foolishness and vexing their hearts with trifling toys. One chases a bubble till it bursts, another plunges into a vortex and is drowned, another, after walking a great ways, looks back and finds himself on the wrong road, too late to retrace his steps; no one seems aware of the means of rational enjoyment & pursuits which unfold themselves to

---

58. Lewis C. Hunt (33d, USMA 1847).

my vision; all are occupied so much with little matters, that the great concerns of life are unheeded. Suddenly the mist clears away and I find myself in the very crowd—lately the object of my pity & wonder.

Oct. 29th

To-day Gen'l Bertrand,[59] the man in whose arms Buonaparte expired, arrived upon the Point, and was received in a manner worthy of his rank & standing; a salute was fired in his honor, the Corps turned out in full dress, and all the officers in dress waited upon him, and invited him to *review* the Corps. Passing along the lines he was recognized by one of the band, a Frenchman. The poor fellow was in ecstasies at beholding him and could not maintain silence, but exclaimed, "Gen'l Bertrand, I have seen you before, at Waterloo!" Bertrand went up to the man and shook him warmly by the hand, and stood several minutes conversing with him.

The general is a middle sized man of about 75 or 80 years, with a head almost bald, somewhat bent, and its few locks white as snow. The expression of his countenance is decidedly pleasant—even jolly—& intelligent. To think that on that breast the head which devised schemes which shook a world reclined as its last lights flickered & expired; to think that in those arms died a genius which Europe could not contain with safety, makes *Bertrand*, in the light of poetry, a hero, in that of history an object of the deepest interest.

He was accompanied by three other gentlemen (French) one of whom was his son. A man of some six or seven feet, with tremendous red whiskers & *moustache*. He was born it is said at St. Helena, and his mother, in presenting him to her husband, remarked that "she could introduce to him *one* Frenchman without first obtaining the consent of the English."

The steamboat arrived while the General was on the review, from which he was obliged suddenly to withdraw. It might be called taking "French leave"! as he stept from the parade ground to the omnibus, made a low bow to the officers—taking off his hat—with the true politeness of a Frenchman—& was soon gone. His visit seems like some vision just flitted across my mind.

I love to shut myself out from the influences at work around me, and in the secrecy of my own heart commune with myself. To *look in* upon myself, to observe how far I am governed by the *little* world whose atmosphere I am at

59. Henri Gratien Bertrand, a skilled engineering officer, was one of Napoleon's most loyal associates. He had served as brigadier general, aide-de-camp, and Marshal of the Palace.

the time breathing, and *look out* from my snug corner upon the *great world* into which I must some day enter, strut my brief hour & move off with the mass. I hardly can determine whether it be wisdom to trouble one's self about the Future, or endeavor to confine one's thoughts upon the well employment of the present. The world, after all the light shed upon it by religion & philosophy, is a mystery, its avenues & highways a labyrinth. . . .

Dec. 31st, 1843

This being the last day of the year I cannot but set myself to the work of reflection. How different are the circumstances in which I now am from those of the last day of the year '42. The object then of my anxious thoughts is now accomplished, viz. my admission into this Academy.

But Oh, what changes have taken place in everything. How many & what varied scenes I have witnessed and participated in. My departure from Detroit for Washington, the emotions of my friends, and my own in relation to that event. My journey with its expanding effect upon my mind; my stay & labors at Washington, the doubt which hung over my success when I left; my return home, & the short, sweet interval of my leave for this place; the dreadful suspense, the welcome reception of my appointment, the leaving of *home*, farewell to friends, the hearts bursting with emotion, tears of a mother, sisters and the warm press of the hands of companions; the journey, the arrival at this place, the admission, the encampment; with all their attendant circumstances these come up into my mind as the fruits of one eventful year.

This year past, this year of years, how shall it tell upon my whole life! How it has changed the current of action in the pursuits of this world! A new profession, a new home, new friends, new enemies, new hopes & fears, new motives, new sins—how few are the new deeds of righteousness!

All has gone well in a worldly point of view, how is it in a spiritual? My God how? I fear I have lost ground. I fear I have had less of the spirit of piety this year than during the last; and yet God's goodness has been signalized more than usually to me this year. How ungrateful! What a poor return!

And in other points have I fallen away. One year ago I had myself under a tolerable discipline, had a good deal of self command, but for the last few months it seems as tho' the reins were entirely thrown away, and I, lost to manly resolution & vigorous self subjection. The many secret determinations to pursue a straightforward course of industry, diligence, virtue, how few of them have been kept. I am almost weary of making resolutions and feel more like giving myself to circumstances.

But no. I must erect new fortifications, build up decayed walls, fill up the breaches and not so easily give up the siege. I am not, thanks to God's Spirit! I am not yet quite lost. But how enviable is my lot on this day. Free from all pecuniary cares both for the present & the future, surrounded by every comfort, bright prospects for the future & dependent upon no one's charity; engaged in the highest pursuits of the human mind—the acquisition of knowledge—& blessed with a good share of success.

Why has not Providence permitted that *I* should be found among those who will be shortly obliged to give up all these advantages & return to their homes in shame? Why have I been blessed with better health than many a one whose constitution is far better than mine? In spite too of my reckless disregard of its demands. Oh how can I but feel that God has been with me! How can I but determine again & again that I will begin the new year with a renewed heart, and lead a new and better life. But how weak am I, how incapable of carrying out such plans! Help, oh Thou who hast hitherto sustained me, that I may make a good improvement of the new year. Not by living entirely to myself, but by preparing both mind & body for serving Thee as circumstances may require.

Standing in Class January 1844:
Mathematicks 8th, French 9th, General Standing 7th.

Military Academy West Point
January 3d, 1844

Dear Eb,
I was examined yesterday, did well. I mean I was examined in Algebra. My French comes off to-day or to-morrow; that is a trifle however. Porter Cole resigned last night; what he is going to do is not yet determined; it was his best plan although he cannot draw money to take him home, which he might have done had he waited to be found; but in the latter case he could never get a re-appointment.

Had no fun at all Christmas or New Years. They pretended to get up a decent dinner at the mess hall, but we had nothing on Christmas but a tough turkey, and the hardest mince pies you ever saw. New Years day nothing but a boiled ham! Old Dick's (Major Delafield's) Christmas Eve *soiree*— (which I wrote Ed about) was a perfect failure—glorious!

But what little things do I write about, while you are overwhelmed with cares. I wish I could bear a part of them for you. I cannot but feel joyful at the idea of my first six months' success, however; how many poor devils would jump out of their skins to be in my place. Poor Backus & Cole, poor Michigan, poor Mrs. Cole, how I feel for them. But it may prove for the best. Backus is not fit for a life of study; he has not got *sense* enough.

You remember I told you that Senator Porter said, when he refused to aid me, that "he did not expect Cole would pass through"; it was a bad place to send him under such circumstances. I hope Michigan will not send another unless he can go through.

[letter continued]

Friday January 5th

My examination in French is over, got through as well as you could wish. I wish I could give you an idea of an examination, one's feelings, &c. Of the latter you can but imagine, but of the former. The officer of the day comes to the different stoops and cries out with a loud voice, for instance, "First section, fourth class, mathematics, *turn out!*" To one who fears being *found*, this sounds much as the cry of *Fire!* which wakes you up in a cold windy night; but to one who has no such fears it is only a little startling.

The section is then formed and marches over to the hall; to give you some idea of the second scene, carry your mind to the Senate Chamber in the Capital in Detroit; in the place of the President's desk place a table a little more elevated than the others and you have an exact picture of the *locale* of the Academic Board. At the highest table in the middle sits the grave superintendent, with spectacles & uniform; before him at another table sits his adjutant, who, with all members of the Board who are officers, are in full uniform.

On each side, forming (as in the Senate) a semi circle, are seated the different members of the Board. There is the knowing mathematician, and the petulant French teacher, and the annalising chymist, and the calculating engineer, and the smooth rhetorician, the serious natural philosopher, and the classic features of the artist Weir—the painter of that splendid picture of the Embarkation.

But let us usher in the cadets to be examined. They enter and take their seats—on each side of the hall. The instructor of the particular section now takes his seat at the adjutant's table, and calls on the name of some one—say Willcox. The General[60] walks out to the middle of the floor, and the instructor says, "Mr. Willcox, you may go to the board and demonstrate such and such a proposition." The General then turns round on his *left* heel *a la militaire*, goes to the black board, puts down his work, faces about and stands in the position of a soldier at attention until called upon to demonstrate.

---

60. Cadets often used the sarcastic "general" when referring to other cadets.

In the mean time several others are called up in the same way and sent to the board, and *one* is kept standing in the middle of the floor and *questioned* in any part of the book, until some one is ready to make his demonstration. The instructor then says, "Proceed, Mr. Willcox." The General casts a timid glance at the Academic Board, and then at the black board and then looks at the instructor, and then begins. "I am required to demonstrate &c &c." His tongue tremulates, his lips quiver, his face changes to every hue as the blood alternately rushes across and deserts it; his knees enter into a most violent conflict and his heart beats time to the Devil's Tattoo! In a short time he acquires a little more confidence (& very little too), and when through his demonstration, walks again to the middle of the floor and undergoes a *questioning.* This last through, he turns upon that identical *left heel* and walks to his scat; happy, oh how happy if he has done well; miserable, no one knows how miserable, if he has done badly.

As soon as each member of the section has gone through this ordeal, the instructor reports to the superintendent that the section is through, the latter asks the Board whether they have any questions to propound, and if not, he says, "The section may retire." It generally takes about two hours to examine each section; the Board commence their session at eight o'clock and sit until three; as soon as a whole class is examined the standing is made out, and the cases of those who are deficient are considered. If there is any doubt entertained concerning any one, he is called up and examined a second time.

I believe they act fairly. Each member of the Board marks down a man according as he does, and if it is found that he gets less than *two*, and that his average mark through the term is likewise less, and his teacher recommends him to be *found*, the die is cast with that man, be he the son of his Celestial majesty, or of Jonathan Swapboots! Last night the result of the examination of our class was read out. Ten poor plebes have been found, Backus among them. I am placed eighth in Math and ninth in French, having risen two files in the former, and ten in the latter.

How are you all satisfied with my progress? For my part I am satisfied with the result. It is a great consolation to me that at the very time you are in straits to provide for the expenses of getting me here, you are not overwhelmed with such news as the friends of Backus and Cole are, but that on the contrary I have done so well and probably stand higher than any Wolverine yet has stood in this Institution. So "tip me your bone" dear brother on my success; I know you feel my *success* a greater recompense for all you have done for me at home than aught else; but some day I may make a more

78 FORGOTTEN VALOR

PRESENTATION OF DIPLOMAS BY GENL. GRANT.

EXAMINATION BEFORE BOARD OF VISITORS.

Examination before the Board of Visitors, West Point. *USMA Library.*

substantial return to you, and if God's providence spares us, likewise to my dearest mother. In the meantime give all the praise to God.

I have taken the pains to see the relative standing of the cadets from the different sections of the country; here is the result. I take the four classes as they stood in June—exclusive of my class—& *first* section in each class. 13 in each section.

1st Class, head man from Pennsylvania.
2d " do do " Connecticut.
3d " do do " Massachusetts.
4th " do do " New Jersey.
In our class (this examination) head man from Georgia.

Thus you see that the *North* furnish four out of five of the head men this year. *Not one* belongs in the West!

1 Sec. 1st Class: 12 North, 1 South (5 of all belong West).
" 2d Class: 5 North, 8 South (1 " " " ").

" 3d Class: 4 North, 9 South (2 " " " ").
" 4th Class: 9 North, 4 South (1 " " " ").
Our class this
examination: 9 North, 5 South (7 " " " ").

Thus you see how small a proportion in the 1st sections are from our Glorious West. My class leads the Western van; there is not a genuine Yankee in the whole of my section! All are either from the South or West, except *one* from New York. The West is *beginning* to show her importance everywhere. Pray with me she may keep it up.

Give my respects to Mr. Hammond, Mr. Duffield, all the folks in the house &c. . . .

Yours forever
Orlando

There is a tale in the Corps that once on a time a young lady who was in the habit of making free with the cadets, came up to a sentinel (in camp) and being challenged, answered "Friend with a kiss." The sentinel said, "Advance, friend with a kiss." Whereupon the lady advanced, intending to whisper the countersign in his ear, but the gallant sentinel gave her a buss and said, "Pass in, Friend with a kiss."

It is said of Mrs. Lieut. Wayne that one night (before she became Mrs. Wayne) she frightened a plebe sentinel out of his seven senses by coming up unawares and marching behind him at a lock step.

West Point
Oct. 20th, 1844
Night before last the order for the relief of Bob Garnett[61] was published. While the orders were reading, the men snapped their fingers and tapped on the floor with their feet, and as soon as the parade was dismissed they broke into three cheers. Garnett was officer in charge and standing near by.

It is said that the next morning when he went into Plebe Hardy's room, Hardy told him he was sorry he was going to leave the corps. "Well," says Bob, "glad to hear that *one* man regrets my leaving. *Gun Lock not snapt Sir!*"

61. Robert S. Garnett (27th, USMA 1841) fought in the Seminole and Mexican wars, distinguishing himself at Monterrey and Buena Vista. Commissioned brigadier general in the Confederate army on June 6, 1861, Garnett was posted in West Virginia, where he was mortally wounded on July 13, 1861, at Corrick's Ford by Federal troops under Maj. Gen. George B. McClellan.

When he was a cadet he was considered one of the cleverest fellows, but since he came back as instructor of tactics he has been hated by nearly every man in the corps for the manner in which he has treated them. . . .

Old Tom [Capt. J. Addison Thomas] came home Thursday night with his bride; next morning, as he came down to his office, about half the men were collected in front of North Barracks to look at the old fellow; he came along with his head down, and as soon as he got into his door, the men set up a general laugh. . . .

West Point
January 1st, 1845
Waked up about 12 by the band playing Auld Lang Syne. Felt perfectly enchanted, the music was so fine. The old year was *played out* in slow strains and *played in* by quick time. The cadets were at the windows, and some on north side of South Barracks, *stagging*, all cheering the band. . . .[62]

And now another year is "numbered with the past" and I look back upon its receding image as it vanishes into empty void behind, and ask myself what mark has the past year left upon my character, my destiny, my soul? It has ushered me into manhood, it leaves me happier than the last did and yet not happy. Happier since I have the near prospect of furlough, and not happy since I stand lower in my class, and have fears of falling from the 1st section.

God's spirit has been with me much this winter, and although I am very wicked and see a great many defects in my religious character, yet I may say that I am more firmly rooted in the faith than I was last New Year's day; for I have seen that God will not desert me though I may desert Him. Last encampment there was little of religion in my soul, scarcely any, and yet God did not give me over to blindness . . . but by His grace brot me back to the light of his favor & countenance.

One year ago I was fearful that I should never see my dear mother alive again. *Now* I rejoice in the hope of seeing her in health next summer. I have been brot to almost to mourn the loss of a brother in law, but he was spared. My sister Julia is married & well settled, my brother Charles is doing a good business for himself, & all things in my family look prosperous & happy. Oh! God grant they may so continue!

And now for the coming year. When I woke up at its birth I immediately sent my thoughts & petitions to Heaven. Happy beginning of the new year!

62. "Stagging" meant dancing with another male cadet.

Oh how my heart swelled! How my wishes for a little show of God's agency of good in this world made it throb! And how I prayed that I might be honored from above with the ability to do something for my fellow man, something for God! And now let my future course have a constant tendency towards this object—to do good. How great an honor it is for man to assist God! God has not the least *need* of man's assistance. He can do everything of Himself. But in His infinite condescension He permits man in many cases to be His agent. But who is *worthy?* No one certainly! Who is able? No one unless God makes him able. And oh, shameful to confess, no one is even willing, unless God's spirit makes him willing!

In order then to become an instrument of God's, I must continually petition God for the honor, and so far as in me lies, I must make constant preparation for the great work. . . . Let these then be my resolutions for the year 1845:

I will keep a perfect, constant, vigilant watch over all my appetites & evil passions.

I will not speak evil of any man. I will pursue an open, straight forward, religious and honorable course in my dealing with all men. Preserve truth as the apple of my eye, and be candid & sincere in even small matters, so as to make it a habit of mind in greater.

I will endeavor for the time I spend here to allow nothing whatever to intrude upon my studies; whether it be pleasure, or thoughts of home, or correspondence.

I will endeavor to cultivate a greater constancy of resolution in all matters and correct this weakness of mind which most frequently makes me a slave to the opinions of those around me. Let me especially guard my independence in thought, will and action, and endeavor to raise myself so far above the fear of others as to become *dead* to what they may think of a good action.

I must improve every moment of the precious time, yielding not even a leizure moment to unnecessary repose, for fear of encouraging indolence & inaction. *The time is short*, let me look upon the moments as *pearls*, as priceless jewels . . . which once lost, can *never, never* be redeemed! Oh happy I am always at the idea of leading a useful life!

I must not allow my mind to revolve upon light topics, but, except in recreation, let my thoughts revolve [around] useful, grand, deep subjects.

Let me make the word of God my frequent *study*. Let me cherish old friendships & strengthen early ties, rather than undervalue them and allow new ones to usurp too great an influence.

For the ensuing 6 months I must make it my aim—for the sake of my dear mother & brother & for the sake of becoming better prepared for God's work, to regain my lost standing in my class, and to rise as much higher as possible. . . .

May I not entertain too high opinion of myself, but think others better. Oh! make me humble. I am *filled* with pride, self conceit, & gross vanity; help me to banish these from my heart, from my manner. And may my heart constantly over flow with the milk of kindness; may I never speak the works of bitterness & scorn, except against sin, and even then with caution, lest I should inflict a wound without effecting a cure.

And now oh God, bless me, anoint me for the coming year. I shall be exposed to temptations; arm me against them. I shall become indolent; incite me renewedly to activity. I shall grow cold, oh warm me with thy love & with zeal. I shall forget thee; oh be thou never far off, Holy Spirit. I shall become attached to the world; oh wean me more and more from it; may I despise & pity & strive to overcome its follies, and from its gilded, fleeting pleasures may I turn towards the golden, eternal joys of Heaven. . . .

May 25, 1845

Long and cruelly neglected journal! Months have winged their way into eternity and no traces of their footsteps have been left upon thy secret, silent pages! Changes have passed over me, events have happened; thoughts have not deserted my hours of solitude and devotion, but there is no monument of their workings erected here. Could I but be free from the constant society of others, free from their "vain babblings" and unthinking mirth and noise, I would not thus have neglected thee, and now there lays my room-mate asleep, and so, my journal, for a moment's chat with thee—

After dinner to-day I visited Tom Neill's room to enjoy his comfortable fire and his sociable pipe of "Benny's best." After other topics were discussed by the crowd gathered there, the conversation (as most usually occurs) degenerated into vulgarity, and with disgust I left them to take a walk.

My faithful walking companion "Mac"[63] was with his mother at the Hotel, and so I went down upon "flirtation walk" alone. Oh how delightful is the fresh breeze that comes down the Hudson, skirting along the most beautiful and fragrant shores and pretty landscapes in the world. How bright the hills appear when decked with "living green," the Highlands of West Point!

63. "Mac" may have been either George B. McClellan or Julian McAllister.

It is here that I drink daily of the pure fountains of Nature; it is here I commune almost daily with the spirit of beauty. Keenly alive to the beauties of woman, it is with nature in such garb as she here assumes that I delight the most. I return to my quarters refreshed in mind and body, and always feel happier, better, stronger. And it seems as though when despondency had settled upon my spirits, there was no bright sunshine of hope to be found anywhere but among the bright hills and on the surface of the brave old flowing Hudson. And her hope basks upon every leaf, and dances along with every wave. . . .

FURLOUGH

Down to the boat at 10 Wednesday eve. 18th June 1845, she did not arrive until about 1— sweet waiting. Ten of us in all. . . . Got aboard *S. America*, some trouble turning out barkeeper; had supper got at the bar, drank all night. . . . Arrived at New York at day break. Took charge of the baggage of the squad. Astor House, corner room, 4th story; all got cockt. Burn[side] wanted to throw a trunk from the window. . . .

RETURN FROM FURLOUGH

Blue devils on board the boat; drank 'em down. Sang, promenaded, played whist and drank liquor until arrived at Buffalo. The idea of returning back from furlough is the worst feeling I ever experienced; had the blues almost constantly. . . . Reached New York morning of the 28th August. . . . Found the fellows in the corner room, 4th story, Astor House, crying for soda water & clean shirts—they left the house 70$ in debt. . . . Landed [at West Point] holding up Cadet B. before old Tom. Walked up the road with Seward. Tom came along with a cit., introduced Seward, cut me because I had no titled father! Felt awful at landing, suddenly dropt from a cadet on furlough to a cadet at W. P., the most miserable devil in the world; went to dinner hooting and yelling. Cut the ball, felt like cutting my throat. . . .

Dec. 7 [1845]

To-night Burnside saw a bumb[64] taking off Mary Lovelace, took up rocks and told the bumb to let her go; after receiving a few whizzing shots the bumb let go and ran for his life, Burnside soon after him, ran for Burt's office, stopt at the door. Burn told him to "strike." Bumb lay his hand to his sabre, another shot of coal and Mr. Bumb run, crying "cadets" "officers"!

64. "Bumb," or "bum" was cadet slang for a regular soldier who was stationed at West Point but who had no relation to the academy proper.

After taps, Heth & Pickett chased the bumb off again. Alden[65] enquires into it. Crazy Stuart[66] (sentinel) says "they may have been playing hide & go seek." Burn says he saw there was difficulty and ordered the bumb to "leave barracks"! . . .

Dec. 14, 1845

Capt. Alden inspected with old Tom this morning and assumed command by the following order this evening. "The undersigned assumes command of the Corps of Cadets."

B. R. Alden

Comdt. Cadets

Quite laconic. Made a farewell call upon old Tom to-day; no more than a dozen others did the same—shameful. . . .[67]

Find my heart in a dark state; not been to the Communion table since last spring; disgraced myself on furlough with others who twit me of it; ashamed to disgrace God by going to His table. Something must quickly be done or I shall be undone. . . .

West Point

April 5th 1846

This evening saw Mr. Parks who sent for me to urge me to come to the Communion. I felt as though I ought to. He said if I did not resume my religion before graduating there was scarcely any probability of my doing so after getting into the army. This being Easter week he urged me to prepare for next Sunday. I promised I would, shedding tears, as is my wont, [in] my *weakness* or *relief*, I know not which. . . .

West Point

January 2d, 1847

Last New Year's day passed away and left no record on these pages. *Superstition* compels me to write something now, for last year (1846) I fear has left no record of good on the sands of time.

<hr />

65. Capt. B. R. Alden was about to become the new commandant of cadets. J. Addison Thomas, newly married, was leaving the Academy.

66. James Stuart (39th, 1846) roommate of George McClellan. Stuart died from wounds received at Rogue River, Oregon, in 1851.

67. Most cadets were delighted to see "Old Tom" Thomas leave. That evening, remembered one cadet, the barracks "shone like a plebe's waist plate," as the cadets put candles in their windows to "show old Tom how glad we are he is going." See John C Waugh, *The Class of 1846* (New York: Warner Books, 1994), p. 62.

I have just been reading some of the contents of this book and how changed are the *tones* of my heart! Oh! it makes me miserable to see how fallen I am! It seems as though my little character was completely gone. I never supposed that trouble *could* affect me so much. To find myself discouraged & almost broken hearted, no enjoyment in the present, no fixed aim, good, bad or indifferent for the future. . . . Oh! the picture is dreadful.

What has wrought this change in an ardent, aspiring mind? Let me examine the events of the past few months. Last spring I thought I had discovered the nature of my mind, and the thing for which it seemed alone fitted. I was told by a friend many years ago that I would one day make an eminent orator, but I never believed it. I thought early I was intended for a painter; later I thought my mind was of a poetic cast. I always thought I should never become a great general, and this is the truest belief of all! But last spring I made a public speech before the "Dy,"[68] and the sublime elevation to which I sprang in my excitement, and the applause of the audience, brought me to the conclusion that *Eloquence* was my gift. The discovery fell like a flood of sun light upon me, it filled me with joy & pride, and I thought that as soon as a convenient opportunity should offer, I would study law.

I was elected through the skillfulness & influence of McAllister (I suspect) to deliver a 4th July oration. My delight was unbounded. I saw distinction "right ahead" and I longed to embrace it. I had but a short time previously made up my mind to do nothing for the mere praise of man. I stifled my conscience and broke my resolution.

But I must go further back. . . . The scene of *sprees* and card playing. I was surrounded then by the most pernicious influence in my class. By giving myself up to the pleasures of the "*crowd*" on furlough, I identified myself with them, losing thereby my previous respectable character of a consistent Christian. My room (no. 17) was the rendezvous for the "fellows" till late at night, partly on account of my roommates & partly my having a light after taps (being sergeant major). I could not drink anything but beer, on account of the parson's pledge, but was in the habit of setting up with the men & playing cards, and they used to procure beer for my special benefit.

I recollect well of sitting up all night long New Year's eve. The score on which my conscience acquitted me of such conduct was that I had no other means of enjoyment. From the trouble which has followed from my looseness let me learn that [having] no pleasure at all is better than that which, however innocent in itself, requires any *excuse* for partaking of it, on account of the uncertainty of its tendency.

68. Referring to the academy's dialectic society.

But in April [1846] I lost my relish for such things on account of becoming more religious, and on Easter Day I took Communion for the first time in nearly if not quite a year. I was so serious that I doubted much whether I should attend the encampment dancing parties, and they are attended by all the members of the church here. However enslaved the heart may be by the customs of its fellows, there are times of unusual religious warmth when it will see clearly through the earthly and even *church* disguises of the truth.

My conscience told me the dancing parties would make me more worldly, and the custom of the members of the church attending them, though it did not serve to blind me to the truth of my heart's suggestion, it succeeded in affording me an excuse: though I promised myself to be on my guard. The author of the Spiritual Converse may say that the best way to overcome temptation is to meet it, but my own sad experience teaches me that the best way to escape temptation is to flee from it. . . . The Devil will meet us more than half way without our seeking him. Veteran saints may boldly meet the "adversary," but the young Christian may excusably show the *discreet* part of valor in such an unequal fight.

The encampment presented a rich view, too tempting for my weak resolutions. I entered it with but one purpose, that of enjoying as much pleasure as possible, in order to make up for the labors of the year. The second day (20th June) was the first of my "pleasure," and the seed of a great harvest of pain, which I am now bitterly reaping, was then sown.

Passing by barracks with Patton, I learned that John Adams was "treating" his friends. I was invited, thought I'd go up to see, not to drink, *saw* that there was to be a *spree*, and endeavored to back out, but I was urged so hard that I consented to drink *one* glass. Having taken one glass, my resolution was dissipated in the fumes of liquor, and the result was that I went to camp excited, fell asleep on a camp stool before Burnside's tent, was seen by Beltzhoover, who put me in as a shower came up, and treasured the event in his heart & memory.

The next event was the 4th July celebration. [The] Corps marched in procession, band, escort (2 platoons), academic board, chaplain & president, orator & reader, corps of cadets, officers, Kinsley's school.[69] Black & Burns carried colors.[70] Stood before altar. Greeted by the smile of Southgates as I entered.

69. Z. J. D. Kinsley's Mathematical and Preparatory School, which was adjacent to the Military Academy.
70. Henry M. Black (24th, USMA 1847); William W. Burns (28th, USMA 1847).

After performance the band struck. Parson took me warmly by the hand; had to hold my breath, felt proud, *grand, lofty.* Yes, I said, my [forte] is eloquence, and I bear the key to unlock the human heart.

Rained all day except when the procession was out(!) After service fired a salute, by which my ears were so stunned that I could scarcely hear for two weeks; found it bad in the evening; perfect [illegible word] at the party; nothing but compliments & congratulations. My God, my happiness, my prosperity was too great! it raised me upon the shoulders of the world and I was borne away. At the party introduced to A.L.C.; very much pleased with her.

A day or two before the 4th went to Fort Put[71] to let out my lungs. Caught spouting *Catalina* by a gentleman & lady, ran down the back wall of the fort to avoid them. On the morning previous to 4th went down by the water among the rocks to practice, was answered from a schooner! . . .

Great compliments at Berard's; gent. & lady of the Point said simultaneously I reminded them of Clay! Great boy among all the girls! See Nora, get interested. Cut her at Brewerton's, meet her in the evening at Alden's. Great flirtation on my knees out on the porch. Beg for a tender token. Refused! . . . Felt bad. Half in love but more than half flirtation. She began it.

Get thick with A.L.C.; never love any one so much like *the character* for my wife, but no idea of getting in love, too young for her, no wish to get married until I could win a *fame* in this world. Ambition ruled my heart, not love. . . .

Nora comes back, walk after taps. Tell her how much I admire [her]. . . . Talk eloquently & poetically. Back about 11. Promise to break off with A.L.C.! Nora gets sisterly[;] advises me not to marry any country girl, that as I had a fine taste I ought to marry a rich girl. . . .

Take A.L.C. to see Nora. "Greek meets Greek." Obvious to my friends that both were trying their best to cut each other out. But both flirting. On my guard.

Morning at band hall. *Swashed* with Nora. Afternoon at Indian falls. Delightful walk. Sudden view of the falls. Charming seat, fit for an angel. Smoke cigar at feet of A.L.C., who fanned me. My Conscience, what happiness! Climbed the fall with her. Soft hand. . . . Think of Nora occasionally, but determine to subdue my passion for her. . . .

The developments of the Court of Inquiry fall upon me while my heart is absorbed in Self & the world. Determine to weather the storm. . . .

71. Fort Putnam, just southwest of the Academy, constructed during the American Revolution under the supervision of General George Washington.

God softens my heart. After the "trial" a relapse into indifference towards God. . . . A feeling of indifference & contempt if not recklessness ensues. Ambition all broken down, disheartened. Mother gets the news, the worst blow of all. . . . Appeal once more to God for support. Dark period. God admits me to his favor but not to the enjoyment of his love. Dreadful feelings. Try to do well in studies. Bad luck pursues me. . . .

The year 1847 is before me. I am almost as ignorant of what I now am (in character) as of what I shall be at the end of the year. This may find me in Mexico or in Oregon, or perhaps in the grave; a better Christian or a greater sinner. O! God, I humbly appeal to Thee once more to lead me. I am blind. Into Thy hands I commit the events of this year. Renew my strength daily. May I learn to despise the world still more and to free myself from the slavery of vanity. O! my mother's God be mine; with weal or woe, be my God & guide.

W. Point
Feb. 21, 1847
The Court Martial proceedings were published Jan'y 24th. *Acquitted of violation of pledge.* Found guilty of 113th Paragraph &c, but "on account of the circumstances which led to and attended the case, and on account of the estimable character &c," "the court *united* in recommending that the sentence be not executed." Thus was my reputation *cleansed* from the stain of dishonor which scandal & persecution had affixed upon it for more than three months. . . .

 THREE

Under Winfield Scott in Mexico

[On May 13, 1846, the United States Congress declared war against Mexico.
Brought about by the U.S. annexation of Texas in December 1845, claims against
the Mexican government by U.S. citizens seeking reparations for personal injury
and property damages incurred in the numerous Mexican revolutions of the
period, and a strong desire by U.S. expansionists to acquire California, the war
would last until February 1848. U.S. military operations began with a
three-pronged plan of campaign. Gen. Zachary Taylor was to invade northern
Mexico and Col. Stephen W. Kearny would occupy New Mexico and California,
while naval forces blockaded the Mexican coasts.

In April 1846, Taylor moved his forces to the mouth of the Rio Grande (which
the state of Texas claimed as its southern boundary). Mexico, however, claimed the
Nueces River (northeast of the Rio Grande) as the boundary and therefore
considered Taylor's move an act of aggression. Mexican troops were then sent
across the Rio Grande, resulting in the battle of Palo Alto, where Taylor won his
first victory, followed by another at Resaca de la Palma the following day.
Consistently pressing the Mexican forces back into Mexico, Taylor occupied
Matamoros (May 18) and captured Monterrey (September 24), eventually
winning a decisive victory at the stubbornly contested battle at Buena Vista
(February 22–23, 1847), ending Mexican resistance in northern Mexico.

In spite of a string of successes by Taylor and Kearny, Mexico refused to
acknowledge defeat, prompting the United States to send an expedition under
Gen. Winfield Scott to capture Mexico City, via the old National Road from Vera

Cruz, on the east coast, which Scott captured on March 29, 1847. Marching west from Vera Cruz, the American forces defeated the Mexican troops under Gen. Antonio Lopez de Santa Anna in a succession of battles at Cerro Gordo, Contreras, and Churubusco, eventually arriving before the city of Mexico itself. After the storming of Molino del Rey and the castle of Chapultepec, the city fell to the Americans on September 14, 1847.

Although Willcox arrived too late to participate in the fighting, his account of following Scott's army to Mexico City is nonetheless a fascinating, often humorous memoir of the life of a soldier on his first campaign. In spite of the hardships suffered and the ever-present frustrations of a junior officer, Willcox's descriptions of the landscape and the people make it easy to see why he and so many other young soldiers fell in love with the strange and exotic country of Mexico.]

‹My classmates and myself desired to go down [to Mexico] as soon as possible after graduating, but the Adjutant General sent us to our homes to await our orders, and consequently none of the Class of 1847 were partakers in those glorious Mexican campaigns. Though it is almost certain that had we been ordered directly from West Point, we could not have reached Vera Cruz in time for the last fighting column which left under [Brigadier General Franklin] Pierce on the 16th of July. Could I have graduated one year earlier, it would have made the greatest difference in my future prospects, but God, who is wisest, ordained it as it was. But the disappointment was great.›[1] The cadets who were fortunate enough to be commissioned for the Mexican War were to rendezvous en-route at Louisville, although their destinations were different—the Brazos, Tampico and Vera Cruz. We were to journey together from Louisville to New Orleans.

We were accorded a fine reception in Louisville at the house of Hon. James Madison Cutts, where we met the celebrated belle of the South, Miss Cutts.[2] In every respect she deserved the title. Tall and queenly but

1. The introduction (and conclusion) for this chapter, contained within the single angle brackets (‹ ›), is excerpted from the closing pages of OBW's *West Point Journal*. The material contained within the double brackets « » in this chapter is excerpted from a journal, written on loose blue paper, in which OBW recorded some of his earliest Mexican War memories (though probably shortly after the war and his return to the States); it also contains entries of his experience on the Plains. This journal is hereafter referred to as OBW *Bluebook*.

2. James Madison Cutts, a nephew of Dolley Madison, had for many years been an official under the second comptroller of the treasury. An able and hardworking man, Cutts rose no higher in Washington politics, as he was without political backing. His daughter was Adele Cutts, whose beauty and charm in Washington society was legendary. She became the second wife of Stephen Douglas on November 20, 1856.

endowed with all the graces, affable and sprightly in conversation, with Southern softness and frankness, it goes without saying that she literally captured that party of bold soldier boys. Yet the rooms were alive with other Louisville girls of marvellous charm. Eager as we were to reach Mexico, this first start in the great world of society, to susceptible youths like ourselves, made us more or less reluctant to hurry off.

But go we needs, and those who remember taking one of the ... Louisville and New Orleans steamers of those days can appreciate the interest and excitement attending the trip: the constant danger of grounding or being blown up [by the boiler], the intense anxiety to beat "the other boat," the cries of the man at the bow bearing the lead, "low water," "by the mark twain," etc., the betting on deck and gambling below stairs, the numerous cocktails and an occasional pistol shot, besides the curiosity we all felt to see Southern life so far as one might judge at the various landings, and new ... passengers with their slaves; these and similar features that characterized travelling down the "Great Mississip'" in the forties, can easily be recalled. No wonder such a trip must have left an indelible mark on the memory and on even the name of one of our best-known authors and humorists, Mr. Clemens. . . .

«Our party consisted of twelve classmates. We came in from Lake Ponchatrain on the morning of the 18th Sept[ember] 1847; drove through New Orleans rapidly to escape the yellow fever—which ravished the city of 100 lives a day—and we found ourselves aboard the [steamboat] *Alabama* four hours before the time.

I have never had such feeling anywhere else as hung over me at New Orleans. It was the city of the pestilence: dirty, gloomy and half deserted. In passing through the street we kept camphor [in handkerchiefs] at our noses. The acclimated probably smiled at us. The newsboys and the "niggers" certainly did.

Some of the party went after a supply of liquors, cigars and *sombreros*. Ours had high peaks, and, slouched on one side, they gave us the look of Guy Fawkes in the parliament cellars, or of the flying Mexican in the barber-shop pictures of Col. May. The down was just beginning to peep from our upper lips and chins, and we thought ourselves very fierce looking fellows.»

Needless to say how eager we were to take the first boats for our various destinations. My steamer, with officers, men and military stores, was headed for Vera Cruz, over the blue Gulf of Mexico. I have never been on the Mediterranean, but I can scarcely imagine any body of water or lovelier sky than our [own] inland sea and its semi-tropical shores.

«There were on board [the *Alabama*] a company of Louisiana Volunteers and ninety sickly, convict-looking scape graces who were shortly to rejoice under the title of M.D.U.S.A. (Mule Drivers U.S. Army). A crowd had collected on the levee when we moved off. They cheered the dirty crowd aboard the vessel. The Volunteers stacked their muskets on the deck, raised a small flag, and answered the cheering vociferously. I tried to feel animated and patriotic, but the mob on the levee consisted of "niggers," apple women and paddies;[3] our heroic Volunteers were drunk, & patriotism was at discount.

But we swept away from the crescent city, leaving the splendid cupola of the St. Charles in the undisturbed possession of its sovereignty over the few churches, that half hide the "diminished heads" beneath the shadow of its greatness.

The teamsters and the soldiers soon got to fighting, but the latter had arms, and a guard was posted over the M.D.'s on the very first row [altercation]. Night came down upon the river and drove us into the cabin, where we began to count noses.

We had Maj. Bennet, a paymaster and a jolly roisterer, with his clerk, Capt. Hale. . . . He had been at West Point in his day, but found it inconvenient to remain. He joined us near Baton Rouge, and was decidedly the hero of our party, for he had been in a fight at the National Bridge, on the Vera Cruz line, and could tell us all about the road, the guerrillas, and other bug-bears.

This Captain had a dispute directly with the third distinguished passenger, the Captain of the Volunteers, with reference to the command. Hale claimed it on the ground of his rank, but the other contested for it on account of his having the only troops on board. Had they proceeded to violence, the latter Captain would certainly have proved himself in the right, unless the teamsters could have been armed and enlisted against him; but M.D.'s are generally of doubtful trust!

Another distinguished character was Dr. Johnson, who talked Spanish, had been a resident, a wanderer and a smuggler in Mexico. He had a long goat's beard, had stories to tell of Waddy Thompson[4] when [he was] Mexican minister, and was an amateur fighter at the Battle of Buena Vista. The

3. "Paddy" was nineteenth-century slang for a person of Irish descent.
4. Waddy Thompson (1798–1868), Whig congressman and diplomat from South Carolina. An ardent Nullifier, Thompson was appointed minister to Mexico in 1842, during which time he procured the release of some three hundred U.S. citizens who had been captured during the war between Texas and Mexico. A favorite of the Mexicans, Thompson was an opponent of the Mexican War.

manner in which he stroked his beard, drew down the corners of his mouth, and decided disputed points, was quite professional.

Besides these gentlemen, there were several whose mien was doubtful, their characters not yet formed, nor their titles known. They might, on arriving at Vera Cruz, become wagon masters and attach a Q.M.D. (Quartermaster's Dept.) to their names; or they might enter the custom house and assist Mr. Walker's[5] agents to work his new tariff, or they might become black-legs. There was no telling; and while in this state of uncertainty as to their exact position in society, they kept their mouths shut, looked down upon their plates when at table, stalked haughtily by the soldier or teamster, and passed an officer deferentially.

A curious class of Mexican heroes this. I may neglect them further on. In Mexico you found them in every train. Many of them without ostensible employment. They were clerks, friends, money lenders, contractors, merchants with small wares and large baggage. . . .

And how they subsisted would puzzle the d[evi]l. Some of them could "ring in" to an officer's mess by the gift of a box of wine, or ham or two, & a cheese. They always offered you part of their lunch on a march, generally had a drop of choice whiskey, and entering the town a little ahead of the column, they would find out where [illegible word] was to be found, pretty women to be seen, and other things useful and curious. They generally managed to be well mounted and look knowing; they were fond of carrying orders, more so perhaps than obeying them, and they seemed to delight in enunciating them loudly to those to whom they were sent.

On the march they were well enough, but in a city or town when you made a stay, they assumed the shape of the hydra, and met you with their hundred heads at every town: Contractors, agents, strikers, wagon masters, gamblers . . . sutlers, interpreters, knaves, fools, bores, cunning chaps, wags, prophets, preachers, news mongers and prison prey of all other sorts.

You enter a saloon. One collars you to drink, another buttons you with a joke, and he introduces to you his friend in leather pants, shabby genteel coat and Mexican hat, with sash and revolver. You all drink, you all laugh; you say something; one of your new friends, who, like Mrs. Croaker, is "all laugh and no joke," thunders his applause upon the bar, and heels it on the floor. . . .

Do you want to purchase anything? Ten to one that they've bought it. Do you go to the fandango? It is crowded with your nondescripts, and you are more likely to get your skull cracked than not.

5. Robert J. Walker (1801–1869) was then secretary of the treasury.

Little did I know the tribe; little did they know themselves, as they sat so demurely in the cabin of the steamer, which was following the winding Mississippi on its way to the Gulf. Yet there were some noble adventurous fellows among those "outsiders," fit associates for any man, and there were likewise some infernal rascals, whom the devil himself would cut in public.

We found ourselves outside the [sand]bar on rising for breakfast in the morning. Which one of the "one hundred mouths of the Mississippi" had cast us into the Gulf, we did not know, but the Balize light house was seen as a speck upon our starboard quarter, and the green water was gradually verging into the "dark blue" of which so much is said and sung.

The vessel began to feel the motion of the billows, [as did] the passengers of that vessel. H—— had laughed over the prospect of seeing us all sea sick; he had crossed the Great Lakes, and could boast of having navigated the Mississippi; he considered himself an old tar; of course he was the first one to suffer. The laugh was on him for the whole passage.

There was an extraordinary teamster on board, extraordinary for his name and nose—the one was so cancered and the other so common—Smith. We had yellow fever cases on board. Smith nursed them, shrived them, shaved them, sewed them up in their blankets and conducted them overboard. Smith showed everybody how everything should be done; that cancer nose was in everything; he was the most active, artful, arduous and ambitious man aboard ship: from the cooking of a meal of victuals in a storm, to the cracking of a skull in a row, Smith excelled all the M.D.s and Volunteers.

Sea voyages are tiresome, yet everybody thinks his sea voyage peculiar: the waves were higher, the people sicker, the captain crosser, the phosphorous brighter at night, and the flying fish flew further by day; the dolphins prettier and the sharks uglier than all those of any other sea voyage on record.

We arrived off the mouth of the Rio Grande & caught a sight [of] the famed chaparral bushes—there was five feet [of] water on the bar. The Brazos is preferable as a harbor; it has eight feet [of] water on the bar. We anchored off here, a lighter was sent out to carry back our paymaster & his coin, as well as two or three of our original party. There was quite a settlement in the harbor, and one at the mouth of the Rio Grande, where none was before. War breeds business, and business breeds Yankees.

A man had been striving to get overboard to drown himself, but Smith was always on hand to prevent the jump, until off the Brazos the poor fellow cries, "Good bye boys, I'm off" and over he went. The water seemed to restore his reason, and he swam for his life. Smith was the first in the small boat which was lowered, and the aquatic adventurer rescued and brought aboard in his sound mind.

Smith was a great man for an M.D.; his name cut off family pride, and he could not turn up his nose, for it was almost eaten off, yet he was a great man nevertheless, one of [Robert] Burns' noblemen. . . .

We drew near Tampico, a few miles from the mouth of the Panuca River— I forget how many. A pirogue came out to us with a pilot and manned by living Mexicans! Descendants perhaps of the old allies of Cortez, the [Campobellians?]; brown & grim; black, soft eyes when beaming over a smile, but fiercely hard & savage when darting from beneath a frown. Straight limbed, broad shouldered, regular featured, between those of the Grecian and those of the North American Indian. Such to me was the appearance of the Mexican native of the *Tierra Caliente*.

They came out in a fleet of boats loaded with fruit as soon as we had cast anchor, and were ready either to carry us ashore or to sell us bananas, etc. My dime dropped into the hands of the "oldest native," and I jumped into the pirogue, just such a log canoe as I had fished in when a boy, and commenced eating and looking *green* at the composed old enemy who was affording me "aid and comfort." One always feels awkwardly in company with one whose language he does not understand. . . . But the old Indian was very *Si, señor*, and I was very mum until we landed upon the shore, which smelt very yellow-feverish, and where I met Bob Wagstaff. He had been a gallant, bluff and burly captain on the Lakes, and was associated with my boyish recollections of all that was bullyish on election days at home, when the Whig sailors and butchers generally visited the different wards for the sake of flogging the dutch Democrats.

Bob was just up from a recent knock down of the "yellow jack," and which he said had nearly "bilged" him. He seemed to be as glad to see any one from Detroit as I was, and he boasted that though he had been unfortunate at home, he was now in the receipt of two or three thousand a year as harbor master. Bob remembered, too, what many Americans in Mexico seemed to forget, that he had a wife in the States, and to her he faithfully forwarded the most of his money.

He took me up into the city; we entered the plaza; there was the foundation of Santa Anna's monument. It was in 1829 that Barradas brought the last Spanish force against Mexico.[6] He occupied Tampico with 3,000 men;

6. General Isidro Barradas, commanding Spanish troops in Cuba, had been sent by King Ferdinand VII to seize Tampico, in response to then Mexican President Vincente Guerrero's recent legislation expelling all Spaniards from Mexico. Santa Anna was sent by Guerrero to

during his temporary absence with 2,000, Santa Anna besieged and took the city with 700. Barradas reappeared. Santa Anna's retreat was cut off by the river. He fooled Barradas into the belief that he had an overwhelming force, and made his escape. . . . Santa Anna obtained reinforcements, delivered Tampico, and drove the Spaniards into the sea, as Gen. Jackson did the English from New Orleans. . . .

On the sides of the plaza were the *fonda*, the stores and the palace. Walk into the *fonda*. There is the usual Mexican quantities of bad mixtures at the bar, and the usual number of tables for roulette, faro, monte and coffee or chocolate. It is a land flowing with *abacinth* and *orzeat*, doubloons and devils; good liquor and good morals are equally as scarce. . . . You would meet nearly every American officer in the place at the *fonda* sometime during the day. . . .

In the evening we attended a *soiree* at Col. Gates',[7] where our vision was blessed with the sight of a few ladies. One, the daughter of our ex consul, a Frenchman who had married a Spanish lady, was very pretty. She looked languishingly from her large, softening eyes, and talked sweetly, but I could understand the eyes much better than the tongue. I talked some bad French to her good Spanish, over a pretty flower, and finally we took a glass of wine, which she "drank to me only with her eyes." As this little circle of ladies appeared to be the last I should see for some time, I regarded the hour spent in it with peculiar pleasure. And there are circumstances which the heart only can appreciate. . . .

On the next morning we left Tampico. Its low built & square houses, whose flat roofs were unrelieved by aspiring steeples—the most commercial are not the most religious towns—disappeared as we made a turn in the

---

reduce the foothold Barradas had established, but he was provided no troops or supplies. As a result, Santa Anna was forced to draw men and resources from Vera Cruz.

Antonio Lopez de Santa Anna, the "hero of Tampico," was first elected president of Mexico in 1833 and eventually assumed a dictatorship. In 1836 he led a Mexican army into Texas, but after some initial success (as at the Alamo) his forces were annihilated by Sam Houston at San Jacinto; Santa Anna was forced to surrender. After a brief confinement in Washington, where he met President Andrew Jackson, Santa Anna returned to Mexico in 1837, deposed but still a hero to the Mexican people. During the period from 1839 to 1844 Santa Anna served twice as president, raising taxes and spending lavishly on festivals and a private army, as he worked his way toward a monarchy.

Overthrown in 1844, Santa Anna was exiled to Cuba. Soliciting aid from the United States, he promised to settle the Texas boundary dispute amicably, if and when he returned to power. Permitted to pass through the American blockade of the Mexican coast, Santa Anna reneged and began to prepare for war. In December 1846 he once again assumed the presidency and in 1847 led his country to war against the United States.

7. Probably Col. William Gates, 3d U.S. Artillery.

river. . . . We followed the coast. The outline was beautiful, now low and rolling back into the interior like a gentle, undulating wave, and now breaking abruptly into lofty ridges, like the piling of mountain billows. But frequently we saw slopes moving evenly down from high mountains to the very sea. One in particular was so regular that you might apparently draw a straight line for miles up an ascent, and it would be tangent at every point. A capital ramp for Jove to descend with his artillery into the squally dominions of Neptune.

The famed peak of Orizaba appeared in its proper time & place, a much talked of and expected friend. There is something elevating at the sight of such a mountain, at such a distance—scores of miles—and so covered with snow. It seemed to rob the clouds of their glory. . . . There is something soul satisfying to see such things. . . .

We were called upon to bury two soldiers. The service was read, the cannon shot, and their blankets, like the Indian and his arrows, bore them company as they were launched into eternity. Who pities the soldier, or praises him, buried at sea or dead by disease? The chords of people's sympathies must be strung with bullets, and yet, perhaps, the least of war's evils are to be found on the battlefield. Bear me witness, ye gallant Volunteers, who, at the call of your country, and for patriotism & politics, rushed down . . . in such swarms to the "Halls of Montezuma." How few of you returned to tell the sickening tale of all your hardships! Perhaps a third might answer the summons, and all covered with glory and the spoils of war & office the escaped appear. Their comrades, where are they? The battlefield can boast of but a few; but the *Tierra Caliente* and its terrible forces, their own carelessness, recklessness & filth have bridged the Gulf, from New Orleans to Vera Cruz, and paved the road to the City of Mexico with their carcasses! Rise, Benton,[8] and collect their ashes; bury them upon the highest mountains, and let Orizaba & Popocateptl be the monuments of their folly, and of the wisdom of the government that sent them thus to die!

The escort not having discharged all their guns at the last round, a few scattering shots were heard after the ceremony was over. "What's that," asked one Paddy of another, who was the wag of the passage. "Och," he replied, "the dead beggars have come up to the top, and they're scaring 'em back, to be sure." This was received with merriment, and the bodies that sank and the waves that covered, and the ownerless names were soon forgotten.

8. OBW refers to Sen. Thomas Hart Benton, an avid expansionist, but who had been initially against a war with Mexico. Benton harbored military ambitions and had hoped to be made general in chief during the war with Mexico.

The Spirit on Orizaba saw our speck of a vessel, animated by the souls of specks of men, burning with specks of hopes and ambition, starting from & cloyed & confined by clay, and the Spirit on Orizaba drew himself upon his proud eminence & laughed, while round *his* breast the rolling clouds spread and eternal sunshine settled on his head.»

Those of our party who were [bound] for General Scott's line, were landed at Vera Cruz—a walled and fortified city that had so long and stoutly resisted the siege of *Los Americanos*, now passively submissive to those left behind when the invading army started on its memorable fighting march to the Halls of the Montezumas.[9]

I reported to General Patterson . . . and was kindly offered a place on his personal staff, which I respectfully declined, preferring immediate line duty in Lloyd Tilghman's battery—my first military blunder, as without gaining any field service under Captain Tilghman I lost the life long influence and friendship of General Patterson.[10]

After a few weeks' monotonous camp life and battery drill on the sands outside the city gates, the battery to which I properly belonged, Co. G, 4th Artillery, arrived to my great joy. It had come from the just-captured City of Mexico. My senior officers were Captain Mansfield Lovell and Lieutenant Fitz-John Porter—afterwards generals of note.[11] They brought

9. Vera Cruz, on Mexico's eastern coast, was the principal port for Scott's army of invasion. He established it as his base of supplies after briefly laying siege to the city, which surrendered to the American forces on March 27, 1847.

Scott's forces began marching inland, following the old National Highway (which Cortez had followed in 1519) through the Valley of Mexico the second week of April 1847, with fewer than nine thousand effective troops. Though greatly outnumbered (by August, Scott's forces numbered no more than thirteen thousand effectives, opposing possibly thirty-six thousand Mexicans), the American forces consistently defeated the inept Mexican forces in battles at Cerro Gordo (April 17–18), Contreras and Churubusco (August 20), and finally before the City of Mexico itself, with assaults on the Molino Del Rey (September 8) and Chapultepec (September 13). American forces entered the city on September 14. OBW landed at Vera Cruz in early October. Although the main fighting was over, guerrilla detachments were everywhere.

10. Maj. Gen. Robert Patterson was a veteran of the War of 1812 who had performed well at the Battle of Cerro Gordo, and in seizing the town of Jalapa, where he won the praise of General Scott. His Civil War career was short-lived and less than stellar; he failed to hold Confederate Gen. Joseph E. Johnston in the Shenandoah Valley, allowing him to unite his troops with Beauregard in time to achieve a Confederate victory at First Bull Run.

Lloyd Tilghman (46th, USMA 1836), then captain, served primarily as an engineering officer during the Mexican War, though he was later given a battery (that never saw action). In the Civil War, Tilghman entered the Confederate service as a brigadier general. He surrendered Fort Henry to U.S. Grant on February 6, 1862. Tilghman faced Grant again at Champion's Hill, Mississippi, where he was killed, May 16, 1863. OBW's service under Tilghman was temporary.

11. Mansfield Lovell (9th, USMA 1842). OBW served under Lovell in Mexico and again on the western plains. As a major general in the Confederate service during the Civil War, Lovell

down two of our six-pounders which had been lost at the battle of Buena Vista and recaptured by our own regiment at the Battle of Contreras, and used in the subsequent fights up to the taking of the Mexican Capital by General Scott. Alas, I had arrived at Vera Cruz too late to participate in that glorious campaign. Scott had cut loose from his communications and the column which brought our guns under Lovell and Porter was the first to reopen the roads. It was commanded by Colonel Joe Johnston[12] [and] escorted an ambulance train of invalided sick or wounded and had come principally for supplies of ammunition, clothing, hospital stores, etc. These were quickly loaded up and Lovell's crippled battery [was] repaired and re-furnished with caissons, horses and ammunition, and the column promptly started for the front. Our route ran over the splendid National Road from the Gulf to the Capital, leading through some of the finest cities and the most beautiful scenery. Old Orizaba first towered in sight over the palm-waving *Tierra Caliente*, and all beyond was more or less mountain and high-land with cities, haciendas and tropical plantations between. We looked for-ward most eagerly to the celebrated pass, described so enthusiastically and well by Prescott,[13] between Popocateptl and Ixtaxahuatl.

This was my first march in a hostile country. It can be more easily imag-ined than described with what exultation I touched spurs to my horse and took up the command, "Battery Forward!" nor with what delight I joined my first campfire and listened to tales of the late campaign, told by intel-ligent officers who had participated in the arduous work and hair-breadth escapes. A finer set of gentlemen I have never met than these....

---

was put in charge of the defenses of New Orleans, which he was forced to evacuate in April 1862—an unfortunate event that earned him the enmity of the South and eventually cost him his command.

Fitz-John Porter (8th, USMA 1845) achieved notoriety as commander of the Fifth Corps in the Army of the Potomac. A loyal supporter of George McClellan, Porter was charged with "disloyalty, disobedience and misconduct in the face of the enemy" by Maj. Gen. John Pope at the battle of Second Manassas. Wrongly convicted, chiefly due to a political vendetta against McClellan, Porter was cashiered from the service in January 1863 and spent the greater portion of his remaining life trying to exonerate himself. In 1878 Porter was exonerated of all charges, but not until 1886 did then President Grover Cleveland reinstate Porter to the rank of colonel (but without awarding him back pay). He died May 21, 1901.

12. OBW's unit was actually a part of Patterson's column, which left Vera Cruz on Novem-ber 1 with some three thousand men. Col. Joseph E. Johnston, a future Confederate general of note, led a detachment of reinforcements that followed Patterson's troops to Mexico City.

13. William H. Prescott (1796–1859), U.S. historian, whose monumental work *History of the Conquest of Mexico*, 3 vols. (1843) was translated into ten languages, and which OBW refers to here.

<<<March from Vera Cruz.[14]

Left Vergara Oct. 30, 1847. Gen'l [Caleb] Cushing in command of the division. Army composed of 4 regiments infantry, 2 squads dragoons, 600 Texian Rangers under Col. [John C.] Jack Hays, Tilghman's battery of 6 pieces and a section under Lt. Gibson: about 200 wagons in the train. Soon after passing [a] little bridge at Vergara, a myriad of birds greeted us. Good omen! Road heavy with deep sand. Chaparrals on sides, trees rather small, increasing in size as we went up....

Took a rest at noon in an old ranch, Gen'l Cushing in company. Saw two dead Mexicans on road side, killed a few days before. They were drivers of a diligence which had brought a Spanish family in from Mexico [City]. Texas Rangers suspected. Halted at sunset at Santa Fe, distance 8 miles from Vera Cruz. Slept out in open air upon the ruins of a burnt rancho.

November 1

Went beef hunting; fine prairie at Santa Fe, gave chase to a herd; five horsemen got separated from party and lost, travelled 3 hours alone, met no human being. Had a fine chase after a calf over hill & through the woods, wounded two & killed a third from my horse with a pistol. Brought in the hind quarters on my horse. In the chase the curb chain broke, horse jammed me against a tree; came near breaking my ancle.

November 2

Gen'l Patterson came up and started us again on the march. Heat great, men dropping down every step. Beautiful scenery, country gradually rising & becoming more hilly; trees larger. Paw paws, limes & oranges in abundance, cactus numerous, large & various. At the rancho on our camp ground at night . . . found a *fence* of growing cactuses! Stopped at San Juan, 2 Spanish leagues (5 miles); battery on bridge, camp in flats on the sides. Supped on some of Santa Anna's beef & bathed under a lemon tree! glory enough for 1 day.

November 3d

Country still rising, getting into a rocky clay soil. Magnificent view winding round a hill near Tolome. Orizaba & Perote in the distance. Valley filled

14. The following excerpts, contained within the triple angle brackets <<< >>>, are taken from OBW's leatherbound journal with entries beginning September 1847, referred to hereafter as OBW *Mexican War Journal.*

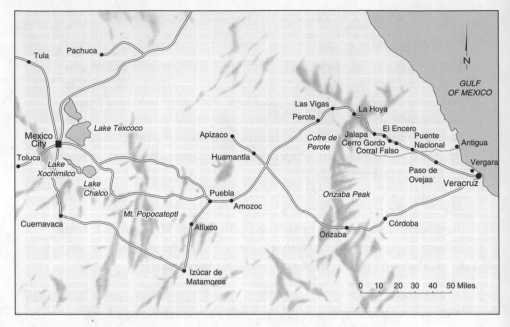

The Road to Mexico City.

with tropical trees. The army winding over the hills &c. Stopped at Passo de Ovejas. Fred Humphreys, Dr. Smith, Lt. Tensfield & myself got poisoned on a Jalapa bean. Slight tingling at throat & puking & purging afterwards.›››

We gathered every night by turns at the respective camp fires, where not only the incidents of the day (fording streams, brushing away guerrilla parties, breaking down of wagons with infinite variations of mule stories and old army jokes) were related, but intelligent criticism from such participators in the war gave one a more satisfactory appreciation of affairs than the book writers ever have. Full justice was done both to the gallantry and skill of General Santa Anna and to General Scott's strategy. That the former had made the most of his resources and, falling back, had seized the best defensive passes in the mountains after each defeat, now goes without saying. Among our own generals, Worth[15] seemed to be the favorite, and Scott's

15. William J. Worth (1794–1849). A veteran of the War of 1812, during which, serving as aide to Winfield Scott, he was severely wounded at Lundy's Lane. At the outset of the Mexican War he served under Gen. Zachary Taylor, as second in command. His action at Monterey earned him promotion to brevet major general. Transferred to Scott's army at Vera Cruz, Worth displayed great enterprise in his pursuit of the Mexicans following the Battle of Cerro Gordo, and again at Churubusco, Chapultepec, and Mexico City.

professional superiority was taken for granted. The dear old chief was accused of being severe to his staff. At Vera Cruz one young officer, having been busy out on the siege lines, came into the mess tent for luncheon when the meal was as good as over, and seized upon some [morsel], about all there was left untouched, when the general lifted his hands in holy horror. "Good God Mr. S.! Who ever heard of tasting such a dish except at dinner." The tired, dusty and discomfited young fellow threw down his knife and fork in terror and dismay. In later days, when our ill-regulated volunteers swarmed at the defense of the Capital, the old General's ideas of military etiquette of course suffered a shock and he became too well-known as "Old Fuss and Feathers," but I always found him concise, trenchant and to the point. Perhaps he showed some vanity over the precise use of words. . . .

The enemy appeared before us at the National Bridge and near Puebla and one or two other points, but to our vexation we could not coax them into a fight. But their display of horsemanship and speed was splendid to see. . . .

JOURNAL ENTRIES, NOVEMBER 1847

<<<Nov. 4
Alarm ½ mile before reaching Puente Nacional [National Bridge], galloped battery forward, but provoked to find it a mistake from guard detail firing from the bridge. I had just stopped to take a look with spy glass at a little mud fort 600 yds. on left and thought I saw a horseman, when Capt. Tilghman rode back & ordered my section forward.

The position at the bridge is the finest for defense I ever saw. Hill above road 300 ft., fort on top. The bridge is the best too; it runs straight 150 feet, then turns to the left; has a circular head at each end, five or six bays, curvilinear abutments with ice breakers, stone parapet, double cross binding on the road way about 45 feet high—all such public works in this country are very superior. The country to-day appeared harder, some little limestone & sandstone appearing. . . . Crossed over the celebrated *Tierra Caliente* and it is different from [what] I supposed. It is not a desert of burning sand, but it is covered with the finest fruit & flower trees in North America. When it falls under the sickle of the American farmer it will become rich (as it now is indeed with wealth) but then in the products, instead of as now with land holders.

Jarote [Padre Caledonia Domeco Jarauta], the Guerrilla chief, sent in to-day with offers of peace for himself & followers, but his demands were so exorbitant that Gen'l Patterson rejected [them]. He demanded security for life and property [in exchange] for simple neutrality. His emissaries wore flat red caps. . . .

November 5
Passed Cerro Gordo. Stronger position than the bridge, right flank protected by a chasm. Mexican batteries were planted on both sides [of the] road, on hills. Approach by the road impossible. Key point [was a] hill near Santa Anna's headquarters, taken by Harney;[16] road cut by Americans two miles off. Six days to cut it. Two hours to reach the hill. Col. Abercrombie[17] states that when the hill had been taken, he turned the guns of the battery on the Mexicans, who were retreating down hill, and swept them away by hundreds. Halted at Plan del Rio. More limestone & some evidence of hydraulic stone along the way.

November 6
Marched to Encero; found a house of entertainment at Corral Falso (false yard); found boiled rice, tortillas, sugars & a species of yam with boiled meat. . . . From Corral Falso the country commences to appear more open and cultivated. . . .

November 7
Marched to Jalapa. Country beautiful. Groves of bananas, lemons . . . citrons, &c at Los [Animas?] where Gen'l Patterson wanted to take a rest, keeping train at a stand in the sun. Jalapa first appears in sight on the brow of a hill close by. Surrounded by orange orchards, cornfields &c. . . . But few steeples in contrast with Vera Cruz. Houses roofed mostly with tiles. Women beautiful. City surrounded by hills. Train created sensation. Saw an old woman as she crossed the street before the battery cross herself.»

One picture remains fixed in my memory that neither war nor peace ever could erase. The view of the great valley of the Aztec City painted by Prescott, with the great snow mountains on either hand . . . Popocateptl, "The Hill that Smokes" and Ixtaxahuatl "P's [the former's] wife 'The White Woman.'" The great monarch rises nearly 19,000 feet, some 2,000 feet above the Mountain King of Europe. The extended summit of Ixtaxahuatl

16. Col. William S. Harney, 2d U.S. Dragoons, was promoted to brevet brigadier general (April 8, 1847) for his action in capturing El Telegrafo hill at Cerro Gordo.
17. Brevet Lt. Col. John J. Abercrombie (37th, USMA 1822).

takes its name from the beautiful robe of snow that covers [it] ... a shape not unlike the human form, extended in repose, on or just below the sky. The pass had not been stained by a battle. Santa Anna had already lost the two great fights [of] Buena Vista and Cerro Gordo and retreated into the Valley of Mexico, which now lay before us, waiting in peace, palm grove, haciendas, gardens, canals, pueblos [and] white cities, a transporting panorama.

This beautiful region had already been fought over and Santa Anna was a refugee in the Island of Jamaica. It will now be remembered that [in April 1853] he returned to Mexico and the presidency, which he lost by harsh government, again became a wanderer, and after several other attempts to regain power, he was finally captured by Juarez,[18] sentenced to death by a court martial, but pardoned by President Juarez on condition of exile, when he settled on Staten Isle and spent several years in conspiracive [sic] cock fighting and card playing until the Amnesty of '72, when he returned home to die—old, decrepit from loss of a leg in battle, with his countrymen disregarded and harmless. He had been, in his prime, a most gallant and skillful officer, but a wrong-headed ruler.

On reaching the historic city, I found a little world of Aztec and Spanish wonders not ever painted in the books—two worlds in fact. Mexican and Spanish streets, walls and ancient buildings, teocalli and cathedrals, hidalgos and Indian—most Asiatic—costumes and manners. Walking one day by the cathedral, I was confronted by a tall, seedy looking Spanish Mexican in cloak and sombrero and evidently a decayed Don, who obstructed the narrow side walk and drew close to the wall. As between equals and gentlemen he should have passed outside. But I had heard that our Mexican friends, taking advantage of American carelessness or ignorance, made it a point not to observe the custom usual among themselves. But we of the younger sort, particularly those of us who had not been in battle, had determined to stand by our rights. So, marching boldly up to meet my rival face to face, I stood waiting for him to begin the contest, when, lifting his sombrero and sweeping it down by his left side with a superb bow of politeness, involuntarily I followed the motion of his hand and gave him the way, bow for bow.

18. Benito Juarez was elected president of Mexico in 1860. Because Mexico was suffering financially and unable to pay external debts, England, France, and Spain chose to intervene. The English and Spanish soon withdrew, but France remained, establishing a puppet empire under Austrian archduke Maximillian, wresting power from Juarez in 1863. In 1867 the empire collapsed, and Juarez returned to power, capturing Maximillian and sentencing him to death. Juarez served as president until his death in 1872. A virtual dictator, Juarez nevertheless had given Mexico its first effective government and a constitution that guaranteed free speech, a free press, and the right of assembly.

As a rule we found all class[es] more polite and friendly than one might expect in an enemy's country. Our veterans rather laughed at than resented Mexican slights on the streets, and we youngsters had the example of such elegant gentlemen as Joe Johnston, Robert Lee and Captain Huger,[19] to tone down our combativeness. And so nothing happened. My old friend McClellan being assistant engineer to Captain Lee gave me the entree among a body of staff officers unexceeded, if not unequaled, in our military history. McClellan himself learned to appreciate the genius and methods of Lee, perhaps a little too highly for his own good hereafter. But we shall see.

Getting our battery and horses in good shape for the field, our stay in the wonderful city seemed only too brief and we were ordered to Cuernavaca, on the road to Acapulco, with a column of infantry and cavalry. . . .

Arriving without hostile adventure we found quarters in an extensive *palacio* built by Cortez himself—with ample accommodations for officers and men and stable room for 600 horses. This, it seems, had been Cortez's country residence. . . .

Our colonel commanding, in distributing his command to the best advantage to keep the peace and to collect the revenues, kept our battery at headquarters for emergency, so that I had little to do but drill, study Spanish and the map of the country and cultivate such Mexican polite society, little enough to be sure, as threw open its doors to los Americanos. Chief of these amiable people was the city alcalde, who had a pretty wife and she a pretty sister. I need not tell you how soon I learned from the latter lady much that is not laid down in the books—not the least of which is how the best part of the Spanish language is made up in signs, looks, fans, and the guitar. Needless to say, that when Don Orlando had to march from Cuernavaca for good and all, he left with a heavy heart, or none at all, with signs of mourning in one fair *señorita's* eyes, and of exasperation on one Alcalde's brow. O thou rascally Cupid, how fortunate for all our sakes that thou dost not always "mean business!". . .

JOURNAL ENTRIES, MAY–JULY 1848

<<<Reached Mexico [City] to-day; passed through San Augustine [gate], where the volunteers[20] gathered around us as though we were Bengal

19. Robert E. Lee and Benjamin Huger (8th, USMA 1825) were then staff officers under Gen. Winfield Scott.

20. As will be observed by OBW's numerous comments, the regular U.S. troops had nothing but contempt for most of the volunteers.

Tigers. Some of the *Voluntarios* amusing themselves by setting Mexican women a fighting. San A[ugustine] [was the] headquarters of Scott before [the battle of] Contreras. An English lady by the name of Benfield was there at the time Scott was. She told Lt. Lovell the most frightful things of Mexican society, incest in every form, young ladies having babies by the peons of their houses, &c. This the 1st Society of Mexico!

Saw the remains of the beautiful defenses from the *tete du pont* to the city. When new, they were perfectly smooth, sodded over and the angles sharp. The American soldiers were cutting down some of the parapet at Churubusco to fill up the holes in the road. Beautiful view of the valley coming down the mount[ain]s. The spires of the cathedral loom up gloriously. In the city [they] put the company in the citadel and ourselves in Gen'l Valencia's house.[21]

May 30

Went to Tacubaya with 3 classmates. Two fine English country houses, Jamisons & McIntoshes, contrasted finely by their lightness & elegance & *chimneys* with the masonry of Mexico. Maguey bushes around Chapultepec riddled with bullet holes. When the Americans were attacking Churubusco, the gentry & ladies in Mex[ico City] were on house tops with spy glasses, cracking their jokes & ridiculing the idea of success, but when they saw the Am[erican] flag run up they rushed down in disgust (& despair), exclaiming *caramba*, &c. Churubusco does look impregnable, but "looks *is* nothing.". . .

May 31st

Fine band [of the] 6th Infantry; that of the 5th not so good as when at Detroit. . . . Went to Bella Union falls, officers, soldiers, teamsters & gamblers dancing with w———s. Such a grand w———e house, gambling & drinking establishment.

June 1st

Started at 4 o'clock; beautiful appearance of the city. The miles of dying lights, the gloomy church spires, the grand outline of the architecture of the buildings appearing in the gray of the morning, the darkness being sufficient to hide the tasteless details. Waited 2½ hours outside the Peñon gate for Gen'l Marshall's[22] volunteers, who came up at last, pell mell. Immense strength of the Peñon hill. A maguey grove & some Mexican houses stuck in one of the steepest sides.

21. Gen. Gabriel Valencia led the Mexican Army of the North.
22. Brig. Gen. Thomas Marshall (1793–1853), former Kentucky state legislator.

Gen'l Marshall came up here. Sensual looking fellow, called Hog Marshall. Tis said he ran for a captaincy & 1st lieutenancy of a company in Kentucky, got defeated, bought 8 votes & got elected 2d lieutenant; company too late for enrollment. He then went to [President James K.] Polk, who gave him a generalcy! . . .

June 2d

Marched out of the Valley of Mexico. Took a farewell view about the spot where, when the army was marching down the mountains, a party of 5 officers viewed the valley [for the] 1st time, 1 exclaimed "how many of us will lay our bones in that valley?" 4 of the party did. Lovell the only one [of them still] alive.

The view of the valley on the south west side is much the finest. Passed over the ground where Twiggs[23] had a stampede. He called up several men & asked what they saw. Several said, "a dead horse," others, "nothing," others "a man's cap" &c. He damned them all to hell, & asking one, who told him "2 dead men & brains in the cap of a third," he yelled, "Hurrah, by G-d that beats Amozoki" (Worth's stampede).

Encamped near Rio Frio. Last night rain broke up the Volunteer's camp. Some got up in their shirts & drove tent pegs; some got up & cursed & laid down, & others turned out by comp[anies] (3 Dragoons) & danced round a huge fire. To-day 3 men were killed & stripped by the bridge between Buena Vista & Cordova, 2 [Kentuckians] & 1 of our teamsters. . . .

June 3d

Difficult rising on account of the cold. . . . A mile or so after leaving camp ground a sudden turn in [the] road brot us so close upon old Ixtac that it seemed as though I could place my hand upon her shroud. A little ways further down the road and a bright slope covered with green . . . with a village nestling in the sun appeared at the base of the rugged hills which rear their cliffs ambitiously towards the old lady. The road side for miles was covered with the trees which the Mexicans had thrown . . . across the path of Scott. . . .

The beautiful valley of Puebla appeared as we rose to the top of the hill at . . . Tezmaluca. The celebrated table lands are really grand, covered with

23. Brig. Gen. David E. Twiggs (1790–1862) led Scott's advance division on the campaign to Mexico City. As a U.S. officer in command of the Department of Texas in early 1861, he surrendered all troops, supplies, funds, etc., to Confederate authorities, accepting a commission as major general in the Confederate army as his reward.

fields of grain miles and miles in extent, green groves from which peep out the spires of churches, with fine *haciendas* looking so exclusive & aristocratic. There is a fine Belgian *hacienda* not far from San Martin, the building of which is the finest I've seen. (Rich foreigners' houses are generally superior.) . . .

Getting in camp at the *hacienda* of San Bartolo, the Company rode one of its members on a rail for stealing liquor from a woman. Four different storms arose, one over Popo, one over the setting sun, one in the south, and one near Malinche, all visible at the same time, while the sky over *our* heads was clear.

Yesterday Lt. Gardner passed us with the peace doc[ument]s. . . .[24] The bridge at Tezmaluca [is] a great place for robbers. Got a glimpse of Coffee Mountain as we came down the road. Saw a little cross which had been lately erected on [the] roadside for some poor murdered devil. . . . Encamped at San Bartolo.

June 4

Before day light, old Sol threw out his lantern to the world and lit up Popo. Then he would change his humor and, shading Popo, fire up Ixtac. The ground became more rolling as we advanced towards Puebla, limiting the view in front. About 9 o'clock came in view of Chohula. It looms up finely, and its fine half moorish church (1 steeple & 2 domes) looks like a tryumphant throne of Christianity over the ruins of idolatry. . . .

A fine Spanish bridge, great place for robbers, 3 miles from Puebla. 2 stone gateways. Church of Loretto conspicuous, perched up on [a] hill on which is Fort Loretto, from which Col. Childs thundered during the siege.[25] City lies in a hollow; as you rise to the top of a hill, you come suddenly in sight of it, though the Cathedral towers are visible over the tops of the hills for many miles. They are 300 ft. high, though they seem scarcely 100 as you stand in the plaza. In general, the churches are handsome, though not so

24. The "peace documents" mentioned here were undoubtedly those outlining the Mexican senate's recent (May 25, 1848) ratification of the Treaty of Guadalupe Hidalgo, officially ending hostilities between the U.S. and Mexico. On June 12 the United States colors were lowered, and the flag of the Republic of Mexico once again flew over the national palace in Mexico City.

25. In mid September 1847, about the time General Scott's troops were entering the City of Mexico, Santa Anna, in an attempt to cut Scott's communications with the coast, decided to besiege the American garrison at Puebla. This, Santa Anna hoped, would force Scott to abandon the Mexican capital and fight his way back to the coast. However, the commander of the American garrison, Col. C. F. Childs, refused Santa Anna's ultimatum to surrender and managed to keep the Mexicans at bay until early October, when Brig. Gen. Joseph Lane's troops, marching from Vera Cruz, forced them to withdraw.

large as those in Mexico [City]. A modern coat of paint would improve them all. Church of San Jose is just partly painted, the contrast is to the advantage of the modern taste. The bells are ringing and every body seems always going to Church.

7 Americans assassinated last night, perhaps as many to-night. Tis said that women have been maltreated in Mexico for their association with Americans. Gen. [Stephen W.] Kearney offers them an escort to leave the country. Left Gen. Marshall 3 miles back; he was afraid to let his men enter the city. Saw the governor enter the plaza. Not a cheer greeted him, although there was a multitude present. . . .

June 5

Saw a *little* girl carrying a *big* boy on her back. Went to the baths. . . . Entered the Cathedral which really struck me with awe more so than when I first saw it. Priests were moving in every direction, praying, confessing, changing vestments &c &c. The Virgin Mary with the gold crown had disappeared.

Left at 1 o'clock. 3 men drunk; dragged them behind caissons. 3 miles out [there was a] terrific hail storm, stones like bullets. Storm came from Malinche. Cortez' spirit mad at the men whose deeds had eclipsed his own! Encamped at Amozoki. Had to put sentinel over the water. Volunteers enraged. Took boy of 3d Infantry [in] to sleep; he was in a high fever all night, raving & calling for water; gave him my buffalo robe and overcoat & had to get up several times for the little rascal. He cried so piteously, "I'll give you a picayune[26] for some water."

June 6th

Went off before daylight in a mist. Volunteers set out yelling as usual. One fellow hollered, "If we ain't getting down into the fog I'll be d——d." Road heavy, country uninteresting. . . . Passed El Peñal with his shaggy mane. Camped at [Nopalucan?]. Rocket thrown among the horses & forge wagon upset. 100 guerrillas could scatter all our horses to the d——l, as we have nothing here but our company and 1 of dragoons. . . . Saw a cross erected where Mejia[27] had been shot, about a mile from Amozoki. He was too honest for Santa Anna. It was erected on a square block of stone. . . . Some friend had lately decked it with flowers.

26. A picayune was a Spanish half real, a coin formerly in use in the southern United States.
27. Col. J. A. Mejia, executed by firing squad in 1839.

June 7

Rose at 3 as usual, off at 4½. Sky cloudy grey. Course due east; gradually mountains lifted the clouds from their tops as *señoritas* lift *rebozos*. Sun warmed up the sky along Coffee Rock and bathed a bed of hills in front with liquid fire; fantastic forms in the sky. . . . No wood; have to purchase it by the armful of little sticks. Encamped at a salt *hacienda*, Vantilla, opposite to which we chased some *guerillas* on the way up with Col. Johnson's [Johnston's] train.

June 8

Perote. Volunteers had stopped at Vereis, had reveille at 12½ by mistake and went by us yelling like savages at about 2½; they broke down at San Antonio, 8 miles back. Misty morning; train looked funny; like the host of Peter the Hermit they went, pell mell, teams, foot & horse. Saw one teamster with hair down to his shoulders, "wet with the dews of the morning," matted & sloppy over his face. Gay set, these teamsters, with such hats as teamsters only know how to wear, & their mules deckt off with ribbons.

Gen'l Marshall went by in his mule coach (he on front seat & jug of liquor doubtless as usual & 2 tumblers on back). He was escorted by a comp[an]y [of] dragoons, who looked like the Spectral Knights of Roderick the Goth as they filed by in the mist.

Heard to-night that 6 women who had been friendly to the Americans & who were on their way down from Mex[ico City] were murdered by the Mexies at Ayotla. They generally brand them with letter P. . . .

Perote a dirty, low, wet place, where the sun forgets to shine. 2 poor churches, but a fine bastioned work which commands the approaches in every direction lies off a mile from town. 105 churches in Puebla, and only 150 free holders besides churches. San Augustine richest & not least rascally. Priests of San A used to take liquor in to the Am[erican] soldiers, which they concealed under their holy vestments. Lieut. P of 4th Artillery says they lie, gamble, steal & get drunk. . . . Sn. Blanco, of Cuernavaca, told me that the 3 priests at that place all kept their women, & he & several others told me that all the priests in the [place] keep their women & that society knows & winks at it.

The plains from here to Puebla not so well cultivated as those beyond. Mirage no phenomenon; whirlwinds of dust flying in vertical columns over 100 ft. high very common; plenty [of] sheep around Perote; fields are ploughed with wooden tools.

June 9th

La Hoya [La Joya]. Left Perote at 4 o'clock. The Indiana Regulars were just turning out, yelling as usual; sounded like prairie wolves. Malinche covered by a cloud all day. Pizzaro looked fine in our rear, his peak only visible over a cloud. Bid farewell to the plains and commenced crossing our 3rd mt. range. . . . Scenery over mts. picturesque, but neither so wild nor magnificent as the range beyond Puebla.

Defile at La Joya was fortified & heights occupied by Mex's in small numbers. [They] fired on Pillow & Cadwallader.[28] Pillow lost a horse & killed a Mexican. "Killed a man," says Twiggs. "Good God! Killed a man? Poor fellow!" The defile is formed by streams of lava, same as [the] pedregal at Contreras.[29] At 1 point [there was a] hill on each side of road with breastworks on top. . . .

Rain came down of a sudden. Volunteers commenced whooping, many men out digging trenches round their tents, & some revelling in what was nearly a primitive order of things. Straw brought to them in the rain for beds. Another yell. Mules unloaded in a giffey. Some [men] rushed out with their pants rolled up to crotch, & *such* grabbing for straw, such pitching into the bundles, such burrowing &c. Rain put out fires; one fellow came out & cursed his fire & then, applying his thumb to his nose, wagged his fingers at the fire and halloed. . . . "G-d almighty d——n J——s C——t G-d d——n all the rains that ever fell." Some men playing cards, others singing psalms, others flying about in the rain, dressed in the most fantastic garments. Night closed in rapidly upon such a ridiculous scene. As one of the Kentucky Captains says, the Generals & Colonels are going home to run for office and so they let the *boys* do as they choose. The fact is, the law ought not to allow them to hold office until a certain number of years after war.

June 10

Jalapa.[30] Volunteers yelling all night. Shooting muskets &c. Drove through their lines as we started off & splashed them finely. . . . Saw a corporal 2 miles from Jalapa who had been stoned & cut & left probably for dead in

28. Maj. Gen. Gideon J. Pillow, a personal friend of Pres. James K. Polk, led a division under General Scott in the campaign from Vera Cruz to Mexico City. As a brigadier general in the Confederate army, Pillow commanded troops at Fort Donelson and Stone's River. Brig. Gen. George S. Cadwallader led a brigade in Pillow's division.

29. The Pedregal was an immense, oval-shaped lava field, some five miles wide by three miles deep. The terrain played a crucial role in the battles of Contreras and Churubusco.

30. The village of Jalapa was the home of Santa Anna; his hacienda, El Encero, was located just east of town.

the bushes. Rolled him over & found him drunk. Tilghman told of a diamond chain of Santa Anna [that] cost $80,000; 17 inches long, wore it from watch pocket to shirt bosom. Santa Anna carried off boxes of wealth, 1 chest full [of] doubloons. His wife got upset in [a] ditch near Encero. 25 [of] Tilghman's men lifted the whole coach & load out upon the road, for which Mrs. Santa Anna made Til's bed for him with her own sheets &c. Find that sick only have embarked. Likely to wait here & enjoy the rainy season some time.

Had to swap overcoats with Tensfield, one of Tilghman's lieutenants, who wanted mine for keepsake, & who told me that Tilghman's life was almost despaired of & that he had arrangements made to elect me Captain of the Company.

June 24

Jalapa. Been here 2 weeks and no prospect of getting off in much less than 3 more. Marshall's division com[menced] to move from Encero to-day. Jalapa abounds in showers, pretty women & fleas. Caught 11 of the latter around my ancles last night, feel as though a dozen were foraging down there now.

Last Sunday went up the hill of ——tepec. Saw the gulf very distinctly, & by means of a glass, Vera Cruz, the Castle & ships in harbor. Just after sunrise is the time to look. The view of the country around is very fine. Lovell thought it finer than that of valley of Cuernavaca. I do not, though it has the advantage of a more pleasing prospect of a coat of green. There is a perfect frustration of a cone of a mt. off a little ways to s.w. and we saw a large mountain far beyond Vera Cruz. Mts. Perote & Orizaba *enormously* beautiful. Have had the pleasure of drinking juleps with ice from Orizaba. The wide & gradual stretch from these mountains to the gulf, comprising the region between the *vomito* and the eternal snow, seems like a gradual ascent, smoothing the irregularities. Such views are worth some trouble, that's a fact. . . .

No dependence placed upon rain. Sometimes clear for 5 days, sprinkling only at night if at all, then an incessant old beaster of 3 days; generally rain every afternoon & night, with bright & clear mornings which invite you out to a ducking.

Our train had 8 men killed [the] day we entered the city, on the road. Old Marshall ordered the black legs[31] out. Peoples, of the *Star*, was heard to dissent. Marshall sent for him by a guard, had him brot to his quarters & then

31. "Black legs" is an archaic slang term for a swindler or professional gambler. Here OBW might be using the term as a derogatory reference to newspaper correspondents.

caned him & sent him to [the] guard house. Peoples went to Vera Cruz next day; on returning brot every body's letters but those of Gen. Marshall.

July 11th

The last division (Worth's) commenced moving down by reg'ts day before yesterday. The other day a Mexican was caught who had bought a carbine from one of the men of "G" Company. He was the owner of a *tienda* quite respectable, & offered 400$ to get off, but he had to take 30 lashes.

There is quite an extensive scale of rascality in operation to get our men's horses, mules & arms. Steptoe's battery was tampered with by an agent of an English mining company; four men & a sergeant were tried. The agent wants to raise a company of 60 men for train guards. He offered one orderly sergeant 100$ bounty and 60$ a month & horse & equipment.

On the night of the 8th a Mex was caught by one of our sentinels, trying to steal a mule. Went over to the Company yesterday & saw him chained by the neck to a caisson. He was a big, burly, cut throat looking rascal, had on a black sombrero with drooping brim, a *serape* falling down from his neck, forming quite a picture.

On going to the Company again I found five Mexs tied up around the yard; one was being whipt, & *yowling* & squirming under the lash, every blow of which brot the flesh up ¾ of an inch. He soon, after 41 blows, was willing to tell what he knew. His whipping had a like effect on the others, & we recovered 2 mules & 2 horses from them. We seized 8 mules, 2 of which helped pull Santa Anna out of the country.

2 women came up & interceded for a man who they said was servant to a *señora*, who came up herself in the afternoon & was very pretty; she got her servant off. Another was a well dressed man who had bought 2 horses & a mule; he said they were out at a *hacienda*. We permitted him to write his friends, who brot in the animals this morning. 2 pretty women brot up his dinner to him, & pale & trembling, asked of me permission to take it to him. He had a horror of a whipping & offered 1,000$ bail, but we kept him tied.

The scene in the yard yesterday morning was rich. 5 Mexs tied hand and neck, one undergoing the lash, officers & men looking on quietly, the fellow's comrades trembling, awaiting their fate, the big Irish corporal with hands in pockets, cooly counting the blows, two blacksmiths at work at the forge & every thing else going on quietly as usual....

July 12th

Left to-day for Encero, 6th & 8th Infantry & Steptoe's Battery & Gen'l. Worth; to-morrow Jalapa will be evacuated by the 5th [U. S. Infantry].

Started alone, ahead of the latter, in company with the *diarrhea*. Stopped by the 2d Dragoons at Los Animas, drunken scene. Heard Saunders' "War that Polk made," an excellent thing. Road bad, stoney & rough.

Encero looks beautiful, covered with green, extensive view of pasture ground, surrounded by mountains, bluff on the right. Santa Anna's *hacienda* on top of a hill. When the army first came up they found it splendidly furnished, but it has been pillaged by the Volunteers. . . .

The Mex whose house we occupied in Jalapa came out for his rent, which the Quarter Master refused to pay. 1$ per day for each room! Sent him back without a cent; served him right.

July 13
Passo de Ovejas (Sheep Pass), commonly, Robber's Bridge. Left Encero 1½ hrs. before daylight; took a final view of Cerro Gordo with its cliff, ravine, its mount. heights and the straight up & down long road where the Americans raked the retreating Mex's from the hill.

Found [Capt. Alphonse] Duperu's Company [of] 3d Dragoons at National Bridge. Martin, with whom I frolicked but yesterday at Jalapa, was dead.[32] For ten miles the road to-day was *swarming* with butterflies. The wild honeysuckle was abundant, but the morning glory showed not its old familiar face. From National Bridge to this place we came down in a rain, pitched our tents in the mud under a tree—I was more used up than I ever was before in my life. Sick & wet, weak & weary after a march of 31 miles. Encero is my evil star.

July 14
Vergara. Gen. Worth started at 2 o'clock this morning and went aboard ship almost immediately (he can no longer laugh at Butler)[33] on getting to Vera Cruz. We started in mud & came down in a norther. The road from Ovejas to San Juan was awful; wagons were stuck & had their tongues standing up like masts of wrecks. They were remains of a train of Kinney's, the escort of which was attacked day before by guerrillas (American);[34] the escort heard a shot, the enemy, with their faces blacked, jumped from the

---

32. Lt. John W. Martin, 3d Dragoons.

33. Maj. Gen. William O. Butler had replaced Scott as commander of American forces on February 18, 1848.

34. Colonel H. L. Kinney, a Texan, was in charge of the mule train. The American guerrillas referred to here were evidently a band of deserters from the U.S. Army who had become outlaws.

chaparral into the road, & the gallant escort turned tail at once, leaving the train at the mercy of the robbers. . . .

Reached the beach before 12. It was covered with hundreds of covered wagons & strewed with camp remains; men were going about picking up wood, & women were roaming round, afraid to stay in the towns where they belong; hundreds have come down with our men in hopes of embarking; futile hopes. Wagon containing our tents detained behind; when they came in, the wind was so strong & the sand so soft, it was almost impossible to pitch them. A sandy scrap for dinner. (Sand assists digestion.)

July 15

Vergara. Went into town this morning to turn in ammunition. Vera Cruz looks better, cleaner than last fall . . . houses have been repaired & painted & show not so much the siege.

Dined with Ensworth on fresh fish & stewed shrimp, & was struck with the superiority of the Mex over the American mistress. Found an old Detroit merchant (Roth) in the Quarter Master's office with Ensworth. They live together in great style. R. said they have both made 10,000$ here. *He* had only been here 8 months. Col. Kinney ½ a million; he buys horses at from 7 to 14$, mules, wagons &c, and sells them [at] 1,000 per cent profit. He gets them at the highest auction bid. Officers of the army have to pay full price. . . .

Gleason, who lived through last summer here & grew fat, has the *vomito*.

July 16

Vergara. Poor Gleason is dead. Learn that we take the *Palmetto*, which will be fitted up for our horses. This is inexpressibly good, but we have been favored by Providence during the whole year. Took an elegant bath in the gulf; did not go far for fear of sharks. A dragoon in Sibley's company was caught by the foot the other day, standing in water only up to his knees. . . .

July 17

Vergara. Dined on green corn, cabbage, &c. Col. Kinney gave me a horse. News that we ship our Company to-morrow on the *Palmetto*. Went into town & aboard the boat.

July 18

Steam Boat *Palmetto*. Vera Cruz Harbor. Came into town 5 o'clock a.m. Commenced taking battery on board by means of a tug boat. Mate damned every heavy thing we had, but I humored him and by dint of curses & pulling & hauling. . . . [We] had all in by 1 o'clock, except the horses; drove the carpenters, drove the Captain, drove the Quarter Master, drove the harbor master until we got the horses along side, & when we thought all was ready, there was 2,000 gallons [of] water [to be put aboard]. Off at 7.

When the forge wagon came on, [a] sailor yelled out, "hello, there's the big bellows, put her upon the poop & blow a gale of wind in the foresail". . . .

Lovell drove a wagon master's mistress (Mex) from the cabin. Capt. Smith got mad too & swore he didn't care a damn if the Quarter Master or Gen'l [Persifor F.] Smith should give an order, he wouldn't carry a whore in his cabin. The Captain really has a formidable nose; it is the crookedest & hookedest nose I ever have seen. Farewell to Mexico.

July 19

New acquaintance named Clark, a sutler, who was at Buena Vista. . . . [He] Saw Zenobia's attack on Col. Miles' train. The Mexican merchants &c whose pack mules the escort was protecting stood on a hill & saw Walker whipt & gave no assistance, though they were numerous, together & well armed. Zenobia made a dash at the pack mules. Clark was driven along with the crowd. Saw a volunteer try to cut the girth to save his pack; a lancer cut his head off at a clip. Zenobia left Clark [as a prisoner] charge of 2 men, [then rode off] to "whip the yankees." Charge in deep files, cavalry toward Walker's, whose forty men dismounted. Walker was at their head; they gave way. Mex's dashed forward & on coming up, wheeled to right & left. While Clark's two sentinels were watching the fight he clapped spurs & escaped to Vera Cruz.[35]

Lovell & Capt. George Woods (Quarter Master to 2d Dragoons) say they saw an Irishman at Churubusco who, being wounded in the leg, cut it off himself, & swinging [the leg] round his head, hurrahed for the victory. . . .»»

‹Took the steamer *Palmetto*, Capt. Smith, for New Orleans, where we took the ship *Palestine* for Old Point Comfort, which we reached August 15th. Sailed for Mobile Point in October, where we found orders for Pensacola, where we arrived Nov. 16 in the brig *Winthrop*. Stationed at Fort McRee in Pensacola Harbor until May 22d, in command of Company M. Ordered to

---

35. Lt. Col. D. H. Miles. Zenobia (first name not known) was evidently commander of a Mexican lancer unit. Walker is probably Capt. Sam Walker, who was killed October 8, 1847, in fighting near Huamantla, Mexico.

Fort Pickens, which I left on leave of absence June 25th, 1849, for Detroit. Got a 5 month's leave from Gen. Scott; travelled through Canada from Quebec to Niagra, and reached Detroit July 20th. Visited Kalamazoo in August, and Chicago in September; reached Detroit 21st October, which I left on the 30th of November for Jefferson Barracks to rejoin my old company, Light Battery "G." . . .>

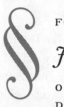

FOUR

Journal Entries

OCTOBER – DECEMBER 1849
DETROIT TO JEFFERSON BARRACKS

*[Visiting his family in Michigan while on leave at the end of the Mexican War,
Willcox remained faithful to his journal, offering some incisive sketches of friends
and neighbors, both prominent and obscure. Yet it is Willcox himself who is
revealed most in these entries, particularly in his diatribe against the Catholic
Church. The religious bigotry here is so intense that the reader is left wondering
whether the remarks are meant as satire, though in all probability they are not.
As a young and struggling Christian, Willcox held some intense views regarding
his faith, and his biases were equally intense toward those who held differing
views. Nevertheless, there is an element of sarcastic, Mark Twain-ish wit here, in
spite of the seriousness of the author and the sensitivity of the subject matter.]*

[Detroit] October 22nd, 1849[1]
Called on [former] Gov. Woodbridge with Mr. Taylor. Gov. said Gen. Cass
had made "another slip" in not attending the St. Louis convention; he
thought the interests of the state much at stake, as the point where the railroad from the Pacific would terminate would make a difference in our commerce.[2] He [also] said a man could not be politically dishonest and privately

---

1. From OBW's *Second Journal*.
2. Lewis Cass (1782–1866) had served in the War of 1812, rising to the rank of brigadier
general. He was governor of the Michigan Territory from 1813 to 1831 and in 1831 became
secretary of war under President Andrew Jackson. Cass resigned that post in 1836 to accept an

honest. He scouted the truckling of Northern men to the South, and declared that when you met a new man from the South, you never need inquire how he stood, he was always true to his own section; you could not say that of Northerners. He gave us some fine pears and invited me to visit him & his family when I could. He has more than once offered to assist me in any way he could, did much towards getting me in to the academy.

Mr. Kercheval[3] told me he would want me probably, to sit up with the corpse of Maj. Robert Forsyth, who died on the night of the 21st.

24th

Had a military funeral. Col. Grayson, Maj. Sproat Sibley, Maj. Denny, Maj. Backus, Lts. Macomb and Scammon pall bearers.[4] One comp'y 4th Inf. & 1 volunteer co. escort. I rode to the grave with Col. Whistler and Capt. [Thomas] Hendrickson. Bishop McCoskry officiated. Forsyth leaves a wife and 5 children; a fine man, a protege of Gen. Cass and much lamented. Heard from Hendrickson of a musket in Prussia which was made so as to admit the cartridge with priming attached, put in at the breach; fired very fast. Got an order transferring me to Light Co. G (now at St. Louis). Know not how this came to happen.

News to-night that active preparations, military & naval, are making in Turkey to resist Russia in case she makes war for Turkey's non-compliance with the demand for Kossuth and his refugee confederates. England & France promise to support Turkey. Spent the evening at Miss O'Keiffe's. Fanny Lee dressed in the greasy old brown frock as usual; if *filth* may merit heaven, she is welcome to a nunnery.

26th

Called on Gen. Cass with Maj. Backus. C. talked mostly of Detroit, touched on the state of affairs in Canada, said he could not understand what men meant by that feeling of attachment towards a man or a family, which

---

appointment as U.S. minister to France. At the time of which OBW was writing, Cass was a U.S. senator, serving from 1845 to 1857, except during his unsuccessful bid for the presidency as the Democratic nominee against Zachary Taylor in 1848. Cass was appointed secretary of state under James Buchanan but resigned his cabinet post in 1860 when Buchanan refused to reinforce Fort Sumter.

3. Benjamin B. Kercheval was a prominent Detroit banker.

4. Capt. and brevet Lt. Col. John B. Grayson (22d, USMA 1826); Capt. and brevet Maj. Ebeneezer Sproat Sibley, assistant quartermaster (1st, USMA 1827); Maj. St. Clair Denny, paymaster (21st, USMA 1822); Capt. and brevet Maj. Electus Backus (28th, USMA 1824); Lt. Eliakim P. Scammon, topographical engineers (9th, USMA 1837).

is called "loyalty." That remark was in bad taste from the ex-minister to France, and the author of *Nights at St. Cloud.*[5]

28th

Attended Henry Whipple's funeral to-day.[6] The widow will be taken care of by the Odd Fellows, each of whom dropped a sprig of spruce, or "live-forever" on his grave. Mrs. W's wailings made me cry as the coffin was lowered. Ed, Rice, Eb and myself remained all the afternoon at Elmwood Cemetery. Ed was very cold towards me, but he has no cause save his own morbid feelings.

29th

Spent the evening at Mrs. Cole's.[7] Lt. Scammon said that Claude Berard, in classifying the books in the library at West Point, placed the *Olive Branch*, a political pamphlet, under the head of "botany"; and *The Scholar Forearmed*, a literary tract, under the head of "military works."....

31st

Spent the evening in a dancing party at Ensworth's; found many young ladies who had grown up from quite young children in my absence. One was a sister of one of my juvenile sweethearts who ran away from home to be married & on whom I waited; another was the sister of an old schoolmate....

November 1st

Went up to Mr. Duffield's to spend the evening but found all out & that they had expected me to tea. I then went to the meeting for the Portuguese exiles from Madiera. About 100 of the exiles were present; they had been forced to leave, some after imprisonment & confiscation of property, & many banished for reading the Bible & then refusing to believe in Saint worship, transubstantiation, &c, of the Catholic church, to which they had belonged. Over 1,000 had been persecuted away from their homes & country.

One was hunted in the mountains by 200 soldiers & standing on the brow of a hill, he had seen his own mother driven from her house, which they

---

5. Referring to Lewis Cass, *France, Its King, Court and Government; and Three Hours at St. Cloud* (New York: Wiley & Putnam, 1841).

6. Henry L. Whipple (1816–1849), auditor general of Michigan.

7. Mrs. Henry Cole, mother of Porter Cole, West Point classmate of OBW.

burnt, and goaded by men with sticks having iron points, such as mule drivers use, to hasten her feeble steps. They put her in prison & confined her & some of her family many months. The man told his sad tale in broken English.

Another case, that of an old man present with them, was almost as touching, and even more exasperating to think it *could* happen in the nineteenth century. The man owned the largest farm on the island, 4 miles in extent; he was thrown in prison & taken out in 2 years & 9 months & only asked whether he believed in "transubstantiation"; he replied "no," and was for that sentenced to death . . . for apostasy, heresy & blasphemy; but the British minister, or consul, had interested himself, & on the case being carried by appeal to the court at Lisbon, the sentence was commuted to 3 months further imprisonment & then banishment.

These persecuted men had reached Demerara, Trinidad & the West Indies, and they are now writing & going to Illinois to settle. They were led, in this case, by two agents of the Protestant Society, which had paid their expenses from New York. A collection was made for them, & over $200 raised. Mr. Duffield said this was really Christ appearing among us. "Fore as much as ye did it unto one of these, &c."

November 7th
Dined with Mr. Chase to-day. Charlotte asked the blessing. I know of no protestant girl who would do the same under the circumstances. I got almost angry with Mr. Chase, who expressed himself with much contempt towards the friends of liberty in Europe, and sympathised with Austria in the affair with Hungary.[8] He is a monarchist & probably an absolutist. The knout or bastinado would do him good.

Mr. Chase is a Catholic—that is, on the side of his wife—so far as he is anything he is a Catholic. This fact tinges his views in the same way that it places many a better Catholic in a false position. In the present grand tendency towards liberty in Europe there is a development of ignorance and superstition, degradation and wretchedness in Catholic countries that presents a melancholy contrast with Protestantism. But Catholics in this country, such as Mr. Chase, tell us that the accounts we get through the papers are false, coming through lying protestant channels, etc.; to be consistent, they say the same of political events in Europe, and this throws them

8. The editor has not been able to identify Mr. Chase; OBW refers here to the Hungarian revolt of 1848–1849, led by Kossuth against Austrian rule. Austria was also suffering from internal difficulties, including a peasant revolt. That too was eventually suppressed, and the new emperor, Francis Joseph, instituted a new, absolutist regime.

into the defense of Catholic despots, with whom, for the sake of Catholicism, they sympathise.

The Catholics are very polite people; they will never controvert your saying; they are too polite to argue; to dispute is excessively vulgar; they leave it . . . to their priests, with whom, they happen to know, you will never be brought into contact. Should you attempt to feed a litter of young puppies, they would all run to the kennel and only take the food at the paws of the old bitch. So with the Catholic lay people. Attempt to give them light and truth, ten to one they bite at you with their ill natured remarks, and will only receive instruction at the hands of "The Church"; that is to say the priests—a class of watch dogs who protect the purity of the faith from new light, guard certain relics of hair, finger & toe nails and bones, devote themselves to celibacy and cluster themselves into abbeys, convents, monasteries and hospitals, with women who are called nuns, and who help them to preserve their celibate vows.

These constitute "The Church," and so confident are the members thereof, that this institution—a long festering sore on the body of Christianity—is the depository of all the true "matter" of the past, the present and the future, that they will receive light from no other quarter. They dare not think for themselves for fear their thoughts should conflict with the Church. They dare not read for themselves, lest they should understand the book differently from the understanding of the Church. And they dare not give their own reasons for their own belief, lest they should not be the reasons of the Church, and some sharp protestant should discover the discrepancy. Thus they turn over their "faith" first, without even investigating it, but taking it in most cases from their parents, and then pin on to the sleeve of the priests their consciences, wills, understandings, tongues and ears. Approach them now with a *fact*, does it shake their system of errors? No, because the layman says go to my priest, he has learning; and the priest, finding nothing in his books, sends you to the infallible pope, and the pope overhauls the former infallible popes, and finding something or nothing, all the same, gives you a . . . piece of paper expressing his opinion, which is most probably that you should not trouble yourself on that which is troublesome to him.

Does this satisfy your Catholic friend? Yes; but suppose you point him out something opposed to it in the Bible, does this startle him? No, he don't pretend to understand the Bible; the priests study that and hammer it out into facts and forms for the Church. But you will explain it to his ears if he will not believe what he reads with his eyes. No, he had rather freeze than rub his hands at any other fire.

There are birds which, at the approach of light, hie themselves to dark places: so with the Catholics; they fly to their heap of rubbish, bones, hair & toenails called "The Church." I will not deny to them learning, the deepest of some sorts, and in past ages the great depositories of learning, but any learning which does not give to the mind the freedom to think for itself is not *soul*-learning, is not light for another world. To speak of mere love, encyclopedism, in this connection, is an irrelevant conclusion, and a logical fallacy. It is a dark lantern which throws light on surrounding objects but hides *the man*. . . .

10th

Dined at Chancellor Farnsworth's to-day. Mrs. Farnsworth pressed me for my opinion of Kate T.—a girl whose education and association have been so highly attended to that she is considered by her relative as the pink of perfection, and not much less by Mrs. Farnsworth and others. I consider her a young prude, or a juvenile *fogy*. She has high cultivation & slim talents: a common pebble which has been worn smooth and become polished by the attrition of constant rolling & rubbing. She would be sweet, though [a] plain, sensible girl, were she not always entrenched behind the palings of a pop eyed refinement, and continually, by her manner, thrusting her notions of propriety in your face. . . .

14th

Party at Lt. [Henry D.] Wallen's last night. Dined, supped and rode out with Marie Farnsworth to-day, and spent the evening at home over a euchre table with Eb [Willcox], Ed and Louise Cole.

15th

Went to Gros Pointe with Eb, Louise & the baby. Dined with Fisher at the old Hudson place. Fisher gave us an enormous squash. Eat pumpkin pie and played with the dirty faced children. Went to Grant's. Found the old Captain & his wife, Louis and Oliver. The old gentleman spoke of father with much affection: the tears came into his eyes. He was at the battle of Monguaga and at the surrender of Detroit by Hull—a lieutenant in Beaufait's Company. When a boy, he was taken by Commodore Grant from the Indians and reared at the old manor house at Gros Pointe.[9]

9. Capt. John Grant had been kidnapped when he was about three by Chippewas, who gave him the name Che-mo-ka-mun. Commodore Alexander Grant bought the boy from the Indi-

At Spring Wells, on patrol duty the night before the capitulation, he saw the enemy crossing opposite the Ecorse River in the morning, and started for the town to convey the intelligence to Hull. He met Col. Miller[10] in a field near the cantonment, very much excited, walking backwards and forwards. Grant inquired for Hull. "Damn Hull!" said Miller, "he is a d——d old ——"

Grant met Hull riding on a large bay horse, told him the news of the crossing. Hull slapped him on the shoulder and said, "we'll show them a Yankee trick." Grant met his company coming down with Capt. Beaufait, near Bloody Run; the men had no flints nor ammunition. Grant procured an ample supply.

There were three thousand men with arms and cannon to defend Detroit against five hundred British with only two six-pounders. The British marched up the old river road by platoons. There were two 24-pounders planted in the middle of the road; a single fire would have swept the enemy like chaff. Besides these, there were two batteries between them and the cantonment, and other cannon. But they marched with confidence until the white flag was raised.

Grant says that Hull's secretary, a Frenchman whose brother's ears Hull had cut off, told him before the crossing that there was "something wrong with Hull." That he had received McIntosh, a Briton from the Canada side,

---

ans, at the insistence of his wife, for a hundred dollars. One who knew him recalled that "Capt. Grant, as he grew up to manhood, understood that he was a native of the United States, and never for a moment wavered in his allegiance, though as the adopted son of a British officer, it might have been supposed that he would have acted differently." Palmer, *Early Days in Detroit*, p. 659; Capt. Louis Beaufait (c. 1760–1854), had served as captain and later colonel of militia during the War of 1812.

10. Col. James Miller, a veteran of Tippecanoe, commanded the 4th U.S. Infantry under Hull at Detroit. He commanded the American forces at the Battle of Monguaga, where he defeated the British and Canadian troops and a large body of Indians under Tecumseh. Miller, who had been endeavoring to reach an American convoy at Frenchtown (now Monroe, Michigan) on the River Raisin, thirty-five miles below Detroit and escort it into the fort, was recalled by Hull, in spite of the victory at Monguaga.

On August 16, 1812, Hull surrendered some 2,500 American troops to barely seven hundred British regulars and Canadian militia and some six hundred Indians, without firing a shot. The surrender included two troops of cavalry, one company of artillery regulars, the entire 4th U.S. Infantry, detachments of the 1st and 2d U.S. volunteer regiments, three regiments of Ohio militia, and one regiment of Michigan volunteers, together with thirty-three pieces of artillery, forty barrels of powder, a hundred thousand cartridges, and four hundred rounds of 24-lb. artillery shot. Though a court-martial found Hull guilty of cowardice, there has never been any proof that he conspired with the British. What was precisely the matter with Hull may never be known, but he may have been suffering from a severe depression.

who crossed the river with muffled oars, several times in the dark; and that Brush and Hunt[11] were parties to the secret intrigue—probably instigators, as they had relatives on the Canada side. Grant says that it was the universal impression among his officers and men that Hull was a coward.

The old man Grant changed his will, so as to divide the front of his farm between Louis and Oliver; the old lady talked French at me, of which I could only understand enough to show me it was bad. I took a drink out of the big tin dipper in the kitchen where years ago I had eaten fritters; *Oliver* made a horrid face and grunted good bye, and we took our departure.....

19th

[Visiting relatives at Monroe, where Willcox arrived with brother Eben and several friends aboard the *John Hollister* on November 17th.] Consented to remain till to-morrow for Uncle Frank. The other party took the stage, and Eb did not reach home until 10½ in the night. Called on Miss Conant, whom I frightened by threatening to carry off her picture. Spent the evening at "Aunt Harriet's" with her and Eliza Cole, whom I conducted across the bridge to her home. Her simplicity and naturalness pleased me, no less than her sparkling black eyes and ruby lips, which I wanted very much to kiss.

20th

Undertook to read a little after breakfast. Little Johnny Tifield was in the parlor with sore eyes and the whooping cough. He sat down near me on the floor and began to pound and whistle. Then he diverted himself, playing with some long bandages which they had just taken from his arm, which, by some unlucky accident, had been broken instead of his neck. On his mother directing to put them away, he ran by me and dragged them across me as he went. Then he seized hold on the door and moved it to and fro, delighted with the murderous melody of its squeaking hinges. I bore this as long as possible, and made him desist. He now got a piece of paper, and gluing one

11. Capt. Henry Brush commanded the supply convoy of some 230 American troops at Frenchtown and was still there when Hull surrendered. No further identification of the officer referred to as "Hunt" can be found. Brush's troops, together with colonels Lewis Cass and Duncan McArthur, who were leading a second expedition to reach the convoy at Frenchtown, found to their disbelief that they had been included in the troops surrendered by Hull. If Cass or McArthur had been present, it may be certain that the surrender would never have occurred. Indeed, Cass was so irate when he learned of the surrender that he refused to surrender his sword. OBW relates, "It was said that he broke the weapon in two on a rock, and in the presence of the officer who demanded it and before High Heaven he uttered an oath which the Recording Angel must have blotted out with a smile." OBW, "Detroit under Three Flags, and the War of 1812," Willcox Papers.

end of it with spittle on his finger, came to me and brushed it across my face. I could endure no longer, but, throwing down my book, rushed out of the house in a state of frenzy. . . .

21st

The Chancellor [Farnsworth] and his lady arrived to-day. I was at the house, but left in the most precipitous manner. Called on Lt. Johnny Newton and wife—they ran away to be married—He relieves Meigs, who has lost most of his own and wife's personal property in the late fire at the barracks.[12]

Spent the evening with some young gentlemen over oysters: from our conversation one would have not thought our minds much "above an oyster."

24th

Part of the evening at Col. Whistler's. Felt unwell, drank five glasses of brandy without any effect upon either head or stomach. Walked over two miles, went to bed sick.

25th

Sunday. Church in the morning, colic still. . . . Dr. Pritcher sent eight blue pills; took only two.

26th

Spent the evening at the Chancellor's.

27th

Took Marie to the lecture delivered by E. C. Walker before [the] Young Men's Society.[13] The address was diffuse and watery, but quite interesting as a discussion of popular events, with reference to the subject set forth, viz., "Education: A work of a *life time*. The orator had only seen twenty odd years; how conceited! Marie and I parted in a queer manner. . . .

12. Lt. John Newton (2d, USMA 1842) later served in the Army of the Potomac, seeing action in every major campaign from the Seven Days to Gettysburg, where he assumed command of the First Corps following the death of Maj. Gen. John Reynolds. He afterwards led a division in the Atlanta campaign. Montgomery C. Meigs (5th, USMA 1836), a native of Georgia, remained with the Union during the Civil War, serving throughout the conflict as quartermaster general of the U.S. Army.

13. The Young Men's Society of Detroit, formed in 1833, was for nearly fifty years a successful debate and lecture club for young Detroit gentlemen. In 1837 the society boasted three hundred members. It disbanded in 1882.

28th

Telegraphed to mother that I should leave to-morrow for Kalamazoo. Made about twenty or thirty farewell calls. Jack Howard and Mr. Duffield asked me to write to them. I am glad such old friends continue to feel an interest in my fortunes. One tenth the trouble one takes with *new* acquaintances would bind *old* friends to us forever.

29th

Thanksgiving-day. The Governor's proclamation is much ridiculed for its harsh official brevity—not one public acknowledgment of Heaven's favor—not one expression of thankfulness for our escape from the cholera. The Governor, it is hinted, had no particular cause for thankfulness himself, as he had not received a renomination and election.[14]

Resolved to take the southern route [from Michigan for Jefferson Barracks, Missouri], and lie over until to-morrow. This will disappoint mother, Julia and the Chicago folks very much, but the northern route is uncertain, and another leave taking would be horrible; it always makes a baby of me and almost breaks mother's heart.

Dined at the Chancellor's with the commissioners to locate Asylums. One is located at Kalamazoo, the other at Flint. Marie had given me a neck comforter of her own knitting. We had another farewell and she manifested much more agitation than I had dreamed of. She said she was "sincere" and hoped I was. I certainly am, sweet creature, a very sincere friend, and hope your husband may be worthy of you when you come to marry—I know few men that would be. I would tremble myself to undertake so precious a charge. It is well we do not love each other, for the garrison is no sphere for one of such exalted merit.

Spent the evening at Rice's with Ed & Eb. I had an attack of colic again, but we had a delicious time, we four old friends that had met so many times together—so many *hundred* times.

En route TO JEFFERSON BARRACKS
30th

Ed came up to the house to see me off. Our breakfast was sad; after the blessing was asked by Eb, I had to go out to wipe my eyes. Louise manifested at parting, more emotion than I ever saw her do towards any besides

14. OBW refers to Gov. Epaphroditus Ransom, who served in that office from 1848 to 1850.

her husband. She said that Uncle Orlando should be the first word little Harry should learn.[15]

We "four," the old set, walked down to the boat. Rucker & Charley Loomis were there. Rice kept bowing his head to me till we were out of sight of each other.

The steamer was the *Arrow*, Capt. Atwood. She threaded her mazy way rapidly down the "silver stream," as the "Swan of Avon" would say. Emblem of my fortunes, fair boat. Shot from the bow of life, once more I go to encounter the chances of my flight. The Capt. is a fat old jollifer; speaks with a twang, and plays euchre with a vengeance.

Col. Grayson was on board, going to meet his wife at Sandusky. Imagine the meeting! after the long suspense about her safety after the explosion of the *Louisiana*. She had taken passage, but was up in New Orleans, making some business arrangements when the accident occurred. Should not such an escape turn the most worldly minded from their worldliness a *little*, cause one to pause a *moment?* Ask her. . . .

DECEMBER 1849

Jefferson Barracks

2d

Intended taking the Louisville packet yesterday evening, but in trying a horse, staid over time and shall wait over Sunday. Went to church this evening, saw [Lt. Charles W.] Field, 2d Dragoons, just graduated, on his way to Fort Leavenworth, on board steam boat *John J. Crittenden* with recruits.[16] He spent the evening in my room, wants me to go on with him to-morrow.

3d

Off on the *Crittenden*. . . . Saw a large bay horse at Crane's, bought him for $100; the man asked $125. Head like an eagle. Had much trouble getting him quiet when on board; he bit, danced, jumped, pawed & snorted; finally got another horse alongside of him; this quieted him. . . .

15. Harry Willcox, son of Eben and Louise.
16. Charles W. Field (27th, USMA 1849) achieved Civil War renown as a brigade and division commander in the Army of Northern Virginia.

§ FIVE

Roaming the Great Plains

RETURNING TO the United States from the Mexican War, our battery took station at Jefferson Barracks, near Saint Louis. It was a famous post in early military annals and was the headquarters of the department, General Mason commanding.[1] There were with us one or two companies of dragoons. Colonel Plympton[2] was a. a. g. [assistant adjutant general], and there was a very lively garrison. Its society was charming. At this distance of time I recall with particular pleasure Mrs. General Mason and Emily Mason, beautiful women, and Mrs. Captain John Love, equally charming.

St. Louis [was] at the gates of the West [and] all its outposts [were] similar to [the] Detroit garrison and city; parties and balls [were] frequent. One ball at [the] hotel [was] attended by garrison officers and ladies in a huge sleigh drawn by battery horses, in great state, bugles blowing as we drove through [the] city. [The] next morning [the] snow had melted and the bedraggled party, on its way out, [was] the laughing stock of the multitude of beholders and targets for the boys' snow balls. . . . Attended Lovell's and Hancock's

---

1. Col. and brevet Brig. Gen. Richard B. Mason. He died July 25, 1850.

2. Col. Joseph Plympton (1787–1860). Plympton began his military career as a lieutenant in the War of 1812. He saw service as a major in the Seminole War and lieutenant colonel in the Mexican War, where he was brevetted colonel for his gallantry at Cerro Gordo.

[weddings] as groomsman. Lovell married Miss Emilia Plympton and Hancock married Miss Russell.[3]

‹8th
Reached Jefferson Barracks about 3 o'clock. Landed by the boat about a mile below; a freed negro man of Gen. Mason's landed with me and took my horse up to the stable. . . . I had a sloppy walk through the slush of snow and mud to the barracks, but the voice of a blue jay bird was the first sound I heard on shore and I accepted it as a good omen.

The first man I saw was Corrigan; he came up to me and said he was very glad I had returned to "G" Company. Lovell I took by surprise, but he jumped up very much overjoyed, and after I had taken off my overcoat he shook hands with me again.

I went to the stable with him at stable call and showed him my horse, which he said was two years older than he had been sold for. We sat up until a late hour, talking. Lovell is in very good spirits, but very "hobby horsical," as Tristram Shandy[5] would say. He has drawn up written details of the duties of all his officers and noncommissioned officers, as he says the battery is a school of instruction, and he is determined to instruct all his subalterns, so that they could command batteries themselves. This is all very clever *bunkum*, by which my friend and captain expects to make capital. He has also drawn up a circular, explaining very clearly the necessity of more men for the batteries, which he is going to send to members of Congress, etc.

9th
Paid respects to commanding officer, Gen. Mason. Introduced to his lady, a young woman of 25 (!) married at 13 to the General, at the instigation of her brother-in-law, Gen. Twiggs. Niece, Miss Hunter, a sweet little girl of 16. Believes everything you say, ignorant of the world, and charmed with

3. Lovell's wife was the daughter of Col. Plympton; Hancock was then serving as adjutant of the 6th Infantry, based at Jefferson Barracks. He married Almira Russell.

4. The following journal entries, contained within the single angle brackets ‹ › in this chapter, are from OBW's *Second Journal*.

5. Narrator and central character in Laurence Sterne's novel *The Life and Opinions of Tristram Shandy, Gentleman* (9 vols., 1759–1767).

the prospect of its gay allurements. May her experience be unpurchased at the price of her happiness! . . .

11th

Tried my horse; he won't do; too clumsey [*sic*]; he slipped down twice with me.

12th

Horse fell again. Visited Mrs. Capt. Love (1st Dragoons). Saw the two Miss Plymptons. One is very pretty, the other good natured. . . .

[No date]

Gen. Mason is a man of uncommon shrewdness and the quickest of plain common sense. His wife is young . . . pretty, smart, fond of show, talkative and quite given to color her narrative to make her facts most wonderful and her conversation most entertaining. . . .

Mrs. Mason was once expatiating in a dolorous manner on the hardships she had once encountered living in a tent, drinking from tin cups and all that, for many months. "Yes," said the General, "it's all very hard, but if you hadn't done it, you would not have had the chance to tell the story over so many hundred times."

I once asked the General what he thought of the Fremont and Kearney difficulty.[6] "I would have shot Fremont," he replied. Again, I said "Suppose Congress should declare that Gen. Taylor's[7] cabinet did not possess the confidence of the people; would it not be necessary for the cabinet to

6. John C. Frémont (1813–1890) had been a national hero since 1842, when he led his first expedition into the Oregon Territory. Dubbed the "Pathfinder," he had helped establish the "Bear Flag Republic" in 1846 and in so doing had taken a leading part in helping to wrest California from Mexico.

Frémont's dispute with Brig. Gen. Stephen W. Kearny began in January 1847, when Frémont was appointed governor of California by Commodore Robert F. Stockton. Stockton, with Frémont's assistance, had captured the town of Los Angeles the previous August and declared California to be a part of the United States. Frémont's appointment as governor, however, was in direct conflict with orders from President Polk, who had appointed Kearny to the post. Stockton refused to recognize the appointment from the president, and Frémont sided with the commodore. Kearny, of course, protested. The issue was settled the following month, when Commodore Stockton was replaced by Commodore Branford Shubrick, who recognized Kearny as the rightful governor.

7. Gen. Zachary Taylor, an old warrior who had fought in every American war since that of 1812, had become a hero during the Mexican War with his victories at Palo Alto, Resaca De La Palma, Monterey, and Buena Vista. He had been elected president in 1848 as a Whig, defeating Democratic candidate Lewis Cass, Free Soil candidate Martin Van Buren, and some lesser candidates. Taylor was a good administrator, holding an average of two cabinet meetings a week. He died in office on July 9, 1850, and was succeeded by Millard Fillmore.

resign?" He replied, "No, I'd tell 'em they *did* possess it and it was none of their (Congresses) business." ...

31st

The last footsteps of the year are lingering in the hall. I feel the rustle of its skirts. The wind is moaning over its departure; my heart feels sad. I am one year nearer the grave, one year further from the innocence of childhood. The ripened old year, marked, like furroughs, with the numerous events of my actions, is giving me one departing, lingering, reproachful look ere it fall from the chronicle of my living days.

Yet have I too much faith in the mercy of Providence to regret the issues of the eventful year. Where I have been fortunate, I feel thankful; where I have been unfortunate, it must be for the best, or it may have been to chasten, and I bow with submission. ...

JANUARY 1850

1st

Called upon all the ladies to-day. Attended a dancing party at Gen. Mason's this evening.

2d

Spent the evening at the General's. Miss Maggy made some attempts at music. She deserves at least the praise of modesty, for she knows she cannot sing, and so does everybody that hears her.

5th

Lovell left for the east this evening in a snow storm. He could not imagine a single point about which he did not leave the fullest instructions, with reference to the company. ...

8th

Euchre party at Capt. Love's; went home with "the sweet little maid at the foot of the hill."

9th

Rode out with Miss Plympton. Took Miss Maggy to the Plympton's this evening to play euchre. The girls teazed her about me. ...

11th

Called on Col. [Braxton] Bragg this evening with Best.[8] Bragg is the Buena Vista chap of "little more grape" memory: lean, dark complexioned,

8. Braxton Bragg (5th, USMA 1837) had won three brevets during the Mexican War. During the Civil War he led a corps at Shiloh and commanded the Army of Tennessee at Perryville,

bright rolling black or dark eye, heavy brows, low forehead but Calhounish in its shape, determined looking, but easy and pleasant in his manners. He is rather a restless, nervous, pugnacious looking "Cassius." . . .

March 2d

The thermometer stood at 46, when it commenced snowing, and gradually fell to 32. It is now snowing hard and thundering at the same time! There was a violent thunderstorm—the first of the season—on the morning of the 28th February before daylight. The coldest weather during the winter was in February; the thermometer stood one day at 8 below zero.

April 1st

Lovell returned to-day. . . .

May 1st

Commenced battery drills. . . . >

Ordered to Leavenworth in the spring, preparatory to duty on the plains, which came in the spring in the way of orders to proceed to the upper Arkansas River [and] halt at a certain point on the northern line of New Mexico and there wait the arrival of [Lt. Col. Edwin V.] Sumner [9] with reinforcements. The object was to quiet, or to quell the Arapahoes.

PLAINS JOURNAL: [10] JUNE–OCTOBER 1850

<<Left Jefferson Barracks on the steam boat *Anna*, Capt. Cheevers, June 13th at about 11 o'clock a.m., with "G" Company battery, 4th Artillery, for Fort Leavenworth. The ladies waved their *mouchoirs*, and we fired a few guns at leaving. I saw my——standing near the flag staff till the last moment. Felt

Stone's River, Chickamauga, and in the battles around Chattanooga, where he suffered a humiliating defeat at Missionary Ridge on November 25, 1863. Clermont L. Best (21st, USMA 1847), then second lieutenant, 2d U.S. Dragoons, made his mark as a Union artillery officer during the Civil War.

9. Lt. Col. Edwin V. Sumner, then commanding 1st Dragoons, became a prominent figure in the Civil War, leading the Second Corps, Army of the Potomac, during the Peninsula and Antietam campaigns, and the Right Grand Division at Fredericksburg. He died from pneumonia on March 21, 1863.

10. The entries contained within the double angle brackets << >> in this chapter, from OBW's "Plains Journal," are found in the OBW *Bluebook*, containing entries relating to the Mexican War and duty on the Great Plains.

quite pensive as we ploughed our way slowly towards St. Louis, thinking, as at least *two* of us did, of "the girls we left behind us." Reached St. Louis at 1. . . . Left the levee and fired some guns at three. The crowd cheered. . . .

14th

Passed the Gasconada River to-day. Saw near it a grove of cotton wood trees growing so thickly that a man could scarcely squeeze his saw between them. . . . The day showery but quite warm. On duty [as] officer of the day.

15th

Rose at 4½ o'clock, just as we approached Jefferson City [Missouri], waked up Lovell to look at the State House. . . .

Two interesting characters on board. One, a Mr. Andrew Robertson of Clay County (near Fort Leavenworth), who gave Lovell some notions on "the gentlin' of horses," and instructed me vastly on the subject of hemp crops. Perhaps he thought me "born for the hemp"! . . .

The other chap was a Mr. Turner, a returned California emigrant [forty-niner], just going home to "*Arrar* (Arrow) Rock," where we landed him after sunset. He drew near home with a heart full of emotion, exclaimed "*thar's* my house" as we came in sight of "*Arrar* Rock"; but though the poor devil was broken down in health, the money he had made—and he had done better than the average—had only incited him to the intention of going out again to the "Diggins" next spring.

The whole village seemed to learn [of] his coming, for they came to the landing, men, women, children and niggers, to greet him. One took his gun, another his canteen; an ox cart carried his trunk up the hill, and so much of a concourse being present, Manning struck up with his bugle as we moved off, which the returned emigrant took *en compliment*.

The heat to-day almost insupportable. The horses have suffered extremely. They stand around the boilers and between the two engines, patient and sweating. . . .

16th

Sunday. Touched at Brunswick after breakfast this morning; small town, not much more than a landing. Most of the towns are inward. Those on the rivers are built on bluffs or hilly eminences.

Saw a prairie some thirty miles below Lexington called Walk-and-Talk prairie. Partly cultivated, ten miles in extent; landing near it; a prairie angel appeared in white dress, blue shoes, black apron, freckled face and green bonnet.

Passed Sabine County; finely cultivated; a Gen. Smith immigrated from Virginia some years ago with 400 negroes; raises tobacco very successfully. Hemp the best crop for the farmer as it is raised with less trouble & care and admits of proper attention to other crops: yield, 800 lbs. to the acre, averages $400. . . .

Talked with some more of the returned California emigrants [miners] today. They say that of a party of 47 that left here together last year, 23 have died in California, and some of the others are broken down in health.

Reached Lexington at 11 to-night. Flourishing town. . . . The effect of torches as we stop to [load] wood or land at night is very fine. A bundle of pine chips, blazing from a grate raised 8 or 10 feet high on a pole and casting its red reflection on the soldiers, boatmen, negroes, water, shore, trees, rocks, boat, horses, passengers and guns, renders the scene quite infernal.

The horses have not suffered quite so much to-day, but the continued heat is reducing them rapidly. I noticed that my steed had been very silent all day and this afternoon I went down, found him hot and stupid; had a couple of buckets of water thrown on him, and I had scarcely got up to the cabin before I heard his loud neigh. The next time I visited him he was quite brisk, neighed a recognition as I approached, and thanked me in his usual way by biting me on the arm. We have to bleed some of the animals, and Lovell is practicing physic on a couple of the men. I find the water and fresh air very invigorating to me: my lank cheeks begin to fill up; the table fare is *not bad.* . . .

17th

Touched at Fort Osage at breakfast time. A small and pretty town at a narrow passage of the river; the first fort built in this part of the country. Found a rapid current at old Independence landing, sometimes too strong for the boats. The new Independence landing, ten miles higher, is a flourishing point of future importance, being the commencement of the Santa Fe route. . . . Got news of the killing of ten men near Santa Fe. We may possibly punish the murderers ourselves.

A monthly mail is to be commenced between Independence & Santa Fe, Oregon & California. Also a telegraph line between St. Joseph—65 miles above Leavenworth—and St. Louis. . . .

The principal points along the [Missouri] River are Jefferson City (160 miles from St. L.), Booneville, Lexington, Independence Landing, Kansas and St. Joseph. The latter said to contain three or four thousand people. The country is mostly rolling with some prairies. Soft wood abounds along the shores, cedar and pine found on the Gasconada.

18th

No sleep last night; rose at three this morning on reaching Ft. Leaven-worth; commenced unloading at once; on duty as officer of the day.

[The] fort [is] situated in a handsome, uneven country. Only two or three fine buildings. The others mostly log; extensive place; fine parade ground with large trees growing over it; houses filled with ladies and women; stables converted into store houses. . . . Found Col. Sumner gone; instructions left for us to start on the 1st [of] July. Invited to quarter with [Lt. Nathan G.] Evans. . . .[11]

20th

Took a ride yesterday in the country; went up a hill immediately in rear of the Fort. The scenery is somewhat Mexican in the regularly rounded shape of some of the hills. . . . Ascended another hill this evening on horseback. The Missouri separates us from the States, where family, friends and C—— [Cornelia Plympton] attract my eyes and heart. . . .

22d

Ben Beall[12] has given me his daguerreotype; it was taken in Mexico. He was at West Point [when he was] 13 years old, from 1814 to 1818 . . . but did not graduate. When on his way to the Academy with his father, he was walking one day in New York in his new "cadet dress," embroidered coat, tights, high top boots with tassels, cocked hat & sword; a boy singing out "there goes a middy on half pay," Beall rolled up his sleeves and was for whipping the urchin on the spot. He landed at West Point equipped with a pointer dog and *liquor flask*.

Beall was a clerk for some years in the War Department . . . and when the 2nd Dragoons were raised he was appointed a captain in them. . . . He is a jolly soul. Comes in every morning and wakes me up, saying "I am the res-urrection and the life" &c. To-day I was lying on my bed in my shirt and drawers, when he came in and, putting my feet together and placing a jug of brandy near one foot, a jug of whiskey at the other, a small looking glass

11. Nathan G. "Shanks" Evans (36th, USMA 1848), second lieutenant, 2d Dragoons. Evans commanded a Confederate brigade at Bull Run, where his timely movement enabled him to block the Union turning movement. He later served at Ball's Bluff and at Second Bull Run, and temporarily commanded a division at Antietam. A drinking problem eventually cost him his career and his reputation.

12. Maj. Benjamin L. "Old Ben" Beall. Originally captain of the 2d U.S. Dragoons, Beall was appointed major, 1st Dragoons, on February 16, 1847. He became colonel of the regiment in May 1861. Retiring from the service February 15, 1862, Beall died August 16, 1863.

at my middle, & crossing a sabre & whip over my stomach, he commenced the service for the dead. . . .

23d

Sunday. Did not go to church to-day: feel like a sinner, but (unfortunately) I have plenty of good company!

24th

Packed the ammunition in the gun limbers to-day; wonder whether I'll get a chance to use any of it against the Indians? Understand that Col. Sumner applied for the expedition himself. Said to be a man of great energy. [He] started from here with a company of raw infantry recruits; they couldn't even mount their horses, so he had the whole party lead them over the hills. Yet he reached the Big Blue (123 miles) in 5 days! . . .

Spent the evening at Rich's with Beall, Lovell, [Lt. John] Kellogg and Evans. . . . Beall told this story once in N.Y. at a dinner party before some British officers. In 1839, when the 2d Dragoons came out of Florida and were at Fort Columbus under Twiggs, the British ship *Andromache* entered the harbor. A lieutenant came to the fort and notified Twiggs that he intended to salute, gun for gun. She [the *Andromache*] gave 21. Twiggs fired 20, when one [gun] exploded and killed a man.

Beall was keeping count. Twiggs asked how many had been fired. Beall answered, "21." The British lieutenant came again & demanded explanation. Twiggs asked Beall what it meant, when the latter stept up to the lieutenant & said, "We gave you 20 guns and killed a man."

"Perfectly satisfactory, sir."

"No," said Twiggs. Sibley[13] run out a gun and give it to them, which was done half an hour after the salute.

29th

Night of the 27th some young officers at the post got on a frolic, serenaded the ladies and fired a six-pounder at three in the morning. A horse was brought into the room, and appeared the most sensible member of the party. The "Night Artillery," as Beall called them, was led by one with a dragoon dress cap on his head, a saddle cloth on his shoulders, and sabre *'en main*. The noise was at first saddled on old Beall, but during the day an order was issued for a sentinel to be put over the Light Battery, in order to prevent the

13. Henry H. Sibley (31st, USMA 1838). Appointed brigadier general in the C.S.A. in June 1861, Sibley commanded the Army of New Mexico during the Civil War.

recurrence of the scenes of the evening before, which was characterized as "a great infringement upon military discipline and reflecting seriously upon the Company & Regt."

An order has been received from Gen. Clarke[14] for Lovell to wait further instructions to be forwarded from Hd. Quarters of the Army to Col. Sumner to establish posts on the route to Santa Fe. As this news was received on the heels of the tidings that the 7th Infantry was ordered to Jefferson Barracks, it is thought that Regiment are to occupy the new posts. We are almost in doubt about our expedition. Some think we will go, others that we shall return to Jefferson Barracks.

A young Englishman by the name of Swier has arrived with a letter from Gen. Clarke to Lovell, and wishes to "rough it with us on the plains." He is from Liverpool. I have received no letters from home yet. . . .

July 11th

On the 8th received the first letter from C—— [Cornelia Plympton] and one from L [Lilly Graham]. On the 10th received another from L—— full of bitter reproaches, caused by mortified pride and disappointment. That from C—— was unsatisfactory on the very point upon which I was most anxious. The letters from the two have made me feel unhappy.

This morning I went across the river with Evans for the sake of diverting my mind from broodings. Went through Weston. A place of 2,000 or more inhabitants. Said to be the best point for starting for California, etc. Ferried over in a *flat*, which took half an hour. Predict that in 5 years there will be *ten* steam ferries between this and Weston. . . .

Found Lovell at the Ferry landing on this side (with the Cockney) looking for Dorothy, who, he said, had stabbed Leroy. He had a party of soldiers scattered round, searching through the woods.

This evening—a night full of rain and lightning—went over with Lovell to take Leroy's deposition. Found him in the hospital, lying on his back with his intestines lying out on his belly where he was stabbed. He was in a clear state of mind. Said he had won some money of a groceryman, with Dorothy, who was coming home with him, when Dorothy came up from behind with a sharp knife, passed a little by his right side, and stabbed him; as he did so, "he shut his mouth tight and grunted." Leroy then ran away

14. Brevet Brig. Gen. Newman S. Clarke then commanded the department, with headquarters at Jefferson Barracks. Clarke had served in the War of 1812, where he was brevetted for gallantry at Niagara, and in the Mexican War, where he was again brevetted (at Vera Cruz) in 1847. He thereafter served on the frontier until his death in 1860.

from Dorothy. Leroy told Lovell "it was hard to die so; if it was a cannon ball he wouldn't care."

I went to the guard house and had Dorothy brought to be identified by the dying man. Dorothy came up close to Leroy and said, "Isn't it false ye are saying?" Leroy was perfectly calm and rational, and gave us a connected and graphic account of all the circumstances, which Lovell wrote down, and Leroy signed without any tremulation of hand. He will die in a few hours; a large intestine is cut. He was sinking rapidly, growing faint and gasping like a drowsy man.

I left the hospital for the cell of the prisoner, whom I had tied hand and foot. Kellogg is still out in the woods, where he went looking for Dorothy (12 o'clock at night).

Received letters from Mother, Mary and Eb yesterday, which gave me pleasure. Mother wished me to read the 144th Psalm, which I have but just done since returning from the beside of Leroy.

13th

Leroy buried to-day; a skull was dug out of the grave they made for him, and it lay at my feet during the burial service. . . .

15th

Marched to Salt Creek; but one man was drunk. Lovell came out in the afternoon and said the appearance, discipline and behavior [of the battery] had been very highly spoken of at the fort. I never felt happier than I did to-day after I got in camp and found myself in the open field; the boundless, "eternal scope of the pe-rai-rah!" Distance from Leavenworth, 3 miles— wood & water; grass tough.

16th

. . . Marched over a rolling country, open, with groups of scattered trees. Encamped on the Stranger [River] in a valley, or . . . basin, with hills circum-scribing us like an amphitheater on all sides except on the side of the *river, which is thickly wooded. Grass & water good. Distance from Salt Creek, 11 miles, Leavenworth, 14 miles. Crossing at the Stranger steep & bad.*

Swier, whom Evans calls Corporal John Bull, went after game but found nothing but a Turkey Buzzard. Met a few Indians to-day, probably Dela-wares or Kickapoos.

17th

Heavy fall of dew this morning; nights beginning to grow cool. Reveille before 4 o'clock. Started at 6½. Rolling prairie country; patches of wood

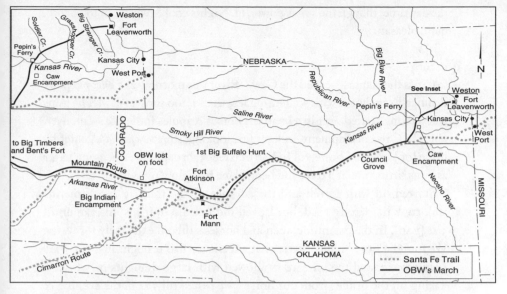

The Kansas Plains, showing the route of Willcox's march. Though in 1850 Kansas was yet a territory, current state lines have been included for the reader's convenience.

here & there, frequently looking like orchards running in lines & forming squares. Much of the time no trees in sight. Trees grow in the valleys of creeks & rivers; country looks as though it had been the bed of a sea, the deep, irregular channels of the subsiding water still appearing, though dry now & for centuries. . . . Reached the Grasshopper [River] at 2. Water & wood; fine camp. Crossing *very* bad on account of the steep banks; distance from the Stranger 24 miles. . . . Distance from Leavenworth 38. . . .

Disappointed to-day in getting no *letters* from home or Jefferson Barracks. The man left at Jefferson Barracks brought the mail to us; got a letter from Col. Beall, who says he's lonesome; cholera at Jefferson Barracks, 5 deaths [on the] 4th of July; news came in a letter to Sergt. Brice from his wife.

18th
Marched to Soldier's Creek to-day. Distance 18 miles from the Grasshopper. . . . Many Potawatomis around here cultivating land & living in log houses. Some of them talk good English. . . . Appearance of country same as yesterday. California road from Independence joins that from Leavenworth about a mile from the Soldier crossing. Some pretty squaws seen. Distance from Leavenworth 56 miles.

Ate one last chicken to-day. I left Leavenworth unwell, but to-day I have felt quite well, and am growing black as an Indian. Fine breeze in the day time, though the sun is powerful. Nights cool & when not too damp, quite pleasant.

19th

Cross the Kansas—called the Caw—River this morning at a Ferry kept by Pepin, a Frenchman with something less than 1,200 sons-in-law. The guns and wagons carried over in a boat; the horses & mules forded & swam over. Found a Caw encampment. Indians fine looking, squaws *squalid!* A chief by name [of] Italice, a powerful Indian of 6 feet 3, brought me a begging letter as I was sitting under a tree, and begged me hard for a picayune.

Started off with Lovell and the advance of the train at 12 M. [meridian], took the wrong road, but Lovell did not discover his mistake untill 5½ [P.M.]. In the meantime, men and horses suffered extremely for water. We found a little "bilge" water that a teamster had brought in a keg *from Leavenworth*, and this . . . we swallowed with large draughts of whiskey. Taking off the bridles from our horses, we rested till 7½ in the evening & then commenced [our] return.

Taken faint and sick from drinking the bad water & whiskey, which preceded our lunch on two bottles of wine and a hungry man's portion of rich old cheese, and laid down in the grass on the side of the road for half an hour's sleep with Evans. Rising after this nap, we found the train had all passed; hurrying to catch up set me to vomiting & purging and we stopped again to lie down. Our orderlies held our horses. I used my canteen for a pillow and Evans rested his head upon my body, and what a delicious sleep that roadside nap at midnight!

We rose after half an hour and got into camp, where we found the tents pitched. During the whole evening march the battery kept up with the dragoons. Our English friend got in a wagon and out again and wandered along with the train without hat or horse, enquiring for the Light Artillery. Some one told him where his horse was, but he said, "no, I belong to the Infantry." The "bilge" water & whiskey & wine was too much for him. In camp he rose in his sleep and was found sitting in Evans' tent over a bottle of brandy, somnambulizing [*sic*].

20th

Started across to strike the new road from the Ferry to Council Grove, taking a road which it was thought must intersect it. After going two or three miles we halted and sent out officers and men in different directions to find it. Lovell being out of humor and thinking he should have gone back all the way to the Ferry & taken a new start, complaining that *we* (the other officers) had persuaded him out of this other course against his better judgment.

One of the dragoons who had been sent to the Ferry, returned with a half breed guide, who told us where we could hit the road. It was a road we had passed, but overgrown with grass, it had escaped our sight. We then started for the point where it crossed Wolf Creek, and came to a Potawatomi village, where there were Indians, half breeds and French people living in log houses and raising corn. We squatted among them and lunched for an hour; got some fine cold water—some got a glass of milk—and then started on an almost obscured trail, only distinguishable by the shade of difference in the grass. The mess wagon was run off with and upset by the mules and my handtrunk smashed to a jam. Following our way suspiciously and watching the compass, we came to the Wacaloosa Creek. Distance from the Ferry, 13 miles, and from Leavenworth, 71.

The Englishman came into camp after sun rise in his bare legs with his two blankets under his arm. He had taken up his bed in his sleep and taken a moonlight promenade. He has been lying sick in the wagon all day. . . .

21st

Crossed a second time the Wacaloosa some 3 miles south of our last camp. . . . Followed the same obscure route all day, wandering out only once for a very short distance, still watching the compass closely to insure certainty; our route lying nearly south.

Got into camp at this Dragoon Creek early, after a fine, breezy, cloudy day, which was almost a compensation for yesterday's sweltering heat, which seemed almost intolerable, and gave several of us swollen, burnt & sore lips. Took a swim in one of the ponds which the creek has left in its almost dry bed. Just now I went out to bathe the sore leg of my horse, which is picketed in front of my tent, and the ungrateful scamp bit my ear nearly off! Distance from Wacaloosa 15, & from Leavenworth 86.

Corporal John Bull says he thought he was going to die yesterday. . . . He is well to-day. One night he waked up and exclaimed that there were two snakes in his bed! He & Kellogg have no bedsteads and both have a constant fear of snakes; they are getting used to the ants, etc., which swarm on them.

22d

March to Bluff Creek, 18 miles, to-day. Corporal John Bull brought two turkeys into camp with much exultation. As it was fresh meat, it was hailed with delight.

23d

March to Council Grove to-day, 12 miles. Passed several creeks contain-ing refreshing cold water. This is on the Neosho River and has an extensive growth of trees. There is a sutler store, and several log houses near it. . . .

We estimated our rate of marching, to-day, by tying a rag to a wheel-spoke & counting the revolutions for a quarter-hour; then, knowing the cir-cumference of the wheel, 5 yds., and noting 310 revolutions in 15 minutes, we found our rate about 3½ miles an hour. I find by taking the estimate of our officers on all the march so far, that Council Grove is 118 miles from Leavenworth. Capt. Easton measured it, & made it 120 or 124 miles.

24th

. . . The men have been washing their clothes. Mine have been washed but ironing is impossible. Among other Caws who came in camp to-day was Kashinga, a fine chief, *begging* with his squaw & 6 children. Another Indian offered Lovell his squaw, but he [Lovell] told black-faced Pander that he had a squaw, and showed him a daguerreotype of [Emily] the beauty of which amazed the savage. Took a fine swim. . . .

27th

Saw three Antelope. Gave chase likewise to a hare, got a shot, long range, with my pistol, and horse ran away with me for a mile or so; bent the bit all up in checking him. I drove the [hare] to the head of the column, where he took the road, Evans after him; but now he threw his ears back and left Evans far, far behind in a twinkling. Marched to the Lost Spring, but found it cool & plenty, *no wood*. . . . Distance from Leavenworth 148.

In the evening [we] all had a sit down in front of my tent, talking over old times till late. . . . Wind stampeded our tents to-day. . . .

30th

Marched to the Little Arkansas. . . . Little Arkansas a mere handful of water now that the season is dry, but quite a stream I should judge when the water is up; the banks are steep & from 10 to 40 yds. apart. . . .

Large number of Caws encamped near us, armed with bows, arrows and spears, with here & there a rifle. They brought in some buffalo meat to swap, tough as sole leather & dried & rather hardened in the sun. They had been out on a hunt a short distance west of the Arkansas; they dare not go so far for fear of the Pawnees. This river is the boundary between the two tribes. We saw trails made by herds of Buffaloes in the grass. Even this en-livened our spirits. Storm of thunder and lightning raging.

31st

Had the morning watch in camp. The lightning played constantly and the heavy artillery bombarded the skies. The Caws likewise kept up an infernal bedlam of sounds, all noises from the "Guard of the Dying" murdered by young ladies at the piano in the "Battle of Prague," to the wailings of the damned, pounded by a Methodist ranter, a sort of *cross* between an Irish wake and a wolf howl. This agreeable discordance of unearthly sounds, with the thunder and lightning "accompaniment," made concert for me till reveille. Marched to Cow Creek to-day. Distance 21 miles; from Council Grove, 110. . . .

August 1st

Another horrid night. . . . The mosquitoes! Bit all over, face, arms, feet & body; *bathed* in ammonia, but they didn't know what it was, as civilized mosquitoes would have done, and consequently didn't mind it. . . .

Saw and chased Buffaloes to-day! I *shrieked* with pleasure and excitement. A party of us dashed into a large herd this morning; they separated into bands, keeping in each band their cows and calves inside, the bulls guarding the flanks. My object was to shoot a cow, and with but two cartridges I chased them for miles; got one long shot; the other went off accidentally; lost my way, but took my pocket compass & steered (rightly) for the road. None of us killed [any] in the morning. Evans shot his mare through the ear. This afternoon two bulls were killed. Kellogg shooting one at 50 paces with his dragoon pistol. One of the soldiers, Godwin, killed his horse—shot him through the neck. The whole camp wild with excitement. . . . Marched to Walnut Creek—branch of the Arkansas, distance 25 miles. . . .

August 2d

. . . Started out this morning after marching a couple of miles with the column and took a young but fleet horse to train for chasing buffalo. Shying off at first when he came close on a herd, he finally gained confidence and gave chase.

[I] wounded a bull early in the action and brought him to bay. With his head down and feet pawing the earth, he awaited me. As I neared him his eyes rolled downwards, displaying the white, and seemed to flash fire; horse took fright and charged off; bringing him up to fifteen paces, the bulls eyes again smoked & rolled and he came pitching at me; horse ran again and the bull resumed his march towards the herd.

Soon I overtook and brought him again to bay, putting another ball into his side. Again he charged & again horse flew; this game I followed, helped by a corporal I took with me, for an hour or so, until I dismounted and advanced towards the bull at bay on foot. When I got to ten paces he charged me, but I gave him a shot in the face, which, without hurting him, brought him to a stand, I, putting off for my safety.

Exhausting all my cartridges, I sent back after more, circling round him meanwhile on my horse, who snorted and turned tail every time the bull charged. Lovell, hearing I had the bull wounded, came out and gave me a couple of cartridges, dashing on by into the herd, but the animal got started again, and ran a couple of miles, in spite of horse & self, for every time I came in front of him, he charged, and then pushed on. Once he got close on the horse's heels, which, by the way, he got full in his face. He got on my horse another time, but turned off, fearing the heels of which he had had a taste. Getting another shot into him, he came to a full stand, charging as before whenever I approached him, tail straight up in the air, feet pawing, nose close to the ground, and eyes rolling in fire; a terrific but noble spectacle.

I now got on one side of him and placed the corporal on the opposite side, and walking my horse round him, keeping him turning, *a la Mexican bull fight;* this sickened him very much, and he fell on his fore knees. Twice I approached where he was down, and each time he rose up to charge me, still keeping me at distance with my horse, from whose back I was determined to kill him, and who began now to behave pretty well, making his circles smaller and smaller and allowing me to fire off his back at a halt, without flinching.

In a short time the bull was unable to rise; still, he made every effort, showing fight to the last; but his eyes grew dimmer and dimmer, and ceased to roll as before when I approached closer. He did not bellow, uttered not a groan, but seemed to be composing himself for death. At last he stretched himself out. I came up to him; he was dead.

Although the chase extended about 8 miles, I found myself near the road at the close, and, the train coming along, I sent for a wagon and one of the sergeants expert at butchering, and secured the nice parts for eating. It was my first achievement and I felt proudly; the best parts of the buffalo are the hump & hump ribs and the fleeces, together with the tongue & marrow bones. At this season of the year the skin is destitute of hair, except from the fore shoulders forward, and down nearly to the feet; they look as if they were *pantalettes.*

Killed another in the afternoon with a six pounder gun at about four hundred yards, with canister shot; he was one of a group of three I shot at. Marched to Pawnee Fork. Distance, 25 miles. Distance from Council Grove 160.

Ye western plains! where roams the dark Pawnee,
  The antelope, wolf, and generous buffalo,
Sweet are your winds, whose spirit fiercely free
  Brave, lordly hearts of independence know.
And I salute the tiny polar tree,
  That, like a compass, providence bids grow,
To guide the wanderer o'er your trackless sea
  of grass, that waves a boundless flowery lea.

I hear one cry "my steed! my steed so fleet!"
  And let me bound again upon thy back,
And flee away with lightning-shodden feet
  Upon the lumbering buffalo's far track;
Ha! the cool breezes whistle loud, and greet
  My raptured brow, and all its tresses shake
With laughter at the dull cold pall of life,
  That glazes o'er their hearts in city's strife.

Hie on my steed! afar the watchful herd
  Snuff the cool air, the scent the coming foe;
Gallop apace, cleave on like any bird!
  Aye, prick thine ears as you behold them now,
And dash on merrily, nor spur, nor word
  May mend thy pace—the wind to thee is slow —
How quakes the turf! how clash the hoof and horn!
  Among them now, wary, brave steed—they turn.

Oh! 'tis a stirring sport, my friends, to see
  A thousand driven by one hardy foe;
Before my foaming horse and frantic me,
  Though hast'ning onward, surlily they go;
Behold they scatter—let the arrows flee —
  Beware, one holds, turn off, see the blood flow!
Come up ye comrades! and ye slaves draw nigh,
  See how a wounded buffalo may die.

With haughty dignity he waits thee now,
  Turns as ye turn, presenting hostile face,
Approach, fierce eyes beneath yon gnarly brow
  Flash fire: stand back, stand back a pace,

T'were silly strife to meet the mighty blow;
   Defiant still he kneels with Roman grace,
Sinks slowly down, his eyes grow white and wan,
   Brave to the last, he dies without a groan.[15]

August 3d

Creek too high to ford; went to its mouth and crossed where it empties in[to] the Arkansas. Got a splendid view as we were on the hill. 300 buffalo wading and sporting in the Arkansas! Met a Santa Fe train. Saw Plympton, Tyler, Dr. Edwards and Maj. Wightman. Lovell left Evans and myself to chat with them, which we did at Evans' camp table a couple of hours on the road in the shade of a wagon and had a glorious time. Scribbled a note in pencil to C. Encamped on the Arkansas 14 miles from Pawnee Fork, 174 from Council Grove. Bathed in the river.

August 4

Sunday. Still marching on the Arkansas bottom; walked on foot 4 hours with the men to spare the horses. Lovell dropped a fine heifer at a single shot near the road. Culled some pretty prairie flowers; the men had them on their horses heads as we came into camp on the Arkansas. . . .

August 5

The first 13 miles to-day [were] dead level, then came to a range of lime stone hills. . . . Walked on foot two hours and a half. Marched 21 miles; encamped opposite a handsome grove across the river, where in 184– three companies of dragoons captured a large band of Texas Robbers. Took another splendid swim in the rapid current of the Arkansas, which here, as usual, is shallow and treacherous. . . .

August 6th

Marched to six miles below Mann's Fort, an old clay and log ruin, built once upon a bend in the Arkansas. Road mostly level, but view mostly relieved by the river with its thin growth of timber scattering along.

[Prairie] Dog villages again and again. These are of holes from 10 to 20 ft. apart, covering sometimes a mile square. There the dog may be seen sitting at the door of his house as you come along, uttering a *rat*iculate [*sic*] sort of bark, and as you get closer, down pops his head, up flies his tail and he disappears. Like many noisy men, *the last thing he shows is his tail.* The owl I find, as

---

15. From "The Pleasures of Retirement," by OBW, stanzas 45–49.

well as the rattle snake, find home and shelter in these holes. The dog, the serpent and the owl—gravity, wisdom and faithfulness—good for a coat of arms. . . .

[Our] camp visited by a party of Indians, headed by Coyota, an eagle-headed Arapahoe & . . . Kiowa, dressed in a motley of American satinet & Mexican and Indian tawdry, who said he was half Arapahoe and half Kiowa: this he expressed by putting one hand on one breast and saying Arapahoe & the other on the other breast and saying Kiowa.

This was a treacherous looking, leer-eyed rascal, but he brought a letter from Fitzpatrick, the Indian agent. Lovell gave them small provisions and plied them with liquor till they got "tight" and we had some trouble getting them out of camp—Kiowa especially wanted to stay all night. A couple of discharges from a six-pounder nearly stunned their ears.

The gestures of the Apache chief were the most graceful and energetic in the world, and he was a powerfully built man. They hugged us like bears, the drunker they got the warmer their embrace. . . . Lovell called me to his tent where I found these chiefs, with their young men & women austerely excluded from the inside of the tent & sitting just outside on the ground. Lovell put his hand on me and said "Chief," whereupon they all uttered a prolonged grunt and something between a "yah" and a "ho ho," and all put out their hands to me in the most d——n rascally friendly manner.

August 7

Marched to a point 1½ miles above the crossing of the Arkansas. Found Indians encamped in large numbers along the other side of the river. A deputation from the "big camp" came across about nine this morning and invited Lovell and his "chiefs" to their encampment, where they treated those who went in the most hospitable manner, and at their departure gave them a large quantity of jerked buffalo meat.

The Indians who were there, some three or four hundred, were Apaches of the plains; Arapahoes and Caywas, pronounced "Kiowa"; men rather good looking, women quite "unpretty."

Coho, Kiowa and half dozen other chiefs visited us in camp this afternoon and swapped a few lies with us in their pantomime manner for some bad brandy and water. They treated their people who came with them in the most arbitrary manner, not allowing them, at Lovell's suggestion, to come into our camp.

Seven miles below the crossing, we came upon a high table land where the heat came like a hot furnace blast upon us. We descended suddenly from this plateau to the crossing, where the river is about 50 or 60 yds. wide, no woods, and, for its amount of interest to us, quite common looking. Distance of the crossing from last . . . camp, 20 miles; from Council Grove 254; from Leavenworth 372 . . . miles. Dis of present camp from the crossing, 1½ miles. . . .

August 10

Delighted to-day at the sight of a train from the states, which has passed over the river on its way to Santa Fe. It is a Government store train, conducted by Aubrey. He sent us [news]papers up to the 17th of July and in the evening came over to our camp, bringing me a letter from Col. Beall, who calls Aubrey the Telegraph of the Plains. His last *run* from Santa Fe to Independence was wonderful—eight hundred miles in 7 days & 16 hours; he caught up 13 horses by chance of the Indians etc. on the way, and on reaching Independence was so exhausted he had to be lifted off his horse. The train we met August 3d was fired upon at Pea's Point near Pawnee Fork the very evening we parted! by either Osages or Pawnees.

August 11

Small stampede last night on my watch; luckily I was near the horses when it occurred. Two or three mules got frightened and came snorting and kicking into the center of the horses with their picket pins and ropes flying in every direction. As Aubrey told us to-day, some Indians had been trying to stampede him only an hour before, & passed on towards us. We presume it must have been the same rascals. And who were they? Coho, Kiowa, etc.! whom we thought half way to Bent's Fort,[16] whom we had treated so kindly and who deceived us so completely. To-day on going to Aubrey's camp, there they were! but they were ashamed to speak to us. Aubrey fears these movements on their part, as they have sent their families up the river, but remain themselves, and he has applied to Capt. Lovell for an escort. Lt. Evans will go with his company. . . .

August 16th

Express from Col. Sumner this morning. He is at the Big Timbers, having left Laramie about 25th of July. The mail from Santa Fe arrived, just in time, yesterday eve; we sent forward our letters this evening by it. Struck our camp and took up the line of march for the Big Timbers. Marched 17 miles. . . .

16. Bent's Fort was an important way station, located near present-day Animas, Colorado.

Yellow Bear, an Arapahoe chief—a "big chief heap"—visited our camp this evening with Coho, Kiowa and a party of young braves, all of which, party & chiefs, got "glorious" as Tam O'Shanter. Yellow Bear is the finest & most *character* looking Indian yet seen. He gave his share of tobacco to his men, & is said to be a "heap" friend to the Americans. Had almond shaped eyes, tinged with red paint & a handsome dress. He is said to have opposed his whole tribe once when they desired to war with the whites. *1st camp above crossings.*

17th
Saw many antelope to-day, *lopering*, as Kellogg says, across the prairies; marched 24 miles. Distance from crossing 44. *2d camp above crossings.*

18th
Marched to *3d camp above crossings*, 25 miles distance, from the crossings, 69. Country uneven; passed through a bad gap in the hills of some length. Attacked soon after leaving it by—flies; glassy, glaring, green headed, sharp monsters that made the blood literally drop from the horses. P.S. *Midnight.* I am officer of the watch. It is Sunday night; the wind is howling out and shaking the tent, while a few spattering drops of rain tap now & then for admittance. I have read a chapter of Proverbs and finished off by mending my coat, under the arm, where it had burst 20 times. . . .

August 19th
Cloudy cold day. After marching 20 miles, Lovell turned off from the road towards some timber on the river, leaving orders for me to march on with the column until he should find good grass, etc., for camping. I watched him & marched on and on for 12 miles before we got to camp, making 32 miles! The horses meanwhile without water, the men without dinner. It was 4½ o'clock when we halted. We fell to downing our lunch voraciously. The jerked meat and whiskey toddy had to suffer!

Soon a hard-feeling, cold drizzle came on, and we turned in to our blankets at retreat. Such a change of weather! Yesterday a sun worthy of the tropics, to-day a drizzle worthy of the D——l in winter uniform. . . .

My attention about 12 o'clock was arrested by a group of officers & other horsemen in front, firing their pistols at something on the ground. Riding up I found a large rattle snake at bay, surrounded by some half dozen foes spitting fire at him, as he probably thought. He was coiled up, with his head crested high, his tongue forking & flashing poisonous fire, making desperate leaps towards any horse that came too nigh. Every shot had missed him; my first ball struck under him, and the flying dirt threw him a little way, but the second shot severed his crested majesty in two, and a teamster coming "in at the death" cut his head with his whip lash. He had nine rattles. Many of these "subtle beasts" are seen daily. This afternoon the quartermaster killed one with eleven rattles. Distance of *4th camp from the crossings, 101 miles.* . . .

20th August

Drizzly day. After marching two miles [we] met an express from Col. Sumner, ordering us to halt and wait for him. He came on about 9 o'clock & we countermarched and made 20 miles on return. He was out of bread, and on his way to examine Jackson Grove (below Fort Mann). He states that the country around Bent's Fort is *deserted* of white men, Indians and game, & he thinks it too far out of the way for a post. Says he will set out to return to Leavenworth about 20th of September. . . . Met Yellow Bear equipped for war. He is going to lead a war party against the Utahs.

21st August

Laid in camp. Assigned to the command of the mounted infantry, about 50 men with the sorriest looking horses I *ever* have seen, just fit to mount Falstaff's recruits. The Indian hunters killed 3 antelope—delicious.

22d

Marched down about 17 miles. Two horses of my Rib Cavalry gave out and I left them on the road.

28th

Camp Mackay, 14 miles below the crossings. Reached here on the 26th, after marching all that day in a rain which soaked me through and through. The Colonel much disappointed at the supply train not being up, and this morning sent Lt. Kellogg with 22 men down to meet it. He is to proceed as far as Pawnee Fork and wait a week should it not arrive before. Kellogg's being gone leaves me alone in my tent, which the 3 days' rain has rendered *rather damp* & uncomfortable. . . . The hunters, John & Wild Cat, kill us a buffalo nearly every day, and when we lie in camp we have bean soup, which, boiled as the soldiers do, is a luxury, but which we have not time to cook on the march. No variety except in court martials, two of which we have blessed the command with.

The Colonel encamps in a square, pickets the animals on the *outside*, and makes the sentinels call out the hour at the guard tent, and "all well" at each post every half hour during the night. He says he never has had a horse stolen on the plains.

Lovell's plan was to enclose the horses by the tents, wagons, etc. on two sides, & this, with the river on the third & a sentinel on the fourth and shortest side, effectually secured the camp. The Indians never attack between tents or wagons, and they could not drive our horses away by a stampede, as there was no other approach or passage through, except one narrow side, strictly guarded, or on the side of the river, where like wise was a sentinel walking, & near which the guard tent was pitched.

We are encamping along the river bottoms in high grass, & when there is rain, or heavy dew, as at night on guard, we get wet almost up to our chins. And Oh! the bugs! No sooner is your tent pitched than a million invade you, or rather resist your invasion upon their dominions. The Lord knows *I* never will trouble them again if *I* can help it! Crickets, roaches, spiders, grasshoppers, ants, tumble bugs, daddy-long-legs and many others with a hundred pairs of legs apiece, run over your tent walls, & settling down, weave their hammock homes, or . . . penetrate into your bed, hop into your face, crawl under your clothes, fall into your water bucket & make themselves fully "at home" by night time, when they commence chirping, squeaking, buzzing & abutting against your light in the most sociable manner.

I have frequently this summer felt the force & beauty of the comparison of "the man who puts his trust in the Lord" to a "tree planted by the side of pleasant waters," for on these desert plains it is only on the margin of the streams that trees can grow at all. After the long, hot march, how delightful these trees look! the only green, living, shady things that meet the eye. Near them we know we are going to encamp and rest; there only is water to quench our burning thirst, and there only is wood & grass. I always feel, in passing a group of trees on the prairie, like a hungry man passing an eating house!

August 30th

Lovell & myself rode down on a sort of *reconnaissance* to the bluffs yesterday, and turned up on the plateau above to look for buffalo. A small herd of bulls came in view. We galloped up to them, dashed into them & separated a young one, but he dodged us both & rejoined the herd which were lopering off.

Lovell took after the herd, I after a single one upon which, with much difficulty, I brought my unmanageable horse, & brought the bull to bay. But as he turned, the horse took fright, & making . . . to the *rear* instead of [to] the left, for which latter I was fully prepared, pitched me head foremost to the ground, my pistol discharging as I fell. I suppose it was about ten feet from the buffalo, but he did not attack me.

My horse put off at full heat. Lovell, in the mean time, had got into the herd, & made a shot, when he heard my pistol, saw my predicament, and took after my horse. I started for camp, some 8 or 9 miles to the west. Lovell soon disappeared, chasing my horse, & [I] was alone & on foot. Fortunately, as I thought, there was one cartridge in my pocket, which I had not been able to get into the holster. Loading the pistol . . . with this, I plodded along, not a tree nor a land mark in sight. I steered for a slight rising of the ground, thinking it towards the river, which I thought ought not to have been more than 1½ miles distant.

The rising turned out to be three or four miles off, and on reaching the top of it, I could see the prairie stretching away beyond until it disappeared in the haze of the distant *mirage*. I now took a new course, which must have been northeast, and went some six miles or more, the very opposite to my course for reaching the river, which would have lead me to camp. But I was deceived by buffalo trails . . . and by the cast of my shadow, which I accounted upon as it would be before noon, when in reality it was afternoon.

I came across an immense wolf, as large I think as most leopards, or perhaps as the Newfoundland dog. He knew not what to make of me. He trotted around in the curve of a circle, towards me, the center of which he kept approaching. I walked away from him in order to encourage him to come up, for I could have killed him easily with my horse pistol, even had he attacked me. But after a quarter of an hour he moved away, looking back at me in a very wistful manner.

I must fairly acknowledge, now, that I was completely lost, and so thought it best to lie down and rest & wait till I could determine the points of the compass with certainty. After an hour or so I started almost due south. Met a beautiful stag antelope with large, branching horns. He stopped, knowing probably that I had no rifle, and looked at me with all the curiosity of a woman, and then trotted off in splendid style, raising his knees nearly to his chin. [I] came near many herds of buffalo, who probably having the same knowledge of my fire arms with the antelope, took but little notice of me. A sly fox even returned to insult me in the same manner.

Walking two hours in the new course brought me to the bluffs about six miles below camp, and as I came down the side of a hill, I discovered a man bringing my horse from camp for me to ride. Lovell had chased him 10 or 12 miles before he could turn him, and then he galloped in, straight for camp, by himself. Here he excited no little wonder & curiosity, not to say alarm. Some thought I had been thrown, some that my horse had got away on my dismounting to cut up a buffalo, while the Colonel even feared that the Indians had killed both Lovell & myself. But the latter got in an hour and a half afterwards & allayed their *fears*, at least, without satisfying their curiosity.

The Colonel *thought* of sending out an armed party after us, but nothing was done until Lovell sent the man down the road with the horse. He had, in running, thrown out the remaining pistol, which I regret, as it was loaned to me by Stanton. After all the fatigues of the day, I inspected my company horses, marched on officer of the day, read till 11 or 12 in the night, and went the rounds of the sentinels at 1½ [A.M.]. To-day feel a little stiff, but well enough to walk 30 miles if necessary, but as it is not, I shall devote myself to my tent, and to thinking of home, sweet-heart & next Fall, which, heaven be blessed! is so near at hand.

September 3d

Now encamped about six miles above Fort Mann, near which the Colonel has decided to locate the new post. . . . On the 30th ult., a train of Oldham's came from Independence & brought the most discouraging news about an ox train so anxiously looked for on account of the mail. On the 31st a train of Dr. Waldo's brought more encouraging news, and to-day we have heard from Chapman, who is en route a few days below. He forwarded an express from Leavenworth, which brought orders to hold the two dragoon companies *out here* in readiness for distant service—probably Santa Fe. The ox train is one day behind him, so that we shall hear from Kellogg to-morrow; and the Colonel talks of leaving me at the new post to be established!!!

Our Delaware interpreter, Dick, whom the Colonel had sent over to the Cimarron to invite in the Commanches, etc., for a talk, came in on the 2d with the Apaches and two Kiowa chiefs with seven old counselors who came with the latter. Coho's son had told the Indians that we wished to kill them, so that, as this party neared camp, only two of them came forward with Dick, while the others got behind a bluff to see how these would be received. The Colonel and Lovell were riding to Fort Mann at the time, & meeting them, went behind the bluff and brought them all into camp in the most friendly manner.

Gathered round the Colonel's tent, we took a smoke with them all, the Colonel ordered the comissary to issue them 50 rations, and they were left to the care of Dick, John, & Wild Cat. A large golden mounted meerchaum pipe we passed around excited their curiosity. In the night we set off some fire works and the savages screamed & laughed with delight and wonder like so many babies.

The next morning, after exhibiting to them, 1st, a revolver which shot itself off the handle at the 2d discharge; 2d, a rifle wall-piece which obstinately refused to fire except by the most assiduous coaxing! and 3d, a couple of brass pieces which behaved very well, we all sat down in grand council. The Colonel sat at the front of his tent on a box, supported on either side by the great Kiowa chiefs, and in a semicircle in front, squatted on the ground, were the others. Dick, who, by the way, is the son of Capt. Ketchum, the head Delaware chief, and John, sat in the center. Dick interpreted for John, and John for the Colonel.

Then spoke the Colonel—the pipe passing from man to man in the party:

> The arm of the Great Father is now very long; it reaches beyond the mountains to the big waters; his eye is upon every one of his red children, and he sees all his white children too; and he will punish his white children when they act bad towards the Indian, as he will his red children when they act bad to the whites.
>
> The Great Father is very angry about the murder of that white woman—Mrs. White—and the killing of those ten white men this spring at Wagon Mound. His eye is upon every Indian who was in those things; there is a mark set upon each one of them, and your Great Father will not rest until those bad Indians are laid under the ground.

He [Colonel Sumner] inquired whether they knew where the band of Apaches were that committed these outrages, and was told they were in the mountains & had not returned down all summer. He inquired whether Mrs. White's little girl was still with them, and was told she was. This they had heard from the Indians who lived at the base of the mountains. The two Apache chiefs said they had heard so much about these bad Indians from the white men, that they had sent a war party into the mountains after them!

The Colonel inquired whether there were any Mexicans in the party that attacked the express at Wagon Mound. They said *there were*, and that they quarreled with the Indians about the plunder, and would let them have none. He inquired to whom the land along the river near here belonged. They told him the Kiowas and Apaches. He said he was going to build a fort here, and soldiers were to live in it, to keep peace between the red children and the white children of the Great Father, and that whenever the white men wronged the Indians, they must come to the fort & complain, & justice should be done; that they must not take vengeance into their own hands, for the whites would retaliate, and then the Indians would always get the worst of it. That there were many white men who did not know the Indians traveling along the road with wagons, and that when they met these white men, they must not rush up toward them in a body suddenly, for that made the white men fire upon them; but that they must approach them few at a time & then they would be well received.

But the Great Father's soldiers all knew the Indians, and they could come upon *them* as they pleased! for *they* were always ready for either war or peace! The Colonel said they would probably see the spot where they were then standing covered with corn next year, to be planted by the soldiers, and that the Great Father wished to see his red children plant corn and live in houses, and that if they behaved well He would make them presents every year. (At this they gave the most sincere *grunt* of approbation evinced during the whole council!)

The Colonel then desired them to tell the Commanches that he wished to see them too, & that he would receive them as he had done themselves. He told them he was going to give them some provisions to take their wives & children, but that he had not much to give, as he had been a long time from home. He then told the big Kiowa chief that if he would send a couple of his men up to the Big Timbers with a letter (to Lt. Evans), he would give them a bag of rice, a bag of flour, some coffee and some sugar.

Then up spake the big Kiowa chief. He would try and send two of his young men to the Big Timbers. His brother was up there & they might wish to go and see him, but he was not certain. He was glad to get a message from the Great Father; he thought it would be for his interest to keep peace with his Great Father, and his people should not attack the Americans any more; that they might travel along the road without fear; what the Great Father had said he would keep on his breast and study over it a great deal. Whenever his people met the white people, they would always shake hands with them, & when he died his spirit would enter his children and they would always feel as he did & be friends with the whites.

He was evidently no orator; he spoke sitting with his elbows on his knees and his head down towards the interpreter. He had a shrewd cast of countenance, a very Caucasian face and head, and his manner, though grave, deliberate & dignified, was businesslike.

These Indians were all fine looking, large men. One grey headed old fellow was a giant . . . in size, and had a head as large as Webster's and a face almost exactly like Franklin's. He was an old Counselor. None of them spoke, however, but the chiefs, and the talk was soon over.

During the day, one of the [Arapahoe] chiefs, Coyota, an old acquaintance, who had quickly recognized Lovell and myself, came to my tent. I offered him a drink, but before he would take it, he went to bring the other chief to share it with him. Not finding him, he brought his daughter, a girl of about 12 years, but she could not stomach it. He made me write his name several times until he learnt the looks of it, as well as that of Lovell and myself; and wished me to give him a letter to a Commanche chief, Short Hair, a great friend of his, who was in doubt whether to come to see the whites. He wished his name, Lovell's and mine on the letter. Accordingly I wrote our three names and drew the figure of a human eye between them and the name of Short Hair, & gave him the missive, which he seemed to understand.

I showed him a picture of C——, which *of course* struck his admiration. He asked me if it was my squaw in the following manner: representing me by one of his fingers, he laid another . . . finger down by the side of it, and said, "*mujer*," the Spanish for woman. I laughed and told him, "yes, my squaw," and he said "*bonita, bonita*," which means "beautiful."

In the afternoon a wagon train came in from Santa Fe, bringing news that Connelly's train had been robbed by the Commanches, near Cedar Creek, of 82 mules. His men were mostly Mexicans, and the Indians dashed upon the animals at 11 o'clock in the broad daylight, and drove them off. The party of Indians was only 30 strong, and there were said to be 35 men with the train! ten of them said to be Americans—which I doubt.

September 9th

Lt. Chapman joined us on the 4th with Co. "F" 1st Dragoons; he had overtaken two expressmen and sent forward their despatches to the Colonel before him. They contained orders to detain the two dragoon companies of our command, subject to further orders for "Distant Service." We got a small mail from the States by the express. Everyone but myself was happy with their letters. The 7th Infantry has arrived at Fort Leavenworth, and [is] waiting [for] orders; all this looks towards the resistance of Texas in New Mexico, but as the papers announce the passage of the Texas bill, buying the land for $10,000,000, and establishing her boundaries, it is supposed the "Distant Service" will be abandoned. . . .

The new post is to be put near Fort Mann. A working party from our command has gone down this morning to break ground. Temporary quarters of sod are to be erected for the winter. Lts. Kellogg & Pleasonton[17] arrived to-day with the ox train and a young surgeon. . . .

12th

. . . Lovell and I are to lay out & put up the weather walls of the [new post]. To-day "D" Company pitched their camp near the work. Two saw mills are to be erected for getting out lumber, and Hall & Waldo, who carry the Santa Fe & Independence mail, are to build houses near it likewise for the convenience of their trains. . . . A Mormon train (women & children in every wagon) have passed us, on their way to the Gila & Colorado. Yesterday morning the Colonel sent off Chapman & his company to meet Evans. He has a beautiful company of gray horses.

One of the camp women was shot dead the other day by the accidental discharge of a gun in a wagon on the road. To-night a teamster died. I am ordered to play quartermaster & commissary. Mule teams, look out!

18th

Mr. Shaw, in charge of a train belonging to Hall & Waldo, came in last night & reported that some 84 of their oxen having strayed off, the Kiowas had got them & refused to deliver them up except on exorbitant charges. Some of these Indians had been met by Dick and promised by the latter some tobacco from the Colonel. They went in to get it yesterday, and of course were disappointed. They passed me at work on Fort Sodom, and looked like great rascals.

After they had left, and after tattoo, Mr. Shaw came in and made his complaint. Capt. Lovell was at once ordered by the Colonel to start for the Indian camp by reveille this morning. I asked the Colonel if he did not want some of my men, and he told me I might go with all I could mount.

Started at 5 minutes of 6 [A.M.], Lovell with two guns and 18 cannoneers; I with only a dozen mounted infantry. As we drew near Shaw's train, we expected, of course, he would come out to greet us & accompany us to the Indian camp. But Lovell had to ride down to him to learn particulars, and Shaw was such a fool that he let 4 Indians, who were in his camp, put out as we approached. He said the Kiowas had promised to deliver the cattle for certain presents, but that when he sent after them, they . . . refused to give them up. . . . He sent some drivers behind us on foot, but did not come himself.

17. Alfred Pleasonton (7th, USMA 1844) was then first lieutenant, 2d Dragoons. His most notable Civil War service was as commander of the Cavalry Corps, Army of the Potomac.

At Jackson's Grove we met a mounted detachment of "D" Co., who had been cutting wood. They said they had heard the Indians passing them in the night, yelling as if drunk. We came to the Indian camp 23 miles [away] at 5 minutes of 11. [Our] Guns [were] behind on the road, but we had the cannoneers, "D" Co. detachment & my men. The Indians had broken up their lodges & sent off their women, children, etc. We saw them scampering over the hills. The chief (the same man the Colonel had the council talk with) and some dozen men remained with the cattle. . . .

Lovell sent the Indian interpreters Dick & John to tell them he was coming to settle the difficulty between them and the white men. We crossed over the river to them. Lovell rode up to them and I formed the command in line, about 50 yards [back,] facing them. The line looked long, and if the red skins had only stood out, how handsomely we could have thrashed them! But they gave up the cattle at once, about 50 in number, and this was all that a Delaware Indian of Shaw's said they had the night before. The cattle were driven off, and Lovell gave the chief two letters: one to Shaw, telling him what presents he must make the Indians, and one to the Colonel, to be delivered in case these terms should not be complied with.

We recrossed the river and pitched our camp in some fine grass. Shortly afterwards, two of Shaw's men came in and told us the Indians had the remainder of the cattle in another herd, back among the hills, and that the chief had told Shaw so the night before. Lovell directed them to hurry up and inform the Colonel, so that, if he thought proper, he might secure the persons of the chief & party, until these cattle should be delivered. The battery got in at 11¼, having made the march and stopped on the way to water the horses, in 5 hrs. & 20 mins.

Last evening I completed the 3d side of Sodom (or Fort Expedient, as Col. Sumner calls it). It is 100 ft. *square*, having two sets of parallel walls 6⅓ ft. high, 4 at the base and two at the top. Lovell and I have laid it all out & built it up so far—Where are the *infantry officers* who should have been here to build their own quarters? Echo! Echo! Echo! Last week I performed duty belonging to four arms of the service, not one of which was my own proper arm, the artillery. . . .

19th

Last night [the] corporal of the guard thought he heard cattle lowing across the river, and, mounting what men we could, we left the six-pounders and wagons and started over this morning. A few miles back we struck a stream, which was struggling through cliffs and ravines, and whose banks were studded with hackberry and cottonwood trees.

We had a romantic march of nine miles, seeing plenty of traces of old Indian lodges, but none whatever of recent ones, nor of cattle. Watered at 11 o'clock [at] a deep spring, whose walls were 20 ft. high & the same in diameter, and struck across for Jackson's Grove, above which Lovell had ordered Sergt. Brice to remove our little camp.

Returned in low spirits, and Lovell and myself confessed in the tent our mutual disappointment, for both had started out in the morning with the expectation of having a fight with the rascally Indians. All we saw yesterday had their arms, bows, arrows, etc., and had we been an hour later, we should undoubtedly have had the pleasure of a chase, and perhaps a fight for the cattle. Best as it was, perhaps.

Grand scene to-night! The river shore sweeps off to the north just above camp, displaying a wide, long tract of bottom land away to the west. This is all on fire. Above this lies a long black line of bluffs, beyond which the country is likewise afire. The remaining light after sunset is reflected from the sky, which forms the background, and is visible through the clouds of smoke. A few large trees standing singly here and there loom through the light and shade like monster spectres; and brightly above all, Venus presides with unusual splendor.

On the opposite side of the sky, the moon is shining in the full, throwing a sheet of silver upon the river, by the side of which the large grove below us so sullenly reposes. And here around the white tents, our animals are grazing, unconscious of the beauty of the whole scene! Poor devils! How much they lose!

20th

Killed a wolf on the road returning to Fort Mann camp; lost a gauntlet by the affair. Lt. Heth arrived by express; a classmate; had a long talk with him on old affairs after we got a bed.[18]

23d

Chapman & Evans came rolling into camp this morning. Was at Heth's fort at the time; on our way to camp, met old Burn,[19] with a tremendous

18. Heth was then serving with the 1st Dragoons, on his way to the "Great Bend" of the Arkansas River, where he was to join members of the 6th Infantry constructing another of the numerous sod posts on the Santa Fe Trail. Willcox later wrote: "I had not met Heth since our graduation. He now commanded his company of mounted infantry and had already laid the foundation for his good repute and experience in Indian affairs. His more brilliant qualities as a soldier developed in the war of the Rebellion during which he became one of General Robert E. Lee's most trusted division commanders, as we shall see in due time."

19. Ambrose Burnside, who was then returning east, via Fort Jefferson, after a year and a half of service with Company C, 3d U.S. Artillery, stationed at Las Vegas, New Mexico.

black beard & head almost bald on top. Col. May, Maj. Peck, Capt. Humber, Lt. Simpson (Topogs), . . . Jerry Folger (sutler) and sundry lap dogs came with Evans, Chapman & Burn. The crowd took a champaigne lunch and got quite merry.

25th
Last night was a night of parting bumpers. This morning camp broke up & Evans & Chapman, feeling like doomed unfortunates . . . started with their companies (& Pleasanton) for Santa Fe (under the late order). The parting was the most painful I have yet seen in the army. We started with our otherwise joyous faces set towards *home*. Stopped an hour with poor Heth, while the commissary took in provisions from a contract supply train, and then rolled on 21½ miles.

26th
Just as our command was rising [over] the hills, we came in view of Ewell's[20] Dragoon recruit (150) train. They drew up & presented arms to us, and we stopped an hour on the road with them. Capts. Ewell & Buford & Bvt. 2d Lts. Johnson, Bingham & Holliday were the officers.[21] They were 29 days out from Leavenworth, delaying on account of an ox train behind.

When the advance sounded, Lovell & myself rode with our commands and left most of the party to have a frolic, which they did have on the road, with champaigne drank at the Santa Fe travelling bar. Marched 26½ miles; the Colonel rode in a wagon nearly all day, but got frisky to-night & ordered some rockets to be set off, but the 1st one nearly stampeded the horses & that seemed to satisfy the old gentleman. . . .

28th September
. . . Killed a buffalo to-day. Encamped on the river between Pawnee Fork and Walnut Creek, at a point a few miles below Pawnee Rock. Chasing the herd, a buffalo calf got knocked down and lay struggling & sprawling as I galloped nearly over him, but I couldn't draw up my horse. Kellogg & the Doctor sick for some days, riding in wagons.

20. Richard S. Ewell (13th, USMA 1840) was then a brevet captain of the 1st Dragoons, on his way to New Mexico. He made his mark as a division and corps commander in the Army of Northern Virginia.
21. These officers were brevet Capt. Abraham Buford (51st, USMA 1841), 1st Dragoons, Lt. Thomas Bingham (29th, USMA 1850), and Lt. Jonas P. Holliday (24th, USMA 1850), 2d Dragoons. Holliday later served as colonel of the 1st Vermont Cavalry during the Civil War, dying near Strasburg, Virginia, on April 5, 1862. The officer identified as Lieutenant Johnson was probably Lt. Robert Johnston, 1st Dragoons.

29th

Sunday. Buffalo in thousands and thousands around us all day. Large districts perfectly black with them. The river from Pawnee Rock very extensive and all the country around alive with herds. Lovell had a fine chase, killing a couple of cows and a calf.

Encamped at the bend below Walnut Creek. The Dr. got out a six-pounder and several buffalo were shot down within short range of our camp. The meat of the calves & heifers delicious; the udder particularly.

My horse mired in Walnut Creek; had to dismount to help him up & I sank down about two feet; the horse, in lunging about, knocked me over, broke off my sabre & lost a pistol. (18 miles.)

30th

The affair at Walnut Creek threw me into a fever; & chills & fever had it, which & t'other, all night. Sick to-day.

October 1st

Determined last night to break my cold & fever, I took off my coat after tattoo & went out to exercise with the sabre for half an hour, got in a glow & went to bed. Got up this morning, took a brandy sling, & ate a hearty breakfast (buffalo meat & red pepper) and my good constitution has thrown the fever. . . . Encamped at Little Arkansas [River]. Found here a small ox train belonging to McCartey. *Hot* days & cold, windy night.

October 2d

7th Infantry came in to-day. We left at 5 P.M. and took an evening march to divide the long march of 26 miles before us, on account of our broken down animals. When the 7th came over the hill they found us drawn up, ready to receive them with appropriate honors, and the fine appearance of the battery took them by surprise. A man by the name of Hardee is carrying despatches to the Gov. of Santa Fe & is escorted by Harrison & a company of the 7th. . . .

October 3d

. . . An express reached us on the way to the 7th last night, with orders for them to *return.* . . . Marched to Turkey Creek. Met 14 recruits for the new post.

October 4th

Marched to the Cotton Wood.

October 5th

Severe frost last night, which made us all suffer; no one could keep warm in bed. Met a train going to the new post. . . . [M]arched 4 miles below Lost Spring. Grouse supper; gloriously fine.

October 6th

Marched to a hill below Diamond Spring, where we found tolerable grazing. . . . Met 3 trains to-day.

7th

Marched to Council Grove, where we halted for the quartermaster to procure grain for our animals. Found there about 50 lodges of Caw Indians. The families of Italice and Kashinga came to us again. Met one train on the road and two others *coralled*, making 3 in all to-day, besides the mail express.

Shortly after we started, a raw, drizzling rain came up and pelted us into camp at Bluff Creek. . . . [A] Mission (Methodist) [has been] started at Council Grove; met a wagon going to it from Union Town. *Country all burnt.*

8th

Marched with a fine wind to Dragoon Creek. Met a large train (30 wagons) with supplies for Santa Fe &c. . . . Fine day & a chance for dry clothes. . . . Distance 20 miles. . . .

9th October

Marched all day through a hard wind & rain. Only two animals gave out (they were mired yesterday & we pulled them on to their legs, neck & heels). Brought them in after reaching camp. Had much difficulty crossing up the bank of the Wakacoosa, where we first struck it. A point little higher up (300 yds.) might be made a better crossing. Grass on the hills all burnt; dreary aspect. . . . Distance 17½ miles. Ate a hearty supper on buffalo meat, which has not yet given out. . . .

11th

Marched to the Grasshopper. Met Indian wagons and one large train.

Asked a man how many days from Leavenworth; he replied "12 or 14." [Actually, Leavenworth was, as the army marched, not more than two days away.]

"What you been doing all this time?"
"*Fooling along.*"

"How many miles you marched a day?"

"Some times one or two & sometimes [I] laid by to eat."

Met the wagon master, who said he knew nothing of the road, nor how long he expected to be going to Santa Fe (800 miles, grass all killed & burnt & winter coming), nor on what day he had started. Some of these train teamsters [are] remarkably ignorant. 5 of them in one train knew not even the name of their conductor. Valley of the Grasshopper beautiful. Water found along the road.

12th

Marched to a point above where we formerly struck the Stranger. Distance 23 miles. . . . Scenery fine to-day: the valleys (well wooded & diversified with autumnal tints) in view all round, and an occasional glimpse of the blue line of the once more welcome Missouri. Hard frost last night; too cold to sleep. Kellogg & myself lay in our beds 2 or 3 hours talking doggerel. A little brandy in our coffee this morning warmed us up & the day turned out a fine, clear, sunny, autumn day. Valley of the Stranger very beautiful. Nothing pleases more than woods after our long pilgrimage on the prairies. Even the horses seem to enjoy it too, for they prick up their ears & quicken their pace, however jaded, as we approach the trees.

13th

Men so pleased at the prospect of getting in to Leavenworth that they were up talking and laughing all night. The battery soldiers commenced scrubbing up as soon as day broke. The country seemed like a new land, so different in its autumn foliage. The happiest day of the expedition. Stopped to lunch (and comb our hair) at Salt Creek. Entered Leavenworth with sabres drawn and bugles blowing. The fort, so far away from the center of civilization, seemed like a home spot, with its white houses and comfortable looks. The ladies were on the porches and waved their handkerchiefs. It was Sunday, everybody in clean clothes; even children and dogs looked tolerable to our prairie-wasted eyesight. Found news of three vacancies in my regiment.››

On return from the Great Plains the battery was dismounted and Captain Lovell, after a short time, was detached and the battery fell to me as a company of foot artillery. We were next ordered to Barrancas Barracks, Pensacola harbor, Florida. With us there was another company of the Fourth Artillery, commanded by Captain (afterwards General) John W. Phelps.[22]

22. John W. Phelps (24th, USMA 1836).

Captain Phelps was . . . awkward and unsociable, but a student. This was the same General Phelps who in Louisiana first proclaimed liberty to the slaves, and armed and organized a body of them for military service—for which he was declared an outlaw by the Confederacy, and his unauthorized proceedings were quickly countermanded at Washington where no coutenance was ever given to any attempt to excite the slaves to insurrection against their masters. The famous, or infamous, John Brown,[23] who had tried that sort of agitation just before the war, drew his inspiration from the atmosphere of Boston, "The Cradle of Liberty"—also of domestic insurrection, rocked by William Lloyd Garrison, Wendell Phillips and Theodore Parker, of which I was soon to know.[24]

The new station at Pensacola brought me into delightful contact with people of the Navy Yard, and Commodore Newton and his charming wife and daughter, who lived near Barrancas. So that, together with Major Chase of the engineers and Mr. Strong, a wealthy government contractor, all living in the neighborhood, rendered Barrancas Barracks less unbearable. Phelps seemed to have no social instincts, and our formal intercourse came within an inch of terminating in a duel, happily averted by his, not my, own good sense. That was the only unpleasant incident connected with our stay at the harbor. Fortunately there were other companies and more sociable fellow officers of the Fourth at Santa Rosa Island, which was [to be] the scene of some operations in the great Civil War not much to the credit of the Northern government.

23. John Brown had led six of his followers (including four of his sons) on a murderous spree along Pottawatomie Creek, Kansas, on May 24, 1856, hacking to death five proslavery adherents in revenge for antislavery settlers killed in the sacking of Lawrence, Kansas. Moving his operations to western Virginia, Brown, backed by prominent New England abolitionists, led a raid on the U.S. arsenal at Harpers Ferry, where he hoped to seize pikes and other weapons with which to arm thousands of slaves in a nationwide revolt. With twenty-one followers (including five black men) Brown captured the armory on the night of October 16, 1859. When Col. Robert E. Lee arrived with a company of U.S. Marines and state militia, Brown holed up in an engine house with his men and hostages. The Marines stormed the building on the 18th, killing two of Brown's men and capturing the rest, including Brown himself, who was wounded. (Eight of Brown's men, including two of his sons, had been killed in a fight with townsmen the day before.) Brown, tried and convicted of treason against Virginia, was hanged at Charlestown, Virginia, on December 2, 1859, and swiftly became a martyr for the abolitionist cause.

24. William Lloyd Garrison, founder of the influential abolitionist newspaper *Liberator*; Wendell Phillips, one of the most vocal abolitionists; Theodore Parker, one of the leading Unitarians.

§

SIX

Reminiscences of the
Washingtons and Early Boston

I THINK it was in 1850 that the regiment was ordered to Northern stations. At Fort [Ontario,] Oswego, New York, I met one of my father's old
friends, Dr. Sprague, father of General John Sprague and Governor William Sprague of Rhode Island; and . . . at Fort Washington, [Maryland],
Major John Pemberton, afterwards the quasi-hero of Vicksburg, and his
lovely wife.[1] Here I was also thrown in contact with some eminent Virginians, notably the last of the Washingtons at Mount Vernon, opposite my
station, and the Masons of Alexandria, further up the Potomac.

The Washingtons were our nearest neighbors. ‹Colonel John Augustine Washington was the last owner of Mount Vernon, and sold it to the
Ladies' Mount Vernon Association for $200,000, after it had been in the
Washington family possession for a century and a half. Colonel Washington was killed about a year later on the banks of his own Potomac, while in

---

1. Dr. Lawrence Sprague, assistant surgeon; John T. Sprague later wrote a book on the
Seminole War (see p. 206, n. 7); William Sprague was governor of Rhode Island from 1860 to
1863, when he resigned to serve in the U.S. Senate, rom March 1863 to March 1875.

John C. Pemberton (27th, USMA 1837) was a native of New York but developed a love of
the South and married a Virginian, Martha Thompson of Norfolk. As a lieutenant general
in the Confederate army he defended Vicksburg, Mississippi, against siege for forty-four days,
eventually surrendering some thirty thousand Confederate troops to U. S. Grant on July 4,
1863.

the Confederate service as an aide-de-camp of his kinsman, Gen. Robert E. Lee.[2] Colonel Washington's father was John Augustine Washington, who in turn was the son of William Augustine Washington, nephew of General Washington. William Augustine Washington's mother was Jane Washington, a niece of the President, so that John Augustine Washington traced a double line of collateral descent from the founder of the great fame of the family. . . .>

Colonel Washington's wife was a Ball, between whose family and his there had been other marriages. They had several children, and they received the numerous visitors that made the pilgrimage to the great President's home and tomb with old colonial courtesy indoors, and all due watchfulness, on the grounds, of the vandal relic hunters. These last would have chipped off every particle of the tomb itself but for an iron railing that at last enclosed it. One of the old Negroes on the place remembered the great "Massa George"—or perhaps he had heard so much of him from his own parents, that he thought he did.

Colonel Washington was a man of medium size, fine dark eyes, broad forehead and somewhat of the General's look, lacking the firm mouth and chin a bit. [He was] about my own age and we had many tastes in common, particularly for books. The family library and his own additions were well stocked. He was likewise a careful and judicious farmer and had an eye to good stock, and the fishing grounds, and like the ex-president, he was not above barrelling the shad for the Alexandria market, after the family and cabin wants were supplied. Here, where the seine was cast and hauled under his own management, I was initiated in the mysteries of that most delicious feast, planked shad, cooked on the beach as soon as caught.

Colonel Washington foresaw and dreadfully deprecated the approaching conflict between North and South. He told me he prayed to Heaven that it might be averted, but that when the crisis came he should have to go with his state—though it would break his heart. He fell in one of the first battles in West Virginia.

My acquaintance with the gallant patriot and consequent knowledge of the estate, perhaps became somewhat useful in the negotiation for the purchase of Mount Vernon by the Ladies' of the Union. My mother-in-law, Mrs. Chancellor Elon Farnsworth, of Michigan, [was] the vice regent for that [organization], and I was able to give some personal facts and incidents in one or two public addresses on the purchase when in embryo. Among all

2. John A. Washington was killed at Cheat Mountain, western Virginia, while making a reconnaissance, on September 12, 1861.

Lt. Orlando B. Willcox,
ca. 1850. *OBW Collection.*

the men [I have met,] I have rarely met the equal of John A. Washington for
lofty patriotism and the characteristics of the gentleman. Peace to his ashes.

We also visited Colross, fine house and ground and the chief residence of
the Masons of Alexandria, much frequented by officers of the army. Here
were several daughters; one of these had married Captain Jefferson Page of
the navy. Her house on F Street was the charming center of a social circle to
which I was privileged through Miss Emily Mason. . . . Miss Emily was
living on Shuter's Hill, devoted to the care of an invalid and widowed sister,
Mrs. Isaac Rowland of Detroit, [and her] children, whose education Miss
Emily personally looked after. . . .[3]

Be that as it may, she was an accomplished writer, and by virtue thereof
and her excellent sense, she saved me from wreaking myself on the public as a poet. Asking her advice on the subject of publication, she read a
lot of my verses, some of which had found their way under sobriquets in
the newspapers, and then she said: "Quite good my dear friend, and if
you think yourself equal, say, to Shelley, publish—otherwise not." I have
always thanked fortune for Miss Emily's advice. The public may be equally

3. Emily Mason was the sister of Stevens T. Mason, "boy" governor of Michigan.

thankful. I have met my fair friend repeatedly since (now 1900), and found her as bright as she was when she appeared to me as the goddess of my boyhood and the wise monitress of my perfervid youth.

One word more as to Colross; with all the hospitality and civility of the head of the house, her demeanor towards officers who buzzed around her daughters drew the line at lieutenants . . . which of course ruled us out. . . . But so far as I was concerned, my matrimonial fate ran in another direction, and I became engaged at Detroit [to] Miss Marie Farnsworth, daughter of one of our most eminent citizens, Chancellor Elon Farnsworth. We were married in the following summer.

While at Fort Washington barracks, I fell under command of Major John B. Scott,[4] a famous army punster, and Maj. John C. Pemberton. . . . One of my fellow lieutenants at this time was Hazzard, a brave and highly intelligent soldier [who was] finally killed in command of a battery at the battle of Malvern Hill, Virginia. Another was Rufus Saxton, now living at Washington and brevetted brigadier general for the gallant defense he made at Harper's Ferry. . . .[5]

JOURNAL: JANUARY 1851–MAY 1852[6]

«We returned to the States in October (14th). Found orders at Leavenworth promoting me out of Lovell's (then Hunt's) battery, and from 2d Lieutenant to 1st, in place of Fahnestock, resigned (April 30). Left Lovell on 21st October; left St. Louis on the 27th for Fort Washington, Maryland, *via* Detroit.

Took Mira from Chicago & reached Kalamazoo about the 1st November. Found my dear mother in poor health; spent a week with her and Julia;[7] visited Detroit with Mira; spent much time with Marie. Arrived at New York

4. Bvt. Maj. John B. Scott (13th, USMA 1821), distinguished at Palo Alto and Resaca de la Palma. He died in San Francisco on November 22, 1860.

5. Capt. George W. Hazzard (5th, USMA 1847), died August 14, 1862, of wounds received at White Oak Swamp, Virginia, on June 30, 1862; Rufus Saxton (18th, USMA 1849) commanded the Harpers Ferry defenses during Stonewall Jackson's Shenandoah Valley Campaign of 1862. The following year, as the military governor of the islands off the South Carolina and Georgia coast, Saxton helped recruit and organize the first officially authorized black infantry regiment, the 1st South Carolina Colored Volunteers.

6. The following Journal entries, contained within double angle brackets « », are from OBW's *Second Journal*.

7. OBW's sisters, Mira Willcox (who married George Davis, an employee of the Michigan Central Railroad) and Julia Willcox McNair.

on 21st. Soon after I left mother at Kalamazoo, she fell & broke the *process* of a shoulder blade.

Reached Fort Washington on the 30th. Waited at Washington [D.C.] until the 19th December for my company to arrive from Baton Rouge. (The regiment had been ordered to the North.) Joined on the 17th December and find myself now (January 1st) quartermaster, commissary & postmaster.

At Washington found Miss Emily Mason. She was at the house of Mrs. Paige, her cousin, who received me for her sake on the footing of an old friend, and took me to see many of the Washington people. There I frequently met the . . . Thompson Mason's of Alexandria, attended with them a *Soiree* at the President's [Millard Fillmore] and one of Jenny Lind's[8] concerts. . . . At Alexandria renewed acquaintance with the Benham's, who receive me much better than I deserve. They and the Masons are my regular visiting places at Alexandria.

January 22d

Went to Washington, found Burnside, dined in company with Tyler and Frost. Took Miss Emily over to Baltimore, left her at Dr. Dunbar's. . . . Spent the evening with Joe Lovell at Barnum's. . . .

23d

Dined with Gen. Walbach[9] and family, treated with the greatest warmth of cordiality. They complain of neglect. Took the evening train for Washington. Supped at the National with Maj. Hunt, who talks of applying for a captaincy in new regiment. Visited. Mr. Buel, who read me a letter he had received from ex-Secretary [of War William L.] Marcy, commending his speech on Union at Detroit. Visited Messr's Conger and Penniman (M.C.s elect from Michigan)[10] in company with Josiah Snow and Walter Dean. . . .

24th

Got up with a severe cholic, got last night from eating [a] cold supper with three Marylanders. McG—— was "three sheets to the wind," said he wanted to introduce me to two friends, both sons of ex-governors of

8. Jenny Lind (1821–1887), Swedish soprano who with the support of the showman P. T. Barnum came to the United States to tour in 1849. Her singing created a furor.

9. Col. (Bvt. Brig. Gen.) John De B. Walbach, commanding the 4th Artillery, had been serving in the Army since 1799. He died on June 10, 1857.

10. James L. Conger, U.S. representative (1851–1855); Ebenezer J. Penniman, U.S. representative (1851–1853).

Maryland, to show me how *they* had fallen! After supper these "fallen" gentlemen left McG in the lurch & cut him cold.

Visited Patent office, saw original Declaration [of] Independence. Dined at Alexandria. Spent most of the evening at Colross; returned with the cholic & took tea and brandy with the Diodatis, and went to bed. The "Diodatis" are sons of the gentleman who owned the house in Switzerland, near Geneva, where Byron dated most of his letters. They are elegant, clever, accomplished fellows.

25th

Returned to Fort this morning, found room carpeted and felt a sense of comfort. Took tea with Dr. Edwards after a sail on the River in the afternoon. . . .

Received a letter from Mary [Taylor]. She is at Galveston, pleased with everything; [it is] not known where they are to settle.[11] Received a letter from Col. [Braxton] Bragg on the subject of returning old rusty staff officers back into their regiments.

Heard a story of a fat man, who came to a toll-gate just as it was closing. "Can I get through here?" asked he. "Guess you can," was the reply, "a load of hay got through!"

Josiah Snow is at Washington, trying to get an appropriation from Congress to establish a line of Telegraphs to California. He had, in company with a Mr. Bangs (from Michigan), made a proposition without his having any sort of knowledge of the route, not even the distance. He asked me [for] information, but I could give him but little, though I gave him two letters of introduction.

February 1st

Passed the evening of this week reading Shakespeare. Hazzard and Nimmo[12] came in after tea and we read till ten, when Pemberton appears and we have hot punch.

2d

Resolved to read three chapters in the Bible every time I swear, so in three days I have read 48 chapters. . . .

11. Mary Taylor and her husband, Charles A. Taylor, had just moved to Texas.
12. William A. Nimmo (10th, USMA 1849) died in Tennessee, March 12, 1856.

March 16th

Yesterday I saw a grasshopper in the door. [I] Stooped down to pick him up, but he jumped out of my hand. I stooped again to catch him, but just in the act, the idea occurred to me that he had some destiny to fulfill, and I said to him, "Go and fulfill it." A few steps [more] brought me to a wasp. I raised my foot to crush him, but just then I thought he might have been sent too for a purpose, perhaps to sting some human being to make him humble or to try his temper; and so I said to the wasp, "Go and fulfill thy destiny, perhaps it is more useful than mine." I then remembered Uncle Toby and the fly, and was glad to have left the insects to their own fate.

[I have] frequently asked myself the question lately, "Am I accomplishing the end for which I was created?" This is a very troublesome question. There is an humble fellow, a soldier, in the garrison, who every night has the musician boys in [his] room and teaches them reading and writing. He is a much more useful man than myself, who am doing no good whatever. And yet I have more talents, more learning, and a higher position than he.

It is not that I have no love for my fellow beings, no desire to be useful, for all my life I have looked forward to some sort of usefulness. But it seems to have been always a great way forward, and on a grand visionary scale. My first desire in life was to be a preacher—I was more religious then, than now—but this I gave up because it would cost my mother more than she was able [to afford] for my education, and I thought besides that there was more ambition in the desire than religion. Besides, I sought the advice of the old pastor of our church—Mr. Duffield—as to whether I should become a minister or a soldier, and after hearing me through, he advised me to become a soldier. There would appear in this advice something inconsistent with religion; but it is not so. Mr. Duffield thought more highly of me than I merited, and believed that West Point would afford me a good education, without expense to my mother; and as an officer has many opportunities of doing good, both my education and position would enable me to be a useful Christian.

I concurred with him fully; and what warm resolutions I formed! and how rapidly they grew cold! and how I put off the time for exerting a good influence! and how soon I found that my sinful course of conduct would render any open effort at doing good as inconsistent as could be in the eyes of my companions! and then how I got to liking pleasure! and how I threw off entirely the profession of a Christian, and gave myself up to the devious courses and evil practices of the irreligious!

Still, after all this, I felt an ambition after something better and higher. "An ambition," ah yes! that is it; my former longings to be good, howsoever imperfect, became almost swallowed up in the ambition to be great.

Now this ambition might have carried me further, ere this, had I ever believed there was the stuff in me of which greatness is made. In moments of excitement, I have performed actions that at the time seemed promising, but afterward, when in cool judgment I have reflected upon them, the delusion has been blown away.

Perhaps I have written things at times, which seemed inspired with some genius; but how soon, after the "glow of composition" has passed off, and I have scanned these "efforts" and compared them with just standards, have I endorsed them "trash"?

Thus, judgment—to say nothing of a knowledge of many infirmities, such as fickleness of purpose, love of pleasure and fondness for women— has curbed my ambition. Thus I find myself, at this moment, without any definite aim of life. I would to God that I could fall on my knees and devote myself from henceforth to the glory of God. But alas, a want of faith, with a knowledge of my ten thousand backslidings, restrain me from a step, which, turning back from, would only throw me in deeper despair; and I humbly wait, perhaps too much, for God's grace to enter my heart & turn me to Him.

But, meantime, there is a path which reason dictates, and religion denies not. Fond of books and given to thinking, I can cultivate my heart, mind and whole character, so as to become the better prepared for the discharge of those duties which Providence may assign to my lot. Not to look for greatness, not to strive for any distinction, but to cultivate humility and content; not to despair of God's returning favor, but to watch my propensities for sin, to avoid temptations, and to employ my time in study, prayer and useful conduct; this may deliver me from the Slough of Despond, and, in God's good time, I may reach the Wicket Gate, where my present burden may roll off, and I may commence anew the *Pilgrim's Progress*. May "Peace begin just where ambition ends."

17th

No sooner had I written the above than something stirred in me to kneel and renew my covenant. One habitual sin has kept me back for several weeks; after kneeling & praying for some time, I gave up that sin in my heart, and promise now to commence a new walk, with God's help. Rising from my knees, I wrote to Miss Emily, asking her to persuade Miss Virginia to be confirmed.

Relieved on the 1st inst. in the duties of commissary and quarter master by Lt. Hazzard, who ranks me. . . .

Received a letter from Marie last week which threw me into great perplexity. I could only infer that something prevents her from corresponding, and even loving me. *Sic transit*. . . .

My last visit to Washington was to get our mail route changed. Attended while up there a reception at Judge Douglass's.[13] The California young men had sent him a watch. Hon. Mr. Wright presented it. Douglass's speech was happy. Gen'l Houston told an undignified, bawdy story.[14] Many Michigan gentlemen present, among others, John P. Sheldon, who knew my father intimately and recollected when I was born. The next morning I was at the rooms of some M.C.s, who were breaking up very much in the humor of college graduates, burning letters, smoking, drinking, packing up, etc.

Went over to Mount Vernon twice last week; was showed a marble sculptured mantle piece captured by an American privateer and presented to Washington; it represented morning, noon and evening in the country. Col. Washington, who lives there, is a great-grand-nephew of the General's, is almost 30 years of age, and has a wife and three children. They are very sociable with us. . . .

March 20th

To-day the board of commissioners for the army asylum landed at the Fort on their way over to Mount Vernon, which they were to examine with a view of selecting a site.[15] The President of the U.S., Mr. Fillmore, & several of his cabinet—Messrs Crittenden,[16] Hall & Stuart[17]—accompanied the Board, with a party of ladies. We fired a salute, showed them around the Fort, and Maj. Scott, Dr. Edwards and myself accompanied the party to Mt. Vernon.

13. Sen. Stephen A. Douglas (D., Ill.).

14. George W. Wright, U.S. representative from California (September 11, 1850, to March 3, 1851); Sam Houston, the hero of San Jacinto, was then a U.S. senator from Texas. In 1861, as governor of the state, he opposed secession, resigning on March 18, 1861.

15. The "Commissioners for the Army Asylum" were looking for a site on which to locate what would become the Soldiers Home, eventually founded in Washington.

16. Attorney General John J. Crittenden had already established an impressive role in the U.S Senate, where he had been first elected from Kentucky as a Whig in 1817. He had most recently been governor of Kentucky (1848–1850).

17. Postmaster General Nathan Kelsey Hall; Secretary of Interior Alexander Hugh H. Stuart.

Mr. Augustus Washington, the occupant of the place, would sell 200 acres to the Government for $200,000, on the conditions that the remains of Gen'l Washington and other members of the family should not be disturbed, and that the property shall never be disposed of to private individuals. A Col. [William T.] Stockton, citizen of Florida & graduate of West Point [1834], was with the party, and we walked around the grounds together. There was a Mr. Duncan, from New Orleans, present, who is going to the Holy Land and wished a flag staff from Mt. Vernon on which to raise the American flag on his journeys. It was selected at about 40 yards from the Tomb by our Maj. Scott; the President cut it down with an axe, which by the by he looked at & handled with the air of a woodsman, and Gen'l [Winfield] Scott presented it. His tall person, as he held the staff in his hand, formed a ludicrous contrast to the figure of Mr. Duncan, a gentleman of about 5 feet. The staff was of cedar. The idea of its going to greet the Cedars of Lebanon, of its carrying the flag of Light & Liberty back to the Land from which Light and true Liberty emanated, is rather touching.

March 31st

What a solemn delightful day was yesterday with me! I went to Washington and escorted Miss Emily to church; on the way she told me it was Communion Sabbath. I went to the table with her; my heart was oppressed to overflowing with joyful emotion; the tears were continually coming into my eyes.

To crown all, I returned to Alexandria in the afternoon and had a long talk with the very person for whom I have been praying during the past two weeks. I pressed her to "come out from the world" and take the same step I had taken. We were both affected; she said little, I poured out my reasons and entreaties in a perfect volume, every word of which came burning from my heart. This morning I saw Miss Emily again and urged her to use all her forces of persuasion. I hope and pray good may come of this, though doubtless, under the peculiar circumstances, it *looks* very queer.

After leaving *her* last night, I passed the remainder of the evening by myself, with but a short interruption, under great excitement of feeling, praying, praising & conjecturing on the subjects of the day; finally I went to bed, slept but little & waked up at 4 in the morning. God knows what may come of all this, but may it result in something good.

Sorry to learn by the papers that Mt. Vernon has not been selected for the Soldier's Asylum. There are two stories for the reason: one that it was too expensive; the other that doubts were felt concerning the healthiness of the place. A place owned by Col. Lorenzo Thomas,[18] near Georgetown, has been selected. . . . Cost, $20,000.

Corporal Cox of our company was buried with military honors this afternoon. I thought of death and wondered whether I was really ready at any moment to enter into the presence of God and all the Angels. One may feel at peace with God and all the world, and ready for any dispensation of His providence on earth, but the idea of passing in a moment into His presence makes me feel the grossness of my heart. There appears some need of purification. It may come by long sickness & expectation of the event, but to be taken out of the world in the twinkling of an eye, it seems as though God *must* prepare the heart for this, *in the very act of death* perhaps. "We shall be *changed*," says Paul.

April 2d
Received a letter from Marie, saying that the words of her last conveyed more than she intended, and many other things which thrill me with joy. Thanks! thanks to Thee, Almighty Dispenser of human benefits. Life is no longer an encumbrance.

13th
Snow storm.

15th
Last night the two Mr. Washingtons staid with me; this morning went over with them to Whital's, who gave us a "plank shad"; very delicious, cooked on a board set up before the fire; saw them hauling the sieve, which was over a mile in length, including the lines. As many as 600,000 herrings have been caught at a single haul on this River. Mr. J. A. Washington saw the haul.

23d
The first warm day since the 13th. Received some good advice from Rev. Geo. Duffield, to whom I wrote confessing my backsliding, ambitions, errors, etc. "The less we look at ourselves and what we do, the better, provided we carry with us the consciousness that we seek the glory of our

18. Bvt. Lt. Col. Lorenzo Thomas (17th, USMA 1823) was then assistant adjutant general of the army. In 1853 he became Scott's chief of staff.

Savior God, and are willing to be anything and everything as he may direct. Some of Satan's severest temptations are addressed to self adulation. Let us forget self, absorbed in the thought of the Savior's worth and glory."

News from home is that George has come down to Detroit to live (on the 1st). Charles[19] has been giving way. Mother is at home and not very happy. Eb writes encouragingly about his prospects, and Gen. Brady[20] is dead; he died on the 15th; he had been thrown from his carriage, his horses ran away frightened at some telegraph wire which had fallen or been left across the road. Detroit is all in mourning; no one's death there ever seems to have been so much felt before.

May 3d

Never knew I such a peace as that I have mostly enjoyed since I renewed my vows to God lately. Perhaps the reason may be that I have attained to a better knowledge of myself, and consequently, thrown myself more upon the strength & mercy of God to sustain me in my feebleness. And it seems as tho' he had come nigher to my heart, opened my eyes to his ways, and unfolded some of those of his excellences which were formerly obscure, as well as presented some means and motives to worship and serve Him, formerly unknown.

Yet must I not boast; for I feel myself, as it were, resting on a mere pivot, held there by God's hand, reclining on his arm, which, withdrawn at any moment, leaves me to fall. But ah! "Though tempest frowns, though nature shakes, how soft to lean on heaven." . . .

The promptings of a wild imagination, to which I am but too much given, prove, when not repressed, a relentless foe to my peace. Ambition and self-adulation revolt likewise against my humility, and sometimes attack me so sorely, that I often fear that the greatest good I can possibly accomplish in this world, will be to bury myself from all usefulness in it. God may not condescend to let me work in His glorious vineyard, in order that I may not have wherewithal to glory or be vain. His will be done! I can only study to improve my heart and understanding by every mean in my reach, and to conform myself to the ways of His providence, in hope that whenever opportunities for usefulness do present themselves, I may unconsciously turn them to the best advantage. . . .

19. Charles Willcox, brother of OBW.
20. Bvt. Maj. Gen. Hugh Brady, of Detroit, had served in the U.S. Army since 1799. He had been colonel of the 22d U.S. Infantry in 1812, transferring to the 2d Regiment in May 1815.

Perhaps I judge too much from the narrow circle of my own reflections, but I have got to thinking lately, that we overestimate the importance of our personal achievements in their bearing upon God's moral government. Though He may work mostly through secondary means, yet He accomplishes the majority of His plans independently of the *wills* of His agents—He can do very well without any of us.

The importance of our actions are much more intimately connected with *ourselves*, their effects falling not only upon our happiness but likewise upon our *hearts*, which are put here and clothed with mortality, for trial and experience, the result of which will determine our future destinies. And when I consider that the action of some one past, or even present moment may possibly affect my whole eternal career, even though I may be saved, it makes me tremble in the midst of that darkness of the flesh in which my spirit is imprisoned, and fervently pray for light, guidance and protection from above.

May 4th, a snow storm: May 11th, the thermometer at 86. . . .

Extract from [a] letter from mother, April 4th. "Dear Orlando, I cannot be thankful enough that you have chosen God for your friend. Although you may depart from him at times, yet I feel that he would keep you in the hollow of his hand. I can see how much better it is to choose God for your friend than all the men in the world; we see it in our every day life."

Extract from a letter from mother, May 18th. "For my part I have seen many years and seen very little quiet, but I am sure my rest is not far from me, a few more setting suns & the place that knows me now shall know me no more forever."

May 23d

Received above to-day. I have been afflicted with a presentiment for several weeks past that her life would not survive the coming summer. Is the above a "shadow cast before"? I know that she would be happier, but her presence on earth has always seemed a link between me & heaven, & to her I owe principally all my advancement on earth. In this same letter she speaks of "*feeling*" that I was in trouble about the 1st of March, & for several weeks she was anxious about me, praying God continually, I suppose, as usual on such occasions.

I have scarcely ever communicated my troubles to her, but never have had a heavy one without her knowing it, at the very time, & who can tell how much her prayers have effected in such cases! Sometimes it comes to her in a dream. Often when no other hope seemed present with me, the hope that her spirit was watching & praying has cheered me. And no one could I ever go [to] for advice on any subject with better profit than to her. Such a strong mind, & so sagacious, so courageous & yet so discriminating & judicious & so much caution & foresight.

I think her most prominent traits are energy of character & goodness of heart. There are two words she scarcely knows the meaning of, viz., impossibilities & selfishness. She kindles with the greatest courage & ardour at the greatest difficulty; but unlike women generally of such masculine minds, her heart melts at the slightest calamity that happens to others. I have often seen her weep over a newspaper paragraph; & yet, plunged in debt, with the darkest prospect ahead, six children to maintain & educate, there was yet no doubt, no discouragement, no tear visible with her. She never felt too poor to be charitable, never too weak to labour for the children; & besides the latter, she generally had some of her relatives' children at her house, supporting them.

Yet she was always strict with us, made us obey her implicitly & promptly too. But she made companions of us; we shared all her trials; her joys were few, & they confined to us. I do not recollect a single joy of hers by triumph or advantage over her neighbors, but I recollect some at the success of her children in life. When we were quite young she seemed to have had but two things in view: our education & our piety. She never turned a beggar away empty. She never was unkind to a servant. Kindness to others was the first moral precept I heard from her. Effort, execution, the first worldly lesson.

Now that the aims of her life seem principally accomplished, though not to her satisfaction, to be sure, but beyond her further remedy, she feels the want of stimulating objects of pursuit; with all her broken down health she feels this still acutely. Many changes too have occurred among her old friends: death, absence, & the extinction of those bonds of sympathy which women have with each other when they are severally bringing up children; these have their effect upon her. Detroit, she says on her last return from Kalamazoo, has lost its charms for her.

Sometimes I think she would be so much happier in heaven that I feel like wishing she were there: yet what a wish! If God keeps her here, must it not be for some good purpose? I know that *to me* her life is of incalculable good; her bereavement would be something more than a mere loss at the time, to mourn over & become reconciled to: it would be the absence of a good influence, of a sympathizing & praying spirit that seems intuitively to discover my troubles simultaneously with their very origin. And yet, mournful truth! "a few more setting suns and the place that knows her now, shall know her no more for ever." I fear I never shall behold that setting sun again, without thinking of thee, O! dearest, best, most wonderful of mothers.

26th

Letter from Mary: more comfortably off; life in Texas hard, but she is *heroic* for the sake of her husband.

28th

Letter from Dave;[21] he & Julia in New York; will be here soon; help me somebody to moderate my transports!

June 6th

The McNair's. They arrived to-day. Dave & Jul & a cousin of Dave's, not pretty but pleasant. Day after day I had expected them & been disappointed, until I had given them up so completely that they took me by surprise. I did not like them to occupy my own quarters with unmarried officers on both sides. [Major] Scott & lady came over & called after we had all dined at the mess, & invited them to their house, but we went over to Mt. Vernon first in the barge; the rowing over & the visit gave them great pleasure. The Washingtons were away, which I regretted as I had spoken to them of Jul & they had expressed a wish for a visit from her. Dave took a piece of stone from the old, crumbling remains of the original tomb, & we got a magnolia flower to press, if possible, & send home for Eb to see.

7th

I have showed them the dell & the great elm tree. They have sat in my room, which they like very much & are surprised to see so well furnished. Jul is delighted; she says she could spend a month; her heart & face are full of pleasure. The Scotts treat them very hospitably. They spent two or three hours in my room to-night. I put on my dressing gown & smoked & showed them exactly how I sat reading by the table, so they could describe everything accurately to mother.

It is a moonlight [night] & everything feels soft & looks beautiful & placid. How much more I enjoy everything with them than when alone. The solitude which I have enjoyed here so much seemed sweet, but to enjoy the very same objects with those we love must be sweeter; & whenever my

21. David A. McNair, a druggist, was brother-in-law to OBW and husband of Julia Willcox McNair.

heart is thus opened, I think of Marie, & imagine how delicious her society will be. Dave & I kneeled down in my room together. He sleeps here in my bed & I take the camp bedstead.

10th

On the morning of the 8th, Sunday, we took the barge up to Alexandria, & after landing went straight to church. Mrs. Thompson invited us all to dinner after service, & we had an agreeable afternoon. I was pleased to see how much they appeared to like the manners of Julia. They told me she was more like a southern lady than a northern.

On going to the hotel, we found that the Masons had called for us with their carriage, so I took Julia out to see them in the evening. They received her with much cordiality, but two young men coming in drew away the conversation of the young ladies. Mrs. Mason took us into the garden & with which Julia was charmed. Mrs. Mason presented her with a large bouquet. Miss Julia Thompson had done the same in the afternoon, & we had them given to us likewise at Mt. Vernon. These flowers carry away pleasant reminiscences.

On the ninth we arose early & proceeded from Alexandria to Washington. Saw the Smithsonian Institute throughout; likewise the Washington Monument & the stones presented by different states & societies. We finally agreed that a plain granite block with "New Hampshire" simply cut on it, was so good a type of the granite state & her simple Puritan origin, that this was the most appropriate stone in the number. There was one from Alexandria likewise presented by the "Descendants of the friends & neighbors of Washington." The stones are not yet set in their places; the shaft or obelisk is going up & has reached 70 feet.

We then went to see the equestrian statue of Jackson.[22] This, perhaps, gave us the greatest pleasure of all. The artist was in the midst of his work, finishing the casting of the horse's head. It is all to be cast in sections. The artist, Mr. Mills, claims the invention of posing the horse upon his hind legs, & having no other support. He was quite enthusiastic & was gratified to see how highly we were pleased.

The cast of Jackson's face gave me a better representation of my own ideas of his character than any bust or picture I had seen. I told him this; he was flattered & said that was what the poet Tupper[23] had told him too, & then it was my turn to feel flattered; so of course we separated mutually

22. The equestrian statue of Jackson would be placed in Lafayette Square near the White House.
23. Martin Tupper (1810–1889), English poet.

pleased with each other: of which I was glad for the sake of my party, for disturbing artists in their employment is seldom productive of good-will.

Julia & I called upon Mrs. Steward & then went to the President's & saw the East Room & the reception rooms. We went to some stores where I got some trinkets to send home to mother & Marie, but they did not suit me much; neither of them care for such trumpery either. My original thought was to get a fan for the first, to supply the place of the one I brought her from Mexico & which she has lost, & a gold thimble for the latter. I believe it would have pleased them both better. . . .

We started to walk to the cars, but I was mistaken in the distance & it was fatiguing, which I regretted particularly as Dave had proposed a carriage. We parted in good spirits. Dave said he was glad at our having been able to see each other so often, & Julia said the pain of parting was destroyed by her leaving me so comfortably & pleasantly stationed & with so many people for friends.

I then hurried down to Alexandria & rode out with Miss Virginia to see Miss Emily's cottage. Mrs. Col. Cooper was occupying it temporarily. It is prettily situated, but the house is old & will require great repairs. Returning in the evening, my horse fell on his knees & hurt them so that they bled badly. . . .

13th

The Marbury's sent to the Fort for us to go out & spend the evening with them to meet some company yesterday; I alone went. There seemed nothing but hills & gates on the road. The Marburys call their place Wyoming; it is seven miles from the Fort.

The company was small but very pleasant. It was united in honor of a Miss Symmes of Georgetown. She seemed so exquisitely soft, graceful & lovely that I was not introduced to her, for fear of breaking the charm her presence carried, by hearing her say something out of character with her appearance.

I had formed a high opinion before of Miss Bettie Marbury, but now I discovered in her much more than I had supposed. She is a creature of the most tender & delicate passion, poetry & music. A being yearning after all the spiritualities of the inner & upper world. She had met once with Geo. Prentice the poet, & he likewise had appreciated her high qualities, & addressed her some exquisitely pretty & touching verses.

I slept in a room with Fendall Marbury & another gentleman; after Fendall blew out the light he knelt down & said his prayers. In the morning we were called in to family prayers. Mrs. Marbury read Scripture & every one kneeled while she prayed. She asked a blessing likewise at the breakfast table & then we sat down: on turning up our plates there was a nosegay under each one. . . .

Such a pleasant visit I have not had in a long time, such a peculiar one never; there seemed so much goodness of heart, piety and poetry assembled under that roof. Oh how everything good & delightful makes me long for Marie.

Oct. 4th

Eben came to see me [on the] 27th [of] Sept. I was across the river at Mt. Vernon; the barge was sent over for me. He was fast asleep on my bed, & as he had traveled all the night before on the cars, I thought I would not disturb him, but after a while [I] got impatient & waked him up.

Few things if any in my whole life have given me as much pleasure as this visit, & I would be glad to recollect every little thing that was done & said—In all my visits home something peculiar has prevented our talking our affairs over as freely as we wished, but now we had nine days, almost uninterrupted. We both felt as though we had renewed our boyhood & come near to the realization of those dreams of confidence & perfection which that season inspired in our hearts.

It is a *rare* blessing to realize early expectations. I believe that we are now more intimate friends to each other than to any one else, & this is not always the case with brothers. One day we went into the country to Church; on another we visited & dined at Mt. Vernon—which pleasure Eb enjoyed peculiarly, so reverent he is to sacred associations—greatness, goodness, worth of any sort; on another we visited Alexandria & Washington; and almost every day we took rambles through the woods.

At Mt. Vernon Eb had given [to] him a bundle of bulbs & slips of plants. At Alexandria we called on Miss Emily Mason, & on Mrs. Steuart at Washington. In the woods we took up a couple of young hollies, which charmed dear Eb, & he sent them home. One of them is for the Chancellor.

Our evenings were spent with all the officers in my quarters—and pleasant evenings they were; the first one particularly, for Eb was fresh from New York & Boston, & happy in his descriptions & incidents. In our walks we found many trees, ravines, hills, etc., which he enjoyed very much. In one glen I recollect he shouted like a little boy or an Indian. It was a wild place & he said the "Spirit of the wilderness" was upon him.

Our conversations were principally about our family matters & our own past, present & future. Many times he put his arm silently around me &

pressed me to him, & sometimes a tear would steal into his eye. I never realized sufficiently before, how completely he feels himself identified with
my interests & happiness. We talked much about Marie, to whose heart
he said he wished he could transfer the pictures forming on his own at every
moment. We talked a great deal about the best course of reading, & divid-
ing his time, systematically, and we drew up a *plan*, which I hope he will
adopt & carry out, as he says he will. He expects likewise to unite himself to
the Church soon. This will be peculiarly gratifying to mother, & will form a
new tie between him & myself, we can more confidently look forward to an
eternity of *friendship*.

After his leaving me I was very lonesome, more so than I had ever been
at this place. But now that feeling is supplanted by a sense of gratitude to
God for the blessing we were permitted to enjoy, by the consciousness that
we are now more closely united in spirit than before, & by the hope that he
will hereafter visit me every year or so.

To no one is Wordsworth's line more applicable than to Eb: "The Child is
Father of the man." He displayed the highest qualities of man when a little
boy: trials, that would have *crushed* any other, may have obscured those qualities since, but now that Providence is lightening his load, they are shining
forth again with a stronger lustre—& brighter for the trial—to me he has
been more like a father than a brother & more like a *friend* than either ——

Dec. 29th

Christmas was spent at Wyoming [the Marbury home]; it was as home-
like as a stranger has a right to expect, more so indeed. I wrote a Christmas
song of home & sent it to mother. It came in a shower of tears. . . .

January 1st [1852] 10 O'clock A.M.

A year has gone out crowned with blessings.

O Divine Power! Jesus Christ, accept the humble consecration of this
coming year's pursuits to Thee. May I take nothing in hand in which religion does not enter. May I live to Thy glory.

Psalm XXXII fills me with hope.

March 12th

On the 20th of January we had the coldest day of the past winter.
Thermometer . . . 6° below zero at daylight. That day Mr. Nimmo & myself walked across the River to Mt. Vernon & dined with Mr. Washington. The season as a whole said to be the coldest experienced in this vicinity
in 15 years. While Mr. Nimmo & myself were at Mt. Vernon, the ice boat

passed & we walked safely over the place she had cut three hours afterwards. She was obliged to lay up some days about that time, the ice had become so thick.

Early last month I spent a few days at the [Mason's] cottage. Every body was busy & I was not inclined to be idle & so went to work on a fence for a chicken yard. I went once or twice to the Theological Seminary close by. Their Library is very interesting with old musty tomes; among others I saw works of Luther, Calvin & Erasmus, Bacon & Raleigh (*History of the World*) that must have been published not far from their own times. I wanted to lock myself up here & live like a worm. There was also a collection of Scriptural works in all written languages—nearly a hundred volumes—that was the donation of Queen Victoria.

March 26th

On my last visit to the cottage I found that the palings of my fence—a work of which I was quite proud considering hanging the gate etc.—were so wide apart the chickens had got through without difficulty. There was one hen, "Susan Betsey" that in addition could fly over without difficulty, notwithstanding her wings were cut. This was one of the little grievances that pure & simple but elegant household suffered. . . .

Week before last we all dined at Mt. Vernon. Eb had sent Mr. Washington some game & fish from the Lakes. The grouse was liked exceedingly, but the gentlemen present of this vicinity thought the fish not so good as their own.

The farmers commenced their spring operations [a] little later this year—latter part of February—than last: ploughing & burning Tobacco beds. For the latter, they select a small space, cover it with brush & set fire. This kills the worms of the soil, takes out any remaining frost, & affords ashes. The bed is then worked up finely, the seed sown, & then the ground covered with brush till the plants come up. When these have attained sufficient growth they are transplanted to the Tobacco fields. Half grown, they look like mullens. . . .

May 16th

Let me thank God this night for enabling me to write something that fills me with hope that my pen may be of use to others. O! Marie would thou wert here that I might read it this moment to thee. . . .»

My company was next ordered to Fort [Ontario,] Oswego, New York, where I [eventually] took my lovely bride. The fort was a small work commanding the entrance to the harbor and the quarters were limited. Fortunately we found an old family friend in the post surgeon, Dr. Sprague. The doctor and his good motherly wife took an interest in my wife in this, her first contact with army life. We lived in the same house. . . . Our commanding officer was Major Chase Ridgely, who acted as judge advocate at the trial of General Scott. . . .[24]

We found Oswego, the "City of Bright Flowers," very hospitable and socially inclined. The society [was] most cultivated and refined, and the young couple, just arrived at the Fort, was given a round of receptions and entertainments delightful beyond our merits and gratefully remembered by me to this day.

JOURNAL: MAY 1852–AUGUST 1853

<<FORT ONTARIO, OSWEGO, NEW YORK

On the morning of the 28th [May], hearing that a portion of my regiment was ordered to the Lakes, I started for New York to endeavor to effect an exchange into one of the moving companies. Found the Chancellor at Washington & laid my plan [to wed Marie Farnsworth] before him; he thought well of it. We spent the evening together, & I was very anxious to learn from him what would most likely be Marie's views. He seemed to think a "winter at the south" agreeable, but told me to do what I thought best, he preferring the Ontario to the Upper Lake stations. I never shall forget how sick & dispirited I felt. I had had the chills & fever irregularly all spring, & everybody thought northern air requisite.

Arrived at New York May 30th. Found Eb at Butts' Hotel. Saw Col. Gardner on Governor's Island; he & all his family thought any of the Lake stations preferable to Fort Washington. Two companies from Charleston arrived in a day or two, about 1st of June. Found that my only chance was to be transferred with Lt. Frank Clarke, a 1st lieutenant on the rolls of "C" company, who could not go to Scott's company in my place, as he was [an] instructor at West Point. As this would take an officer entirely from Fort Washington, Col. Gardner said I must obtain the sanction of the Adjt. General.

24. Referring to the court of inquiry held in regard to charges made against General Scott by generals Worth and Pillow at the close of the Mexican War. Beginning in Mexico, the court reconvened in Frederick, Maryland, but the charges were eventually dropped.

Left New York on the 2d, saw the Adjt. General[25] on the morning of the 3rd at his dwelling house. After some conversation he said, "Tell Col. Gardner I don't think the commander in chief would have any objections; none suggest themselves to me; on the contrary, I hope it will be done." "You might be ordered back in the Fall," he added, but "no," continued he, "that would not be necessary, for I can assign a graduate to Maj. Scott."

I thanked God in my heart, proceeded to Fort Washington, gathered part of my baggage, left the rest to be shipped, & was back at New York on the 5th. My hurry was on account of fearing my new Company would leave New York immediately, as the Quartermaster had said he had just received the requisite orders for their transportation. This latter proved a misconstruction, & we were in New York in a great state of anxiety & suspense until the 7th, when the orders finally came, & we left on the evening of the 10th on the steamer *Troy*, for Troy [New York]. There were three Companies, Ridgely's, McCown's & Getty's.[26]

Our Company (Ridgely's) arrived here on the morning of the 11th. We relieved Col. (Brevet) Wright, who had Co. "F," 4th Infantry. He left on the 15th, together with one company from Sackett's Harbor (& the band) & one from Niagara. The regiment (4th Inf.) are to resort to Governors Island & proceed thence to California.

November 1st

Am a married man. Marie is now mine, & lights up my soldier quarters with a flood of golden joy.

On the evening of Oct. 6th left here for Detroit, & was married there on the 21st by Bishop McCoskrey at [St. Paul's Episcopal] Church.[27]

Nov. 19th

Four weeks last evening since wedding & not yet a cloud so big as a man's hand. The weather a week previous to the nuptials was so fine for the season that everybody seemed struck as if it augured happiness for us. Caro Farns-

25. Col. Roger Jones was then adjutant general of the U.S. Army, a post he held from March 7, 1825, until his death on July 15, 1852.

26. Samuel Chase Ridgely (9th, USMA 1831) and John P. McCown (10th, USMA 1840). George W. Getty (15th, USMA 1840), who had established himself as an excellent artillerist during the Mexican War, continued to do so during the Civil War, commanding batteries on the Peninsula and South Mountain. At Antietam he commanded the Ninth Corps Artillery, and at Fredericksburg he led the Third Division, Ninth Corps. Getty led a division of the Sixth Corps in the Wilderness (where he was severely wounded).

27. The original says "Christ's Church," though OBW later described St. Paul's Church as being the "church of our baptisms & marriage & where both our Fathers had been vestrymen." Rev. S. A. McCoskrey served as minister of that congregation from June 1836 to October 1863.

worth & Ellie Blake, William Wilkins & Bethune Duffield waited on us at Church.[28] There was a very large reception party at the house immediately after. On the next night a party at Eb's, & on the next one at Mira's. We left Detroit on Monday the 25th in the *Mayflower*, & arrived here on the evening of the 26th.

There was a carriage & a cart from the Fort waiting at the cars & the first prominent object we saw on alighting was the moon rising full in front of us. We regarded it as a pleasant omen. In great changes in one's life how apt we are to regard omens. It was a cold evening; Marie was tired & grew more & more silent as we drew near our new home; I felt it painfully, fearing she might be dreading the realities of life now dawning upon her. We thought we should have to depend upon Dr. Sprague's family for our tea, & the coldness & silence of my quarters hung upon my imagination. Fancy our delight & surprise at finding a cheerful fire in our front room, & a hot supper got ready for us by one of my acquaintances, Miss Patten. She had come down on that day, brought her mother's [illegible word], crockery, victuals, &c, & prepared to receive us in our own home, which we quietly took possession of & here we are so comfortable & happy; thank God.

January 1st, 1853

The happiest new year's day in all my life so far. I think I am as near *contentment* as any one on Earth can be. I have been prospered & blessed beyond my deserts. Marie makes me grow happier & happier in her society; to this result the perfect openness & sincerity of confidence that exists doubtless contribute; may this always continue.

Friends at home are well, so I feel but little solicitude for them. Charles has got married, & as it meets with mother's approval, it is well. I wish I could feel a greater *spiritual* progress, but I hope I am more contented to be what God wills than before. My Marie is full of trust in God, & borrows little trouble.

Intellectually I hope to have advanced during the year. As I can read & think with more *composure* than ever, I hope it is done to better purpose. I hope to make something out of a little poetry written during the year, as well as the Latin I've studied.

With reference to the future year, one knows not what it may bring forth. I leave all to God, determined to do my duty in all things by the assistance of His grace, without which blessing all we do is vain. . . .

28. Caroline "Caro" Farnsworth, sister of Marie; D. Bethune Duffield (1821–1891), noted Detroit attorney and educator, son of Rev. George Duffield.

June 1853

On the 3d of this month I went to Syracuse to meet my mother & sister Mira, & brought them home with me; they had left Detroit on the morning of the previous day. This happiness I had been looking forward to several weeks. Mother's health had been very poor during the winter & spring & a trip East it was expected would do her much good. Mira had never been across Lake Erie.

We gave them a little room looking out on the Lake, took them to dine daily, [and] fed them on white fish; the bracing air & sense of happiness & relief from care seemed to do them good quite fast. Luckily there was a regular tea party while they were here. Mira attended with me at Mrs. Murrays & saw some nice people; others too called.

They staid with us till the 13th & enjoyed great satisfaction at the manner in which we were living, both seeming to have formed a strong attachment for Marie, who did her best to make them feel happy. As for me, it was like realising at once some long dream of pleasure, & nothing occurred to mar the enjoyment of all parties. . . . Their pleasant visit, & two or three from the Chancellor, have shortened the separation from home beyond calculation. Indeed, I can scarcely acknowledge how much we are blessed beyond deserving; soon we shall have Marie's mother & Caro with us.

July 12

Another pleasure. Mrs. Farnsworth & Caro have come to-day. Marie was delighted to receive them, & her mother could scarce restrain her emotion. We are all very happy. Riches never could make us so happy, nor fame, nor eminence of any sort.

Fort Ontario, Oswego, N.Y. July 24th, 1853
2 o'clock at night.

Praised be God. Marie was safely delivered of a fine girl at 5½ p.m. to-day. Blue eyes; long, wavy, dark hair: weighs 8¼ lbs.[29]

Three little things on Earth,
Are all other blessings worth;

The sweetest thing in life
Is a loving little wife;

29. The baby was named Marie Louise Willcox, nicknamed "Lulu."

And the next to that in joy,
Is a noisy little boy;

But if you cannot have this,
Why a quiet little miss.

At 2 weeks of age weighed 9 lbs.
At 5 weeks, 11½ lbs.

August 4th, 1853
Change of Stations.
Received orders to take the company to Fort Hamilton. Commenced packing at once. Mrs. Farnsworth, Caro, our excellent nurse (Mrs. Eleanor Allen of Syracuse) & all hands at work.

August 8th
Dr. Sprague died suddenly & in the midst of our confusion incident to packing up; a deep gloom fell over the garrison.

August 9th
Moved Marie over to Mrs. Patten's. I carried her down stairs in my arms & a red headed, tall Scotch recruit carried [her] up stairs at Mrs. Patten's. . . . Mrs. Farnsworth left. I slept at the hotel last night & will do so to-night.

August 10
Left Oswego with Co. "C."

August 12
Yesterday reached Fort Hamilton; found we had been ordered to Fort Mifflin, Pa.; took steamer *Delaware* & came by the way of Cape May.

August 19
Having heard from Howe[30] that I would be detailed this Fall for the Battery at Fort Leavenworth, I started for New York to get the order changed; succeeded.

---

30. Capt. Albion P. Howe, adjutant, 4th Artillery. Howe remained with the 4th Artillery during the Civil War, eventually winning promotion to brevet major general.

August 20

Arrived at Oswego this morning. Brought a servant girl, Miss Sarah Cobb, to go back with us in case Ann demurred. Found Marie quite weak. Mr. Farnsworth came this evening.

August 21

Delightful Sunday with Marie, who enjoys her father's presence very much. He seems pleased with our baby, who is to be called Marie. He had heard of the Battery detail & written to Marie, offering to take her to Detroit till we were ready to go. He wishes now to take her [and] for me to come after her in Oct. Marie & I think [it] unnecessary.

FORT MIFFLIN, PA.

August 25

Left Mrs. Patten & kind friends at Oswego yesterday morning. Had rain all the way to New York. Baby travels well. Mother not so badly as feared. Find nothing prepared in the quarters, but hope to get settled in a few days....>>

For the next few years our home was in Boston, the company being stationed at old Fort Independence in Boston harbor, except for its participation in the last Seminole War, which will be recounted in an ensuing chapter. Here we for a time vegetated for the most part, with some literary browsing. For society we were thrown upon our own resources. Beacon Street people were never famous for cultivating the military folks down in the harbor. But there were compensations. The Athenaeum library, lectures, concerts, etc., [were] available to the outside barbarians. At one of the evening lectures at some hall, I, a total stranger, was requested to introduce the Reverend . . . McBurn, author of *What a Blind Man Saw in Europe*, whom I had once met at Detroit. When the curtain rose, my good friend stepped forward with his hands folded, waiting to be introduced to the audience. But I was seized of a stage fright and shamefully failed to appear. The experienced speaker and traveller, however, was equal to the emergency, and after rolling his sightless eyes around for a moment, he waded right into the smooth waters of his subject and soon became interested and interesting, as he always was, and is now for that matter, as Chaplain of the Senate. I hope that his prayers for the politicians will meet with favor without prefatory remarks, though people profanely think the politicians are past praying for.

I called on Mr. Longfellow and walked with him under the Washington elms at Cambridge, and afterwards met him and sat with his new and beautiful wife at the Tremont Theatre, during a performance by Charlotte Cushman, whom the poet applauded warmly.[31] His tall form, simple yet cordial manners, with an air of serenity and interest in all things, nature, art and human welfare, rendered him to me the most interesting man I had ever met. Saw Oliver Wendell Holmes[32] frequently. But I shall always regret not seeing two other Bostonians of scarcely less note than Mr. Longfellow himself, viz. the great philanthropist, Dr. Samuel Gridley Howe, and his wife, Julia Ward Howe. During my stay at Fort Independence they were the nearest of our neighbors at South Boston, where the doctor had charge of the blind asylum, which gave him his greatest fame. Mrs. Howe was a cousin of my most intimate friend at West Point, Julian McAllister. But I little dreamed of it until years after I had marched with thousands of my fellow soldiers to her soul-stirring "Battle Hymn of the Republic." In all respects she was one of the best and most remarkable women of our country, as her published Reminiscences best show. However I met some of the eminent Bostonians, not least of whom was Oliver Wendell Holmes. [He was] on the street and browsing over books and joking with James Field and others at the book store. A small bustling man, with any look but the look of an *Autocrat of the Breakfast Table*. Occasionally I saw Anson Burlingame, my old Detroit school fellow, rapidly rising as a politician in Massachusetts, where he had married and settled. He was a graceful-tongued orator, with the look of an Indian and some of the blood. He had studied law at Detroit with an obscure lawyer named Tryon, noted for his shifty ways and avarice. But he took a fancy to my friend and sent him to Harvard University, and at Cambridge [Burlingame] met and married the daughter of a prominent and wealthy gentleman. He had Indian blood in his veins, which was manifest in his complexion and profile. His success as minister to China and his denunciation in the House of Representatives of the Brooks assault on Charles Sumner[33] on the floor of the U.S. Senate, have given him a wider reputation than he had when I last saw him in Boston during the Anthony Burns Riot in 1854, of which I will next speak.

31. Charlotte Cushman (1816–1876) was considered one of the leading tragedians of her day.
32. Oliver Wendell Holmes, Sr., (1809–1894), writer and physician. Holmes was a professor at the Harvard Medical School when OBW met him. His fame as a writer was purely local until 1857, when his series of articles "The Autocrat of the Breakfast Table" was published in the *Atlantic Monthly*.
33. Sen. Charles Sumner (Massachusetts) became one of the leading Radical Republicans.

§ SEVEN

The Anthony Burns Riot

FIFTY YEARS ago I was stationed as a lieutenant of the United States Army at Fort Independence in Boston harbor. During my service there the Anthony Burns Riot occurred, at the time a very sensational and widely discussed episode. Burns was a slave who had escaped from Richmond or Alexandria to Boston on board of a sailing vessel and who found employment with a clothing merchant at the Hub. He was a shrewd-looking fellow, about twenty-seven years old. His story of the manner of his leaving his master was that it was accidental. According to his account, one day while tired, he lay down to rest on board of a vessel, went asleep, and during his slumbers the vessel sailed. He said he was willing to return to his master.

His frankness was drawn out of him by a reporter soon after his arrest under the Fugitive Slave Law.[1] The arrest no doubt frightened him into talking. Later he became reticent. He was arrested at Boston on Wednesday evening, May 24, 1854, locked up in the United States Court House for the night and brought before a commissioner for examination. The examination proceedings were conducted by Benjamin F. Hallett, district attorney for the United States, and the claimant's counsel, and were hotly contested by volunteer counsel for the negro. The latter was Richard H. Dana, author of *Two Years Before the Mast*, who was a brilliant attorney. He was assisted by

---

1. The Fugitive Slave Law was an integral part of the Compromise of 1850. The law declared that northern officials were responsible for returning fugitive slaves to their owners.

C. M. Ellis, equally learned in the law. The hearing lasted eight days, under stress of the fiercest excitement, and tumultuous efforts to rescue the prisoner by force.

A mob of some thousands stood surrounding the court house, when our two companies of regular troops, under Major [Samuel Chase] Ridgely, reached the square. The west door of the court house had been broken open by means of a stick of timber used as a battering ram. One of the deputy marshals, James Bachelder, had been killed, and the marshal himself had a narrow escape. But the mob had not succeeded in gaining entrance. We found the door already repaired and fairly barricaded.

On the previous night a public meeting was held at old Faneuil Hall, where fiery speeches were made by Wendell Phillips and Theodore Parker, a noted preacher of the Gospel of Peace.[2] Both were notorious abolitionists, denouncing the arrest of the slave on the sacred soil of Massachusetts and within the purlieus of Faneuil Hall, and urging an attack on the court house by the "Children of Adams and Hancock." This attack Parker proposed to make at once, but Phillips advised waiting till daylight—thinking, no doubt, that it might be more effectually organized. With morning came the attack, but there was no apparent organization, and neither Phillips nor Parker put in an appearance. But a murder was committed that gave the law-abiding citizens a pause and lent a bloody ghost to the occasion.

I have always remembered and profoundly respected the U.S. marshal, Watson Freeman. As a man he sympathized with the poor fugitive, but as an officer of the law he did his utmost to guard him until the trial was over, and then to prevent bloodshed following the decision of the court, as we shall see.

By the aid of our troops from the fort and two companies from the Navy Yard, the marshal felt that he could hold the court house, but that there would be more danger of an attempt at rescue and consequent blood letting on the streets on our way to the revenue cutter at the wharf with the prisoner. Our military chief, Lieutenant Colonel Dulaney, called a council of war over the emergency. The colonel fell asleep during the conference and no decision was arrived at. Our chief reported sick and returned to the Navy yard next morning, leaving matters in Maj. Ridgely's hands. The major had

2. Wendell Phillips (1811–1884) was an abolitionist lawyer, an orator, and a crusader for human rights. Rev. Theodore Parker (1810–1860) was then chairman of the Boston Vigilance Committee, which aided runaway slaves by operating the "Underground Railroad." He was indicted for his role in endeavoring to release Anthony Burns from prison but was never brought to trial. Parker had befriended John Brown while the latter was operating in Kansas and had been an early advocate of making Kansas a free state.

such a severe cold that he was unable to talk over things with the marshal, and he directed me to go ahead as his adjutant and do everything I could to cooperate with the civil authorities and report from time to time for further instructions. But while he concurred with the marshal in the opinion that our force was inadequate, he would not ask the War Department for more troops. It may be remembered that Mr. Jefferson Davis, of Mississippi, was then Secretary of War.[3]

The marshal had already obtained a small number of assistants and they were a resolute and brave set of fellows. Many more guards, civil if not military, were needed, but he was afraid any further appeal would be refused. I must not leave the reader to infer that Major Ridgely shirked the responsibility, for as there were many in garrisons within a few hours' call and none were ordered, he inferred that the responsibility lay with Mr. Davis.

However, when the marshal came to me in his perplexity over his position, I thought that as a last resort he might appeal to the attorney general at Washington, reporting the emergency and telegraphing for authority to employ one hundred additional deputies. The suggestion staggered him. But with a doleful face he said, "I'll try, and if it is refused, the responsibility will rest where it belongs." And try he did. Much to his surprise the authority came.

The next point was where to get the men, as public opinion was so strong against us that it would be difficult to find responsible men who would fire on their fellow citizens. This problem we solved together, and he sent down to the lower and back streets among the bruisers and shoulder hitters and tempted them with the bait of liberal pay and meals at Parker's restaurant.

This was ample, and one hundred lusty fellows applied, one or two at a time, and were forthwith sworn in as deputy marshals. They were armed with carbines and drilled, on the open square, at every lull in the storm by young officers, in loading, firing and marching. Jibes were not wanting in the newspapers and nightly meetings. "Rag tag and bob tail" and "Falstaff recruits" were the mildest terms flung at the new supporters of law and

3. Jefferson Davis (23d, USMA 1828), former U.S. congressman (1845–1846), and veteran of the Mexican War, where he served as colonel of the 1st Mississippi, and of the U.S. Senate. Davis served as Secretary of War during the Pierce administration. Reelected to the Senate in 1856, he served until Mississippi left the Union in January 1861, resigning his seat on January 21. On February 22, 1861, he was inaugurated as president of the Confederate States of America, which position he held until the defeat of the Confederacy in 1865. Captured while attempting to flee in Irwinville, Georgia, on May 10, 1865, Davis was imprisoned at Fort Monroe, Virginia. He was to be tried for treason against the United States. Two years later Davis was released on bail, and the charges against him were eventually dropped. He died on December 9, 1889.

order. But their solid and threatening appearance had its due weight in the bosom of the outside rabble. While the motley enlistment was going on, events still more exciting transpired daily, if not hourly.

On the second day threats were made against Phillips and Parker themselves, and their dwellings were guarded. The Boston Cadets, under Colonel Amory, were called out to keep the peace, and paraded near the court house square. Then ropes were drawn across the side streets by the chief of police. General Edmands[4] established headquarters at Albion. The only incident at the court house door was a scuffle with a well-dressed woman, who insisted upon entrance as a lady to see the unfortunate prisoner. She tried her hand for more than two hours. Various individuals were arrested for riotous proceedings elsewhere. Certainly the mayor took all the necessary measures to keep the peace outside the square.

Negotiations were going on for the purchase of Burns, and at eleven o'clock it was confidently stated that he would be purchased by Wendell Phillips and others for $1,200, and that the money had been raised. Wendell Phillips's name seemed to be on every tongue. But the negotiation collapsed and excuses were made. It would be "a covenant with Hell" to admit an ownership in slaves under the shadow of Bunker Hill. "And to plank down the money for it," was another objectionable feature on the tongues of wags.

It turned out that most of the money was raised by the colored people themselves. The negro's owner, Col. [Charles F.] Suttle, was willing to sell, but the negotiation fell [through].

In the evening a mob again gathered around the "slave pen," as it was called, and some stones and bricks were thrown. One of them struck a member of the New England Guards. Many riotous patriots were arrested by the police and locked up in the central station. The excitement was intense on the Sabbath night. But Mr. Taylor, chief of the police, kept cool and preserved the peace without military aid.

About the same state of things continued during the ensuing week, and several of the newspapers had their fling. The *Boston Post* tried to pour oil on the troubled waters. Not so the old *Commonwealth*, one of whose headlines was as follows:

ANOTHER MAN SEIZED IN BOSTON

BY THE MAN HUNTERS

THE DEVIL BILL RENEWING ITS VIGOR

AND GETTING UP A JUBILEE AMONG US

ON THE PASSAGE OF THE NEBRASKA BILL.

4. Brig. Gen. B. F. Edmands, Massachusetts State Militia.

The same issue of the paper learnedly "surmised" that the men who were guarding Burns were "the identical men who passed resolutions in a Democratic convention in favor of the extension of slavery into Nebraska and fired guns in honor of such extension. They are probably paid by the Custom House."

Such spurious information had the effect to mislead the credulous, but it arrayed Free Soil and old line Democrats openly on the side of public order and the enforcement of the law.

During most of the week, train loads from the country churches, armed or expecting arms, came in daily and marched up in comical bravado to the square and there dispersed. Anson Burlingame told me that not much was to be expected from these loose arrays of Christian fighters. But he added that secret clubs were organizing, arming and drilling, that meant real business. There was, he said, one such in the city of one hundred young men with which he was connected, and he coolly advised me not to make myself conspicuous, or do more than I was actually obliged to do, and no harm should come to me. Of course I thanked him for his personal interest, but on the other hand I advised him to look out for his own head when the conflict should come. I told him literally that if he showed himself on the street in riot, I would have him shot, the first man. A poor return for his friendly intent, perhaps, but hasty, and "all haste comes from the devil," according to the Turks.

I soon found that the city authorities evinced a disposition to do no more than preserve the peace on the streets and protect their own citizens at their homes. Up to the night of the last day of the trial, when the decision was announced that the defendant was a slave and must be returned, I could hear of no steps [taken] by police or local soldiery to join in the bodily escort of the slave to the revenue cutter. The situation was perhaps more threatening than ever as the secret and other organizations were more forward; and by the advice of Marshal Freeman and Major Ridgely on that night, early, I called upon Mayor [J.V.C.] Smith to request his cooperation. He declined to go any farther than he had done. In fact he was adverse, and he politely declined. After informing him of the decided views of the commanding officer and the marshal as to the emergency, I finally had to say, "Well, Mr. mayor, if the streets of Boston are flowing with the blood of its citizens on the morrow, the responsibility will fall on yourself."

His honor, the mayor, yielded at my last warning, and inquired what cooperation we wanted. This was very little, only a rear guard of cavalry and police patrols on the side streets coming into State Street, which led to Long Wharf. And this was granted.

The truth is that the danger of a bloody conflict was greater than any of us supposed—it was not so much from the mob that howled around the court house as it was [from] unseen forces. There were sturdy, "dyed in the wool Democrats," who had always stood by the South on the slavery question, the large shipping interests, owners, masters and sailors engaged in Southern trade, and the merchants likewise interested therein, together with Southern men, dealers and others actually on the spot. Even the Free Soil Democrats wanted to see the compromise law fairly executed in the North. These, to say the least, were antagonistic to the mob and their violent spokesmen. A warning had already been sounded in the street that Theodore Parker's house was in danger. Besides the above, there were the number of Southern students at Harvard College, few, or many perhaps, [of whom] were notoriously handy with pistol and bowie knife, that might have been fairly matched against Burlingame's organized "one hundred young men of the best blood in Boston."

One of the foolhardy and illegal acts committed by the abolitionists was an attempt to arrest Col. Suttle, owner of the slave, and his witness, William Brent, of Richmond. Even Chief Justice Wells, of the Massachusetts Supreme Court, lent himself to the scheme, and issued a writ of replevin on Marshal Freeman, who disregarded it. The attempt increased the indignation of the party just mentioned and turned the plot and plotters into public ridicule.

I did not know, nor do I know now, to what extent the various elements of opposition were combined, if at all. But the fact that the whole military were held in readiness betrayed the anxiety of the Boston officials.

Next morning, Court Street, in front of the court house, and the immediate vicinity was filled with a mass of human beings, and large numbers thronged the sidewalks on State Street. The mayor had posted his proclamation, directing General Edmands and the chief of police to make the necessary disposition of their respective forces, to secure order throughout the city, and urgently requesting all well-disposed citizens and other persons "not to molest or obstruct any officer, civil or military, in the lawful discharge of his duty."

Thus the die was cast at last, with all the civil and military weight of a great city and center of abolitionism in favor of law and order. Both respectable sides may be said to have grounded arms at the crisis. But during the forenoon the excitement increased, and reached its highest pitch at 2 P.M. Meantime, efforts were renewed to purchase Burns and failed.

Every avenue leading to Court and State Streets was cleared by the chief of police, supported by General Edmands. The U.S. troops were marched out of the court house and their arms carefully inspected. Next came the deputy marshals with pistols and drawn swords and [they] were formed in hollow square. After these appeared Marshal Freeman and some half dozen aides with the fugitive—who at first appeared to be utterly indifferent to the proceedings. He had been furnished with a new suit of clothes.

The marshal and his group took position in the center of the hollow square, and amid mingled execrations, hurrahs and hisses of the multitude, the silent procession moved off. Major Ridgely and our two companies from Fort Independence were at its head. Following the square of marshals with the negro, who now may be said to be "escorted," came the marines, next a six-pounder gun under Lieutenant—afterwards General—Couch,[5] of the Fourth Artillery, and finally a rear guard of city cavalry.

At the corner of Court Square and Court Street, the demonstrations of the baffled mob were most uproarious, and all the way down Court Street we were greeted with theatrical-like thunder, a bottle or two of vitriol and cayenne pepper from the windows, and from the office of the *Commonwealth* newspaper were thrown a little shower of cayenne, cowitch and other noxious missiles. But no bones, and scarcely any flesh parts, were broken, and we continued to move in utter silence and indifference, more apparent than real, waiting to see what should happen next. The person most alarmed and the one who felt most relieved, as we reached the revenue cutter, was Anthony Burns. As he leaped on deck, he slapped his hand on his thigh, laughed and said: "No nigger ever had a whole brigade escort him afore." He was quickly placed out of sight in the cabin.

But one attempt had been made to break into the column, and that was foiled by a detachment of the National Lancers and others of the Massachusetts volunteers. After some delay occasioned by the labor of getting the field piece aboard, the word "cast off" was given, and the cutter, at 3 P.M., June 3, 1854, started for the South with her precious charge on board, and the troops returned to their stations.

Was the lesson lost on the Southern mind? Judging from what I soon learned of the feelings of Jefferson Davis himself, I came to think that the Southern mind was not easily satisfied. For the leading Democrats of Boston, Benjamin F. Hallett, Charles C. Green and others, who knew of the active part I had taken in the comparatively peaceful rendition of Burns to

5. Darius N. Couch (13th, USMA 1846). Couch later distinguished himself in the Army of the Potomac as a division commander on the Peninsula, in the Second Bull Run and Antietam campaigns, and as commander of the Second Corps at Fredericksburg and Chancellorsville. In December 1864 he would lead a division of the Twenty-third Corps at the Battle of Nashville and in North Carolina.

his master, advocated my promotion to a staff appointment, [which was] then vacant. I soon went to present their letters to President Pierce and Secretary Davis, thinking I would have a "walk over," particularly as I believed that I had a warm friend in the Cabinet, Robert McClelland,[6] Secretary of the Interior. But to my extreme astonishment, I found that Mr. Davis was "disappointed" in the issue of the Boston affair, and not in the humor to reward those who had contributed to its success. This I learned from a close friend of the administration, Henry N. Walker, United States attorney for Michigan. So I pocketed my papers and returned to my post.

Come to think of it, there might have been any one of several reasons for Mr. Davis's "disappointment." He may have thought that the execution of the law by force was not a fair test of government sentiment, as tomorrow there might be a government opposed to the execution of that law. Or he might have thought the hostility manifested in New England was nothing more than one might expect from the whole North. Or he might have felt chagrined because our employment of one hundred deputy marshals was a reflection on himself as the military commander. Or possibly he was already hoping if not scheming for pretexts looking to the dissolution of this great and glorious Union. At any rate, such chances were freely discussed by the young Southern hotbloods of the day, who looked towards a Southern Empire, which should not only cut loose from the non-slave-holding states, but embrace the sister republic of Mexico.

JOURNAL: JUNE 1855–MARCH 1856[7]

Left New York June 17th, 1855 for Corpus Christi with recruits under Capt. Marcy[8] for Texas. Ship *Middlesex*, Capt. Parmalee. Orders to return to my post, Ft. Independence, on recruits being turned over at Corpus Christi....

On going to New York to embark for Texas in June, carried the manuscript of *Shoepac Recollections*. It had been previously declined by Phillips & Samson in Boston. It was accepted by Bunce & Brother, N.Y.

Returned to Fort Independence early in August, passing through Detroit, whither Marie had gone in my absence, uncertain about the time of

6. Robert McClelland had served as U.S. representative from Michigan, 1843–1845 and 1847–1849. He was governor of Michigan from 1851 to 1853 and for four years, beginning March 4, 1853, was secretary of the interior under Franklin Pierce.

7. From OBW's *Second Journal.*

8. Capt. Randolph B. Marcy, future father-in-law of and chief of staff to Maj. Gen. George B. McClellan.

my return from Texas. Went to Detroit in October. Delivered a poem there before the Young Men's Society [on] November 20th, subject "Solitude in Society."

Little Elon born at Detroit [December] 6.[9]

Returned to Fort I[ndependence] with Marie & Elon, leaving Lulu (as they have begun to call little Marie) with her Grandma Farnsworth, January 2d.

Renewed study of Blackstone.[10]

Shoepac Recollections published about 1st March/56. . . .

9. Elon Farnsworth Willcox, first son of OBW and Marie Farnsworth Willcox. He graduated thirty-ninth out of forty-three, USMA class of 1878, served in the 6th U.S. Cavalry and as aide to his father in Arizona.

10. Referring, of course, to Sir William Blackstone's *Commentaries on the Laws of England*, 4 vols. (1765–1769), which for more than a century served as the foundation of all legal education in both England and the United States.

§ EIGHT

The Last Seminole War

[By the autumn of 1856, Orlando Willcox was already well aware that army
life could, at times, become monotonous. Boredom, homesickness, and the
accompanying alcoholism were then the greatest enemies of the American
soliders, not a foreign army.

For Orlando Willcox, the Florida campaign would illustrate just how
monotonous a soldier's life could become. His previous tours of duty, in Mexico,
on the plains, and on the East Coast, had all had their benefits: the beauty and
excitement of an exotic and foreign land; the thrill of chasing a thundering herd
of buffalo; the opportunity to socialize with prominent and sometimes famous
citizens. The malaria-infested swamps of Florida, however, would try the
patience of officers and enlisted men alike, and many young subalterns and
company-grade officers, disillusioned and disgusted with the army, would resign
their commissions when it was over. Orlando Willcox was no exception in this
feeling. Yet, somehow, in spite of these hardships—in spite of the boredom and
disease, the pettiness of superior officers, and disgust with army red tape, Willcox
managed to retain his sense of humor, venting his disgust and despair in a caustic
wit that flowed from his pen and into the pages of the journal reprinted in this
chapter. His satire on "modern war" is a jewel in itself. There is sadness too, in the
recorded deaths of enlisted men and civilians who otherwise would have been
forgotten. If the Florida campaign of 1856–1857 gained nothing militarily, it
at least produced this illuminating history of a campaign that failed.]

THE SEMINOLES began their forays on the American white settlements as early as 1819, when they raided over the border of Florida, then a Spanish colony, into Georgia. They were promptly chased back by General Andrew Jackson. He did not hesitate to cross the international boundary line, for hesitation was no part of his compound.[1] This scare and the demands of Georgia no doubt led to our acquisition of the Orange Peninsula in 1821. But the savages, from their so-called impenetrable everglades, broke out from time to time against the "repeated aggressions, false promises, neglect and abuse of the whites."

The Seminole War lasted seven years, from 1831, and continued at intervals up to 1849.[2] According to General Jesup,[3] the government had committed the error of attempting to remove the Indians when their lands were not required for our own agricultural purposes. The Seminoles were not in the way of the few white inhabitants of the peninsula, and the greater portion of their country was unexplored wilderness; yet the government undertook to banish them to another unexplored wilderness beyond the Mississippi River. For this purpose, during the struggles, repeated treaties were forced upon the savages after each notable campaign. But, as might have been expected, the treaties were long evaded and postponed by the body of the warriors. This happened through the influence of such wily chiefs as Wild Cat, the son of King Philip, and Osceola Powell, son of a white man and a squaw.[4] The injudicious treaties themselves kept the war going.

Strange as it may sound, under Spanish and English rule, the Indians of Florida had roamed unmolested throughout the peninsula, enjoying the confidence of, and association with, the white inhabitants, mostly Spanish; and the officials had treated them with "kindness and distinction." Be-

1. Actually, the seeds of enmity between white Americans and the Seminole people predate the War of 1812. Escaped slaves from Southern plantations often found new homes among the Seminoles; they even intermarried with the Indians, forming a race called the Maroons. Some blacks, however, were reenslaved by the Seminoles. Slaveowners, pressing the government for the return of the slaves who had escaped, were the primary cause of the disputes with the Seminoles.

2. The first Seminole War is actually said to have lasted from 1817 to 1818, though that time frame is misleading, as open hostilities between white Americans and the Seminoles began much earlier. The second Seminole War lasted from 1835 to 1842, the third Seminole War from December 1855 to 1858.

3. Gen. Thomas S. Jesup (1788–1860). Distinguished as an officer in the War of 1812, Jesup had served in Florida since the beginning of the Seminole War and succeeded Gen. Richard K. Call as commander of the Army of Florida in December 1836. Wounded at Jupiter Inlet on January 24, 1838, Jesup was succeeded by Col. Zachary Taylor.

4. Legend had it that Osceola was the son of one William Powell, an English trader. Osceola himself, however, declared, "No foreign blood runs in my veins; I am a pure-blooded Muskogee."

sides the Seminoles, there were also the Mickosukies, Tallahassees and some Creeks in Florida.

The Seminoles, or "Runaways," were a migrating branch of the Creeks. They had abandoned the main body of that Indian nation in 1750 under a noted chief named Secoffee. Another band of Creeks came over to them in 1808. One of Secoffee's sons was named Bowlegs and the last chief of the tribe in Florida was our friend, the Enemy, Billy Bowlegs, of 1856–57. The tribe had taken possession of the middle part of the peninsula, unopposed. They held slaves and cultivated the soil until driven to the everglades by the stress of war. I can well remember the sallow faces and emaciated bodies of officers and men coming up from the sickly field from time to time, particularly after the year 1836. They told us of old Micanopy, the fat and lazy.[5] He was nominally the war chief, but usually an advocate for peace. He had to be pushed on by the young and ambitious chiefs, and the bolder men of the tribe. These were Little Cloud, a great hunter and warrior; Tustenugge, or Alligator, crafty and politic, the most intelligent of the chiefs; Jumper, Tiger Tail, and Chief Abraham, the latter a negro. These names were familiar town talk all over this country during the long struggle of the Seminoles.

I think I have a weakness for Indian heroes. Perhaps I inherited a love for them from my father, who had extensive dealings with the Indians of our own peninsula of Michigan, and had trading posts at Detroit, St. Clair and Mackinaw. He generally found them more honest than the average white man, and less forgetful of a face or a kindness. The chiefs were frequent visitors at our house at Detroit, where my oldest sister sometimes entertained them with music. One of the young chiefs, a handsome fellow, too, had the audacity to demand her hand in marriage—an act which threatened ill consequences for a time. He reasoned well. White men took squaws—why should not he, a chief, a hunter and a warrior, have a white squaw?

I took particular interest in the fate of Osceola, bad as he was. It was he who laid in wait for Major Dade and his command in the woods. He was the murderer of General Thompson and others.[6] He was seized finally by order

5. Micanopy was chief of the Oconees, a major branch of the Seminoles, and head chief of the Seminole Nation.

6. In June 1835, U. S. Indian agent Wiley Thompson had Osceola arrested and put in irons. The following day, Osceola agreed to sign a treaty in order to win his release. He took his revenge in two separate but coordinated attacks on U.S. soldiers on December 28, 1835. While marching from Fort Brooke, near Tampa, Maj. Francis L. Dade and some 110 officers and men were slaughtered in an ambush about forty miles northeast of the fort. Only a few soldiers escaped. Some fifty miles to the northwest, at Fort King, Osceola himself, with some twenty Seminole warriors, ambushed the agent Wiley Thompson and a dinner guest, killing both. The

of General Jesup, while on a peaceful errand for a talk, and imprisoned in Fort Moultrie, where he long languished, his proud spirit broken ere it took its flight for the happy hunting grounds. He had met craft by superior craftiness; but pray what right had the white men he hated, to rob and to banish the nation to which he belonged from their own soil?

One feather in the cap of the long-warring Florida Indians was the fact, often recited, that the blacks, many of whom had been their slaves, took their part, and fought in the ranks with equal ardor. Some became chiefs, the most noted of whom was Chief Abraham.

On our own side, General Jesup's name figured notably as an able officer and a just man. In 1837 he succeeded so well that nearly the whole body of the Indians and blacks were assembled at Tampa Bay to migrate, under Micanopy. A fleet of vessels lay ready to receive and carry them to the Mississippi, when, at the last moment, the *reconcentrados* vanished, as it were, in a night. Wild Cat and Osceola, both of whom had come in and agreed to migrate—the better to play their usual game—had won over the warriors and stampeded the old chiefs and head-men of the tribes. This stupendous failure, after all his successes, together with his troubles over the supply department and the ill-disciplined volunteers, made General Jesup tired of a war which, in every sense, he considered unwise. There certainly need have been no excuse for the frequent want of forage, and it must have rattled the old general to hear the hungry jackass brays imitated by the Georgia volunteers, thuswise: "Gen'ral Jesup, Gen'ral Jesup, Corn, Corn!" At any rate, he pressed his demand to be relieved, and retired from the field universally respected, if not beloved. For more detailed particulars of the early stages of the Seminole War, the reader is referred to Colonel Sprague's veracious history of the Florida war.[7] There will be found therein some notable likenesses of participants in the struggle. The cynical half-grin on Osceola's face recalls to me the face of Voltaire on his statue near Geneva.

To best illustrate the difficulties and prolongation of the war and the heroic obstinacy of the tribe, it is only necessary to give the names of the generals who successively took command against them: Zachary Taylor, Macomb, Worth, Armistead, Clinch, Call, Gaines[8] and even the great Scott,

---

"Dade Massacre" caused Congress to appropriate money the following January for the complete subjugation of the Seminoles.

7. John T. Sprague, *The Origin, Progress and Conclusions of the Florida War* (New York: D. Appleton, 1848).

8. Bvt. Brig. Gen. Walter K. Armistead (1st, USMA 1803), father of Confederate general Lewis Armistead; Brig. Gen. Duncan L. Clinch; Brig. Gen. Richard Keith Call, a protegé of Andrew Jackson's, served two terms as territorial governor of Florida (1835–1840, 1841–1844); Edmund P. Gaines.

with about all the artillery, infantry and dragoon regiments in the army, and the gun boats and marines of the navy.

General Taylor, before he succeeded General Jesup, had fought a famous battle in the very section of the peninsula where Billy Bowlegs confronted General [William S.] Harney in 1856–57, and whither I went as an officer of the old Fourth Artillery. The regiment was well known in Florida and many of our officers and men had been killed or sickened and died there. Among the former West Point men, I shall always remember Lieutenant O'Brien,[9] author of our song:

> In the land of Sun and Flower, his head lie buried low.
> No more to sing Petite Coquille and Benny Havens, O!

All our artillery command was ordered to proceed by sail via Tampa under Brevet Major John B. Scott. The major was something of a wag, and he made things very pleasant for us on the long voyage. Among my fellow officers were Lieutenant Swallow, Captain J. P. McCown, of Tennessee (afterward a general in the Confederate service), [Major] Thomas Williams,[10] of Detroit (afterward brigadier general in the United States Army, who fell heroically at the battle of Baton Rouge), Lieutenant [Joseph H.] Wheelock[11] and Surgeon McLarren.

The voyage was one of the usual length for sail ships, with fogs, contrary winds off the Carolina capes and the reefs of Key West. I may be forgiven for quoting from the diary of a gushing young lieutenant:[12]

<On the 24th day of Oct. 1856 set sail five companies of our regiment [4th Artillery] from Boston Harbor for Fort Myers, Florida. The whole regiment was ordered into the field, together with the 5th Infantry. The old play of The Florida War was to be repeated that winter. Our Government

9. John P. J. O'Brien (16th, USMA 1836) died on March 31, 1850, at Indianola, Texas.

10. Thomas Williams entered the war as a major in the 5th U.S. Artillery. Promoted brigadier general in September 1861, he served in the North Carolina expedition in October and later was given command at Fort Hatteras. He also served under Maj. Gen. Benjamin Butler in the operations against New Orleans, Louisiana. Commanding at Baton Rouge, Williams was killed during a Confederate attack on the city on August 5, 1862.

11. Joseph H. Wheelock (6th, USMA 1850) was then post quartermaster. He died in Washington, D.C., in 1862 (exact causes and date unknown).

12. In this chapter, originally written for his memoirs, OBW simply paraphrased entries from his journal. The editor has taken the liberty of quoting directly from the original, a leatherbound journal titled *Florida Journal, 1856*. The entries for this chapter are contained within single angle brackets < >. Entries within double angle brackets << >> are comments made by OBW in the paraphrased version of his journal that the editor feels are appropriate to insert into the original entry.

never does anything in earnest. There is something facetious about our government.

It may be thought that hardy, well drilled, & well disciplined troops would be ordered into Florida. By no means. Our government filled the companies up with raw, undrilled, undisciplined recruits on the very eve of their departure. It must be [thought] that, . . . if they were in earnest, our government would [have made] use of all the skill & experience acquired by the troops already in the field. No, our waggish government ordered them out of the field; recruits could keep up the play well enough. Behold us gallant warriors of the North, embarked in this noble cause. . . .

The 10th November the Warriors of the North landed on terra firma, on the soil of Billy Bowlegs—William Cruikshanks, *alias* Billy Bowlegs. [We] did [not] land, however, until we anchored off Charlotte Harbor,[13] tumbled, or threw ourselves with impetuosity overboard, leaving the best part of our baggage on the ship.

We, Uncle Sam's men, never do anything with deliberation. The landing was effected with as much haste as if we had been an army under full retreat before the enemy, leaving most of our baggage on board. The steam lighter which received us thus lightened was the *Jasper*; the nice, low-pressure [boiler], slow, single engine boat, which, of all boats, was the best calculated to do the job worst, which no business man would have employed in such business at all. The river Caloosa Hatchee was [a] narrow, shallow channel, winding intricately, so that the *Jasper* labored hard with her [deep] sea keel & single engine.

Passed Punta Rosa (Old Fort Delaney) where stores are often landed from ships, situated at the mouth of the river, 18 miles below Fort Myers. Half way up [we] passed the scene of "Harney's Massacre," where the Indians made a night attack on his company in the early years of the war, 1849–50, & he fled in his night clothes for his life, swam out to a boat in the river & escaped narrowly. The spot is still called "Harney's Massacre," & the incident always mentioned with a smile at the hero's expense, who swears dreadfully to this day over it, & always vows revenge.

Just below Fort Myers & hiding it, is a point called "Point Disappearance," which, sure enough, like many other fine points, disappears as you approach it. The shore at Fort Myers is [a] bluff & presents a pile of rocks which relieves the eye after passing the low sandy shores on either side. A long

13. Charlotte Harbor lies on the Gulf Coast of Florida, at the mouth of the Caloosahatchee River, near Fort Myers.

wharf . . . built on slender piles, & supporting a hand car railway, projects from the shore. At the end of this wharf we saw Col. Harney, Brown (Maj. of 2d Artillery), Capt. Pratt, Capt. Hancock[14] & other officers, & a meagre, motley clad number of sallow-faced soldiers. But they told us their appearance was fine compared with that of the soldiers we should find at Fort Deynaud.

After landing our baggage, packing it in six covered wagons, dining with Capt. Pratt's mess (where the soup was beyond praise & where we saw Bananas, Roses & Heliotropes . . .) the officers, on horse back, & men, on foot, set forth for Fort Deynaud under Maj. Williams at 4½ P.M.

The country was sandy but hard under foot, covered with pine & palmetto trees wide apart, & small palmetto & mangrove undergrowth, in which an Indian might hide within the toss of a jackknife. Marched 8½ miles to a place called "Horse Hole," where we found water & which afforded a beautiful spot for a night camp. It was a very bright moonlight night, & the dark tops of the surrounding pines looked like trees of paradise in whose branches the stars were hanging like glittering jewels. I was officer of the day that night & what with the novelty, the bright moonlight, wayward fancy, my barking dog [Scotch terrier] Pincher & a strong cup of coffee, I scarcely closed [my] eyes till reveille bugle sounded at 4 o'clock.

November 11th.

Moon still bright when we marched out of camp & for two hours afterwards the trees of paradise still hung over us, & then came the rosy hues which precede a fine sun rise. But here the sentiment ended. The day proved hot, the road grew heavy & rough with palmetto roots, & water lay more than ancle deep over many a road. To us on horseback it was as nothing, but the men, most of them recruits & unaccustomed to marching, were sorely put to it to keep up, although the gait required was slow & the halts frequent. One great evil was continual eating & drinking.

Coming to within three miles of Fort Deynaud, the road plunged into deep sand, not hard like that already passed over. Found the Fort to consist of a cluster of sheds, which in the distance looked as if the roofs were of new shingles, but which proved on coming nearer to be palmetto thatch. The place now looked like a Hottentot village, & the garrison like scarecrows. They had been long reduced by fever & diarrhea, scarcely a corporal's guard fit for duty; but their deep sunken eyes brightened at sight

14. Capt. Henry C. Pratt (20th, USMA 1837), 2d U.S. Artillery; Winfield Scott Hancock.

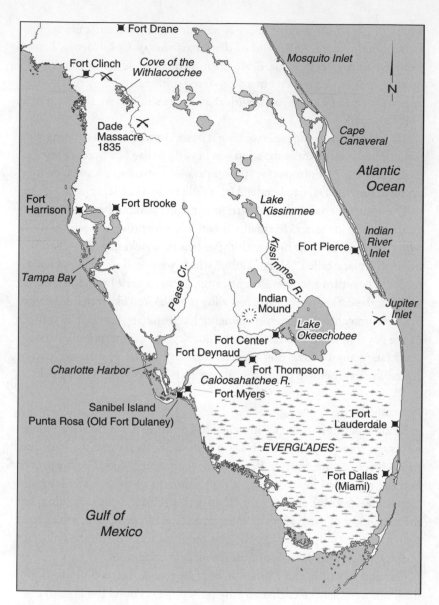

Florida during the last Seminole war, 1856–57.

of us who had come to relieve them. They little reckoned the disappointment in store.

There were two officers & a citizen surgeon at the post. Capt. Gibson, Lieut. [Frank] Larned & Dr. Blair. Under one of the long sheds (at the south end of which was the hospital) our men were quartered. Our officers [were quartered] beneath two sheds opposite the men's; two of us, Williams & myself, in log rooms, & the others in tents, stretched over frames, with their walls raised by 18 inches over clapboards at the base. There were log huts for the guard & prisoners, the sutler, & the laundresses, a small picket enclosure for a block house, now occupied by the village blacksmith, some corn, the rats, & a tank of rain water.

A huge disgust fell upon us, but afterwards we learned to appreciate the advantages of these thatched cottages, being so thick they resist the sun at noon & the dew hanging like mill stones from the sky at night. <<If this is a specimen of the Florida "forts" and their garrisons, how I envy Billy Bowlegs in the Everglades.>>

15th November

Great was the excitement of Capt. Gibson on going away. He rattled on all night with his choice vocabulary, stumped in & out on his splay foot, babbling like Vulcan, & started his command away at 3½ in the morning, advising those who had the prospect of staying in the country "to blow out their brains."

The first day or two we rested & cleaned up. Many of the men stiff, but few foot sore from the march (28 miles from Fort Myers). Rowing being heard the day after Capt. Gibson departed, there was a sensation. It proved to be a party from his command who had returned for "Bruce." Bruce was the officers' cook. Bruce had got drunk & was missing. But he was not here—possibly he had gone alone through the woods & been killed. The chances were for it. Men had been killed under the nose of Punta Rosa: a herdsman had been shot one morning while at the cattle pen, here, a stone's throw from the guard house; a wood [cutting] party of seven soldiers were attacked near the landing ¾ of a mile below us, & it was considered unsafe to hunt, however near the post now. In fact, the officers of the late command visited their guard at night armed to the teeth, so no hopes were felt for Bruce. But the rascal turned up safe next day at Fort Myers.

Another & more important fear to me is the illness of Mrs. Wilson's child; it has croup & water on the brain & the Doctor has no hope for it.

20th November

The little one is better—a strong constitution aided its recovery. Kelly, while sentinel on post the other night, stumbled & shot himself through the foot. The thermometer ranges up towards 80, the water is bad, & the men are being attacked by diarrhea & other diseases, mostly bilious.

There have been some inconveniences not owing to the climate. The men have had no camp kettles & no mess pans. That was the fault of those who hurried them away [from Fort Myers] unprovided. But the women have been no better off, & washing is done without ironing. There was no necessity for either.

But something white is seen through the trees. Wagons, by Jove! Everybody is sure he has letters, & that the [items] most needed of every sort are at hand. The stir in the village is without parallel. The trains comes in. The contents known. The wrong things have come & the right [things have] been left behind. There are but few letters & many turn away disheartened at it. But when we come to hear the news that some of the companies lately so rejoicing over the prospect of leaving the country are actually to remain [e.g. Capt. Gibson's men], we consider ourselves happy, we who have no hopes of any kind.

Yet I have kept back the greatest ill of all our fortunes—the fleas. They eat us up & make us feel like exclaiming —

"This world is all a fleeting show?"
"Say rather, a shooting flea!"

They cover the body like body lice in Egypt. . . . [T]he wicked flea, whom no man pursueth, simply because catching is out of the question. There is no rest sitting or lying down, no escape standing or running. Poor Pincher has lost his appetite. You call him, he runs part way & suddenly drops as if shot, & scratches. He jumps into the air & falls back scratching. <<Our best story teller, the Major, pauses just at the critical point of his army tale to hunt the flea. The Major was on General Scott's staff in Mexico—and wishes he were there now and so do we, for that matter.>>

It is too customary to speak [slightingly?] of the flea, & to reckon a flea bite proverbially as next to nothing, just as we speak of a drop in the bucket. A flea bite is a very respectably-sized nuisance—a flea bite is no trifling matter, as one can assure you who knows & who speaks feelingly at this moment. Some times you feel as if they had fairly hitched on to you & were running you like a hackney coach over a rough pavement. The soil of the Seminoles has avenged the owners by its fleas. They breed in the sand so fast that one would think Florida a great maggoty cheese. On going to bed the rule is to strip stark naked & make a flying leap for it: on rising in the morning to plunge into a tub of water. But the fleas of this country can jump further & hit surer than the fleas of any other land. It cannot be said there is any lack of energy in the inhabitants of this country. To the deuce with the whole of it!

On Saturday evening the 22d [November] the *Ranger* arrived. The *Ranger* had been expected so long that it was thought there was no such boat in existence except as a phantasmagorian fancy or exhalation of the brain arising from miasmatic influences. The *Ranger* was a real double-engine, flat bottomed steamer such as ply the Mississippi, & well calculated to ply the Caloosa Hatchee. She brought most of the baggage & Lieut. Terrill[15] for the post. The lieutenant is called "stud.". . . She [the *Ranger*] started back on Monday, expecting to return in a few days with Genl. Harney.

On that day [Monday, November 24] occurred one of those events peculiar to military service. Our post chief [Major Thomas Williams] rides a hobby. He apes the English & French governments & military establishments. His hobby is a little curvetting cross breed between English & French. He has drawn up a system of instruction in aiming and firing, very well for regular service, but not so well for bush whacking. I fell into a discussion with the Major as to the best mode of instructing my own company, which I ventured to assert was a matter of my own province. But I was *ordered* to say nothing to him about it, & hushed up instanter.

This made me mad, but I said nothing. I was forbid to instruct my company in any other way than after the hobby, being told moreover that an order for the hobby would be issued. Feeling that this mode of action was ungentlemanly (though by no means unmilitary) I made arrangements to withdraw from all intercourse with the Major & form a company mess. <<Internal discord begins and even Pincher knows that the Major and I are "out." He will not be coaxed to go near him.>>

Next morning the Quarter Master informed me that he was ordered to furnish me that day with other quarters, anticipating the arrival of Genl. Harney, & to communicate the fact to me. My reply was that if this came as a request I would comply with pleasure; if as an order, I required it to come in writing. The Major's reply was he would not give a written order.

I moved over to the platform where the other officers' tents were pitched & occupied the quartermaster's, who moved in with Dr. Blair. Meantime I

15. William R. Terrill (16th, USMA, 1853) was then post adjutant. Beginning the Civil War as captain of the 5th U.S. Artillery, Terrill rose to the rank of brigadier general, as chief of artillery for the Second Division, Army of the Ohio. He was killed on October 8, 1862, at the Battle of Perryville.

felt like fighting the Major, or, as an agreeable alternative, dying from shame under such insults. But considering discretion &c, & that the Chief warrior & myself both had families living at Detroit, I resolved to request an explanation.

The interview took place in the warrior's office. The Quarter Master & even the orderly was summoned to witness it. The turning out of quarters was not alluded to on either side, but the hobby horse affair was mutually explained & peace ensued. The Chief gave me his hand & invited me to dine with him that day, which I did. . . .

Lt. Terrill had brought a request that day from Col. [Gustavus] Loomis that white flags might be hung out for the Indians. And on the night of the 25th the mail express arrived (two horsemen) at 2 o'clock, bringing orders for hostilities, except defensive, to cease, & a flag, two plugs of tobacco & some wampum were sent, to be posted [for the Indians]. For this purpose a spot was selected about two hundred yards beyond the upper bank of the river, & the articles were deposited next day by Lt. Wheelock (Quarter Master).

Yesterday I was sent to see whether any change had taken place, or whether any Indians would be there to talk. The following will explain the affair:

«Fort Deynaud Fla.,
November 26, 1856.
Sir:

The Brevet Major commanding this post directs that you proceed at 11 A.M. tomorrow to the tree to which the flag of truce was attached this morning by Lieut. Wheelock.

The tree is a pine one on the opposite side of the river, about a quarter mile distant, on the right hand side of the road: You will take with you three men selected by yourself. You will be careful to take exactly the number specified. Wait until the hour indicated by the pine stick planted by Lieut. Wheelock. Should any Indians present themselves you will apprise them of your friendly feeling; request them to visit the Commanding Officer of this post. And inform them that General Harney desires to see them in Council. Lieut. Wheelock will give you all information with regard to the position of the flag, etc., that you may desire.

I have the honor to enclose you the circular from the Headquarters, Department of Florida, and a copy of 'Directions for the Use of Signs';

both of which you will return to this office so soon as you have performed your mission.

> I am, Sir,
> Very respectfully,
> Your obedient servant,
> Terrill,
> 1st Lieut.,
> 4th Artillery,
> Post Adjutant.»

These "directions" were furnished from Head Quarters of the Dpt. of Florida. The following were my instructions:

Directions for use of signs.

I. Blaze a conspicuous pine tree near the post, nail the flag to it, & tie the package (tobacco & beads) under the same, protect the package from rain by palmetto leaves.

II. Make a clear, flat place in the sand, describe a circle about two feet in diameter, at the centre plant a pine stick, not painted or stained, three or four feet high, inclined to the sun at any hour you choose: this is a sign that every day at that hour you will send there for an answer; tie to the stick a white string with (say three or four) knots; these knots will indicate to the Indians how many will be in your party at the expected visit.

Wheelock, [Richard] Wilson (my orderly sergeant) & Carroll (a great rogue but a brave fellow of my company) went with me. We were taken across the river in a scow. The men returned to this bank & waited with their arms. The whole command was kept under arms till our return, which took place in half an hour. The tokens had not been disturbed, nor was there any other sign of the presence of Indians.

This duty became the daily routine. On my going, as it was the first day after depositing, some of the officers jocularly bade us farewell. Yet it was thought possible we might be fired upon, a contingency that soon ceased to be thought of.

Meantime however the calamity which seems necessary to this ill fated region has begun. Sickness. The heat is intense, ranging upwards of 80, the nights filled with miasma. To-day, [November] 28th, there are sixteen sick in my company with the malaria. Among them is Harms, the cook of my mess, a good, devoted, handsome fellow, in whose charge my wife placed me. Amid the sickness the hobby rages. This evening all caps except the uniform are forbidden. Down with straw hats, felt hats, comfortable hats of all kinds, & hurrah for headaches, sun strokes, & other most military discomforts! There is something noble about a tyrant, but a *tyranette* is more petty than even a martinette. *Vive la bagatelle!*

THE RIVER CALOOSAHATCHEE

This post is on the Caloosa Hatchee River, which twists snake-like between its banks of pine, live oak & palmetto brake & brush, almost doubling itself between here & Fort Myers. It is not a cheerful stream, although the live oaks are quaint & crooked & the palmettos oriental, & flocks of paraquettes [parakeets] occasionally fly over it. But the oaks are shrouded in heavy draperie of long pendant Spanish mosses, which sway to & fro, casting sombre shadows on the dark waters. The chief birds that frequent these gloomy shades are a species of rook, or raven perhaps, black as Hades & eternally cawing. Here I sometimes wander & catch the melancholy mad fever. . . .

November 29th

This evening Maj. [Hiram] Leonard (paymaster) & a small escort arrived. [Lt. Edward F.] Bagley, who it was thought had deserted at Boston, came with them, also Magilton.[16] Mather still hot. Nineteen men of my company on the sick report. Harms better. Wilson's child worse, threatened with inflammation on its lungs.

November 30th

This evening visited the child, found its chest filled with phlegm, oppressed for breath, gasping, & fluttering its little arms for breath, as if it would use its wings & fly. Asked Mrs. Wilson whether she had . . . Epicac to throw off the phlegm. She said no, that none could be had at the hospital. Antimonial wine? Didn't know but that would be good.

Then I went to Dr. Blair, who said he had none of that, not in fact anything, even castor oil, quinine or the most necessary & common medicines, nothing in fact to give the child or the men, not even soda . . . nothing at all save Epsom salts & turpentine. He went over to see the child & returning said it had now congestion of the lungs, which is a stage lower than inflammation.

16. Albert L. Magilton (18th, USMA 1846).

Here is a post long established in a climate notoriously sickly & no attention paid by the ruling powers to supply medicines; not a dose of oil or quinine, nothing but turpentine & salts. God! where is thy thunder! Why sleepeth thy wrath! Such is one of the destitutions of "distant posts."

A refreshing shower this p.m.

Twenty-two reported sick in my company. Harms removed to the hospital. Sergt. Wilson sick.

December 1st

Thermometer 82 in the shade. Swallow came to me about ten o'clock & said that Mrs. Wilson's baby was dead. He was present when it died. Soon afterward I went over to her. Found her calm. The baby was placed upon the large bed in a clean frock, looking very natural & little emaciated. Mrs. Wilson said she would feel better about it if there had been more medicines to give the baby. The Sergeant was standing in the door.

When I turned away from the couple my emotions became uncontrollable & I was forced to sit down & weep. The Sergeant very decently left the house. I thought of my instrumentality in advising Mrs. Wilson to come with us to Florida, as well as the desolation of these parents. The sea voyage & lack of medicine probably had killed the child.

To-day the Doctor himself is quite sick. There has been great trouble getting men to work in the hospital. Quigley, the cook, drunk, & Thayer, an attendant, refusing to nurse the sick, both sent to the guard house. One would think the men would do anything to help each other under such circumstances, but they exhibit perfect indifference.

In my company there has been great difficulty finding a competent cook. Had just installed Partridge when he is taken sick [on the] first day. Twenty-four sick in "C" company, 15 in "L." Walsh & Forrest quite low. I heard the Steward telling the Doctor of one of them. The Doctor said, "Here is a case where oil is needed." Should the man die for want of oil who will be to blame?...

A case of petty tyranny. The Lofty has conceived a prejudice that Connelly (my fifer boy) neglects his clothes & person. This eve at parade he ordered the adjutant to have him taken to the river & policed, said he stank so he could smell him from there (100 feet). Parade over, while guard was falling out, I called up Connelly. He looked clean as his clothes, which were worn on ship & on the march, could allow. [I found his] Shoes blacked, face washed, hair combed. Opened his coat, person & shirt clean. Our tyrannette said, "Look at his belts. Pugh! Go to the guard house."

Connelly's own manner is impudent. He looked like a mad hyena & as soon as he got near the guard house, threw his sword into the sand. The Major ordered him to be "tied up by the thumbs until he winced." After supper he [the major] sent word to me to "take him in charge & punish him as I liked, but *he* would have him switched." But for the sword part of the affair I should do nothing.

At midnight [the] Express came in bringing me a long sweet letter from my wife. My children well & all happy—poor Mrs. Wilson, poor Mrs. Wilson.

Next day the child was buried. The mother seemed inconsolable. She wept over & clung frantically to the corpse, crying, "My poor little baby, my dear little baby, such a nice baby." She had made a pretty shroud herself. There were no women with her. The coffin was lined & covered with bleached cotton. Few followed the remains. [Lt. Herbert A.] Hascall & myself among them. I read the burial services with a thick voice. My thoughts were so full of what would be my Marie's feelings under such a deprivation that I could scarcely read.>

I scarcely dared to write my wife that Mrs. Wilson's baby was dead. The top of a trunk was the little angel's coffin. We all anxiously looked for a visit from General Harney in hopes of some sort of relief. Sickness was increasing from day to day. Thirty-two were sick at once in my company. The major himself, taken down with the ague, orders the sentinels (at last!) to be posted in the shade.

<Forrest of "L" company died & was buried to-day from bilious diarrhea. Walsh of "C" is very low. Musician O'Brien has been brought over, & lies all comfortably dressed & tucked up in my back tent. Saw a soldier fall backwards this p.m. as if he had been shot. Top Lofty refused the Doctor's application to have the corpse of Forrest removed immediately from the sight & smell of the other patients, out doors into a tent proposed to be pitched.

All the officers seem disgusted at the conduct of the tyrannette. Duty instead of being rendered pleasant by the comdg. officer is only irksome to the most zealous. So saith the Quartermaster. Furthermore, the Qr. Master says, "What is the use of complaining of d——n fools at Washington when we have them in the field."

December 3d
At Tattoo last night Sgt. Callahan reported that two men in quarters were very sick. I asked the Doctor to let them go into the hospital. He replied

there was not room enough. I told the Sergeant to have a couple of men set up & tend them, & asked the Officer of the Day to let them have a light. Top Lofty saw the light & ordered it to be put out.

To-day a fine rain at daylight & a shower at noon make the air fresher. No new men taken sick except Lt. Hascall. The Doctor, however, has given up sick. The morning report of both companies show forty-six, & there are four camp women sick. Found Mrs. Wilson & her husband lying on the bed & no one to attend them. [Illegible name] was so delirious the other night he threatened the life of his wife. She is now the only woman able to help the others.

Sgt. Wilson sent me a letter to forward [to] Maj. Ridgely, asking his influence for a discharge. I did so, saying to the major I could not deny the Sergt. any avenue of escape from this infernal country. I hope to-day the sickness has reached its crises.

Two companies with regimental Hd. Quarters arrived at Fort Myers Dec. 1st. Gen'l Harney gone around to Fort Dallas. . . .

4th December

Poor Walsh died to-day. He was buried with the honors of war. A miniature of some lady found in his pocket book I laid on his bosom. The earth is limestone just beneath the sandy surface, requiring hard work & a pick axe. One stone that could not be removed at the bottom of Walsh's grave seemed to jut into his side. We buried him in his blanket. There was not lumber enough at the post to make a coffin. So said the quartermaster. A post established two years & not lumber supplied sufficient for a coffin! *Vive la bagatelle!* . . .

December 6th

My boy's birth day; sent for a bottle [of] champaign; invited Swallow to dine & drank [to] the youngster's health. Swallow "wished he might be a good boy." Hascall, "many additions" «which made us all laugh considering the size of a lieutenant's pay.» Bagley "concurred in both." . . .

Last night, as I sat watching the camp, the moonlight & full star light was so fine, with Orion just over the men's quarters & the trees lifting upwards their dark tops, that the words of Tennyson came to my lips, with "*palmetto*" instead of "*ivied* casement."

"Many a night, from yon palmetto casement, ere I went to rest, Did I look on great Orion, sloping slowly to the West. Many a night I saw the Pleiades, rising through the mellow shade, Glitter like a swarm of fire flies tangled in a silver braid." . . .

Sunday was celebrated by the arrival of a herd of cattle with some volunteers under Lt. Parker & Capt. Hooker, the beef contractor from Fort Mead. The Captain is an ex-volunteer, & thinks the Indians are cowed by the skirmishes on the *14th & 16th* July. Some of his own company took part in those affairs & the Captain describes the cutting of a prisoner's throat with great *sang froid*.

Tuesday at reveille it was reported to the Commissary that all the cattle had escaped. Four volunteers left out of those who lately came & passed on to Fort Myers offered to go in search. In the evening they returned with one or two, & were annoyed at finding themselves ordered to the guard house for firing off their pistols!

Field, the sentinel on [Sentry Post] no. 2, says he saw the cattle breaking out from the pen at taps & reported it to the corporal of the guard. Louis believes the Indians did it, & says one of the volunteers, Mooney, saw Indian tracks. The Board, who sat to-day on the affair, could come to no conclusion except that the Commissary was not to blame, which is the main thing always expected of a Board.

Fort Thompson, which lay on the route of the volunteers from Fort Mead, has been burnt up by the volunteers, who set the woods on fire. To-day large volumes of smoke has canopied the sky, & as the wind has blown strongly from the fire (7 miles off) towards us, some alarm felt. We are persecuted but do not wish to be burnt. . . .

The other day Louis conducted Terrill & me to a fine sulphur spring about ¾ mile below the landing, on a branch of the Caloosa Hatchee. Afterwards Terrill, the Doctor & myself visited it again & brought away one canteen's full. The place is a good one for the Indians to murder a small party, but the spring is tempting.

Why did the Major keep that orderly waiting outside his quarters that coldest night till long after taps? No wonder men break down when every duty becomes so uselessly onerous, every burden grievous. One never knew a more completely depressed, disgusted set of officers & men than this command. I asked the orderly why he had not brought over his overcoat? He replied, "I might as well bring blanket & all." Wheelock gave him a blanket. The last few verses of the 5th chapter [of] Galatians come in play at this place.

Felt hugely inclined to be sick last night. Had the usual symptoms of the prevailing fever: headache & sickness at the stomach. Took a shanghai quickstep & got up some perspiration. We must have looked frisky to the fairies themselves last night. All the young officers went running to & fro in the moonlight *à la shanghai* to keep warm. . . .

Jan. 1st 1857

Fort Center. By what concatenation of events I find myself here I scarcely know how to detail. On the evening of the 22d [December] came Gen'l Harney to Fort Deynaud. He did not stick his nose inside the room from which I had been three weeks previously ejected "in anticipation of his arrival." He criticised the manner in which the men were dressed & drilled in the heat of the day. There was a talk of moving the post to some healthier spot if found in the vicinity, & the General made an arrangement to meet Major Tom at the lower Steam Boat landing at 9 the following morn to look at a site near there.

On [that] morn the Major was an hour behind his time, & the General had shut himself in his state room, mad. When the former appeared, the latter stormed, & made some disparaging remarks about drilling in the sun, & the uniform hat which the General denominated "fog-stacks." <<I fancy that the General's mind had been running on the days when Tom was an airy aide on General Scott's staff in Mexico and now needed "taking down a little." *C'est possible.*>> It was said the General had ordered the Captain of the steamer to put off, telling him "he wouldn't wait longer for Jesus Christ himself." But this is apocryphal—though characteristic. . . .>

Having been summoned to attend a Court Martial at Fort Myers, I had intended to take the *Ranger,* but arrived at the wharf too late. Thinking the official visit would last some time, I turned off the road to visit a little sulphur spring. And so took the "mail express" and shot an opossum on the way down, for the Fort Myers mess.

I interviewed the general at Fort Myers next day and reported the condition of my company. The general questioned me in a quizzical way, but I assured him [that] if suffered to move my company I could quickly make it more efficient for the field and thereupon I volunteered for the first rough service. The general smiled but gave me no satisfaction. Next morning I left for Punta Rosa and spent nearly a week [on Sanibel Island] with Captain McCown, hunting and fishing—with spiritual rappings at night communicating with a spirit that had lived on the island, but was neither fisherman, Spaniard nor gentleman in search of health. The spirit admitted itself finally to be a "woman," but not a Yankee—rapping hard. The spirit predicted among other things that I should join Capt. McCown with my company for Cape Sable. Surely there was something in the air, but the spirit had not caught on.

On returning to Fort Myers the first news I heard was that my old Company C was ordered to Fort Center and Co. L, Major Williams' company, down to Fort Myers! "Glory to God!" I exclaimed and I never have spent a happier Christmas holiday than I did next day, notwithstanding the gloomy predictions of the staff that I could not have this or that, as everybody, even the doctors, and everything, trains, tools, etc., were held back at Fort Myers for the great move into the big cypress contemplated by the general himself. Yes, I could have two supply wagons for Fort Center and, leaving them to catch up, I took horse for Fort Deynaud.

<On the morning of Sunday the 28th [December] <<my lucky day in all the wars>> I started my company for Fort Center. There was some delay getting off in consequence of a drunken teamster who had suffered three mules to get loose. I had him dragged at the wagon tail during the day's march, which quite sobered him, & taught him a useful lesson. The soldiers all carried their guns loaded, & knapsacks & forty rounds ammunition. We encamped at Half Way Hammock, distance from Deynaud about 15 miles. The tramp seemed little to me, but Hascall was quite glad to reach camp.

I determined to make it a rule to set my men their example, & preferred marching on foot with them to riding horseback. The effect was good. Even Hascall, whose legs are short & quarters fat, declared next day he was glad we had walked; he felt so much better for it.

Another march of about the same distance brought us to our destination. As we came to the point where the road touches close to the river we saw a beautiful grotto formed by the branches & dependent Spanish mosses of one huge live oak over another. The breeze swayed the long airy gossamer stalactites, till it seemed as if some beautiful cave had become alive in every part, lost its cold stiffness & swung its weird like arms & vaulted chambers to some melodious chant.>

We found Fort Center lying near a great Indian mound rising, with a green tree on its top, from an immense tract of saw-grass, prairie and swamp, with clumps of palmetto and lines of live oak, bordering on Lake Okeechobee, and looking both oriental and tropical. But the site of the old fort itself was so choked up with weeds and scrub palmetto that we had to cut and slash our way up to it, [where] we [rested], got out our camp kettles and mess pans, ate dinner and pitched tents while Pincher went nosing and snuffing around for rats and other small deer. Water fowl, gull and duck, came wheeling over us in single file or battalions as if to reconnoiter the invaders of their vast solitude and fishing grounds.

Of course we had brought along a sutler boy. His name was Gus. He had fine black eyes and yellow hair, an inconvenient memory for debts and a hobby for snake root, which he freely presented to the men for all their ailments. But now as the men were too busy to mind him, Gus went fishing.

Whatever the cause, it is astonishing how the men picked up without a doctor. The sick report, over which I had to preside in my ignorance, soon fell down to the small digits. The medicine chest consisted of anti-bilious pills, quinine, and a morning salutation. The men, of their own accord, mostly, seemed to learn how to shoot and they were never refused to go hunting—at their own risk. I brought along a few books. I was pleased to learn that Fort Center had been named for the lamented Lieut. Center,[17] adjutant of the Infantry, who I had often seen at Detroit.

The battle of Okeechobee ranks among the most noted Indian contests known to our history, and as one of the severest since Wayne's[18] battle of the Miami, and I felt that I stood on classic ground at Fort Center. Col. Zachary Taylor says in his report of the battle that he moved down the west side of the Kissimmee River, towards Lake Istokpoga, which empties into Lake Okeechobee. He took this route partly to cooperate with the general's movement, but mainly "because he knew a portion of the hostiles were to be found in this direction."

Late in the evening of the first day's march, the Indian Chief, Jumper, his family, part of his band, and a few negroes came in. Alligator sent word that he was coming in. But placing no confidence in that treacherous chief, Taylor put himself at the head of all his mounted men and pushed on, crossing at Istokpoga Inlet—just above Fort Center. He soon heard that not only the Miccosukees but the Coacoochee and Alligator, with other chiefs and a large body of Seminoles, all well armed, were encamped at a hammock near the cypress swamp. He found their fires still burning, quantities of beef lying on the ground and other evidence of sudden hasty departure.

A young Indian warrior, well armed, was captured and he pointed out a dense hammock only a mile off where the hostiles were formed for battle, "with a swamp in their front impassable for horses and nearly covered with a thick growth of saw grass, five feet high and about knee deep in mud and water, which extended to the left as far as the eye could reach, and to the

17. Lt. John P. Center (30th, USMA 1833) was killed on Christmas Day, 1837, at Okeechobee, Florida.

18. Referring to Gen. "Mad" Anthony Wayne (1745–1796) and the Battle of Fallen Timbers, where on August 20, 1794, forces under his command defeated the Miami Indians of the Ohio Valley. The battle led to the treaty of Greenville, by which the Indians ceded the land that now makes up most of Ohio and parts of Indiana, Michigan, and Illinois. Wayne commanded at Detroit in 1796.

right a part of the swamp and hammock we had just passed through (he says) ran a deep creek."

At this place the final disposition for attack was made. The volunteers and Morgan's spies, under Col. Gentry, formed the first line in extended order, instructed to enter the hammock and in the event of being attacked and hard pressed, fall back in the rear of the regulars of the Fourth and Sixth Infantry—the First Infantry being held in reserve. At the borders of the hammock the volunteers and spies received a heavy fire from the enemy and fought well until Col. Gentry fell mortally wounded, when they broke for their baggage and horses—instead of the rear of the second line, nor could they again be brought into action as a body.

The weight of the enemy's fire was principally concentrated on five companies of the Sixth Infantry, which not only stood firm but continued to advance until their gallant commander, Lieutenant Colonel [Alex R.] Thompson, and his adjutant, Lieutenant Center, were killed, and every officer and most of the non-commissioned officers of those companies were either killed or wounded—one of the companies having but four members left, when that portion of the regiment retired to a short distance and again reformed.

Lieutenant Colonel [William S.] Foster, of the Fourth Infantry, with six companies, amounting in all to but one hundred and sixty men, gained the hammock in good order. Here he was joined by the two remaining companies of the Sixth and a company of volunteers, continued to drive the enemy for a considerable time and by a change of front kept on driving until he reached the great lake, Okeechobee, which was in the rear of the enemy's position and on which their encampment extended for more than a mile.

Meantime, Captain Allen, with two companies of mounted infantry, had been ordered to examine the swamp and hammock off to the right and in case he should not find the enemy in that direction he was to return to the baggage and advance on hearing heavy firing. As soon as Allen was found advancing, Taylor ordered the First Infantry, Colonel Davenport, to move to the left and gain the enemy's right flank, "which order was executed in the promptest manner possible." Then the enemy gave one more fire and retreated, being pursued by the First, Fourth and Sixth Infantry and some of the rallied volunteers, until near night, and until these troops were nearly exhausted. The enemy was driven in all directions.

This account of the battle is given as nearly as convenient in the words of Taylor's modest official report—he does not take half the credit that was his due, first for the masterly movement around the lake, by which the enemy were compelled to fight with the lake in their rear and second, for the conduct of the battle itself, over ground next to impassable, by arrangements made and orders given before hand to meet every emergency.

Far from self glorification, he praises only his officers and men and mourns their losses, adding "Here I trust I may be permitted to say that I experienced one of the most trying scenes of my life, and he who could have looked on it with indifference, his nerves must have been differently organized from my own. Besides the killed, there lay one hundred and twelve wounded officers and soldiers, who had accompanied me one hundred and forty-five miles, most of the way through an unexplored wilderness, without guides, who had gallantly beaten the enemy in his strongest position and who had to be conveyed back through swamps and hammocks from whence we set out without any apparent means of doing so."

He carried his sick and wounded back "on rude litters constructed with the ax and knife alone, from poles and dry hides fortunately found at the enemy's encampment." Verily, as General Sherman once exclaimed: "War is Hell!" and of such was the first Florida war.

A block house roost, ascended by a ladder, was all that remained of old Fort Center, and thither Lieutenant Hascall and I climbed to survey the country by day and to sleep at night. The lake is a shallow affair, but broad. Fort McRae, on the opposite, eastern side, was invisible. It was commanded by our old instructor in philosophy, Joe Bobs (Captain Roberts) of the Fourth Artillery, and we were to supply and keep up communication with that invisible post, and be ready for the next movement against the invisible enemy, whose forefathers raised this mound, and held their ghost dances hereabouts and on Istokpoga, or "Dead Man's Lake," nearby. The presiding genius over the scene seemed to be a solitary crow, perched on a cabbage tree, which o'ertopped the mound.

Winter passed monotonously by. We planted our radishes, lettuce, tomatoes and peas, and tried to be contented over the books and newspapers—which furnished food for conversation, which latter sometimes lagged. The Florida "crackers" told us of a tradition that the Indians had fixed their final stand against the whites at one of the mounds. We hoped it might be this one.

We grew tired of everything, tired of wading in the water for game and tired of each other, nearly to the point of fighting. Such was life at a small outpost in Florida at intervals. The region seemed to be a land of water, and this lake the end of a chain of lakes and rivers stretching far up into the peninsula, inviting connection by canal with the river of St. John, that might be navigable for light-draught steamers connecting Jacksonville with Tampa and thus connecting Charleston with the city of Havana.

Spring came and everybody was in motion. Troops had been sent out from every other post, south, east and west of us, and here and there a skulking savage was shot and now we hailed the order for us to make ready as part of a movement to envelop and drive the refugees *en masse* to a final stand, either to fight or to make peace and quit the country.

Major Williams came up with his own and another company and took command for a scout on the Kissimmee. Mackinaw boats and dugouts were accumulated, and thirty days' rations issued (the boats could hold but thirty) for a searching expedition as far up the great chain of rivers and lakes as hostile signs might warrant.

A soldier on water is very much like a sailor on horseback and the grinning alligators seemed to leer at our frantic attempts at rowing. Fortunately the Thalopopokatchee, which we soon entered, ran up stream, as it seemed, and the wind was accommodating. So that with a little practice we made headway and reached the north shore of Okeechobee just before night and went into camp. Nothing could be more beautiful than our canopy of cypress trees with their Gothic arches of branches and long hanging mosses, lit up by the camp fires and stars. And here we rested our tired limbs and slept after supper and tattoo—as much as the mosquitoes would let us, guarded by the scouts thrown far out, and the sleepy camp sentinels.

Next day, nearing the mouth of the Kissimmee, for which Lieutenant Bagley of the Fourth and Captain Mickler, the guide, had been marching on the shore, we saw the two row back post haste. We soon heard that the enemy were nearby, only a few hundred yards distant. Most of the command was immediately put ashore and deployed. The men dashed ahead fearlessly enough, but terribly encumbered by the thick, tall saw grass and palmetto roots, which soon broke up the line somewhat, and put every man of us to his trumps.

For my part, trying to lead as best I could, sinking to my waist and deeper, I slashed away with my sabre for a path and sometimes threw myself back-forwards to lead my men. But the fleeter enemy had skedaddled out of sight. It seems that two of them were fishing from a canoe, when discovered by Bagley and the guide, whose boat party gave chase, firing as they went. The Indians made for the shore for dear life. One of them was hit and seen to fall just as their canoe struck bottom, but he scrambled to land and the two ran through the woods yelling like fiends.

The only trophy of our pursuit was the captured canoe, containing turtle and fish enough for a considerable camp. But no vestige even of a camp rewarded our subsequent search. The two Indian fishermen may have come from a distance, or the main party, if there were one, might have escaped in their light canoes by the numberless shallow streams, which coursed through the hammock. The only hope that we could entertain was that the troops operating on our flanks might intercept the fugitives.

And so, next morning, our little fleet, led by Major Williams in the cutter *Page*, with Captain Mickler, the guide and pilot, rowed away into and up the Kissimmee and the lakes, scouting betimes, with little or no satisfaction. On the way we had come precious near swamping the boats and contents several times, and as it was we lost clothing, equipments and ammunition galore, and nearly stove in our boats in bad weather. Compared with Colonel Taylor's battle of Okeechobee, this scout may seem a small matter, but it is written to show what is little known of the minor obstacles in the way of campaigning in Florida.

In order to cover as much ground as possible and to gain a more intimate knowledge of the country, making maps and taking notes, our command was divided and continued the work up to Lake Cypress. At the completion of this work, Major Williams established a new post on Lake Kissimmee and I returned with my company to Fort Center. Then, with the knowledge gained by the various scouting parties, the troops had picked up and killed or captured so many small parties of the guerrilla bands that General Harney was relieved and ordered to a more important command in Utah, leaving Colonel Gustavus Loomis, a West Point graduate of 1811, with the Fifth Infantry, Fourth Artillery, "crackers" and mounted volunteers to finish the work. This the old soldier did so effectively that, during the year 1858, the remainder of the Seminole tribe was brought in and nearly all sent to the Florida Indian reservation in Arkansas.

The last black slave of the Seminoles was living in 1901, an ugly wench named Hannah—once owned by one of the last of the chiefs, Tallahassee. Quite a few of the Seminoles still live in the Everglades now as peaceful and indolent as they once were formidable and warlike.

AN INCIDENT OF THE FLORIDA CAMPAIGN[19]
<On the 4th [of] March, 1857, the little garrison at Fort Center, Florida, was considerably stirred by the sight of an Indian scalp. A volunteer Captain (Johnstone) held it up by a braid of hair a foot or so long. The scalp itself was two or three inches square. The sight of it shocked more than one.

19. This incident, recorded in OBW's *Florida Journal*, is apparently a detailed account of an event also recorded in a small leatherbound diary for the year 1857. In the entry for March 4, OBW comments that the sight of the scalp was "revolting. Such practices by white men are a poor comment on white nature."

The commanding officer shuddered at the sight & exclaimed "Horrible! horrible!—Sit down, captain, sit down."

Another officer contracted his brows at the sight & turned away in disgust, muttering between his teeth, "Ask a man to sit down with you who has scalped an Indian!"

"Where did you take it?" asked a youngster.

"About ten or twelve miles north of the Ford. The advance guard saw him as he was crossing from the sawgrass to a little hammock. They surrounded the hammock & sent word back to me. We rode up & charged the hammock. Two or three of the boys fired at him, & he snapped at them."

"Why didn't you take him alive & get the $5,000 reward?"

"We wanted to. I told him to come out, we wouldn't hurt him; but he snapped back his gun at me & I drew up & hit him just here"—pointing behind his left side.

Some gentleman just now spoke about scalping Indians. "I didn't know it was contrary to the regulations. They have often been scalped before."

"I don't know anything about it," said the commanding officer.

The Captain was a shrewd-looking man in a brown coat & red face & whiskers, with settled shoulders & a square topped hat. Around his waist was buckled a revolver. His antecedents were that he was Captain of a Company which he had employed to drive cattle. For a long time then no one knew where he was. While others had been riding hard, sleeping wet, & going hungry through the campaign & so far without seeing or catching an Indian, this shirk, on his way to his company, had the luck to fall in with & kill "the first Indian."

I heard from a Floridian guide at the post who it was that finished the life of the victim & had him pointed out to me. He was a tall, well-looking youth in a dirty white felt hat, soldier's blue jacket, nondescript pants, one spur & holes in his stockings. The guide also learned some particulars of the last scenes.

The Indian had five balls in him when he fell. They asked him if he could live. He shook his head, but looked them calmly in the face. They put many questions concerning his tribe. He refused to answer.

"God d——n him," said one. "I'll make him answer," & pointed his gun toward his heart. The Indian started, turned his face toward the speaker, & threw a fierce look at him.

"Let's scalp him," said another of the gang. At this likewise the Indian started. But these were the only two occasions in which he evinced any emotion. There appearing no hope of his recovery, they put an end to his suffering and took his scalp.

On the 5th of March Fort Center was again aroused. A party of volunteers came stringing in, carrying on an animated conversation with the soldiers. The day after the events just recited happened, Lt. Johnstone, son of the Captain, was returning from a scout to the northwest of their camp on the Ford of the Thalopopokatchee——

"When," said one of the volunteers, "we struck a trail. It led to a sawgrass swamp. We dismounted from our horses & came to an island on which was a pretty little Indian garden & a hut, fire & so forth. Then we saw the squaw. As soon as she saw us she snatched up her baby & ran screaming as loud as she could scream. She ran right fast too. We had to run her down three or four miles, she screaming all the time. Sergt. Stanley caught her. When the boys came up she gathered her baby to her bosom & looked frightened to death. She thought we were going to shoot her. We gave her two blankets. She doubled up one of them——

"What did she have on?"

"Nothing but a short skirt." She tied the blanket round her neck & that covered her well. Then she took the other blanket, folded it in three, put her baby in it & threw the little thing over her back & shoulders.

"Is she handsome?"

"Very good looking—about twenty or twenty-two. In the camp we found a whole hat full of beads, some skins, old fashioned coffee pot & cooking utensils. There were tracks of a man & another child. She said she had three children."

"Would she talk?"

"Not for a long time; she was frightened. Every time one of us came up she would hug the child & look towards Sergeant Stanley as her protector. And when Stanley was out of her sight she looked terribly frightened till he returned. She held up her three fingers when Duke—Duke talks Indian a *leetle*—asked her about the children, but I don't believe she's got but two. When we brought her a horse to ride she just touched her foot to the stirrup & lit on the saddle like a bird. She rode part of the way & walked some."

"When I met her," interposed one of the bystanders, "she was just sitting on her horse suckling her baby."

"Is she the wife of him killed the day before?"

"I don't know. When we showed her his scalp, she burst out crying—she knew it, but whether it was her husband's ——"

"Showed her the scalp?"

"Y-a-i-s—I felt sorry for her. I felt sorry for the man. But, lieut*ai*nant, when I saw him lying thar dead" (this is the scalper speaking now) "I couldn't help a-thinking of my uncle, aunt & cousin whom the Indians murdered & cut all to pieces. I couldn't help feeling glad to see him when I thought of them."

"Well," said another, "the Indians follow close. We found a blanket in their camp which one of Capt Johnstone's men had lost the day before. That 'ar Indian was a good looking chap; he was about my height (six feet) & not over eighteen or twenty. He had on a hunting shirt with a fringe & new buckskin leggings sewed tight to his legs so as not to come off."

"What sort of gun?"

"He threw that away so we couldn't find it."

The party was mostly broken by this time. But one old pioneer said as he turned away——

"That chap's family'll be revenged on somebody yet to pay for this."

They took her [the squaw] to Fort Myers. Passing through Fort Deynaud the ladies clothed her & the child in white ladies' frocks, which she took off in the guard house, resuming her own simple apparel. They dressed her up in one of the frocks to appear before Gen'l Harney. But she doffed it again. She saw a string on one of the men's hat's which had tied the hair of her little girl & she burst out crying & cried till they gave it her. When she reached Fort Myers the General threatened to hang her to the tallest tree in the cypress swamp if she didn't tell all about her people. Alas! poor squaw, what will become of thee, for if thou don't betray thy people, will they not burn thee, or what not?

MODERN WARFARE
[A Treatise]
An army in modern warfare means a brevet officer with his brevet command. A brevet officer is commonly a soldier who has reaped laurels by going where other soldiers go & who, by a discriminating Congress, is designated as one who forever after is fit for no practical purpose whatever, except to clamor for a brevet command, tyranise [*sic*] over his former equals, & abuse his superiors.

Warfare under such men consists in disgusting those under them, keeping their own feet dry in all swamp operations (now the field of military achievements), while they heap unnecessary labor on others, & making long papers giving learned reasons why nothing has been accomplished, called reports.

The object for an army in modern warfare consists in the fifty-two blank forms of the Quartermaster Dpt., & one thousand & one blank forms pertaining to the other departments, a bale of red tape to each officer (called officers' baggage), one horse in case of need for provisions, i.e. when alligators or other indigenous food of the climate gives out, & a musket to each man, purchased from the Chinese government.

A Depot is a place where necessary clothing is left while troops are in the field, modern improvements having changed the ancient meaning of the term, which was a place from which clothing & other supplies were furnished to troops in the field.

Reinforcements consists in picking up raw recruits least acquainted with the use of fire arms or horses, & sending them to the most sickly places at the worst seasons of the year—this being considered a great improvement on ancient usages.

This certainly has its advantages. It brings into play the foreign element of national greatness, an emigrant from frigid Norway being of great use in the torrid zone of Florida. Another advantage is the opportunity it affords a bountiful government to spend money, one of these recruits costing as much as a native & lasting but three months, the government thus multiplying its generous donations twenty-fold every five years. . . .

Head Quarters in modern military dictionaries means a paper factory. The mother factory being at Washington, & the smaller ones wherever brevet officers command. To these factories all the army is busily engaged forwarding paper rags [called] uniforms. This forms the test of military ability, buttons having engaged the profoundest researches of our chief military men [of] this century.

As a first requisite [the] uniform must not be adopted to the sort of service required. It must be proved to have been tried in Algeria by the French—if it answered there it must needs do here, on the same principle that, as the porters in Smyrna carry a load of eight hundred pounds on their backs, every American must do the same, & because John Chinaman eats rat pies, this should form our national dessert.

Campaigns. These are conducted on political principles of Expediency—there being no sort of difference in this respect between ancient monarchs who made war at their soverign wills, & modern administrations which order campaigns whenever an election is to be carried. A campaign closes with equal caprice & facility.

Thus, to carry the election in Florida, a vigorous campaign is ordered there against the Indians that for twenty years have served this political pretext, & a vigorous general is ordered to the spot. The election carried, the campaign is over, the vigorous general is ordered to another field where political expediency requires the display of energy, & from there on to the end of the chapter. Thus it turns out that military men become the best politicians by governmental influences, & aspire to the presidency in due course of time.

Military Education. The ancient maxim that "money is a good soldier's mill ore [illegible word]," is now reversed. A young man finding he cannot make money in civil walks is provided with a commission & gets on as well as the rest of them, the military profession having become reduced to little other than the paper maker's trade, at which any fool can serve & make a living.

This article cannot be wound up more gracefully than by the following conundrum & epitaph. What resemblance is there between the celebrated Eastern Conqueror Genghis Khan & a modern commander? Ans. One is Genghis Khan, the other Genghis Khant.

Epitaph
Here lies great Genghis buried low,
All men are shams says he.
And he of all men ought to know,
For *chief of shams* was he.

Camp Humbug, Kissimee River Florida, May 28/57.>

NINE

The Coming of the War Storm

[In mid-June 1857 Willcox's company joyously received the news that it was being recalled from the malarious swamps of the Everglades to Fort Myers, on the Gulf coast. After eight long months of fighting mosquitoes, yellow fever, and boredom, Willcox had had enough of Florida and the army. Realizing that the service, with its slow promotion and long absences from home, was no place for a family man, he resigned his commission, departing Fort Myers July 9, on leave of absence pending the effective date of his resignation.

Returning to Detroit, Willcox undertook the study of law and the life of a regular citizen, only to find it was a life for which he was entirely unsuited. He soon became miserable. Civil life, and civilians in particular, proved altogether too civil for his tastes. The fact that the Panic of 1857 hit just as his resignation took effect only added to his disillusionment.

Facing the daily drudgery of the law office, Willcox longed for another kind of life, the life of a writer. Although he had achieved a degree of success with the publication of his first novel, Shoepac Recollections, *a semiautobiographical sketch of his life in old Detroit, his subsequent works would not prove as popular.* Faca: An Army Reminisce, *about the sister of a young officer, would be his last novel.*

Unhappy as a civilian and frustrated by his lack of literary success, Orlando Willcox, like so many other former officers (Ulysses S. Grant among them) was in the end rescued from obscurity by the coming of war. On May 1, 1861, as one of

*the leading military men in his state, Willcox was commissioned colonel of the
1st Michigan Infantry.]*

I RESIGNED my commission of first lieutenant in the Fourth Artillery,
U.S.A. [effective] September 10, 1857, after ten years of interesting service
but slow promotion. My taste for books, often interrupted, returned to old
Blackstone and the law, and the law became my new profession in partnership with Eben N. Willcox, my brother, at my old home in Detroit. Here I
studied and practiced with little or no distinction professionally but with
keen interest in public affairs—an interest particularly owing to the alarming drift of politics toward disunion. . . .

CITIZEN WILLCOX: LIFE AMONG THE LUNATICS
JOURNAL ENTRIES, 1857–58[1]

Reached Detroit & rejoined my family on the 24th July. Meantime "Faca"
was published in Dec./56, & "West Point" was begun in monthly series
in *Stephens' Illustrated New Monthly.*[2] The story ended with the October
number.

July 27th
Began study in a law office with a view to the legal profession, & from
this time a new life begins.

RULES FOR THE NEW LIFE.
To remember that the period of work has come, that idleness, even when
there seems nothing to do, is to be done away with.

That, whereas before one's manners had little bearing, now they are
everything, next to one's principles.

The old habits must be subjected to the most severe pruning & every
weed pulled out by the roots.

1. These entries are taken from OBW's *Second Journal.*
2. Like OBW's first novel, *Shoepac Recollections, Faca: An Army Reminisce* (J. French & Co.)
was published under OBW's pseudonym "Walter March." The book did not actually appear
until 1857. The fictitious "West Point: A Tale" is the story of three West Point cadets. The
main character, Philip Smith, is based largely on Willcox himself, and the other cadets bear the
characteristics of OBW's friends. Both *Shoepac Recollections* and "West Point" are semiautobiographical, while *Faca*, the story of an army officer's sister, bears little resemblance to OBW's life.

Care comes, let it not be anticipated. Past experience teaches trust in Providence, which ought to lighten the burden.

Never to forget that the old was renounced for its evils, not dreaming there were no evils to be met with in the new, but expecting many.

Guard well the heart: nourish but not pamper the body: & resist to the uttermost all injuries that threaten the brain. Fort Myers, Florida, June 28th 1857.

Sept. 9th
Caro Farnsworth married.

Sept. 10th
My resignation as an officer of the army takes effect to-day.

In order to gain success, certain rules must be followed—though success may happen, or light upon one, as it were, by accident. But one should look to Providence to bless his diligence. In the general affairs of life, many things are effected, with little knowledge, by acting upon public credulity. This is unworthy, for even success without consciousness of merit or ability cannot be satisfactory.

On the whole, it seems that in order to succeed, sober & continued labor must be followed, & nothing is truer than the maxim that labor is its own reward. The mind is apt at delusions. One of these is a certain disposition to put off learning or doing a thing thoroughly until some other opportunity. This will breed a superficial way of learning & doing. Better do a little & well, than much & not well. Some successful scholars owe their excellence to having studied a single book. Review & review & review.

HINTS LEARNED BY HARD TIMES
On the 24th Aug. 1857, a panic began with the failure of the Ohio Life Insurance & Trust Co., which bred the hardest times yet known in my life.[3] Through it I observed men narrowly, & found how changed they become by pecuniary changes.

A few lessons might be improved as beacon lights, viz., not to publish your own losses, but rather conceal them. That when things look darkest, light may be at hand. Never to put yourself in a situation of the dearest friends *dependent*, nor assume a controversial attitude on the *defensive*.

3. The Panic of 1857 and the depression that followed brought a dramatic end to more than a decade of U.S. growth and prosperity, and it had worldwide consequences.

The worst feature of these bad-faced times is the grossly apparent ugliness & selfishness of the human heart. A certain demoralisation seems to have taken place, so that men do what I am sure many of them would scorn to do were it not for the cover of hard times.

December 3rd

At a meeting of the citizens of Detroit this p.m., a proposition to authorise the Common Council to buy a site for an Alms House & a Work House on the Melcher farm was voted down in the most disorderly & violent manner. The author of all the opposition, who by false representation of every sort had stirred up this hostility, remarked triumphantly to Dr. Russell on coming out of the meeting, "Now we shall have a Work House!"

There is no end to human calamity. On the same day with the above, a meeting of the stockholders of the D & M R.R. Co., voted out its president, H. N. Walker,[4] & voted in N. P. Stewart in the most uncourteous & hasty manner. Walker has just returned from Europe where he has brought nearly to completion the negotiation for a loan of L150,000 from the Great W. Canada R.R. Co. It has looked squally for some time. Circulars & requests for proxies have been flying freely. But no one knew for what mysterious purpose till now. Walker thinks himself a much abused man.

At times I am sick of the state of things in civil life. I seem to have missed the principal things for which I resigned. Home seems a place all artificial & conventional, & the social beauties, so attractive to one wandering at a distance, are like the flowers of a garden on a dusty street.

From the necessary restraints of the army I have fallen, it would seem, into the unnecessary provincial limitations of a watchful, envious, jealous, fault-finding, money-making neighborhood. Almost every day I feel it so strongly as to bring myself nearly to the resolution to apply for a new commission in the army. Still I do not know how much of this dissatisfaction may not arise from the universal excuse these days, viz., Hard Times. Then I stifle my indignant insurrection of feelings, & plod on in the mazes of the law.

O! what a very proper set they are at home! The fact is I am not a proper man. I never dare hope to be. It makes me feel at times as if I were in a straight jacket, to look on the very faces of the polite lunatics.

4. H. N. Walker (1813–1886) was a leading member of the Detroit bar, Michigan attorney general (1843–1845) and state representative (1844). In 1849 he was one of the founders of the Detroit Savings Fund Institute.

If there is a man whose memory haunts me it is Charles Lamb.[5] I envy the rogue more than any king or kaiser that ever lived. A picture of him in an elegant morning robe (& slippers to match), sitting at a mahogany desk with his rich & sparkling pen just poised like a falcon to pounce on some gentle, quaint, dove-like conceit & fly away with a laugh, is ever before me.

I agree with Tristram Shandy, a cleanly shaved chin & a fresh shirt for an author. I would have every thing around me neat & trim, rich & elegant, & be an author. No love for a garret. I wrote the last chapters of "West Point" in a garret & ill luck betide it!

Oh a diamond pointed pen

And a seat in a rich boudoir!

Me thinks I could fling pearls & rubies every time, like bubbles from a gold-mounted meerschaum pipe. I'd have sliding satin wood panels, open only to the touch of Marie, & one side of my room should be of glass & look out on a flower garden with two rows of trees in the middle of it. And far far away would I banish every polite inanity with a man's face, or a woman's either. I begin to hate the frigid manners of the north. Let me go south & die of wantonness.

Tis said the sculptor dies a hard death, because he makes faces—and *busts!* I do not wonder at it. Most busts are horrid things. You think they must take cold in their bare neck & shoulders. Poor Washington looks as if he'd lost all his teeth & tried hard to conceal the defect by keeping his benevolent lips well closed. Byron is always turned around so far that you think his neck is almost twisted in two.

Passed the Bar by examination on the 23rd Dec. 1857, at Circuit court. . . .

December 30th

Maj. Maclin, paymaster U.S.A., urges me to apply for a majority in the new regiments.

December 31st

A very pleasant tea party at home last night. The Bishop, son-in-law & daughter, Captains [George G.?] Mead & Scott & ladies, & the Whipples [were] present. Army society has an invincible charm.

5. Charles Lamb (1775–1834), English essayist, critic, and poet. His most popular work, *Essays of Elia* (1823), contains such memorable essays as "A Dissertation upon Roast Pig" and "The Praise of Chimney Sweepers."

On the morn. of January 4th [1858] a telegraph to Eben & me announced the death of poor George Davis. We started for Chicago at 12 M. with mother, took up Julia at Kalamazoo.

George died with a song on his lips. His heart was diseased. Was buried in the most solemn manner with both Christian & Masonic rites. He left poor Mira with seven children. . . .

June 28, 1858. Our second daughter was born this a.m. at about six o'clock, at the house of her grandfather.[6]

Sept. 26, 1858
RESOLUTIONS & REVOLUTIONS

Times are these for resolutions new, when revolutions of feeling sweep over my heart. I pause, after a year's experience in the new life, not to mourn over the change, but to turn that experience to account.

I have tasted the cup of civil life. I have gone through the shock. I have seen how completely men esteem you for your rank in life & read in their eyes my decline, as if they were letting me down, link by link, into the well where they drop the things they wish to forget.

And yet my resolute purpose survives. Yet do I despise the flesh pots of Egypt. The desert will not always last.

I feel that my wife & little ones are made happier. That my mind is [illegible word] by the change. That the future is widened.

The Law, my new profession, is nobler & greater than the profession of arms. And the same elements of success & satisfaction are to be found in each, with this advantage in the former, that it will never admit of the consuming rest that eats out the latter. More diligence, more study, more temperance, more reliance on work than on fortune, calls now for *sleepless* effort.

It is on this step I pause, finding that the habits of a life must be revolutionised. That the labor is so great & the time so small, that heart, mind & body must cast its slough—the cumbrous accretion of too much leizure & too little labor [are] the carcase of idleness.

To come to the point. Indulgence in meats & drinks must be cut off as indulgence. Fitful reading, surface skimming, day dreaming, word spinning, must be dropped. The love of display must give way to the necessities of each case. Growth must begin on the solid foundations of stability. So much for the mind.

6. Little is known of OBW's second daughter, named Caroline "Caro," after Marie's sister. She died sometime before January 1860.

No new life without a renewal of the Spirit. The heart must change. Here I must fall back on the beginning of my Confidence. Days of my innocent, noble boyhood come again! Days of holy seeking, nights of retrospection & prayer, rekindle your torch. Light of the world, shining in the dark, O religion, shed your pure lustre on my bowed head, sanctify my waiting heart.

RAISING THE REGIMENT

Having been intimate with army officers from the South, and stationed long at Southern posts, I knew the earnestness of the Southern people, and deprecated the anti-slavery agitation and the bitterly uncompromising spirit exhibited on both sides. As a Democrat I took my stand with Stephen A. Douglas, who seemed to me to inherit the mantle of Henry Clay for the Union and its compromises.

It may now seem strange, but many men of the rank and file of the Republican Party in Michigan, who denounced the South most frantically, thereby provoking hostilities to the extent of their influence, leaned over on the shoulders of William H. Seward[7] in the belief that there would be no war, that the South was bluffing (as if they were not bluffing, too!) or that if hostilities should break out it would be a "sixty days affair."

This sentiment I had occasion to test in the winter of 1860 and 1861. Having taken some interest in the militia and being at the time just mentioned a member of the State Military Board, I was called upon to go before the legislature out at Lansing to urge necessary preparation for the coming crisis. In the course of my address, after speaking of my somewhat intimate knowledge of Southern sentiment and inviting attention to the obvious drift of affairs, I urged the raising of at least two regiments by our state to meet the expected call of President Lincoln for the preservation of the Union. The majority of the legislature listened incredulously and although the influence of their great party leaders, Ex-Governor Moses Wisner, Governor Austin Blair, and perhaps Zachariah Chandler,[8] was exerted for

7. William Henry Seward, governor of New York (1838–1842) and U.S. senator (1849–1861), was the front-runner for the Republican presidential nomination in 1860 but was defeated by Lincoln, who named him secretary of state, a position he retained through the Andrew Johnson administration as well.

8. Moses Wisner, noted Detroit attorney and Michigan governor (1859–1861). He served as colonel of the 22d Michigan Infantry, posted in Kentucky. He died of typhoid at Lexington on January 5, 1864.

Austin Blair, war governor of Michigan (Republican). A strong supporter of Lincoln, Blair had at the outset of the war no funds (due to theft) to raise troops. Raising money through

legislative action, yet members seemed to be so much under the spell of Mr. Seward's "sixty day" optimism that they would go no further than to authorize the governor to muster in companies sufficient for "one or at most two regiments," and did not appropriate a single dollar even for such a purpose! Indeed, one prominent member of the senate had moved to amend the bill by inserting the word "cornfield" instead of "field" officers. Whether the well-known fact that the majority of the military board were Democrats had any influence in the opposition of the legislature, I am unable to say. But, at any rate, in consequence when the First Regiment was afterward raised, it had to be clothed and fitted out for the field by private subscription. I was appointed colonel.

While raising, or rather organizing, the First Regiment in Michigan for the War of the Rebellion, I received a hurried dispatch from [Chancellor] Tappan[9] of the University of Michigan, calling me to Ann Arbor "at once," as the students were clamorous for joining my regiment in a body. This action on the part of the students, it was thought, was probably the result of a military address made by me at the University a short time before. So far from believing that the "war scare would not last," as some public men taught, the University people seemed convinced of a prediction that I had made to them in the address, that there were Southern reasons and Southern resources for a war most likely to last as long as the War of the Revolution lasted.

I had advised that the students should form a military corps and look for commissions instead of joining the ranks as private soldiers. Fortunately this advice, combined with the influence of Chancellor Tappan and the faculty, prevailed. I am very happy to add that many of the graduates took commissions during the war and brought military distinction upon their alma mater and themselves. In reviewing the checkered course of my life, and seeing how little good I have done in the world, I must confess to some pride in the incident just mentioned.

And yet before reaching a wider field, other things occurred at home likely to puff the vanity of a young lieutenant suddenly lifted up to be a full-

---

donations, he was finally able to send the 1st Michigan Regiment to Washington ahead of schedule. He served in the U.S. Congress during Reconstruction. Zachariah Chandler, Republican senator from Michigan (1857–1874, 1879), one of the staunchest of the Radicals, and a member of the Committee on the Conduct of the War from its inception in late 1861. Following the war, Chandler pressed for the impeachment of President Johnson. Chandler served as secretary of the interior under President Grant (1875–1877). Reelected to the Senate in 1878, he died shortly after taking office, on November 1, 1879.

9. Henry P. Tappan (1805–1881), president of the University of Michigan (1852–1863).

fledged colonel. My native townspeople, with the exception of a few "dyed in the wool Democrats," who accused me of inconsistency and undue zeal, heaped more honors upon my head and the regiment I commanded, than any of us deserved before the trial of our mettle.

The war spirit was up and the earliest regiments in all the states North and South received like attentions. Sword and flag presentations were going on all over the country and the stirring notes of drum, fife and bugle were heard in every town, despite the skepticism of Northern politicians as to the earnestness of the South. Could these gentlemen but have known the correspondence then going on between the governors of Southern states, and between other leading men in that section, and even between the Southern officials and the War Department's head, John B. Floyd,[10] or could they have seen the train-loads and ship-loads of ordnance and war supplies that were being sent to Southern arsenals from towns and harbors, now revealed in the Rebellion records, it might have opened their eyes—if anything could.

In fact, not a few of our bureau officials and naval officers did know—indeed it was an open secret. Yet so blind was partisanship that some Republicans at home predicted that my regiment would be recalled before it ever reached Washington. Nevertheless, such persons were ignored and the leading men of both parties, General Cass, Henry A. Hayden, Senator Chandler, James F. Joy[11] and others, advanced their money and credit to fit out the First Michigan Regiment for "three months service." This was the period fixed by President Lincoln—probably at the suggestion of Mr. Seward, who was Secretary of State and head of the Cabinet. I do not believe that Mr. Lincoln shared those optimistic views, but, as he said later on, he "hoped to have more influence with the next Administration."

Let me quote from a careful address delivered by my dear friend, the lately deceased Colonel W. H. Withington,[12] before the Michigan Loyal Legion:

10. John B. Floyd, former governor of Virginia, served as secretary of war under President James Buchanan from 1857 until his resignation in December 1860. As a general in the C.S.A. he commanded troops at Carnifax Ferry, Western Virginia in May 1861, and in February 1862 at Fort Donelson, Tennessee. He died on August 23, 1863.

11. Henry A. Hayden was a prominent figure of the Michigan Central Railroad; James F. Joy was a noted Michigan attorney and one of the principal founders of the Michigan Central Railroad. He served as state representative from 1861 to 1862.

12. Originally a captain in the 1st Michigan Infantry, William H. Withington was mustered out on August 7, 1861, but was subsequently appointed colonel of the 17th Michigan Infantry, which he led with distinction at South Mountain (September 14, 1862). For that action he was made a brevet brigadier general (March 13, 1865).

The governors of the Cotton States took forcible possession of the forts, arsenals, navy yards and custom houses and other property, in some cases even before the states seceded. The only forts not seized were three in Florida and those in Charleston Harbor, whose final capture opened the slow moving eyelids of the North to the fact that the South knew and meant what it was doing. On the secession of Texas, the last state to go out, occurred General Twiggs' treasonable surrender in February 1861 of all the Federal military posts and property in Texas. There were eighteen of these posts and stations, with arms and stores to a large amount.

"All through these preceding overt acts, which were nothing less than levying actual war," as the gallant Withington said with emphasis, "the North stood still." This paralysis was due in part to President Buchanan's weakness towards such traitors in the Cabinet as John B. Floyd. But Buchanan's manners in the White House were very charming. The first official notice and proclamation of insurrection was made even before Lincoln's election in a message sent by the governor of South Carolina to the legislature of that state. Andrew Jackson would have hanged him higher than Haman. The Confederates' turn for surprise soon came, however. They too had failed to forecast the future. The unexpected suddenly loomed upon them in the towering form of an Awakened and United North! Let me add, in the language of Governor Blair, that "when the call came for volunteers the question was not who should go, but who should go first."

The country was ablaze. Military spirit was native in Michigan, growing up as our frontier state under so many ensigns of war, Indian, French, English and American, and tutored by so many and such brilliant war chiefs as Pontiac, Tecumseh, and soldiers like Gladwin, Hamtramck, Scott, Wayne, Harrison, Cass, Brady and a score of heroes of the War of 1812.[13] Her young men and men who had fought in Mexico were already imbued with military ardor. More or less attention had always been given to the militia and we had already a small body organized and uniformed with some field officers and twenty-eight companies, one of which, the Brady Guard of Detroit, was a crack company of fame throughout the U.S. These companies were lo-

13. Maj. Henry Gladwin, British commander at Fort Detroit from 1763 to 1764, successfully defended the post during the Ottawa Chief Pontiac's rebellion; Col. John F. Hamtrammck, a Canadian who joined the American army in 1775, commanded at Fort Detroit in 1796 and again from 1802 until his death in 1803.

cated at the principal towns and mainly sustained themselves, although they had the aid of the state government to some extent.

During the summer preceding the war the state encampment at Jackson had been well attended and fairly instructed under Colonel, afterward General, Alpheus S. Williams,[14] a Mexican veteran of repute, aided by some other men of experience. Fortunately for myself, I accepted an invitation to take a hand in the camp exercises, and I thus became acquainted with some of the noble fellows who served with me later in the war.

I had to smile as I remembered my first introduction as a boy to the old militia training—a nondescript, "hay-foot-straw-foot" affair, under Captain Cicotte.[15] The rank and file mostly spoke *patois* and were armed with old swords, shotguns and some pitch forks. As I stood by, a laughing spectator, I was suddenly ordered into the ranks and found myself a "corporal." This was, so to speak, the first "step" in my military career. And now, many years later, and almost as suddenly and unexpectedly, I found myself at the head of a fine regiment, marshalled on the Campus Martius, very near the spot of the long-ago militia training. But instead of Captain Cicotte and other rough militia officers in cocked hats and motley array, on horseback or afoot, were seated General Cass on a grandstand in company with [Colonel] Williams, the adjutant general, and the quartermaster general of the state, the mayor of the city and other officials, with a hundred or more pretty girls.

At old Fort Wayne, below Detroit, the First Michigan Infantry Volunteers had concentrated as fast as the companies were completed. I like to recall their old names: The Detroit Light Guard, Captain Lum; Jackson Grays (color company), Captain Withington; Coldwater Cadets, Captain Butterworth; Manchester Union Guard, Captain Clarkson; Ann Arbor Steuben Guard, Captain Roth; Detroit Hussars, Captain Roberts; Burr Oak Guards,

14. Alpheus S. Williams, a native of Connecticut, graduated from Yale University in 1831 and settled in Detroit, Michigan, in 1836, where he practiced law and held numerous public posts. A veteran of the Mexican War, Williams had also served as major in the Detroit Light Guard; when the Civil War came he was commander of Michigan's camp of instruction at Fort Wayne. Promoted to brigadier general in August 1861, Williams led a division in the Twelfth and later the Twentieth corps, and he commanded the Twelfth Corps at Antietam (after the fall of J. K. F. Mansfield) and at Gettysburg. He led the Twentieth Corps from time to time during Maj. Gen. W. T. Sherman's Georgia campaign and in the March to the Sea. To his men, he was "Old Pap." After the war, he served as U.S. minister to San Salvador (1866–1869) and as a U.S. representative from 1874 until his death on December 21, 1878.

15. Captain Francois Cicotte, early settler of Detroit and veteran of the War of 1812.

Captain Abbott; Ypsilanti Light Guard, Captain Whittlesey; Marshall Light Guard, Captain Hubbard; Adrian Cadets, Captain Graves.[16]

Our days at the Fort were passed in drills, dress parades and learning how to take care of ourselves on soldiers' commons, of the state. General Scott soon telegraphed to Governor Blair for "the regiment commanded by Colonel Willcox," and my friend, Major William D. Wilkins,[17] hastened to provide for transportation.

Ah, how many wives', sisters', and children's hearts quickened and how many tears started when the day came for the soldier boys to start! In the histories of regiments and campaigns, even in the biographies of officers, there is little mention of the deeper undercurrent of family bravery, suffering and fortitude, or of struggles of the hearts at home. Notwithstanding

16. Capt. Charles M. Lum, Company A, was wounded at First Bull Run. Mustered out on August 7, 1861, Lum reentered the service on November 20, 1861 as colonel, 10th Michigan, serving until October 18, 1864.

Capt. Ebenezer Butterworth, Company C, was mortally wounded at First Bull Run and died in a Confederate hospital at Charlottesville, Virginia, August 17, 1861.

Capt. Isaac L. Clarkson, Company D, served until mustered out August 7, 1861. He reentered the service six days later as captain, Company B, 17th Michigan. Wounded at Antietam, Clarkson served until October 19, 1863.

Capt. Horace S. Roberts, Company F, a Mexican War veteran, served until mustered out on August 7, 1861. He reentered the service as a lieutenant colonel in the reorganized 1st Michigan. Appointed colonel on April 28, 1862, Roberts was killed at Second Bull Run, August 30, 1862.

Capt. Ira C. Abbott, Company G, served until mustered out on August 7, 1861. He reentered the service ten days later as captain, Company B, in the reorganized 1st Michigan Infantry. By March 18, 1863, Abbott was colonel of the regiment. Wounded twice at the Battle of Fredericksburg and again at Gettysburg, he was discharged on December 22, 1864. On March 13, 1865, Abbott was brevetted brigadier general, U.S. Volunteers, for gallant and meritorious service during the war.

Capt. Franklin W. Whittlesey, Company H, served until mustered out on August 7, 1861. He reentered the service three days later as major in the reorganized 1st Michigan. Whittlesey was promoted to lieutenant colonel on April 28, 1862, and to colonel on August 30, 1862. Resigned and honorably discharged, March 18, 1863.

Capt. Devillo Hubbard, Company I.

Capt. William H. Graves, Company K, served until mustered out on August 7, 1861, reentering the service ten days later as a lieutenant colonel, 12th Michigan, and made colonel on September 1, 1862. He was discharged on June 10, 1865.

17. Maj. William D. Wilkins was inspector of the First Brigade, Michigan Militia, at the beginning of the war. Captured at the Battle of Cedar Mountain, August 9, 1862, while serving on the staff of Brig. Gen. Alpheus Williams, he spent a hellish six weeks in Libby Prison. He was exchanged but again captured at Chancellorsville; he may well have been the last Federal officer to speak to Stonewall Jackson before the Confederate general's death. Imprisoned again in Libby, for one month, Wilkins was again exchanged, but he resigned his commission August 29, 1863, due to ill health. He was brevetted lieutenant colonel and then colonel in March 1865 "for gallant and meritorious service during the war."

the flowers strewn on your path, or the tumult and *eclat* of preparation by the dear ladies, how their hearts sink when they see you go away! How anxious they are to hear the news of every battle! What exquisite anguish in the families of the killed and wounded or captured! Yes, the time had come for me to leave my aged mother, my brave and devoted wife and two little children, and I was but one in six hundred. Little did we know then of what the future had in store, when we tore ourselves away from our families, promising to be "home again in three months."

§

TEN

On to Washington

TO GOVERNOR Blair's call for a regiment of volunteers to march for Washington, Michigan responded with alacrity, and a few days discovered "the flower of our manhood" in rude quarters at Fort Wayne, "waiting for orders." The first move was to be by boat to Cleveland. In answer to the inquiry made of Duncan Stewart, the chief dock and vessel owner of the day, that gentleman promptly replied: "I can move the First Regiment tomorrow morning. All you have to do is to notify me of the hour."

But there were certain complimentary ceremonies to be performed. Saturday, [May 11], 1861, was a gala day in the old city. The Campus Martius was a parade ground already renowned from the days of Cadillac[1] and Hull, to say nothing of more recent "hay foot, straw foot" militia drills under Colonel Brooks[2] and Captain Cicotte. There were now assembled the state and city dignitaries together with a host of my fellow townsmen and a bevy of the pretty girls of a city always famous for the beauty and grace of its feminine *habitans*, and other American ladies.

1. Antoine de la Mothe Cadillac (1656–1730), French soldier, who in 1694 was given command of the post at Mackinac, then the most important position in New France. On July 24, 1701, four years after the French had abandoned all posts in the west, Cadillac landed at the site of what became the city of Detroit.

2. Edward Brooks, who had been an officer under Harrison at the Battle of the River Thames, was chosen captain of the City Guards, the first uniformed infantry company in Detroit, in

Our city recorder, Judge Henry A. Morrow,[3] who afterwards won distinction also as a soldier, made a parting address. This required a response from the new colonel in behalf of his regiment. At the conclusion of these formalities the pretty girls stepped forward and pinned a rosette on each warlike breast and a cockade on each hat amid the cheers of the multitude and martial strains by the regimental band.

Then the Jackson Grays, Captain W. H. Withington's company, were marched to the front of the stand for the acceptance of a stand of colors that ought to have been given us by the state, but was contributed by our fellow citizens, the ladies. The presentation speech was handsomely done by our talented, learned and poetic young lawyer, the late D. Bethune Duffield, son of my dear old dominie, Rev. George Duffield. Of course the gift had to be "accepted" by the regiment's colonel with compliments all around, but whose allusions to the ladies, in whose name and behalf the flag had been contributed, deserve more than a passing mention. It was this:

But of you fair sisters, beautiful daughters of Michigan, what praise can be told that is worthy of you? Ever since the first drum beat of the war and the first volunteer stepped forward to encounter the privations of camp life, you have been busy contriving comforts for the soldiers. We have been crowded with tender and generous offers, and ingenuity has been pressed and taxed to suggest something or anything that might contribute to our good, or kindle our martial zeal. Soft underclothing, convenient "housewives," blue scarfs to encircle our necks as with loving arms, Bibles for our spiritual help in the hour of temptation, these starry cockades and this flag of lofty state and national significance—all rained upon us with smiles and tears of sisterly love and devotion. We thank you for them all, and, ladies, we enlist under your colors.

After a touching benediction pronounced by Dr. Duffield, the mayor of our city, Mr. C. H. Buhl, proposed "three cheers for the flag," to which I supplemented "three cheers for the girls we leave behind us." Needless to say that both were greeted "uproariously" by the regiment.

The ceremonies were concluded by the U.S. District Court Judge, the venerable Ross Wilkins, who gave us one of the ablest arguments ever made

1830. Brooks was appointed colonel of the 1st Regiment Michigan Militia during the Black Hawk War.

3. Henry A. Morrow, later colonel of the 24th Michigan of the Iron Brigade.

Presentation of colors to the 1st Michigan Infantry, May 11, 1861. Colonel Willcox is barely visible in the center of the photo, astride his horse, just behind the tree. *Burton Historical Collection.*

on the right and duty under the Constitution of the general government to suppress the Rebellion. He said: "So far then as your relation to your consciences and government is concerned in going forth to this war, you are not called upon morally or in your duty to God to make any further inquiry."

This had been a ticklish point with many of us during late political agitations on the stump. But there seemed no question now, and Democrats and

Republicans in the regiment felt equally strengthened by the learned judge's patriotic address. From that day I never heard the question raised, and yet it was a question that had taxed the most gigantic minds on either side of the Dixie border.

When mustered into service for "three months or the war," the field and staff were composed of myself as colonel; Loren L. Comstock of Adrian, lieutenant colonel; Alonzo F. Bidwell of Coldwater, major; surgeons William Brodie and Cyrus Smith; Adjutant John D. Fairbanks; Quartermaster Edward Gray and Chaplain [Edward] Meyer.[4] The company commanders were Charles M. Lum, Detroit; William H. Withington of Jackson; E. B. Butterworth, Coldwater; Isaac L. Clarkson, Manchester; William F. Roth, Ann Arbor; Horace S. Roberts, Detroit; Ira C. Abbott, Burr Oak; F.W. Whittlesey, Ypsilanti; [William H. Graves, Adrian] and Devillo Hubbard, of Marshall. The non-commissioned staff was: Sergeant-Major C. Fred Trowbridge; Quartermaster Sergeant William I. Stephens; Drum Major Selah Riley (who was short and fat); Fife Major James D. Elderkin, a Mexican [War] veteran who was tall as a mountain pine.[5] The men of the regiment looked the brave and sturdy soldiers they afterwards proved themselves so well to be. As may be easily imagined I felt very proud of the representation of my native state by such officers and men.

We were all impatient to be off for Washington and take a hand in the fight before it was over, i.e. the "sixty days only" predicted by Mr. Seward.

4. Lieutenant Colonel Comstock, a Mexican War veteran, served in the 1st Michigan until mustered out, August 7, 1861. Reentering the service on May 29, 1862, as captain, Company A, 17th Michigan, he was commissioned lieutenant colonel March 21, 1863. Comstock was mortally wounded at Knoxville, Tennessee, on November 25, 1863, dying that same day.

Maj. Bidwell was mustered out on August 7, 1861, reentering the service on January 11, 1862, as a captain, Battery D, 1st Michigan Light Artillery. He resigned and was discharged on August 2, 1862.

Dr. Smith, the assistant surgeon, served until mustered out on August 7, 1861. He reentered the service September 10 as assistant surgeon, 9th Michigan, and was appointed surgeon October 10, 1862. He was discharged on October 18, 1864.

Lieutenant Fairbanks served until mustered out on August 7, 1861. He reentered the service on August 21 as a major, 5th Michigan. Mortally wounded at Glendale, Virginia, on June 30, 1862, Fairbanks died at Washington, D.C., on July 25, 1862.

Quartermaster Gray served until mustered out on August 7, 1861. He reentered the service on September 5 as a major, 3d Michigan Cavalry. He resigned and was discharged on September 28, 1862.

5. Sgt. Maj. Trowbridge served until mustered out, August 7, 1861. He subsequently became a career soldier, commissioned a captain in the 16th U.S. Infantry in January 1863. He transferred to the 2d Regiment on April 17, 1867.

Elderkin served until mustered out on August 7, 1861, reentering service on October 16, 1861, as bandmaster of the 5th Michigan. He was mustered out on January 2, 1862.

In connection with the raising of the Michigan First, a second regiment was being organized. Governor Blair came to me one day and said that a man by the name of Israel B. Richardson, of Pontiac, had applied for a commission in the Second. "But," he added, "the Pontiac people think he is crazy." He inquired if I knew the man. "Not personally," I replied, "but I know something of him as a West Point graduate. He has seen service in Mexico." "Well," the governor said, "he is modest anyway. He says he had resigned a captaincy in the regular army and thinks he might fill the office of major in the volunteers. Will you please see him?"

I soon found that Richardson was so far from being insane that he was as sound a nut, but he was slouchy and slovenly, something of the style of cadet that Stonewall Jackson was and also quite absentminded. He went about Pontiac looking queer perhaps and certainly unsocial. But in talking over old times, the Mexican war and the coming strife, I found him clear and alert and up to the occasion. It did not take me fifteen minutes to "size him up," and returning to the governor I reported most emphatically: "That is your man, not for major, but for colonel, the man to drill your Second regiment." It may be unnecessary to add that Richardson led the Second Michigan and a brigade at the opening of the fight at Bull Run, rose to be a famous major general and nobly fell at Antietam in command of a division.[6]

But to resume the story of the First. . . . At Fort Wayne our spiritual welfare was looked after by Bishop McCoskrey, and our kit was supplied by the women of the state—God bless them all. The oldest governor of Michigan, General Lewis Cass, and the war governor, Austin Blair, and the latter's staff, put us to our paces in reviews and parades, and we were quite packed up and satiated with honors and equipments and ready for the start. This took place by steamer on the morning of [May 13], 1861, for Cleveland, after last farewells to those we left behind.

I never have forgotten how brightly La Belle Riviere shone on that eventful morning, nor how beautiful were its banks—the tall Lombardy poplars at Sandwich, planted in the time of Louis XIV, the vines and orchards all along the way from Spring Wells—where the white fairies used to dance, with the ghostly arms of the old white windmills, where the *Habitans* used to

6. Israel B. Richardson (38th, USMA 1841), fought in the Seminole War and earned brevets as captain and major for gallantry in Mexico. Originally colonel of the 2d Michigan, he led a brigade at Bull Run. Leading a Second Corps division during the Peninsula Campaign, Richardson earned promotion to major general in July 1862. He led his division at South Mountain and Antietam, where he was mortally wounded in an attack on the Bloody Lane. He died on November 3, 1862.

grind their corn; the beauty of Put-in-Bay, where Perry[7] had proclaimed "the victory is ours"—what a cluster of associations to cheer the hearts of departing soldier boys—some of whom were never to return!

At Cleveland we took [railroad] cars amid the applause of new multitudes. We were received all the way to Baltimore with the most complimentary newspaper and other allusions. Even farmers in the field and the women at their homes waved their hats, handkerchiefs, etc. as we sped along. One dear Ohio lady in the excitement of the moment, having neither bonnet, shawl or handkerchief handy to wave, grasped at parts of her dress without avail and finally tore off a bit of petticoat and waved it frantically.

On arrival of the train at Altoona about breakfast time, imagine our surprise at finding long tables spread with "the best the country afforded" for the hungry soldiers, with the city authorities primed for "speechifying." While the colonel found it difficult to find words adequate to the occasion, one of the regimental wags, Orderly Sergeant B. G. Bennett,[8] of Company G, was quite equal to the emergency, and on the call of his fellows he stepped forward and fired off a *feu de joie* of fun. Of course no such "breach of discipline" could have happened in a regular regiment. Bennett afterward became a commissioned officer and was killed in battle.

On arrival in the vicinity of Baltimore we considered our holiday jaunting over—for the Sixth Massachusetts had been assaulted a few days before on their way through the streets on changing stations. [It was] quite a little distance then from the Philadelphia station to the depot for Washington, and I now made arrangements to march through Baltimore *vi et armis*. The men in each passenger car were arranged so that one half a company with accoutrements on, and guns loaded with ball cartridges, marched out at either end so as to form a connected line outside without delay. There was no great amount of baggage as the men had most of it strapped on their own backs. But there was a wagon or two.

United States Marshal Kane—of somewhat unenviable notoriety and doubtful loyalty—was the first man to meet us at Baltimore. He accosted me on our alighting from the cars and politely offered to "escort" the regiment

---

7. Referring to Admiral Oliver Hazard Perry's victory over the British at Put-in-Bay (also known as the Battle of Lake Erie), off the coast of Sandusky, Ohio, September 10, 1813. What Perry actually said was, "We have met the enemy and they are ours."

8. Benjamin G. Bennett, of Burr Oak, Michigan, mustered out of the regiment on August 7, 1861. Reentering the service as a captain, Company D, 11th Michigan, he was commissioned a major in the regiment on January 7, 1863, and was killed at Missionary Ridge, Tennessee, on November 25, 1863.

through the city. Declining his escort, all I asked was to be shown the way. As he glanced at the prompt and military manner in which the men had stepped from the cars and formed ranks, I saw that he knew we meant business and his somewhat patronizing manner vanished.

The regiment marched up the street in column of companies with colors flying and the band playing national airs—the first of which was the "Star Spangled Banner," which as you may remember had its birth at Baltimore, and with Marshal Kane piloting the way, we met with no actual opposition. At one point, however, where the street crossing was crowded, the mob began to hiss. General Abbott, then a captain in the First, says there were "cheers for Jeff. Davis," but I do not remember that. What I do remember is that some hissing took place just as the head of the column reached the crossing. I turned about and gave command loudly, "First Company right wheel, Ready!" intending to fire down the street, when the crowd broke out into cheers, and we marched on playing "Yankee Doodle," and reached the train for Washington without further interruption.

It took us but a few minutes to unload baggage wagons under guard, to put the men aboard the waiting train at Calvert Station and push through for Washington, where we arrived [May 16th], being the first regiment from across the Alleghenies to reach the Capital. We of course received much attention. Some said "the city began to breathe more freely," but this was said *en compliment* perhaps. However, only a few days before we came, "special orders" had been issued for "the defense of the city." The Washington newspapers and the Washington correspondents of the New York newspapers all spoke in warm praise of our appearance, and we were by no means insensible to the complimentary comments.

But we soon had sterner business on hand. We were first marched up Pennsylvania Avenue to Fourteenth Street and bivouacked in the rear of the old Willard Hotel until provided with quarters for the night in town, not knowing when or where we were either to go into camp or to take the field. Neither the quartermaster's department, which under Major William D. Wilkins had hitherto made such admirable arrangements all the way from Detroit, nor any of the adjutant general's staff "knew anything," for reasons which you shall see presently.

While thus waiting we kept up the usual routine of drill exercises, including a parade in front of the White House and a call made by the officers on Uncle Abe, as the men called the President, who, by the way, now perpetrated one of his "little jokes" on us. After shaking hands in his hearty manner with the officers and complimenting us, he walked out to the band and stepping up first to its leader, Elderkin, who was about his own height, he pounced down on our Drum Major—who though short in height, weighed some three hundred pounds—and exclaimed: "Sir, you are the biggest blower in the U. S. Army!"[9]

I next reported to the renowned [general]-in-chief of the armies of the Union, General Winfield Scott. The tall, majestic hero of Lundy's Lane and Mexico drew me up like a boy to his broad breast in an affectionate embrace, and spoke of how pleased he was to see me with "such a fine regiment." This was not wholly in token of appreciation of the present visit, but as a renewal of an old acquaintance at West Point, where, before the Mexican war, he had last heard my class singing "Changing the Gray for the Blue"—a song composed for the class by Mrs. Scott. As soon as General Scott released my arms he inquired, "Where do you want to go into camp?" I promptly replied "across the Potomac, sir, if you please." This evidently pleased the old soldier, for the next day I received orders to report for duty to General Mansfield[10]—commanding the Department of Washington, by whom all further uncertainty was ended.

The First Michigan and the Eleventh New York, Ellsworth's Fire Zouave regiment, were ordered to pack knapsacks, etc., for Alexandria.[11] I was directed to be ready by twelve A.M. on the 24th. [An hour later] my command

9. Capt. Ira Abbott writes in his journal, May 22, 1861:

In the evening [the] colonel with band, field & staff & line officers called upon Gen'l Winfield Scott. The old Gen'l was in full uniform & appeared very feeble. From there we marched down to the White House, Band playing Hail to the Chief. As we arrived in front of main entrance, Presdt. appeared on the balcony, a few well chosen words of welcome, retired. Usher appeared & all conducted to East room, officers east side, band north side. Mr. Lincoln came in accompanied by Mr. W. H. Seward. When we were introduced by our colonel they passed from the officers to the band. After shaking hands with the members [the President] passed back to the leader, who was a fat old Dutchman weighing over 275 lbs. The President, looking down upon him, said, "I declare, sir, you are the biggest blower I ever saw." This brot the house down. The Band struck up Yankee Doodle & we marched out all pleased, & gratified with the honor of having grasped the hand of the old veteran hero of the battle of Lundy's Lane & War with Mexico, & of introduction to the President of the U.S.

Notes and Journal of Capt. Ira Abbott, copy in OBW's hand, Willcox papers.

10. Brig. Gen. Joseph K. F. Mansfield (2d, USMA 1822), then commanding the Department of Washington. He was mortally wounded while commanding the Twelfth Corps at the Battle of Antietam, September 17, 1862, and died the next day.

11. Ephraim Elmer Ellsworth, who had gained a measure of fame drilling his Zouave Cadets of Chicago in exhibitions across the Midwest and had studied law under Lincoln in Springfield, Illinois before the war. When Lincoln was elected president, Ellsworth accompanied him to Washington. Ellsworth had hoped to procure the position of chief clerkship at the War Department and had written OBW requesting a letter of recommendation in January 1861. The outbreak of war, however, caused him to abandon the effort, and he went to New York, where he recruited the 11th New York Fire Zouaves from members of the city's fire department and was appointed colonel of the regiment.

stood at Long Bridge, waiting its turn to cross. Senator Zachariah Chandler had marched with us that far, but he was not suffered to cross. But in place of the stalwart Senator who had become famous—or as they said in the South, "infamous," for advocating "a little blood letting," there had come Captain George Stoneman's troop of cavalry and lieutenant of the artillery, [George], with a section of six-pounders to join me.[12] Then we advanced across the historic old structure, still standing, and not greatly altered, on to the "sacred soil" of the most important [and] celebrated of the Confederate states.

LETTERS: MAY 1861

Washington
May 17, '61
My Dear Marie
I am tired to death this Eve. Arrived last night at Eleven & got abed at 2. Marched through Baltimore with colors flying to the tune of Yankee Doodle, had a few groans but tremendous cheering all the way. Marshal Kane was polite as a basket. He said we were the finest appearing regt that had passed through. The regiment seems to attract as much attention here as elsewhere, cheered every time we appear, etc., papers full of praise. New York *Herald*, *Times*, Baltimore and Washington papers & others. Drilled & had a dress parade this Eve. on Pa. Ave.

Mr. [Zachariah] Chandler still here, says we go to Fort Monroe in a few days to operate outside in the Virginia contiguous region, probably with the New York regiments. He has gone down to Fort Monroe to-day. Saw Dr. McLarren, Maj. Sibley & others at the War Office. Dr McL. is Medical Director of the District.

Good night & God bless you. Are quartered on D St. just where it comes out on Pa. Ave. Saw Capt. [Montgomery] Meigs to-day. Love to all.

Orlando

Washington
May 20, '61
My Dear Chancellor [Farnsworth],
I write you instead of our Marie this evening a hasty line, to say we are still here, expecting either to go to Fort Monroe or in Camp here in a day or

12. It was not Stoneman but Capt. A. G. Brackett, Company I, 2d U.S. Cavalry.

two. My health is good, cold wearing off. It is a wonder I have not broke down, but ten minutes rest refreshes one completely. My Coldwater horse is come, a perfect beauty & strong as a steam horse. Love to mother & Marie

Orlando

Washington
May 21, '61
My dear Marie & Lulu & Elon,

I hope you are all well and as happy as you can be when I am away from you. My nice new horse came yesterday. He is a beauty, dappled grey, each spot as large & round as a dollar, with very long white mane & tail. He is the most beautiful horse I have yet seen in Washington.

I am in good health. Shall go into camp perhaps tomorrow. Have not yet heard from Mama. God bless you, kiss baby.[13] Your loving husband & papa,

O. B. Willcox

Washington
May 23 [1861], night
My darling wife,

We march before daylight for Alexandria. Heaven is my shield of War; to God I commit my self, my regiment, my wife & darlings.

Having but a moment to spare, you must give love to mothers, Father, Eben and all friends. The telegram will carry news before this reaches you. I hardly expect serious conflict.

Adieu till to-morrow.
Thine, Orlando.

13. OBW refers to his daughter, Almira Cora Willcox (called "Ali"), born March 9, 1860.

ELEVEN

The Taking of Alexandria

THE FIRING on Fort Sumter having cleared the political atmosphere, President Lincoln issued his first call for volunteers on April 15, 1861.[1] But the occupation of the nearest points in Virginia, opposite Washington, by Federal troops, did not take place until late in May.

Meantime, the Capital of the Union was endangered and more or less in a state of siege. There were various hostile designs upon Baltimore, which, if they had prospered, would have isolated Washington from the North, and possibly paved the way for its fall. There was constant correspondence between Baltimore and Charleston, and afterwards with Richmond. There were open, as well as secret, meetings. A recruiting office was opened by Louis T. Wigfall[2] in March, and not only recruits but cannon, arms and

1. OBW wrote two separate accounts on the capture of Alexandria. The earliest, written on November 26, 1881, and originally titled "Occupation of Alexandria, 1861," forms the basis of this chapter; it was written partly in the third person, partly in first person. The editor has taken the liberty of standardizing the point of view in the first person, to match the style of the rest of the memoir. The second version, titled "The Taking of Alexandria," was written about 1903, but it is in some ways more complete than the earlier version. Excerpts from this later version have been included here within single angle brackets < >.

Fort Sumter was fired upon by Confederate troops on April 12, 1861. The Union garrison formally surrendered on April 14. On April 15, Lincoln proclaimed a state of insurrection and called upon the states to furnish 75,000 troops.

2. Louis T. Wigfall served as U.S. senator from Texas from 1859 until he was expelled in July 1861. A fervent secessionist, Wigfall urged the Southern state governments to take over Federal military installations, especially Fort Sumter, South Carolina, and Fort Pickens, Florida. At

ammunition were shipped South, while attempts were made to "carry the state out," and to obstruct the passage of Union troops. In fact, Baltimore and Maryland were nearly engineered into the Rebellion. Fortunately, the Governor of the state, Thomas Holliday Hicks,[3] and the majority of the people, were Union-loving men.

Nevertheless, Washington was long in great danger. On April 19th, the same day that the 6th Massachusetts regiment was assaulted by a mob in Baltimore on the one side of Washington, Harper's Ferry Arsenal, on another side, had to be burned by Lt. Roger Jones, to prevent its falling into the hands of the Virginia troops, with all its arms and military stores.[4] These two events, with the blockade of both the Philadelphia and the Harrisburg routes, raised a loud cry all over the North, "the Capital is in danger," and quickened the impulse and movements of volunteers towards the threatened point. On came the 7th New York and 8th Massachusetts, by way of Annapolis and Annapolis Junction, and "Tom Sherman's Battery"[5] of regulars to reinforce the beleaguered garrison, and Washington breathed a little more freely.

By the 28th of April there were ten thousand troops present for duty, and the Military Department of Washington was formed. General Joseph K. F. Mansfield assumed command of it; still it was considered that 10,000 more troops would be necessary to give security to the Capital.

On April 26th, General Scott issued an order from Headquarters of the Army, stating that "From the known assemblage near this city of numerous hostile bodies of troops it is evident that an attack upon it may be expected any moment"—and the [General] in Chief proceeds to detail measures, and posts of officers, to be taken "for the defense of the Government, the peaceable inhabitants of the city, their property, the public buildings and public archives."

Fort Sumter, Wigfall rowed out to the beleaguered fort and called for its surrender. Elected to the Confederate senate, Wigfall became a bitter opponent of President Jefferson Davis's military policies.

3. Thomas Holliday Hicks (1798–1865), loyal governor of Maryland from 1857 to 1862. His efforts were largely responsible for keeping Maryland in the Union. Hicks later held a seat in the U.S. Senate, dying on February 13, 1865.

4. The 6th Massachusetts was attacked by a secessionist mob while switching trains in Baltimore, en route to Washington. Exact casualties are unknown, but at least four soldiers and nine civilians were killed. The U.S. Armory at Harpers Ferry, West Virginia, was actually burned on April 18, by retreating Union troops, though much of the machinery was left intact and was later used by the Confederacy.

5. Thomas W. Sherman (18th, USMA 1836) then commanded Battery E, 3d U.S. Artillery. He later became a brigadier general, commanding bases on the Atlantic coast for the blockading squadron. He led a division at the Battle of Port Hudson, Louisiana, where he lost a leg.

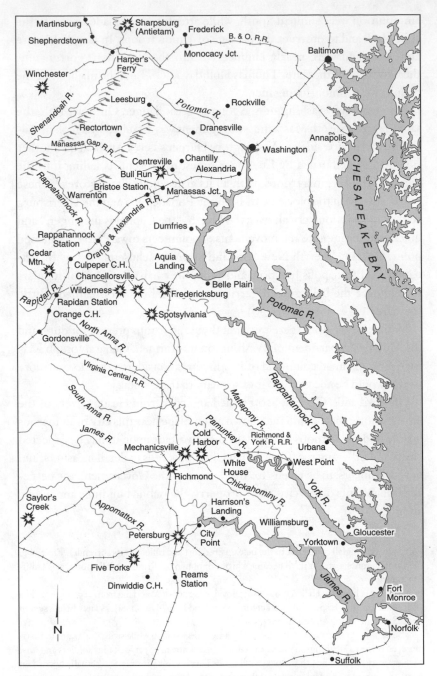

The eastern theater of war, 1861–65.

The dangers increased on all sides until May 13th, when General Butler,[6] with the identical 6th Massachusetts and other troops, numbering, however, only 1,000 men, seized Baltimore; fortified Federal Hill was quickly reinforced, and Baltimore was "corralled." "My Maryland" began to show a sweeping reaction and to give independent regiments of volunteers to the Union, and all the routes by Philadelphia, Harrisburg and Annapolis at last were safe.

Now it became high time to pay attention to the Virginia side; danger threatened from Fredericksburg, Culpeper Court House, Harpers Ferry, Fairfax Court House and more immediately from Alexandria and Arlington Heights, just across the river, at all of which points Southern troops were reported. Fortunately their armament and organization were not equal to their spirit and numbers, and no attempt was allowed to be made to capture the "Government &c" from the Virginia side. General Lee,[7] who commanded the "Virginia forces," under the "Governor and a council," adopted "a defensive policy and began a methodical and thorough military preparation."

General Philip St. George Cocke[8] first commanded on the Potomac, with headquarters at Culpeper Court House. His Department included the whole line of the Potomac, and of course embraced the forces opposite Washington.

On May 5th there had been a "scare" at Alexandria, which for various causes and reasons induced Lieutenant Colonel A. S. Taylor, commanding, to evacuate that point with his forces, among which were Powell's and Ball's

6. Brig. Gen. Benjamin F. Butler, a powerful Democrat and state legislator from Massachusetts, suppressed the riots in Baltimore and secured the movement of Federal troops to and from the capital. The first major general of volunteers appointed by Lincoln, Butler served as military governor of Louisiana from May to December 1862, earning the everlasting hatred of many of the Southern people, who dubbed him "Beast Butler." Commanding the Army of the James in May 1864, he failed in his attempt to seize Richmond, largely through his own bungling. He soon found his army bottled up at Bermuda Hundred and was removed from command in November 1864. Butler led a failed expedition to seize Fort Fisher, North Carolina, in December 1864, his last major effort of the war. He later served as U.S. representative from Massachusetts (1867–1875, 1877–1879) and governor of Massachusetts (1882–1884), and he was an unsuccessful candidate for the presidency in 1884.

7. After refusing command of the U.S. forces on April 18, 1861, and resigning from the U.S. Army on April 23, Robert E. Lee was appointed commander of Virginia forces. He served in that capacity until August 31, when he was appointed a general in the C.S.A. and special military advisor to President Jefferson Davis.

8. Philip St. George Cocke (6th, USMA 1831) later commanded troops during the First Bull Run Campaign, at the Battle of Blackburn's Ford (July 18, 1861), but committed suicide December 26, 1861.

companies of Virginia Cavalry;[9] and for which he was called to account by General Lee, and, though not arrested, he was ordered back by General Cocke.

On May 10th, Colonel [George] H. Terrett, of the "Provisional Army of Virginia," was assigned to the command of Alexandria and troops from Alexandria, Fairfax, Loudon, Prince William and Fauquier counties. On May 21st General M. L. Bonham of the Confederate States Army was assigned to the command of the troops on the line to Alexandria with orders to post his brigade of S.C. Volunteers at Manassas Junction;[10] Colonel Terrett's command, in Alexandria, and General Cocke's, at Culpeper Court House, were included in Bonham's Department of Alexandria.

Thus matters stood on the Virginia side of the river on May 23rd, when the orders came from General Mansfield for the offensive to begin, and for the "invasion of the sacred soil of Virginia by the Goths and Vandals of the North." The command moved in three columns, viz.: by the Aqueduct, by the Long Bridge, and by steamer; General Heintzelman,[11] then colonel on General Mansfield's staff, and who superintended the crossing at Long Bridge, said in his report two months afterwards, that, "on the afternoon of the 23d, I went with General Mansfield to the Engineer Department, and he there explained to me the plan of operations. This, I understood from him, did not include the occupation of Alexandria."[12]

And in this Colonel Heintzelman was mistaken, for at about noon on that day Colonel Ellsworth and myself were summoned to meet General Mansfield, and at one P.M. we received instructions for the capture of Alexandria. But as these instructions came direct from the general, they may have formed no part of those assigned to Colonel Heintzelman's superintendance, and may have been omitted to him at the first interview. Besides,

9. Capt. E. B. Powell and Capt. Dulany Ball, 13th Virginia Cavalry.

10. Brig Gen. Milledge L. Bonham, South Carolina lawyer turned soldier and a veteran of both the Seminole and Mexican wars, was a U.S. representative and major general of militia at the outbreak of the Civil War. Bonham commanded troops in Charleston harbor just prior to the commencement of hostilities and participated in the First Battle of Bull Run. In January 1862 he resigned to serve in the Confederate congress, and in December he was elected governor of South Carolina.

11. Samuel P. Heintzelman (17th, USMA 1826) began the war as colonel of the 17th U.S. Infantry. He commanded the Third Division at First Bull Run, where he was wounded trying to rally his broken command. He thereafter commanded the Third Corps, Army of the Potomac, during the Peninsula Campaign and at Second Bull Run, where he performed poorly. Heintzelman served out the war in less distinguished assignments.

12. See "Report of Maj. Gen. S. P. Heintzelman, U.S. Army," July 20, 1861, in *The War of the Rebellion: A Compilation of the Official Records of the Union and Confederate Armies*, 128 vols. (Washington, D.C.: GPO, 1880–1901) ser. 1, vol. 2, pp. 40–41 (hereafter cited as *OR*).

there was great secrecy enjoined on the respective leaders of the movement; Colonel Heintzelman does not mention General Sandford[13] at all in his report, but General Sandford accompanied the Arlington column, in command of it—according to his own report of May 28, 1861, while Colonel Heintzelman, in his report dated July 20th, mentions the movement "By the Aqueduct (route)—staff commanding Captain Wood,"[14] and "By the Long Bridge—staff commanding Colonel Heintzelman."

The troops that crossed at the Long Bridge for Alexandria were the 1st Michigan Volunteers, Stoneman's troop [of the] 1st Cavalry, and a section of two guns under Lieutenant George, of my old regiment, the 4th Artillery—while Colonel Ellsworth's regiment of "Fire Zouaves," now the 11th New York, went down by the steamers *Baltimore* and *Mount Vernon*.

The orders to Colonel Ellsworth and myself were the same, viz., to act in concert, to communicate by signaling each other at or near the Half Way Creek at early dawn next morning, and so to time our movements as to march on Alexandria simultaneously, Ellsworth by the river front and my [command] by the Washington Pike. We were to cut off telegraphic and railroad communications with the interior at once and attack whatever force should oppose us, and take military possession of the town and tear up the track and bridges of the Orange and Alexandria R.R. from the depot, as far out as practicable.

I never understood the object of the last part of the program and General Mansfield never explained it, nor did it look like an early movement toward Manassas. So the whole movement probably emanated from General Scott himself, to balk a speedy return of the enemy in force to threaten Washington.

The little column which marched down by land left their quarters in the city at midnight of the 23rd, and rendezvoused at Long Bridge at one o'clock [on the] morning of the 23rd, ready to cross. General Mansfield was there in person. Senator Zachariah Chandler of Michigan accompanied me as "Volunteer Aide" and Captain Owen, of Washington, reported as guide.

There has been much dispute as to what regiments first crossed the Long Bridge. The First Michigan never claimed the honor. The whole movement across was led by an advance guard of a battalion of the District of Columbia Volunteers, commanded by Captain J. R. Smead, 2nd Artillery.[15] The

13. Maj. Gen. Charles W. Sandford, New York Militia.
14. Capt. William H. Wood (37th, USMA 1845), 3d U.S. Infantry. Wood was later commissioned major, transferred to the 17th U.S. Infantry, and appointed to General McDowell's staff as acting inspector general.
15. John R. Smead (15th, USMA 1854) was killed at Second Bull Run on August 30, 1862.

12th and 25th New York and 3rd New Jersey followed, also the 7th New York, which encamped near the bridge. A regular field battery and a troop of cavalry filed in rear. These were for Arlington. My own regiment then pushed across.

<The jurisdiction of the Federal government extends over the Potomac River. There is no boundary line of demarcation in midstream. Therefore, the First Michigan, in its advance on ancient Alexandria, did not reach the soil of the old Dominion until it came to the Virginia end of the old Long Bridge.

As the regiment was crossing, all minds were full. This was, for us, the actual beginning of the long, bitter story of the Civil War. The "invasion" was made cheerfully enough. The officers and men were full of enthusiasm and zeal, conscious that their cause was just and determined, that their duty should be done. But, looking back over the long retrospect of more than forty years, I cannot help recalling the grim fate that awaited so many of the bright, brave boys of the first regiment that ever came under my command. So many of them fell on the soil of the state which we were that dark night "invading." Others died in hospitals and noisome prisons. Some of them still sleep in old Virginia. A handful of the veterans yet survive, to whom their colonel's hat is off with due pride, mingled with tender remembrance!

At the Virginia end of the Long bridge, Col. Charles P. Stone was stationed with a battalion of District of Columbia guards, which greeted us in passing. This officer afterward gained fame at Ball's Bluff, and was subsequently a distinguished pasha in the army of the Egyptian Khedive.[16]

Several regiments had already crossed and right-wheeled up to Arlington Heights, where General Sandford commanded. We turned down to the left, marching as far as Half Way Creek, towards Alexandria, which was then considered "the danger point" most eminently threatening our capital. There were other "war clouds": Manassas, Culpeper, Harpers Ferry, Fredericksburg, etc.—but these were all more remote. . . .>

The 12th New York, Colonel Butterfield, accompanied the 1st Michigan as far as Four Mile Run (the Half Way Creek in question), which we reached

16. Charles P. Stone (7th, USMA 1845) was then colonel of District of Columbia Volunteers, responsible for the safety of Washington. As a brigadier general in overall command of Union troops at the disastrous Battle of Ball's Bluff, Virginia, on October 21, 1861, Stone was arrested by the Congressional Committee on the Conduct of the War; he was imprisoned without cause for 189 days. He later served in the Port Hudson and Red River campaigns but resigned from the army in September 1864. Following the war he was chief of staff of the Egyptian army for thirteen years.

Long Bridge over the Potomac. *U.S. Army Military History Institute (USAMHI), Carlisle Barracks, Pennsylvania.*

at the peep of day. We found the enemy's videttes on top of the hill just beyond the Alexandria and Georgetown canal viaduct, and skirmishers were thrown forward from the advance guard of Michigan infantry. As the order of march had prescribed "cavalry in rear," it was surmised that a pursuit by Stoneman's horsemen driving the rebel videttes pell mell into Alexandria might prematurely alarm the garrison of that ancient city. . . .

<At Half Way Creek we had to wait for Colonel Ellsworth's steamer on the Potomac, whose signal we looked for to renew our route. . . . But as the steamer hove in sight and moved right on and much faster than our legs could carry us, the "simultaneous" part of the business collapsed. It was imperative that Ellsworth should "slow up," instead of which my gallant young friend impatiently paddled ahead, landed at the old King's Street wharf, where, leaving Lt. Col. [Noah L.] Farnham in command of the regiment, he marched up the street with one company, not for the railway depot, but for the Marshall house Confederate flag, in the capture of which both he and Jackson lost their lives. . . .>

The enemy were not without warning—although the videttes in front of us did not seem to scamper off to give it. For Colonel Terrett commanding at Alexandria reports, from Manassas Junction to the Adjutant General of his Department that, on the morning of the 24th inst., about 1.30 A.M., Captain Ball came to my quarters and reported that one of the videttes, stationed at the Chain Bridge, about three miles west of Georgetown, D.C., had informed him that a squadron of cavalry had crossed over to the Virginia shore. I immediately ordered my command under arms, to await further orders. About 5.30 A.M. an officer was sent from the steamer *Pawnee*, Northern Navy, to inform me that an overwhelming force was about entering the city of Alexandria, and it would be madness to resist, and *that I could have* until *9 A.M.* to *evacuate* or *surrender.* (!!!) [OBW's italics.] I then ordered the troops under my command to assemble at the place designated by me on assuming command in Alexandria, that I might either resist or fall back as circumstances might require. . . .[17]

But Colonel Terrett was mistaken as to the time of day. We actually entered the city in the midst of a glorious sunrise. . . .

‹Without firing a shot—except at long range—my command entered the city. On approaching King Street, by good luck, I had taken the lead with the guide, Owen, and an advance guard, while Capt. Stoneman swung around to the rear of the town. On approaching King Street, Owen reported a troop of Confederate cavalry. We halted and I ordered up the two field pieces, wheeled one of them around the corner toward the troop, and, dashing up to them, I thundered, "Surrender or I'll blow you to H——!" I hope the "Recording Angel" wiped out the "bad words" although I doubt it, & why should she if a female of spirit? I think it was the only cuss word I exploded during the war.

The Secesh troop seemed paralyzed; most of them were in the saddle while others stood stock still with one foot in the stirrup. But the captain rode forward, saluted, and tendered me his sword.

"Your name, Sir," I demanded.
"Captain Ball."

"Ball," I repeated to myself, "a family connection of George Washington, now in the rebellion!" I treated him as courteously as I could, bidding him keep his sword, but turning him and his troop into the old Alexandria [slave] pen, which stood nearby—for I had no time to spare at the moment. My orders were for the Orange and Alexandria depot.

And yet I was detained. A soldier came running out from the Marshall house with the shocking news that Colonel Ellsworth was killed. One com-

17. "Report of Col. George H. Terrett, C.S. forces, commanding at Alexandria," dated "Manassas Junction, Virginia, May 28, 1861." *OR*, vol. 2, pp. 43–44.

pany that he had brought with him was left standing, waiting orders, and this company I placed in charge of the pen and Captain Ball's people. I had no time now for further investigation, [but we continued] on our way to the depot.

I deeply mourned the loss of such a gallant soldier and trusted friend as Colonel Ellsworth. He had bright prospects of good services to his country and glory to himself. But how could he have rushed to such a fate or fallen into such a trap? The secret of his eager haste to reach Alexandria was to be first to secure a rebel flag, and that before my troops could arrive on the spot, for the "flag question" had been discussed among the boys of both regiments in Washington.

Needless to say, the news of Ellsworth's tragic fate fell on the North with a shock scarcely less than the subsequent news of our disaster at Bull Run. My telegram to General Mansfield—"Alexandria is ours, but Ellsworth is killed," spread like wildfire, but in the excitement of the occasion my own small part in the taking of the first city south of the Potomac very naturally was overlooked except in my native state. . . .>

The Orange and Alexandria Depot was quickly reached and found to be evacuated, and our skirmishers ran out on the line of the road on foot and in handcars. We commenced tearing up the track according to orders, one or two little bridges were burned, and the work was carried forward with some precaution, until we came in contact with what proved to be a party of the enemy engaged in similar work, on their own side, where-upon we discontinued, and pushing forward, exchanged a few shots with their vanishing rear guard. Finally we saw what proved to be the last train of rebel troops making off under steam. They had been rushing trains out ever since the unfortunate message from the *Pawnee*.

Colonel Terrett, in the report already mentioned, says further:

As soon as the troops were formed which was promptly done (i.e. that we might either "resist or fall back") I repaired to the command, and then ascertained that the enemy were entering the city by Washington St., and that several steamers had been placed so that their guns could command many of the principal streets(?) I ordered the command to march and proceeded out of the city by Duke Street, Captain Ball accompanied me as far as his quarters, a little west of the rail road Depot, where he halted, and I proceeded to the cars which were about ½ a mile from the Depot, where I had ordered them to be stopped; and, from orders given before marching out of the city, the Cavalry was to follow in my rear for the purpose of giving me information in regard to the movements of the enemy, Captain Powell followed my instructions, and why *Captain Ball* did not I am unable to report.

Certainly there is no pretence here that Captain Ball was captured in violation of the message from the *Pawnee*, nor does it anywhere appear that the *Pawnee's* offer was accepted; on the contrary, the troops were assembled at a place designated in orders that Colonel Terrett "might either *resist or fall back as circumstances might require.*" Furthermore, if either General Bonham, who commanded the Department of Alexandria, or General Lee, Commander in Chief, ever felt that Ball's troops were captured and held as prisoners of war in violation of any truce or agreement whatever, he would certainly have claimed their restoration. As it was, they were lionized in Washington, whither they were sent that afternoon, under the guard of Ellsworth's Zouaves, and made much of by their Southern friends as heroes, and by no means considered as the victims of "Yankee fraud——"

General Bonham, in his report to General Lee of the capture of "Ball's Dragoons," same day, from Manassas, made no complaint. On May 25th Bonham reports that "Colonel Terrett, with as many of his troops as he could bring off with him, arrived at 11 oclock." And in another report of same date he says, "The Alexandria troops are here, without cooking utensils, and many without arms," which indicated more haste than Colonel Terrett seemed willing to admit.[18]

I do not know how many troops Terrett had, but there were with Colonel Taylor in Alexandria on May 7 about five hundred. Ball was ever treated with suspicion after his release and return to the Confederacy, unjustly I think, as disloyal to his cause, and as was hinted in Colonel Terrett's report, he was supposed to have voluntarily lingered with a view to fall into our hands. In my opinion he and his command were surprised by the rapid movements of our advance, and paralyzed by the proximate muzzle of a field gun; and it would have been madness to resist, and cruelty to his men to attempt to run, after being so surprised. But the matter remains buried in the limbo of the mysteries and blunders of the war. . . .

‹I left a strong guard with cavalry outposts at the Mills, and rode back to King Street and down to the wharf, followed through the now peaceful city by a single orderly. And fearing lest the Zouaves might break out and sack the city in revenge for the loss of their leader, I ordered Lieutenant Colonel Farnham, commanding, to march the regiment out to a field near

18. See "Reports of Brig. Gen. M. L. Bonham, C.S. Army, commanding at Manassas, Virginia," *OR*, vol. 2, pp. 42–43.

by and there wait my visit to inspect them. But to my utter surprise, little or no indignation was expressed, much less threats. And some of the men complained of too much fancy drill, and . . . essentials neglected. And sure enough, on inspecting the ranks, I found that some of the Zouaves scarcely knew how to load and fire. Perhaps the fault lay with the company officers.

On proceeding up town again, I shook hands with his honor the Mayor, Lewis Mackenzie, an old friend, who told me of "the truce," as he called it, with Lieutenant Rowan, and as the hour named had not expired, he claimed that "neither hostilities nor military possession could fairly be the thing." . . . I replied to the mayor:

I cannot recognize your right to bind the military, but you may be assured that nothing shall be done by myself further than to make provision for the security of life and property in a city where I have already so many friends and acquaintances. And how are the Masons, the Fairfaxes, Benhams, and other old friends? Besides, very dear sir, we have restored you and your people to the Union.

And, in secret thoughts, I believed the old gentleman—who was a rich forwarding merchant—was really glad of it. However that may be, he had afore time made no little *lucre* by Uncle Sam's troops at Fort Washington below, and now had on hand some "bad debts" contracted with the Confederate officers who had flocked in from Manassas. That there had been many of the latter visitors I felt assured from the reports of our spies and from the frequent puffs of the locomotives running in and out of town during our morning march and, sure enough, as it subsequently became known, not only officers, but military supplies and troops, under command of Colonel Terrett, were rushed out. He had ordered out likewise what organized forces there were under Captains Powell and Ball, but the latter was not quick enough, and ended up by getting the [slave] pen.

On revisiting this slave pen [and] auction house, I found it a decent enough, substantial looking building now guarded by our Michigan fellows. There were kept the auctioneer's descriptive book of slaves received and sold, [and] their owners' names. Prices ranged from $50 upward. Some of my officers reported that they had found several slaves, including a man, a "likely looking $1,800 girl," and a boy, *in durance vile*, and waiting either to be sold or to be taken away by their respective masters or mistresses. My men set all three prisoners free, and on the appearance of a well-dressed gentleman to "claim his property," the negro man, whom he grabbed by the coat collar and attempted to take with him, resisted, and the master was hustled off alone amid the jeers of the Michigan men. That slave took free service and became company cook in Company C. After the war he went to Michigan with Captain Butterworth, at whose home he finally died.

The first thing to do in order to secure peace and tranquility was to appoint a provost marshal, and I named Captain Devillo Hubbard. One of his orders was in case of doubt concerning the peaceful intentions of any citizen, to tender him the "oath of allegiance," and if the party declined, to report the case to me. And what was my amusement, in one case, at least, to find that the zealous provost—not knowing himself exactly the terms of the required oath, made certain citizens of Virginia swear to "bear true allegiance to and obey the orders of the Governor of Michigan!"—in language of the captain's own commission.

In his search one day with a patrol, Captain Hubbard found in one house a Confederate flag. Capturing it, of course, he marched the owner of the same up to my headquarters, dragging "the rag," as he called it, in the dirt, with the stars and stripes flying overhead. Who could blame him?

Doubtless there still lingered some Confederate officers in the city in disguise. . . .

Nine years had passed since, as a lieutenant of artillery, stationed at Fort Washington opposite Mount Vernon, I had made frequent visits at Alexandria and formed many acquaintances. To some of these I had given written protection of their persons and property. But with one exception, the Mason family, which I had known at Detroit and which had furnished two governors of Michigan, they rather gave me the cold shoulder. But public tranquility being the main object, I quickly issued a sort of proclamation of peace . . . in token of which I camped the troops and reinforcements, as fast as they arrived, out on [Shuter's] Hill, detaining only a small guard in town near my headquarters at the Everett house and at the slave pen guard house.

On the whole, I am gratified to boast that "order soon reigned in Warsaw" and that in the capture and occupation of Alexandria, no blood was shed, except in the tragedy at the Marshall house.>

I understood from Lieutenant Colonel Farnham, left commanding [the Fire Zouaves] on the wharf, that the steamers with the regiment on board had swept straight down and reached Alexandria a little before sunrise, neglecting, or perhaps forgetting, to "lie-to" off the mouth of the Half Way Creek and signal the land troops. When they arrived, there was a sentinel at the wharf who fired off his gun and fled. As near as I can make out, Colonel Ellsworth landed at once with Company A, Captain Coyle, and started for the telegraph office, while Company E, Captain Leveridge was ordered to the R.R. Depot (probably the Alexandria, Loudon and Hampshire Depot, as we found no Zouaves at the Orange and Alexandria Depot), and the rest of the regiment were left to land and await further orders.

The circumstances of his [Ellsworth's] death are well known. How on his way he caught sight of the Marshall house flag, and with Chaplain French, Lieutenant Winser, Francis E. Brownell, and one or two other privates, he stepped across to the hotel, leaving the company halted on the side-walk. How he entered, and meeting a man in the hall, demanded, "Who put up that flag?" The man answered, "I don't know, I am a boarder here." How Colonel Ellsworth went up on the roof, cut the flag down himself, and winding it around his body, was returning down the stairway, when the same man who had called himself a boarder, but who was the landlord himself, J. W. Jackson, now met the party in the hall with a double barrel shot gun in his hands, and fired the fatal shot, and was himself shot down by Brownell, just as his beloved colonel fell forward, exclaiming only, "My God!"

Colonel Farnham's dispatch to General Mansfield was dated twelve minutes before my dispatch was written, and was as follows:

> Alexandria Va. May 24, 1861
> 5.18 A.M.
> Sir:
> It is my painful duty to inform you that Colonel Ellsworth, late Commanding Officer of the First Fire Zouaves Regiment New York Militia, is no more. He was assassinated at Marshall House after our troops had taken possession of the city. I am ignorant of the details of the order issued to the regiment, I await further instructions. My men are posted advantageously in the streets.
> Noah L. Farnham
> Commanding Fire Zouaves

It seemed that Jackson was warned of the coming of the troops, and could have escaped, but that he stayed behind with the avowed intention of killing any man who should take down his flag.

I found that the Colonel's body had been tenderly cared for by his comrades and carried on a litter of muskets to the steamer. But I felt apprehension that his men would break out and seek a terrible retribution on the city, and, assuming command, I ordered the regiment to be collected and marched into an open field where they were kept occupied with inspections and other military details, until the fearful stress and excitement were calmed down and the officers had acquired full control over the ranks.

The death of young Ellsworth created a horror of indignation in the North next only to the firing upon Fort Sumter, particularly as it was, or appeared to be, applauded throughout the South enthusiastically, and, as it was heard, subscriptions for the support of the assassin's family were eagerly and widely circulated.

In Alexandria the feeling was divided, many, probably most of the citizens deplored the act as not only a violation of the laws of war, but uncalled for, if not brutal. Still, others considered it as a patriotic deed, and it was accepted and adopted as an open declaration to the North of the desperate resistance to be expected from citizens as well as soldiers. Still, was it not a political mistake? President Lincoln, in his super human patience, knowing the South better than most men, was waiting for the Confederates to place themselves flagrantly in the wrong. There was still much hope of reconciliation, but those who remained sanguine after Sumter had their eyes fully opened by the applause in the Southern newspapers that followed the fall of Ellsworth, as if the South assumed the act as [its] own.

By direction of the President, Ellsworth's bleeding body was transferred to the White House, and thence buried with floral decorations and all the military and civic honors that could be lavished upon the martyr and hero of a nation. On the other hand, in the South it was considered that Jackson had fallen in defense of his flag, and in the eyes of his fellow countrymen, he, too, had his apotheosis as a hero-martyr, so that this and Sumter, the very transactions which mostly stirred the innermost bosom of the North and satisfied that section that "coercion" was necessary, "fired the Southern heart" also, and swept away the last vestige of "passive resistance." In Alexandria, then, and under these apparently minor and insignificant operations, a spark was kindled into a flame which raged on both sides for four years.

«To return to my unfortunate friend, Col. Ellsworth, I had made his acquaintance in the winter before the war at Detroit, whither he had come in the course of his tour with a company of Zouaves on exhibition drills. He was barely twenty-four, an enthusiast for the new tactics, coupled with athletic exercises & the French Zouave uniform. As a drill master he excited much interest, & young men organized Zouave companies wherever he went. Such a company was organized at Detroit, & had me nominally for its captain.

The newspaper men were his friends, & some thought he might be the young Napoleon of the war. Unfortunately his military education was not equal to his zeal, & even when he came to command & drill his regiment, mostly firemen of N.Y. City, he shot beyond his mark. There are a thousand and one things about the progress, care & discipline of a regiment of volun-

Col. E. Elmer Ellsworth,
11th New York Volunteer
Infantry (Fire Zouaves).
USAMHI.

teers which cannot be learned in a day; much more in actual military operations is some experience needed to comprehend & carry out your orders.

In the occupation of Alexandria, much was left by the general commanding to the colonels. As Ellsworth saw it, his idea was to get there as soon as possible. It is said that he heard [of] the flag at the Marshall house & of Jackson's boast that he would kill the man who should attempt to haul it down. Whether or not, I do not know. But it seems that immediately on his steamer's reaching the wharf, the eager colonel took the first company that landed & made for the Marshall house, leaving his lieutenant colonel, Farnham, as the latter told me, & the regiment without orders.

But it turned out in the providence of God that this act of seeming rashness & youthful impetuosity was the best card that could have been played in the game of war at the time. The death of Ellsworth fired the Northern heart, united all parties, & gave a fiery impetus to the war. States, cities & counties vied with each other in raising "the sinews of war," & young men & old hastened to enroll & were eager to march to Washington or anywhere to defend the flag. After all, there is something near to the American heart in Old Glory. A Confederate officer of high rank once told me that the Confederacy had made their first & greatest blunder when they adopted a new flag. Be thus as it may, no wonder & no blame to young Ellsworth when he saw that *that flag* had been hauled down, & a hostile rag was flaunting in its place—there, of all places, over the home & church where Washington himself had wrought & worshipped!

His remains were carried reverently to the Capital of his country & lay in state at the White House. The whole country was in mourning—not least of all Alexandria itself, whose citizens, it is said, had been forced into the subscription for purchase of the flag, & who shuddered or shrugged their shoulders as they passed by the Marshall house. A sadder man than Mayor MacKenzie was seldom seen. . . .

[With] The remains of the youthful . . . soldier lying in state in the East Room of the Executive Mansion, President Lincoln & his family shed genuine tears over the blasted hopes that he himself had entertained. For the President had known him & he had accompanied the Presidential party from Illinois to Washington as, in a sense, the manager of the expedition—at a time of great excitement & dread of peril.

The funeral was conducted in as great state as if the corpse had been that of a cabinet officer, escorted by a corps of troops & attended by the military & civil dignitaries of the Capital.

At the same time, Ball's troop of cavalry were smarting under their disgrace; they had been shipped to Washington under a guard of Ellsworth's own men—by whom it was falsely reported that they had been captured. The incident was sufficient to [warrant] a newspaper paragraph. But the whole circumstance of the capture of Alexandria got into the newspapers by gross work, & the troops that did the actual work & restored order quickly afterwards were not even attended to. Such is the lying tongue of Rumor—to say nothing of Fame. Very naturally, under the dark pall of gloom, everything was overlooked but the capture of the First Secession Flag, & the fate of its captor. Alas! how soon did we become accustomed to the death of our heroes!>>[19]

As for the remaining incidents connected with the day, they seem trifling compared with the ghastly tragedy we have mentioned. I soon received an unconditional surrender of the town at the hands of the Mayor, Honorable

19. The above remarks on Ellsworth contained within the double angle brackets << >> are excerpted from OBW's notebook, "War Notes, 1861–1865," pertaining chiefly to the events described in this chapter.

Lewis Mackenzie. Immediate steps were taken to ensure order and security, a military police was established, pickets thrown out, and a sort of Proclamation, headed "Orders No. 2," was issued and printed by some Michigan soldiers, Galloway and O'Donell, in the office of the venerable Alexandria *Gazette*—which was found deserted of its editor. The *Sentinel* newspaper office was equally deserted and silent, except in an echo in the last issue, as follows: "We are able to meet our foe eye to eye, front to front, column to column, and chase them back from our soil &c &c," in which the doughty editor reckoned without his host, another little mistake to be added to the chapter of incidental history. . . .

‹On the first Sabbath day following I walked up to the venerable brick church where George Washington had been wont to worship. There I could almost feel his imposing presence—a sorrowful countenance enough, mourning, perhaps, over the fact that Virginia, his native state, his home, and the home of Patrick Henry and Thomas Jefferson, had broken its sacred bond with the Union—a bond cemented by four years in the Revolution and not to be restored again without a fratricidal war that was to last another four years. But thanks to the Lord of Hosts our reunion is come to stay, and is stronger than ever.›

LETTERS: MAY 25–JULY 20, 1861

Alexandria, Virginia
25 May/61
My dear Marie,
I have not had a moment's time to write you a report of the capture of the town. But here I am with 2 regiments, a Light Battery & Co. of Dragoons with Alexandria in my fist.

Love to all,
Orlando

Will write more fully.

Camp Willcox
Near Alexandria
May 31, 1861
Dear Chancellor,
Your kind letter of 27th inst. is received, & I hasten to acknowledge receipt of it with the draft enclosure. The kindness of the act brought the tears to my eyes. I will send on my May pay accounts as soon as I can get

some blanks. I wrote Marie the last news yesterday. We are in camp on the same hill with the Fire Zouaves & on the best terms with them. The "wolves" & the "lambs" lie down together literally. It is perfectly amazing how extremely well my men behave. Perhaps it is partly owing to the fact that there are so many respectable men in ranks & partly to the fact that I never see the least violation of good behavior of any kind without rebuking it & appealing to the pride of the regiment.

My successor in Alexandria, Col. Stone, keeps my Adjt., Surgeon, Provost Marshall & City military police (one company) because he cannot fill their places elsewhere, although he has 4 regts. to select from. The respectable citizens of Alexandria actually petitioned that the Mich. troops might be kept in town to guard it. Of course all this is gratifying.

Your former letter was received in my busiest moments when regulating Alexandria, or I should have answered it. In regard to the commission, I think that my Michigan friends, [Zachariah] Chandler, etc., do not work heartily, for fear of the consequences to the regiment. Gov. Blair has behaved queerly too about the 3 years business.[20] He promised he would have recruits ready to fill us up for 3 years & now writes that the pressure is so great outside that he cannot designate us or any regiment for three years unless 4 are accepted. I wish I had one good influential friend at Court.

I am glad you make it so tolerable for our dear Marie. God bless her & the children. We have alarms of threatened attacks every night. But I think of home last thing before going to sleep.

Thine,
Orlando

Alexandria
June 3 [1861]
Dear Chancellor,

I enclose my pay accounts for May. I hope the Sec. of War will make arrangements for speedy payment. Otherwise they will not be paid till Congress appropriates. I hoped to spare $100 for Marie, but the express charge on the horse was $79.25 [and] used up my surplus. I am sorry to have her dependent, & especially have some debts unpaid. But I hope to live to bring

20. OBW hoped that the 1st Michigan, originally a three-months regiment, would be redesignated as a three-years unit, though it would be up to each man whether he wished to reenlist for that period. The regiment returned to Michigan following the expiration of its original term of enlistment and was mustered out of service on August 7, 1861. The regiment, however, was immediately reorganized as a three-years unit, returning to the Army of the Potomac with 960 officers and men. It served until the end of the war.

things up. You see how the vile newspaper reporters yesterday glorifying me are now circulating outrageously false reports, caught up from secession sources.

I am behind hand in correspondence, having scarcely time to write Marie, & poor Eb & Mother must feel deeply injured. But I will write them both to-morrow. Some important movement is close at hand. In haste. Love to all.

Thine,
Orlando

Shuter's Hill, Alexandria
June 4 [1861]
My darling Marie,

I have been busy all day lifting a load of letters & papers of all kinds that threatened to bury me. Some of those which I think might be interesting to refer to at a future day I have put in packages & shall mail them to you.

I have had a delightful letter from Caro, & another from you. You must keep calm & hope for the best. God's blessings in the past are the best assurances for the future. I am quartered in the most beautiful ground about Alexandria, surrounded by flowers, & in the house of Mr. R. S. Ashby. I wish you were here. But in a few days we shall march.

I mailed the Chancellor my pay accounts for May last night. I feel very much worried about your financial condition, although Father is so kind. I know his means are cramped too. . . .

Col. Comstock is in great trouble. His wife is sick & his house & furniture sold & he can get no pay. He thinks of resigning.

The three years business is not yet settled. Gov. Blair ought to have designated us at once as one of them. I cannot yet find time even to go to Washington.

Henry calls the horse "Henry." He is a good servant & takes good care of things—generally keeps them locked up so tight I have to go without! The horse is at present lame but will soon be over it. He excels everything. The mess chest does very well. It is so well furnished with good things that the servants waste. The first evening they poured a can of those splendid strawberries into a tin pan & put them on the table, & they went like smoke. Speaking of strawberries, the gentleman & lady of the mansion which forms my Hd. Quarters had flowers & strawberries in abundance & we have them every day. Just in front of the house is a tree under which the Adjt's tent is pitched. The whole of my camp is in a beautiful grove.

Give much love to my little Lu & Elon & tell them to write me letters. Pren Sanger[21] is acting Adjt., & makes a capital officer.

Kiss the Baby twenty times & take a thousand kisses for yourself. Direct to Alexandria via Washington. Yours devotedly, my heavenly love,

Orlando

Shuter's Hill, Alexandria
June 14 [1861]
My darling Wife,

Day before yesterday I went to Washington & found that my application for three years, although endorsed strongly by Col. Heintzelman, Gen. McDowell[22] & Genl. Scott in very handsome terms, was stayed in the Adjt. Gen's office because it did not come through the Governor of Mich. I telegraphed to him. But fearing as Col. Stockton was pressing hard for his regiment that something might happen, I went to the President & he cheerfully ordered it to be accepted & wrote an order to the Sec. of War on the spot, saying if any regiment was accepted from Mich., it should be this one, "by jings!" This was "truly gratifying," as Caro would say.

To-day I got Father's telegram saying the Governor had named it as a 3 years regiment. This last relieves me, as I feared that some bother might be made by the circumlocution office. A great many of the present men will go out, but not too many I hope. As soon as I get orders with regard to the muster I shall know how many more will be regained & send word to the Governor. I am much obliged to Mr. Chandler & all our friends.

The last papers from home, [the *Detroit*] *Tribune*, contain more slang about the [men's] fare. I have done everything but write about it, & there is not any truth in the charge. No regiment in the field fares better, none have been favored so much, in every way, & if the men thought less of pies & cakes, who write the complaints, they would relish more manly food better. As it is, the complaint is confined to a *few* of our city boys. The country companies are perfectly content. But enough to say that I neglect no means to have them all well fed.

I am sorry you feel badly darling & hope to have you with me a little while before the summer is over. I am glad you let the house & like

21. 2d Lt. Joseph P. Sanger, originally of Company F, 1st Michigan Infantry.

22. Brig. Gen. Irvin McDowell (23d, USMA 1838) commanded the Union forces at the First Battle of Bull Run. Following that defeat, McDowell was superseded by Maj. Gen. George Mc-Clellan. McDowell relived the nightmare of his first defeat while leading a corps at Second Bull Run in August 1862.

your arrangements entirely.[23] Hope to get time to write Eb & Father to-morrow.

Good night. May all the blessed host wait on you & our little ones. Your Husband

O.B.W.

Shuter's Hill, Alexandria
June 18 [1861]
My darling Wife,

I write you on the Eve of "great expectations" to-night, an attack being apprehended towards morning. I meant to write Father to-day as well as yourself at length. Give my love to all. I am well & trust in the shadow of the Almighty. Your darling,

O.B.W.

Shuter's Hill
June 24 [1861]
My darling Marie,

I wrote a pretty full letter to Eben this p.m. & find time to write you to-night. The letter to him described a few of my perplexities. . . . I will not bother your little hairs & heart about such things. I have had a lady guest for the last few days. Mrs. Capt. Clarkson. The Capt. has been sick & she attended him in his tent, but I invited them to my little honeysuckle house where he has now recovered & goes up to Washington tomorrow. Both she & Mrs. Withington have been some time at Washington, visiting their husbands here often. Both are good officers. I fear Clarkson cannot remain in the reorganization. Withington, who is one of the best Captains, just received news from his partner this p.m. that enables him to stay. All the other captains will most likely remain and fair expectations from all the companies except "A"; the best of the non-commissioned officers remain & most of the best soldiers. Unless I have some outside interference, the new regiment will probably be a very fine one.

In regard to my own wants I have none. You fitted out my clothes & mess chest so completely that I need nothing. If you have a chance to send on some of that good tea, I would like it for the mess. How often I have fancied you at the mess table instead of Mrs. C. Griff. Owen went up to Washington

23. Marie Willcox had recently rented out the family's house on Larned Street in Detroit (which they had purchased in May 1860) and took up quarters with her parents.

to-day. He has been unwell, but declines to return to Detroit. The Dr. thinks it nothing serious. . . . The Dr. is constantly at work over or for the sick. To-day Dr. Macgruder, the Medical Director of the Eastern Virginia District, inspected his arrangements in every respect & pronounced them superior to all others here. In good health & love to all & hoping to hear good news from the Baby, I remain, your ardently devoted husband

O.B.W.

In Camp on top of Shuter's Hill
Alexandria, Va. June 24 [1861]
My Darling Lulu,

I received your nice little printed letter with a great deal of pleasure. I wish you & Elon were here a few days. If Grandpa comes on to Washington he must bring Mama. Are you good & obedient to Grandma? I hope you & she are as devoted as ever. I have a nice little cat & there is an old negro man that pickled the strawberries & takes care of the garden, & you would love him.

Tell Elon to be a good boy & grow up to be a *good* and that will make him a *great* man. Tell him that papa is away from you & him to fight for our country; that is, that you & all the little children of America may have all the blessings that your papas and grandpas have had. And tell him I want to have him think more of his sister than he does of himself, & learn to love God & Christ and all the neighbors. I hope to come back to Detroit after a while & expect to see you very much improved. Are you not glad to get in the old house?

Your papa

In Camp Shuter's Hill
Alexandria, Va.
June 27/61
My Dear Mother [Mrs. Farnsworth],

If you will excuse a few lines only on a poor scrap of paper I will write just to say that I have been trying to write you for a week. I should certainly like to hear from you as often as possible, as your affection & ambition keep pace with mine. I hope you will make Lulu as much like you as possible, and am thankful to you for devoting so much time to the glorious little creature. I am sorry that I forgot to write her in my letter how glad I was to get the needle book and the quarter of a dollar. Tell her I needed them and thank her very much. Tell Elon he must try to learn all he can.

I was horribly shocked at the news in Marie's letter of the death of Orry McNair. I had great hopes of influencing his future career. But Heaven's will be done. The blow might have struck nearer home.

We had a visit yesterday & dined Bishop McIlham, Bishop Clark of Rhode Island and Dr. Butler of Washington. Tell Bishop McCoskrey I would like a visit from him. . . . My regards to the Bishop family & the Trowbridges. Will write Marie in a day or two. Can spare her part of this month's pay. Love to Father and the children.

Your devoted son,
Orlando

Sunday night
Shuter's Hill, Va., June 30, '61
My darling Wife,
On Friday I went to Washington to make further arrangements for reorganization, & drew my June pay. Maj. [Cary H.] Fry, the Paymaster, accommodated me with a draft for you & I enclosed it forthwith to you. It was $122 and I hope you received it. Make what disposition seems best. I would rather pay small debts first, then parts of larger ones, but keep a little till next remittance.

Near the War Office I met Gen'l McDowell, & he was very cordial indeed. He said he was going to put me in command of a brigade of either two or four regiments, according to circumstances, & that he was glad to have an opportunity to show that he did not relieve me on account of dissatisfaction at Alexandria but in consequence of a general arrangement for putting all the brigades under regular officers. (Tell Father that Col. Howard[24] was mistaken about Stone's being my junior. He ranked me in consequence of his regular commission, which always takes precedence over volunteers of the same grade.)

I have not heard further about the brigade & it may all fall through. One thing is certain, there is a great lack of competent colonels & generals, and all the regiments require drilling badly. At present I am bothered about the 3 years preparations, but I should like to have two or four regiments to handle. Breathe not a whisper, lest it should be thought I am trying to cut

24. Col. O. O. Howard (4th, USMA 1854). Originally colonel of the 3d Maine, Howard was appointed brigadier general in September 1861. Losing an arm from wounds suffered at Seven Pines, Howard recovered to command a division and corps in the Army of the Potomac, and he eventually led the Army of the Tennessee during Sherman's March to the Sea.

out [Col. Alpheus S.] Williams. I sincerely hope he may have his appointment, & have urged him to come after it himself, besides applying for him at [the] War Dept.

McDowell spoke of giving me one of the other Mich. regiments, but they are neither over on this side [of the Potomac]. But adieu to ambition. My heart yearns towards you & the children. It would be so delightful just to see you only half an hour. I feel much concern about Baby. You must keep quiet & calm yourself & feel no concern for me. If it becomes necessary to have more bracing air for her, go where you can to get it. I suppose I might take the regiment home to reorganize. But I fear that if I do they might order me to Cairo;[25] and Washington is a better place to be near. But I hope to see you before Fall in some way. . . . Tell Father I will answer his last very soon. Write me all that is said about the regiment & the recruiting for it. I think Eb might as well copy that song (except last verse) & have it published in the *Advertiser.* Mother has it. Call it "Recruiting Song, for 1st Regt."

Your letters give me more delight than anything else I have. Everything you have done about [the] house & children pleases me & I am sure it is the best. Tell me all you can about the house hold. Miss Dix [was] here yesterday & Senator Trumbull & Grimes to-day.[26] Congress will be fierce for an advance in Va. God bless you all.

Orlando

Shuter's Hill
July 6/61
My dear Marie,

I have not been able to write you in some days—having the honors of a brigade thrust on me without any means to organize the staff except two fresh young graduates from West Point. One is Mr. [George A.] Woodruff, who is from Mich., very smart & direct. He is Asst. Adjt. Gen'l. The other is Mr. [John R.] Edie, Aide-de-Camp.[27] My regiment is brigaded with the Zouaves. We had a grand turn out.

---

25. Referring to the Union base at Cairo, Illinois, a staging point for troops in the western theatre.

26. Dorothea Dix, U.S. superintendent of women nurses; Sen. Lyman Trumbull, Radical Republican from Illinois; Sen. James W. Grimes (R., Iowa).

27. Lt. George A. Woodruff (16th, USMA 1861) later commanded Battery I, 1st U.S. Artillery. Mortally wounded at Gettysburg, July 3, 1863, he died the next day; Lt. John R. Edie (14th, USMA 1861), 2d U.S. Cavalry.

I enclose a check. I advanced money on to one of the men in June. Father can collect it. I received his letter & the pay accts to-day. Will attend to it first time I can get to Washington. Love in haste to all,

Orlando

Shuter's Hill
July 10 [1861]
My darling Wife,

I received your note of July 4 yesterday. I was very glad to hear from you but sorry to find you in rather low spirits at the time. Can you imagine that God is not with me here as well as at home? But I know how hard it is to cast off anxiety. I am glad the 4th of July is over, & hope no more guns or rockets will be heard at Detroit until they announce our victory. It cannot be many days before we march, probably ere this reaches you. I feel confident of our troops & our cause.

I had got thus far when an order was sent for me to repair forthwith to Col. Heintzelman's Hd. Quarters, where I found Gen'l McDowell, & soon all the colonels of the Alexandria Division were assembled & the order of the advance discussed. One satisfactory fact is there are no old fogies.

[Alpheus S.] Williams & Wilkins arrived here and dined. Williams is promised his Brigadiership as soon as the bill is passed. Wilkins is offered the Lt. Colonelcy of the 2d [Michigan] & is foolish I think not to accept. He prefers staff duties.

I am sorry Eb feels the war excitement so much. It would be such a good time to bring up the odds & ends of the office & his own affairs particularly.

The prospect for reorganization keeps brightening, although I suppose enlistments are dull during harvest time.

Prof. Williams' son in law, Richards, is seeking a lieutenancy in the army. I was glad to forward a recommendation & Chandler endorsed, & thinks he will get it. Poor McNair! how heartrending all their troubles in a heap. He would be glad to get even a sutlership in the army. But I advise him against that. . . .

I am glad you like the new tenants, but hope you will get Judge Bell or some Collector to look sharp after the rent. I am delighted that the Baby is well, & that you like Mary.

You are a capital finance manager. Do not starve or go naked! I am very glad you take such kind care of Mother. I will write again before we start. I expect my fourth regt. tomorrow. God bless you all. Kisses to Lulu, Elon & the Baby.

Your husband,
Orlando Willcox

Strawberry Hill
July 13, '61
My dearest Wife,

You perceive that Hd. Quarters of the "2d Brigade" are shifted to an euphonious hill. It is two miles out (on the Fairfax Road) from Shuter's Hill. The camp moved day before yesterday to Cloud's Mill, & I moved last evening to this point one mile below Cloud's Mill. The Zouaves are camped at the base of my hill, & the 38th [New York], Col. Ward,[28] are two miles nearer town. These, with a light Battery, Capt. Arnold,[29] which is in town, constitute my brigade, but I hope to have the Mich. 4th added in a day or two.

Strawberry Hill is owned by a Mr. Watkins, one of the F.F.V.'s [first families of Virginia]—late a butcher. It is a beautiful spot, commanding a railroad & turnpike, & gives a view of a great many camps, Maine, Vt., N.Y., etc., besides a white spot of the Potomac in the distance. The rail can now run 8 or 10 miles & it is cheerful to hear the whistle & the rattle after the dead stillness of Alexandria.

Mrs. Watkins is a prolific lady, having added 14 to the race (in one instance three at a birth), of which her husband is boastful. There is a farm of 100 acres, to which is about a negro per acre as a working force. They give us two rooms & a [piazza] & feed us for the few days we shall tarry. Mr. Meyer is at camp, & Dr. Brodie, Lt. Woodruff, Lt. Edie & Lt. [Francis H.] Parker constitute my military family. One important item is stable room for the horses.

We are all alive for the grand move which cannot be put off long. I have a new servant, colored, Dogan, & shall probably take him & leave Henry to bring up with my baggage, as he knows all about it & Dogan seems to be a good [orderly] & takes care of "Henry" & the other horse. I shall have to start with nothing but a blanket & pair of socks. I would write more of our arrangements & plans but it would not be prudent, & what I know is official.

28. Col. J. H. Hobart Ward, 38th New York, was appointed brigadier general in October 1862. He fought at Gettysburg, the Wilderness, and at Spotsylvania Court House, where he was wounded. Ward died in 1904, hit by a train.

29. Capt. Richard Arnold (13th, USMA 1850), commanding Battery D, 2d U.S. Artillery.

I am not so full of glorious "pomp & circumstance" as to forget for half an hour my faithful little wife & my pretty little ones. But I am quite sanguine of returning to you all well. I see Gen'l McClellan is succeeding finely.[30] We shall probably have tougher work, but I have no fear of the result. The only serious apprehension in my mind is about lack of good water, for which we shall probably suffer on our marches.

Much love to Father & Mother & kiss the children over & over for your dear devoted Husband,

O.B.W.

Fairfax Road
July 16 [1861]
My glorious Molly,

Off once more on the march. This day we go no further than about 8 miles & anticipate no opposition. To-morrow we go to Fairfax & expect there may be fighting. Keep as calm & trustful . . . as possible.

I received Father's kind letter, but for the last few days have been too busy to write any thing but business, orders, etc. The 4th Mich. has joined my brigade, also a light battery, D, 2d Artillery, Capt. Arnold.

It is impossible to say or conjecture what will be the event of the campaign. It seems to be thought the enemy will fall back. If not we must drive them back.

My heart is too full for my eyes, surrounded as I am by my staff, to trust writing the impulses of the moment. I can only say God bless & keep you & bring us & the children all together soon.

Love to Father & Mother, Caro, Frank, [Albin?] Wm. Blodgett[31] & all. Kiss my children.

Orlando

In Camp
Centreville, Va.
July 20, 1861
My dear Marie,

I have received a letter from your beloved pen & it gave me supreme pleasure. It was written in such a calm, cheerful spirit. It has no date (don't

30. Referring to McClellan's recent victories at Rich Mountain and Corrick's Ford, which secured western Virginia for the Union and brought "Little Mac" instant fame.

31. William T. Blodgett, a wealthy New Yorker who had made a fortune in the varnish business, was an intimate friend of OBW. Blodgett's daughter, Nelly, was to be the godmother of Franklin Delano Roosevelt.

forget to date your letters), but you say I will have left Alexandria before receiving it.

We marched from Alexandria on the 16th with the whole brigade of 12 regiments, [Capt. James B.] Ricketts' Battery,[32] Arnold's battery (in my brigade) & C Company, 2d Cavalry, all composing Col. Heintzelman's Division. The Brigade commanders are 1st, [Brig. Gen. William B.] Franklin, 2d, O. B., 3d, Howard. The next day we marched: Franklin for Sangster's Station & I for Fairfax Station, both points on the [Orange & Alexandria] Railway. The roads did not diverge for some distance, so that I was kept back by Franklin, who moved very cautiously & slowly, till 12. At 12 I overlapped him by chance & got on to Fairfax Station & took eleven prisoners & a Secession flag & pushed on towards Fairfax Ct. House, but found it already occupied, & turned back & camped at the Station. Had I been able to march straight from the Pohick, alone with my brigade without being delayed by Franklin's brigade, I might have caught a thousand of the rebels at least.

As it was, the rapidity of a single hour secured for my brigade the only prisoners taken & only flag that I heard of being captured by all the army. Ten of the captives were caught by Capt. Butterworth & one by Sergt. Beardsley of F. Co., son of Beardsley [the] hotel keeper of Detroit. (They were brought up to Gen'l McDowell, who questioned them yesterday & attracted thousands of eyes.)

The next day we all marched to this point. Our division, as well as most of the troops, are camped on the long sloping sides of the hills overlooking Little Rocky Run. Centreville stands on top of the Western Ridge opposite me. We are right on the Blue Ridge & the scenery is magnificent. Just now there are thirty or forty thousand troops bivouacked almost in sight, & Gen'l McDowell is reviewing a Division of 12,000 men on one slope.

All are in good spirits. The affair of Tyler's was but a premature & mistaken attack & was not a repulse.[33] It showed the enemy's position in a thick wood about 2 miles from us, & displayed our artillery to great advantage. Nothing could have been handsomer [than] the action of Ayres' Battery.[34] Ayres is a classmate. There [are] quite a number of my class here, all in con-

32. Capt. James B. Ricketts (16th, USMA 1839) commanded Battery I, 1st U.S. Artillery. He was shot four times in the Battle of Bull Run.

33. Brig. Gen. Daniel Tyler (14th, USMA 1819), commanding the First Division in McDowell's army, engaged the Confederates at Blackburn's Ford on Bull Run, July 18, 1861. Col. Israel B. Richardson led Tyler's Fourth Brigade, which was the chief unit engaged against the Confederate brigade of Brig. Gen. James Longstreet. Tyler lost eighty-three men, while the Confederates lost sixty-eight.

34. Capt. Romeyn B. Ayres, commanding Battery E, 3d U.S. Artillery, took part in the affair at Blackburn's Ford.

spicuous positions. Ayres, Burnside (not a general as you suppose but like myself a brigade commander), [Capt. Otis H.] Tillinghast,[35] chief quarter master, & [Capt. James B.] Fry, adjt. gen'l. The latter does everything he can for me at Hd. Quarters. He is an old friend. His offices were useful yesterday. I got him to appoint Parker to muster in those of the present regiment who wish to remain & the number is already quite respectable, & hourly increasing.

There is a rumor at Fairfax & Alexandria that I was killed the other day, but Prof. Cooley who is here goes down to-day & will telegraph you.

Love to all, & kisses for babies. The 2d Mich lost but 5 or 6 killed & wounded.[36]

Orlando

35. Capt. Otis H. Tillinghast (13th, USMA 1847) was mortally wounded at Bull Run, dying on July 23, 1861.

36. Referring to losses suffered by this regiment (which belonged to the Fourth Brigade of Tyler's Division) at Blackburn's Ford.

§

TWELVE

The Battle of Manassas

[In early July 1861, Orlando Willcox was given command of the 2d Brigade of Col. Samuel P. Heintzelman's Third Division of the army then being formed under Brig. Gen. Irvin McDowell in and around Washington, D.C. It was a significant step in Willcox's career, recognizing both his professional experience and his earlier action in capturing the town of Alexandria. Consisting of the 1st and 4th Michigan and 11th and 38th New York Infantry regiments, and Capt. Richard Arnold's Battery D, 2d U.S. Artillery, the brigade numbered more than three thousand officers and men. Less than three weeks after his assignment, Willcox led his new command into the first major battle of the Civil War—the Battle of Bull Run, where he was wounded and taken prisoner.]

‹The First Battle of Manassas or Bull Run is commonly said to have been one of the best planned but worst fought battles of the Civil War. General McDowell's plan was strategically excellent. After the enemy's left was turned, I never witnessed better work than the fighting that took place on some parts of the field. This fighting would have given us the day but for one or two tactical misadventures. And this to say nothing of the confusion and delays owing to the blocking of the columns at the Stone Bridge over which we all crossed Bull Run.›[1]

---

1. The introduction for this chapter, contained here within the single angle brackets ‹ ›, is from the chapter "The Battle of Manassas," written by OBW in about 1903. For the main part

[The following is transcribed from a notebook that General Willcox kept while in prison. The account is prefaced "Strictly Private, & written for my family."]

[WE] LEFT Alexandria July 16, 1861. There were 3 brigades, Franklin's, Howard's & my own. We took the old road & marched to the Pohick.[2] The last of the column got in at midnight. Heintzelman, in command, then sent for brigade commanders & read his orders from Gen. McDowell. Franklin's brigade was to march next A.M. for Sangster's Station, mine to Fairfax Station. Howard [was] held as a reserve.

Franklin preceded me till within 1½ miles of Fairfax Station, where his route branched to the left, mine to the right. Gen. McDowell expected Fairfax Station to be reached by 8 A.M., but Franklin moved slowly . . . & it was 12 M. before he turned off. On reaching the woods near Fairfax Station, I sent forward scouts, followed by 3 companies of skirmishers (Butterworth's & a company [of] Zouaves) all under Maj. [Charles] Leoser of the Fire Zouaves. These were followed by an advance guard, then the main body.

The road was found obstructed by felled trees; these were quickly cleared away for Arnold's battery to pass. The enemy fled at our approach. Capt. Butterworth succeeded in capturing a sergeant & 10 men. A masked battery was found in the woods, deserted, & a small earth work at the station commanding the R.R. track. Two camps [of] infantry were found, with fresh fires, victuals half cooked, a flag of blue silk, embroidered "Tensas Rifles" (Alabama) & a small cavalry camp. Many articles were found hastily thrown into the flames, among which was a fine case of medical instruments, also clothing, etc.

Firing being heard in the direction of Fairfax Station, we rushed on about half way towards that place, but found the ground occupied by [Col. Dixon S.] Miles' division, & the shots were from Garibaldi's (Blenker's) men, who were foraging after turkeys.[3] My skirmishers saw, on their approach to the station, large numbers of infantry & some cavalry retreating in the distance. The people of [the] neighborhood said the place had been

---

of the chapter, as published here, the editor has reverted to OBW's earliest account of the battle, written in a notebook while he was yet in prison, hereafter referred to as OBW *Prison Journal*.

2. Heintzelman's route followed the old Fairfax Road, which ran south of, and parallel to, the Orange & Alexandria Railroad, to the point where it met the railroad at the crossing of Pohick Creek, about three miles east of Fairfax Station.

3. Col. Dixon S. Miles (27th, USMA 1824) commanded the Fifth Division, in reserve at Centreville. Col. Louis Blenker commanded the First Brigade of Miles's division. He was mortally wounded while defending Harpers Ferry on September 15, 1862, dying two days later. The 39th New York (Garibaldi Guards), commanded by Col. F. G. D'Utassy, was part of Blenker's command.

occupied by 2 or 3 troops, most of whom left in the train of cars at 11 A.M. Instead of reaching here at 8 A.M., I was not allowed to get up till 1 P.M.; otherwise we might have had a smart brush.

We lay at Fairfax Station until 4 P.M. next day, when, by orders of Col. Heintzelman, we left 4 companies, under Major Childs, 4th Michigan, to guard the depot, & marched the command via old Braddock [Road] to Centreville. Just as we turned off on the Braddock Road, an order came from Gen. McDowell (by Maj. Wood) to detach the rest of [the] 4th Michigan to Fairfax C. H. This done, we proceeded & camped at Rock Run, opposite Centreville, along & above which the Army lay. Heintzelman, with Franklin & Howard's brigades, arrived half an hour after me, by a road direct from Sangster's.

The transportation was short, & not rations enough. We had started with 4 days rations in the haversacks. One wagon was allowed to each regiment, as well as an ammunition wagon & an ambulance. We lay at Centreville the night of the 18th, & the whole of the 19th & 20th, during which time rations came in. On [the] afternoon of [the] 18th, Tyler, pushing his reconnaissance too far perhaps, was checked at Blackburn's Ford (Bull Run). We heard the firing from our march on Braddock Road & felt chilled on hearing the result, particularly as a New York regiment behaved shamefully. Ayres' (formerly Sherman's) battery behaved nobly.

On the 19th I obtained an order from Gen. McDowell to muster in the [1st Michigan] Regiment for 3 years. Lieut. Parker, U.S.A., of my staff, procured rolls & swore in about 75 officers & men. But there was great disposition to go home for a short time. I had had much trouble with regard to re-enlistment. First, at Detroit, the regiment, after voting by acclamation for 3 years, came on to Washington before the thing could be perfected. The subject was again broached at Alexandria, but though many of the men now held back, all the recusants said they would re-enlist, if their services were needed, & if they could obtain short furloughs. Besides, the Adjutant General refused to muster us in for the war or 3 years unless the governor of the state nominated the regiment for the service. This he did not do, although I telegraphed & wrote him until just before we left Alexandria—nor, in fact, until after the President had, at my request, accepted the regiment independently of the governor, & an order was then issued for me to reorganize the regiment for the war. All this had a poor effect.

On the afternoon of the 20th, forming the skirmishers who had attacked Fairfax Station as an escort, we carried the captured flag first to Col. Heintzelman, & then to Gen. McDowell's headquarters, where it was deposited with some *eclat*.

The division & brigade commanders were ordered to assemble at Head-quarters on [the] night of [the] 20th at 8:00 o'clock for orders, the Army being ordered first to march this P.M., which [was] countermanded; we were to start at 2½ A.M. the 21st. Arrived at headquarters; the officers were not called into Gen. McDowell's tent till about 10 o'clock, when the order of march was read. It was a long document & no copy was furnished any of us, & there was a general ignorance of the topography of the contemplated field of operations across Bull Run to the rear of Manassas.

The order was substantially as follows: [Brig. Gen. David] Hunter[4] was to make a long detour by Sudley Church Ford, which crossing he was to drive in any opposition & turning towards the left, advance towards Manassas, [and] at [the] same time effect a junction with Heintzelman. He [Heintzelman] was to take a road crossing the Run between Sudley's & the Stone Bridge, & Tyler's division was to cross at or near Stone Bridge, after the left flank of the enemy was turned by Hunter, & the left center shaken by Heintzelman. This programme was not carried out, as it was found that there was no road between Sudley's & Stone Bridge, & consequently Heintzelman's division had to follow after Hunter to Sudley's Church.

At 2½ A.M., my brigade was promptly under arms & ready to start, but we were delayed by the troops in advance until 5:45, when we moved forward, & after a very hot march & incessant delays & halts, reached Sudley Church ford about 1 P.M. Tyler opened fire on our left at 6:15 A.M., & Hunter on our right (in advance of our division) at about 10. The different columns formed long clouds of dust. The puffs & clouds of the discharge of fire arms had been visible to us some time before we reached the ford. Franklin's brigade was just crossing the ford before mine.

The first order I received while the men were halting & looking for water to fill their canteens, was to post Arnold's Battery, with a regiment to support it, on a hill [to the] left of the ford, but not across it. This done, the brigade (consisting now of only the Zouaves & 38th New York regiments) crossed over, marched up a hilly road by the church, in front of which the men threw off their overcoats & blankets, & many their jackets. Taking a winding route to the left & front, we marched about 1½ miles, when we came by a piece of woods where Burnside's glorious brigade was resting & caring for their wounded.

A little further to the front & I was ordered to form in line of battle & sweep across the ground. The 38th had already formed in fine order, the Zouaves coming up on their right, when the order was changed, & I was

4. Brig. Gen. David Hunter (24th, USMA 1822) commanded the Second Division.

directed by an aide to send a regiment over to support a light battery now firing from a hill by the house known as Dogan's house, ½ a mile to our right & front & overlooking the Warrenton Turnpike. I took the Zouave regiment to this hill & here came first under fire. A cannon ball struck within 3 ft. of my horse & ricocheted over the Zouaves, who ducked their heads & look[ed] back at the projectile with childish wonder.

Thus, when I came into action, my brigade was divided up into detachments, no two regiments being together, & from ½ to 2 miles apart. Under such circumstances I thought it my duty to be with the foremost regiment, the Zouaves, & send for the others when necessary.

Col. Heintzelman now came in person & directed the battery, which proved to be Ricketts', to cross a field to our left & open fire from an elevation across the Sudley & Brentsville Road & near Mrs. Henry's house, & the Zouaves to support it. On the banks of [a] little branch [creek] on our route, we met [Capt. Charles] Griffin's battery in confusion, retiring from a position in which, without supports, the men & horses had been picked off by the enemy in the woods near by.[5]

Arriv[ing] on the right of Ricketts' battery, which was firing to the front blindly, we found it planted on a most unfortunate spot, the ground rising directly in front, a broken line of second-growth pines forming a curve or pocket, extending, within range of small arms, from our right around until the extreme point intercepted our front view of the field.

Col. Heintzelman rode up from our right to the front & suddenly exclaimed, "Here they are, here they are!" & waved his arm for the supports. I ordered up the Zouaves at once. They moved forward in good order with a reserve in rear of 2 companies. The woods were bristling with the enemy. It was now 2 o'clock, & according to Beauregard's report, the remains of Bee's, Bartow's & Evans' brigades had here formed & [were] strengthened further by Jackson's Brigade,[6] & with Waltham's, Imboden's & another light

5. Capt. Charles Griffin then commanded Battery D, 5th U.S. Artillery.

6. Brig. Gen. P. G. T. Beauregard (2d, USMA 1838) commanded the Confederate forces at Manassas. Although Gen. Joseph E. Johnston, who ranked Beauregard, arrived with reinforcements from his Army of the Shenandoah while the battle was in progress, Beauregard remained in command on the field. OBW, though in prison when he wrote this account, was familiar with Beauregard's report, as it had been published in the Richmond newspapers. See Beauregard's Report, OR, vol. 2, pp. 484–505.

Brig. Gen. Thomas J. Jackson commanded the First Brigade, Col. F. S. Bartow the Second Brigade, Brig. Gen. Barnard E. Bee (33d, USMA 1845) the Third Brigade of Johnston's Army. Both Bee and Bartow were killed during the battle. Col. Nathan G. Evans, an old acquaintance of OBW, commanded a temporary brigade in Beauregard's army.

Samuel P. Heintzelman.
USAMHI.

battery, with Stuart's cavalry[7] posted at this very point, his left having been driven back thus far & now reinforced from the center, in all 6,500.

But just as the Zouaves came to the crest of the rising ground & ere the enemy were visible to them (although visible from a horse's back) the fire burst upon us from the whole pocket of woods which partially enclosed us, & at the same time Ricketts' cannoneers, horses & drivers began to fall. The weight of metal against us was as of ten shots to one, of every class of projectiles. Amid the din not an order could possibly be heard. I shouted "charge bayonet!" but although [I was] among the file closers, my voice could not reach the files in front of me, & the whole regiment was swept

---

7. Maj. J. B. Walton (CSA)   incorrectly given as "Waltham" by OBW—commanded a battalion of the Washington Artillery (New Orleans); Capt. John D. Imboden commanded the Staunton (Virginia) Artillery in Beauregard's Army; Col. J. E. B. Stuart (13th, USMA 1854)—incorrectly spelled "Stewart" in original, but corrected here—commanded the 1st Virginia Cavalry of Johnston's army.

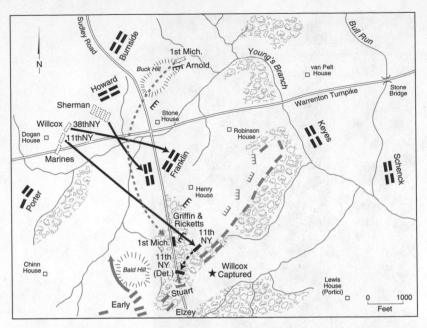

First Manassas (Bull Run), July 21, 1861. The progression of events involving Willcox's Brigade is as follows: 1) Having dispatched the 1st Michigan to support Arnold's battery on Buck Hill, OBW marches the remainder of his brigade to a point just south of the Dogan house. 2) Dispatching the 38th New York to support Franklin, OBW leads the 11th New York forward to support Ricketts's battery. The 11th strikes the left front of the Stonewall brigade. 3) As Stuart's Confederate cavalry regiment moves up the Sudley Road, it strikes the detachment of the 11th New York left to support Ricketts. The detachment is overrun and retreats, along with the rest of the regiment. 4) The 1st Michigan marches to the front, forming behind a fence along the Sudley Road. OBW leads the regiment in a charge, when he is wounded and captured.

back as by a tornado. They fell back to their post on the right of Ricketts' guns a confused mass of men & officers, the latter, with Col. Heintzelman, myself & Maj. [James S.] Wadsworth[8] of Gen. McDowell's staff, striving to form the ranks.

The fire from the woods still kept up on our right. The enemy not visible to Ricketts' officers & men, I dismounted & pointed one of his guns. Al-

8. James S. Wadsworth was then serving as an aide to General McDowell. He was appointed brigadier general in August 1861, and the following March he was made military governor of Washington, D.C. Wadsworth's major Civil War service was as commander of the First Division, First Corps, Army of the Potomac, which he led on the first day of the Battle of Gettysburg, where the division was virtually destroyed. Given command of the Fourth Division, Fifth Corps, in the spring of 1864, Wadsworth was mortally wounded on May 6, 1864, at the Battle of the Wilderness, dying two days later.

ready every cannoneer except the one who was loading had been shot down at this piece, as the latter informed me, saying, "Colonel, I'm the only man left here." With Col. Heintzelman's approbation and a promise of reinforcements, I then took a small detachment of the Zouaves & attacked at the point from which the fire proceeded closely on our right. The movement was successful, about 20 of the enemy were killed & wounded, a few prisoners taken & the woods were cleared. Posting the men so as to hold the point & observe the return of the enemy, I rode back for reinforcements.

But, meantime, Stuart's cavalry charge had taken place upon the Zouaves left to support Ricketts, these supports had disappeared, the gallant Ricketts, his first lieutenant, Ramsay, & many of his gallant men had fallen, killed or wounded, & men & horses now lay about the guns which the enemy had not yet taken possession of. On the same field lay many gallant Zouaves; their spirits had fled to join their Colonel [Ellsworth], in whom dwelt the soul of the regiment. Col. Heintzelman, in his report, mistakes in saying that this regiment was repulsed by the 4th Alabama. The 4th Alabama had entirely withdrawn from the field at the time we came up, having, with Hampton's Legion, been effectually cut to pieces by Hunter's division in the morning.[9]

As Col. Heintzelman had promised, I met a reinforcement coming up in my own darling regiment, [the] 1st Michigan. This regiment I led back to the field. But, meantime, the enemy had gained possession of Ricketts' battery, & drew a line of skirmishers to receive us. We opened fire from a fence on the roadside. At the first fire, the right wing of the 1st Michigan fell back under the orders of some officer. The left stood their ground & drove the enemy out of sight, their number not being considerable. At this moment, Col. Heintzelman again came up & I proposed to him to go forward with this regiment to the point of woods already gained, & seek to turn the enemy's left flank. He told me to push on & he would send me another regiment.

As the regiment moved forward, the enemy were engaged with [Col. William T.] Sherman's brigade,[10] their front was changed, & with more force on their flank the day would have been ours. Between my regiment & Sherman's brigade was a regiment I took to be one of Franklin's Massachusetts regiments. But there was a lack of concert of action. We were attacking

9. See "Report of Col. Samuel P. Heintzelman, Seventeenth U.S. Infantry, Commanding Third Division," *OR*, vol. 2, pp. 402–4; Col. Wade Hampton commanded "Hampton's Legion," a South Carolina regiment consisting of infantry, artillery, and cavalry.

10. Col. William T. Sherman (6th, USMA 1840) commanded the Third Brigade of Tyler's First Division.

the enemy's strong-hold & what had now become his main body, strengthened from the center & reserve & Johnston's reinforcements, numbering in all 7 or 8,000 men, by bringing up our forces one regiment at a time.

In the course of the day Ricketts' battery was retaken again by another regiment of the 2d (my) brigade, viz. [the] 38th New York, which was ordered up probably in pursuance of Heintzelman's intention of reinforcing me. For Heintzelman, coming up as we regained it with [the] 1st Michigan, ordered me to push forward & said he would reinforce me. At this point in his report, Col. Heintzelman only says the 1st Michigan was brot up & fell back "in considerable confusion." This is only true of the right wing, but, as I have said, the left wing stood firm & cleared the field of the enemy, & when Col. Heintzelman came up, I exclaimed, "Col., the 1st Michigan has retrieved the day!" With regard also to the 38th, which the gallant colonel does not mention at all, besides what I have said of it, it also repulsed a charge of Wheat's Battalion, the New Orleans Tigers,[11] who dashed at them at charge bayonet, & with Bowie knives (some say in their teeth) but I did not witness the feat.

Meantime, to return to the 1st Michigan, without waiting for the right wing we pushed on rapidly & regained my former position in the point of woods, & soon the rest of the regiment was led on in line & good order by Maj. Bidwell. My hope was now to turn the enemy's rear, especially as I saw a regiment of ours in grey uniform moving on their left & front.[12] We advanced to the point of woods, my men giving a loud cheer as I rode up to the right wing, & pushed to the rear of the enemy, now hotly engaged with the regiment in grey, as well as another, probably one of Sherman's, further towards the center, the enemy's line stretching out diagonally between my troops & Sherman's, their rear rank exposed fairly & within 150 yards to our fire.

We availed ourselves of a slight ravine, or gullet, & fought partly under cover. As soon as the enemy discovered our fire, their rear rank faced about with utmost coolness & began to return it, & it was during this sharp prac-

11. Major Chatham Roberdeau Wheat commanded the 1st Louisiana Battalion, or "Louisiana Tigers," of Evans's Brigade. Wounded at Bull Run (shot through both lungs), Wheat nevertheless survived, continuing to command the regiment until he finally fell with a mortal wound at Gaines' Mill, June 27, 1862.

12. Though dark blue was the predominant color for uniforms in the Union army, early in the war many Northern regiments outfitted themselves in some rather unique uniforms, including cadet gray, which was, of course, the prevailing color of Confederate uniforms. This, of course, caused fatal confusion on the battlefield, but nowhere more so than at First Bull Run. Following that battle, few Union regiments wore anything but dark blue, though a few regiments (the Zouave units, for instance) continued their peculiar forms of dress until late in the war.

tice that my horse was shot in the front & lower part of the neck, & I was shot in the right fore arm. Within ten paces of me were Capts. Whittlesey & Graves, 1st Michigan, with muskets, loading & firing in the coolest possible manner. One of the enemy crept over towards us on hands & knees, loading & firing, until he was killed within easy pistol range. I saw men firing at me very deliberately, but I had passed through such hot work already that I had scarcely a faint idea of being hit, until suddenly I felt a severe shock, like that of electricity in my arm, which began to spin around like a top. This was followed by extreme faintness, such that it was with difficulty I could hold the rein in my left hand & guide the horse to the rear even a few steps.

At this moment Capt. Withington came up to convey intelligence that a new force of the enemy had just appeared, probably across the field in our rear & left, where the battery was, & were engaged with their backs to us, and, I think, on the left of the Henry house. But observing my condition, the captain took the rein & led my horse to the woods nearby, where I dismounted & the captain bound a handkerchief tightly around my arm above the elbow.

It must have been with great difficulty that the 1st Michigan cut their way back from their position, for the enemy were now on two sides of them, & I soon found were approaching on a third side.[13] These were the 28th Virginia. A party of their scouts or skirmishers were coming up a road in the woods, when I discovered them & ordered the three or four men who had gathered about me to fire upon them, & shouting at the same time "bring up the whole regiment!" as loudly as I was able, the enemy's party beat a hasty retreat. The men said one or two fell.

This little affair roused my strength a little, & had my horse not been wounded, possibly I might have been bound on him & escaped. The poor steed (a magnificent dapple grey stallion) followed me like a dependant child. But I had scarce strength enough left to form a plan; my only purpose was to get to the rear before the regiment, still fighting manfully, knew that I was down.

With Capt. Withington's assistance, I now crossed a fence & was going across a bit of open field holding my right arm with the left, & Capt. Withington's right arm around my waist, when in this helpless condition we were assailed by Col. [R. T.] Preston,[14] who charged on horseback at us,

13. See "Notes and Journal of Capt. Ira Abbott" for a detailed first-hand account of the 1st Michigan's escape from the field, App. A, p. 687.

14. Col. R.T. Preston commanded the 28th Virginia. OBW indicates in his little black *Prison Diary* (not to be confused with his *Prison Journal*) that he was captured at 5 P.M.

William H.
Withington.
USAMHI.

thundering loud oaths, pointing his revolver & demanding our surrender. Of course there was nothing left us but to comply. The stout colonel (for he was a stalwart man with a grizzled huge beard & loud, gruff voice) then demanded who I was, & when I told him, he hallowed like a bull, "You're just the man I've been looking for." I replied, "I am an officer & a gentleman, sir, & expect to be treated as such." He assumed a milder tone & politely told us [to] keep our swords.

While this parley was going on, a party of the colonel's men came out of the woods close by where he came at us, & escorted us to the rear, into a hollow a few hundred yards off, passing on our way [two] long lines of the enemy lying on their arms, & probably waiting for orders or posted there waiting the approach of our troops. This is a confirmation of the fact that Beauregard had at & near the plateau a sufficient force to meet all we could show & largely out numbering the troops we did bring up. But he pretends in his report that we came upon him with overwhelming numbers.

In the hollow we found a surgeon of the 1st Maryland (Secession), who gave me some whiskey & roughly dressed my wound using the cloth of the sleeve as a sort of plug, & to staunch the blood, which flowed profusely, he used as a compress a fragment of corn cob picked off from the ground. I do not complain of this, for he probably used the only means at his command.

They then started with me to go further to the rear when, after taking about ten steps, my head began to swim, the air grew black, & I fell to the ground, fainting. They carried me back to the foot of the tree where the wound had been dressed. I lay there some time in semi-consciousness, & then sat up against the trunk, while they poured more vile whiskey down my throat.

The party [of Union troops] who [had] stood around me in the woods, & drove off the first of the enemy, were now brought here as prisoners. One of my fellows, when he saw my condition, said, "What is this, the colonel?" & leaned over me some time, weeping. A Secession officer—happening by with some of his own wounded & learning my name, asked if I were the Col. Willcox who commanded at Alexandria, & finding me the same, he said I should be taken care of, as I had been kind to his friends in Alexandria, & procuring a blanket, had me placed upon it. Five soldiers, with the help of Capt. Withington, took me up, then carried me by a circuitous route nearly to Mr. Lewis' house, when we met another Marylander, a Dr. Meredith, who, learning who I was, stopped the party to look at my wound, & said I had shown some kindness to friends or relations of his at Alexandria. As my mode of conveyance was painful, he sent for a litter, & while waiting for it he took off the rude dressing on my arm & dressed it with cotton bandages. It was here, I think, that someone asked if he should remove the map— a large doctor—from my bosom. I nodded my head, & he took it. This was a large topographical map of the country about Manassas furnished officers of divisions & brigades, & a letter appeared afterwards in the Southern papers from someone claiming that I had given him the map on the field, as a present in return for his kindness to me. In the same manner my spurs and field glass disappeared. The surgeon who first dressed my wound took my sword & promised to take care of it & return it to me. But although he afterwards called upon me at the Lewis house, I have never seen the sword again to this day. In regard to the map, a Col. Moore of Kentucky called on me afterwards at Richmond & said it was he who took it & meant to return it, but that Gen. Beauregard had ordered him to give it up to him. I do not know but dare say he [Col. Moore] may have been the author of the letter, as there were several letters & stories, equally false, claiming for their fabricators to be my captors, & describing particulars, minutely & romantically.

As soon as the litter came, they placed me on it & carried me to Mr. Lewis' house,[15] the same Maryland surgeon going with them, & although the building was crowded, even in the halls, with the wounded of both sides, he directed that no one else should be put in the room assigned to me; it was a pleasant square chamber in the 2d story & overlooked the battlefield, in the west. Thus, by the goodness of God, I had been kindly dealt with by the enemy & I shall never forget or cease to be grateful to those who saved me from the horrid exposures of many, who lay, even for days, in the sun & rain, their wounds undressed.

Soon after reaching these comfortable quarters, Capt. Withington saw Capt. Ricketts lying in the hall at the foot of the stairs & had him brot to our room. In the evening Dr. Grey of the regular Army took up his quarters with us, & next day we had Dr. Lewis, 2nd Wisconsin, & Drs. Howmaston & Swalm, 14th New York (Brooklyn Regiment). Refreshments that night were out of the question, & I lay all night enduring great pain, especially as my arm had been bandaged so tightly as to prevent all circulation.

A Dr. Darby of Wade Hampton's South Carolina Legion came in, there being many of his regiment lying wounded in the building. He very kindly asked to see the wound, dressed it & put on a more comfortable bandage, just in time to save the arm from amputation. The wound was an ugly looking affair, 3 inches by 4, grazing but not breaking the bone. The doctors all thought it was a shell wound, but I think it came from a large minie musket ball, which, touching the bone, revolved in the flesh, & coming out it struck one of my coat buttons, denting the latter & tearing it nearly off. Had it not so happened that my arm was up, holding the bridle rein in the right hand, the ball or bit of shell must have penetrated my side & taken life itself. The contemplation of my narrow escape & kind attentions made me calm & resigned to the good providence of God.

Col. Hampton, Ex-Gov. Manning, Ex-Gov. Allston & other South Carolina gentlemen visited us almost daily.[16] They were full of praise of Ricketts' Battery & the 1st Michigan, from both which they frankly acknowledged having suffered much on the field. Col. Evans (now Gen'l Evans of Leesburg) also came in with Capt. Tillinghast's watch, which he thought of de-

15. The Lewis House, "Portici," located on the field southeast of Henry Hill, served as Johnston's headquarters during the battle and as a hospital afterwards.

16. John L. Manning, thirty-seventh governor of South Carolina (1852–1854), and Robert F. W. Allston, thirty-ninth governor of South Carolina (1856–1858).

The Lewis House, "Portici," on the Bull Run battlefield. Willcox and Ricketts were taken here immediately after they were wounded and captured. *USAMHI.*

positing with me for Mrs. Tillinghast . . . Tillinghast being one of my class-mates & Evans was in the next class below.

But the most distinguished visitor of all was Mrs. Capt. Ricketts [Frances Anne Pyne "Fanny" Ricketts], who arrived from Washington a few days after the battle, encountering great trouble & some insults after leaving our lines, but was equal to any danger. But she did not confine her nursing cares to her husband, but administered those sick room blessings to me which a lady only knows how to confer, sharing the duties with Capt. Withington, who bathed, fed, dressed & tended me like a loving brother.[17]

Dr. Darby came in daily & brot us many necessaries such as towels, shirts, blankets, etc., some days riding 18 miles to reach us. In short, he treated us as if we were of his own people. Mrs. Ricketts also went about constantly among the wounded men of both sides like a ministering angel, & her coming was always greeted with a smile from faces drawn with pain or closing in death. Mr. Lewis brot us many little comforts—though the battle had ruined him.

Among our trials was the dearth of the most common refreshments, hard bread & bacon of doubtful odor being almost our only stay for some days, &

17. Withington was awarded a Medal of Honor in 1895, "for remaining on the field to suc-cor his superior officer at Bull Run, July 21, 1861."

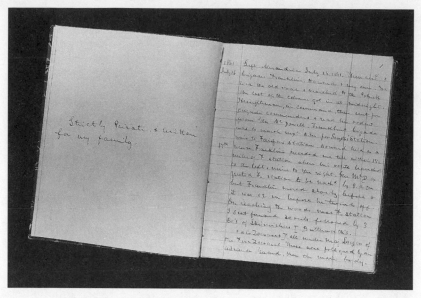

OBW's prison journal. *OBW Collection.*

even these so precious that some times we knew not where the next morsel was coming from. But we fared as well as the enemy's own, & after a few days a commissary dept. was set up in the barn & the actual necessaries such as bacon, bread, sugar & coffee were obtained. As for cooking, there were no vessels, nor dishes to eat from. One by one we gradually obtained a tin plate, tin cup, knife, fork & spoon, & Mrs. Ricketts' ingenuities in preparing our meals added greatly to their relish.

Some of the officers encamped in the neighborhood sent us an occasional chicken, egg, or bit of butter, which were obtained with great difficulty within the circuit of many miles. In one of our greatest straits, Maj. [Archibald] Gracie,[18] an acquaintance of Mrs. Ricketts, traveled far & wide for something eatable & finally returned with a goose, which his camp cook converted into soup—than which no turtle [soup] ever tasted better.

The surgeon who now took us in charge regularly was Dr. Lewis of [the] 2d Wisconsin, who remained to look after his wounded on the field, where he also dressed wounds of some of the enemy, & after [the] fight took an

18. Maj. Archibald Gracie (14th, USMA 1854). A New Yorker by birth, Gracie was at the outbreak of the war a cotton broker in Alabama. His allegiance remained with the South, and he was promoted to brigadier general in November 1862. Seeing action at Chickamauga and the siege of Knoxville, he was severely wounded at Bean's Station, Tennessee, on December 14, 1863. He was killed by Federal artillery at Petersburg on December 2, 1864.

ambulance & brot in the suffering both that night & next day, through the rain. The driver refusing to stay, he [Dr. Lewis] drove the team with his own hands. He was one of the most humane men & tender surgeons in the world, & at [the] same time full of good humor & wit. He is one of the salt of the earth; his very touch was healing.

The piazzas were strewn with amputated limbs for several days; dead bodies were lying under the trees in the yard. . . . the stench of the sloughing wounds in the house & from dead horses & men on the battle field was loathsome; the worms got in many of the wounds & whole quarts were removed at a time from living sufferers—they crawled on the floor & fed their dreadful ways into sound parts of the body with death in their train.

During all these melancholy days there was also great dearth of pure water—the springs being constantly stirred up by thousands of soldiers. Withington & Dr. Swalm roved for miles in quest of this common necessity, exposed to, & some times bearing the insults of the [Southern] soldiers. Both these gentlemen were assiduous & constantly busy in their attentions to our various needs. Night & day the house was filled with groaning, some times shrieks, & prayer for relief or death. Some were out of their head & constantly raving.

Among our visitors who were numerous & mostly for curiosity, were a few of my old Army friends, generally polite but not one of them did me any good & some were insulting. Almost every stranger inquired, "What did you come down here for? Do you expect to subjugate us?" But, after all, it was from strangers that I experienced most courtesy & most tangible comfort. Col. Lay, formerly of the U.S. Army but now on Gen. Beauregard's staff, came to inquire about the handcuff story which [had] created so much noise in the South. The story was that 30,000 handcuffs designed for the rebels were brot by Gen. McDowell & were captured. Both Ricketts & I denied it point-blank, & offered, if they could find them, to be the first to wear them. Lay afterwards came back & expressed Gen. Beauregard as satisfied, but to this day the tale never has been corrected, but has been kept alive to foment the passions of the South.

A day or two after the battle a Mississippi colonel called & said my horse was still alive & in his camp, & he politely sent me my overcoat, comb & brush that were attached to the saddle.

Capt. Withington had a parole limited to the boundaries of Virginia, & often visited the battle field. He went to the spot where the 1st Michigan was last engaged, & found that this regiment penetrated further than any other into the enemy's lines. In fact it was generally acknowledged by Secession officers.

We lay at the Lewis house almost two weeks, until Friday, August 2d, when Capt. Withington, Dr. Grey & myself were sent to Richmond, where we arrived on Saturday evening, August 3rd, my wound bearing the jolting of the cars with pain but not so ill as I feared. At the Richmond depot Gen. [John H.] Winder[19] met us, & politely furnished me with a cushioned carriage to the hospital, Dr. Gibson's, & at the latter place he directed a separate room for me. As the building was already crowded, this was a great courtesy. Here Capt. Withington & myself lay down, not as at the Lewis house on the boards & a single blanket, but on comfortable cots.

In a day or two Capt. & Mrs. Ricketts & Dr. Lewis joined us; they arrived in the night, the captain in great pain & exhaustion, & Mrs. Ricketts with feelings bruised beyond even her heroic powers of endurance, by the brutal insults she had received on the route, even at the hands of her own sex, who poked their heads in at the doors & windows of the cars & shouted "Where is the Yankee woman! Is she a laundress? Does she work for the soldiers?" & some even shook their fists at her. As soon as she came into the room she shook hands with me without power to utter a word, but burst into tears.

A day or two afterwards Lt. [Bernard] Mauch, of [the] 1st Michigan, was brot to the hospital & occupied an adjoining ward with Capt. McQuade, 38th New York, & Lt. Dickinson, 3rd [U.S.] Infantry. Mauch was wounded in the thigh, which was broken, but not yet amputated, although more than 2 weeks had now elapsed since the battle; had it been done even now his life might have been saved, but it was still neglected from day to day (our own surgeons not being allowed to perform such operations) till, finally, when the amputation took place, he sank rapidly & died.[20]

Mauch was a brave man with splendid & forceful muscular development. He (as well as Capt. Butterworth, 1st Michigan) received his wound while trying to get over to me just before I was wounded. His body was interred in the cemetery opposite the hospital by some Germans, & not, like the rest of the poor fellows who died here, thrust into the negro grave yard like dogs, without service, in holes, one of which was opened daily for all who died that day. In this hole the coffins were piled one on top of another till night, when the hole was closed.

19. Brig. Gen. John H. Winder (11th, USMA 1820) was then provost-marshal and commandant of Richmond prisons. In June 1864 he was placed in charge of Andersonville Prison in Georgia; in July he was given command of all Confederate prisons in Alabama and Georgia. In November of that same year he became commissary general of all prisons east of the Mississippi. He died on February 8, 1865, in Florence, South Carolina.

20. Lt. Bernard Mauch belonged to Company F. OBW indicates in his *Prison Diary* that Mauch died August 13, 1861, "after long neglect."

Poor Mauch bore his sufferings manfully, but just after the amputation, Dr. Peachy gave him one of his cold-blooded thrusts. Dr. Peachy was the principal house surgeon under the general superintendence of Dr. Gibson, & very bitter against us all. Just as he had completed his too long deferred work with Mauch, he turned & said, "I would do more for you if I thought your government treated our prisoners half as well." On another occasion a Zouave asked him for a bullet which the doctor had extracted from his wound. Dr. Peachy replied, "No sir, you can't have it, & if you make any fuss about it I'll put you in irons."

The appearance of Dr. Peachy in our room always gave us a shudder. Although outwardly polite, we felt that he was a spy & that he hated us one & all. He once handed a letter I had written to Capt. Butterworth around to a bevy of his friends on the door steps outside, & they all read it unblushingly.[21] He frequently ordered people who brot milk & newspapers on sale, not to sell any to the Yankees. His spying propensities were not devoted exclusively to us, but he was always hovering near Dr. Gibson, on some pretence or other, when that gentleman visited the hospital & had any business with strangers outside the usual routine. But Dr. Peachy had one weakness, or blindside, by which you could reach his heart, if heart was his, viz., his vanity. He had studied in Paris, & any sly allusion to his Parisian skill would conciliate the wretch at once.

Except what is connected with Peachy, few bitter associations rise in my mind with the recollection of the Richmond Hospital. But from the morning after my arrival, when he gave my wounded arm a rough dressing, until my departure, of which he was very impatient, he was an object of distrust & dread.

Such too was the feeling generally among our wounded officers. Occasionally he took a look at Ricketts' wound, but always passed it over slightingly as a small affair, altho Ricketts suffered acutely, & at one time an amputation of his leg was seriously discussed. We were cautioned against this creature by a lady who told us that he was in the habit of speaking about the Federals under his charge with great vituperation. I will do him the

21. OBW's letter to Butterworth was evidently in reply to one Butterworth had written to him. Butterworth, who had received a "bad wound in the thigh and a slight one in the hand," had been captured and imprisoned at Charlottesville, Virginia. On August 4, 1861, he wrote OBW "under very trying circumstances." As the regiment's term for enlistment was up and those not captured had gone home, Butterworth asked OBW if there was a chance that he and the men who were with him might be released or exchanged. "I should like to go home as I think I should improve so much faster than I do here. If you can do any thing for me or tell me how the matter stands please let me know by return of mail." Butterworth was not released, and he died in Confederate hands thirteen days later.

James B. Ricketts. *USAMHI.*   Fanny Ricketts. *OBW Collection.*

justice to say, however, that no warning was necessary to place us on our guard against him—his very looks invited distrust. However, he had some friends among the men.

Contrasted with Dr. Peachy stood Dr. [Charles Bell] Gibson[22] & Dr. Newton, who were both true gentlemen. Dr. Gibson is a gentleman of the old school, about 55 years of age, his father a physician of great repute in Philadelphia. His visits brot sunshine into the wards; he showed so much care for our situation in all respects, was so courteous & tender of our feelings, & ready to do everything in his power for us consistent with his duty & was withal so skillful in practice, that our feeling towards him amounted almost to veneration.

Dr. Newton was a young gentleman from Augusta, Georgia. He seemed to take quite a fancy for me & showed it by coming every evening to see what I or any of our party required. His care even extended to my reputa-

22. Dr. Charles Bell Gibson, formerly a professor of surgery at Hampden-Sidney College, had served a brief stint as surgeon general of Virginia before becoming head of the Officers' Hospital in Richmond.

tion, for on hearing a report in Richmond to the effect that before leaving Alexandria I had addressed my men holding up the beauty & booty of Richmond as an incentive to their zeal in the cause, he came to me at once, & was so well satisfied with my contradiction of the slander that he seemed to take great pleasure in correcting it.

As soon as Dr. Lewis arrived he took surgical charge of our party. We all ate, slept & lived in the same room, Mrs. Ricketts using her shawl as a screen in the corner near her husband. Although in the same room with three strange gentlemen, Mrs. Ricketts evinced the most becoming sense of the situation, & with infinite tact relieved us of all embarrassments, while she managed, imperceptibly to us, to guard her own retirement. She soon put herself in good accord with the Sisters of Mercy, who managed the cooking & interior economy, while they also did the duty of nurses. There was a general waiter named Patrick, who bought little necessaries for us at the market & shops, which, added to hospital fare of soup, maize bread, tea & coffee (such as are found nowhere else but in hospitals), under the magic influence of Mrs. Ricketts, gave us the nourishment we so greatly needed.

There was a lady of Richmond who sent us a bounteous dinner every Sunday regularly. Mrs. Gen. [Samuel] Cooper[23] also called as often as the bitter prejudices of Richmond Society would allow, & contributed considerably to our comforts. Through her Mrs. Ricketts procured a chafing dish so that we were able to cook for ourselves, & never have the rarest delicacies tasted so good as our little chance meals, made in a [hodgepodge] of all we possessed, & cooked by Mrs. Ricketts.

Her influence extended still further; with her capital power of conversation, wit & mimicry, she sped along the lagging hours rapidly. All over the hospital she soon became known, & was greeted with smiles of welcome by the saddest patients in the wards. She knew many by name & listened to their various complaints only with a mind to alleviate, so that the little bounties which occasionally fell to our lot from one friend or another were miraculously enlarged by this wonderful woman & extended to many others. As the men grew better & began to walk about, they found their way to our room & formed a coterie of admirers that any lady might be proud of.

Visitors, in fact, were never wanting. Dr. Gibson found it impossible to keep out the throng that almost every day, certainly on Sundays, wandered

23. Gen. Samuel Cooper (36th, USMA 1815) was a native of New Jersey and former U.S. adjutant general. He resigned from the U.S. Army in March 1861 and became the highest-ranking general in Confederate service, serving throughout the war as adjutant and inspector general of the Confederacy. Mrs. Cooper was the great-granddaughter of Revolutionary statesman George Mason.

through the wards. Our own room had no door, & we hung up a green blanket, which was frequently thrust aside rudely, & strangers would stalk in or stare at us without ceremony. One day a party came under the guidance of one who had been there before. This person lifted up our blanket curtain & exhibited us to his friends in the manner of a showman. "Here are Ricketts & Willcox," said he to his audience of some half dozen. "That's Ricketts lying down & there's Willcox with his arm in a sling." The curtain dropped after a long stare & the audience retired; two of them had officers' shoulder straps on their chivalrous shoulders. Ricketts & myself made it a rule to decline discussions with visitors; & after delivering themselves of a few choice epithets at the expense of "Old Abe" & "Old Scott," accompanied by a chaste flow of tobacco spittle deposited on the floor, our silence prevailed over their loquacity, & they withdrew.

Some of our visitors were of the better sort, & old acquaintances. Among these was Gen. [Simon B.] Buckner,[24] who expressed profound regret at the situation of affairs, but denounced the President for keeping bad faith with him in regard to the neutrality of Kentucky, accused Gen. McClellan of falsification, & yet said he should take no part in the war unless Kentucky seceded, in which case he should side with her & the South. He said he came to Richmond with no view of entering the service of the Confederacy, & offered to carry north any letters we might have when he left, which would be in a few days. He promised to call for the letters, but that was the last we saw of him, tho' we heard a few days afterwards that he had left town a brigadier general of the C.S.A.

<Captain John McGruder [Magruder], "Prince John," as he was called in the old Army, [also] came to see us—Ricketts more particularly—to talk over old times and to enquire [after] our wants. He was quite friendly and very entertaining, and we were loath to complain of our poor fare and destitute condition and tried to hide it in a jocular way. But the Prince saw through that disguise, and finally said: "Well, gentlemen, it is really too hard but I haven't a cent of money myself, though if my note at the bank can be of any use you are welcome to it," adding with a comically lugubrious expression, "but it never has done me a bit of good!">

Dr. Lewis was always devoted, not only to the party in our room but to all our wounded requiring his services. In a couple of weeks, Dr. Lewis went home with other surgeons on a parole, & Dr. Swalm took his place, prefer-

24. Simon Bolivar Buckner (11th, USMA 1844) was commissioned brigadier general in the Confederate army on September 14, 1861, though he had probably received notice of his pending appointment earlier.

ring to remain rather than leave the suffering. Our surgeons labored under many disadvantages; their instruments were taken away & their practice liable to interference on the part of the Confederate surgeons; in short, their duties were pretty much those of dressers & attendants.

Dr. Swalm was, however, indefatigable; night & day he was among the wounded until he was very near brot down with a fever himself. The typhoid had broken out in the hospital & several died, including a Confederate surgeon, & we began to feel apprehensive of danger to ourselves, reduced as we were. As fast as possible our wounded were removed & Confederate patients brot in—the convalescents went to the tobacco company factory, where our prisoners were confined in large numbers. I was, in fact, ordered there myself, but at the interposition of Dr. Gibson, was kindly permitted to remain with my friends, the Rickettses, until the 10th Sept., when I was ordered to Charleston, South Carolina, with Capts. Withington & [Capt. Edward W.] Jenkins[25] & a large party of officers & men from the tobacco factory.

25. Capt. Edward W. Jenkins, of the Naval Brigade.

THIRTEEN

Touring Southern Prisons

AFTER A painful separation from the Rickettses, to whom I had become as fondly attached as if of the same family, I left the hospital with the two captains in an ambulance, escorted by a common detective policeman, for the depot.[1] Here I found Col. Corcoran & the other prisoners under charge of a guard of Louisiana soldiers & Capt. [George C.] Gibbs.[2] I saw Dr. Barney a moment, & Dr. Gibson came down with a heavy blue overcoat & a bottle of whiskey & bade me farewell. I shall never cease, while life lasts, to remember him. But for leaving the Rickettses, I liked the move, particularly as we were assured of every accommodation at Castle Pinckney in the harbor of Charleston. I wanted the Rickettses to go with us, but the captain

---

1. The opening of this chapter is continued from OBW's *Prison Journal*, quoted in the previous chapter. Because OBW did not continue the story of his confinement in this earliest memoir (having stopped writing the account while yet imprisoned in Charleston), the editor finishes the chapter by quoting from a later memoir, entitled "Touring the South As a Prisoner," written by OBW in about 1890. Material taken from that memoir is enclosed within single angle brackets ‹ ›.

2. Col. Michael Corcoran, an Irishman who had emigrated to the United States in 1849, became colonel of the 69th New York Militia in 1859. After his release from prison in August 1862 he was appointed brigadier general and raised the "Corcoran Legion," a brigade of four New York regiments composed mostly of Irish immigrants. Corcoran served as a division commander in the Seventh Corps at Suffolk, Virginia, in April 1863, and later led a division in the Twenty-second Corps occupying the defenses of Washington. He was killed December 22, 1863, when his horse fell on him in a riding accident; Capt. George C. Gibbs, 42d North Carolina, then commanding the prison guard in Richmond.

feared for his leg, & it was perhaps as well that he remained, as the journey was the worst by far I ever took.

The first disgust was experienced at Petersburg, where the town turned out *en masse* to stare at us & evince various tokens of hate, from depot to depot, as we marched—a mile or more. The crowd was not made up of men & boys, as usual, but the women & girls of the city honored the melancholy procession with their faces.

At Weldon, North Carolina, the train laid over for the night. The men were lodged in a warehouse & the officers permitted by the indulgence of our commander, Capt. Gibbs, to stay, on parole, at the hotel, where we were very comfortable, but I was quite unwell from weakness, etc. The next day [we] traveled as far as Wilmington, still in North Carolina. It was very hot & we had no refreshments along the road, save the inevitable salt bacon & hard bread, the former nauseating my stomach. Gibbs promised a supper & lodging at Wilmington, but soon after arriving announced that his arrangements had failed, & we were compelled to remain packed in the cars all night in the depot, experiencing little less than the horrors of the hole of Calcutta.

No one slept or scarcely breathed; there was no air & not space enough for stretching a leg. The night was one of the hottest of the climate, mosquitoes bled us freely, the cars were densely packed, no water could be had until morning, & when that came, such a haggard set of wretches I never beheld. Leaving Wilmington breakfastless, we passed the day rather delaying than running on the R.R., until we reached Florence [South Carolina] in the evening, & lay there still cramped up in the cars, till nearly morning, when we started again & reached Charleston, South Carolina, about 6 A.M. 12th Sept.

At Charleston we found a large force of infantry & cavalry waiting at the depot to escort us, as we supposed, to the wharf to embark for Castle Pinckney, but to our consternation & disgust we were marched up to the city jail. ‹I must confess that this fell on us like a clap of thunder from a clear blue sky, and that even I, with my equanimity intent to give all fair allowance for the exigencies of war, was almost beside myself. But in vain I protested. Most of the fellows were boiling over with indignation, and cried, "What next?" There was some talk in the newspapers of retaliation for something or other that had happened out west, and we presumed that perhaps we might be the selected victims.›[3]

3. At this time the Confederacy was deciding whether to hold a number of Union officers as hostages for Confederate guerrillas who had been captured in Missouri. This matter, however, soon took another form. See note 10, p. 314.

Here again we were crowded like cattle in pens. The officers were as-signed to their rooms on the 1st floor, with a small hall shut in by an iron-grated door. The rooms were about 10 x 12. The one I entered with a dozen others was marked over the door by some previous inmate, "Bummer's Re-treat." It was a corner room & fortunately contained two windows, iron grated.

‹Colonel Michael Corcoran, of the 69th New York, and most of the pris-oners, put on a stolid look, before the guard at least, as we moved in, but my friend, Major James Potter,[4] of my brigade, seemed broken-hearted. I soon noticed him kneeling on the floor at the end of our floor, with his elbow on the window and his face in his hand, looking out on the jail yard, woebegone enough.

I walked up and said to him: "Well, Jim, what is the matter?"
"Look down there, colonel," was his reply.

Looking down, I saw the high stone wall which fenced in the place, and in the middle of the yard an ugly black gallows looming up ominously, re-minding me, of course, of the retaliation possibilities.

"Fortune of war, major," I said, as reassuringly as I could. "But I hardly think our government will let it come to that," pointing to the ugly black thing below.

"Well colonel," he burst out, "when I was a boy, my father sent me out to live with an uncle in Pennsylvania on a farm. The old fellow said I was a worthless chap, and would come to the poor house, and be damned lucky if I escaped the gallows. Now they put me in the poor house hospi-tal at Richmond, here I am in jail, and confound his infernal soul—there stands the gallows."

This was said with such a tragical sob that we all broke into a laugh, which relieved the tension of our feelings on the spot, and we began to form groups and spread out our little belongings on the floor.›

Here we were confined without beds or other articles of furniture what-ever, not even dishes of any description to eat or bathe from. But most of my comrades had brot their tin cups, some had a knife & fork & plate, & we washed our faces at the pump in the yard when let out for half an hour, morning & evening. We stretched our blankets on the dirty floor

4. Maj. James Decatur Potter, 38th New York.

& rested our weary & famished bodies, consoling ourselves with tobacco & pipes, until about noon, when some bread, meat & coffee were brot in for breakfast. . . .

‹Then we began to discuss the situation generally—for so much depends upon one's jailers, and in this case still more on the local commanding officer. We congratulated ourselves at least on escaping the clutches of "the infamous Winder," as we called the Confederate provost marshal at Richmond, who was notoriously indifferent, if not over-zealous in his hostility to us.

As a matter of course our letters for home had to pass muster at the Commandant's office to see that no military information was conveyed, but our fare was better than it had been at Richmond—thanks to the commissary . . . lieutenant, Boag was his name. Let all my descendants bless his memory, for we had rice occasionally as a change from hardtack, especially at Castle Pinckney, where in the course of a week we found ourselves, and in a better atmosphere, and we were allowed to purchase things to eat. No letters reached me from home until October 10, but we had an occasional glimpse at newspapers, as, for instance, one morning at Castle Pinckney Lieutenant Boag asked me if I would like to inspect the rice—pointing into a barrel and leaving the room to which he had escorted me. On lifting the lid I was only too glad to find the morning paper, and to report "the rice" as excellent.

We had very little sickness and only one death at Castle Pinckney. One of my "boys," Porter, of Company D, died in the hospital of typhoid fever. But his course to a better world was smoothed by Chaplain Eddy, of a Connecticut regiment—who, together with Chaplain Dodge, held regular services, including the communion.[5] Chaplain Eddy was a big, noble-hearted specimen of "muscular Christianity," and he had to give his weaker brother Dodge an occasional shake down when the latter complained of things that could not be helped. I soon began to notice that despondency was but a step to illness and the graveyard. "To find a soldier's resting place beneath a soldier's blow" is one thing, but to curl up and die in a rebel prison, like a dog, as one fellow expressed it, became unpopular and looked silly.

Our greatest suffering [occurred] after our return to the [city] jail October 30, with literally nothing to wear; we were pretty much a ragged lot of beggars, and clamored to our friends and even to the Northern government

5. According to OBW's *Prison Diary*, Porter, Company D, 1st Michigan, died of typhoid fever at Castle Pinckney, South Carolina, on October 2, 1861; H. Eddy, chaplain, 2d Connecticut; G. W. Dodge, chaplain, 11th New York.

Castle Pinckney, South Carolina. This photo may have been taken at the time of OBW's incarceration there. The prisoners in the courtyard are chiefly those of the 11th and 69th New York, captured at Bull Run. Note the Confederate guards on the roof. *USAMHI.*

to send us clothing and blankets—which indeed came at last, in government boxes marked Q M Dept., and consigned to myself for the Union prisoners. The rolls were made out and duly signed and forwarded to the Quarter Master General, and, unlike some of my other government accounts, I have never heard of them since.

But there were other drawbacks left, in what I must call the meanness of superior officers now and then. In Richmond we were rather persecuted by General Winder, who is so often mentioned in our accounts of Libby Prison, etc. He was not of the manor born—i.e., not a citizen of any of the seceding states, but from Maryland, and therefore, to show his zeal, he was all the more down on Northerners. But as ill-luck would have it, we found at Charleston a commanding officer who could out-Herod Herod, and the change in the situation was from Scylla to Charybdis, to say the least.

One of our old unpopular West Point instructors, General Roswell S. Ripley, was in command of the Department.[6] He was of Ohio birth, and for

6. Brig. Gen. Roswell S. Ripley (7th, USMA 1843), then commanding the Confederate Department of South Carolina.

that reason, perhaps, also over-zealous in the Southern cause. We soon learned that he had already given stringent orders for our fare and keep. The lieutenant in charge of us, a type of the real Southern chivalry, quietly ignored all the orders that were of unnecessary harshness. I soon found that all the Northern generals who were serving with the South, were more or less despised by the high-toned gentlemen of the Confederacy. . . .

PRISON DIARY[7]

October 30th
Remanded back to the city jail leaving a few sick at the Castle.

November 1st
Poor Brink of the Michigan First died at the Castle.

November 2nd
Brink buried at Magnolia Cemetery, near the city. By the courtesy of [Lieutenant] Boag, I was permitted to attend the funeral, in company with himself and Reverend Mr. Taylor.

November 5th
Commotion astir due to the news that Commodore Dupont's fleet was at Port Royal with possible intentions on Charleston Harbor.[8] Good! Received a cheering letter from home and wife; all there well but anxious, naturally. But her anxiety [was] only perceptible between the lines. However, the letter has the cheering news that the government promises us clothing, if it can be gotten through. But so far, so sensitive are the Confederate authorities over the belligerent-rights question that there are no exchanges, not even chaplains or surgeons can be exchanged.

November 19th
Orders from Richmond that the field officers in prison, Corcoran, Neff,[9] Major Potter and myself, should be locked up in solitary cells.

---

7. The diary entries included here are as paraphrased by OBW in his memoirs, though it is clear that he was referring to his *Prison Diary*.

8. Flag Officer Samuel F. Dupont then commanded the U.S. South Blockading Squadron. On November 7, 1861, a combined land and sea operation consisting of Dupont's fleet of seventy-seven vessels and Brig. Gen. Thomas W. Sherman's infantry, some twelve thousand troops in all, seized Confederate-controlled Port Royal, South Carolina. The Federals, however, did not exploit their success, and Dupont made no movement toward Charleston.

9. Lt. Col. George W. Neff, 2d Kentucky.

Colonel Michael Corcoran's name had been drawn by lot while we were still in Richmond, as a hostage for one Smith, convicted of piracy in Philadelphia.[10] We were also informed that ten of the field officers in the hands of the Confederacy, and three captains, to be selected by lot, should be held as hostages for thirteen men on trial for piracy in New York. Besides Corcoran and myself, there were included Colonel Woodruff,[11] Lieutenant Colonels Neff and Bowman, Major Potter and Major Vogdes, U.S.A. Captain Ricketts, lying wounded in Richmond, was also included, and Captain Thomas Cox, of the 1st Kentucky, who was of our number, offered chivalrously to take his place, but was refused. Ricketts' name was afterwards withdrawn from the list by the Confederate Secretary of War [Judah] Benjamin.

Major Vogdes, who had been my classmate at West Point, had but recently joined us in prison.[12] He had been captured in a night attack on Santa Rosa Island, Pensacola Harbor, under peculiar circumstances, that is to say [because of] his voice, which was a notorious organ, celebrated at West Point . . . for its peculiar twang. It seems that in the darkness and confusion of a night conflict in the woods [,] both parties claimed the victory and the Confederate leader (I think Colonel John Pegram)[13] called out, "Surrender, Yanks!" "No," yelled Major Vogdes, "you're our prisoners. Lay down your arms!" Whereupon the Rebel leader exclaimed, "Vog, is that you?" and a colloquy followed, which resulted in the surrender of the weaker party, and the appearance of the gallant "Vog," as a prisoner of war in our jail.

10. Fifteen Confederate privateer commanders were eventually captured by Union forces, including Capt. Walter W. Smith, of the privateer *Jefferson Davis*. All were sentenced to death as pirates, as the United States did not recognize them as legitimate prisoners of war. The Confederacy retaliated, and on November 9 it ordered a like number of captured Union officers, chosen by lot, be held as hostages for the privateers. Besides Corcoran (held for Smith), the list was to include six colonels, two lieutenant colonels, three majors, and three captains, all of whom were placed in condemned cells and sentenced to hang if the privateers should be executed, as the Federal government had ordered. OBW was chosen as one of the hostages. In the end, the United States decided to treat the privateers as regular prisoners of war, the Union hostages were taken off the condemned list, and there the matter ended.

11. Col. W. E. Woodruff, 2d Kentucky.

12. Maj. Israel Vogdes. OBW is mistaken, in that Vogdes was not a classmate of his but graduated eleventh in the class of 1837. However, OBW doubtless knew him from his prewar service. Vogdes had been captured in a Confederate attack on Santa Rosa Island, in Pensacola harbor. After being released from prison, Vogdes spent most of the remainder of the war on engineer duty.

13. John Pegram (10th, USMA 1854) was to be captured July 11, 1861, at Rich Mountain, western Virginia.

For my own part, I enjoyed the major's society immensely—not only for old association's sake, but for his vast knowledge of the science of war, of which I had still so much to learn, and there was no end to his oddities—and no discount on his voice.

The new order stated that we should be treated in every respect as "pirates and common felons," as hostages for the captured Confederate privateers, who were being tried by the U.S. Court at Baltimore for piracy on the high seas. Lieutenant Boag brought us the news with a sorrowful face, and tried his best to cheer us up with the information that President Lincoln had been notified and warned that we and eight other prisoners of war—the highest in rank in the hands of the Confederates, were to be held as hostages for the privateers and treated accordingly. "Your government will never suffer you to be hung, and your confinement cannot last long," added our good friend, the courteous jailer, and he kindly put off the dungeon business until nightfall.

We received the bitter tidings as best we could—in painful silence for the most part; at any rate, no word of reproach against our own government escaped our lips in the presence of Lieutenant Boag, and we began at once to pack up our duds for removal to our new bedrooms. Even my excitable comrade, Potter, did credit to the Potter family by his self control, and this gave him a newly acquired dignity. Our fellow prisoners "below the gangway" were by no means as reticent. The news spread among them like wild fire and we soon heard volleys of execrations fired off at the head of "Jeff Davis." Our own chief executive and the War Department at Washington were also pretty freely discussed, until the cooler heads checked the barbecue.

Lieutenant Boag returned at night and led me to one of the sixty-four brick-walled and stone-floored cells, barred by an iron door, where, to my surprise, I found a little table and a cot bedstead. They were furnished by the good jailer as extras, on his own responsibility. He told me also that his orders were to search me strictly and remove every utensil and convenience about my person, down to a penknife, [to] put me on bread and water, and to treat me in every respect as a condemned felon. "But," the lieutenant added, "I'd see Jeff Davis d——d first! You are a gentleman and an officer, sir, and I am not a common jailer," or words to that effect. Further on, the lieutenant—after a plain but sufficient supper, brought me a Bible and a pack of playing cards, remarking with a smile, "After a game of solitaire you can read your Bible, colonel, and then take the other refreshment." He then said "good night."

Taking his advice, I must confess that I [slept] more easily than any one might imagine. I had, however, first prayed for my more distressed family, and for an early release from *durance vile*. I had some dreams, of course, and one of them was a little odd. I dreamed that I had become an old man and returned to Detroit after a very long absence to visit my own grave. After poking around on some moss-covered and dilapidated stones in the family lot at Elmwood Cemetery, I found the right one. The name and dates were quite obscure. But there was the number "76," but whether this meant [my age] or the year of our Lord, I could not tell. But on awakening from the dream, I took it to heart as a message from the Almighty, or from some guardian angel, that my days were to be prolonged into the seventies, as they have actually been. Another comfort was that "things might have been worse."

Daylight brought me no cheer; the grated door admitted not quite light enough to read . . . and I could scarcely sleep. But I said to myself, "They have spared me the degradation and suffering of chaining me to the floor." Perhaps I owed the indulgence to Lieutenant Boag, but I have since thought that no orders came from Richmond to inflict fetters upon the hostages. Mr. Davis was too noble a man for that, as I learned afterwards.

In the morning we were let out for exercise and the wash basin. I did not like to ask my fellow hostages how they had fared, for fear of betraying Boag's partiality to myself, which would have made them feel badly. At any rate they uttered no loud complaints. I don't remember exactly our daily diet, nor how long we were kept in close confinement. But it did not last long, for as soon as President Lincoln received the notice from Richmond, he must have ordered criminal proceedings stayed at Baltimore and the privateers were placed on the footing of either ordinary or extraordinary prisoners of war, and we were released from strict confinement. This was the second diplomatic triumph for the Confederacy. The jailing of prisoners was, however, continued, and only a few exchanges took place for some time.[14]>

PRISON DIARY[15]

December 1st

Dr. Griswold of 38th N.Y. died in jail last night, buried to-day. No officer suffered to go. 138th Hymn [sung]. Had a rose in my window.

14. The final decision to treat Confederate privateers as prisoners of war was not made until February 3, 1862.
15. These diary entries are transcribed directly from OBW's *Prison Diary*.

December 12th

A great fire broke out [in Charleston] last night at 8½ & burnt all night. An awful sight. Door locked at 3 A.M.

December 18th

Received letter from wife & brother. Great joy.

December 20th

Anniversary of South Carolina Secession. Gen'l Evans called.

‹On New Year's day, 1862, we found ourselves on board a train of box cars bound for another jail. Our party numbered one hundred-seventy, and on reaching [the] Columbia jail, South Carolina, we found one hundred-forty other prisoners—among them W. C. Moore[16] and [Pvt. Charles] Kauffman, First Michigan—in the jail, making in all, besides the guard, 310 guests of Southern chivalry.

The prison was a stone affair, 60 feet by 40, and there were a dozen of us in one small room. But it was on the first floor, [which] gave us a peep, at least, through iron bars, [of] the outer world—a narrow back street. But the fortune of war again favored us with a gentleman for our keeper, Captain William Shirer, and another light broke in upon us shortly: one of our wretched number, Captain Sprague, of the 7th Ohio, was exchanged and left us January 5, with congratulations on our part and promises on his part to "work for our exchanges." Ohio had put her shoulder to the wheel and the good work had begun. Three cheers for Sprague and three more for Ohio, was our parting salute. I wonder now whether this quasi-acknowledgment of belligerent rights was not received at Memphis, Ship Island, and other horrid dens where Confederates were confined, with equal uplifting of brave hearts. No question of it. And then to think of its effects on the dear mothers and wives at home, praying on their knees for captive sons and husbands!

Thinking now that there was some prospect of our separation, a Prisoner's War Association was then and there formed—with the consent of Captain Shirer for the meeting. The dear fellows did me the honor to elect me as their first president. This looked like business, and each prisoner began to reckon up his chances for recrossing the border with a longing that is inexpressible. But . . . many months passed sluggishly along before many of us were exchanged . . . [or] before general exchanges began, owing

16. Pvt. William C. Moore, 18th Michigan, captured at Bull Run. Moore was later exchanged and served as lieutenant and captain in the 18th Michigan.

to various questions of dispute; terms of parole, some of which were repudiated; treatment of civilians—such as Congressman Ely,[17] who was captured at Bull Run and thrown into the Ligon Tobacco Factory among the "common herd"; the status of Southern citizens confined at Fort Lafayette—whose release on writs of habeas corpus had been refused by the sturdy Major Burke, commanding;[18] and above all other questions was that on the effect that exchanges might have on European powers, for whose recognition Confederate embassies had been sent abroad, and which were jealously watched by Mr. Seward and our own embassies.

Besides these matters, the blockade of Southern ports affected the rights of foreign merchant vessels, and the rights of the Confederacy to purchase arms, clothings and provisions abroad. If belligerent rights were accorded, both sides were equally entitled to purchase materials to carry on the war [from] any country—if not, the blockade runners were worse off than ordinary smugglers, in that their persons were held, and as these were foreigners, you see what a ticklish question was this.

But there were points in our favor to urge against foreign recognition of the Confederacy. First, the antislavery feeling; second, the size of our navy to enforce the blockade and prevent the shipment of cotton; and third, the Beecher family. The power of Harriet Beecher Stowe's *Uncle Tom's Cabin* and of Henry Ward Beecher's speeches at a subsequent period in England, were very great.[19] I think it was at Manchester [that] Mr. Beecher brought down the house in a repartee. While telling of the superior strength and resources of the North and the certainty of our success, one of the audience

17. Rep. Alfred Ely of New York, a spectator at Bull Run, was captured during the battle and held in Richmond until late December 1861.

18. Fort Lafayette, New York, became one of the principal Union prisons for political prisoners, including members of the Maryland legislature who had done nothing more than express sympathy for the South but who had been imprisoned because it was feared they would lead the state out of the Union. General Scott also intended to use the prison for incarcerating former U.S. officers who had resigned their commissions to serve the Confederacy, if and when they should be captured. Most political prisoners were denied the privilege of the writ of habeas corpus, which Lincoln first suspended on April 27, 1861, "for reasons of public safety." By September 15, 1863, Lincoln, with the previous approval of Congress, authorized suspension of the writ throughout the nation.

General Scott said of the commander at Fort Lafayette, "Colonel Martin Burke is famous for his unquestioning obedience to orders. He was with me in Mexico, and if I had told him at any time to take one of my aides-de-camp and shoot him before breakfast, the aide's execution would have been duly reported."

19. Harriet Beecher Stowe (1811–1896), who had published *Uncle Tom's Cabin* in 1852, and Rev. Henry Ward Beecher (1813–1887), her brother, were vocal opponents of slavery.

arose and said: "Now sir, I would like to ask you a question: if your side is so much the stronger, why has the war lasted so long?" "That is easily explained," quoth the Orator. "It is because we are fighting with Americans."

It was my good luck to see and hear Mr. Beecher more than once. He was a stout man of florid complexion. He had a fearless look and stood well on his pins, as the boys say, vehement in language but holding back his gestures for the most emphatic points.

But to return to our prison experiences. One morning while in Columbia Jail we heard a tap on the window. On our raising the sash a newspaper was slipped in to us by some person outside, who kept his face out of sight and said not a word. On opening the paper, imagine our delight to read [of] the battle and capture of New Orleans by the Union forces under General Butler.[20] Underneath the pleasure of my own heart came a little tinge of sympathy for General Mansfield Lovell, the battery captain under whom I had served so pleasantly in Mexico and on the Plains, a very gallant, dashing and loveable [officer]. Of course the South were not sparing of their censures, but the chances of war were against him, as the fickle Jade [of Fortune] was afterward against General John C. Pemberton for the fall of Vicksburg, although he had held out bravely and with great military skill & science for more than a year—the longest siege of the war. But both were Northern men, and I shall always esteem it an honor to have served under both when they were company commanders in the Fourth Artillery. Pemberton was a tall man of elegant manners, while Lovell was shorter and more of the *beau sabreur*, and he rode any wicked horse like a centaur. . . .

On a bright Sabbath day, January 5, 1862, Captain Shirer came in and announced that one of our number, Captain Sprague, 7th Ohio, was exchanged, and that if he wished he could be gotten off immediately. This was the first break in the gloom. Imagine our joy! It took but a few minutes to make him ready for the Northern train which left an hour afterwards. A few days after, Lieutenant Connolly, one of Corcoran's officers, was released and was followed next day by [my] most intimate friend, the gallant Christian soldier and gentleman, Captain Withington, and half a dozen sergeants

20. OBW's memory has failed him here, as the U.S. capture of New Orleans occurred on April 25, 1862, while he was in Libby Prison. The event was not recorded in his vest-pocket *Prison Diary*, which he referred to constantly while writing this chapter. Maj. Gen. Benjamin F. Butler was not involved in the capture of that city, which surrendered to naval forces under Capt. David G. Farragut, but assumed command there in May 1862 as military governor of Louisiana.

and others were exchanged before the field officers were placed on the same footing as company officers and men.

On Tuesday, February 18, we heard of the capture of Fort Donelson, and men began to inquire, "Who is General Grant?"[21] Next day I received a letter from Lt. Col. John Pegram, C.S.A., who, at the instance of my father-in-law, had been sent over the lines to be exchanged for me. But alas! he said that the Confederate government had refused the exchange on the grounds that he was not my equal in rank. However, on the 23rd came an order for all our party to be shipped in three lots for Richmond for exchange. Colonels Corcoran, Woodruff and myself drew lots for priority, and the first lot fell to me.

Accordingly next day, one third of the "old gang," as we had begun to call ourselves, started under Captain Shirer himself. The party consisted of myself, at the head of the Michigan men, 40 in number, together with Major Potter, Surgeon Stone, Captain Ross A. Fish, [32nd New York]—"the life of the gang," . . . Captains Austin and Gordon—called Fatty Gordon—Lieutenants Kent, Worcester, Gordon—called "little Gordon"—Walter . . . and Chaplains Eddy and Dodge.[22] Our train took the Weldon route and we arrived safely at Richmond and put up at the Tobacco Factory[23] on the 27th—and there our troubles began.

The officers signed their paroles not to attempt escape but, next day, when some of us requested permission to visit friends in town, we were refused point blank, and furthermore, no one was allowed to visit us—such were Winder's orders. On the same day, Colonels Corcoran and Woodruff and party arrived and now there were over a hundred of us pent up like sheep in a pen, with the cheering intelligence on March 1st that we were to be detained for some time yet.

Next morning we were awakened roughly for roll call. Our paroles were returned to hold until further orders. Not even the officers were allowed to "go to the rear"; one of our own surgeons was driven back [from the latrine].

21. Fort Donelson, at the head of the Cumberland River, fell to Union forces under Brig. Gen. U. S. Grant on February 16, 1862. This followed the capture of Fort Henry, on the Tennessee River, on February 6. The fall of these two Confederate forts opened Kentucky and west Tennessee to Federal control and catapulted Grant to national prominence.

22. Capt. George Austin, 2d Kentucky; Capt. Leonard Gordon, 11th Massachusetts; Lt. Jacob Ford Kent, 3d U.S. Infantry, later served on OBW's staff; Lt. Frank Worcester, 71st New York; Lt. D. S. Gordon, 2d U.S. Cavalry; Lt. Charles Walter, 1st Connecticut.

23. OBW indicates in his *Prison Diary* that this was the Tobacco Factory Hospital, on Main Street. This was undoubtedly the Moore Hospital, formerly Ligon's tobacco warehouse, at 26th and Main Street in Richmond.

On another morning two . . . of our room-mates, Austin and Kent, had the honor of being prodded with sabre scabbards to hasten roll call. You have often heard of our little roll caller, a nice boy—but the officers of the guard were some times brutes in shoulder straps. On the 4th of March—auspicious day we thought—Colonel Bowman, Major Vogdes and myself united in a respectful letter to . . . General Winder, remonstrating on the breach of our paroles, and the petty annoyances of our extraordinary confinement, and we requested an interview. Next morning came an answer, the general promising to call in the afternoon—which he failed to do and we never saw the man's face. Perhaps the General did not know of our indignities. We might have said more than we did—for instance Chaplain Eddy and two fellow officers [Walter and Worcester] were "wipt," says my little diary, for light [on] after taps, playing chess, and later on, March 17, some of our people were put in irons for resenting insults that no one, least of all a soldier, could pass unnoticed without putting his manhood to blush.

We received one or two calls from clergymen: the Reverend T. G. Dashiel, to see me, at the instance of an old friend, Mrs. Commodore Newton, whom I had known at Pensacola Navy Yard, and Reverend Mr. Burrows, to "visit the prison." I hope the good Samaritan was allowed to see the six prisoners who were in irons, but I have doubts. During the month we had the pleasure of shedding our ragged underclothing and worn-out shoes, etc.—a consignment of these articles having been received from Washington and issued to some thirty of the most ragged, on regular receipt rolls, duly signed and witnessed. One of our number, Lieutenant Downey,[24] was allowed to "red tape the thing through," and the rolls were probably forwarded through the proper Confederate channels to Washington. The business was one with which I had long been familiar and I do not think it miscarried, because our letters from home had come through and were duly delivered—except in one or two instances, and these were doubtful.

On March 26th we were ordered to "pack up" and were straightway marched with beating hearts, that beat like drums, not to the dawn of delivery, but to the chambers of the famous, or infamous, Libby Prison—an old tobacco factory that had been kept by Messrs. Libby and Sons on Carey Street, below 20th, opposite the Canal. I understand that the building has been purchased since the war, and set up as a curiosity for morbid souls in Chicago. Queer taste, but comment would be stifling. By the way, one part of the building where the officers were packed—officers quarters—smoked

24. Lt. John Downey, 11th New York.

incessantly from the guard house [chimney], until we began to feel like a box of smoked herrings.>

<<Here . . . [we] were placed in a fair-sized room with a rough floor and bare brick walls, without a stick of furniture, in company with fifty other officers. . . . We all soon began to break up into little cliques and messing groups and I was allowed a prisoner from the ranks to wash our few tin dishes. As for cooking, there was nothing to cook, except the given-out "dunder-funk"—as the hard-head compounds given out were called. Perhaps we missed coffee and tea [more] than any other thing. But we gave new Delmonico names to every menu!

Several of the Irish lieutenants evinced some hostility against me, for no apparent reason other than that the captain of the prison, the somewhat notorious Turner,[25] seemed to treat me as the head of the party, instead of Colonel Corcoran. But they gained no headway, as Corcoran and I ignored all divisions and tried to keep the peace among all prisoners.

I found the colonel to be courteous on all occasions, notwithstanding the abuse which had been heaped upon him for refusing to turn out his regiment to receive the Prince of Wales, now Edward VII, at New York City. Notwithstanding our miserable prison fare, and sleeping pretty much on the rough boards used for drying tobacco leaves, I had nothing to complain of, except the ceaseless tread of one hundred of our fellow prisoners from the ranks overhead, and, after a while, their noisome carelessness of sanitation, from which streams of filthy matter began to filter down the walls. But most loathsome of all was the vermin which infested our bodies in spite of all personal precautions, confined however to ablutions from the dishes in which we cooked and ate our meals. There was a grim humor in our evening concerts and morning exercises, "hunting for gray backs," enlivened by endless and fruitless scratchings and volleys of execrations. What few supplies we could purchase came in by the roll caller, a good little chap. The newspapers we occasionally saw, came by petty bribery or by a string let down from the windows.

One the whole, I think we had no cause of complaint compared with the sufferings of our fellow captives at Andersonville. We were not even as badly treated as some of the Confederates were in one or two of our own prisons, notably Memphis, where the Confederate prisoners were kept in cellars, chained down to the floor, and starved. And notwithstanding our prolonged confinement of some thirteen months at Richmond and elsewhere, we encountered little illness and but few actual deaths, which is

25. Capt. Thomas P. Turner, commanding Confederate military prisons.

(*Top*) Libby Prison in 1862, as photographed by Charles Rees. The Union prisoners are clearly visible at the windows. *Chicago Historical Society.*

(*Bottom*) An idealized painting of captured Union officers in Libby Prison. Willcox and Corcoran stand in the center (Willcox is on the left). *Anne S. K. Brown Military Collection, John Hay Library, Brown University.*

nothing to compare with the fortune of a party of Union soldier prisoners who landed at Wilmington, 9,000 in number, of whom a quarter died from the effects of their confinement.>>[26]

<On Good Friday, April 18, we saw a little boy fall into the canal. One of our men, walking outside the prison on some errand for the cook house, threw off his coat and was about to jump in and rescue the unfortunate, but the guard threatened to shoot him, and the boy was drowned before the sentinel's eyes and in sight of all of us, amid cries of shame! We heard that the little fellow's name was "Francisco," and it was W. J. Clark, of a New Jersey regiment, who might have saved him. I do not know what action the officer in charge or the city authorities took, if any, to punish the sentinel. One Easter Sunday the men were all put on bread and water for some unexplained reason for "tumultuous conduct," i.e., cries of shame on Good Friday.

On Tuesday of May 2nd, my too brief little vest diary jots down an interview which I held with the Honorable John H. Reagan, of Texas, who probably called at the instance of my sister, Mrs. Taylor, then living in Texas, but I had nothing to ask except the speedy exchange of our Bull Run prison party.[27] Although Mr. Reagan was, I think, at the time, a mem-

26. The above material, within double angle brackets << >>, is from an early chapter by OBW entitled "The Battle of Manassas," which details some of his early prison experiences. These experiences at Libby Prison, however, he relates as having occurred while he was first incarcerated in Richmond; however, he did not enter Libby until he was transferred to Richmond from Columbia, in February 1862.

27. John H. Reagan, former U.S. congressman from Texas, had originally been elected as a member of the Provisional Confederate Congress but resigned to accept the position of postmaster general in March 1861.

OBW's half-sister, Mary Taylor, had made a harrowing trip from her home in Texas to visit her brother in prison. Obtaining a pass from her brother's old friend, Gen. Mansfield Lovell, in New Orleans, Mary proceeded northward, through the Confederate lines, for Washington. Passing on to Richmond, she was eventually directed to Charleston. Although Mary managed to reach Richmond, she was apparently unsuccessful in her quest to visit her brother. OBW makes no mention of such a visit in his prison journals or reminiscences. Mary was greatly moved by her experiences. In an incomplete memoir, she wrote:

I reached the city of Charleston at night—found her in *sackcloth* and *ashes*, and the smouldering embers of the great conflagration of the day before my arrival—Through ruins and debris, I groped my way silently, with throbbing heart, to where I remembered the old jail once stood. By the glinting of the moon, I reached for the bell pull, not realizing what I was doing. I only intended to reconnoiter a little, and on the morrow, to call on proper authority, and if possible obtain permission to see my brother—but, in my *frenzy* at the door bell, I had called the jailor to his post. I explained the object of my visit and restless impatience that brought me at that hour to the jail, only to see the cruel place where a dear brother was incarcerated. I will not dwell on what transpired during my stay—and the effort made for the prisoners—and return to Fortress Monroe and Washington, but, even

ber of Mr. Davis' Cabinet, nothing was effected beyond the exchange of two of our members, Capt. Favish and Lt. Dempsey of Colonel Corcoran's regiment.

By the way, I may as well tell you of a little incident that had just happened. It seems that my irrepressible friend Major Vogdes had been particularly indiscreet and severe in denouncing his compulsory association with the Irish members of our party, and Lieutenant Dempsey had overheard it. At this his Gaelic blood was roused and the Lieutenant forthwith raised a picked crew of choice spirits to toss the major in a blanket after taps. The secret leaked out and over to me just as we had all turned in for the night, and I arose and went over to Colonel Corcoran, who lay on the floor near by, and denounced the proceeding as disgraceful to us all, and I requested the colonel to nip the thing in the bud—which he alone could do. I found him also very much put out with the major, and he flatly refused to comply at first, saying that "the d——d 'Jew' deserved a rousting," and it was not until we had quite an argument and I convinced him that the major was "but a half-crazy mathematician," that he consented to interfere, saying it was only to oblige me.

On the 15th of May the long agony of hope deferred over the exchange negotiations was terminated in the most unexpected shock—we were all put aboard the cars for Salisbury, North Carolina! Our disappointment can scarcely be realized, much less described at this late day. How little did we know of the strenuous exertions that were being made in our behalf, or of the difficulties that stood in the way, nor that the time would ever come when I should want to forget the whole painful subject, as I certainly wanted to do later on.

We found the Salisbury enclosure least irksome of our prison limits. It was in fact a merciful relief from close confinement—several acres of Mother Earth compassed by a tall fence, inside of which there were wooden houses of different degrees that had been used for offices and quarters for the officers . . . and hands of some sort of a factory. The guard house stood at the gateway and we found sentinels in gray duly posted along the fence. There was plenty of room and to spare for all of us in the vacant houses, in which we arranged ourselves in messes of mutual choice,

---

in these perilous and exciting times, I remembered and *wept* over the ruin and desolation of this once proud and chivalrous city!

Returning to Texas, Mary and her husband found that their home had been ransacked and plundered. Treated as Yankee pariahs, the couple left the Confederacy through Mexico, eventually making their way back to Washington.

and were told that we should have the liberty of the grounds by day, subject only to the usual restrictions of a military post, such as call to quarters, roll call, taps, etc.

But "what," I asked one of the gentlemanly Confederate officers, "is that other inclosure inside our bounds that has no cover?"

"Oh, that is for our own people, citizens, deserters, and others."

"Poor fellows," I said, "they seem to have no shelter from sun or rain or snow."

"Not at present," he replied, as he shrugged his shoulders rather significantly.

And sure enough, shut up in that exposure was a lot of human beings worse off than ourselves; worse off not only in respect of rain or shine, but some of them [were] half starved. It was not long—though against the rules, that our men, on the sly, managed to hold communication with them and to toss hardtack over the fence for a scramble.

Our own fare was meager enough, but as we took up our quarters, each mess managed to make the best—in other words to cook the best—of the situation. My own little mess of four or five officers and a soldier who volunteered as chief cook and bottle washer, could boast of some cash to help things along. One of the greatest luxuries in the camp was the new accession [of] a wash tub, and perchance a bath. No wonder that the silent guards seemed amused with the joyful exclamations, bursting into songs and sailor hornpipes. But in a few days, of course, we began to feel the limitations. "Man never is but always to be blessed," and it was perfectly ridiculous for us to expect too much, as some of my compatriots did, and I am sorry to say that, slight as was the restraint, a few of our men violated the rules. But the punishments were by no means so brutal as those of Libby Prison, thank Heaven.

One bright day in August, all of our captains were summoned to the commanding officer's quarters. Curiosity was on tiptoe to learn what for. They were told that a party of Confederate guerillas were held *in durance vile* by the American government, and as two of them [had been] condemned as spies and ordered to be hung, two of the captains present were to be held as hostages. The lot fell upon Captains Austin and O'Meara[28] out of the

28. Capt. Timothy O'Meara, 42d New York.

25 present, and the two were then marched to the Guard House and put in limbo. The next event was more encouraging to our hopes; . . . a small number of Union prisoners captured at Shiloh had been exchanged—although it had been effected through the influence of a Mr. Cashmeyer.

On June 14th, quite an acquisition, socially, was received at my mess, viz. Colonel Sir Percy Wyndham, of the First New Jersey Cavalry, a gentleman adventurer from England, who had been captured in the Shenandoah Valley Campaign, probably in a head-long charge at the head of his regiment. He was a very handsome man, with blue eyes and fair complexion, trim built and altogether one of the dashing sort. He reminded me of my old Battery commander, Mansfield Lovell, and we became friends from the start—a happy-go-lucky fellow, though he chafed a good deal at the present turn of the wheel. What he most dreaded seemed to be the hostage imbroglio, particularly as the very next day after his arrival, two more of our number, and surgeons at that, Doctors Hoffman and Slocum,[29] were mewed up as hostages. Should he [Colonel Wyndham] become one of the unlucky number, there might arise a ticklish interposition of the British Lion's paws, he said, and an embarrassing investigation of his right to quit the Old Country to accept his commission. . . . At any rate, I think Sir Percy's [luck] piloted him home safely [in] the end.

From the date last mentioned at Salisbury, no incident seems to have occurred worthy of record in my little waistcoat pocket diary until the month of August, when exchanges were actually put in motion, after a heap of rubbish correspondence between the two governments on the *quid pro quo*, during which the [Confederate] officials refused to accept Lt. Col. Pegram for [myself], but did [accept] the lieutenant colonel for Brevet Lt. Col. Bomford.[30]

But on August 15, our Adjutant General, Lorenzo Thomas, was notified by Robert Ould, adjutant for [the] Exchange of Prisoners at Richmond, that an agent had been appointed to receive and deliver prisoners at Vicksburg, and that he [was sending] on Colonels Corcoran and Willcox, Major Vogdes and one or two other officers, meaning Colonel Bowman. Accordingly, on the same day, General Thomas writes Colonel Ould that he had duly received the three colonels and Major Vogdes aforesaid. You may

29. John B. Hoffman, assistant surgeon, U.S. Army, captured at Strasburg, Virginia, on May 25, 1862; Capt. George D. Slocum, surgeon, U.S. Navy, captured at City Point, Virginia, May 19, 1862.

30. Lt. Col. James V. Bomford, 8th U.S. Infantry.

be sure that it was a warm "reception" on both sides, but you can scarcely conceive the joy of our release and all that it meant, or the delight with which we hailed the Old Flag when we first came in sight of Aikens Landing [Virginia]. Vain, vain the attempt to sing—"Our flag is there, our flag is there / We hail it with three cheers," for it was as much as any of us could do to keep down the sobs, tough customers as we were, after almost thirteen months' imprisonment.

We arrived at Fort Monroe next day and were happy to learn from General Thomas that he had started a steamer to Aikens for 130 other of our officers confined at Richmond.

Query? The circumstance that the Adjutant General of the army himself was exchanging the prisoners [made it look] as if the President himself had at length taken the matter in hand, and determined to "push things," particularly when he found that "Barkis was willin'"—as he expressed it.[31]

The Honorable Hamilton Fish and Bishop Ames[32] had gone on a mission to Fortress Monroe, and communicated with the Confederate authorities at Norfolk, and on their return to Washington reported that the Confederates were ready to negotiate a general exchange, and what is more, to parole any excess that might be left in their hands. Our newspapers almost unanimously advocated it. One of them said: "We would be glad to hear from any quarter one good reason for not exchanging prisoners." Another exclaimed:

> Think of the crowded and filthy tobacco ware houses, the brutal keepers, the rotten food, the untended wounds, the unmedicated disease, the miserable marches through the blazing south, and the reincarceration in other jails more remote than the first. . . . The Country has cried out against this cruel anomaly. We have hoped that the supposed "political necessities" under which it is justified, had yielded to the claims and instinct of humanity. . . . The President has given his hearty approval to the proposed policy. Still it is not carried into effect.

31. A paraphrasing of the quotation "Barkis is willin'," from Charles Dickens's *David Copperfield*, chapter 5.

32. U. S. Rep. Hamilton Fish, New York, had been appointed by President Lincoln to the Board of Commissioners for the Relief and Exchange of Union Prisoners. Bishop Edward R. Ames also served on the board.

For some reason . . . it seems that there had been a "balk" in the negotiations so far, and Heaven only knows what gratitude the prisoners owed to Hamilton Fish and Bishop [Ames]. At the conclusion of immediate exchanges, it was found that the South held a surplus of "three hundred," whom they released on parole, according to their chivalrous agreement. . . .>[33]

33. Capt. Withington later stated, under oath, that "throughout this long imprisonment, with its privations, squalor and uncertainty with the apparent indifference of our own government and the weary days, weeks and months of hope deferred, Col. Willcox never let down from his high bearing as an officer, a Patriot and a gentleman. He was the recognised [sic] leader and kept up the *morale* of the body of prisoners with whom he was associated. By his precept and example he saved some, and better fitted all to serve their country as soldiers and as citizens." Deposition of William H. Withington before Deputy Clerk, Circuit Court, Jackson County, Michigan, February 8, 1886.

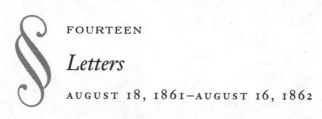

FOURTEEN

Letters

AUGUST 18, 1861–AUGUST 16, 1862

[Marie Willcox to O.B.W.]
Framingham, Mass.
Aug. 18/'61
My dearest Husband,

It is four weeks today since the dreadful news came that you were "killed." Afterwards, at midnight, the telegram was that you "still lived, though badly wounded." Eben and I came on in the morning train, and after twelve hours vexatious delay at Harrisburg, reached Washington on Thursday, where we met Father and Mr. Harrison.[1] A more wretched and perplexed party never existed.

Washington [was] in such a state of confusion, all panic-stricken. It was dreadful to be within a few miles and yet find it impossible to go further. It seemed as if I *must* go at all hazards and was only persuaded to control myself by the thought of the dear little children, whom I had left at home, the baby quite ill. It was the most fearful struggle between instinct and inclination and what seemed the stronger claim of duty. I consented to wait until the return of a gentleman from Alexandria, who went over to Manassas at the request of Dr. Brodie on Wednesday. He returned Friday with the statement that "he had seen a classmate of Col. Willcox, who assured him that his wound was not severe and that he had gone to Richmond where he

1. Frank Harrison, husband of Caro Farnsworth Harrison.

would receive every attention. This seemed very encouraging, and they would not listen to a word of my attempting to go on alone. I do not know how it might have proved, but I think I should have been sustained and reached you in safety. As it was, all hope gone, the reaction resulted in a total prostration. It was with difficulty that Father got me over to N.Y. and after several days of suffering I came here, where Caro is spending the summer.

It is only within a few days that I have been able to set up at all. I am still very weak. The attack was similar to that I had at Fort Independence. No one can imagine who has not experienced it. . . .

Father is now in Washington. I hope he will be able to ascertain if there is any hope of your being restored to us. I am getting very anxious and impatient that we do not hear from you. Direct letters have been received from other prisoners. I hope our letters have reached you. I wrote from Washington and from N.Y. through friends of yours who kindly offered to forward the letters to Richmond. . . .

[Marie Willcox to O. B.W.]
Framingham [Mass.]
18th [August]
My dearest Orlando,

I have just received your letters, I was going to say, but I mean a letter written by someone for you, which fills me with contending emotions. Oh my dear Husband to think that you should have lain so ill all those weary days and *I* not with you. No power on earth would have prevented me my attempting to reach you could I have known that you were there. But we were misled, and thought you slightly wounded and in Richmond. Dr. Brodie told me I would "only be in the way, and add to your annoyance if I should go," and *all* so protested, that I, fearing to trust my excited nerves, really was persuaded to abandon the hope.

Why it should have been so ordered by an overruling Providence I cannot tell. That I was not permitted to be with you will always be a regret. Time, instead of softening, seems but to increase the overwhelming sense of mortification and grief. I had with me every comfort that love or ingenuity could devise, a little black bag that would have been like Fortunatoe's wishing cap, capable of promoting the means of every want. There was a clean linen pillow case for your head, bandages, and salves, and lotions, and wine, and brandy, and lemons, and jelly, and tea, and fresh-eggs and [illegible word] to turn milk into custard for you, a dressing wrapper of the gayest French prints, and all had to be taken back to N.Y., where I made a donation to Mrs. Garish.

Marie Farnsworth
Willcox, wife of OBW.
OBW Collection.

Do not think I really mind this, but I want to make you laugh now [that] it is all over; to me it was dreadful! Mother sent the last bottle of cologne water that Father brought from Cologne, to bathe your head, and Mrs. Scotten her wedding chemise, to strip into bandages. Dear little Lulu had no end of things to send. It was a sad parting that morning when I went to their little beds to wake them, to kiss good bye. Elon, who had sobbed himself to sleep praying his "Father in Heaven to take care of his dear Papa who was killed," jumped up, and seeing me with my bonnet on, exclaimed, "Oh you are going to get Papa! You are going to get Papa!" hugged and kissed me and danced around the room for joy. Lulu seemed more deep in her joy at the hope that her dear Papa might be restored to her. She has the heart of a woman. Her affection for you is something extraordinary for a child.

As we drove down to the depot all the flags were at half mast for you, and while waiting in the cars I read your *obituary* in the morning paper, and all along the route we met men whose "dearest friends had seen you on the field," some dead, some fainted, and in every imaginable position. All this was so trying! Every paper had a different account. "That you were last seen wounded on the field" so filled me with horror and indignation. That the regiment for which you had sacrificed everything should turn and leave you without an effort to rescue the leader to whom they owed all the prestige they have gained.

I believe Mr. Pitman is to be colonel in the new organization and Roberts lieutenant colonel.[2] I saw many of the regiment in Washington. I do not think the importance of their position was appreciated by Col. Heintzelman. His report was not satisfactory to me. Burnside's was the only report that seemed to me what it should [be]. McDowell said that you "were captured in the thickest of the fight," which is more than he said of any-one else. I hope if you are permitted to write again you will tell me exactly how ill you have been and how you are at the time. To Capt. Withington I cannot be grateful enough, and also Mrs. Ricketts, for their kind care and attention to you. Mrs. Ricketts has not been out of my mind since I heard of her having gone to Manassas. "If I could but have reached Washington in time to have gone with her" is the one thought by day, and when my head rests upon the pillow I dream of it. I am getting strong [and] I shall soon be able to travel. If you are not exchanged I shall try again to reach you. You can never know the misery of these four weeks to me.

> Your affectionate wife,
> Marie

[Fanny Ricketts to O.B.W.]
General Hospital, Richmond Va.
Monday Sept. 23, 1861
My dear Colonel,
My silence must be no criterion for apparent negligence; reasons beyond our control or explanation must account for the tardy expression of our daily unceasing regret in the separation, after so many trials shared together in such companionship as a lifetime of vicissitudes seldom affords!—We can never forget each other; there are mutual memories which can never die, al-though years may elapse before our next meeting, God grant under happier auspices! ——

We heard of your arrival at "Castle Pinckney" through the newspapers, and trust the privilege of mutual correspondence will not be denied.—Here all remains "in status quo." Capt. Ricketts' health improves very slowly since you left; he has never even hobbled into the next room; his leg is much

---

2. John C. Robinson became a colonel, commanding the 1st Michigan as reorganized for three years' service. Horace Roberts served first as lieutenant colonel but was promoted to colonel April 28, 1862.

swollen, continuing to discharge freely, attended with great soreness and of course a constant drain on his much weakened system.

Do you remember our last happy evening, there was no foreshadowing of coming events to mar our little cheerfulness, and we often [refer] to it. My own health and spirits gave way to many combined influences, & the Friday & Saturday after your departure I was obliged to lie in bed, fighting against depression and atmospheric ills!—now I have revived, blessed with a long letter from my dear Mother, who had received mine sent by Gen'l Magruder, which assures you of the safety of yours also. Your cousin, Mrs. Herow, had been to see my Mother, anxiously enquiring about you, which reminds me that I wrote to your wife and also to Mrs. Withington, thinking it might be a slight consolation to them! You will be glad to hear that our poor amputated men will be allowed to return to their homes this week, and those cases which their mutilated condition and impaired health demands. Would to God the same humanity could be extended to our hopelessly wounded, whose want of clothes, money to procure any little comforts, & depression of spirits with exhausted strength offers an appalling prospect for sufferings during the coming winter!

Poor Metcalf, the Zouave who was amputated & recovered so rapidly, has relapsed, must endure another amputation & will die. Briggs is convalescent & goes home. Shephard is not considered well enough. Shillinglaw also goes but McQuaid is not sufficiently recovered nor indeed out of danger; his life hangs on a thread & gives us constant anxiety from our interest in his indomitable nerve. Eukin [?] is out of danger, and all are improving although we have had two amputations last week. Francis, who had fourteen bayonet wounds, had his leg taken off last Friday, & Whitehouse lost his arm.

How gladly the 800 released on parole & now here would be exchanged & how easily it might be effected & so many made happy! . . . Eleven of our surgeons were sent home on parole, we are told, but of course we know nothing beyond the report. I wish my husband could be released on parole; he will be useless for the next eight months and our fate is so uncertain, we know not what a day may bring forth; as soon as his wound heals, however, I shall never leave him. It lightens his trials by sharing them. D. Swalm has again refused to go from those he sees benefit by his surgical attendance & now performs a self-sacrificing duty; he still sleeps in the same cot, & yours has not been removed, a silent reminder if we needed any! My next letter will be to Capt. Withington, who I hope remains with you. . . . All here unite in kindest regards to you, Capt. Withington, and our other friends, who may be with or near you.

Let us hear from you, dear colonel, if possible; you know our address & the pleasure it will give us—Adieu, God bless & guard you for those brighter days in store for us all is the daily prayer of

> Your ever warmly
> attached friend and
> sister in affliction,
> Fanny Ricketts

Columbia, South Carolina[3]
February 17, 1862
My dear Brother,

I hope you & your family are all well, that the office & the Farm are flourishing & that our dear mother is still alive & well. This morning I received a letter from our secession sister, who had got back to New Orleans after visiting Richmond & enduring terrible fatigues, long delays & numerous accidents of travel. She writes full of hope of my speedy release under the supposition the settlement of the Privateer question was at hand & would settle all. How disappointed she will be if the story is true that I & others are to be held for a new class of men.[4]

But Marie & Mother, how must they feel when, for the fourth time, they are called upon to count my life in peril! It is perfectly heart-rending. To them as to me, it almost seems as if my death would be a relief. And yet, my dear Eb, if this story be true, I do not wish any humiliating concessions made to save a life now so little valued, except for my wife & children's sakes & not valued above my own or my country's honor, for their sakes even.

The report seems incredible, as such a threat cannot effect its object as it did in the Privateers' case. Then the judiciary & the public were in favor of treating them as other prisoners of war. But as I did not even then sue for governmental interference, much less do I ask it now. I clearly foresee that when blood begins to flow it will flow in torrents. Let the bitter consequences fall where they are justly due, but let no friend of mine seek to save my life at the sacrifice of my country's honor & the dignity of the law. But the whole affair seems unworthy of belief.

3. This letter is extracted from a copy made by OBW in his *Prison Journal.*
4. Although the privateer crisis had been settled, it was supposed that OBW and other Federal officers might be held hostage for Confederate sympathizers who had burned bridges in Missouri.

Your last favor was from Lansing. Write often in hopes that some letters may get through. With love to all

> Your devoted Bro.,
> O.B.W.

Richmond, Virginia
April 2, 1862
My dearest Wife,

I have been here ever since last of February with no more apparent probability of exchange than ever, & without even the consolation of hearing from home. I can only say that I am well, & entirely in the dark as to the cause of longer detention. It is [learned] our government has broken off negotiations. We are confined as usual in large numbers in warehouses, without egress to even a yard for air & exercise. All the Columbia party are here. I hope you are able to bear up under this misfortune & that the dear little ones are well. Kiss them & give my love to Father, Mother & Eb. I hope you have some light from your side to sustain hope. I can see none here.

> Ever your devoted Husband,
> O. B. Willcox

Richmond
April 30 [1862]
My darling Wife,

I entrust this letter to hands that I hope will get it to you without the surveillance of the authorities. Although I have nothing contraband to communicate, yet I can express myself more freely than when I know official eyes are to coldly peruse.[5]

My darling! how can I ever express the thousandth part of the love I feel & the consolation even of that love in moments most dire & frightful. The fact of your devotion has supported me under all circumstances, & had I never appreciated you before[,] this bitter absence . . . has revealed our union in a holy light—as if I were, even in this world, linked to an angel, for such you are & ever have been to me.

But it seems, as if to try me at the tenderest point, I have not been permitted to receive but few of your precious letters—none at all since February 3d, altho I hear thro Withington of at least one of mine reaching you. I was

---

5. The original, written on very thin paper, perhaps onionskin, has many creases, indicating that the letter was folded numerous times, to enable the bearer to conceal the secret missive from prying Confederate authorities.

treated with some consideration at Charleston & Columbia, but it looks as if the Richmond authorities had some particular spite against me, for not only is my correspondence with home cut off, but none of the friends who visited me when I was here in the hospital have come to see me this time.

Even my former credit for being at least *a gentleman* seems lately to have worked a disadvantage, for the blackguards of the prisoners have had their letters quite regularly. As one instance, Col. Corcoran, whom these people profess to despise, & who has certainly less claim to their respect than any prisoner here of equal rank, has his letters every week. How omnipotent is humbug! The Irish Lion is as near an ass [as] can be, & yet he not only overshadows us all at home but has more privileges here than any one. I can speak my heart to no one but you on this subject, but it galls me to the quick to have a low-bred, uneducated, selfish, cunning foreigner toadied by our too generous people on all occasions. When I add to that he came into the war with no love for the country but at the instigation of Bishop Hughes[6] to practice himself & his countrymen in arms for acting in Ireland, you can judge still better of my indignation. Yet his name is mentioned in Congress & every where before mine & every other. Why, my dear, he has not expressed one intelligent idea, even on the subject of the war, in the whole nine months I have been with him.

But a truce to this subject. I keep all these things to myself & wish you to do the same. The tale of my wrongs & suffering as a prisoner I will keep till we meet, which I trust will now be soon, notwithstanding that it has seemed as if I never were destined to be liberated. The repeated hopes & disappointments have not broken my spirit in the least, but I have, I hope, learned some useful virtues such as patience & caution. But it wrings my heart to think how this suspense must have cruelly consumed your precious heart. Keep up. Keep young & bright as ever for my sake, for God will assuredly bring us together. Write me your views, Father's & Eb's about my reentering the service & send the letters to Rowland Trowbridge[7] to keep till my arrival at Washington. All my fellow Michigan prisoners go in a day or two. Be polite to them—particularly Bolio.[8] Of course Eb & Father will keep a bright eye to my exchange. God bless them both. Love to all

Thine,
O.B.W.

6. Archbishop John R. Hughes (1797–1864), of the archdiocese of New York, was a native of Ireland.

7. Representative Rowland E. Trowbridge (R., Mich.).

8. Pvt. Franklin Bolio, Company A, 1st Michigan Infantry, wounded and captured at Bull Run. Bolio later served in the 27th Michigan Infantry.

Richmond
May 2, '62
Mrs. O. B. Willcox
Detroit, Mich.
My dearest Wife,

While I write, the men are preparing to go home, but the officers have no idea of their prospects. Father is at Ft. Monroe, waiting the result of the proposition for my exchange, & has written me. If it fails & he has to wend his melancholy way home & see you without me by his side, what will you do my darling! But you must be prepared for the worst as I am, being involved in this everlasting snarl on the exchange question, like the two cousins in *Jarndyce & Jarndyce*.[9] If we do not all go mad or become idiotic it will not be the fault of the circumlocution office. I am glad the men get off. Some of them may call to see you particularly Bolio, son of my old french acquaintance, Gideon Bolio. He has been my faithful attendant, cook, waiter, clothes-washer, & pipe lighter & will tell you & the children all about it. You will encourage his visits & trust the children to walk with him, as he is a very well-behaved boy & seems very much attached to me.

I wish you would call on Mrs. Mauch & tell her I would not like to entrust her noble husband's ring to any other hands but her own, & for this reason have not sent it, but hope soon to deliver it in person. When I get out I hope to meet Father & consult with him before taking any steps as to the future, & I wish you to write me on the same subject, & send the letter to Rowland Trowbridge, or still better, Gen'l Meigs, to keep till I reach Washington. Tell the children I look at their pictures very often, particularly Sundays, & wonder whether they will recognize Papa when he gets home. Kiss them all for me & give my love to both Mothers, & Eb, Louise, Scottens, Duffield, Bishop McC & Mr. Trowbridge. Courage, Courage! Keep young & bright as ever.

Your devoted,
O.B.W.

Salisbury, N.C.
June 12, 1862
My dearest Wife,

I was made very happy yesterday by receipt of yours of May 17 [and] 24 from Detroit & N.Y., & again to-day one of April 18th arrived giving full

9. Referring to characters Richard Carstone and Ada Clare, cousins, in Charles Dickens's *Bleak House*. The cousins were wards of the court in the distribution of an estate that had gone

news of home. The idea that you are in N.Y. waiting for me! Your heart must have sickened indeed on hope deferred, & I fear it is destined to the same misfortune a long while yet. Notwithstanding that a general exchange was believed some time since to be consummated, yet the long delay has destroyed my belief in it, & you must not suffer yourself to be a prey to alternate expectations & disappointment any longer, but not expect me until you hear of me across the lines. Disgusting business!

Pained to hear you were unwell in the spring. I hope the air of N.Y. will strengthen you, but do not confine yourself too closely; tell Father & William [Blodgett] I charge them to [tote] you out *nolens volens*. Eb on the farm & the NcNairs at Chicago are changes indeed. From the reception of your letters here I hope to hear from you now often, at least once a week.

The courtesy & kindness of Capt. Godwin here are in marked contrast to Richmond authorities & you can at least think of me now as better treated, & more air & exercise. I am in a nice room with Maj. Vogdes, Maj. Potter, Lt. Kent & Dr. Williams, looking out on a garden, where the roses are just dropping off & peaches are coming, & we have the freedom of an enclosure embracing the different quarters & prisons. When first arrived I had no strength left & it takes little now to knock me up, but the change has been salvation. My constant effort is to banish unruly thought & try to think this long captivity ordained for some wise purpose.

One of my best friends, Capt. George Austin of Kentucky, has lately been put in close confinement as hostage for the Guerrillas, a hard case for him as he is one of the oldest prisoners & already lost his sight in one eye. We have forwarded an application to Washington in behalf of him & his fellow hostage, Capt. O'Meara. There are several new Michigan prisoners here, among them is one of my own regiment but now of [the] 1st Cavalry, wounded in the head. His name is Huntly.[10]

A thousand thanks to Father for his indefatigable devotion. It is worth the suffering to see it but I am unworthy [of] so much pains. I am all eagerness to go home & see you & the little ones, for no man ever had a more lovely family, but we must wait & hope. With love to all the delightful circle in N.Y., I remain with undying love

Your husband,
O. B. Willcox

on so long that it had become the subject of endless joking; court costs eventually absorbed the entire estate.

10. Sira Huntly, formerly of 1st Michigan Infantry, had enlisted in the 1st Michigan Cavalry in August 1861 and was wounded and captured at Bull Run.

Salisbury, N.C.
June 14/'62
Hon. E. Farnsworth
New York
My Dear Father,

Received your letter of May 13 with following endorsement: "This letter was delivered by the flag officer & received by my A.D.C. [aide de camp] Lt. Preston who on examining it found that $25 mentioned was not enclosed & he handed it immediately to me—no money was enclosed (signed) Benj. Huger, Maj. Gen."[11] I fear the money was abstracted on the other side as Gen. Huger's word is *unquestionable*.

New complications again postpone exchanges. One of my best friends, Capt. Austin, is one of the hostages; do all you can for him. Marie will feel terribly disappointed again. Who knows what will happen next in this war? I hoped to meet her in New York ere this & still hope that calm & sensible views will prevail. But why are *we here condemned* to be the foot balls for every petty mistake & blunder? Nothing can ever recompense me for the torture inflicted through me on my family. As long as we are in the enemy's hands we prove a good card which they will not hesitate to play, regardless of consequences. But you know all this. Believe me, nothing can daunt me, but I feel indignant over this perpetual fool's play, while Marie's pale face haunts my mind & our mental longings are raised & disappointed by feeble diplomacy & chicanery. But we hear from you at least. A few more such men as you might have saved all this suffering.

Your devoted Son,
O. B. Willcox

Salisbury, N.C.
June 22, 1862
Mrs. O. B. Willcox
New York
My dearest Wife,

Very happy to acknowledge receipt of your letter of 10th inst. telling me that another officer, Col. Baldwin, had been forwarded for me. I hope he has been sent across the lines so that he can exert his personal influence, for several exchanges have been effected in that way. But the indifference, if not positive opposition manifested here, fills me with little hope. Of course

11. Maj. Gen. Benjamin Huger (CSA) (8th, USMA 1825), then commanding the Department of Norfolk.

there is an ulterior design. At any rate they have had every opportunity presented for exchanges & yet hold on to the hostages & thereby block the way to general exchanges.

I say this to keep you from being again disappointed; whatever flourishes you hear, do not put too much faith in them. I have made up my mind for bearing a prolonged period of captivity with all due fortitude. The worst feature of it is my separation from you. But I am glad to hear that the children are so well & that you are in N.Y. Father's goodness & devotion affect me deeply. I hope both of us may be spared that I may repay in part at least. I am sure you have borne up wonderfully my pretty little heroine; preserve your equanimity a while longer.

It suits my plans exactly to meet you in N.Y., where I would like quite a visit. Dr. Moody never made his appearance. Col. Sir Percy Wyndham is in my mess. There are in all some 180 officers here living on the breath of rumor & looking for exchange, as ship-wrecked mariners strain their eyes for a sail. Yesterday completed my eleventh month. Glad to hear of Caro's housekeeping & should like to nestle a few days on Murray Hill. The money enclosed by Father may have been retained at Fort Monroe as Gen. Huger wrote that it did not come in the letter. I wrote Father [a] few days since, care of William. A thousand loves to you who form the sunshine behind this cloud. Remember me to each & all.

Thine Ever,
O. B. Willcox

[Marie Willcox to O.B.W.]
July 28th [1862]
My dearest Husband,

As the newspapers assert that "beyond doubt a general exchange of [prisoners] has been arranged," and every day, in anxiously scrutinizing the lists of returned prisoners, I fail to find that name so long sought in vain, I am kept, of course, in a state of most painful suspense.

It seems too good news to be true, that you should really be permitted to escape from the clutches that have so long held you fast. It is better to write though, in case you may come out ignorant, as you must be, as to the status of affairs in your own state, and at Washington, and without any clue to the expectations or the wishes of your friends.

There have been so many changes in the charge of the War Dept. that any personal influence gained previously is of no avail now. I do not know how the present *chief* may regard your claims to consideration. I know that all your friends here, and at home, think that at least you should demand a

Brigadiership, dated from the day of your capture, which is but just, as it is well known that your name was among the *first* for that position, and that you would undoubtedly have received it, had you come back on the run with the rest, instead of going forward and doing your duty. Gen. McDowell said that he heard the subject discussed at the War Dept. and that it was agreed that your promotion should date from Bull Run; he moreover said to Father that you behaved with more gallantry than any officer on the field. I merely state these facts, to let you know that in the winter, that was the state of your case.

I hear from William Blodgett that Mr. Follet,[12] and some Michigan men seem to expect that you are to go home and use your personal influence to raise a brigade. The Democrats talk of you for Democratic candidate for governor. But you will not wish to identify yourself with that organization as it at present stands in Michigan. A colonelcy in the regular army might do, if you thought best. It may not be necessary to decide at once.

But as you go to Washington, it is better to take the position you intend to hold. "You know my character gentlemen, my services, and sufferings. I think myself entitled to so and so, or nothing." You would not place yourself in such a false position as to accept a Brigadiership where you would be ranked by every political fool in the service.

I write this, taking it for granted that your sense of duty prompts you to continue in the field, and that your health will permit it. I almost wish it were otherwise; to escape from this horrible anxiety only to experience new apprehensions of your safety, is torture, but there is no choice. These are dark days for America and her people.

I am in New York at 21 Park Ave., Murray Hill. Elon is with me. Father brought him on last week as far as Albany and returned with Caro and her children. Mr. Harrison taking charge of Elon here. His health has not been good this summer. Change of air seemed desirable. If I do not hear of your being on this side of the line, I shall go on Wednesday to Framingham and stay until I hear from you by telegraph, when I will meet you in N.Y. at Frank's (who is at home and keeps the house open). William and Abbie [Blodgett] would like to have us go to Forestdale, but I thought you would want to get home. If the idea of a few days recruiting in the bracing air of the green mountains strikes you favorably, advise me to that effect, and I will meet you there.

On the 21st of this month, I enclosed a certificate of deposit for fifty dollars; did it reach you?

12. Probably Martin P. Follett, former Michigan state representative.

I trust this hope is not doomed to disappointment. Congress has adjourned, so you will not meet our delegation. You need place no dependence upon them. They have forfeited all claim to public respect, and will advance only those whom they can *use*. You will *burn* this, when read, and hasten to the embrace of your own true wife

Marie.

Salisbury, N.C.
July 30, '62
Mrs. O. B. Willcox
21 Park Ave., New York City
My dearest Wife,

I have received your letter of 10th last enclosing your carte & mother's 4th July account of the children & home. You can little imagine the thrill of pleasure which both give. The likeness shows that you are physically well but looks sad, as I feared. Remember your old philosophy of cultivating expression & don't yield to habitual sorrows in the face or the heart. To hear so much of the dear, dear little ones, in such vivid picture-writing as mother employs, brings them with more reality before my mind than they have yet appeared. How I long to be with them again!

Almost a week has elapsed since I last wrote you by Dr. Grey & none of our party have commenced moving homeward. It cannot be many days for our patience to be taxed & within the last week a strong fit of homesickness has seized me. I certainly hope that the Hostages & the July prisoners, after all the fuss made about us in Congress & elsewhere, & after our long stay & repeated disappointments, will not be the *last* exchanged, when every thing claims that they should be the *first*. I know of nothing exposing the cartel[13] to a rupture, but should such an event happen after a partial exchange & *we* be left, a gross injustice would be done us.

But away with these dismal fears. I hope for the best. In fact from the latest advices from Richmond it appears that the commissioner had not [arrived?]. It would do us no harm for you to write Gen. Meigs inquiring about the matter & stating it to him in as strong light as possible.

I hope to meet you in New York. Meantime you had better observe Mother's hints about the wants of the little flock at home & provide their wardrobe, not forgetting some handsome presents for herself.

13. Cartel of U.S. representatives (Fish and Ames) negotiating for an exchange of prisoners.

It is somewhat queer that, after his fair promises, Dr. Moody should have neither visited me nor sent me the money you entrusted to his care. But no matter, I have been able to procure funds through Higgins. With unspeakable love,

Thine,
O. B. Willcox

Love to Caro & Frank

[Marie Willcox to O.B.W.]
Framingham
August 1st [1862]
My dear Husband,
You perceive that I did not forward the letter written in N.Y. There seemed some hitch in the exchange of Prisoners, so I thought it more safe to wait. I see by the Boston papers that Gen. Buckner[14] and the other prisoners from Fort Warren went forward yesterday to be exchanged, so I send this on, though I have little faith that it will reach you.

I came over on Wednesday the 30th July, found the family here all well, and very glad to see me. It is just a year since I came here last year. Elon is delighted with the country, the hay making, hillsides, and berry picking, and improves daily in appetite and strength. The change was just what he required. He says, "Oh I do hope we shall get a letter to say that my dear, dearest! Papa has got away from the rebels, and for us to go meet him." His temperament is very much like yours, a fine noble-spirited boy, sensitive, generous and affectionate. His relatives in N.Y. were quite taken with him. William and Brown took him to the Central Park, showed him the deer, swans, &c.

I met several Detroit gentlemen coming over here. They say you are very much wanted in Michigan. Mr. Chandler is getting up a regiment which he intends to lead into the field. Mr. Morrow is also getting up one, and Gov. Wisner. With these various influences I do not think I should try recruiting. It is stupid that they do not fill up the old regiments, instead of sending such a lot of green officers into the field. But they are all selfish, they want the rank, and the pay.

If you do come out you will want some clothes; do not get much until you get to N.Y. and let Frank or William get you a respectable citzen's rig. I brought on your military coat, pants, and a black silk vest, which you will find in a trunk at Caro's, but do not be seen in bright buttons. I am so dis-

14. Brig. Gen. Simon B. Buckner had been captured at Fort Donelson.

gusted with the volunteer officers flourishing round in their toggery, that I should be mortified to see you with it on. But can it be possible that I am to see you at all? It seems a happiness too great for belief or realization. I shall watch the papers, the post and telegraph. How terrible the disappointment if it is in vain. Your own true and loving wife

Marie L. Willcox

American Telegraph Company
By telegraph from Fortress Monroe Aug. 16.
To Mrs. O. B. Willcox Care Cyrus Blake.[15]

I am coming under the old stars. Shall start for Washington this Evening and will send word from there to New York when you may expect me.

O. B. Willcox

15. Cyrus Blake was the father of Hannah Blake Farnsworth, wife of Elon Farnsworth.

§ FIFTEEN

South Mountain and Antietam

On August 16, 1862, the day Orlando Willcox was officially released from prison, the Union Army of Virginia, under Maj. Gen. John Pope, began converging with elements of Maj. Gen. George B. McClellan's Army of the Potomac, now shifting north after evacuating the Virginia Peninsula. Robert E. Lee, however, was also shifting his troops northward, and on August 29–30 his Confederate forces defeated Pope's army at the Battle of Second Manassas. As the retreating Federal forces fell back on Washington, demoralized and in great disarray, McClellan was once again placed at their head. Setting out at once to reorganize them as they filtered back into the capital, "Little Mac" prepared to intercept the Confederate forces as they crossed the Potomac and moved north into Maryland.

Willcox, of course, realized the peril his country was in and was eager to return to duty in spite of his recent inprisonment. After a whirlwind trip back home to Detroit, where he was accorded a hero's welcome, the newly appointed brigadier returned to Washington and reported for duty.

Given command of the First Division, consisting of two brigades in Maj. Gen. Jesse L. Reno's Ninth Corps, Willcox set out with the rest of the Army of the Potomac on the campaign that would terminate in the battles of South Mountain (September 14) and Antietam (September 17, 1862), the bloodiest single day in American history.

UPON EMERGING from imprisonment, I felt like one "born again." We were whirled [into] a waiting carriage through a crowd to the Willard

Brig. Gen. Orlando B. Willcox shortly after his release from prison. *USAMHI.*

House, where the multitude were clamorous for speeches. Colonel Corcoran thanked them and made some patriotic remarks, in his usual brief and modest way, but Major Vogdes and the writer launched out [at] the impotent manner in which the war was being conducted—an indiscretion on my part that made some enemies for me in the Congressional Committee on the Conduct of the War.[1]

At night, Mr. George W. Childs, publisher of the *Philadelphia Ledger*, called and asked for a written narrative of our prison experiences. And here I committed mistake no. 2, for Mr. Childs had guaranteed me a profit of $10,000, a sum that would have come handy to me and mine for the rest of our lives. But I was most anxious to be rid of the prison nightmare that overshadowed my memory, and to get back into the field as soon as possible, after seeing my dear ones at home.

The next day was memorable, not only from the warm greetings of friends in Washington, but likewise by a personal call from the President in

1. In Washington on August 18 Willcox gave a lengthy speech, stating among other things that the government had been waging "a brainless war" of ineffective, "isolated expeditions." Much of the war's reverses he blamed on "men without principle, and without patriotism," who had urged impractical and unmilitary plans on the government. He further accused contractors of graft and declared that "the blood of our men, the groans of the wounded . . . the wails of the widow, have been coined into money."

his carriage, and an invitation to an informal dinner that evening, which, of course, we were proud to accept. I never shall forget that dinner at the Lincoln cottage—[the] Soldiers' Home. The face of the great President and Father of his people, when it was in repose, had that faraway sad and anxious look which has been so well described by Winston Churchill in the *Crisis*, as if it bore the seal of his destiny.[2] And for once the facial expression was scarcely alight with the usual gleams of his proverbial humor, for the reason perhaps that he was both anxious to hear about Libby Prison, and still more concerned over the exigencies of General Pope's army at Bull Run, on which the lives of so many officers and men, and perhaps the safety of the Capitol, depended.[3]

The furniture of the room was quite simple. Sitting opposite the President as I did, at a small table with but two other guests, gave me an excellent opportunity to study his remarkable features, wonderful as the expression of Christ's face in some paintings by the great masters. But I was also curious to see how the President's wife, a Kentucky woman, felt about the war. But while the conversation was apparently intended to interest Mrs. Lincoln, for I noticed that the President often turned towards her as he queried us, or otherwise speaking of the war, the lady herself kept silent, and looked unsympathetic —to say the least. And I could but fancy that here was one more great burden for our host to carry, viz., the wife of his bosom, the Lady of the White House, while she could not but share some of her husband's anxiety, was perhaps, at heart—a "rebel"! But I may have been mistaken.

Aside from this, no wonder that the President felt deeply anxious for Pope. General Halleck[4] evidently distrusted Pope's abilities and had ordered McClellan to report in person at Washington with a view to contin-

2. OBW had dinner with President Lincoln on the evening of August 18, 1862, along with Secretary of War Stanton, Maj. Gen. Henry W. Halleck, Gen. George A. McCall, Col. Michael Corcoran and Col. Alfred M. Wood, the last three having also been recently exchanged; see Earl Schenck Miers, ed., *Lincoln Day by Day: A Chronology, 1809–1865* (Washington: Lincoln Sesquicentennial Commission, 1960). OBW here refers to *The Crisis*, a novel of the American Civil War (McMillan, 1901) by the American novelist Winston Churchill (not to be confused with the future British prime minister).

3. Elements of Maj. Gen. John Pope's (17th, USMA 1842) Union Army of Virginia commanded by Maj. Gen. Nathaniel P. Banks had been defeated on August 9, 1862, at Cedar Mountain, Virginia, near Culpeper. By August 18 (the day OBW dined with President Lincoln) Pope was pulling back to the north bank of the Rappahannock and awaiting reinforcements from the Army of the Potomac, which was then withdrawing from Harrison's Landing on the Peninsula. Lee finally defeated Pope's entire army at Second Bull Run (August 29–30, 1862). As the Union troops retreated toward Washington, the temporarily deposed McClellan was once again called upon to reorganize the dejected troops, to head off Lee's impending invasion of Maryland.

4. Maj. Gen. Henry Wager Halleck (3d, USMA 1839) was then general in chief of the Union army.

gencies, but exactly for what purpose the latter could only surmise—he guessed that it was not friendly. It appears in his letters that he was haunted by fears [of] some jealous hostility on the part of the Administration.

When he arrived at the seat of government waiting orders—as still commander of the whole Army of the Potomac—it seems that the President wanted him to direct Pope what to do—but that he declined. In his letter of August 21st, written at Fortress Monroe, where he was superintending the transportation of his troops up the Potomac, he says—"Just received a telegram from Halleck stating that Pope and Burnside are very hard pressed, urging me to push forward reinforcements and to *come myself as soon as I possibly can!*" Pursuant to these instructions, he sent the 9th Corps up the Rappahannock to reinforce Pope and, next day, the 22nd, he writes, "I am confident that the disposition to be made of me will depend entirely upon the state of their nerves in Washington."[5]

On the 23rd he is still more explicit, and writes: "I take it for granted that my orders will be as disagreeable as it is possible to make them, *unless Pope is beaten*, in which case they will want me to save Washington again."[6]

Yes, to save the army and the Capitol of his country, even as a *Pis-Aller*, as if that were not a sacred duty in any event. But why need the Little Napoleon have placed himself on record in such a light? Imagine General Washington or General Grant expressing such language on any contingency, and then publishing it to the world!

And yet there was no other man in the army who could have done the work in such a handsome manner as "Little Mac" certainly did it—picking up the shattered remains of a ruined army, inspiring the men with new confidence and his own enthusiasm, refitting the ragged, barefooted columns, and marching them on to victory. Meanwhile, it was part of my own good fortune that, having been just promoted to be a brigadier general,[7] I met my old West Point friend, McClellan, in Washington, and to be offered the command of a division in his army, "say, in the 9th Corps?" And how soon could I join? I need not tell you that I jumped at the chance.

As you may well imagine, I lost no time in starting for home and a quick return to the field. The good people of Detroit and some other parts of Michigan, always so partial towards my poor desserts, gave me what was

5. McClellan to his wife, in George B. McClellan, *McClellan's Own Story* (New York: Charles L. Webster, 1887), p. 470. This quote was paraphrased in OBW's original manuscript; it is given accurately here.

6. Ibid., p. 471.

7. OBW was promoted to brigadier general on August 20, 1862, the commission to date from July 21, 1861.

described in the newspapers as an enthusiastic public reception. But the joyful welcome of my devoted and long-suffering wife and that of my patriotic [and] proud mother, with that of the rest of my family, cannot be described.

Going home by way of Brandon, Vermont, where, at Grandfather Blake's house, my wife waited me, I was loudly greeted by a patriotic crowd at the depot, together with a committee inviting me to speak at a "war meeting." The Brandon newspaper of August 23, 1862, gave this flourishing account of the whole proceedings:

At an early hour that evening . . . our mammoth Town Hall, which it seems some thought would never be filled, was crowded to its utmost capacity, with an intelligent mass to hear a war speech from a war man. To say that the speech was eminently a speech for the times, brim full of logical conclusions and practical hints, stirring incidents and telling appeals and replete with passages of touching eloquence, surpassing beauty and richness, and that it far overleaped the highest expectations of all, would but faintly tell the story. To be appreciated it must have been received entire as it came from the Heart and lips of the gallant hero. General Willcox left town on Monday for his home in the west.

My children [were] scarcely old enough to remember that a like ovation met our return to our old home—a poem of welcome by Mrs. E. H. Hall in the *Detroit Gazette*, and a platform reception on the campus martius where sat dear old General Cass, Senator Chandler, Robert—afterwards governor—McClelland, and other friends. And, drawn up in the crowd, stood a detachment of my old Michigan First comrades, whose excited, enthusiastic cheers were the sweetest part of that public reception at Detroit, my native city.

But after a few days enjoyment of such rare transports, I was off to the wars again, and returned to Washington in time for the Antietam Campaign; was assigned to the 9th Corps, commanded by my old classmate Burnside,[8] to whom, and to General McClellan, I reported at Frederick, Maryland, where I took command of my division [the First Division], said to be at the time one of the best in the army—and a noble set of fellows they certainly were. . . . I was glad to find two good Michigan regiments, and six from Massachusetts, New York and Pennsylvania, together with a couple of

8. Burnside was then in command of the right wing of the army, consisting of Maj. Gen. Joseph Hooker's First Corps and Maj. Gen. Jesse L. Reno's Ninth Corps.

light batteries, and that they had already smelt powder in the field under my predecessor in command, the late notable Isaac Stevens.[9] This general had graduated . . . at the head of his West Point class, over such men as Halleck and Ricketts, entered the Civil Engineer Corps and had already won fame as a great explorer, lately in the extreme northwest. He reentered the service in the present war as Colonel of the 79th New York Highlanders, a crack regiment, rose to the command of the division, which he handled with great skill and bravery in the recent Manassas Campaign. He lost his life in the brilliant rear guard action at Chantilly, where he led his troops with the colors of the 79th Highlanders in his hand. The words seem tame enough to wind up the career of one of the most brilliant men in the army. And yet it was a seat in his saddle that I was called to fill! I never felt less worthy or more humble over any lift in my career. But I determined to follow, so far as I knew how, so worthy an example, as a standard to which I always pointed the brave men who fairly worshipped him, especially the New York Highlanders—with whom I have ever since kept up a warm connection, for the sake of Auld Lang Syne.

The shattered ranks were rapidly repaired and refitted, their clothing and equipments were fairly complete, and in a few days after a review by Burnside, my two brigades—commanded respectively by "Old Ben Christ,"[10] and Thomas Welsh of Pennsylvania—with the two batteries, were ready for the march to the South Mountain region. . . .

The town of Frederick in Maryland is only 44 miles from Washington. Lee had camped his army in a line between the town and [the] Potomac River, and recruiting offices were opened for "My Maryland." His foraging parties, driving in all the horses, cattle and hogs and sheep in the neighborhood, rather dampened the spirits of the "truly loyal" Southern sympathizers, and the General's proclamations must have read rather flat, although the road to Washington lay open some days to the invaders, during which time McClellan gathered up the fragments of Pope's army and reached Frederick on the night of September 10[; there] he found the recruiting offices closed, [and] Lee's army in retreat to the passes of the South Mountain range. McClellan moved on with precaution to protect the lower fords of the Potomac *en route*, and thereby ensure the safety of Washington.

It appears that Lee's programme was to live on the country for several months, to capture Harper's Ferry and Martinsburg and their garrisons, to

9. Stevens (1st, USMA 1839) had served with distinction on Winfield Scott's staff during the Mexican War. His support of Franklin Pierce in 1852 brought him the governorship of Washington Territory in 1853.

10. Col. Benjamin C. Christ; Col. Thomas Welsh.

Celebration honoring the return of OBW to Detroit upon his release from prison, August 27, 1862. *Burton Historical Collection.*

threaten Washington and Baltimore, [and] to draw the Union Army from [the] south to [the] north side of the Potomac and away from their base of supplies—in case he entered Pennsylvania. Of course he had counted on the virtual destruction that Pope's army had suffered and he counted on the loyalty of the Marylanders.

Meantime, his first object was Harpers Ferry, against which he sent [Maj. Gen. Lafayette] McLaws[11] and Stonewall Jackson—the latter to capture Martinsburg and with a view to cut off retreat of the Harper's Ferry garrison. The bulk of his army occupied the South Mountain passes, which D. H. Hill[12] occupied along the Hagerstown and Boonsboro road, his [left] resting at Turner's Gap—the terminus of the National Road from Frederick, as well as a road to Sharpsburg.

Following [Brig. Gen. Alfred] Pleasonton's cavalry in pursuit, the 9th Corps arrived opposite Turner's Gap on the morning of September 14, and began the attack, General [Jacob D.] Cox[13] leading at the head of his division, supported by my division. Next on our right was Hooker's corps—and still further to [the] right, our other corps were extended . . . [with] Franklin's corps, whose instructions were to look out for Harper's Ferry [on the left of the army].[14]

<But as it turned out, Franklin was either too late or not near enough to assist the brave Colonel Dixon Miles [commander of the Harpers Ferry garrison], whose last words as he fell mortally wounded in defense of Harpers Ferry became memorable: "I have done my best, and what I thought to be my duty. This is a fitting end for a soldier." This catastrophe, the loss of a great arsenal depot and strategic fortress, and that of a grand old soldier, happened early next morning, September 15.>[15]

By Pleasonton's advice, confirmed by Reno, [now] commanding [the Ninth Corps], I was posted at the junction of the road leading up to Cox's troops and another to a gap on his right, called . . . Fox's Gap. The enemy

11. McLaws (48th, USMA 1842), then commanded a division in Lt. Gen. James Longstreet's command in the Army of Northern Virginia. McLaws's troops occupied Maryland Heights, overlooking Harpers Ferry from the north bank of the Potomac, during this phase of the campaign.

12. Maj. Gen. Daniel Harvey Hill (28th, USMA 1842) then led a division under Stonewall Jackson.

13. Brig. Gen. Jacob D. Cox then commanded the "Kanawha Division," the Fourth Division, Ninth Corps. He succeeded to command of the Ninth Corps following the death of General Reno.

14. Maj. Gen. William B. Franklin's left wing of the army, consisting of his own Sixth Corps and Maj. Gen. Darius N. Couch's Fourth Corps division.

15. This entry, encased within single angle brackets < >, was originally meant as a footnote by OBW.

were partially hidden on the ridge among rocks and trees above us, and I had scarcely got into position with Cook's battery[16] advanced some hundred yards in front of the left battalion, before the Confederates wheeled a battery into view and opened a plunging fire of canister and shell on Cook, which soon "knocked him into pie," and compelled him to withdraw two of his most exposed pieces to refit. The other two pieces kept pegging away, and became the object of the enemy's desultory attention down to our final charge, Cook's first lieutenant, John N. Coffin, doing fine work against heavier guns. There were several attempts by the enemy to capture the guns with infantry covering, [of] which there are published, as usual, several conflicting reports.

Meantime, my old classmate, John Gibbon, was "thundering away" with his batteries, and demonstrating with his [brigade] with as much noise and display as if the whole army were at his heels, on the pass in his front. . . .[17]

While my own artillery duel was going on and I was momentarily expecting orders from Reno to advance, there came up a new regiment of Michigan troops [the 17th Mich.] for duty with the division. Happily it was commanded by Withington—my old friend and fellow prisoner of war.

"Glad to see you, Colonel. But what can you do?"

"We can march by a flank and load and fire, General."

"All right, sir. You see that battery up in the gap? Now if you can steal up through the woods and pick off some of the cannoneers, that will help a good deal."

"All right," was his reply, and moving round . . . one side, he led his Wolverines like stealthy savages through the woods, where the crack of their rifles was soon heard, causing an evident abatement of the enemy's artillery fire, and some mysterious movement of his infantry. In fact, they were getting in line to charge down on my whole front just as my orders came to make a main attack on Fox's Gap, and we promptly moved forward to meet them, the gallant Welsh in front, leading his brigade, with the Highlanders on their right.

. . . When the grand movement of the day began, Withington had his regiment drawn up in a hollow, partly masked by a stone fence which overlooked the field at the very point where my division finally met the enemy in line of battle. . . . At the critical meeting of the two lines, the enemy marching down the hill and giving into us with a plunging fire, while we were

16. Capt. Asa M. Cook commanded the 8th Battery, Massachusetts Light Artillery.

17. Brig. Gen. John Gibbon then commanded the famous "Iron Brigade," the Fourth Brigade, First Division, First Corps.

pushing up, firing for the main part over the heads of our own men, a mutual charge bayonet began; Withington, after one good volley, roared out, "Over the wall and at 'em!" Whereupon the lusty 17th fellows leaped the stone fence, clubbed their muskets, and, with the Highlanders, soon threw the Confederate left flank into confusion and the day on my part was practically won. . . .[18]

But one event saddened our rejoicings. As soon as my people were relieved by General Sturgis's division,[19] late in the afternoon, General Reno went forward to a tree in front of the skirmish line to reconnoiter. But the Confederates were still sullenly firing chance shots from some points of vantage, and some way or other Reno was struck down by a stray musket ball. As he was being brought to the rear, passing my headquarters, I stopped the litter and inquired, "General are you badly hurt?" "Oh yes, Willcox," he said in feeble voice, "killed by one of our own men."[20] The attending surgeon shook his head as he moved on with the litter, and I knew the worst. The great leader died that night, to the inexpressible loss of the 9th Corps— as was evinced in the coming action at Antietam. Listen what General Pleasonton said of him in his report:

He was eminently successful in driving the enemy until he fell at the moment he was gallantly leading his command to a crowning victory. The

18. In 1891, OBW received a moving letter from Isaac Steely, a veteran of Company C, 45th Pennsylvania, which had fought under his command at South Mountain. Steely wrote: "And be jabers did you see the performance of the 17th Michigan on the right of the road. I was of course somewhat occupied on our own side of the road. Yet I could not help keeping one eye on the Brave 17 Michigan *God Bless Them;* I never saw the like; and not drilled troops either." Isaac Steely to OBW, July 13, 1891, OBW Collection. The 17th Michigan lost 132 officers and men that day, and Steely's own 45th Pennsylvania lost 134, these two regiments each losing more men than any other single regiment in the Ninth Corps.

19. Brig. Gen. Samuel D. Sturgis (32d, USMA 1846) then led the Second Division, Ninth Corps. Sturgis, a veteran of the Mexican War, where he was captured at Buena Vista, was in command of Fort Smith, Arkansas, when the war began. He refused to surrender that post to Confederate authorities and evacuated the garrison and much of the Federal property. He fought at Wilson's Creek, Missouri, assuming command of the Union troops after the death of Brig. Gen. Nathaniel Lyon. In July 1863 he led the cavalry of the Army of the Ohio. On June 10, 1864, a combined infantry and cavalry force under Sturgis was decisively defeated by Maj. Gen. Nathan Bedford Forrest's rebel cavalry at Brice's Cross Roads, Mississippi. After the war, Sturgis would command the 7th Cavalry for a time. His son, James G. Sturgis, was killed with Custer at the Little Big Horn.

20. Reno also met Gen. Sturgis while he was being borne to the rear, greeting him with similar words: "Hallo, Sam, I'm dead!" Reno's voice was so natural, almost cheerful, that Sturgis thought he was only joking and quipped that he hoped it was not as bad as all that. "Yes, yes, I'm dead," Reno assured him, "good by!" It may well be that Reno died believing he had been shot by his own men.

dear judgment and determined courage of Reno rendered the triumphant results obtained by the operations of his corps second to none of the brilliant deeds accomplished on that field. At his loss a master mind had passed away.

Later on in that glorious but saddened day, a still more singular incident occurred on my front. The officers and men of one of the regiments were eating their suppers in the dark in a little field or court yard enclosed by a stone fence, not far from the pike, while I was visiting the boys to see if rations had come up from the rear, where [the] cooking was being done out of the enemy's sight. Tattoo had sounded about 8½ o'clock that night and [it was] so dark that from my horse's back I could scarcely discern the men squatting in groups on the ground, when all at once there came a roar and blaze of musketry from [the] top of the fence. The men seized their guns and were about to scatter when I shouted, "Steady boys, fire at the blaze." Fortunately I had not lost my head, and the bullets were whistling around me and above the men who . . . began pegging away, and the attack was miraculously repulsed with little loss. Although the bullets came like a hail storm, the number of Confederate bodies found next morning shot in the head was a marvel to the whole command.[21] This incident, like one that happened on my front afterwards at Cold Harbor, goes to show that such attacks sometimes fail from troops coming up suddenly and firing hastily because they shoot too high. But as I remained on horseback, I owe my miraculous escape to a merciful Providence. I think that this little affair was what McClellan alluded to in his report as "a night attack on our left," as I heard of no other.

By the following morning, the whole enemy on our front had vanished in the direction of Antietam, as was revealed by a general advance of our victorious army. Incidentally, it seems that McClellan had directed Burnside to put his corps upon the old Sharpsburg road "early in the morning," and that "about mid day the 9th Corps had not stirred from its bivouac. I sent for Burnside for an explanation," says McClellan, "but he could not be found. He subsequently gave as an excuse the fatigued and hungry condition of his men."[22] This was the beginning of an estrangement between

21. Isaac Steely wrote OBW of the carnage he witnessed after the fighting: "Perhaps you remember how the Dead Rebels were draged End Wise to each side of the Deep cut road, and then nearly touched Elbows; and that behind the stone fence in front of our (45th Pa) last Position the Dead Rebels lay five deep, all shot in the head." Isaac Steely to OBW, July 13, 1891, OBW Collection.

22. McClellan, *McClellan's Own Story*, p. 586.

Maj. Gen. Jesse Reno.
USAMHI.

the two friends, who had up to that time been on such good terms, perhaps too familiar for subordination, an estrangement that never healed. [At South Mountain] we had met with a dreadful loss, over 1,800 in killed and wounded, including 355 of [my own men], but the enemy must have lost more heavily in killed, wounded and a large number of prisoners.

One little incident had touched my heart more than all the corpses that strewed the ground where Withington had charged. Sitting on the stone fence, a little higher up, was found the body of a little boy in gray, a musician, perfectly dead and rigid, his arm extended and finger pointing towards our lines.

Before entering upon my own experiences and observations at the battle of Antietam, let me take a wider scope on some peculiar phases of the campaign. According to *McClellan's Own Story*, on the morning of September 1, General Halleck verbally placed [McClellan] in command of the defences of Washington. [McClellan states:] "On the 3d, the enemy had disappeared from the front of Washington, and the information which I received induced me to believe that he intended to cross the upper Potomac into Maryland." [McClellan] therefore, on the 3d, ordered three corps out beyond the line of works, and reported the same to Halleck, for which it seems he was rebuked by Halleck, who told him that his command "included only the defences of Washington" and did not extend beyond the line of works; "that no decision had yet been made as to the commander of the active army." Nor was any one named subsequently.[23]

From this it plainly appears that McClellan entered upon the coming campaign without authority, or as he expresses it,

> with a halter around my neck; for if the Army of the Potomac had been defeated and I had survived I would, no doubt, have been tried for assuming authority without orders, and, in the state of feeling which so unjustly condemned the innocent and most meritorious Gen. F. J. Porter, I would probably have been condemned to death. I was fully aware of the risk I ran, but the path of duty was clear and I tried to follow it. It was absolutely necessary that Lee's army should be met.[24]

Acting on this brave and generous impulse he promptly began the advance, covered by Pleasonton's cavalry, which soon came in contact with the enemy's cavalry, our right wing under Burnside moving on Frederick, supporting Pleasonton all the way up to Turner's Gap—as we already have seen.

But our good friend Halleck, meantime, [complained to McClellan] that "you are wrong in thus uncovering the Capitol." But why General Halleck neither took personal command nor ordered some other commander to the front is one of the conundrums of the day, unless he meant to give McClellan rope enough to hang himself; a solution too horrible to believe, for it really does appear that Halleck was honestly most anxious to ensure the safety of Washington, which he thought was endangered by McClellan's "precipitate movements." For he, Halleck, telegraphed McClellan as late as the 13th, "I am of the opinion that the enemy will send a small column towards Pennsylvania to draw your forces in that direction, then suddenly move on Washington." Even on the 14th, the day of South Mountain, he telegraphed [that] "scouts report a large force on the Virginia side of the Potomac. If so I fear you are exposing your left and rear."[25] I scarcely need remind my military readers that McClellan moved up between the Potomac and the B & O Railroad, keeping his columns in touch with both sides [of the river], thus forcing Lee to either face and fight him or recross the Potomac by upper fords. But there always appeared some hallucinations about the safety of Washington—as when at an earlier stage of the war, McDowell's corps was held back from the Army of the Potomac contrary to McClellan's wishes and expectations, with evil results.

23. Ibid., p. 549.
24. Ibid., p. 551.
25. Ibid., pp. 555–56.

So much for some of the larger incidents of the campaign, as revealed by telegraphic correspondence published since the war, but of which we subalterns were, and most people are now, more or less ignorant. If they show a feather in the cap of my much maligned friend McClellan, so much the better.

Leaving the bloody battle field at Fox's Gap with a loss of 355 killed and wounded, my division was posted in reserve at the Burnside bridge in front of Sharpsburg, on the morning of September 17 [during the] battle of Antietam, while Crook and Scammon[26] and finally Sturgis, were assaulting the bridge, which the latter finally carried by the gallantry of the 51st Pennsylvania, Colonel [John F.] Hartranft, and 51st New York, Colonel Potter.[27] Meantime, Rodman's[28] division crossed Antietam Creek at a ford not far below, and after several hours of artillery dueling these divisions were formed in line, General Cox commanding, and advanced towards Sharpsburg by scarped roads, passing to the higher land above through ravines and woods filled with the [enemy's] infantry and sharpshooters, the turns of the roadway covered by rifle pits and breastworks, including one strong stone fence, and crossing two ridges, before reaching Sharpsburg.

. . . General Cox's report . . . [of] September 23 . . . goes on to say:

At about 3 o'clock, the necessary changes in the line having been completed, the order to advance was received from General Burnside and the whole force, except Sturgis's division, was put in motion. General Willcox on the right, his whole division in line supported by Colonel Crook, was ordered to move on Sharpsburg, which lay about a mile distant to the right of our front. General Rodman, supported by Colonel Scammon, [Cox's Kanawha division] was ordered to move in the same direction, first dislodging the enemy from his front, and then changing direction to the right, bringing his command *en echelon* on the left of General Willcox. The advance was partly covered and followed up by [Capt. Seth J.]

26. Col. George Crook (38th, USMA 1852), then commanding the Second Brigade, 4th (Kanawha) Division, Ninth Corps; Col. Eliakim P. Scammon, formerly commanding the First Brigade of the Kanawha Division, moved up to command the division following the Battle of South Mountain.

27. Col. John F. Hartranft would eventually rise to division command in the Ninth Corps. After the war he would be a special provost marshal during the trial of those accused in the Lincoln assassination and would serve two terms as governor of Pennsylvania, 1873–1879.

Col. Robert B. Potter would also rise to division command in the Ninth Corps. He would be severely wounded during the final assault on Petersburg, April 2, 1865.

28. Brig. Gen. Isaac P. Rodman commanded the Third Division, Ninth Corps.

Simmonds', [Capt. Charles P.] Muhlenberg's, [Capt. Joseph C.] Clark's, and Cook's batteries. . . .[29]

The troops moved forward in perfect order and with great enthusiasm. On the right, General Willcox and Colonel Crook quickly repulsed the enemy and drove back their artillery, pushing victoriously forward nearly to the village. On the left, General Rodman and Colonel Scammon likewise advanced rapidly, driving the rebels before them. The enemy, however, were manifestly in much greater force than ours, and massed their troops heavily on the extreme left. . . . Batteries were accumulated against us upon the semicircular ridge in advance, and the advancing line was subject to a most trying and destructive cross fire of artillery. The enemy now brought up still more fresh troops upon the left, and while General Rodman was making disposition to meet them by a change of front of a part of his command, he fell, desperately wounded by a ball through his breast. The loss of their commander at a critical period caused confusion in a portion of the division on the extreme left.

The Second brigade of his division, Colonel [Edward] Harland commanding, was forced to retire after an obstinate contest, in which they suffered terribly. . . .

The whole line was now engaged, the supports being brought to the front, except the reserve division of General Sturgis at the bridge. This now was ordered up, and came promptly, though much exhausted and weakened by its previous exertions during the day.

The mass of the enemy on the left still continued to increase; new batteries were constantly being opened upon us, and it was manifest the corps would, without re-enforcements, be unable to reach the village of Sharpsburg, since the movement could not be made to the right whilst the enemy exhibited such force in front of the extreme left, and the attack both to the right and left at once would necessarily separate the wings to such an extent as to imperil the whole movement unwarrantably.[30]

This account agrees in the main with my own report and recollections, but it needs to be filled up with some details of our proceedings on the right, belonging to my own memoirs.

29. Simmonds led the Kentucky Battery, Muhlenberg led Battery A, 5th U.S. Artillery, and Clark (9th, USMA 1848) Battery E, 4th U.S. Artillery.

30. "Report of Brig. Gen. Jacob D. Cox," *OR*, vol. 19, pt. 1, pp. 423–27. For OBW's report on Antietam, see ibid., pp. 429–31. OBW originally paraphrased much of the excerpt from Cox's report; it is quoted accurately here.

On the falling of Rodman and consequent confusion and partial disintegration of his command, I rode over to his division, and, with the aid of Scammon, rallied the broken ranks, and pointing to what appeared to be a clear road from my front to Sharpsburg, I succeeded in restoring confidence among the officers sufficiently for another joint movement forward. With two batteries on the roadway, my two brigades on either side, and a similar formation under Scammon, the command was ready to start, when I received an order from Burnside forbidding the move. I sent back an aide-de-camp to explain the situation—a clear front and signs of confusion at Sharpsburg, and to insist upon our going ahead. When the aide returned, he brought another order to halt, with a message that McClellan concurred—for the reason that he expected an attack on our left from A. P. Hill, coming over from Harper's Ferry. I do not remember seeing General Cox during the day, but suppose that he was fully occupied on the left. But this was the time when we felt the loss of Reno. As for my friend Burnside, I do not know how he was handicapped, but I did not see him among us after our crossing the Antietam.

The following letters from General Sackett to McClellan, of February 20 and March 9, 1876, partially explains the situation. In the letter of February 20, Sackett says:

Gen. Burnside ordered assaults to be made on the bridge, which were for a time unsuccessful. I had been at his headquarters for fully three hours, when Col. Key[31] arrived from your headquarters with positive orders to push across the bridge and to move rapidly up the heights; to carry the bridge at the point of the bayonet, if necessary, and not stop for loss of life, as sacrifices must be made in favor of success.

And again, after the capture of the bridge, he says: "Gen. Burnside at once issued instructions for the move in the direction of Sharpsburg, but for some unaccountable reason things moved slowly and there was a long delay in getting the troops in motion." And Sackett then adds, "Often since that time I have thought what a serious mistake was the death of the noble and energetic Reno."

31. Delos B. Sacket served as McClellan's inspector general during the campaign. For the letters quoted here (paraphrased by OBW in the original manuscript but quoted correctly here), see McClellan, *McClellan's Own Story*, pp. 609–11.

Col. Thomas M. Key, of McClellan's staff, was basically McClellan's eyes and ears on Burnside's front, reporting back to McClellan concerning the operations on the army's left.

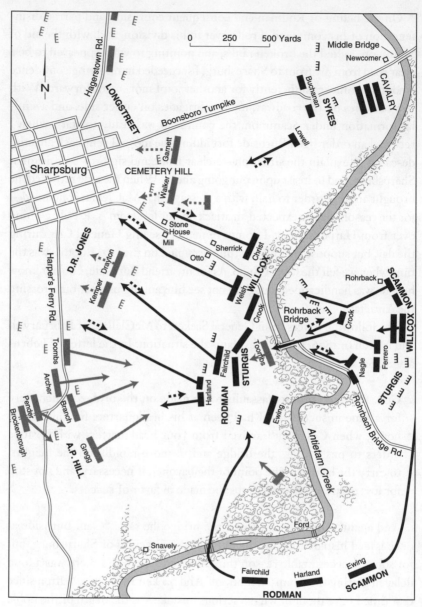

Attack of the Ninth Corps at Antietam, September 17, 1862.

In the letter of March 9/76, General Sackett writes in relation to an interview between McClellan and Burnside:

... [L]ate in the evening of the day of the battle of Antietam I was with you in your tent when Gen. Burnside entered. The position occupied, and the condition of his command, became at once the topic of conversation with you two.

As I understood the matter, Gen. Burnside desired to withdraw his troops to the left bank of the stream, giving as a reason for the move the dispirited condition of his men; stating further that if he remained in his present position and an attack was made by the enemy, he very much feared the result.

You replied: "General, your troops must remain where they are and must hold their ground." Gen. Burnside then said: "If I am to hold this position at all hazards I must be largely reinforced"—and if not much mistaken, he mentioned the number of men necessary for the purpose at 5,000.

These letters probably explain, among other things, the halt which was ordered of Scammon's and my commands at the time when success seemed most assured. As for the fear of an attack on our left, the story had been started as the partial reason for the halt of the line under General Cox, and still remained as a bee in the bonnet to prevent our crowning success, for the two-fold reason that neither any reinforcement nor appearance of General Hill ensued.[32]

As it was, we bivouacked on the field for the night and slept on undisturbed. I fastened on one end of the halter strap to my horse's bridle ring, the other to my foot, and the noble animal never once awoke me—much less did the enemy.

On the following December and without my knowledge at the time, my name was sent to the Senate by President Lincoln for promotion as full major general. But as luck would have it, I had a canny and unscrupulous enemy in the ranks of the Senate, by whose tactics the confirmation was postponed, and never came to vote.[33] I may add on the authority of

32. OBW was greatly mistaken in believing that A. P. Hill did not reach the field. Hill, whose troops made a forced march from Harper's Ferry, began to arrive at about 3 P.M. and proceeded to give Rodman's men a very hard time indeed. Hill's troops are undoubtedly those referred to by Jacob Cox in his report as the increasing "mass of the enemy on the left." In fact, by the end of the day Hill's men had taken a position directly in front of Willcox.

33. Referring to Sen. Jacob M. Howard.

[Col. John C.] Kelton,[34] that my name, with that of General Hancock, went up from headquarters at the head of the list. This incident explains a remark reported to have been made by General McClellan, viz., "that if some other generals had acted as Hancock and Willcox did, the battle of Antietam would have been a greater success." But I have no proof that the remark ever came from McClellan, and I certainly consider that any such remark would have been an unjust aspersion upon the more distinguished generals, Sumner, Mansfield, Sedgwick,[35] Richardson and others, who, on our right, successfully upheld our flag in the "bloodiest one day's fight of the whole war," during which we lost in killed, wounded and missing, over 15,000, and the losses of the enemy were about the same.[36]

The question of the day that never has been satisfactorily settled was "why did not McClellan at once follow up Lee, who abandoned the field on the night of the 18th?" The first reason that presents itself to my mind was the loss of so many general officers. Rodman, Mansfield, Hooker, Richardson, Sedgwick, Crawford, Dana, Hartsuff and others killed or wounded in the battle of the 17th.[37] And not to go into other [particulars], we have it on record that he had but one day's supplies in his wagons with which to move at once, that the enemy remained in force on the Virginia side of the Potomac with a large body in ambush back among the woods, as [was] revealed by Porter's reconnaissance. And the President himself, on a visit shortly afterwards, became satisfied that McClellan's reasons for not moving either at once or for some days, were sound. But the length [of delay thereafter] was not so satisfactory to the President. In Hapgood's life of Lincoln,[38] you will find the record of those urgent letters and dispatches pushing McClellan ahead in Virginia down to Warrenton, which prove the President's superior force of character and common sense knowledge of strategy.

34. Kelton (26th, USMA 1851) was assistant adjutant general, U.S. Army.

35. Maj. Gen. John Sedgwick commanded the Second Division, Second Corps. He received three wounds in his division's attack on the West Woods, north of the Dunker Church.

36. Losses for the one day of fighting at Antietam were actually about 12,401 for the Federal army (25 percent), and some 10,318 for the Confederates (31 percent). Stephen W. Sears, *Landscape Turned Red: The Battle of Antietam* (New York: Ticknor & Fields, 1983), pp. 294, 296.

37. Of these general officers, Hooker was wounded in the foot; Joseph K. F. Mansfield (commanding the Twelfth Corps), Israel Richardson (First Division, Second Corps), and Isaac Rodman were mortally wounded; John Sedgwick, Brig. Gen. George L. Hartsuff (Third Brigade, Second Division, First Corps), Brig. Gen. Napoleon J. T. Dana (Third Brigade, Second Division, Second Corps), and Brig. Gen. Samuel W. Crawford (First Brigade, First Division, Twelfth Corps) were wounded.

38. Norman Hapgood, *The Inner Life of Lincoln* (New York: Chautauqua Institution, 1900). However, the reader might find it more convenient to consult Stephen W. Sears, *George B. McClellan: The Young Napoleon* (New York: Ticknor & Fields, 1988), pp. 318–43, for a sound analysis of Lincoln's post-Antietam prodding of McClellan.

Brookville, Md.
Sept. 10/'62
My dear Marie,
Being delayed this morning in getting off, I drop you a line. We shall start in an hour or two, but I don't know yet where will be the next camping ground. Write me care of Gen'l Burnside as often as you can, send the letters to Col. Rucker[39] who will forward to Burnside. Neither the 17th nor the 20th has yet joined, but I understand Withington is at Leesboro, one day's march behind.[40] I hope you will not stay in Washington if you feel uneasy, but leave at once. It does not seem likely I can see you until after the present campaign immediately in hand. . . . I shall write you frequently. I hope that unfortunate trunk will come along, & that Romeyn with Arndt & the horse will not be long. I wrote you from Leesboro about a cook but don't bother yourself. Adieu. I will direct to care of Mr. McNair. Yours in haste,

O.B.W.

Near Frederick [Maryland]
Sept. 13/'62
My dear Marie,
We have taken Frederick with slight fighting. My division entered New Market first but Gen'l Reno thought Cox & Rodman were (as they ought to have been) ahead of me and so ordered them first to Frederick. Otherwise I should have been the first in Frederick. Rodman is now driving them over the range of hills making a reconnaissance in force towards Hagerstown. All well in haste,

O.B.W.

Blue Ridge
Sept. 15, 1862
My dear Wife,
We have had a glorious victory. Though I have had many narrow escapes personally my command mourns 377 killed & wounded. The 17th Mich. &

39. Col. D. H. Rucker, assistant quartermaster of the U.S. Army.
40. The 17th Michigan did in fact join Willcox's division later that day; the 20th Michigan would not join until September 24.

45th Pa. covered themselves with glory & wreaths of victory. No officers of 17th killed but I fear we shall lose one or two.

God be praised for his mercy.

O. B. Willcox

Telegraph this home.

Mouth of Antietam
25th Sept/62
My dearest Marie,

I write you by every mail that goes. After writing yesterday I received a very nice long letter, enclosing William's letter, paper extracts. It is certainly provoking that all details (& more than all) were reported in the papers of the operations of every corps but our own. I claim that my division has been the most successful in its work of any in the corps. It was attacked at South Mountain & beat the rebels off from their own ground, so that when Sturgis came up the thing was decided & he had nothing to do but relieve my regiments (exhausted of ammunition) & stand their attempts to stampede us at night. At Sharpsburg I commanded on the right of the attack made by Burnside's corps & my division won another complete victory, carried the heights on the right & [nearly] entered the town.

I wish Bailey Myers or some New Yorker had been with us, for it seems as if the trumpet of fame were held alone by New York. My officers & men feel that we have not had justice at the hands of the newspapers.

In regard to Eb I am glad you sent the $100. If possible I will send you the necessary paper by this mail to get pay for the Manassas horse. At any rate those taxes must be paid before the 1st of [Oct.]

We march at noon three miles nearer to Harper's Ferry. As we draw near there I shall hope more to see you. As in prison so now you & your letters are the greatest blessing of my life. I earnestly desire to see you before you go home & talk over events that you & the children & all the family would like to remember. Father's letter & mother's are excellent. Tell Father I am really careful & never expose myself unnecessarily. When poor Rodman was shot his division at once became partially demoralized & probably nothing but my presence prevented it from falling back disastrously. Scammon, who commanded Cox's old division, stood manfully by me. My right was *all secure* but Rodman & Scammon were pressed, & the extreme left, Sturgis, was in danger. I told Rodman's brigade commanders that we could hold the ground & would, & agreed with them & Scammon to assist the left by a charge bayonet (our ammunition being exhausted) along the whole line, when we were *ordered* to fall back near the bridge. I had my Washington horse killed in the same battle; he was being led with my escort. I called him "Reno." Another horse, "Burnside," was disabled, & Roebuck came up just in time. Burnside [the horse] is nearly well. Arndt keeps them in splendid order. Adieu. God bless you & the children. Tell William I wish he would have a thick uniform coat (long) & thick vest, such as I told him of, & sent on to you. Also send me 3 flannel drawers & 3 thick flannel shirts.

Thine,
O. B. Willcox

In Camp near Antietam
Sunday, Sept. 28, 1862
My dearest Wife,

It is a soft mild lovely Sabbath afternoon. We have had an interesting day. I assembled the chaplains, four in number, of two brigades (Fenton's[41] & Welsh's) & told them I wanted to have both brigades meet for divine service, & that instead of the ordinary sermon I wanted each chaplain to make a short address, commemorative of God's goodness in giving us the late victories & saving our own lives in battle.

Accordingly seven regiments formed around my head quarters at eleven o'clock & we had a most impressive service. First, I told the troops I had thought proper to call them together that we might thank God for his protection, that I wanted them to stand up in prayer & singing & that they might sit in ranks during the reading & speaking. [The hymn] "Old hundred" was then performed by the band of the 45th Pa. Chaplain Piatt, 79th New York, then prayed. Then a hymn was sung, Mr. P. giving off two lines at a time. Then a chapter was read. Then Chaplain Caufield spoke. He is of the 100th Pa. Then a hymn. Then the German chaplain of the 46th N.Y. prayed in the German language. Then Chaplain (Rev. Dr.) Brown of the 36th Mass. spoke (very eloquently). Then the German chaplain spoke in English. Then Chaplain Caufield prayed. Then the hymn "Liberty" was sung & benediction pronounced. The regiments then filed off in perfect order, one at a time. You never saw anything more grand. Dr. Brown said it reminded him of the Armies of Heaven assembled around the Throne Above. My heart was moved to tears several times. The men all looked so sturdy & clean considering all things, & behaved with so much propriety. The scene grew more & more impressive & interesting till, towards the close, those in rear stood up to hear the speaking & remained standing.

41. Col. William M. Fenton, formerly commanding the 8th Michigan Infantry.

I wished that you & our families & the Bishop could have been present. The chaplains were all delighted. No such public recognition of God had ever been given in this division of the army before, & they feel strengthened for the future. I hope to acknowledge God in all my ways. This afternoon Gen. McClellan had service at his Hd. Quarters & sent invitations around. I could not go, but Brackett[42] & Romeyn of my staff went, as well as Col. Fenton, Col. Withington & some others of the division.

Last evening Dennis the cook got up [a meal] with the nicely chosen things [you sent]. How considerate you are for me! I am sure your thoughts must be occupied entirely with your cares for me. Dennis starts off well. I must have one thing more, viz., a camp cook stove, which I would thank Capt. Dana[43] to select, if I have not already exhausted his good offices, & send me by 1st opportunity. I hope he received the papers in regard to my Manassas horse. There will be less difficulty about the one killed at Sharpsburg. Roebuck is frisky but not vicious. I shall use him in camp & on the march & keep him back in rear in battle.

I hope it will be so we can meet in a short time. If I knew when you could be at Harper's Ferry or Sandy Hook I could go over after you.

Robert[44] is waiting for me to send a line to William in his letter, so God bless & keep you.

Your devoted,

Orlando

In Camp near Antietam Iron Works
Oct 2, 1862
My dearest Marie,
Your notes containing Eben's letter, the list of mess chest etc. came today. Lieut. Ford arrived this eve & says the chest is with his regimental baggage in the car & expects to have them tomorrow, so I dare say all will arrive safe. The newspaper extracts are amusing. I will send you copies of my reports soon. It must be trying to be away from the children, but they are just as well, & while you continue to receive good accounts from home do not worry yourself. You do not know what amount of consolation I derive from your neighborhood, & from hearing so often, besides the absolute good

42. Lt. Levi C. Brackett, 1st Lt., 28th Massachusetts, aide-de-camp to OBW from September 1862 until the end of the war. OBW later called Brackett his "favorite aide."

43. Capt. James J. Dana, assistant quartermaster, formerly of the 4th U.S. Artillery.

44. Capt. Robert A. Hutchins, assistant adjutant general to OBW from September 1862 until the close of the war. Hutchins, a favorite, was severely wounded at the Battle of the Wilderness; he earned two brevets for gallantry during the course of the war.

you do by sending what I need so promptly & well. . . . I sent Capt. Dana the papers relating to the Manassas horse & as soon as I hear from him I will make out those for the Sharpsburg loss. Roebuck is under [the] weather to-day with a bad cold. The change is very great for him.

In regard to your enquiring about the rank of Cox, his date as brigadier is from May 1861, so that he fell in command of the Corps by seniority. But Burnside says he, Cox, will soon leave for Western Virginia, & Burnside gave me to understand I would succeed to the command. But *nous verrons.*

The President is here somewhere to-day & visited the Sharpsburg battlefield with Burnside. I hope he will learn if he did not know (as nobody seemed to) that our Corps did *some* fighting on the left. McClellan stated in his report that no arms were picked up at South Mountain, & I to-day sent him a written report of one of my officers showing that I had gathered there *1106* stand [of rifles and muskets] & sent to the provost marshall at Frederick. We also took some hundreds of prisoners that were turned over without count. In regard to young Pell, I cannot get him a commission, but if his friends will do that I can find a place on my staff.

Did I write you of the review on Tuesday, 30th Sept.? I reviewed my whole division & it made a very good appearance. Gen. Cox was present, but Burnside was called away just at the time. The Division is improving in tone & every thing very fast. There is good feeling & perfect order & subordination & all that. It was completely run down after its long series of what in fact amounted to disasters, but the late fights & all our efforts have brought it up wonderfully. I hope God will direct me & give me the necessary wisdom. You don't say how you like the *carte [de visite].* I wish you would send me a dozen. Also your own in a locket & the children's when you can. I have now three brigades, forming the largest division in the Corps. Good night! May the Angels guard their sister.

Thine,
O.B.W.

I enclose some original lines by Gen. Sturgis.

[Though there is no signature, these lines, dated 1862 and found among General Willcox's letters, may be those composed by General Sturgis, as mentioned above, though the handwriting is unmistakably that of General Willcox:]

Argument—a la Milton

A great nation is struggling for existence—its fluttering hosts are drawn up in battle array to meet the foe—the battle rages as n'er battle raged before—The mighty columns now advance and now recede, like mighty giants as it were to breathe—& thus while victory seems to perch now here—now there—the cry is heard above the roar of war—"Seize the Bridge! or all is lost!"—"Seize it soon and all is sav'd!"

Acrostic

[Antietam Bridge]

"Advance my boys (such was the cry)"
"Nor lag behind one valiant man!"
" 'Twere cheaply won though we all die"
"In gaining thus the ancient span."

Each heart with noble throb did swell
To know the goal of glory near,
And far away through glade & dell
Might then be heard the echoing cheer.

By those brave men sent up on high,
(Righteous men! who fought for Right)
Inspired with patriot zeal they fly!
Down o'er the Bridge!—Then up the height!
Great God! What slaughter! Yet 'tis braved.
Encore! hurrah! the Day is sav'd!

Tuesday night, 3d Oct/62
My dearest Marie,
I cannot go to bed without dropping a line to tell you of our review. The President with Generals McClellan & Burnside reviewed all four of our divisions. Gen. Burnside said that mine looked the finest, was drawn up in best order, cleanest, & showed most care & labor. The President remarked to Gen. Burnside in the hearing of McClellan, "Is not Gen. Willcox a very faithful officer?" Burn said "Yes sir, that's just what he is." In these corrupt times that's a recognition. I had my division drawn up in column of regiments & the others had theirs in brigade lines. I had also the satisfaction of settling a misunderstanding, that threatened something serious between three of our generals, two of highest rank, that gave me infinite pleasure. But I must reserve the details till we meet.

So I think I can go to bed "satisfied & happy," as Caro says. Good night.
Orlando

[Letter from Marie Willcox to her mother, while visiting O.B.W.]
Camp Israel Oct. 8th [1862]
My dear Mother,

Here I am in camp at last. After writing you from Washington on Friday I received a letter from O. B. again expressing the wish to see me, but not fixing a time. In the evening I spoke of the feeling which impelled me to go, and yet [I had] the fear that they might move, or some contretemps occur if I ventured. A gentleman who was calling said that his friend, Major Dodge, paymaster, was going the next morning at five, and that he would go and ask him if he would not be my escort, the reply to which was that he would call for me with his carriage at five in the a.m.

I was ready, and came on to Harper's Ferry without trouble. There we found the town in terrible confusion, a mass of army transportation wagons, and the debris of the fire of battle. We were landed on the track, nobody knew where to turn. Major Dodge hailed a gentleman, Captain Ruggles, who proposed that we should go to the Provost Marshall's, so they took my basket and satchel and there we went. After a time we found a lieutenant from Burnside's corps, who seemed willing to do what he could, but doubted the possibility of reaching Gen. Willcox's head-quarters that afternoon. I said I could ride on horseback if no other way was found. After a few minutes he came with the good news that a party of gentlemen were going over the road that led past the General's camp, and he had secured me a place in their carriage.

I arrived there about dusk, we drove up to his tent. He was standing in front, looking on. I quite took him by surprise, although he said from the time he saw the carriage coming toward his tent, he thought that it must be me. The camp was near the battle field of Antietam (about two miles) rather pretty country; the tents of thousands of men scattered over the fields, with the camp fires blazing and the flickering figures around them is a scene worth the looking at. I took tea in the tent, and spent the evening pleasantly. Col. Withington, Robt. Hutchins and Col. [Henry] Bowman came in. Col. Bowman was a [prisoner] of War in Richmond, is now in command of the 36th Mass., a very fine regiment which has a glee club which came during the evening and gave me a charming serenade. They sing wonderfully well.

The next day Orlando rode over the battle field of Antietam with me, and showed me the exact position of his command and the enemy's of the fight on his division. It is a great shame that he was not permitted to drive the enemy as he wanted to. They were fairly beaten, and running! panic-stricken, his men having gained all the important positions and the crest of the hill when, because Sturgis was pressed hard on the left, he was ordered to retire, which order he received three times before he obeyed it. It would have turned a doubtful fight into a glorious victory, and probably would have bagged a large number of the rebels. Such a chance only occurs once in a life time. If you would only see the ground you would understand the whole thing perfectly.

As to the bridge, they never retired to that at all. That night he slept on a hill ever so far this side of it. If my coming had furnished nothing more, I should consider the pleasure of seeing this field worth ten times the trouble. I rode a horse of Capt. Hutchins, with a side saddle borrowed in the neighborhood. Sunday evening several officers came in to see me. Charly Mc-Knight[45] was there during the day. Tell Sarah he is looking very well and thinks this war has been the making of him. He expects soon to be promoted to a captaincy.

Monday Orlando was busy and the day hot, so I did not ride on horse back, but at evening parade walked round and saw the various brigades. His command numbers about five thousand men. Gen. Sturgis called during the day. He is rather fine looking, seems honest and plain spoken. He said that the camp was to move next morning at daylight. Accordingly, the order came from Gen. Burnside, and at day break the whole corps was in motion. I went [on] a quiet road with Lt. Brackett of the staff (aide de camp) a nice fellow. The ride was about ten miles, through one of the most picturesque and beautiful countries in the world. Robert's horse went very nicely, so I did not need to change for the ambulance, which accompanied us in case I might tire of the saddle.

We rode up to the house of a Dr. Boteler, who has a fine place in the "pleasant valley" just behind the Maryland heights which command Harper's Ferry, about which so much has been said lately. This valley runs along for miles through Maryland; it is wide and rolling, and on each side is shut in by very high ranges of mountains. The scenery is the most picturesque possible. This valley had been selected as the camping ground. Troops were right in the fields around his [Boteler's] house. He and his family (wife and five daughters)[46] are all Secesh, but received me very politely, came out and assisted me to dismount, and escorted me in in true *chivalry* style. The ladies showed me a room where I took a bath and went to sleep, having gotten up at four o'clock and breakfasted by moon light (in a

45. Lt. Charles A. McKnight, 7th Michigan, aide-de-camp to OBW.
46. Dr. Boteler actually had seven lovely daughters, which of course delighted the young men of OBW's staff.

grove outside the tent, quite romantic). I dressed in time for dinner with the family, after which I sat with them and looked out upon the assembling and camping of the army.

General Burnside rode up with a large staff and escort, and was loudly cheered by the crowd of soldiers who gathered to see him pass. He came in to see me. He looked just as rough and careless as when I saw him in Washington. He said that seeing me made him feel as if he would like to have Mrs. Burnside come out. About five [P.M.] Orlando rode up for me to go over to his head quarters, he having got his tent pitched &c. So we bid adieu to our Secesh hosts, and rode over on horseback.

The position of the camp is so picturesque, that I wish you would look in upon the valley so rightly named "pleasant valley." On the high rolling ground through the center is the head quarters with a little grove running down the knoll on the left, from which, on all the hill sides, may be seen the tents and campfires, as far as the eye can reach. On each side of the valley high mountains rise abruptly, looking like great walls reaching to the Heavens. On one side the height is historic in its association as the ground on which the battle of South Mountain was fought and won. The other is the Maryland heights commanding Harpers Ferry, which alas was not fought, and the capture of which the rebels claim as the great object of their invasion of Maryland. It is again in our possession, and is used as a signal station; during the day a flag waves, and at night there are lights of various colors displayed. Last evening, as the signal light appeared on one height, the moon rose over the other, contrasting its soft light over all the red blaze of war.

Today I have been very quiet, as the weather is too hot to move. It is like August, rather than October. The tent is a large hospital tent in which is a rough camp-table, a camp bed stead, which serves for a lounge. A tick filled with straw and spread with blankets occupies one corner and is the resting place at night. The trunks, two crotch sticks to hang coats on in the corner, and a couple of boxes . . . complete the furniture.

I have generally taken breakfast and tea in the tent, and dinner with the mess. The servants seem all very useful in their places. Arndt keeps the horses looking splendidly. Roebuck is petted and rubbed and talked to more than ever in his life before. There is another horse, Burnside, that seems more reliable, and which Orlando uses more. He has also another common horse, a coincidence of names, in the horse "Reno," killed in the same battle that the General for whom he was named lost his life. The cook Dennis, as black as the ace of spades, does very well, and there is a man, Fred, that seems to be a sort of waiter and *valet de chambre* who is invaluable.

Robt. Hutchins fills his place, which is a very important one, with satisfaction to himself and the General. Romeyn was at first very green, and it does not seem to rub off. He is a useless appendage, but I hope not disposed to do much mischief. I shall remain a day or two. Direct to Capt. Dana as usual. The dear children are quite well I hope; love to Father

Marie

Pleasant Valley
Oct. 18/'62
My dearest Molly,

After you left I mused for a long time on the vanity of honors & glory compared with the few days of perfect happiness I enjoyed while you were with me in camp. I could not for a long time restrain the tears. And then what a blank succeeded! I could not remain at the tent, but ordered up Roebuck & dashed away till nightfall. About 9 o'clock I went over to [General] Burnside & staid till midnight. To-day he & I dined with Dr. Boteler, who gave us a good dinner, bragging as usual over every dish in the style of true chivalry. I hope to hear from you very soon.

Received a letter from Eb to-day. Says the Chancellor did not give him money for the taxes, & is greatly distressed. He says Father told him he was not in a situation to help him. He must be helped. You may send him $100 out of the pay accts.

Burn says that from what McClellan told him he had no doubt I would have permanent command of the Corps.[47]

Not heard yet from Dana—but this is perhaps a good sign. Expect Sturgis & [Brig. Gen. George W.] Getty[48] tomorrow. Rob is tenting with me.

Good night Darling,
Yours Ever,
O. B. Willcox

Pleasant Valley
Oct. 23/'62
My dearest Wife,

I was very much annoyed yesterday to find that a letter I wrote the day after your departure had laid in my *escritoire* ever since. But you never need feel alarmed at not hearing from me, it is only a sign that I am very busy & well. I think of you more constantly even, than ever, since your delightful visit. All is now hurry & busy preparation.

47. OBW had assumed command of the Ninth Corps on October 8.
48. Getty assumed command of the Third Division, Ninth Corps, on September 25, 1862.

Stoneman[49] has not yet actually joined although assigned to the Corps.

He is below the Monocacy. But Sturgis & Getty have both returned. I send you Col. Bowman's *carte*. He wishes mine in return, for Mrs. Bowman. Will write you her address so you can send one. He is one of my favorite colonels, you know.

Dennis & Fred have a tent in rear of mine for a mess tent, & they are delighted. I have given up the big tent for the office & taken a small one. It has been terribly windy & cold ever since you left. Have received no letters. Want some money, but don't send it by mail. See that Eb gets his $200. Write Father & both Mothers for me. R. N. Rice[50] spent the night with me lately. Send worlds of kisses to the children. . . .

> Thine Ever,
> O.B.W.

Pleasant Valley
Oct. 25 [1862]
My dearest Molly,

Night before last I received your two first letters. Coale[51] has not come yet. Brackett says you promised to send a photograph of me for him.

Got Burnside to *telegraph* yesterday for Dana, & hope to fetch him.

> All well in haste,
> Orlando

Pleasant Valley
Oct. 27/'62
My dearest Molly,

Part of my corps went across to Lovettsville [Va.] yesterday & I am just about to transfer my Hd. Qrs. over.[52] Will write as often as I can. Meantime direct as usual through Burnside & write me often. No mails, but a terrible storm for two days of rain & wind. But it has cleared off. Last night my tent blew nearly down. Had to call the guard to keep it from going over. A thousand kisses,

> Your Husband,
> O.B.W.

49. Brig. Gen. George Stoneman served briefly with the Ninth Corps before being promoted to major general and assigned to command of the Third Corps.

50. Onetime superintendent of the Michigan Central Railroad.

51. Capt. John H. Coale, recently appointed commissary officer to the First Division.

52. After much prodding by President Lincoln, McClellan at last began to move his army across the Potomac, between October 26 and November 2. The Ninth Corps crossed at Berlin, Maryland. Lovettsville, Virginia, was the next village beyond the Berlin crossing.

Oct. 30/'62

My dear Marie,

I write you at 3½ A.M. from Bolington. Am just going out ahead of Sturgis & Getty to get a position for them at Wheatland.

I have enclosed to Dana the August pay accts. properly made out in place of the others, & those for September. Sorry to hear of poor little Maud's illness. Express my sympathy to Caro.

Better make no change in arrangements at present. We must either have a big fight, or go into winter arrangements ere long.

In haste darling,
O.B.W.

Monday Nov. 3d, 1862

My dearest Wife,

A long march yesterday for the men—especially the new troops. My command is south of the Snickersville & Aldie turnpike. Thursday was warm & bright. To-day we rest in camp & other troops are moving. I saw both Ricketts & [Brig. Gen. George G.] Meade[53] yesterday; both inquired after you. It is cold with wind, no signs of rain.

Gen'l & Mrs. Wright at Wheatland (8 miles from Berlin) were both very polite to me, altho secesh, they are peace-making people for the neighborhood. They said they would be glad to see you &c. Yours in haste,

Orlando

Near Upperville
Nov. 4 [1862]

My dearest Wife,

Here we are moving down this side the Blue Ridge in splendid style, shutting them [the Confederates] off from the gaps. McClellan & Burnside are in the advance with Pleasonton to-day.

53. Meade (19th, USMA 1835), then led the Third Division, First Corps. Meade was a veteran of both the Seminole and Mexican wars, having been brevetted in the latter for bravery at Monterrey. OBW had known Meade while the latter was on engineering duty in Detroit. He had performed similar work in the early stages of the Civil War, aiding in the construction of the Washington defenses. He led a brigade during the Peninsula Campaign, where he was wounded at the Battle of White Oak Swamp. He participated in the Second Bull Run campaign and at South Mountain and Antietam, where he assumed command of the First Corps after the wounding of Maj. Gen. Joseph Hooker. He assumed command of the Army of the Potomac three days prior to the Battle of Gettysburg.

For two days my corps pressed up after Pleasonton. To-day we rest. All well & good spirits. Hunter & [Col. Orlando M.] Poe[54] just called & wish to be remembered.

Wish my love to Father, Mothers, Eb & children a thousand kisses for you & the latter.

In haste,
Orlando

Near Rector Town
Nov. 5, 1862
My dearest Wife,

One more day's march further from you & yet nearer as we have struck the Manassas railway which will soon be in operation to furnish us supplies as we move on. I have my own Hd. Qrs. in the most sequestered little nook in the world, a stream running around it—a branch called Goose Creek. Yesterday morning Gen'l [William W.] Burns[55] took command of my old division. He graduated in the same class with Burnside & myself. I have appropriated his quarter master, Capt. Chambloss, who takes hold well & has already ingratiated himself with Genl. Ingalls.[56] This disposes of the command of the division & Col. [Daniel] Leasure[57] takes a brigade. I wanted Gibbon very much but am very glad to have Burns. Now if I only could have got Dana I should have been satisfied all around. Poe would like to come in with the 2nd Mich. but Stoneman may object.

Young Hutchins of the 6th Cavalry has just come in from Pleasonton's front in high spirits. Pleasonton is thrashing Stuart finely, especially to-day, when he took several officers & 70 men prisoners. Young

54. Col. Poe, formerly colonel of the 2d Michigan, was soon to be given command of First Brigade, First Division, Ninth Corps.

55. A captain in the commissary department at the beginning of the war, Burns was later appointed brigadier general of volunteers and led a Second Corps brigade with distinction during the Peninsula Campaign, where he was wounded. Commanding the First Division, Ninth Corps, under OBW at Fredericksburg, Burns was detached from the corps and attached to Maj. Gen. W. B. Franklin's Left Grand Division. OBW later praised Burns for his "promptness, coolness, and good judgment" during the battle. The horrors of Fredericksburg left Burns with no taste for field command; he resigned his commission in the volunteer service, reverting to his regular rank of major in the commissary department. He died in Beaufort, South Carolina, April 19, 1892.

56. Capt. Chambloss had recently replaced Capt. Harry Porter as assistant quartermaster for the First Division; Lt. Col. Rufus Ingalls.

57. Leasure commanded the Third Brigade, First Division, Ninth Corps.

[Lt. Alexander C. M.] Pennington[58] has a battery with Pleasonton & has distinguished himself highly. Good night.

Thine, Orlando

Orleans Nov. 7/'62
My dearest Wife,

We arrived here yesterday after a long & fatiguing march from Piedmont & Rector Town via Salem, got in at night. It was a bitter cold night for the men & this morning it is snowing fast. We shall move on perhaps in the course of the day. The bridge at Waterloo being burnt it may delay us a few hours.

My Hd. Qrs. wagons not coming up in time, I took quarters for the night at the house of a Dr. Chapman, where I am now with Staff waiting orders from Burnside to march. Burnside is in the village. My host is an old gentleman, with his nice old wife & a widowed daughter. That box which Coale was to make up has not yet come. It was expressed to Harper's Ferry. If Dana has an opportunity, I wish he would have it brought back to you, as you may get it to me by another route. Love to all & kisses for yourself & children.

Thine,
O.B.W.

Gaskin's Mills
near Waterloo
Nov. 9 [1862]
Dear Molly,

I ordered prayer to be made this morning for the continued triumph of our arms & the success of Burnside, his officers & men.[59] We are bearing the hard weather well enough. The only thing I need particularly is thick red flannel under shirts, which if you have a private chance send.

With love unspeakable,
Orlando

Near Waterloo Nov. 10 [1862]

This letter was delayed by a move. Meantime I have written & telegraphed, so I suppose you know I am well. Have you heard of the change in the command of the army? The postman goes down to-day & will give this

58. Pennington (18th, USMA 1860) led Battery M, 2d U.S. Artillery, attached to Pleasonton's cavalry division.

59. Burnside assumed command of the Army of the Potomac upon McClellan's dismissal, November 7, 1862.

Maj. Gen. Ambrose E. Burnside with some of his generals, November 10, 1862. *Seated, from left:* Brig. Gen. Henry J. Hunt, Brig. Gen. Winfield S. Hancock, Maj. Gen. Darius N. Couch, OBW, and Brig. Gen. John Buford. *Standing, from left:* Brig. Gen. Marsena M. Patrick, Brig. Gen. Edward Ferrero, Brig. Gen. John G. Parke, unidentified aide, Burnside, Brig. Gen. John Cochrane, and Brig. Gen. Samuel G. Sturgis. *OBW Collection.*

to Dana in person & bring back anything from you. Send all home letters & those from Caro, & two red flannel undershirts & one drawers. Also Rob's package—a buffalo robe he expects from William through Capt. Dana.

> Thine Ever,
> O. B.

Outside defenses of Army at Warrenton
Near Waterloo, Nov. 14/'62
My dearest Molly,

[Daniel R.] Larned, private secretary to Burnside, promised me some days ago he would telegraph you whenever he did Mrs. B. I thought you would like to hear often & quicker than the outrageously tardy mail. I have [had] charge for some days (ever since the 9th) of the whole of our most exposed flank, & been kept in a constant state of worry, besides, for want of supplies, scarcely sleeping or eating with any satisfaction.

I suppose that in the general arrangement I shall fall back to my own corps only, but I have been responsible lately for 28,000 men, including [Brig. Gen. Amiel W.] Whipple's & Stoneman's divisions—about twice the number of Scott's army in Mexico, with Longstreet & Jackson watching for a chance at us & constantly reported to be near me. So far nothing has happened, & I trust that God will continue to protect & guide me & our arms. But for this consolation I could have no rest or comfort whatever. My main business has been to sustain Pleasonton—who . . . calls for brigades & divisions as he requires them. I should like to attack Culpeper at once & think we could cut off there a large depot of their supplies. In fact, I offered Burnside to do it, if he would supply me with provision & forage.

I wrote a long letter to Father the other day & Eliza Davis. You must write *often* to Eb & Mother for me.

If you receive Larned's telegram I wish you would reply & let me know that all are well. My regards to James & Mrs. Dana. Capt. Chambloss is bringing up the Q.M. Department. Under Porter it was so completely ruined that even Ingalls demanded a change. It was an outrage upon Dana not to let him join after so much was done by me, & Burnside too, to get him. Of course now Chambloss will expect promotion if I am promoted. Send my love to Caro & Frank, William & the Browns. . . .

Thine Ever,
O.B.W.

Kisses for the children & a big one for *thee*.

Near Warrenton Junction
Sunday p.m. 16 Nov./'62
My dear Molly,
After much trouble I have got my corps together & we are thus far "South." Had an artillery affair yesterday at Sulphur or Warrenton's Springs.
Monday a.m.
Too tired to write last night. Am well. Passed through Fayetteville & part of the corps thro Bealton yesterday. The artillery affair at the Springs was quite a little attack made by the enemy on Sturgis' train as he was leaving for Fayetteville. It lasted about one hour & a half. The enemy drove in pickets & got a perfect range of fire on the wagons & for a time there was a brisk fire. They were nearer to us & had a better position for their artillery than when they attacked Sigel[60] last summer in the same vicinity. [Maj. Sidney] Willard's[61] 35th Massachusetts repelled a charge of their cavalry. Gen'l Getty got up a little before me, but I reached the spot before his troops ar-

---

60. Referring to the action of August 23, 1862, between Union Maj. Gen. Franz Sigel (commanding First Corps, Army of Virginia) and Brig. Gen. Jubal Early's Confederate brigade.
61. Willard was killed at the Battle of Fredericksburg.

rived. [Lt. Samuel N.] Benjamin's battery[62] was got into position & opened upon them with effect quite charming to behold.

Sturgis' guns were of smaller calibre than the rebels, who had two 20-pounders like Benjamin's, but all were handsomely handled. They had a brigade of infantry, a regiment of cavalry (probably of Stuart's), two 20-pounder & one or two lighter pieces. The infantry, except Willards', were not engaged, though [Col. Rush C.] Hawkins' brigade[63] was deployed to cover a ford (Porter's Ford) higher up. They did us little or no damage altho the attack was on Sturgis' rear & train. But we lost a valuable young officer of Durell's Pa. battery, Lieut. McIlvaine, & a few wounded, before they were finally repulsed.

Couch's corps[64] left this point yesterday morning, & I shall leave to-day or to-morrow. To-day we are getting off our sick & taking in stores at Warrenton Junction.

With regard to promotion, before Burnside took command he told me that he & McClellan had recommended me to the President, but made me promise not to say anything to you. I should think there ought to be little trouble about it now & secrecy no longer necessary. If Father can get it for me I wish he would, as it would put an end to talk of a young brigadier commanding a corps. But Burnside is so fearful of being accused of partiality that I fear he will scarcely do me justice, & he seems to feel the same way towards his old corps. Did you receive the autographs & Henry's sketches? Write a telegraph to Father as you see fit. Give love to all. The order directing corps commanders to send in lists of their staff for appt. did not include me for some reason best known to Burnside himself. Poe has joined with the 2d Mich. & has [temporary] command of my old division.

Thine ever & with true heart,
O.B.W.

62. Benjamin (12th, USMA May 6, 1861) led Battery E, 2d U.S. Artillery.
63. Hawkins commanded the First Brigade, Third Division, Ninth Corps.
64. Gen. Couch then had command of the Second Corps.

§ SIXTEEN

The Battle of Fredericksburg:
"My Only Object Is to Do Right"

ON NOVEMBER 7, 1862 the Army of the Potomac lay encamped at and around Warrenton, Virginia, whither it had dragged itself by dilatory movements of nearly three weeks duration from Antietam, notwithstanding the lash of President Lincoln's vigorous pen. Burnside was still in command of a Grand Division, leaving me commanding the 9th Corps, with which I had followed Pleasonton's Cavalry Corps so far in advance, supposedly towards Richmond. General Pleasonton having discovered that A. P. Hill was isolated at Culpeper Court House . . . proposed that we should attack him with our two commands. There certainly was a fair chance for success, but the enterprise was disapproved at headquarters, and there the 9th Corps lay sucking [its] fingers, as it were, in camp, awaiting further orders.

But on the morning of November 7, very early, I was awakened in my tent by a message from Burnside to come over and see him immediately. I found the general sitting with the Bible on his knee in a state of prayerful anxiety. Without the least sign of exultation, he handed me a letter to read and asked my opinion. The letter had come from the President, accompanying an order for McClellan to turn over the command of the army to my classmate. And the President wrote that Burnside should not refuse the command, for reasons which General James Wadsworth, the bearer of the letter, would verbally give.[1] The principal reason given was that if Burnside

    1. This meeting between Burnside and Willcox most likely took place on the morning of November 8, Burnside having received the previous evening his copy of the orders relieving

382

declined, the President would have to appoint General Hooker, whom he distrusted. From all I could learn, the President apprehended a *coup d'etat* in case of Hooker's military success.

"Well, Burn, do you not want the command?"

"No, under the present circumstances I don't feel equal to it. I cannot expect the hearty co-operation of the McClellan element, but the worst of it is that I cannot decline, according to Wadsworth."

Of course there was nothing more to be said. I very much pitied my friend for the honors thus thrust upon him, and I withdrew, leaving him to pray for Higher Help. General Halleck was to be down next day with Quartermaster General Meigs to proffer their support, and this was a gleam of light.

On Halleck's arrival, the first question discussed was the line of march to be pursued. Halleck advocated the line so far pursued by McClellan, by way of Culpeper and Gordonsville. But Burnside proposed to take the Fredericksburg and Rappahannock River route, in preference, and the reasons he gave were so strong that the President coincided with him by telegraph, only advising him "to lose no time." The principal feature of the plan was the prompt dispatch of pontoon trains from Washington, sufficient to span the Rappahannock at two points; and this General Halleck promised should be attended to, and that at least one train should leave as soon as he arrived at Washington. But on November 22, Burnside complained in a letter to General Cullum,[2] chief of staff at Washington, that no train had arrived up to the 19th, when

the whole of General Sumner's[3] column—33,000 strong—would have crossed into Fredericksburg at once over a pontoon bridge, in front of a city filled with families of rebel officers and sympathizers with the rebel cause, and garrisoned by a small squadron of cavalry and a battery of artillery which General Sumner silenced within an hour after his arrival.

Had the pontoon bridge arrived even on the 19th or 20th, the army could have crossed with trifling opposition. But now the opposite side of the river is occupied by a large force under General Longstreet, with

McClellan and turning command of the army over to him. OBW errs in stating that Wadsworth was the bearer of the orders; it was Gen. Catharinus P. Buckingham who delivered them. Wadsworth, however, did visit Burnside shortly after the latter's ascension to the top command.

2. Brig. Gen. George W. Cullum (3d, USMA 1843) was then chief of staff to General Halleck.

3. Maj. Gen. Edwin V. "Bull" Sumner then commanded the Right Grand Division, consisting of the Second and Ninth Corps and Pleasonton's division of cavalry.

batteries ready to be placed in position to operate against the working parties building the bridge and the troops in crossing.

The pontoon train has not yet arrived, and the river is too high for the troops to cross at any of the fords.[4]

This letter furnished the first key to our ultimate defeat at Fredericksburg, where we found the whole of Lee's army in the city and on the heights. Meantime, viz., November 15, the 9th Corps started on the new line and marched to Fayetteville, one mile beyond Sulphur Springs, where we had quite a brush with the enemy. General Sturgis was attacked just as his train moved out, by a regiment of cavalry with two 20-pounder rifles and one lighter gun; but General Getty's coming up with his division, throwing out Hawkins's brigade, and with Benjamin's battery opening on the enemy, we forced the single column slowly out of sight, and we went into camp, picketing the roads and river crossings in all directions. But the campaign did not fairly open until after the promised pontoons had arrived in front of the city, and in December we got ten ready to be laid, in the face of the enemy.

The scene was most picturesque from our headquarters at the Lacy house immediately opposite Fredericksburg, premising that the weather was extremely cold and views were blurred with [the] vapor of men's breaths. Major [Ira] Spaulding, with the engineer brigade, constructing the pontoon bridges, worked under fire of the enemy's sharpshooters; the work was so slow that volunteers from the 9th Corps were called for, and the 8th Connecticut and 89th New York successively responded. These worked with a will on the central pontoon, suffering heavy losses every moment in killed or wounded, until finally Burnside ordered Colonel [Harrison S.] Fairchild, of the 89th New York, to send one hundred men with four officers to cross in boats and dislodge the enemy. A battalion of the 89th then pushed across in four boats and performed their duty in the most daring and successful style, and Colonel Fairchild crossed with the rest of the regiment in like manner and the first bridge was laid.

The 46th New York Regiment of General William W. Burns's division also crossed on the same evening, and these, with [Brig. Gen. Oliver O.] Howard's[5] division of the 2nd Corps, occupied the lower part of the town. Meantime other commands in like manner came over.

I trust this will give you an idea of the manner of our entrance into the city of some 8,000 people, occupied, and more or less entrenched by Lee's

4. Burnside to General G. W. Cullum, Chief of Staff, Nov. 22, 1862, *OR*, vol. 21, p. 103.
5. Howard then commanded the Second Division, Second Corps.

army—already a historic town of some note. It was here that Captain John Smith had fought the savages in 1608; here that Washington's boyhood days were mostly spent, and from this place Washington started to join General Braddock's disastrous expedition. Near this place was opened the first iron mine that ever was worked in America, from which mine the cannon and balls were cast that were fired against the British in the War of 1776. And from those very heights a rebel flag was now unfurled. We found the city itself thinly occupied by sharpshooters and light batteries, but fairly barricaded and enfiladed by walls, ditches and marshes. But scarcely an inhabitant was found remaining, Sumner having given due notice of his intention to shell the place on his arrival, in certain contingencies.

From the monthly return of the Department of Northern Virginia, we know now that Lee's army arrayed in front of us consisted of Longstreet's and Jackson's Corps, 152,842 men and 186 pieces of artillery.[6] From right to left, our army was posted in three Grand Divisions, the 2nd and 9th Corps under Sumner on the right, Hooker with the 3rd and 5th Corps in the center, and Franklin on the left with the 1st and 6th. My old friend, Colonel Couch, commanded the 2nd Corps next on my right, and my left extended in front of the town over Hazel Run to Deep Run. I was ordered by Burnside himself to support Sumner on the one hand, and to engage the enemy on my immediate front sufficiently to prevent them from detaching troops to the right or left, where the main attacks of the day were to be made. I think Hooker's orders were similar. From this it will appear that Burnside expected Sumner and Franklin to do the decisive part.

Couch's attack to gain the heights began about noon of the [13th] under his two division commanders, [Brig. Gen. Winfield S.] Hancock and [Brig. Gen. William H.] French.[7] Supported by my right division under Sturgis, the first crest beyond the city was gained, and when Couch's left began to break, Sturgis advanced [Brig. Gen. Edward] Ferrero's brigade,[8] which, with the assistance of [Lt. George] Dickenson's battery[9] posted near the "brick kiln," drove back the enemy to their cover of stone walls and rifle pits, which, by the way, were quite plentiful. But our attack was quickly renewed.

6. This figure is ridiculously high; it sounds more like an estimate of McClellan's than Willcox's. The December 10 return for Lee's army gives his "present for duty" as 78,513. Deducting the usual noncombatants, sick, and two brigades of cavalry not then present with the army, Lee's effective strength was roughly 58,500. *Battles and Leaders of the Civil War*, vol. 3, p. 147.

7. Hancock had the First Division, Second Corps, while French (22d, USMA 1837) commanded the Third Division.

8. Ferrero commanded the Second Brigade of Sturgis's Second Division, Ninth Corps. Howard's Second Division also made a disastrous assault, suffering severely.

9. Dickenson commanded Battery E, 4th U.S. Artillery. He was killed at Fredericksburg.

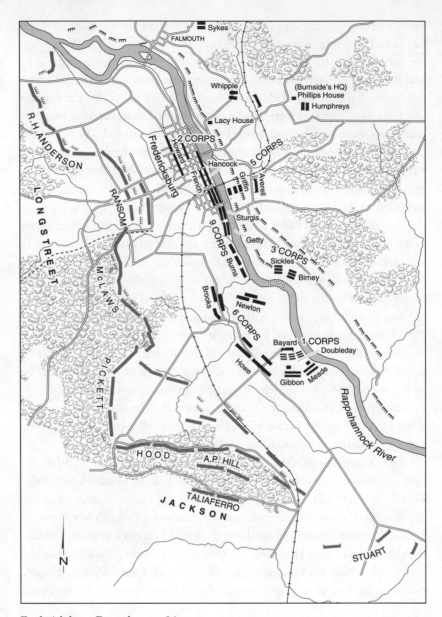

Fredericksburg, December 13, 1862.

[Brig. Gen. James] Nagle's brigade of [Sturgis' division] dashed forward, supported by my gallant old classmate, Charles Griffin, of [Brig. Gen. Daniel] Butterfield's Corps, the celebrated 5th, commanded afterwards by Warren.[10] These brigades were assisted by [Capt. Stephen H.] Weed's and [Capt. Charles A.] Phillips' batteries[11]—Dickenson's having suffered so severely in the previous conflict in which the brave and skillful Dickenson himself had been killed.

And now, although our joint attack under General Couch almost recovered the crest of the hill, we were forced to retreat before superior forces. Then Getty's division started on his own front, hoping to find a weak point in the enemy's line.[12] His route lay over broken fields, crossed by a railway cutting and an old canal ditch which could only be crossed by the street bridges. He formed his division under a concentrated fire that rapidly increased as he advanced, but he pushed on through it all and had nearly gained the crest beyond, where he met with so destructive a fire that he was forced back. And there it was that [Lt.] Col. [Joseph B.] Curtis fell, "waving his sword and cheering on his men" of the 4th Rhode Island.

And I had but one other division and that had been detached to support Franklin, so that both Couch and myself found ourselves rather *hors de combat*, with nothing left for us to do but to keep up a threatening attitude. I have since wondered whether, instead of the desultory manner in which the troops had made their attacks, a combined advance of both corps under Sumner, in person, would have not been better, especially if Hooker, with his two corps, had moved upon our left at the same time, i.e., as soon as Franklin became engaged.

But it seems that Burnside's main reliance was on Franklin, and there has been much dispute over Franklin's conduct on that day, and in fact, over the fealty of that gallant officer, whose ability never has been doubted. And who, though he was a strong McClellan adherent, certainly could not afford to sacrifice his own reputation and imperil the country's cause, out of love for any man. We must judge him fairly by his own report, as Sumner and the other Grand Division commanders have been judged.

10. Griffin then commanded the First Division of Butterfield's Fifth Corps. The corps was later commanded by Maj. Gen. Gouverneur K. Warren (2d, USMA 1850), during the war's final year.

11. Weed (27th, USMA 1854) was chief of artillery, Fifth Corps; Phillips led Battery E, 5th Massachusetts, First Division, Fifth Corps. The battery took a pounding on December 13, losing fourteen horses killed or disabled. Amazingly, however, just one man was killed and one wounded.

12. Getty's division occupied the center of the Ninth Corps's position, with Burns (detached) on his left and Sturgis on his right. Each division was initially formed in two lines of battle.

But giving due credence to Burnside's instructions and reports, it seems that the enemy had built a road from Hamilton's, in rear of the crest on Franklin's extreme left, which enabled them to communicate from any part of their line to another. This was the point on the heights that Franklin was ordered to seize in order to place our forces in a position to move down the old Richmond road in rear of the crest and force its evacuation by the enemy, with at least the loss of their artillery. For this purpose Franklin was ordered to send at once a column, with a division, at least, in the lead, and well supported. His command consisted of the First Army Corps, Gen. John F. Reynolds; Sixth Corps, Gen. "Baldy" Smith; Third Corps, Gen. Stoneman; and Burns's division of the 9th.[13]

Franklin says in his report (Series 1 Vol. XXI, page 449):

About 7.45 o'clock on the morning of the 13th (Saturday), Brigadier-General [James] Hardie arrived from general headquarters, and informed me verbally of the designs of the commanding general in reference to the attack. . . . These orders arrived soon after 8 o'clock. In the meantime I had informed General Reynolds that his corps was to make the attack indicated by General Hardie, and he ordered Meade's division to the point of attack, to be supported by Gibbon's division. As Smith's corps was in position when the order for attack was received, and as a change in the line would have been attended with great risk at that time, and would have caused much delay, I considered it impracticable to add his force to that about to make the attack. I thought also that Gen'l Reynolds' force of three divisions would be sufficient to carry out the spirit of the order. . . .

At 8.30 o'clock General Meade's division moved forward about 500 yards, and, turning to the right, pushed toward the wood near the Bowling Green road. It was met by a severe fire of artillery. . . . In the mean time the two divisions of General Stoneman's corps which had been detailed as supports, and were then at the bridges, I ordered over to the support of General Reynolds. . . . Meade passed into the wood, carried it, crossed the railroad, and gained the crest of the hill, capturing two flags and about 200 prisoners. . . . At the same time Gibbon's division advanced, crossed the railroad, entered the wood, and took some prisoners, driving

13. Officially, Stoneman's Third Corps belonged to Hooker's Center Grand Division, while Burns's First Division, Ninth Corps, was part of Sumner's Right Grand Division. These units had been detached to assist Franklin and were now under his command.

back the first line of the enemy; but the wood was so dense that the connection between Meade's and his line could not be kept up. In consequence of this fact, Meade's line, which was vigorously attacked by a large column of fresh troops, could not hold its ground, and was repulsed, leaving the wood at a walk, but not in order. . . . Gibbon's division was also repulsed shortly afterward. Just as Meade was repulsed, two regiments of Berry's brigade, Birney's division,[14] Stoneman's corps, which had just arrived, were thrown into the wood on Gibbon's left. They also were soon driven out. While Meade's division was getting rallied, the remainder of Birney's division came up and drove the enemy from the front of the wood, where he had appeared in strong force. This division, with the aid of the artillery, soon drove the enemy back to shelter, and he did not again appear. . . . Gibbon's division then fell back in good order to its position of the morning, and was relieved by General Sickles' division,[15] of Stoneman's corps, which took the position Gibbon had previously held.

As the enemy made a serious demonstration on Reynolds's left, as soon as his disposition of Meade's division was discovered he ordered General Doubleday's division to that part of the field.[16] This division soon drove off the enemy's artillery, forcing him to leave the river bank on this side of the Massaponax. Our troops advanced on the left, and occupied the position held by the enemy in the morning. . . .

When Birney's and Sickles' divisions were placed in position it had become too late to organize another attack before dark, and all of the troops under my command had either been engaged or were in line, except Newton's division,[17] Smith's corps, which was held in reserve. . . .

Burns' division, of Willcox's corps, was guarding the bridges, and on many accounts it would have been imprudent to have taken it away. . . .

This ended Franklin's efforts to turn the Confederate line. Meantime, let us hear from Burnside. Referring to the heights on the crest, his report reads: "He (Franklin) was ordered to *seize these heights, if possible, and to do it at once.* [OBW's italics.] I sent the order by General James A. Hardie, a member of my staff. It reached Franklin at 7:30 A.M. At 9 A.M. Hardie reported, 'General Meade just moved out'; and again at 11 o'clock 'Meade

14. Brig. Gen. Hiram G. Berry commanded the Third Brigade of Brig. Gen. David B. Birney's First Division, Third Corps.
15. Brig. Gen. Daniel E. Sickles commanded the Second Division, Third Corps.
16. Brig. Gen. Abner Doubleday (24th, USMA 1842) led the First Division, First Corps.
17. Brig. Gen. John Newton commanded the Third Division, Sixth Corps.

advanced half a mile and holds on'; and later, in the same despatch Hardie says, 'Reynolds has been forced to develop his whole line.'"[18]

At 10:30 Burnside had sent Capt. [Philip M.] Lydig to Franklin to ascertain the condition of affairs. Lydig's written statement is as follows:

I found General Franklin in a grove of trees in the center of his command, and, on delivering my message, I was informed by him that Meade was very hotly engaged; that Gibbon had just gone into the fight, and that his men were by that time pretty generally engaged. . . . I then inquired if any of General Smith's corps were engaged, and was told they *were not* [OBW's italics]. I returned to headquarters . . . and reported the information I had received to General Burnside, who seemed at the time annoyed at the smallness of the force engaged, and expressed his surprise that none of Smith's troops had been put into the fight.[19]

Then, says Burnside:

I next sent Capt. [James M.] Cutts with an order to General Franklin to advance his right front. Capt. Cutts states in his note book that he carried the order to General Franklin and the General said to him that "it was impossible to advance." I then sent Capt. [R. H. I.] Goddard with this message, "tell General Franklin, with my compliments, that I wish him to make a vigorous attack with his whole force, our right (i.e. under Sumner) is hard pressed." This order was delivered to General Franklin in the presence of General Hardie before 2:30 P.M.

[Goddard] says:

Either General Franklin or General Hardie told me that all the forces were engaged except Burns' division, which was guarding the bridge. Sickles' division was just going into action. The left had been very seriously threatened, but that now the attack was changed to the front. It was impossible to remove troops from the left to the center at that time. As soon as an opportunity presents itself, a vigorous attack should be made along the lines, as General Burnside wished. I stated also, just before leaving, that General Burnside was very explicit in giving this order

18. See "Report of Maj. Gen. Ambrose Burnside, Commanding Army of the Potomac," Operations from November 7, 1862–January 25, 1863, *OR*, vol. 21, pp. 82–97.

19. See Lydig's statement, *OR*, vol. 21, pp. 127–28.

to make a vigorous attack. [Which taken in connection with the previous message to use his whole force, leaves no doubt as to what Burnside meant.] [20]

As Franklin's main attack took place at his extreme left, Burns's division was not called into action, but on the following morning that division recrossed Hazel Run and the 9th Corps was selected to make [a] second main attack, for which it was accordingly formed with our six batteries in position under my friend Capt. Weed. But the order was countermanded and little or nothing more was done during the day except the repulse by Getty and Burns of a Rebel movement meant to gain an enfilading fire on our troops and batteries. The main credit was due to Getty, who had anticipated the movement.

On the same night a council of war was convened at headquarters, in which the question of further proceeding was discussed. Burnside felt that he had not been supported by certain of the leading generals, and he now proposed to place himself at the head of his own corps and make a night attack. This was put to a vote, and my opinion being required first of the corps commanders, I being the junior, I said, in substance, that a night attack by a whole army against another army doubly entrenched, such as Lee's, was a thing almost unheard of and most likely to result in a terrible disaster; but that if it were ordered, I claimed to lead the 9th Corps myself, leaving Burnside to direct the general movement from his proper position, [that of] commander in chief. I do not think that there was a single vote for the proposition—in fact the discussion went all one way and the question was dropped.

That night the main body recrossed the Rappahannock, my corps [numbering] 16,000 men with five batteries, except the pickets. We crossed without confusion in less than two hours under silent passive exposure to the enemy's sharpshooters and artillery, for which feat the main credit is due to Major Crosby, my provost marshal.

Now, having set forth the essential points on both sides of this famous controversy, I leave you to form your own conclusions without giving any opinion of my own. Let the facts speak for themselves. [21]

20. Statement of Capt. R. H. I. Goddard, *OR*, vol. 21, p. 128. OBW in the original manuscript mistakenly identifies the quote as that of Captain Cutts.

21. Losses for the Ninth Corps during the battle were 1,330. This figure, however, includes the casualties for Burns's First Division, which was detached (Burns suffered only twenty-seven casualties). Total Union losses at Fredericksburg were 12,653. Confederates suffered about 5,309 casualties.

But to continue the narrative. On December 20th, Generals Franklin and Smith wrote a letter to the President (Rebellion Records, Series 1, Vol. XXI, page 868) advising an abandonment of the campaign, and recommending the James River route to Richmond, the route which was afterwards followed by Grant.

Burnside was undoubtedly "a failure" in the estimation of the gentlemen who wrote that letter, but he still had something to say. Concerning those gentlemen and other officers whose names are published in the famous General Orders No. 8, January 23d, 1863, paragraph IV reads: "It being evident that the following named officers can be of no further service to this army, they are hereby relieved from duty and will report in person without delay to the Adjutant General U. S. Army:—Major General W. B. Franklin, Commanding Left Grand Division; Major General W. F. Smith, Commanding Sixth Corps"; and others including Generals Sturgis, Ferrero, John Cochrane, and Lieut. Col. J. H. Taylor of Sumner's Grand Division.[22]

The same order recites that Major General Hooker "having been guilty of unjust and unnecessary criticism of the actions of his superior officers, and of the authorities, and having by the general tone of his conversation endeavored to create distrust in the minds of officers who have associated with him . . . is hereby dismissed the service of the United States as a man unfit to hold an important commission during a crisis like the present. . . . This order is issued subject to the approval of the President of the United States." Paragraphs two and three dismiss Generals [William T. H.] Brooks[23] and Smith and Newton for similar reasons to those given for the exodus of Hooker.

But this extraordinary order was not approved by the President, and was not issued, nor does it appear that charges were preferred against the mischief makers for trial by court martial. And the result was that Generals Franklin, Smith and Newton and some others were recommended for dismissal from the service, and what is still more astonishing, if true, according to Franklin, Burnside "recommended to the President the dismissal of the Secretary of War himself!"—sufficient proof to Franklin's mind that Burnside was "crazy."[24]

22. Brig. Gen. John Cochrane led the First Brigade, Third Division, Sixth Corps, at Fredericksburg; Lt. Col. J. H. Taylor was then acting chief of staff and assistant adjutant general to General Sumner. For General Orders No. 8 see *OR*, vol. 21, pp. 998–99.

23. Brig. Gen. William T. H. Brooks (46th, USMA 1841) commanded the First Division, Sixth Corps.

24. Burnside did in fact write Lincoln, requesting the dismissal of both Secretary of War Stanton and the general in chief, Halleck. See Burnside to Lincoln, Jan. 1, 1863, *OR*, vol. 21, pp. 941–42.

Be this as it may, Burnside himself was relieved from duty in the Army of the Potomac, together with Franklin and others. Hooker was placed in command of that army, and my old classmate yielded most gracefully. In General Orders No. 9, January 26, he announced the transfer in words that do credit to his mind and heart:

> By direction of the President of the United States, the Commanding General this day transfers the command of this army to Maj. Gen. Joseph Hooker.
>
> The short time that he has directed your movements has not been fruitful of victory, or any considerable advancement of our lines, but it has again demonstrated an amount of courage, patience, and endurance that under more favorable circumstances would have accomplished great results. Continue to exercise these virtues; be true to your country, and the principles you have sworn to maintain; give to the brave and skilful general who has so long been identified with your organization, and who is now to command you, your full and cordial support and co-operation, and you will deserve success. . . .[25]

No sign of insanity about that! but a spirit of self sacrifice and devotion to the cause of his country.

Burnside, with the 9th Corps, was ordered to Cincinnati in command of the Department of the Ohio, and Franklin to New Orleans to command the Department of the Gulf—as good an arrangement as could be expected or wished by all the high belligerents, to avoid further scandal, and to preserve the *morale* of the army itself; and for which no end of praise is due to that wonderful strategist, Abraham Lincoln.

LETTERS: NOVEMBER 19, 1862–MARCH 1, 1863

Opposite Fredericksburg
Nov. 19, '62
Dearest,
Here we are at the "jumping off place." But first to answer your last letter's [question]. The infortunate box by Coale never has seen daylight. We sent several times for it to Harper's Ferry, even from as far back as

---

25. Burnside's farewell address was published as "General Orders No. 9, January 26, 1863," *OR*, vol. 21, p. 1005.

Wheatland, but failed. Coale himself was so much mortified that he started back to Washington, where he has been sick ever since. The money you "have left" keep for your own use, & by the time I need more I can send another pay acct.

Gen. Burns, who commands my old division, is one of my classmates & a first rate soldier. Every thing works smoothly & well in the division. Poe relieved Fenton in the 1st brigade & Fenton started for Michigan day before yesterday to try & get more men.

The army take the new change [Burnside replacing McClellan] kindly enough. Although I think that the general opinion is that it hardly does justice to either general, relieving one while succeeding & putting the other in his shoes to take up his plans, substantially without having time to form new or different ones of his own. I like both men; both have great elements of success, though in different ways.

With regard to Dana's joining me & gaining rank, I tried every way to get him & after every effort failed, & the quarter master dept. was nearly smashed up & ruined in the sight of Ingalls. I took Chambloss on the recommendation of Burns, who brought him with him for himself, but gave him up for a higher position than he could confer. Now if Reynolds has applied for Dana & can secure him a lieutenant colonelcy, he had better go with him. And not only for the above reason but because Biggs is still quarter master of the 9th Corps on paper, & no recommendation of mine can effect anything. It may be so long before my own promotion that Dana had better not wait if he can secure it through another corps commander. I would rather have Dana than any other man in the world, both for his ability & for his kindness to you. To tell you the grand truth of all, I should not wonder if some major gen'l yet succeeded in ousting me. I will see tomorrow who Sumner has for quarter master, & if the post is vacant will put in an oar for my friend.

Rob [Hutchins] has just come in & says that it was reported at one of the camps in Couch's corps that Sedgwick was to have this corps. Sedgwick is an old division commander under Sumner & there may be something in it. For some reasons I should regret it. It would seem to the public like a reflection upon me. But for others, I would prefer some other command less liable to contention, particularly in the West. On the whole, I shall not bother myself, for Providence determines all things & He will provide the best for me & for thee & for our children, because we put our trust in Him.

Congress will soon meet & I hope my friends will get me nominated as major general & confirmed promptly. I sent you some autographs the other day when I happened to be at head quarters as your letter was handed me, among them Burnside's, Parke,[26] chief of staff, & other chief of depts., & Sturgis & Ferrero, two of my own corps generals.

I wrote you last from Warrenton Junction. The next day we marched to a little village on the Stage Road called Hartwood, & arrived here about noon to-day. I am quartered in a very grand old-fashioned mansion called the Lacy house.[27] It overlooks Fredericksburg, & has been successively the head quarters of McDowell, King,[28] & Burnside. This afternoon the rebel pickets across the river & our men have been bantering each other in the most amusing manner. My corps is just opposite the town, while Couch's is at Falmouth, a mile or two further up.

Capt. Parke, commissary for head quarters, will carry this & bring back any answer, or "other small packages" you may have to send. The flannel shirts & Henry's pencils arrived safely, for a wonder. Have you seen Maj. Crosby? The shirts are just the thing. I would like some maccaroni, some common pickles, a keg perhaps (more economical), a few small boxes sardines & a can or two of pickled oysters by way of grandeur. We shall probably be opposite this place some days. Fred suggests that you might have a few dozen eggs put up for me. Tell Mother she must not get *entirely* out of patience for your return. Regards to the Danas & McNairs.

Thine,
O.B.W.

Lacey's House. Opposite Fredericksburg
Nov. 21 [1862]
My dearest Molly,

After a rain of two days steadily & four nights, the sky is clearing up. I received this morning the vest & letters from you & that [letter] enclosed of Mother's. The dear little children, how it touches my heart to be so far away from them so long. But it delights me to hear the least of the details

26. Maj. Gen. John G. Parke (2d, USMA 1849) later commanded the Ninth Corps in Kentucky and during the siege of Vicksburg. He again served as Burnside's chief of staff during the Wilderness and Spotsylvania campaigns, in 1864. When Burnside was granted a leave of absence (which turned out to be permanent) on August 13, 1864, Parke resumed command of the Ninth Corps, leading it during the siege of Petersburg and until the end of the war (except for several absences, when the corps was commanded by OBW).

27. The Lacy House (also known as Chatham) on Stafford Heights, east of Fredericksburg, on the left bank of the Rappahannock River, later served as Maj. Gen. Edwin V. Sumner's headquarters during the Battle of Fredericksburg, and as a Union field hospital. Robert E. Lee had visited the home while courting his future bride. Today the house is the headquarters of the Fredericksburg and Spotsylvania National Military Park.

28. Brig. Gen. Rufus King (4th, USMA 1843).

concerning them. Mother is doing wisely & well with them, all that we could wish. How I sigh to settle down again ever so humbly & enjoy their society & yours. Nothing compensates for this absence from all I hold so dear. Nothing but a stern sense of honor & duty. Send me all the letters from home. Your letter of 16th frightened me about Caro & her little cherubs, but as nothing later had been said by Frank, I hope all is passed over.

In regard to what has arrived & what not, I received the flannel shirts & things for Henry, who was astonished & delighted. . . . The iron lozenges will be faithfully taken. I am much better now, & have an appetite. Rob received his overcoat, but thinks his robe has little chance. If the box turns up from Harper's Ferry, do not send it without it can be placed in some one's hand belonging to my corps. . . .

You know I have told you of the jealousy existing on account of my having so high a command. Sturgis yesterday sent in a claim for the command on the ground that the President could not date back my app^t prior to a session of Congress, & that therefore he is my senior. He was put up to it by some meddling gentlemen elsewhere, but I hardly think he will succeed. The whole thing gives me very little trouble, & must not worry your precious little brain either.

I wrote you quite at length by Maj. Crosby, also a letter by Capt. Parke. If we are detained here any great length we may be able to see each other, but if the weather sets in dry again we shall soon cross. Meantime keep calm & hopeful as ever & write me something every day. The mails have begun to come in.

You had better open the box & take out my blankets if there are any in it. Those sent already are sufficient. I send you back the grand Consular letter as a memorial from Europe. He has written me again & I wrote him to-day. Kindest regards to the McNairs & Dana's & kisses for all the children.

Thine,
O. B. W.

[Opposite Fredericksburg]
Nov. 21 [1862] Evening.
I have been principally busy writing letters this rainy day, occupying a quaint old-fashioned room with green high wainscoting, in one end of this huge old-fashioned building called the Lacy House. At night, by the fire in the grate, in the perfect stillness & with the old time furniture, I can scarcely help falling into fantastic reveries. It is such a room as would please an author. But I have changed the tenor of my thoughts so much into soldier life that sentiment & revery flit only like shadows over my mind, once so

contemplative & abstract. If *you* were only setting by my side with your fair cheek lit by the fire & your soft hand in mine, how delightful it would be. And still more so if we were at home with Lu & Elon & Ali at our knees, & Father & Mother quietly sharing our bliss, how inexpressibly better that!

But away with such delicious yet provoking thoughts. The enemy are just across the river with their guns in position & their troops hid back in the woods. A few days & what a change from the quiet of this place & this still evening. God grant that I may survive it all & that we may be still victorious.

Allen, the mail messanger for the corps, will leave this at Capt. Dana's office with word what time he will leave Washington. He will put up at the Richmond House. . . . We sent over a message to-day by flag of truce. The flag was an old towel which I found in my trunk & which I used at the Lewis House & afterward in prison & given me by Mrs. Ricketts. The *Herald* reporter asked for a piece of it. Gen'l Patrick,[29] provost marshall general, was the bearer.

The overseer left in charge of the house by Maj. Lacey (Confederate service) called upon me this evening, & offered anything he had. His family occupy the other end of the building. At all places where I make my head quarters the people are very civil & I find that they generally speak well of me. Gen'l Sumner occupies a house called the Philips house near by. Gen. Burnside first thought of staying here, but his head quarters now are too numerous a body for one house, except it were an Astor.

One sweet kiss * & then good night. Let the world go as it will, neither time nor death itself can work any change in our hearts. We are, & shall remain; we have met, & never can be apart; we have know[n] each other & shall never cease to love.

Thine,
O.B.W.

Opposite Fredericksburg
Nov. 25, '62
My dearest Love,
To-day I received your letter of the 17th only acknowledging my [letter] date of the 15th, since which time I have written three letters by private hands, viz. by Maj. Crosby (who returned to-day), by Allen the mail messenger (likewise returned to-day), & by Capt. Parke, by whom I hope to hear from you in two or three days. Allen leaves in the morning again & will

29. Brig. Gen. Marsena Patrick (48th, USMA 1845).

hand this in at Capt. Dana's office & leave word where he may be found & when he is to return. Capt. Coale has received word from the express that the wonderful box is there at Washington & awaits his orders; he will send for it immediately. I have moved my head quarters from the Lacy House back about a mile and am in camp again, in a pine grove where it is sheltered from the wind & frost, & the spicy smell is very fresh & fragrant. The little head quarters camp at one end & the office tent (the one *we* used when you were with me at Pleasant Valley) at the other. Capt. Shillinglaw,[30] my Scotch aide, has come on; he is a picture of an old knight in armor, & looks very grand & dashing.

How delightful an hour's chat would be *vis a vis;* but do not come on yet. The rebels are in great force across the river & are working like beavers putting up breastworks, & an attack cannot be delayed long. Had the pontoon bridges been sent as agreed from Washington we [would have] crossed the first day or two. Now it will cost a tremendous battle. I wish with you that [Maj. Gen. Nathaniel P.] Banks' enterprise could be sent to cooperate in the attack on Richmond—perhaps it may be.[31] Meantime the fine weather is going fast & the roads breaking up & the winter may be upon us with its icy claws. To-night it begins to sprinkle just as it did just before the late heavy rains which nearly ruined our roads. I wish we had sought the enemy at Culpeper & thrashed them there. But let the "grim visaged god" go.

I saw Larned[32] last night again & he said he continued to send your telegrams, promising letters &c. You ask whether McClellan came to take leave of the 9th Corps. No, I was away at Waterloo while the other corps were just around Warrenton, but he sent me his regards personally. The Administration could hardly have chose a more inopportune time to relieve him from command.

Gov. Blair has at last written—saying he had not had *time* before to answer my letters! Blamed as the army is, what can be thought of the conduct of the governors in sacrificing the old regiments for new appointments? Did I tell you that on my way through Fayetteville lately Col. [Henry A.] Morrow[33] & his officers called upon me? I was waiting an hour at Gen'l Doubleday's head quarters for a guide. They all expressed a strong wish to join my corps. Morrow was very demonstrative.

30. Capt. Robert T. Shillinglaw, 79th New York.

31. Banks had recently been appointed commander of the Department of the Gulf. He would later cooperate with Grant in the Vicksburg campaign.

32. Daniel R. Larned, private secretary to Burnside.

33. Morrow was colonel of the 24th Michigan of the Iron Brigade, which belonged to the First Corps.

By the way, [Brig. Gen. Thomas F.] Meagher[34] has succeeded in getting one of my Irish regiments transferred to his brigade, viz. the 28th Mass. I find Gen'l Sumner very amiable so far & hope we shall have no trouble. I do not altogether discontinue visiting Burnside, but his time is so engrossed & there is so much jealousy in certain quarters that I seldom go except on business, when I find him as ever, but perhaps *a little* restrained. He lunched with me the day we arrived here & continues to camp near the old 9th Corps. My own camp is now about half way between his & Sumner's.

The little camp candle sticks are very nice & convenient. I will try to make Fred take good care of them & keep them as relics for Lu. I wish Lu might write me as often as possible, & Elon too. I am glad to hear that they get on well at school, & hope they do not make their dear Grandma any more trouble than they can help. How I should like to hear Elon & Ali sing a duet! The dear little treasures, I never read an allusion to them without a tear starting to my eyes. It is cruel to be separated so long from them.

I am anxious to hear whether Reynolds has nominated Dana on his staff. But Reynolds is not a major general & it is questionable whether his appointment would make him [Dana] lieutenant colonel. Sometimes I feel as if I *must* nominate him myself, but I think it would do little good at present, & then after all what can I do with Chambloss?

Pray to have the war soon over & the old household images set up in their places again. But first of all pray for a *successful* ending. Is not Mother's patience worn out? Have you heard from Father? How are poor Caro & her little ones? My love to them all & kind regards to the Danas, particularly James.

Thine ever,
O.B.W.

In Camp Opposite Fredericksburg
Eve. Nov. 27/'62
My dearest Molly,
This has been Thanksgiving Day. I wonder how you have spent it? Last year I was in the Charleston Tower as miserable as mortal well could be, & it was sad enough for you at home. Much cause as we have for anxiety &

---

34. Meagher, a native of Ireland, commanded the Irish Brigade, which he had raised in New York and led during the Peninsula Campaign and at Second Bull Run. The brigade was shattered in its heroic assault on Marye's Heights during the Battle of Fredericksburg. Meagher died on July 1, 1867, falling overboard in a drinking spree aboard a steamboat near Fort Benton, Montana Territory.

trying as it is, both to be away from home, still it was worse last year & we ought to be thankful & trustful.

I had some visitors to-day. Gen'l Hobart Ward, who was one of my colonels at Bull Run, & several Michigan officers, delaying my dinner till after 3 o'clock, when Rob & I sat down to a leg of boiled mutton & rice, & some potted corn, which Capt. Shillinglaw presented. Last evening I had a guest from Michigan, viz. Rev. Mr. Taylor, a Methodist minister whom you may remember our seeing on the steamer when we took the trip to Lake Superior. He is newly appointed chaplain to the 8th Mich. Capt. Parke also arrived, bringing the drawers & a letter, a good long one, full of your thoughts & feelings, anxieties & speculations. I am a prey to just such things, but struggle & strive until I get the better of them—by divine help.

I am much more concerned about you & am anxious to see you, but not yet. Since Louise does not go to Detroit I also fear that Mother will find it very lonely & irksome to be chained down to the children. If Father comes on, perhaps you had better make your mind to return with him in time for the Holidays, before which time I hope to slip over to Washington & see you.

I inquired to-day of Seth Williams[35] whether Reynolds had applied for Dana & was told he had but that Meigs refused to spare him. I think it perfectly outrageous. Washington is a great center of *disgust*, which radiates in every direction. A fearful accumulation of responsibility rests *there* for many things—I will not venture to say what, nor do I wish you to say a word, but truth will [come] out some day. Meantime feel no uneasiness about me. . . .

Gen'l Sumner reviewed my corps yesterday. It was after an awful rain & the troops were cold & stood up in the mud in many places, so that it was not a brilliant affair. Unless we cross over very soon I will get up something better soon.

You see I have written a letter to Lulie. I hardly know how to talk to her, she has so much more sense & feeling than children usually. I must write to Elon. It seems to me they do not write many letters from home. Send my kind regards to Louise Blake & all the family. [Capt. Giles W.] Shurtleff gets on very well, is indefatigable & systematic. Rob has his valise & overcoat but not the robe. Brackett is well & sends regards. Dennis complains of a headache to-day. Maj. Crosby is unwell again. You must not wonder at not seeing him, he was sick. The officers all go to Washington & return post haste.

35. Brig. Gen. Seth Williams, assistant adjutant general, Army of the Potomac.

I saw Burnside the a.m. He is still as kind & obliging as ever. He showed this yesterday by telegraphing to the Secretary of War for me . . . to allow [Lt. O. M.] Dearborn[36] to remain with me after he had been ordered by the latter to South Carolina where his regiment now is. The Secretary consented.

If Father comes on, the points of the case [for my promotion] are these. That I am almost, if not quite, the senior brigadier in the service. That I commanded a division in two actions & have been recommended by both McClellan & Burnside for promotion. That I have had command of the 9th Corps since Oct. 13. That during part of the time I had also charge of the line of the upper Rappahannock with both Stoneman's & [Brig. Gen. Amiel W.] Whipple's[37] divisions under me, besides the corps, during which time I crossed part of my command over the river & successfully sustained Pleasonton's operations, withdrew it again without loss, stood a rear guard attack on Sturgis at Sulphur Springs, & finally performed a flank march along a large part of the river. That is, in brief, the record, you little politician!

Now good night & don't bother your little brain about this wicked world. Give my best regards to Capt. & Mrs. Dana & little May.

Thine Ever,
O.B.W.

[Opposite Fredericksburg]
Saturday
Nov. 29/'62
My dearest Molly,
Last night I was visited by Gen'l Burns & Col. Taylor (adjt. gen'l for Sumner) until a late hour & prevented from writing. I send you a line to acknowledge receipt of the can of oysters & tooth brush. We discussed the oysters last night & pronounced them delicious. Glad to hear Caro returns to health. A change is making [in] the mail arrangements; I don't know whether it will ensure more promptness. I send this by an orderly after Allen.

In haste,
O.B.W.

36. Dearborn was aide-de-camp and ordnance officer to OBW.
37. Whipple (5th, USMA 1841) then had command of the Third Division, Third Corps.

[Opposite Fredericksburg]
Wednesday Dec. 3/'62
My dearest Molly,

Our mail arrangement is changed so that the matter of both corps is to come in one mail & I fear we shall not have it so regularly. Allen goes up today to settle his business in the dept., & I hope he will bring back a long letter from you. The work of making major generals is going on at Washington. We hear of Reynolds, [Brig. Gen. George] Sykes,[38] & Hancock, but I don't hear of O. B.

The box with stove & blankets etc. & your last with pickles etc. arrived yesterday. Last night had an oyster supper with my division generals. You are very thoughtful & lovely.

In haste,
Orlando

Opposite Fredericksburg
Dec. 4/'62 Eve.
My dearest Molly,

The nights are getting very cold indeed, though the days when the sun is out are moderate. You have doubtless seen Lieut. Brackett, who I hope will be polite & show you some attention. I have taken Charley McKnight[39] as acting aide, much to his delight & probably to the satisfaction of Sarah. What will the Romeyns say?

This morning Hooker reviewed Sickles' division & I saw several redoubtable heroes for the first time. Sickles himself & Meagher. Capt. DeRussy, my old friend, also has returned. His battery is in Sickles' division, but he will probably have command of the reserve artillery. The camp is full of rumors of new major generals & of their probable commands. I don't know how many are to have the 9th Army Corps. I take it all very coolly & wait my promotion; meantime am expecting new troops to fill my corps up to 20,000. I fear we have lost Benjamin, transferred to the Reserve Arty.— "temporarily" the order says, but [Brig. Gen. Henry] Hunt[40] has been talking of it so long I guess its done for good. Cook's battery is mustered out, & I have two others assigned in the place of the two gone.

I received a very nice letter from Julia yesterday, which I will take great pleasure in answering. I see they have published one of my orders in some of

38. Sykes (39th, USMA 1842) then led the Second Division, Fifth Corps.
39. Lt. Charles A. McKnight, 7th Michigan.
40. Hunt (19th, USMA 1839), a native of Detroit, then commanded the Artillery Reserve of the Army of the Potomac.

the newspapers. What does Capt. Dana think of the President's message?[41] Don't it look like taking the war easy, dropping salt petre & taking to milk?

I hope to hear of Father's arrival just in the very nick of time. Rumor says I am to be appointed, but I suspect that Halleck may have me in his breeches pocket, with a good many others.

Night before last I invited my three division generals & we had an oyster feast. Your box of good things are a god-send, I assure you. The butter is delicious & the only butter I have *enjoyed* in the field. The wonderful Coale box has also arrived & Fred & Arndt have got their things. All are "satisfied & happy" except Rob—whose robe has not turned up. The cigars are just the thing & I hope Dana will remember the brand if it is not too long since he bought them. Sometimes I think I cannot let you go home. But what shall we do about dear, kind Mother & the children? Good night & God bless you, my life's blessing.

Orlando

Opposite Fredericksburg

Dec. 11, '62

My darling Mother,

The canonading has begun. It is probable that I shall be engaged to-day in a very bloody battle. I hope God will shield me from harm, but if His will be otherwise I can meekly submit. I can only convey to you my trust which you have taught me & to crave your blessing, Thanking you for all your great love & care, & asking your pardon for all my faults.

With love to Eben & all my sisters & their families, I remain

Your devoted son,
Orlando

Opposite Fredericksburg

Dec. 16, 1862

My dear Wife,

It is with a sad heart that I sit down to write you to-night—the first moment I have been able to command for the purpose. Without pretending to

41. Referring to Lincoln's message to Congress, delivered on December 1. Lincoln reported that foreign relations and commerce were in good shape. He also recommended three constitutional amendments: first, that every state which abolished slavery before 1900 would receive compensation; second, that all slaves who gained freedom during the war would remain free, and loyal owners would be compensated; third, that Congress would provide for colonization outside the country for all free black people who desired it. Roy P. Basler, ed. *The Collected Works of Abraham Lincoln* (Brunswick, N.J.: Rutgers University Press, 1953), vol. 5, p. 518–37.

be a prophet, I can truly say the failure of our bold, impracticable attempt upon the enemy's fortified lines was not unexpected. The season, the roads, the reality were all against that rapidity of execution which was required. Burnside was compelled by the force of public will—if nothing more—to make the attempt at all hazards & against every obstacle. We dared the lion in his very den, & skulking behind his lair he held us at bay. Finding we could not rout him, we withdrew under his teeth with [the] most graceful manner, & wait now in good condition for another spring at him.

I hope the judgment of the nation will be suspended until it can act rationally & not condemn us without a hearing. It is Providence, not man, after all, that rules in the armies of the earth, & the force of events is guided by Him more than we are apt to consider.

In preparing for the attack my corps was stretched between Couch's attack on the right and Franklin's on the left. One third, Burns' Division, was diverted from my immediate control by Franklin, & I had but two divisions left to cooperate with Couch's columns. Each of these divisions was thrown against the enemy immediately in their respective fronts and fought with great determination to gain a foothold on their batteries. But the enemy were too strong for us to penetrate at any point. Their guns enfiladed us, their infantry had their stone walls & earthworks for a cover, & as many men as we besides. They do not dare to meet us in the open field. We gained the ground up to the very base of their works & held so much as we cared to hold all the next day.

The next day my corps was selected by Burnside to lead the new attack. I had every preparation for it, troops & batteries in position, a column of 35 regiments, with three field batteries on each flank—but all the general officers decided against it. Gen'l Sumner requested Burnside to suspend the movement until the Grand Division & corps commanders could be consulted. We all thought it would be a useless slaughter of our men, & could not lead to anything *decisive*, even if we pierced the first line, as the enemy had a new line of artillery in rear, with flanking batteries, & all their infantry in position, fresh to fall upon our men when blown; & so Burnside yielded his own judgment, wisely as I certainly think; for a failure would have certainly entailed the most terrible disaster of the war, while a success could have led only to partial results. In other words, with a tremendous sacrifice of life we could only have succeeded in pushing back the enemy on a new line of defense & won an indecisive victory; while if we failed we were utterly gone ourselves. The boldest men, such as Sumner, deemed the case too critical for experiment—partly because *all felt* that success was next to impossible, & with such *feelings* it is impossible. To fight a battle with a river

Opposite Fredericksburg Va
Dec 16. 1862

My dear Wife.

It is with a sad heart that I sit down to write you to-night — the first moment I have been able to command for the purpose. Without pretending to be a prophet, I can truly say, the failure of our bold impractable attempt upon the enemy's fortified lines was not unexpected by The season, the roads, the locality were all against that rapidity of execution which was required. Burnside was compelled by the force of public will — if nothing more — to make the attempt at all hazards & against any obstacle. We dared the lion in his very den, & stalking behind his lair he held us at bay. Finding we could not route him we withdrew under his teeth in the most graceful manner, & wait now in good condition for another spring at him.

I hope the judgment of the nation will be suspended until it can act rationally. & not condemn us without a hearing. It is Providence, not man, after all, that rules in the armies of the earth, & the force of events is guided by Him more than we are apt to consider.

Letter from OBW to Marie, December 16, 1862. *OBW Collection.*

immediately in rear is one of the most hazardous things, on equal terms. To fight it on unequal terms would be an act of unmitigated folly, especially when the stake is the safety of the Capitol & the existence of its army of defense.

I hope you will send this letter to Father & Eben & let them show it to any of my intimate friends. I feel deeply for the cause & for Burnside, but not despondent for either. We still envelope & press the enemy all over the theater of war, from here to Louisiana, & have not by the movement, nor by withdrawing, which was an act of common prudence, done any harm, nor lost any useful ground, unless the croakers & traitors place us in a false position by misrepresentation, misleading the timid public mind. I am willing to bear my share of the responsibility like a man, although never could I have thrown myself into battle or died more gloriously than when directing the charge of the 9th Army Corps.

I have not space left to speak of our all recrossing the river. It was most beautifully done. With my love to all & gratitude for safety & prayers for ultimate success

Your devoted husband,
O. B. Willcox

Opposite Fredericksburg
Dec. 19/'62
My dear Father,

You will not charge me with neglect on account of my seldom writing you, as your own large experience in important affairs will suggest the necessary excuses of my situation. Besides, I often charge Marie to send you my letters—one lately in particular in regard to our recent repulse across the River. I understand the Hon. Z. Chandler (& co.) is in camp. Don't it remind you of the French Revolution when divers members of the Assembly accompanied & dictated to the generals? I suppose this is a smelling committee. Is it likely they can comprehend the cause & above all provide the remedy? I never heard of a committee that could do anything but white wash, & we need no white washing. History will set the thing all right.

In regard to myself, I never said a word against crossing the river to Burnside, nor against the whole affair, and Hooker & everybody thought as I did. An attack on the 14th was actually ordered & I was directed with my corps to make it. I came over to Sumner's head quarters & waited there for Gen'l Burnside to get directions from him as to the precise point of attack—having my columns ready formed and six batteries of artillery ready, with their positions selected. But I told Gen'l Sumner that I had no faith in the grand result, even if my own attack succeeded, because if we carried the first line of entrenchments, the second awaited us with the bulk of the enemy's infantry to contend against. Sumner said then that he would advise the general to call a council of the Grand Division & corps commanders to advise.

While these were assembling, Burnside went to a private room & sent for me & then I strongly advised against the battle, for the simple reason that our success could be but partial, while if we failed the disaster would be decisive against us. I think now that all military men will sustain this view, & that it is lucky Burnside yielded—which he did with the greatest reluctance. After that, the withdrawal was a matter of course, or we should have become demoralized, if not worse. I thought that men risking the uneven chances of

the only good army we had, or could have for a long time, was impolitic. Here you have the secret history & the great reasons of the whole affair. It was a great responsibility for me in my inexperience to assume, & I am curious to learn whether you approve of it.

Christmas is near by & I am sorry Marie & I could not be with you all at home. But she is of the greatest comfort & use to me so near. I hope in fact to have her in camp again in a few days. If the rumors of Sedgwick taking the corps had proved true, I would have applied for a leave of absence & got some consolation by going home. But Dana saw Sedgwick yesterday & was told by him that he was not assigned to the corps. Indeed, if things grow much worse, I don't see as I can be of any service at all, & the question may possibly arise whether I had not better, in that event, abandon the whole concern. What do you think of the proposition?

The question would then be what should I do to support my family in civil life? The law I am told yields small recompense. I think I could superintend a railway—or at any rate do something. I would like your views on the whole subject. Having fairly won my promotion, I think it is a shame that it is witheld. I understand the President is in favor of it, but there are many conflicting interests, & he, poor man, must steer a course to avoid rocks.

But independent of this, what encouragement is there in the field? Poor Marie is perfectly miserable & distressed, & can any salary or glory compensate this absence from home, which seems to be of no avail even to the cause for which I am willing to lay down my life, if by so doing I can do any good. It is a very intricate question. Pray let me have all the light your superior wisdom can furnish. With Love to mother & kisses to the children.

Your devoted Son,
Orlando

Head-Quarters, 9th Army Corps
[Opposite Fredericksburg]
January 2d, 1863
My dearest Molly,

Strange to say the weather has been so fine that you might have staid longer without any risk. I received news of your safe arrival on board the boat & suppose Brackett will be down this p.m. with the report of your passage up to Washington, which I anxiously hope was not so dreary & uncomfortable as your trip down. I received Dana's reply to my dispatch the morning you left & suppose a vehicle awaited you at the wharf. I watched you in my "mind's eye" every step you took till safely reclining on your couch beneath the hospitable roof of the best & kindest of men, without danger of chill or fever.

Evening.

Brackett has just returned and affords me gratifying intelligence of your trip. Do not overexert yourself now, but do as you promise. Keep a brave heart during the long months to come. I may see you.

I hope my letter to Father will quicken his movements. Trowbridge (Rowland) spent the day before New Years with me. All seems to be fair so far as the delegation goes. He is at least a warm friend. It is probably determined, however, not to promote any of us until the army has "done something." Next time I think they will do something worth while. The telegraphic news from Rosecrans is just received here & so far was favorable.[42] I hope the bravery of our effort lately will fire them out West to mighty deeds.

Yesterday was spent very finely. A good many called to see me but I was out all day with my staff. Called on Sumner, Sedgwick, Hancock, Howard & the 79th [New York], who gave a grand regimental collation. Speeches were made to toasts, etc. Good night now. Keep calm & be hopeful for the best & don't borrow alarm. Kind regards to the McNairs & Danas.

Thine ever,
O.B.W.

Monday January 4/'63
[Opposite Fredericksburg]
Molly darling,

The Deuce is in the mails again as I have not heard from you but once since you left my "bower" & that was by Brackett. No change yet in affairs since you left. Burnside was to review my corps yesterday, but countermanded the order on account of its being Sunday, but tomorrow I shall offer him one. I saw both Meade & Whipple to-day at Stoneman's review. They always inquire after you with much apparent interest, & both say they would have come to see you had they known of your being here. Strange to say it was known through the *Herald* that you visited me—the very thing I wanted to avoid.

I wonder how your health is. If Father is as long starting as he was making up his mind, I fear you may be detained some time, but I would avail myself

42. Referring to Gen. Rosecrans's recent victory at the Battle of Stone's River, Tennessee, December 31, 1862–January 2, 1863.

of the first good opportunity of going to *New York* without waiting for him. Once there I shall feel easier about you than I do now. I think that with Caro, Abby & Ellie, your thoughts would be diverted & your cares lightened. Still, even there I would not stay any longer than to get a good rest & renewal of strength for the still more fatiguing ride to Detroit.

I would give anything if I could be induced to take a more cheerful view of things. You are so young & bright & lovely, that life ought to appear more charming, and for my part, I have hopes of pleasant days ahead for us & our little ones. You will soon shake off the sombre gloom that has pressed upon you from the very surroundings. It is for this reason that I am impatient to have you leave the foul atmosphere of Old Washington. I wish I were brighter myself. I feel preoccupied & must be the most uninteresting individual extant.

Meade has got his promotion, the only one that has. His appointment arrived a day or two before the crossing of Fredericksburg. I understand that mine is made out, but still lies in the Secretary's drawer with the others. O! for some wide awake friend to give it a lift! Father ought to know of it. But you had better burn this letter lest, if he see it, he should think I censured him for not starting from home. One thing I ask, as a special favor of you, [is] not to bother your head by a single thought further on the subject. . . . I value all things as dross compared with your peace of mind.

Yesterday I made a reconnaissance, along with Gen'l [Daniel P.] Woodbury of the engineer brigade, & had the pleasure of making his acquaintance. He is a fine Christian gentleman, such as one rarely finds in the field. I discovered it in five minutes conversation.

I must close now, as Henry will have to take this up to head quarters tonight. The pay accts. have not yet arrived.

> Good night Sweetest,
> Thine,
> O.B.W.

Headquarters, 9th Army Corps
[Opposite Fredericksburg]
Wednesday night, 7th January 1863
My dearest Molly,

To-day I was so uneasy at not hearing from you that I telegraphed Capt. Dana to inquire after your health & whether Father had arrived, but have not yet received a reply. To-night, however, the mail brought in your welcome letter enclosing Nina's & Mrs. Fink's. To crown the day I have also received a very nice letter from your dear good Mother, telling me all about

Ali, the core of her heart. Mother seems quite lonely & misses young society. You will soon be with her though. She regrets Louise not coming to visit. If one of the Davis girls would be agreeable, perhaps Nina might spare Julia a short time.

I have no particular news but a report that Sumner's Grand Division is to go to Washington. This seems to be a Washington rumor. Would it not be provoking if it turned out true *after* you should have left! By this time I suppose Father is with you.

Yesterday we made another attempt at a review for Gen. Burnside, but the day was squally, & just as he arrived it rained & nearly spoiled the affair. . . . But the troops looked splendid & cheered him heartily. Gen. Burns is quite unwell with an attack of pleurisy.

I am glad your finances turned out so well. It is about as I told you. Chambloss got my account for the Antietam horse allowance, so I shall soon have $175 from that source. The Bull Run horse claim was suspended for inquiry as to paying for horses *captured!* The news from Rosecrans turns out right after all. It is cheering in the midst of our gloom in this camp. I hope Sherman will have Vicksburg.[43] The war prosperous & you well & I should be the happiest of mortals. I am so glad you are "gaining," even though it may be "slowly." You must not expect too much as you are terribly pulled down. Cheer up, my brave little Soul! Our Heavenly Father never yet has deserted us.

Thine Ever,
Orlando

Do not bother about things to send me.

Headquarters, 9th Army Corps
[Opposite Fredericksburg]
January 9, 1863
My dearest Molly,
Last evening & this both brought me letters from you, so I feel doubly rich. I enclose Mother's letter as well as one from our little Caro. This evening I also received from Lieut. [James] Gillis a box containing half a dozen magnificent & delicious pears which came for you, intended as a New year's gift, but were delayed somewhere *en route*. I don't think I can afford to forward them to you! They were sent by Mrs. Gillis. You can thank her in my name instead of your own. I wrote Gillis a note.

43. OBW had apparently not yet learned of Maj. Gen. W. T. Sherman's defeat at Chickasaw Bluff on December 29; by January 2, 1863, Sherman had deemed the campaign a failure, and he withdrew from the Yazoo.

Yesterday was a blue day with me. I tried to ride it off but failed, & finally shut myself into the back tent by a warm fire & the "Orpheus C. Kerr Papers,"[44] which I borrowed of Genl. Burns, & read assiduously through, poor jokes, bad poems & all—but there are some capital hits contained in the thing. And by the way, as we shall have some in-door weather necessarily, if you know of any agreeable books, I would like something for a dark day. It never rains but it pours, & the mail has brought me the blank pay accounts which I send enclosed likewise, signed for December to Capt. Dana, along with this.

I must close for the mail at Burnside's head quarters.

> Thine Ever,
> O.B.W.

[Opposite Fredericksburg]
January 10/'63
Night rainy
My dear little Marie,

Had I suddenly heard the singing of a bird it would not have surprized or delighted me more than your cheerful letter received this evening by Allen. Father's coming & your better health together have put you in spirits again. I am very glad you came to see me before leaving, & am especially glad Father has come on for you. I shall now feel comparatively easy.

The basket arrived safe. Tell Julia to get me some sort of a metal mustard pot & some good mustard. If you have time I want some patent collars, wide, turn-down, 14½ inches long. The assortment in the basket are fine. I send up by Allen the requisition for the ambulance to Dana. . . .

Be of good spirits & write me often.

> Thine Ever,
> O.B.W.

[Opposite Fredericksburg]
January 11/'63
My dear Molly,

I wrote you & Father by Allen who left this a.m. early. The adjutant general (or Secretary of War) has appointed Rob lieutenant colonel, asst. adjutant general of the 9th Corps. Also Kent, whom I recommended, as asst. inspector general with same rank. This looks favorably.

44. Orpheus C. Kerr was the pseudonym (a play on "office seeker") of humorist Robert H. Newell. Lincoln said of the *Orpheus C. Kerr Papers*, "Anyone who has not read them must be a heathen."

The storm has cleared off & it is pleasant again. No news of importance. It is three times as lonely since you left. I have a sudden greed for reading, to kill time & divert thought. Rob is down with remittent fever, but not a bad attack. It will be over in a few days. The things in the basket are very nice. I will send back the basket to Julia. . . .

If the weather continues fair, Father may visit me. He can judge . . . from the appearance of things whether I shall want to make any change in my plans, & if so, of course I ought to see him. Hope he will see the President. At all events he & you will write me *very fully* before you leave Washington. Love to him & all. Send me some stamps.

Thine,
O.B.W.

[Opposite Fredericksburg]
January 14/'63
My dear Molly,
Allen arrived in the night & leaves this a.m. in a few minutes. He brought your nice long letter with the joyful news of your reinvigoration of strength. Father's interview with Stanton[45] reveals a volume. But I do not wish him to soil his fingers too much with such people. The saddest part of the whole business is that the cowards at Washington try to shirk their responsibility on us, refuse to give Burnside an order or a glimmer of advice, & yet exclaim "Why don't the army do something!" The course of the Administration at Washington refusing promotions & brevets for past services is fearfully demoralizing the officers.

However this is little to the point. Couch has turned up or will turn up here to-day or to-morrow, & then, as I am not a major general, I suppose I must lose my gallant corps, unless some other disposition is made of Sedgwick.

Burnside said last night that when Couch went away he thought he was going to resign. Now if Sedgwick takes my corps, I shall get a leave & see you. Burnside says he thinks it can be arranged so I may not lose the corps. Both Stoneman & Reynolds are my juniors—but as Sedgwick is in this Grand Division, he would naturally (or unnaturally) take [over] according to his rank.

I have pretty much smothered out all my indignation at the outrageous course things have taken for a long time, but now I *am* disgusted—after that remark of the Secretary's [Stanton's].

45. Edwin M. Stanton became secretary of war on January 15, 1862, replacing Simon Cameron.

Love to Father & tell him to let Chandler know I am likely to lose my command for want of the rank. But I fear the feeling is too strong against the Army of the Potomac for any body to care.

Thine,
O.B.W.

[Opposite Fredericskburg]
January 19/'63
My dearest Molly,

I hope you are well & having a delightful visit with Caro. No news at all yet, nor am I in a hurry for any change until the present cloud over the army clears away. Am satisfied that all will turn out for the best, because I always try to do right, & every body seems well-disposed toward me. Father's visit to Washington will tell at the right time. *At present* I do not see how the President can make any promotion, so do not let your thoughts run on the vexed question. Your mind now needs quiet & rest for a long time, as much as your body needs change & the calm atmosphere of home. Again I say let nothing distract you.

Mrs. Burns is down here. She [was] as you were & as desperate but now [is] happy & better. [She] is quite a pretty woman. Tell Father I appreciate his pithy note & shall mind his good advice & write him fully. Love to all. . . . Much obliged for Mother's letter. . . .

Thine Ever,
O.B.W.

[Opposite Fredericksburg, undated letter to Marie. The beginning appears to be missing.]

I am painfully alive to the outrage the authorities will inflict upon me if they refuse my promotion. At the same time I have never had high expectations on the subject. The claims of everybody will be furiously urged & there are many in the army who would tear down everybody for themselves, but they cannot hurt me because my only object is to do right, & he who lives for this cannot be hurt. They may prevent my rising, but if God will only let me *live* & spare you & the children, how really insignificant [is] all else in comparison! I would not exchange a hair of your precious head for a crown. Your truthfulness, purity, & devotion are infinitely to be preferred above the world. At the same time for your own sake & the children's sakes, I desire a good name & the means to make you comfortable & happy. The additional pay of maj. gen'l I greatly need for you, for so far our expenses seem to have absorbed the pay.

I wrote Mr. Chandler the other night. What course he will pursue I cannot tell. Perhaps Eb's opposition at the late election may disaffect him . . . although I never opened my mouth on politics but abstained scrupulously—in fact have none. But a truce to the thing. The great desire of my heart is to see you & I really hope to do so. . . . Meantime do not worry. I hope to hear more cheering news from Caro. How anxious you & all at home must have been kept about her. Write her how much concerned I too have felt about her. . . .

Eben complains that he sees but few of my letters. Please have them shown to him when you send any home, as I have so little time to write anyone but you. . . . Good night my darling.

Thine,
Orlando

[Opposite Fredericksburg]
January 22/'63
My darling Molly,
After two days' severe work in the storm between here & one of the upper fords, I have been lying idle to-day. Our efforts have been thwarted by the infernal mud-powers. We can well swear now by all the "Powers of mud!"[46]

I received yours of the 18th this evening. Poor Caro. I hope her child is recovered. She has had a "winter campaign" of her own, hard for the poor child to bear. Express my most heartfelt sympathy to her & Frank. I shall look for the next tidings from New York with double interest.

You probably wish to know how I mess, etc., in my present transition state. I am still in my old quarters. Genl. Sedgwick tents with me & is anxious to have me remain with him awhile. I still keep my own mess going with Kent & Brackett [&] additional members.

Shillinglaw I have relieved from duty & sent to his regiment. He has behaved badly for some time. I hear to-day he has resigned. He first tried to get on Burnside's staff & he has been trying to vamp himself up with letters from everybody. I dare say he will turn up in some high post.

---

46. On January 19, 1863, Burnside began to shift his army upriver in an attempt to cross the river and outflank Lee's army, still occupying the heights above Fredericksburg. That night, the grand divisions of Hooker and Franklin were near U.S. Ford. By the next evening the rain had begun, and the army quickly found itself bogged down in the mud. Guns and wagons sank deep into the bottomless roads, horses and mules dropped dead trying to pull them out, and the morale of the men disappeared. By January 22 the campaign, which the men dubbed the "Mud March," was declared a failure, and the army began to struggle its way back to its camps at Falmouth.

My duties as Burnside's assistant chief of staff are but nominal while things are quiet. B. has gone up to Washington to-day.[47] Will write you again on his return, especially if I can get anything definitely fixed about my hereafter. Love to Father, Frank & Caro.

Thine Ever,
O.B.W.

[Opposite Fredericksburg]
January 29/'63
My dearest Molly,

Arrived yester[day] even[ing] in a baggage car & snow storm. It is awful to see the troops in camp, especially the pickets. As for the roads, there are none, they have all sunk in beds of bottomless mud.

Saw Julia, the Gillises & Danas at Washington. Saw Gen. Hooker this a.m. & have written Father & William [Blodgett]. It is all right so far as he is in command. Now let William go ahead. He is the personification of success. The proudest leaf in the chaplet of my military records would be owing promotion to W.T.B. Have written Trowbridge & Parsons. The latter is wide awake & zealous.

All glad to see me in camp. Rob well. Arndt & the horses needed my return. . . . Brackett & Shurtleff gone to Washington. Charley [McKnight] not yet returned. He has overstaid his leave. Thine with love to Caro.

Orlando

January 30/'63
Dear Father,

I wrote both you & William yesterday by the mail. All seems favorable so far as Hooker is concerned. He promises me a corps, but evidently under the impression I am to be maj. gen'l. He seems to think highly of me. I gave William a list of persons to see in Washington in connection with his own people. Now is the golden opportunity if ever.

I wish you would see Burnside & ask his advice. Tell him *for yourself* that you fear my being relieved of command of the 9th Corps. . . . And *for me* say that I was sorry to miss him at Washington. Also ask whether I was included

47. Burnside visited the president to urge him to implement General Orders No. 8, dismissing Hooker, Franklin, and others from the service, stating that he could not continue in command of the army if it was not carried out. The president agreed: meeting with Burnside again on the morning of January 25, he formally relieved him of command of the Army of the Potomac, replacing him with Hooker.

in the leave of absence granted his staff (as I was, nominally, perhaps, assistant chief of his staff). The Grand Divisions will probably be broken up & the corps reestablished as they were.

My love to Marie & Caro. When do you expect to leave NY?

Thine,
O.B.W.

P.S. The *Herald* reporter brought down a *rumor* this evening picked up at Willards, that Gen. W. was to have command of the 9th.

Washington
Feb. 5/'63
My dearest Molly,

I have not had a moment's time since arriving here to write you. Came up yesterday morning. Found William had gone, but the good work which he had begun was watched & followed up closely by Mr. Parsons & all looks well. A new & powerful ally is unexpectedly found in Mr. Kellogg. I will write you full particulars in a few days, but have scarcely seen Julia & must return to camp early tomorrow morning. Have written more particulars to William.

Later.

After spending an hour with the Julias I have more news. The 9th Corps has been ordered to *Suffolk*, *Gen. Smith* in command & Gen. Sedgwick has been assigned to command of Franklin's Grand Division.[48] I learn this by a note which Allen brot up from Robt. [Gen. Daniel] Butterfield (chief of staff) has telegraphed for me to come & take my old Division.

What it all means I cannot tell until I get down there. It seems the order was for them to go at once. I knew that Sedgwick was offered a Grand Division, & perhaps had I been on the spot I should have resumed command of the 9th. There is either some arrangement which will still result in this, or else some one has been false, as Hooker expressly *authorized* me to say here that he wanted to give me a corps, & I have said it everywhere.

Will write you as soon as possible from below. I return to-morrow, but it may be some days before you hear again, as all will be hurry & movement. Do not delay longer in New York than for fair weather to travel. Say noth-

---

48. "The Julias" refers to Julia McNair and her daughter of the same name. The Ninth Corps did not go to Suffolk, but to Newport News. Maj. Gen. William F. Smith had taken temporary command of the Ninth Corps but would be replaced by Maj. Gen. John G. Parke in March.

ing of the Suffolk movement, & if any one inquires after me, say I have taken my old division for the present. In much haste,

Thine,
Orlando

One consolation—the promotion appears all secure. I enclose a check for $296.38.

Washington
Feb. 5/'63
My dear Father,

I have already written Marie & William, whose letters you will see. I expected to stay over at least to-morrow, but must leave in the morning & trust affairs in an unfinished state to Mr. Parsons & the Delegation. I think I have done no harm by coming up. On the contrary, Mr. P. thinks that my presence has fired up both Kellogg & Beaman[49] to the warmest state of interest. Will write again in a few days. Meantime Mr. Parsons will probably write William.

Very truly thine,
Orlando

Newport News, Va.
Feb. 13[?]/'63
My dearest Molly,

Your note of the 12th was gladly received yesterday. Your reception home must have been very welcome. This has been a sad day to me. Arndt, my devoted groom, injured himself on board the transport by a strain producing a severe hernia from which he is not likely to recover. I fear he cannot survive many days even. I had no house to put him in on arriving here & he is [in] a hospital tent with both Fred & North taking care of him with other assistants & all we can do for him. I feel dreadfully. He inquires for Roebuck, takes hold of my hand, squeezes it & calls me his dear General. He has some idea of his danger. Gangrene has commenced.

Poe has returned a brigadier general & is temporarily commanding my division while I keep the Corps until Gen. Smith returns. It is queer how many rumors I am the subject of just now—the last is that I am to be Military Governor of Washington. I think I should clean out old Sodom some.

49. Congressman Francis W. Kellogg (R. Mich) and Congressman Fernando Beaman, Michigan, one of the founders of the Republican Party.

It gives me great pleasure to hear you are so well. Do not overtax your strength in any way. Mind & stop before you get too tired.

Officers & men here seem equally pleased at getting away from the mud & the Army of the Potomac. Here we are on the banks of the river, on hard ground, beautifully encamped, about ten miles from Fortress Monroe.

Gen'l [John A.] Dix,[50] by the way, is very fearful Burnside is going to relieve him from his Dept. None of us know yet precisely what the Corps was sent here for: will know by the 25th probably, when Burnside's leave expires.

With much love to all,

Thine,
O.B.W.

[Newport News, Va.]
Feb. 17/'63
My dear Father,

I enclose Parson's last letter, fearing you may not hear from either him or William. But perhaps you have seen him already. I see by the papers the entire list is sent back to the President. Tell Marie to call on Mrs. P. & show every appreciation of their truly great & wonderful kindness & interest in me.

Poor Arndt is very low; it will be a great blow to me to lose him. He wants his remains sent to Detroit. Have written Marie this mail. Love to dear mother.

Thine,
O.B.W.

Newport News
Feb. 18/'63
My dearest Molly,

The rain storm continues to rage—dreary enough. But Arndt is better & the Doctor begins to hope.

Poor Robert—the reduction of the Grand Divisions reduces him & he is no longer lieutenant colonel, but captain, & belongs to me again. The wise people at Washington do everything for the army, of course, everything that is bad. The Ninth Corps don't know whether it is on its head or its heels, don't know whether it has a head. So many changes make them dizzy.

Roebuck & I were out to-day in the rain. I rode him down & we opened the tent for Arndt to see him & he was wild with flattering delight. I fear

50. Maj. Gen. John A. Dix, then commanding the Department of Virginia.

that one of our schooners is lost with some men & twenty-eight horses. I have not entirely given her up. Smith is expected back to-morrow.

I hope mother will not allow you to write me all the letters. Her pen should never rest no more than a star should dim. Love to all the little ones.

Thine,
Orlando

Newport News
Feb. 24/'63
My dearest Molly,

Another & most fearful storm has vexed our coast. Look out for news of shipwrecks. Last night I met Admiral [S. P.] Lee,[51] who, with Capt. [Pierce] Crosby (fleet capt.) took tea informally with me. They give cheerful encouragement of the prospect of the gun boat attack on Charleston, but there will be more *delay*—of course—why not?

Rumor points the 9th Corps to North Carolina, but nobody knows nor can tell till Burnside comes down.

Newport News consists of a promiscuous old rat hole of sutler sheds, offices, log houses, shanties, etc. I pitched my own tent temporarily at the Corps head quarters, but to-day have moved down to my Division camp on a pretty bluff overlooking the river, & have as usual with me a pretty camp.

Poor Henry is in disgrace for getting tipsy & has been sent back to his regiment, or I would have him make you a sketch.

Gen'l Smith now wields the baton of the Corps. Col. Withington, who has just returned from seeing "that baby," is getting up tents for his wife to visit him. But I reckon her stay here will be short & sweet. Arndt is gradually sinking. Indeed, with his injury, life would be a burden. But everything is done for him as if he were an officer.

There is a stoppage of my letters somewhere. Have not received one from you since more than a week ago. . . .

Gen'l. Dix is a perfect gentleman—his assistant adjutant general, [Daniel T.] Van Buren, is one of my old classmates. Gen'l Smith & I are on good terms. We attended a grand dinner given by the 51st New York to Col. Shephard, who presented them with a stand of colors—toasts & speechifying on hand. . . . My best love to Father, Mother & the darlings.

Thine,
O.B.W.

51. Lee commanded the North Atlantic Blockading Squadron.

Newport News
Sunday Night
March 1/'63
My dearest Molly,

To think that I have but just to-day received answer to a letter two weeks ago & more from Acquia Creek makes me sigh again that you are not as near me as when you were at Georgetown. Two letters, nice ones, one of the 20th, the other of the 22d—good you write often, & they will come regularly now they are fairly started.

To-day has been a happy day, both in the two letters & in a sense of comfort in my double tent with a board floor & a glorious fire place, in knowing that you & the three little banditti that steal away all your time are well, & that God has been merciful, spared me, & blessed me, & given me consideration & honor, & saved me from thousands of ills common to humanity.

And yet poor Arndt, we buried him with all the honors of war yesterday near my head quarters. I do not know that I shall send his body on yet. Everything is so extortionate, & if he has any family connections at Detroit, they would probably expect to have the balance of wages due him paid to them. But I think he has no family in this country. Ought I, for my own gratification, to bear this expense at this time? No. Still, it was his wish & if the weather permits I may have it done.

I am about a mile above the landing of Newport News, on the high bank of the river, with as pleasant a camp as I ever had. The division have splendid hard ground & enjoy it hugely. I am close above the river & hear its washing on the beach. Fish, oysters & eggs are plenty. Mrs. Poe, Mrs. Withington & other ladies are expected. Some officers' wives are here already. Monitors, iron clads & other naval craft lie off, waiting for Merrimac 2d, etc.

Burnside is still expected & it is conjectured we go to N.C. Your details concerning the children are very interesting. Lulu is just entering on the awkward period. Do not be impatient with her. Grace & softness will round her angularities in due time. Little Alli must be charming. Tell her I love her dearly & want to see her very much. I see by your letter that old Pincher still stretches himself on the library rug before the fire. I wish I was with him there this Sunday night. Raymond's book bill is probably right. Get some volumes he bound for me—biographical sketches, etc. Embrace all the family for me.

Thine ever,
O.B.W.

 SEVENTEEN

Kentucky & Indiana
Operations, 1863: A War of Giants

[On March 19, 1863, the first two divisions of the Ninth Corps embarked at Newport News and headed west for the Department of the Ohio, now commanded by Ambrose Burnside at Cincinnati. The Ninth Corps itself, however, was soon shipped to Lexington, where from April 10 to June 9, 1863, it fell under Willcox's jurisdiction as temporary commander of the District of Central Kentucky.]

THE CHARMING little city of Lexington, in the blue grass region of Kentucky, remains one of the greenest spots in my memory of the Secession War. Here the 9th Corps was encamped during several weeks in the spring of 1863. My command embraced not only the Corps itself, but other troops more active in the District of Eastern Kentucky, down to the Tennessee border, where the Confederates were organizing and starting raids and committing depredations under Forrest, John Morgan and others.[1] I took up my quarters at the town in which, and thereabouts, many of the most charming and cultivated families of the state were residing—the Crittendens, Breckenridges, Brands, Dudleys, Clays, etc., including quite a sprinkling of people whose husbands and brothers were fighting on the other side. The feud between the two parties was so bitter that they were no longer on speaking terms—even at church. One of the most delicate duties

---

1. Brig. Gen Nathan Bedford Forrest, the renowned rebel cavalryman; Brig. Gen. John Hunt Morgan.

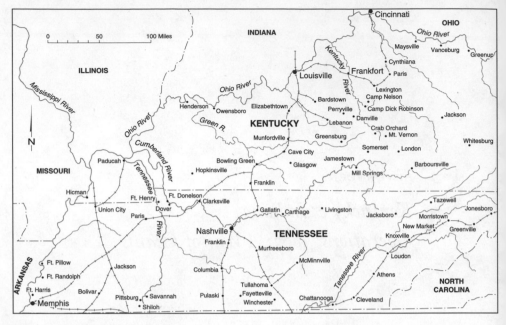

Kentucky and Tennessee.

that lay before me was the execution of an order that had been issued by my predecessor, General Quincy A. Gillmore,[2] for the banishment of two prominent "rebel" ladies, Mrs. Morgan, mother of Gen. John Morgan, and another lady, I think her name was Warfield, who was not only a leader in Kentucky society, but a writer of some note, the author of the *Household of Bouviere*.[3] These two ladies had been charged with communicating "military information" in their correspondence with kinsmen in the vicinity of Mount Sterling, where Morgan and his able lieutenant, Col. [R. S.] Cluke, were operating with success.[4]

There had certainly been an extraordinary amount of knowledge of the locations and movements of our troops shown by the enemy on both sides of the border. But in a country like Kentucky, where the people were secretly, if not openly, divided on the Union question, there must have been

2. Brig. Gen. Quincy A. Gillmore (1st, USMA 1849).

3. Catherine Anne (Ware) Warfield, (1816–1877), poet and novelist, was a native of Natchez, Mississippi. She later moved to Lexington, where she married R. E. Warfield. Some of her most prominent works were *The Household of Bouviere* (1855), *Romance of the Green Seal* (1867), and *Hester Howard's Temptation* (1875).

4. Col. R. S. Cluke had on March 22, 1863, captured Mount Sterling, along with the Federal garrison of three hundred men.

many avenues of information besides ladies' letters. Anyway, the ladies denied the charge. Their last few days at home were drawing nigh. They could not live in the shifting field of war, and they knew not where else under the sun they could live. And now an appeal came up to me through a very prominent Union lady, Mrs. Charles McAllister, to remit the sentence. This lady brought with her a petition signed by some forty Union ladies, and she warmly urged it on social grounds. She was noted for hospitality to Union officers, and I had been a frequent guest at her house, famous for good breakfasts, which were quite [welcome] after our long sojourn in camp. "Kentucky breakfasts" are as good as a passport to society. Besides, her friendly advice had been of some use to me in the conduct of affairs in a state like Kentucky.

I had learned already how bitterly society and even family membership was divided between the Union and Southern sympathizers at Lexington, and I now noticed that not a single "rebel" name was signed to the paper. I asked Mrs. McAllister "why not?" "Oh, they would scorn to petition a Yankee general. Those whom we have known intimately from childhood, have been to school with, and communed with at the same altar, now turn their backs on us at the church door. And as far as your own officers, you must be aware how the Secession ladies treat them, sweeping their skirts aside as if to avoid contamination. No, General, you cannot expect them to sign. You must do this as a personal favor to me."

I told her how it grieved me to refuse, but that "I must have some official reason for granting such an official matter, and if the Secession ladies asked it, that would look at least like an implied promise of their better behavior in [the] future. At any rate, if you will bring me a petition similar to this one, but signed by the same number of Confederate sympathizers, I will consider it favorably!"

"Oh, you hard-hearted man," she exclaimed, "you know they will not do it."

"Well," said I, "that is their own affair, if they choose to refuse an act that would save the ladies of their own social circle from exile and wandering, they cannot blame either you or me," and with that forlorn hope she turned away, vainly striving to hide a tear.

A few days afterwards Mrs. McAllister did bring me a paper signed by ladies of the Secession faction. "Here it is at last," she said, "though I cannot get quite the same number of names, but this they think is humiliation enough for their proud spirits—and oh, if you refuse!" But I did not refuse. Putting both petitions together as the basis of action, I repealed the order then and there.

Now mark the result. A fortnight or so afterwards, the young officers of the 9th Corps gave a ball at the most fashionable hotel, inviting all the pretty girls in town, and their mothers, to attend. And to the surprise of everybody they all came, passed under our flag, which had been arched at the front hall door and over the stairway, and they danced with our handsomely dressed young officers to the stirring music of our best bands, and to the tunes of "Yankee Doodle" and "Dixie" alike. It must be needless for me to add that this social reunion restored peace and harmony throughout the city; and that had been so badly disrupted ever since the cruel war began in dear old Kentucky.

Much of the credit I received was also due to ex-Senator John J. Crittenden, who came over from Frankfort occasionally to see me. I had known one of his sons at West Point, and had seen the Senator himself at Washington. But what a change in his looks! The tall, erect form was bent, his face was seamed and haggard, "beneath a crown of sorrows," as Col. A. K. McClure[5] so happily expresses it. He had struggled for years in the Senate for the Union, and he was now a member of Congress, fighting for conservative treatment of the South against fiery odds. Both of his sons had gone to the war and were battling against the Union; and of all his great compatriots, from Henry Clay down, "who was there now to honor Logan?" Verily, the old man's case seemed pitiful, but he still cherished hopes for Kentucky, and thought that, with the success of our arms and the prudence of our rulers in the state, Kentucky might yet be kept in line.

But there was one man on whom he had set high hopes that had already disappointed him, my old West Point friend, Simon Bolivar Buckner, who after artfully posing for some time as a "neutral," finally declared for Secession. And with strange inconsistency, Buckner was now in the field fighting against his own state.

I must not forget to chronicle another "popular" event due to Mr. Crittenden's advice. In the midst of predatory raids going on in different parts of the state, it had become necessary to build a fortified supply depot called Camp Nelson, on the road to Cumberland Gap, but not very far from Lexington. And my predecessor had ordered out all the farm and plantation negroes to labor on the work, no matter whether their masters were Union or Confederate. This seemed a hardship on the Union slave owners of eastern

5. Col. Alexander K. McClure (1828–1909), journalist, attorney and politician from Pennsylvania. McClure served as a delegate to the 1860 Republican National Convention, where he helped nominate Lincoln for the presidency.

Kentucky, and these gentlemen petitioned me to repeal that order, so far as they were affected. The Senator [advised me] to do it, and I went even further in the published orders, limiting the laborers for Camp Nelson to those whose masters were Confederates, especially to those who were fighting against the Union. Both of these mitigations of my predecessor's orders appeared to myself so expedient that I think my friend, General Gillmore, would have granted them in time.

But the world moves on, and my "pacific policy" was but a drop in the bucket on the great military operations that we had to prosecute with inadequate force. The limits of the department embraced Indiana, Ohio, Michigan, Illinois, the most of Kentucky, and all of Eastern Tennessee that we might occupy. The troops were necessarily few at any one point, even with the addition of . . . two divisions of the 9th Corps, and out of these, guards had to be taken for the Louisville and Nashville [rail]road, which supplied Rosecrans's army, and for other railroads in the state. The lines occupied by the troops were constantly disturbed to meet frequent attacks of the enemy's cavalry and the guerrillas. Since the defeat of Pegram[6] by Gillmore, and during the month of April, nothing of any importance had occurred along the lines, although skirmishing with the enemy's cavalry was of daily occurrence, except the destruction of the enemy's supplies at Celina on [the] Cumberland River, in the zone of military operations conducted under General Hartsuff[7] and myself. . . .

I was in the midst of preparations for Sanders' raid into Tennessee, which I had proposed to Burnside,[8] and which the latter says in his report of March 25, 1865, "was one of the boldest raids in the war," and which indeed proved very successful, destroying railroads and bridges and a vast amount of public stores, capturing ten pieces of artillery and some four hundred prisoners, and spreading almost to the very gates of Knoxville. [While I

6. Brig. Gen. John Pegram, at the head of 1,500 horsemen, had made a move toward Danville, Kentucky, forty miles southwest of Lexington, on March 23, forcing the Union defenders there back to the Kentucky River. Gillmore set out to attack Pegram on March 28, driving the rebel cavalry fifty miles, finally bringing them to a stand near Somerset on March 30. Pegram made a desperate defense, but Union infantry finally broke his line, forcing the Confederates to withdraw back across the Cumberland River. Though he lost nearly five hundred men, Pegram did manage to retain over five hundred head of beef, the real object of the raid.

7. Maj. Gen. George L. Hartsuff (19th, USMA 1852), then commanding the Twenty-third Corps.

8. Col. William P. Sanders and raid into Tennessee, June 1863. Willcox misspelled the name as "Saunders" in his original manuscript. OBW first proposed this raid to Burnside in a letter of May 31, 1863; the original is in the OBW papers.

was] engaged preparing for Sanders' raid, and in connection with a similar movement I was making for sending General Carter[9] on a similar movement into Tennessee, I received an unexpected visit from Burnside, who brought me a most singular order. The 9th Corps was to report to Grant before Vicksburg, but General Parke was to go in command, and I was to be switched off into Indiana on a very singular secret mission.

It seemed that Governor Morton of that state had usurped, or at least assumed, the functions of military commander,[10] and this had produced a controversy with Secretary Stanton, which not only disturbed the relations of the two high officials, but interfered with the despatching of reinforcements to the armies of the Mississippi valley, which fracas I was expected to settle; and in order to do this I was to take command of the district and be clothed with authority to suspend the Governor, if necessary; in other words, to turn him out of office. It was a war of giants, for these were, *par excellence*, the stalwart members of the party in power; and poor I, an obscure brigadier general of the army, was called upon to end the matter at all hazards. Of course I objected, and most strenuously too, for I felt like a lamb led to the slaughter. And to be relieved from command of a corps just ordered into the field, to take command of a petty district in the peaceful North, was a humiliation in the eyes of the army, that nobody could understand.

Nevertheless, here was an order given Burnside to "select a general officer who knew something of law, and send him at once to Indianapolis." As a sop to Cerberus, Michigan was added to the district. I had no alternative but to go, so with my two aides-de-camp, Brackett and Richards, I took a train for the capitol of Indiana, with feelings that can be more easily imagined than described.[11]

9. Brig. Gen. Samuel P. Carter had recently been placed in command of the newly organized (but provisional) Fourth Division of the Ninth Corps.

10. Governor Oliver H. P. T. Morton (Republican) was the most powerful of the Union war governors. In early 1863 Morton found himself faced with a legislature dominated by Peace Democrats, threatening to limit his war powers. Unwilling to allow that to happen, Morton directed Republican legislators to remain at home, thus preventing a quorum in the state congress and effectively shutting down the Indiana government. Morton, however, immediately set up what proved to be a dictatorship, running the state in part with private donations, but chiefly with funds from the Federal government. In spite of his extreme devotion to the Union and his general support of the Lincoln administration, Morton nevertheless opposed several of its measures, including the draft.

11. OBW officially assumed command of the District of Indiana and Michigan on June 10, 1863. Besides Brackett and Richards, his staff at this time also consisted of Maj. G. Collins Lyon, 17th Michigan infantry (originally 2d Lt., 1st Michigan) acting assistant inspector general and provost marshal, and Lieutenants W. V. Richards and Charles A. McKnight, aides-de-camp.

If [worse] should come to the worst, how was I to know whether I would be sustained in suspending the governor of a sovereign state in peaceful relations with the Union? Perhaps I was to be made a cats-paw and then dropped. It was not until years afterwards that I learned from [Maj. Thomas M.] Vincent, who was Stanton's confidential secretary and assistant adjutant general in the war, that the great war secretary fully intended to uphold me and take the whole responsibility of an act which would have been an illegal transaction.

Fortunately for all parties, I learned how to steer my course soon after my arrival at Indianapolis. The state was infested with home rebels, Knights of the Golden Circle, or, as they now called themselves, Sons of Liberty, who were resisting the enrollment proclamation of the President, and the draft enrolling officer had been assaulted and some had been killed.

There were two orders of membership in the disloyal clubs, the larger one composed entirely of initiates for political purposes; the smaller of the higher number, or "Knights," was military in its structure and purpose. Its ramifications extended through most counties of the state. Their creed was the absolute right of secession and of unlimited slavery. Their object was to defeat "coercion" and to disrupt the Union, [urging] the separation of the northwestern states from the Union, and their formation into a separate government, i.e., into a part of the rebel Confederacy. They were in close communication with the disloyal elements in Kentucky, civil and military, where treason had worked in disguise as "armed neutrality," or had committed war openly, as we have seen. In cooperation with one or two of their movements, one or two outbreaks had happened in Indiana on the Ohio. The penalty [for breaking] any of the three or four oaths contained in their "ritual" was a "shameful death." The strength of the order was variously estimated at from seventy-five thousand to one hundred-twenty-five thousand. In some counties it embraced every member of the political party opposed to the war, and the disloyal elements, all of whom were better known as "Butternuts."

But this state of affairs was not disclosed to me on my arrival at Indianapolis, nor until some weeks afterwards. On paying my respect to Governor Morton, I found that large and bulky statesman rather taciturn—his look seemed interrogative—"What are you here for?" There had been some friction between himself and General Hascall,[12] my predecessor, which I suppose resulted in Hascall's relief by the War Department; and the governor now had a very convenient military tool in his place, viz., the

12. Brig. Gen. Milo S. Hascall (14th, USMA 1852).

mustering and disbursing officer, H. B. Carrington,[13] a colonel absent from his regiment that was fighting in the field, a man of little or no experience as a soldier, but just the man for a political mine expert. And this the situation seemed to demand. His spy system extended somewhat through the secret orders, and it was said that he himself had joined the treacherous "Order" to unravel its schemes. At any rate he claimed to have exploited it. But whether he had not exaggerated its numbers and its danger to the state, for the purpose of being useful, and to be kept out of the field where his regiment was fighting, was a mooted question.

At all events, he was "useful" to the governor, in as much as in the absence of the district commander, Carrington was the ranking officer present, and could throw military affairs into the governor's hands. And this I suppose had been one cause of the friction between Morton and Stanton, and this was "what I was here for." Another cause of complaint was that the governor was detaining Indiana soldiers till after the state elections, which would occur in the autumn, and this had been alleged by loyal Democrats.

Finding that citizens were being brought before courts-martial, or "military commissions," for which there was no law, as the state had not been proclaimed under martial law, I consulted Senator Hendricks,[14] [Col.] Rose, and other good Union Democrats, and determined to put my foot on the illegal practice; and accordingly issued a general order forbidding it in future, and directing that citizens charged with violent opposition to the enrollment act, or other violations of United States laws, should be brought before the United States Civil District Courts for trial. This removed one cause of discontent, and it was so obviously the correct thing that no remonstrance came from the governor, who certainly was too good a lawyer to object.

But in order to check the detention of United States troops in Indiana, I directed the recruiting officer to send me copies of all extensions of furlough that might reach his hands, as it was part of his business to account for and return absentees to their regiments. In compliance therewith, I soon received a furlough extended by Lars Noble, adjutant general, "by order of the Governor of Indiana." Here was the very evidence most needed, and there was nothing for me to do but address a note to General Noble, requesting a copy of any written authority he might have from the War De-

13. Brig. Gen. Henry B. Carrington.
14. Sen. Thomas A. Hendricks of Indiana, elected vice president under President Grover Cleveland in 1884.

partment allowing such a procedure. The general told my aide, who took the message, that he would look the matter up.

Soon after I heard the heavy tread of the governor himself in the hallway, and he came into my office appearing somewhat flustered, but cool and unusually polite, and assuring me that he was sure he had the necessary authority from Washington, received from either the War Department or the President himself, but that he could not lay hands upon it just then. To this there was but one reply: "I do not pretend to question what you say, sir, but in as much as I am personally responsible for every U.S. soldier who may be in the district, and as I am particularly ordered to expedite the transmission of troops to General Rosecrans in Tennessee, it is and must be obviously necessary that I should know the cause of any detention. Rosecrans is on the eve of a battle with Bragg."

I thought he felt as if I ought to take his word as sufficient authority, but he did not say so, and he bowed and left me, confident that he could find the missing document. But he never did find it, and there was no further trouble with the War Department, no more furloughs were "extended," and there were no more complaints that Indiana soldiers were held back from Rosecrans.

‹All troops possible to be spared were ordered into the field, leaving available only Col. [James] Biddle's 71st Indiana, a detachment of [the] 51st and 63d Indiana Infantry guarding the rebel prisoners at Camp Morton, [Capt. James H.] Myers' 23d Indiana Battery, and a squadron of cavalry under Capt. [John] Patton, 3d Indiana [Cavalry], all stationed at Indianapolis, except a company at Madison and two at Evansville.[15]

Disturbances [continued to occur] at various points where the enrollment was resisted, but [were] easily quelled by sending a small force of infantry or cavalry to the spot promptly, and making as little noise about it as possible.

15. OBW wrote three versions of his account of Morgan's Raid, and extracts have been taken from each of those accounts. First there is the account of the affair written specifically for his memoirs, but it appears quite incomplete. That material, written about 1901, forms the basis for this chapter. Second is his "Report of Operations of Indiana Troops," dated November 20, 1865, and addressed to Gen. W. H. Terrell, then adjutant general of Indiana; OBW referred to it as an "informal sketch" of the affair. Excerpts taken from this account appear within single angle brackets ‹ ›. Finally, there is his account entitled "Morgan's Raid Through Indiana and Ohio, 1863," written in 1891. It formed the basis for his article "The Capture," published by *Century Magazine* as part two of the series "A Romance of Morgan's Rough Riders," December 1891; the published version, however, differs in several respects from the original, which was consulted in completing this chapter. Excerpts from that version appear within double angle brackets ‹‹ ››.

Persons arrested were turned over to the civil authorities for indictment, and in a few weeks but little excitement or opposition to the laws was manifested. The most serious outbreaks occurred in Sullivan, Greene and Monroe Counties. About the 25th of June I sent Col. Biddle with his regiment, a section of artillery and [a] company of cavalry to Bloomington to operate in these counties, where government officers and loyal citizens had been killed, and where it was credibly reported that some fifteen hundred Butternuts were in arms and drilling.

Col. Biddle met with no organized resistance. He dispersed the misguided malcontents and arrested some twenty or thirty petty ringleaders. . . . [T]he more important chiefs, who, by their speeches and intrigues had stirred up the strife and bloodshed, never appeared with any of these armed followers, but invariably sneaked off, leaving them to their fate, without any intelligent head or directing mind. I examined most of the prisoners myself, and found them for the most part ignorant, and acting under a mistaken sense of party zeal. Some of them were discharged, and some turned over to the U.S. marshall. . . .

On June 19th I received a telegraphic dispatch that a guerilla band of rebels under Capt. [Thomas H.] Hines had crossed the Ohio at Leavenworth, and were moving into the interior, or perhaps up towards New Albany—this was probably the first actual raid made by the enemy into Indiana.

The [Indiana] Legion [i.e. state militia] in the vicinity were already collecting to attack this band of plunderers, whose numbers were estimated at two hundred. A party was sent out from New Albany. Capt. Patton took the cars immediately from Indianapolis with his cavalry, arrived early at Orleans, and started scouts out in advance—the farmers in the neighborhood all volunteering. Hines found himself soon baffled in his object, whatever it was, for the Indiana Legion—men and armed private citizens—were soon swarming around his path, and he recrossed the Ohio with considerable loss and infinite disgust. He killed the sheriff and a citizen of Crawford County, and lost seventy of his men with their horses, arms and plunder.

Troubles on the border and raids from Kentucky were whispered among the members of certain secret societies, who were thought to be in communication with Southern traitors, and Hines' raid, though it terminated ingloriously, gave some color to these rumors. About this time I issued an order against secret organizations, which alarmed the more moderate and opened the eyes of the ignorant to such an extent that for a time, at least, their meetings were suspended. . . .

We had information that some of the conspirators were importing arms into the state for their societies, or "circles," which were organized on a military plan. A few persons were arrested [and] charged with this offense. Stringent measures were adopted, restraining the purchase and sale of arms and ammunition, a few arrests were made, and some bonds required of guilty or suspected parties. But the authority of the district commander was quite limited for the want of clear instructions or positive policy from higher authorities.>

My "mission" was accomplished, and I was able to get away into Michigan for a few days, to visit Mrs. Willcox, unto whom a child had been born on July 4, day [after] the victory at Gettysburg. The infant was a female, and in commemoration of her birthday we gave her the name of Grace North. . . .

<On the Fourth of July I received a telegram from Gen. Burnside to send the 71st Indiana Infantry, Col. Biddle, with all my available artillery and cavalry to Kentucky, to report to Gen. [Jeremiah T.] Boyle. The rebel Gen. John Morgan was marching through that state towards the Ohio, with four thousand cavalry. . . .[16]> On the Fourth of July, the last day of all others for treason to do its worst, Morgan, starting out on his great raid, appeared at the head of a division and demanded, in writing, the surrender of the Green River bridge stockade, and of its garrison, which consisted of a single regiment, the 25th Michigan Infantry, under Col. Orlando H. Moore. Most of the defense took place, not behind the stockade, but in the woods at a ford near by. Col. Moore says in his report:

The battle raged for three and a half hours, when the enemy retreated, with a loss of over 50 killed and 200 wounded. . . .

The conflict was fierce and bloody. At times the enemy occupied one side of the fallen timber, while my men held the other, in almost a hand-to-hand fight. The enemy's force consisted of the greater part of Morgan's division. My force was a fraction of my regiment, consisting of 200 men, who fought gallantly. I cannot say too much in their praise.

Our loss was 6 killed and 23 wounded.

16. General Boyle then commanded the District of Kentucky at Louisville; Morgan, leading two cavalry brigades under Col. Basil Duke and Col. Adam Johnson, crossed the Ohio into Indiana at Brandenburg, Kentucky on July 8, 1863. He had no more than 2,500 troopers, but one dispatch to OBW reported that Morgan's force was "said to be six thousand (6000) strong." Telegram from Capt. Budd to Willcox, July 10, 1863, OBW papers.

After the battle, I received, under a flag of truce, a dispatch asking permission to bury their dead, which request I granted, proposing to deliver them in front of our lines.

The detachment of 40 men under command of Lieut. M. A. Hogan, Eighth Michigan Infantry, held the river at the ford near the bridge, and repulsed a cavalry charge, made by the enemy, in a very creditable and gallant manner.[17]

Truly this was "a very pretty fight." It taught John Morgan a lesson—a lesson which, however, he learned more fully afterwards, in his gallant raid through Indiana and Ohio, as we shall see in due time.

<On the morning of the 5th, Morgan captured the Union troops at Lebanon. Part of the Indiana Legion were ordered to Louisville, and Col. [Charles V.] Deland's 1st Michigan Sharpshooters were ordered down to Indiana from Detroit, together with the 12th Michigan Battery.

On the 6th Gen. Boyle reported cannon firing heard at Louisville. On the 8th he reported Morgan as having crossed the Ohio at Brandenburg with two steamers which he captured. He was now known to be on the soil of Indiana.>

<<When we heard at Indianapolis that Gen. Morgan . . . had gotten through Kentucky and crossed the Ohio, the city was panic stricken. The state had been literally depleted of my troops to assist Kentucky and everybody knew it. The very worst was apprehended: that railways would be cut up, messengers and freighters robbed, bridges and depots burned, our arsenal pillaged, 2,000 prisoners at Camp Morton liberated and turned loose upon the community, Jeffersonville, with all its government stores, and possibly Indianapolis itself destroyed.

Nor was this all. It had been reported and partly believed that the state was undermined with rebel sympathizers. The coming of Morgan had been looked for, and his progress through Kentucky watched with breathless anxiety. It was predicted that hundreds, perhaps thousands of Knights of the Golden Circle and Sons of Liberty would flock to his standard and endeavor to carry the state over to the Confederacy, or to start an independent Confederacy with Missouri, the northwest and Canada. Such stories had been spread for party purposes by the ultras.

17. "Report of Col. Orlando H. Moore, Twenty-fifth Michigan Infantry (District of Kentucky), of engagement at Green River Bridge, Ky.," *OR*, vol. 23, pt. 1, pp. 645–46. Original was paraphrased somewhat by OBW; the extract is quoted precisely here.

There may have been some political object in this extraordinary advance across the Ohio, known now to have been forbidden by Bragg; and it is believed to this day that Morgan had some secret object based upon secret information. He had already run great risks, first in crossing the Cumberland in the face of a force equal to his own, and now he had left a much larger force behind him, and he probably had fair reason to believe that his ranks would at least be largely recruited in the southern counties of Indiana. But whether he had come to stay or only come to steal, here he was, with the country all open before him.

Governor Morton was one of the four great war governors—perhaps the greatest—and he went to work with all his tremendous energy and indomitable will, in the face of the fiercest opposition that had been encountered in any northern state, amounting, just before, almost to open rebellion. He had been accused of usurping war powers of the state and of encroaching upon those of the U.S. Nevertheless, he did not hesitate now.>> Our city papers of [July 8th] announced that Governor Morton had issued a call for one hundred thousand volunteers to repel the invaders, which forces he intended to command himself as commander-in-chief of the militia.

This action seemed all the more plausible as the number of United States troops in the district was indeed insignificant, but I could not understand why myself, as the district commander, had not been . . . consulted, and as the messages were coming in thick and fast, I sent an aide-de-camp to the governor, requesting him to meet me at the telegraph office. This invitation the new commander-in-chief declined to do, but we soon met by chance in the hall of the building.

After bidding each other good morning, with rather an independent air on his side, I said that the reason why I had wished to see him was to learn from himself at which points he proposed to concentrate his regiments, in order that I might know where and how to cooperate with what few United States troops were under my command, and there were precious few of these indeed!

His reply, after some hesitation, was, "Well, general, I had not thought of that"; and after still more hesitation, "Where would you post them if you were in my place?" To this I said: "If there is a map of the state handy, sir, I will show you with great pleasure." Thereupon he led the way into a room on the hall, where we found a large map hanging. Then I gave him my views, which were simple enough, ignoring the likelihood of a revolt in our southern counties, which some people would have us believe was the object of the raid. I pointed out the railway lines, and showed the governor at what points I thought Morgan would be most likely to cut them in order to prevent our sending reinforcements to Rosecrans (who, by the way, was on the eve of a battle with Bragg)[18] and how the lines could be cut most directly, by the raiders marching straight along the road from Jeffersonville towards Indianapolis. Therefore that the first points for concentration of Indiana troops would be at the intersection of that line with the lines running east and west. And I added further, that in my own opinion the raid had been planned, and perhaps by Bragg himself, for the very object of crippling Rosecrans in this manner.

"Therefore, sir, if you can place a considerable body of men at Seymour, where the railway from Jeffersonville intersects the Ohio and Mississippi Railway, that depot would be safe, and Morgan would probably sheer off, as he could not afford to stop to fight."

"Why not?"

"Because General Hobson[19] is coming upon his rear with a force about equal to his own." Then, feeling very much as I used to feel at West Point when making a "demonstration" before Professor Church, I turned to the governor for his approbation.

It seems I was mistaken in the supposition that the raid had been planned according to concert with General Bragg. On the contrary, Bragg "expressly stipulated in orders that it [Morgan's raid] should not extend beyond the Ohio River." The vim and dash of Morgan "impelled him frequently to over-ride the orders of his superior. He liked to make his own and conduct independent expeditions, which was one secret of his fame and the charm by which he led his young and reckless followers." So that I was mistaken in part of my explanation. But my advice concerning the best way to meet the raid was so manifestly correct that the governor adopted it on the spot and requested me to carry it out myself, i.e., as fast as he could raise the troops.

Fortunately, the latter was an easy matter. Various border alarms—particularly the recent "Hines's Raid"—and various discoveries of plots for uprisings by the Sons of Liberty and Butternuts—had led to rapid concen-

18. On June 23, Rosecrans began moving southward from Murfreesboro, Tennessee, toward Bragg's army at Tullahoma. Rosecrans would finally succeed in turning Bragg's position and forcing the Confederates back to the Tennessee River. The campaign ended in early July with little fighting, but it was a precursor to the Battle of Chickamauga, fought the following September.

19. Gen. Hobson, commanding the Second Brigade, Third Division, Twenty-third Corps, aided by Gen. James M. Shackleford, commanding the First Brigade, Second Division, Twenty-third Corps, and Col. Frank Wolford, led a force of some four thousand Union cavalry and mounted infantry in direct pursuit of Morgan's raiders.

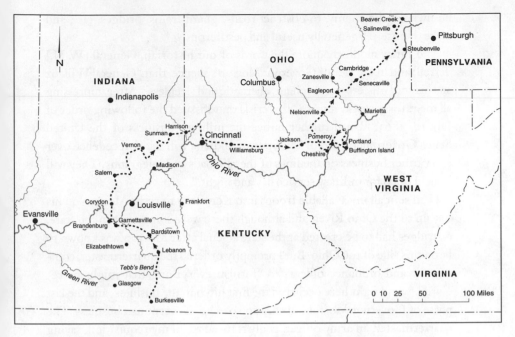

Morgan's Raid, July 1863.

tration of minutemen and the Indiana Legion, and now regiment after regiment was quickly raised and distributed at suitable points. Some experienced officers, such as Generals Lew Wallace,[20] [James] Hughes, and Milo S. Hascall came forward to assist.

«The three great junctions of the Ohio and Mississippi Railway—over which troops and supplies were shipped from all points to Rosecrans, viz., Mitchell, Somerset and Vernon, were first in my thoughts to be made secure; for surely Morgan must have some military objectives, and these were the most likely. The westerly junction was Mitchell. This was quickly occupied and guarded by Gen. Hughes, with Legion men, reinforced by the new organizations rising in that quarter. Seymour was the most central, and lay directly on the roads from Cincinnati and Indianapolis to Louisville, and to Seymour a brigade was assembled from the center of the state, with Gen. John Love,[21] an old army officer, to command, and [with instructions] to have an eye to Vernon likewise. To the latter point Burnside ordered a battery from Cincinnati; and what few troops I had in Michigan, though half organized, came down to Vernon and to Gen. Love. Besides these thus rendezvoused, the people of the southern counties were called upon to

20. Maj. Gen. Lew Wallace, future governor of New Mexico and author of *Ben Hur* (1880).
21. Gen. John Love (14th, USMA 1841).

bushwhack the enemy, to obstruct roads, guard trains, bridges, etc., and make themselves generally useful and pestiferous.»

And I may modestly quote the words of our historian, General [W. H.] Terrell, and in the face of Governor Morton's silence, that "General Willcox and his staff officers were vigilant, energetic and sleepless." After impressing all the railway stock, it was at this crisis that I issued the following order of July 19, 1863: "Until further notice the military business of the United States Government and of the State of Indiana will take precedence over every other business on the lines of the railroads and telegraphs. They will be held open for military service day and night."

I had sent all my available troops into Kentucky to resist Morgan on his way up to the Ohio River, and although there were some arms in the state, cartridges had to be created at the state arsenal after Morgan was known to be on this side of the Ohio. But I promptly ordered the quartermaster, commissary and ordnance officers to "furnish everything that might be required." And right here occurred the first hitch in the business, and the last phase of Governor Morton's absorption of U. S. Government business. The quartermaster, an army officer, cooly refused to fill my requisition, saying that he had been ordered to report to the governor of the state. I think I gave him but fifteen minutes to decide whether he would obey my orders or go in arrest. That red tape official soon yielded.

«Our people first came in contact with the enemy opposite Brandenburg, where he crossed. This point was guarded by a detachment of the Legion and one field piece, and as the fog lifted from the river just before noon on July 8th, they opened fire on the two steamers [of troops] that were crossing.

This staggered as well as surprised the rebels but for a moment, however, when Morgan answered with his Parrott guns from the Kentucky shore, and scattered the obstruction, the men abandoning their guns, falling back and giving the alarm. The next interruption came from the [Union] gunboat *Elk*, Lt. Fitch commanding, that hove in sight just after the two steamers had landed their loads of Morgan's men, and opened with her three guns on both shore and steamer and threatened to become, as Basil Duke said she might have been, "mistress of the situation": for "a single, well-aimed shot would have sent either of the steamers to the bottom," the crossing cut in twain, and further proceedings at least delayed until Hobson or [Brig. Gen. Henry M.] Judah or both got up.[22]

22. The gunboat that first encountered Morgan was not the *Elk* but the *Springfield*, a "tinclad"; Judah, commanding the Third Division, Twenty-third Corps, was in overall command of

For the first time in his life, Morgan is said to have lost his presence of mind, and ruin stared him in the face. But after an hour's contest, chiefly with the Parrott guns and without apparent injury, the gunboat drew out and steamed up the river. She reappeared about five o'clock with a consort, exchanged a few shots with the Parrotts, hovered in sight till dark, and again disappeared. Morgan got everything across during the night, and burning his steamers behind him, proceeded inland. Hobson got up next morning. He had halted for the night within ten miles, and it now took him 24 hours to cross. Thus Morgan had a start of 24 hours from the river.>>

Morgan crossed at Brandenberg, fortunately neglecting New Albany and Jeffersonville, where there were stored about $4,000,000 worth of government property. We surmised that his object was to burn the bridges and break up the Ohio and Mississippi Railway. Anyway, there were some fears that the Butternuts, who had already resisted the enrollment and killed a number of officials, would rise. But perhaps the enthusiastic and overwhelming display of our loyal militia dispelled that fear. And yet, alas, we had little or no cavalry except that brought by General Hobson, who had pursued the great raider through Kentucky, and was now following him up under the disadvantage that Morgan was seizing all the fresh horses and leaving his broken down stock for Hobson's remounts—literally, "Hobson's choice."

<<Our militia made the first stand at Corydon Junction, where the road runs between two abrupt hills, across which Col. Jordan threw up some light entrenchments. Morgan's advance attempted to ride over these "rail piles" rough shod, but . . . some 20 troopers were unhorsed. They brought up their reserve and artillery, flanked, and finally surrounded Col. Jordan, who, after an hour's resolute resistance, surrendered.

This gave the raiders the town and the citizens the first taste of Morgan's style. The town was given up to plunder, the ladies bantered, threatened and levied on for meals for the whole command; the most respectable gentlemen were marched at the head of columns with pistols at their head, all in the most chivalrous manner, as if Beauty and Booty were inscribed upon Morgan's banners. This disgusted somewhat the numerous class of Southern sympathizers, and gained Morgan no recruits.

Throwing out columns in various directions, Morgan pushed for Mitchell, where no doubt he expected to cut the Ohio and Mississippi Railroad,

---

the pursuit for Morgan, but his troops were trapped by flood waters behind the Green River; the initial pursuit was actually led by General Hobson, aided by Gen. James M. Shackleford and Col. Frank Wolford. The quotation of Basil Duke here is paraphrased by OBW from Duke's article entitled "The Raid," part one of the series "A Romance of Morgan's Rough Riders," *Century Magazine*, December 1891.

got as far as Salem in that direction, captured or dispersed a few squad of badly armed minutemen, who were guarding depots and bridges, which he burned, and doubtless, hearing from his scouts, sent out in citizens' clothes, of Hughes' force collected at Mitchell, he discretely turned off. . . .>>

<Moving square to the right, he crossed the Louisville and Indianapolis Railroad at Vienna and rode into Lexington that night. His plans were already foiled, and the only question with him now was how to get back into Dixie. The most available point for him to strike the Ohio was Madison, where he might hope to burn the city and cross the river with an air of triumph. But Col. [B. F.] Mullen was at Madison with some two thousand muskets, and Morgan was apprised of this fact by the appearance of a body of Mullen's mounted scouts, who came up the Madison road and dashed through Lexington just before break of day on the 11th, and found Morgan's men asleep in the court house square.

Morgan again changed his course and turned north towards Vernon, where the Indianapolis and Madison Railroad crosses the Ohio and Mississippi Railroad, and where there is a considerable bridge, which it was his object to destroy. But as soon as Gen. Love, at Seymour, became satisfied that Morgan was moving eastward, he dispatched Colonel [Hugh T.] Williams' and [J. H.] Burkham's regiments, with four pieces of artillery, to Vernon by rail. I telegraphed Burkham to hold the place at all hazards, and I also ordered Gen. Love to the threatened point with the balance of his command. Leaving Col. Burkham at North Vernon, Col. Williams took his own regiment, one company of Burkham's, and two pieces of artillery to old Vernon, and posted his small force so as to defend the bridge and the town.>

<<Here Morgan next turned up, planted his Parrotts, and demanded surrender. He was . . . defied until Love's arrival with the rest of his militia, and then he swept off in a hurry from Vernon, followed by our men, who captured his pickets, rear guard, etc.—but having no cavalry they were soon out-marched.

Morgan seized all the horses and left none for the militia or for Hobson. This gave him great advantages, which enabled him always to gain on his pursuers, and he would have left Hobson far out of sight but for the Home Guard, who obstructed the roads and bushwhacked his men from every hedge, hill, or tree, where it could be done. The sudden appearance of the militia in ranks or behind breastworks annoyed and delayed him. But the trouble with all our people was that we could not attack him in sufficient organized numbers—which his feelers enabled him always to avoid.

After his leaving Vernon, we felt safe at Indianapolis. "Defensive sites" were abandoned, and the banks brought back their deposits, which they had expressed off to Chicago and the north. Some fears, or hopes, were now entertained for Madison, towards which Morgan next bent his way. Fears for the safety of that city, and hopes that we might, with the help of Judah's troops and the gun boats now on the way up the river, put an end to the raid. From Indianapolis we started Gen. Lew Wallace with a good brigade of minutemen, and with high hopes that either at Madison or Lawrenceburg, Wallace might "capture them." The people ahead were telegraphed for cooperation. But after going down that line as far as Dupont, Morgan turned northeast for Versailles, where we next heard of him threatening the Cincinnati and Indianapolis Railway.

This was a nice bit of work. He baffled all our calculations and did some damage on both the Ohio and Mississippi and Cincinnati [rail]roads, sending off flying columns in a dozen directions at a time for this purpose, and to throw Hobson and company off of the scent. Some of these columns looked like travelling circuses, adorned with useless plunder and an excess of clowns.>>

‹There was every variety and contradiction of report with regard to Morgan's movements and intentions. But he himself was utterly confounded. Hobson was pressing on his rear. Our Indiana levies, as if springing from the soil, headed him off when he turned north. Southwardly, the towns on the Ohio—Madison, Aurora and Lawrenceburg—were guarded, and gunboats and steamers armed with artillery and infantry patrolled the river. Nothing in fact prevented his [capture] in Indiana but our lack of cavalry—we had but two hundred in the field and a company organizing at Indianapolis.›

Thus [the enemy] went through Pierceville and Milan to Harrison, on White[water] River, and on the Ohio line. Here Hobson's advance came upon them, but unfortunately it paused to plant artillery, instead of dashing across the bridge and encountering the robbers until the main body should arrive. This lost us the bridge, which was burned before our eyes, and many hours' delay marching round by the ford.

Their next demonstration was towards Hamilton [Ohio]. Here there was a fine railway bridge over the Big Miami. Hobson followed in such close pursuit through New Baltimore, Glendale and Miamisville, that the raiders did little damage. Their attempt to burn the bridge at Miamisville was repulsed by the Home Guard. My troops were dispatched from Indianapolis to head them off at Hamilton....>>

The division for this purpose was given to General Carrington, with orders to get away within an hour. At the expiration of the hour he had not started, although his men and provisions were aboard the train and everything was waiting. I soon discovered the reason for this extraordinary delay.

The conductor refused to take the train with a "drunken officer" in charge! It seems that the general had mounted a high horse in full field outfit, haversack, a big field glass and an overcoat, and started for the depot; but that on his way he stopped to accept the congratulations of his friends and a parting cup, and had taken a drop too much. Fortunately, the lately displaced General Hascall, happening to be at my hotel headquarters, offered to go in Carrington's place, and he started the whole outfit in about ten minutes . . . «"just in time to be too late." He proceeded through Hamilton, Ohio, as far as Loveland. But Morgan had sent only a detachment towards Hamilton to divert attention from Cincinnati, towards which he made a rapid march with his whole united force.

Governor [David] Tod of Ohio had already called out the militia and proclaimed martial law. He raised men enough, but left Burnside to organize and arm them; consequently things went slower. But Morgan found the great city guarded and passed through the very suburbs by a night march around it, unmolested. He crossed the Little Miami Railway at daylight, and came within sight of Camp Dennison, where [Lt.] Col. [George W.] Neff half armed his convalescents, threw out his pickets, dug rifle pits, and threw up entrenchments. His fiery old veterans saved a railway bridge and actually captured a lieutenant and other rebels before they sheered off and went some ten miles northward to Williamsburg. From that point they seemed to be steering for the great bend of the Ohio at Pomeroy.

In the vicinity of Cincinnati, Col. W. P. Sanders, who [earlier] made the splendid raid in East Tennessee, came up from Kentucky with two troops of Michigan cavalry and joined Hobson in pursuit, and these were about the only fresh horses in the chase. Sanders had come up by steamer and, landing at Cincinnati, had been thrown out from there, it was hoped, ahead of Morgan, who was too quick for him. They met later on.

Under the good management of Col. [August V.] Kautz,[23] in advance with his brigade and Sanders', the men now marched more steadily, and gained ground. Kautz had observed how the other brigade commanders had lost distance and blown their horses by following false leads, halting and closing up rapidly at the frequent reports of "enemy in front," stopping to plant artillery, etc. Marching in his own way at a steady walk, his brigade forming the rear guard, he had arrived at Batavia two hours before the main body that had been "cavorting round the country" all day—"misled by two citizen guides"—probably Morgan's own men.

23. Col. August V. Kautz (35th, USMA 1852) led the First Cavalry Brigade, Third Division, Twenty-third Corps.

Not stopping to draw the rations sent out for him from Cincinnati, Hobson urged his jaded horses through Brown, Adams and Pike counties, and under the lead of Kautz, reached Jasper on the Scioto at midnight. Morgan had passed through Jasper at sundown. This was on the 16th. The next day [Hobson passed] through Jackson at noon, where the ladies stood ready to lunch the whole command. [On the] Eighteenth, Hobson, at Rutland, learned that Morgan had been turned off by the militia at Pomeroy, and had taken the Chester road for Portland and the fords of the Ohio. The chase became animated. Our troopers made a march of 50 miles that day, and still had 25 miles to reach Chester. They reached Chester without a halt. Eleven at night, and still 15 miles to reach the ford. On, on, till dawn of the 19th, and they struck the enemy's pickets.

Two miles out from Portland, Morgan was brought to bay—and not by Hobson alone. First [came] the militia. "Our experience in Ohio," says Duke, "was very similar to that in Indiana. Small fights with the *militia* were of hourly occurrence. They hung about the column, incessantly assaulting it; keeping up a continuous fusillade, the crack of their rifles sounded in our ears without intermission, and the list of killed and wounded ever constantly swelling. We captured hundreds daily, but could only break their guns and turn them loose again. They finally resorted to one capital means of annoyance, by felling trees and barricading the roads."[24]

Then came Judah. His division had . . . pushed up the river in steamers, parallel with Morgan's course, landing reconnaissances at Madison, Lawrenceburg, Cincinnati, Maysville and finally, with only mounted men at Portsmouth, whence he marched with the latter up the Scioto valley, then eastward between Morgan and the Ohio. Lt. John O'Neil, afterwards of Fenian fame, with a troop of Indiana cavalry, kept up the touch on Morgan's right flank by a running fight, stinging it at every vulnerable point, and reporting Morgan's course [to Judah] in the neck-and-neck race. Aided by the local militia, O'Neil now dashed ahead, and now fearlessly skirmished with the enemy's flankers from every coign of advantage. From Pomeroy Judah communicated intelligence with Hobson, and like Hobson, travelled all night. He reached the last descent to the river bottoms near Buffington Bar, and near the historical Blennerhasset's Island, early on the morning of the 19th.

Finally, the Ohio River was up. It had risen unexpectedly. But here Morgan must cross, if at all. It could not be forded by night, when he got here.

24. The editor has not been able to identify the source from which OBW drew this quote of Basil Duke.

He tried the ford at Blennerhasset. Failing in this, his men collected flat boats and set to work caulking them, meantime sending a party to Buffington Bar, where they found a small earthwork and its guard[25]—and these things delayed them until morning . . . their flankers and rear guard strung out on every road.

Judah attempted a reconnaissance in the fog with a mounted detachment and a field piece down a lane, where he was surprised and stampeded and lost his gun by a volley from the enemy, who were equally surprised, but masters of the situation for a moment, and who killed and captured some officers and men. But the check was brief. The 5th Indiana [cavalry] deployed and moved forward, supported by the 14th Illinois, while the 11th Kentucky swung round on the right of the Indiana regiment.

Meantime, the sun rose, and now the advancing lines saw O'Neil dashing over ditches and fences towards the river, saw him driving the rebel guard from Buffington, pell mell. This inspired Judah's skirmish line that now charged with its supports, drove the enemy in his front back on the river, recaptured the lost gun and took two others and some prisoners. On the skirmish line fell Maj. Daniel McCook, father of the famous fighting family, who pushed himself in, against remonstrances, to find the slayer of his son, [Gen. Robert L. McCook, whose killer] was reported to be with Morgan.[26]

Morgan's troops, on Judah's side, were now driven back on the main body. A battery was planted and Morgan crowded to a point where the river road ran by a steep, high bluff, in the direction of Hobson, and at 9:30, Hobson's guns were heard pounding on the Confederate rear, beyond the hills.

Kautz came first, with his advance of two hundred men, against perhaps a thousand. He was asked by an officer if he meant to attack. "Certainly," he said, "that's what we've come for." And fortune favors the brave, for just as he deployed along the edge of some timber on a ridge in front, Sanders arrived, and opened with two guns, our men crowding in now on all sides. The whole Michigan cavalry now charged with the Ohio cavalry, or fought on foot, the Michigan men, with their Spencer repeating rifles doing especial havoc and magnifying their apparent number, until most of Morgan's force was crowded into a "cat hole." Other parts dissolved like mist before the sun. Their ammunition was nearly exhausted. The enemy thought

25. Unbeknownst to Morgan, the volunteers manning this earthwork had abandoned it upon his approach, dumping their cannon into the river.

26. Brig. Gen. Robert L. McCook had been killed August 6, 1862, in an attack by a party of Confederate guerrillas while he was riding ill in an ambulance near Decherd, Tennessee.

they saw eight or ten thousand infantry around them, where never an infantryman was, for Judah had left his infantry behind him, and Hobson never had any.

They began to surrender in large numbers. Sanders' cavalry alone had captured 700 when Morgan, at the head of a few horsemen, dashed through the narrow pass by the bluff before mentioned, reached Blennerhasset Bar, and crossed to the Virginia side. He had scarcely reached the shore before the *Elk* gun boat, or its apparition, as it might have seemed to Morgan, rounded the bend, opened fire on the fords, and stopped all further crossing. Thus left alone, Morgan recrossed and made a gallant effort to reorganize what was left of his late command. . . . His brother Dick, Gen. Duke, his chief support (Duke was called "Morgan's brains") and most of his officers were captured, killed or wounded.[27]

Yet, with a considerable force, he succeeded in making an escape, and started like a fox for cover, into the interior. Passing around the advanced columns of his enemy, he suddenly came upon the end of Shackelford's column, under Wolford, whom he at once attacked with his usual audacity. Shackelford reversed his column, selected his best horses, and gave pursuit. He overtook the enemy at Backum Church, where Wolford's Kentucky fellows rushed upon Morgan's men with drawn sabers and yells, and chased them until next afternoon, when they were found collected on a high bluff, and where some hundred surrendered; but Morgan again escaped, and with over 500 horsemen, who yet gave our fellows a long chase by the dirt road and by rail.

Continuing north through several counties, he veered northeast, toward the Pennsylvania line, showing his teeth, burning car loads of freight, buildings and bridges by the way . . . though hotly hounded by Shackelford and flanked and headed off by troops in cars.

Among the latter was Maj. [W. B.] Way, 9th Michigan, with a battalion of his regiment. Way had left the cars at Mingo and marched over near to Steubenville, where he began a skirmish which lasted over 25 miles, towards Salineville, away up in Columbiana County. Here he brought Morgan to bay. The latter still fought desperately, losing over 70 of his men killed or wounded, and slipped away. Another detachment had come up by rail, under

27. The gunboat was not the *Elk* but the *Moose;* Colonel Duke, along with Col. Richard C. Morgan (the general's brother) and most of Morgan's staff, had surrendered with some seven hundred men. Col. Adam Johnson had managed to cross the Ohio with about three hundred men and managed to escape, leaving Morgan himself with roughly seven hundred men.

Maj. [George W.] Rue, 9th Kentucky Cavalry, joined Shackelford at Hammondsville, and took the advance with 300 men.

At Salineville he found Morgan, pursued by Maj. Way, pushing for Smith's Ford on the Ohio. Breaking into trot and gallop, he outmarched and intercepted the fugitives at the cross-roads near Beaver Creek, gained the enemy's front and flank, when a flag of truce was raised and Morgan coolly demanded his surrender! Rue's threat to open fire brought Morgan to terms, when another issue was raised. It was now claimed that Morgan had already surrendered, viz., to a militia officer, and been by him paroled. This "officer" turned out to be a prisoner of Morgan's, Capt. [James] Burbick, of the Home Guard. It seems that Morgan himself did not claim the parole that his negotiations claimed, but simply said to Rue that he had already surrendered. The latter took in Morgan with 364 officers and men and 400 horses, and held them . . . till Gen. Shackelford came up, who shipped them off to Camp Chase as prisoners of war.≫

And this ended one of the longest and most remarkable raids and successful . . . pursuits of the war, all through Kentucky and Indiana and across into central Ohio. ≪It had no bad effect upon the movements, communications or plans of either Rosecrans or Burnside, as I learn from Gen. Rosecrans himself, other than to delay Burnside's march into East Tennessee. This delay, during which his raw cavalry had become veteranized in pursuing Morgan and sluggish organizations were completed in Michigan, Ohio and Indiana in consequence of the scare, actually benefitted Burnside, and rendered his success more certain in East Tennessee. But I doubt his being delayed long by the raid. On the 17th of June he telegraphed Halleck that he was "organizing," and at that time the 9th Corps, his main reliance, had not returned from Mississippi.

On the other hand, Bragg lost a fine large division of cavalry, wantonly wasted and uselessly destroyed, that, if added to Buckner's force—already equal to Burnside's in East Tennessee—might have defeated Burnside; or that, if thrown across Rosecrans' flanks or along his lines of supply and communication, or, used in reconnaissance on the Tennessee River, might have baffled Rosecrans' plans altogether. As it was, he was able to deceive Bragg by counterfeit movements that could easily have been detected by Morgan. But those whom the gods would destroy they first make mad.≫

Morgan was straightway put in the penitentiary at Columbus, from which he made an almost miraculous escape. . . .[28] His pitiful gang scarce

28. Morgan escaped with several of his officers on November 27, 1863, only to be killed near Greeneville, Tennessee, on September 3, 1864.

knew what fate might await them, but Uncle Sam was just, if not magnanimous, and their restraint, though strict, was not unduly severe either at Columbus or at Camp Morton, Indianapolis, whither they were soon conveyed, unshackled and unshorn.

They were a wild-looking set of fellows when they arrived at my bailiwick, but most of them belonged to good families in Kentucky, and I was soon besieged by letters and visitors from their friends, beseeching me to "be merciful," and to admit the bearers into the camp to see the boys and relieve their dire necessities. I did manage to secure the admission of one very nice party of ladies and gentlemen from Lexington and Louisville, who had brought underwear and other necessary articles, and doubtless some love tokens from sweethearts and wives.

These excellent people had been so successful in their mission, that on their return to the hotel they were in very gay spirits, and they gathered after dinner in the parlor where they not only manifested their gushing thanks to the "General," but invited him to hear some music and join their entertainment—which latter token was, of course, declined. One very pretty lady who presided at the piano had a very rich and melodious voice, and as I paced the hall listening to the singing and enjoying an occasional glimpse of the jollity going on within, my attention was suddenly arrested by a dreadful scream within, and on stepping to the door, what should I see in the general confusion, but the fair singer herself, in a faint, with a little infant clasped to her unconscious body, while a number of agitated voices were calling for a doctor.

It seems that the dear little infant was the lady's own child, had sprang from an upper window in its glee, and fallen on the balcony opposite the piano, and now lay equally unconscious with its mother, on her breast. A physician was soon found and restored the lady's senses after a succession of fainting spells, but the little one's white wings had flown to a better land.

‹There was little or nothing left for me to do in Indiana. The opposition to the conscription was completely quelled, and the citizens all enrolled. And all disloyal or opposing elements were fused in the immense heat of patriotic excitement caused by the late invasion. Gen. Burnside was ordered in August to take the field in Tennessee; it was my wish to join my old division of the 9th Corps, and so I expressed myself to the adjutant general of the department. But I received no orders on the subject until the 11th of September, when there came a telegram from Washington for me to report to Gen. Burnside at Knoxville, and the District of Indiana and Michigan was broken up.

Head Quarters District of Central Kentucky
Lexington, Ky.
April 15/'63
My dearest Marie,

Yours of 9th is received. It is sweeter than the breath of the south wind to hear from you. Night before last I had the honor of a serenade by a band of Lexington—& enclose you an extract from the "Lexington Observer & Reporter," published to-day. Mrs. McNair writes the ladies arrived safely at Washington.[29] I feel relieved. This morning I received a beautiful bouquet from some ladies at the hotel.

[I] work hard as ever, stampedes from the front every night regularly. My relaxations are but snatches. The horses are in splendid order. Roebuck never looked so well. I rode him through town this evening, out as far as Ashland.[30] Hope Father will come. Love to all the children & a kiss to each.

Thine,
O. B. W.

Lexington, Ky.
April 22/'63
My dearest Molly,

Just received your sweet little note of the 20th. Mr. Sayre, a humorous & rich old banker here, has just come in & says to tell Father to come right to his house. He has no small fry, only one or two ladies in his house, a big one, & he will really take it as a compliment. He hobbles in here every day. I hope Father will not put off coming *any longer*.

You seem to have had a house full. Don't exert yourself too much. . . . Would like very much to have seen Lulu in her spring bonnet & dress. I didn't like the turn-up thing she wore. Kiss my lovely Ali for me first thing every morning. Glad Father paid church notes & glad they were no more. Parsons wrote me my major general business was defeated on account of Corcoran, & that Howard was provoked about it. He thinks it will still come through Kellogg.

Thine always,
O.B.W.

29. OBW's mother, together with Mrs. Farnsworth, had recently left on visits to Washington and New York.

30. Ashland was the home of OBW's idol, the late Senator Henry Clay.

Lexington, Ky.

April 29/'63

My darling Marie,

We have had two disagreeable rainy days, causing the grass & buds to start forth, but interfering with military operations. We had an expedition across the Cumberland in contemplation under Gen. Carter. But the rise in the water prevented infantry & artillery [from] crossing & all we could do was to swim some 300 cavalry over, which made a dashing reconnaissance almost as far as Monticello.

[Same letter continued at later date.]

I am sure you will think, my pet, that I neglect you . . . but I have had my hands full. The troops of the 9th Corps are in motion again & I have not known which way to turn. Every moment interrupted by the citizens. I expect to leave Lexington in a few days, but where I cannot tell. The movement began yesterday is countermanded to-morrow for one in some other direction. I stole an hour for church this morning. It was thinly attended. The probability of my leaving Lexington seems really to cause some feeling. The people seem to have taken a fancy to my ways of doing things. Your husband has the credit of being called a gentleman by both Unionists & rebels. I think I could do much good in three months, but these frequent changes keep the people uneasy & wavering in their confidence. Kiss each little darling for me. I am delighted to hear your health is so good. Write me more often, even if the letters are short. Love to Father & Mother.

Thine,

O.B.W.

Lexington, Ky.

May 3/'63

My darling,

Do not fret yourself if you are not able to write so often as you used to when not so busy. I do not want you to tax your eyes & your strength when worn out & weak. Only write when it is not too trying. I always know there is some good reason if I do not hear from you—the only annoyance is that I fear you are not well. I am glad the children are so well. Tell Ali I received her sweet little message & it makes me very happy. I wish I could see her to-night.

Tell Father not to fear about my making enemies of newspapers & women. I have almost converted some of the secesh women here. Eighteen ladies have pledged themselves to good behavior to save a Mrs. Higgins from being sent away. I presume [Wilbur Fisk] Story, of *Chicago Times*, will swear vengeance, but the order did a world of good in these parts. I believe if I had sole control in Kentucky I could make it one of the most loyal states.

I am sorry the photographic group is a failure. I have not seen any of them. Some of the single ones promised to be very good. I have not heard a word from William Blodgett. The Grose Isle scandal is the most amusing thing I ever heard. Tell Mrs. Scotten that with Davis' consent, I wish she could keep me posted in Detroit gossip.

Our respective mothers seem to be on quite a frolic. Glad of it, dear souls. I hope they may never know a shade of sorrow in this world. They have selected the two great *metropoli* to visit, & while one is enjoying the fashion & grandeur of New York, the other seems to be made much of by the Rickettses, Gillises, &c in Washington. . . .

Robert is quite a bean & Brackett a favorite. In fact all my staff seem in high favor with the fair sex of Lexington. I expect to get off this week for the front. We have changed the tune with the rebels & are driving them beyond the Cumberland down into Tennessee. Love to all.

Thine ever,
O.B.W.

Lexington, Ky.
May 6/'63
My darling,

Just received your note of May 3d telling me of Father's departure with Lulu, leaving you all alone. I fear you will be [illegible word] somewhat but pretty busy. Ali is a little tea party in herself & Elon a perfect hop. Speaking of hops, I send you a ticket of invitation. I wish Mrs. Scotten could be present to describe it. It is expected to be a more extensive affair than anything we have had, the former ones being but hotel parties. All the Union ladies are invited & some of the secesh, no doubt, as society is intermixed. The affair is got up on the expectation of my leaving Lexington, which is yet postponed. When I do go it will be in command of the 9th Corps, which now forms but a part of my command.[31]

They are at present somewhat scattered, one brigade, the Michigan brigade, being out of the district in [the] western part of state, below Louisville at Columbia. But I don't know when we shall get into the field. Unless we take East Tennessee we shall be here or somewhere in Kentucky some time.

---

31. OBW would not be given command of the Ninth Corps, however, as in June it would be shipped off to assist Grant at Vicksburg under General Parke.

How I should like to share your labor & enjoyment in the garden. Be very careful of your precious health my darling, & avoid fatigue. I do not see a child but what I think of Elon & Ali & dear old Lu.

Thine always,
O. B. W.

Lexington, Ky.
May 9/'63
My darling Mollie,

I received a letter from you yesterday. The sad news from Fredericksburg created perfect consternation among the citizens here, requiring all my tact & calm assurance to keep within bounds.[32] I never betrayed my anxiety & the next morning news greatly relieved the public mind. I am just receiving reports through the telegraph operators from Buffalo & Pittsburgh that Richmond is captured!

The complimentary Hop was quite a brilliant affair. I only wish you had been present. The staff had just begun to invite people for Friday night when the news of Hooker's defeat interrupted proceedings till some night next week—if we are here. Do not feel uneasy about me. I will write you quite often.

Thine with love,
O. B. W.

Lexington, Ky.
May 13/'63
My Darling Wife,

Last night I received your letter of May 10th enclosing Mother's letters from New York to you & Lulie. They seem to be enjoying themselves on their travels, and I am very glad they went. Have you received a draft for $150? I sent the money to Cincinnati by Capt. [Varness?] to get a draft & forward it. I meant to send you $200, but had to spare $70 to Julia on David's life insurance.

I have heard several times from the gay Washingtonians, & your name was duly honored. Tomorrow Mr. Sayre, the rich eccentric banker who said Father must come to his house, leaves for New York. I have given him a letter to Father, who will find him quite an amusing character.

You have heard of the death of Gen'l. Whipple.[33] I feel very much grieved over it, for Whipple was a warm friend of mine & always anxious to get into

32. Referring to the Battle of Chancellorsville.
33. Maj. Gen. Amiel W. Whipple was mortally wounded at Chancellorsville.

the 9th Corps. I hope you will write to Mrs. Whipple. I have lost another friend in Capt. Weed of the 5th Artillery, formerly of the 4th, killed in the late Fredericksburg battles.[34] It is sad to think of these things. I understand [J. Ford] Kent was wounded. You will remember he remained with Sedgwick. You can easily understand what I think of the late disaster from what you knew before of my opinions of Hooker. Good night, kiss the little folks.

Thy husband,
O.B.W.

Lexington, Ky.
May 15/'63
My darling wife,
I received a letter from you this morning and thank you very much. Yesterday I had a review which passed off very well. Spent the evening at the house of a corner neighbor. About eleven o'clock the city band came & gave us a serenade. I am again on the *qui vive* for the rebels who are threatening us on the Cumberland, near Somerset. They want to prevent our expedition into East Tennessee.

Mr. Sayre, the old gentleman who wanted Father to come & stay with him, has gone to New York to spend a month or two. I gave him a letter to Father. I wish I could see the old place in its spring beauty. You are playing "Proserpina among the flowers, herself the fairest flower." It will no doubt serve to amuse & give you fresh air. Give Ali & Elon a good hug for papa, and send my best love to Lulu & her good grandparents.

Thine,
O.B.W.

Lexington, Ky.
May 27/'63
My darling Wife,
The day after my last we had a fire in which the hospital was burnt. All the sick & wounded were moved without injury, but it was a painful sight. Of course there was excitement & confusion as usual. I stationed myself on the steps & but for the large columns, would have been smashed from the things thrown from windows. The *Cincinnati Commercial* nearly killed me with a bedstead—but it was a bed that struck me—pretty good for the

---

34. Referring to Capt. Stephen H. Weed, commanding the Fifth Corps artillery. Weed was not killed at Chancellorsville; he survived, only to meet his end on July 2 at Gettysburg, defending Little Round Top.

newspapers. By the way, I must send you the Cincinnati papers, for they have all the Kentucky news.

The weather has been very hot & dry for some days; the streets and roads are awful dusty, but I ride nearly every evening. The only place to ride to escape dust is the cemetery, which is handsome & modern & has a tall monument of Henry Clay. By the way, Mrs. H. C. speaks very highly of me for protecting the Ashland property &c. I meant to send you an invitation to our grand affair, but they were all exhausted & some more had to be written. They were elegantly printed on long lozenge-shape cards. I enclose [a] list of dances for Lulu's curiosity cabinet.

I expect Burnside tomorrow by way of Louisville, where he is to-night. A Mr. Elliott, merchant, gives us a party Friday night. O why cannot you be with me to share these honors, they are *painful* without you my love.

I see the Macalesters [*sic*] more than anybody; they invite me to breakfasts & teas very often. Much obliged for Mother's letter. Has Father seen Mr. Sayre? Kiss my two darlings.

Thine,
O. B. W.

Lexington, Ky.
May 29/'63
My darling Wife,

I received your letter of [the] 26th to-day. I envy you the garden & the flowers, the river & old home, so delightful to all. Then Father has returned. Did he see Mr. Sayre? I shall always regret his not visiting here. Give him my best love.

Hartsuff will be here to-morrow. Whether he will interfere with me or not I don't know, but suppose not. But the command will be pretty well mixed up. The papers say he is to command all the Kentucky troops except [the] 9th Corps & Carter's division, which I suppose will remain under me. I prefer not to have him so close, not admiring his character.

I hope the Kirklands will find you well & strong enough to entertain them. Give them my kindest regards.

Do you wish me to come home *early* or *late* in July? Of course I cannot expect to stay very long, but I long to see you more than ever. Sometimes the absence seems too intolerable to bear. But we must keep up a brave heart & hope for the best. . . . I wish you were here to eat strawberries. They are abundant & fine, & the people are more hospitable than one can be equal to.

To-night there is a grand party at Mr. Elliott's, said to be in our honor. I wish I could transfer all such honors to you. How are my little darlings. Tell

Ali her little papa will come to see her this summer, & tell Elon we'll have some grand rides & walks.

Thine,
O.B.W.

Lexington, Ky.
May 31/'63
My darling Marie,
This is Sunday night. I expected to start for Stanford to-morrow morning, but have to wait till Wednesday to see Gen. Burnside. Will write you again before leaving. I never saw anything like the regret people seem to manifest at our leaving. Hartsuff is here & the District commands are to be broken up; when I go it will be in command of the 9th Corps & Carter's Division. It will be some days yet, as it is so difficult to accumulate supplies over the bad roads. Poe has Mrs. Poe with him. Col. Bowen left Friday for Mrs. Bowen & will be greatly disappointed in not having her with him. Of course he will not think of taking her to Stanford. I suppose we will make at least a raid across the Cumberland River into Tennessee. I hope to have a little more rough service before going home. Love to all.

Thine,
O.B.W.

Head Quarters District of Indiana
Department of the Ohio
Indianapolis, Ind.
June 24/'63
My dear Marie,
. . . You & Father probably saw the newspaper reports of a big raid into Indiana & destruction of Ohio & Mississippi railway. Not a word of truth in it.[35] Glad to hear of the return of dear Grandma & little Ladie Lulu. Give my best love to them. I should have sent Lu something by Eben had I known [of] her return. But will remember her when I go home.

Every day has its new excitement in this state. To-day it is armed resistance to the conscription near Bloomington, Monroe Co. They have stolen the rolls, are armed & drilling, & I have sent down a regiment of infantry & company of cavalry. As soon as all these alarms are over I will trot over to Detroit; will try to be with you next Sunday but cannot promise anything

35. Referring to the Hines Raid, which did little damage.

certain. I do not think you write me very often, do you? Are you quite well? Love to all.

Thine,
O.B.W.

Indianapolis, Ind.
Friday, June 26/'63
My darling Marie,

I have received your letter but Lulu's picture was not in it. I hope you will send it. . . . I received a nice letter from Gov. [James F.] Robinson of Kentucky this morning, which I will send you. Am impatient to get over to Detroit, but another Sunday will probably pass over without it, as the trouble in Monroe County, although quelled, has extended to Greene County. But I apprehend nothing serious. One would think that under the awful sense of an invaded & bleeding country, home strife would hide its head, but party spirit knows no bounds, no shame. My God! what a picture we present now to the world! Still, I am not in despair but think Lee will soon meet a reverse in Pennsylvania or Maryland.[36] Love to all.

Thine,
O.B.W.

Indianapolis, Ind.
July 1/'63
My darling Mollie,

I received a nice letter from your precious ladyship yesterday, & am perfectly delighted to find how well you are. If you only knew how much I think of you & long to be with you & with *les enfans* you would fully appreciate the keenness of my wish to spend the 4th of July at home. But it is extremely doubtful whether I can get away from these Hoosiers. I do not know how they will behave on that day, with their rival celebrations & chance of collisions. Still I will come if possible.

Caution Elon about running around the streets—in fact, don't trust him out alone at all. Tell Darling Lu I am sorry she is bilious. She must keep out of the sun.

There was a war meeting last night at which I spoke with more or less success—nothing seems so sickening as to have to urge men to defend their own country.

36. Lee of course was already marching north, with the van of his army already across the Potomac, heading toward its destiny at Gettysburg.

I have come out with an order against *all* secret political societies, & both the leading party papers here have endorsed it, as you will see by those I send you. It is fortunate for me that I enjoy in so short a time the confidence of both parties. Voorhees[37] really went to work in his congressional district to prevent resistance to the enrollment, as he promised; & it will soon be completed successfully in the whole state. Love to all.

> Thy own,
> O.B.W.

Indianapolis, Ind.

July 10/'63

My darling Marie,

We are in the midst of one of the great excitements of the war, Morgan being across the Ohio & actually in Indiana. What a contrast it must be to your calm, quiet bedroom. You need not have a moment's apprehension; it will only delay my visit to you. I was too busy to write yesterday, and you must not think strange if you seldom hear for some days to come.

How is the little 4th?[38] Does she begin to smile yet or is she reserving that angelic impulse for her Father? Kiss the little amazon goddess. How do the other children take it?

> Thine,
> O.B.W.

Indianapolis, Ind.

Sunday, July 26/'63

My dear Mollie,

How I should like to be with you to-day above all days, it would be a little paradise with our own little cherubims that I hope do continually *not* cry. How is the patriotic, & the little old lady, & the little man with a saddle. . . . Last Sunday I was with them, which reminds me that I have not heard from you since I left.[39]

Gen'l & Mrs. Love will leave here middle of next week for Detroit & other "places of interest," perhaps as far as Quebec. You may be able to call

---

37. Congressman Daniel W. Voorhees (D., Ind.).

38. Referring to his as-yet-unnamed daughter, who would eventually be christened Grace North Willcox, in honor not only of the Union victory at Gettysburg but of OBW's great-grandmother, who bore the same name.

39. The allusion here is from the *Te Deum Laudamus*, of the Anglican liturgy: "To thee Cherubim and Seraphim continually do cry." OBW had just returned from visiting his family (including his newborn daughter) at home in Detroit. He had apparently set out soon after Morgan was out of his jurisdiction.

on them and I hope Father & Mother will too, for the Loves are very polite & hospitable to me. Last Friday night they gave me a very pretty little party indeed—dancing, & very pleasant; the governor adorned it with his graceful presence.

I have over a thousand of John Morgan's men at Camp Morton, & the Kentuckians are beginning to come up to see their relatives. Of course our own prisoners are treated so meanly at Richmond that I can grant them but few privileges, & it is hard to refuse my noble Kentucky friends anything. I mean the loyal people who come to see the prisoners. Their manners contrast rather strongly with those of Hoosierdom, I reckon.

Weeks seem to glide along without my being ordered to the field. Were it not for being so near you & having chances to see you & to have you with me this would be too intolerable. It is contrary to all my tastes & inclinations. But as Neistetler, the Dutch quartermaster, says, "now don't make a fool of yourself & get shot," & there is something in that.

Have you settled quite upon the all-important name? My kind regards to Mrs. Baker, for whom I shall ever entertain the highest regard. If it don't tax Mother too much, can you not have the Loves & Hardings to tea, & invite a few nice people afterwards in the evening? Shall I send you some soldiers to go out on the highways & press in some decent cooks, etc.? I want the aforesaid Loves to see my children.

Thine always,
O.B.W.

Indianapolis, Ind.
August 4/'63
My dearest Mollie,

I am quite desperate at not hearing from you but once in two weeks. . . . I hope you have had no set-back in health. My little trip to Detroit gave me so much pleasure & satisfaction that I have borne the ills of Hoosierdom quite comfortably, & I think I can make your visit here very agreeable.

I have had the present of a large cake, which I undertook to remove from the glass in order to send it to you. It was from the rich baker's daughter who takes so mightily to my staff. She is now quite struck with Brackett. The cake wouldn't stir without breaking & I don't know what to do with it.

How do Lu & Elon get on with their horses? I hope Father gives them some attention. How did you like the Loves? Roebuck is quite lame. He is hoof-bound & has a bad corn. I think I shall have to send him back.

Charley [McKnight] left for his regiment last week. Of course he hadn't money enough & I lent him fifteen dollars to pay traveling fare. I came very near sending Richards to his regiment too. He became quite thick with a rebel young lady, against my express wishes. But for his mother, I should have shipped him, & as it was [I] administered a reproof he will not be likely to forget. Now write me if you love me & give my love & kisses to all.

Thine,
O.B.W.

Indianapolis, Ind.
August 5/'63
My dearest Mollie,

This evening a sad, heart-rending calamity to a Kentucky lady happened at this hotel. There was very joyful singing in the parlor & I had just stepped to the door & saw it proceeded from two ladies at the piano, & was part way back to my room when I heard a scream & several others proceeding from the parlor, & people began to rush in. I returned & met Mr. Holton, the landlord, with a pale & insensible child in his arms, & one of the ladies who had been singing the moment before, screaming in her brother's arms. The piano was close by a door opening on a balcony & the child had dropped from the bedroom window, two stories above, & fallen on the balcony, just within a few feet of the mother. All heard the fall, but no noise from the child, & for another moment the mother continued her singing. It was too dark outside to see what it was that fell, but a lady stepped upon the balcony, & as the child was picked up the poor mother recognized the dress of her child. It seems that she had left the child asleep upon the bed. It was only eleven months old, could not walk; must have fallen out of bed & crept to the window, & by means of a carpet bag under the window, climbed upon the sill.

It is now an hour; the child continues to breathe badly. I have sent to Camp Morton for the lady's husband; he is a rebel prisoner of the name of Cunningham. Dr. O'Connell & another physician are with the child & everything will be done. The greatest sympathy is manifested. The people are from Paris, near Lexington. I never was more suddenly or greatly shocked at anything before. The room from which the child fell was my old quarters previous to my last visit to Detroit.

I received your Sunday letter this morning, relieving me from my desperation at not hearing from you. I am glad it was nothing worse than the hot weather, though that is prostrating enough. Thank Mother very very much for the handsome manner in which she entertained the Loves on short notice. . . . I am glad the children looked & behaved so well. Tell Lu it is quite a compliment to me to have it said she looks like me.

Of course you cannot think of paying me a visit at present, but you looked so well & promising when I saw you that I had got up quite a fever of expectation to have you here after a few weeks. And now I must devise how I can get to see you at home. I am tied down here as much as ever, every day having its new duties. But I expect to see Burnside in a day or two. Much love to all.

Thine,
O.B.W.

The child has breathed its last.

Indianapolis, Ind.

August 21/'63

My darling Mollie,

Here I am this eve at my old quarters, Bates House, which I did not reach until tea time, instead of breakfast as I expected.[40] The train did not connect at Sydney for seven hours. We got through at early day break. After breakfast a number of the citizens called & asked me to address the people. I was tired & unwell, but they insisted notwithstanding, & at half past ten conducted me to the street corner & put me on a dry-goods box, where I held forth for almost fifteen minutes, very little to my own satisfaction I must say. A few of the gentlemen returned with me to the Inn & sat there till one o'clock, when the train left.

Robert did not expect me till next week & I was almost sorry I did not stay over Sunday with you & Mother, for I find it much lonelier here than ever, & you two forlorn ladies seem to need me so much. I hope you will both go out every day with the carriage or buggy. Lulu will soon be well enough to drive out. Write me at least a word every day until she is up & about.

We had the honor of young aide-de-camp Howard's company as far as Sydney, & his father was at the depot to see him off. He was quite cordial to me. I think you had better call on Mrs. Howard & manifest some interest in her health. Remember me to Father, Frank & Caro whenever you write. Much love to Mother & kiss Lulu, Elon, Ali & the baby for

Thine with more love than
tongue or pen can express,
O.B.W.

40. OBW has just returned from Detroit, his second visit there in a month.

Indianapolis, Ind.

August 25/'63

My darling Mollie,

Received your first letter to-day enclosing Thesta's curiosity of literature. Yours was a nice satisfactory production, cheering me with good news of Lulu. I have had a day's hard work, particularly on a large number of court-martial cases. . . .

My love to our talented mother. Tell her that she has enough left in her composition to make up six young modern ladies, and that I want her to gild the setting rays of the old home, lighting up every cloud, and brightening all the beloved horizon. She can make the place pleasant & interesting as ever if she will not take the atrocities of the new age so much to heart. I fear, otherwise, that servants & boys will be the death of her.

In haste, thine with kisses for the little birds,

O.B.W.

Indianapolis, Ind.

August 25/'63

My darling Mollie,

A turn in the weather gives me more energy. Maj. McClure & Gen. Love are both absent & my evenings are silent & solitary for the most part. My eyes do not admit of much reading and if you were here you would be the object of my devoted attention. However, to-morrow night I am invited to a Methodist party & a Presbyterian party, which I wish you could attend. The fall of Sumter is reported to-night.[41] I hope it is true, but it comes as a sort of matter of course. By & by people will forget that it is God who giveth the victory. Good night. Kiss Lulu for

Papa

Indianapolis, Ind.

August 28/'63

My dearest Mollie,

You will see by the enclosed that Sergt. Wilson has at last got a commission. Col. Smith telegraphs me that Vallandigham is at Windsor [On-

---

41. On August 17, Federal forces began their first great bombardment of Fort Sumter, pounding the works with nearly a thousand shots, including some from a two-hundred-pounder called the "Swamp Angel." Sumter's brick walls began to crumble, but the fort would remain in Confederate hands until February 1865.

tario].[42] I have ordered him to be arrested if he crosses, but hope he will not attempt it. Maj. McClure has got back. Rob Hutchins has gone down to Lexington to see after his horse & very likely his sweetheart. I hope Lulu continues to mend. Write daily. Love & kisses to all.

> Thine,
> O.B.W.

Indianapolis, Ind.
September 1/'63
My dear Mollie,

The first day of Autumn! Is it a melancholy reflection or a pleasant one? For my part, I am glad to find the "heated term" coming to its close. We have had here a cold snap, but to-day it is quite warm again. I have received but one letter from you & a paper since I left home. Vallandigham's reception looks to me like a fizzle. I suppose he is gone now. Judge O. Flynn! Pah! Now I have Judge Perkins on my hands; he has issued a *writ of habeas corpus* which I declined to do anything more than return without producing in court the body of the soldier. Soon will come a question of conflict of jurisdiction between the military order of Gen. Burnside & the civil process of the Supreme Court of Indiana. . . .

I may go over to Detroit in a short time again. I am very restless & dissatisfied here alone. I hope Lulu is getting well fast. You & Mother must dine out to the market often & get plenty [of] peaches & good things to eat. Make it a point for one or the other to dine out daily.

Write me when you expect Father home. Robert has returned from Kentucky quite flattered with his reception there. Everybody, including clerks in the stores & even the negroes greeted him heartily, & all people & the 9th Corps seem to wish for my return there.

If you don't write I shall think you are indifferent. Kisses to all. Mrs. Love says the children are "splendid."

> Thine with love,
> O.B.W.

42. Clement L. Vallandigham, former congressman from Ohio and leader of the Peace Democrats, had been arrested on orders from Burnside at Dayton Ohio on May 5, 1863, for a speech on April 30 at Columbus, in which he had made derogatory remarks about the president and the Union war effort. Tried by a military court and denied a *writ of habeas corpus*, Vallandigham was sentenced to two years in a military prison. Lincoln himself later commuted Vallandigham's sentence to banishment to the Confederacy, from where he later traveled to Canada. Operating from Niagara Falls and Windsor, Ont., Vallandigham conducted a campaign for governor of Ohio but was defeated in the October election.

Indianapolis, Ind.
September 2/'63
My dearest Mollie,

I received your Sunday letter to-day with great joy & satisfaction. Am sorry Lu is so slow in recovering. Tell her she shall have an album to put all her photographs in very soon. You may mail the documents Miss Campbell left for me. I have the manuscripts.

Caro's letter was very entertaining. I wrote her a few days ago. Write Ellie & congratulate her for me on the safe arrival of the new damsel. Extend my congratulations also to Fanny McDonald. I hope her husband will find a good man for the house. You had better send Mr. McD word again or he may forget it. I was astonished at getting a letter from Mr. Taylor to-day. He was over at Matamoras, Mexico—near Brownsville—on business, & says letters can reach him & Mary through the American Consul at that place.[43]

I reviewed the six months troops to-day & shall review the batteries to-morrow. Col. Biddle left this evening, expressing eager hopes of coming under my command again. Lizzie Hutchins is again disappointed in her esposo, that is to-be—He has written he cannot be on till the last of the month. The marriage was fixed for the 5th, I believe. . . .

Good night, my love. Kiss my little sweetheart, Lulu, Elon & the name-less one, & love to Mother from

Thine,
O.B.W.

Indianapolis, Ind.
September 3/'63
My dearest Mollie,

This afternoon I spent reviewing & inspecting the batteries. The 12th Michigan cut rather a poor figure, but it is improving. Its Capt. Hillier[44] is being court martialed & it is at present commanded by an old West Pointer, Capt. Robertson, who is getting it into shape.

My staff present rather a fine appearance on horse back. Robert, Rich-ards, Brackett, [and] Maj. Lyon are all handsome men & dashing on horse back. There was a band mounted on horses present, which played toler-ably. We took tea at the artillery barracks with Capt. Myers, & came home at dark.

43. Referring to Charles and Mary Taylor, brother-in-law and sister of OBW.
44. Capt. Edward G. Hillier, 12th Michigan Artillery (formerly of the 1st Michigan Ar-tillery).

This evening I was honored with a visit from Mr. Voorhees, the celebrated Democratic congressman. Gen'l. Love, a Gen'l. Blythe & three or four colonels—quite a soiree. Voorhees seems very friendly, & though he has the most rebellious district in the state, he controls them. This evening he said he had lately traveled among his constituents & that the spirit is much more quiet & peaceful than it was a few weeks ago, that he had used his influence for submission to the laws & told them I was a just man. Which is better than to have him opposing me.

To-morrow I am going a fishing with Gen'l. Love, Maj. Hall, Col. Rose & some other gentleman, a very agreeable party, & next week I think of going to Terre Haute, which is said to be the most agreeable town in the state.

Good night,
Ever thine,
O.B.W.

EIGHTEEN

Campaigns in East Tennessee

DURING MY absence in Indiana, the 9th Corps had gone to Vicksburg, thence to Jackson, Mississippi, and finally to East Tennessee—the scene of active field operations against Buckner, which had no inconsiderable bearing on the great struggle between Bragg and Rosecrans in West Tennessee.[1]

The direct road to East Tennessee, from the north, lay through Camp Nelson and Cumberland Gap. My first orders after the Morgan Raid . . . took me to Camp Nelson, where I arrived on September 21, specifically to assume command of all reinforcements and march to Cumberland Gap, in order to assure the security of that gateway, and to operate therefrom until further orders, i.e., until I could rejoin my division at Knoxville.[2]

1. The Ninth Corps, having participated in Grant's siege of Vicksburg from early June through July 1863, had been ordered to return for service in Kentucky and eventually east Tennessee on August 3.

On August 16, 1863, Rosecrans began moving his Army of the Cumberland from the area south of Tullahoma toward Chattanooga and the Tennessee River. This move forced Bragg to abandon Chattanooga on September 9; Buckner had the responsibility of guarding all of east Tennessee and protecting Bragg's right flank, including the all-important East Tennessee and Virginia Railroad, the most direct line of communications between Chattanooga and Virginia.

2. Burnside began advancing his forces from Kentucky into east Tennessee in mid-August, in concert with Rosecrans's advance, protecting the latter's left flank. Burnside's troops occupied Knoxville on September 2, cutting the East Tennessee and Virginia Railroad. Leading elements of the Ninth Corps were just then joining Burnside at Knoxville from Jackson, Mississippi.

462

The troops were nearly all new; one regiment, [the] 116th Indiana, was without firearms.[3] We started on the 24th [of] September. The country was rocky and hilly, the roads rough, and our marches were slow, with my inexperienced and footsore soldiers and wagons breaking down daily. But persimmons were ripe and grew wild in the open. Consequently the men kept up their spirits—in fact, whenever a tree was sighted bearing the luscious fruit, some fellow would sing out "Persimmons!" and the ranks would break incontinently, in spite of orders, guards, or provost marshal. This was particularly the case with the 116th Indiana, until their arms overtook them.

Finally, I believe each regimental commander had to detail foragers to march along the flanks to preserve order; and yet whole regiments would be allowed to break ranks "to forage." This went on less and less as discipline obtained the upper hand, and it ceased finally when we got down between Somerset and London—Morgan's old neighborhood in the noted "hill country of Kentucky," where spies and bushwhackers lurked behind rocks and trees. At Pittman's Station we found Capt. Dudley of the 11th New Hampshire, in command of 150 men to hunt bushwhackers, but handicapped by "strict regulations." However, I gave him discretionary authority to hire scouts, and we had to leave him to do the best he could, untrammeled, but sore at being left behind.

The particulars of that march may seem unimportant compared with the movements of armies and battles we read of in history, but I give them to show some realistic elements of [a] soldier's experience in obscure corners of the nursery of war, on which veterans from the ranks will dilate afterwards a hundred times, where they speak once of their great battles and show how fields were won.

Those Indiana boys of mine who were taunted along the march as "persimmon knockers," have now assumed the sobriquet for their organization [as] something to laugh about in their yearly gathering at Indianapolis—not forgetting to invite their old commander, whom they had at first spoken of as "that old regular."

But also to show you that "the old man" himself had some worriments, permit me to add that during the march I received some annoying dispatches, being as I was unfortunately *not* out of reach of the telegraph. For instance, reporting my slow progress to General Parke, commanding the

3. OBW's command consisted of approximately three thousand untrained troops, primarily the 115th, 116th, 117th, and 118th Indiana infantry regiments (all six-months volunteers); Hoskins's brigade of the Twenty-third Corps; the 12th Michigan, 21st Ohio, and 23d Indiana batteries; and two companies of the 3d Indiana Cavalry.

9th Corps, he "hurried me up," so to speak, and I had to hurry up, outfooting our raw cavalry reinforcement, struggling with their own difficulties to overtake us from the rear. Of course I began to "push things," but met with so many petty breaks in the machinery that General Parke finally consoled me with the command "*not* to make forced marches." And as is not infrequently the case in handling raw troops, some of the officers would stand between their men and the provost marshal or the officer of the day. But such cases were settled on the spot and gradually disappeared.

Forage questions likewise arose, as the inhabitants refused to sell; but our energetic assistant provost marshal, Lt. J. F. King, found a way under the "conscription law" to gather about all that we needed. We had some 200 wagons in the train, some of which had the bad habit of sliding off at steep and shelving rocks—particularly after a rain, on the road from Flat Creek to Cumberland Ford, and some wagons of the supply train consequently were left miles behind with a rear guard.

Before reaching the Gap, our orders were modified by General Parke, so that making but little halt at Cumberland Gap, we closed up and started for Blue Springs [Tennessee], which place we reached on October 8, brushing away some of the enemy's cavalry enroute, and crossing two large streams, the Clinch and the Holston rivers—infantry by ferry boats, cavalry by the fords.

Burnside had been slowly driving Buckner through East Tennessee until the latter made a stand at Blue Springs. The Kentucky brigade under Buckner was made up, according to the *Louisville Democrat* of a contemporary date,

> of young unthinking men drawn from nearly every county in the state, whose parents were themselves loyal. Upon one man more than all others their curses will fall. We have a feeling of the profoundest sympathy for those whose sons have been enticed away from their homes by the archtraitor Buckner and who now are plunged into the deepest anxiety to know of the fate of their children.

These words may or may not have been written during the crisis of our East Tennessee campaign, but those young Kentuckians gave a good account of themselves during the Battle of Blue Springs. They occupied a series of elevated positions fronted by a dense wilderness, through which ran a narrow, winding road, compelling our advance brigade, under Col. Carter, to deploy through thick timber and thorny brush.

After an hour's rest, "General Burnside closed up the column by ordering forward the 9th Corps, with the division of reserves under General Willcox." The new position occupied by the "Johnnies" was on the edge of a belt of woods which bounded the further side of a cleared piece of ground.

Again Col. Carter pushed forward to attack, but midway of the clearing was checked by a sudden and dashing charge of the Kentuckians, compelling General Ferrero's division[4] and finally the whole 9th Corps under General [Robert B.] Potter to advance, Ferrero's troops pouring volley after volley into the rebel ranks. Astounded at this unforeseen occurrence, they fell back once more, and left us masters of the field. The artillery again came into position and kept up a desultory fire until sun down.[5]

Next sunrise they had vanished, leaving me to follow up their shattered forces. Burnside, with his corps, started back to Knoxville to look out for any further detachment from Bragg's army. I found that the enemy had stubbornly contested over 2 miles of ground. Following in pursuit, we overtook them at Warm Springs, across the North Carolina line, where they turned and attacked Col. [James A.] Smith, leading our advance, on October 20. They were repulsed "after a skirmish of two hours," in which we had but one killed and five wounded. . . .

On the night before, our advance had captured a picket of ten men. Withdrawing from the North Carolina line, I established headquarters at Greeneville, a pretty little town on the railroad, inhabited, for the most part, by Union people, chief of whom was Andrew Johnson's family. The future president himself was military Governor of Tennessee, then living at Nashville, but his sister, Mrs. Patterson, invited me to make my home at her house, an invitation that was so cordially urged that I accepted—although it separated me from the whole of my staff.

Those charming little homes had been so frequently raided by Confederate cavalry that they were almost "cleaned out" of the necessaries of life: food, blankets, clothing and even of household utensils, and so you can imagine the joy with which we were welcomed. Most everything that had been left was hidden away in the most unlikely places. On being shown to my bedroom, I noticed that the bedding looked unusually high up, the secret of which I discovered next morning. . . . I was awakened early by the colored maid, who first knocked, and as she proceeded softly to turn the

4. Brig. Gen. Edward Ferrero was then in command of the First Division, Ninth Corps.
5. The action at Blue Springs took place primarily on October 5, 7, and 10, 1863, between Burnside's troops and some 1,500 Confederate horsemen under Brig. Gen. John S. Williams.

door knob, I closed my eyes and awaited events. Slipping into the room, she came to the bedside and, opening a little trap door beneath the bed, she drew out a fowl of some sort. Having already heard the clucking of chickens, quacking of ducks, and something besides that sounded to me like little pig notes, I could scarcely guess which of the lot was withdrawn.

And then, before dressing for breakfast, on investigating the contents of my bedstead, I found betwixt the feather bed and mattress, quite a quantity of corn and other grains, and some few potatoes and onions; so that between the savings from the chamber and some coffee and white sugar sent over by our own commissary, we enjoyed the "best breakfast," so Mrs. Patterson said, they had had "since the war began." As for sugar, that was less appreciated than the coffee, for they were never short of the maple product.

One of the staff tells the story that the good old woman who presided at table where they were breakfasting, asked the officer who sat opposite her, "Will you have long sweetening or short sweetening, sir?" In some perplexity of ignorance, he replied, "Either, but long if you please, as I have a big cup." At this, the woman, reaching up to a shelf, took down a bowl of thick maple molasses, and stirring it up with her forefinger, she drew out a twist of the "long sweetening," and dropped it into his cup. The next gentleman replied to her question, "I believe, madam, I will take it short"; whereupon she drew from the shelf a cake of maple sugar, inserted [it] between her black gums, broke off a mouthful, and dropped it into number two's cup. Needless to add that this ended "sweetening" for that meal. The story may seem too good to be true, but it went the rounds of the camp and was well attested by every member of the staff, excepting the two victimized, who laughingly submitted to no end of chaffing throughout the campaign.

Of course, considering the utter destitution of the poor whites particularly, I had to order . . . sales of pork and flour rations to them, and the upper classes were by no means too proud to ask for a little tea and coffee, in exchange for which all classes were glad to give liberally of their snuff and tobacco, a luxury to ourselves, particularly the young officers, among whom snuff taking became the vogue.

But these bright days were drawing rapidly to a close. November 6, on hearing of Colonel Garrard's defeat and heavy losses at Rogersville,[6] I gave

6. Col. Israel Garrard, 7th Ohio Cavalry, held Rogersville with his own regiment, a regiment of Tennessee mounted infantry, and an artillery battery. On November 6 Garrard's troops were caught by a pincer movement of two Confederate brigades, conducted principally by Brig. Gen. William E. "Grumble" Jones (10th, USMA 1848). Garrard lost his battery and some seven hundred men, mostly veterans, forcing Willcox to withdraw from his advanced position at Greeneville.

orders to pack up, and on the 7th we started for Cumberland Gap, by way of Bull's Gap and Tazewell, scouting well towards Knoxville on our way. It had long been the desire of the government to secure the loyal inhabitants of East Tennessee from the hands of the rebels, who fully appreciated the importance of continuing their hold upon that country, with its large quantity of agricultural products. Our plan likewise was to cut off rebel connection with North Carolina and Virginia, and this being so far accomplished by Burnside's troops; the corollary to the proposition was for us to secure the mountain passes.

At any rate, pursuant to Burnside's order, I marched the whole of my command for Cumberland Gap, the importance of which point, lying in the angle which forms a junction of the states of Tennessee, North Carolina, Virginia and Kentucky, you can easily comprehend. Moreover, the Gap was the gateway for retreat into Kentucky, in case Knoxville, already threatened, should fall into Confederate hands. The Confederate generals had fully appreciated the importance of this point and fortified and garrisoned it accordingly. It was perhaps the strongest mountain fastness on either side, and, as you would imagine, it had been a difficult one to take.

The first Union commander who undertook the feat was Col. John F. DeCourcy, who moved an inadequate force into the passes on the Kentucky side, and after marching the same troops among and around the rocks, and on the roads and by ways, and making as much display as if they were thrice their number, he demanded the surrender [of the forces opposing him.] General [John W.] Frazer, the Confederate commander, opened up not his guns, but a parley as to "terms," during which negotiations General Shackelford arrived with a stronger command and some guns, mortars and implements for a regular systematic attack, and he also demanded the surrender, pointing out the helplessness under circumstances of a useless defense and sacrifice of life; and while he was parleying with Frazer, General Burnside came up in person from Knoxville, and he also sent a message. His presence certainly portended "business," and General Frazer gracefully yielded up the fortress with all its guns and stores and 2,000 prisoners.[7]

I fancy, however, that since our large armies had gained a secure foothold in Tennessee, the place ceased to be one of sufficient importance to the Confederacy for a stubborn defense at great cost of life and material.

7. Brig. Gen. James M. Shackelford then led the Third and Fourth Brigades of the Twenty-third Corps. He would be appointed to lead the Cavalry Corps of the Department of the Ohio in October 1863; Colonel Frazer (his appointment to brigadier general was never confirmed), commanding Confederate troops at Cumberland Gap, surrendered September 9, 1863.

Prisoners of war are easily exchanged, and guns can be bought or manufactured, but human life cannot be restored.

My own previous stay at this mountain eyrie had been brief, but this second "occupation" gave me plenty to do. In the first place we were short of provisions and were expected to live on the country; grain had to be gathered by foraging pastures and taken to mills on the little streams to be ground, and taken away under the eye of a watchful foe. But the latter were likewise straitened for food, and it soon got to be a laughable occurrence that while we were grinding at a mill, the enemy would coolly look on and await their turn. Neither side could afford to destroy the only resource on which we both depended for subsistence. And this "reminds me of a little story," in short, a practical joke played at the "old man's" expense. Fresh meat was not only a scarcity but almost an impossibility, but one day a forager brought me a suckling pig, which he had found astray and captured. I was only too glad to receive the only fresh bit of meat of the season; and to make a jollification over the same, I invited several colonels, but to our dismay, the *piece de resistance* of the feast was missing! Some years afterward one of the "Indiana boys" called to see me at Washington, and remarked with a chuckle of self-satisfaction, "General, did you ever find out who stole that pig?" "Never until this moment, you rascal," was my response, whereupon we took a drink to old times and the lost pig.

But foraging for food was not the most serious occupation of the season, for upon Longstreet's advance from Chattanooga, and particularly after the fight at Campbell's Station, Knoxville became besieged, and squadrons of Wheeler's cavalry were jealously watching the Cumberland Gap passes to prevent reinforcements and succor from [coming from] Kentucky; and while making sure of holding the Gap, my business was to keep open communications with Knoxville and incidentally to aid Burnside all I could.[8]

On November 20 I had received at Bean's Station, on my way up, a dispatch from Colonel [Felix W.] Graham, commanding my cavalry protecting my right flank and scouting in direction of Knoxville, a dispatch saying that his "advance scout had got within 5 miles of that city, and within a quar-

8. Following the Federal defeat at Chickamauga, September 19–20, 1863, Rosecrans was forced back into Chattanooga, which was then besieged by Bragg's army. Lt. Gen. James Longstreet, sent west from Lee's army in time to assist Bragg at Chickamauga, was dispatched northeastward on November 4. His force of twelve thousand infantry and five thousand cavalry under Maj. Gen. Joseph Wheeler moved up the East Tennessee & Georgia Railroad, intent on crushing Burnside's force in east Tennessee. Arriving at the Little Tennessee River, near Loudon, on the fourteenth, Longstreet began to probe the defenses of Knoxville. Following an engagement at Cambell's Station on November 16, Burnside fell back into the defenses of Knoxville, and the siege began.

ter of a mile of the rebel pickets, and found that the road on this side was already blockaded, citizens reporting that there were 80 to 100,000 rebels around Knoxville; steady and heavy firing during the afternoon."[9]

Of course my telegraphic communications were cut off from General Burnside. My last message from him had been that "the security of the retreat of your forces to Cumberland Gap was the first object," and this probably was the reason why he had not ordered my command to join him at Knoxville before the siege began.[10] Of course I was now left to my own discretion, subject to orders from higher headquarters.

General Grant had relieved Rosecrans and was now in command of the Grand Division embracing the Departments of the Ohio, Cumberland and Tennessee.[11] My first message came from Grant at Chattanooga [on] November 20, and reached me at Tazewell, where I was detained by a rise in [the] Clinch River. It read as follows: "If you receive no further instructions from General Burnside, follow those he has given you. Retreat should not be allowed . . . but can you not concentrate your forces and *raise the siege of Knoxville?* [OBW's italics.] This I know would close the route to Cumberland Gap for us, and would probably not compensate unless entirely successful in expelling Longstreet." His [Grant's] views were more fully shown in [his] next message, same date:

If you can communicate with General Burnside, say to him that our attack on Bragg will commence in the morning. If successful such will be made as I think will relieve East Tennessee. Longstreet passing through our lines to Kentucky need not cause alarm. He would find the country so bare that he would lose his transportation and artillery before reaching Kentucky, and would meet such a force before he got through that he could not return.[12]

9. Dispatch of Graham to Willcox. Graham was colonel of the 5th Indiana Cavalry. The actual strength of Longstreet's Confederate forces besieging Knoxville was approximately seventeen thousand. Burnside had about twelve thousand Union troops in the city, exclusive of recently recruited loyal Tennessee volunteers.

10. The editor is unable to find a dispatch with the exact wording used here. It is probable that OBW is paraphrasing the following dispatch from Burnside, dated Knoxville, November 17, 1863: "We have arrived here with no considerable loss, no loss of artillery. Shall hold this position til the last—*take all measures to render your position secure—and to ensure your safe retreat to Cumberland Gap if it becomes necessary*" [editor's italics]. From OBW's copy, Willcox papers.

11. Grant assumed command of the Division of the Mississippi on October 16, 1863. The following day he replaced Rosecrans with Maj. Gen. George H. Thomas. Grant reached Chattanooga on October 23.

12. The above two dispatches from Grant to Willcox can be found in *OR*, vol. 31, pt. 3, p. 207.

The two dispatches were rather contradictory, the first directing me to carry out Burnside's instructions, which were to hold the Gap, and the second to ignore them. But both messages from Grant contemplated my raising the siege of Knoxville. The general was not yet aware of my message to Halleck that "Wheeler's whole Corps and one division of Longstreet's is reported this side of town."[13] Nor did he know that Wheeler's Corps alone was more than sufficient to cope with my heterogeneous mounted force. Wheeler had led the advance of Longstreet's army. He first moved up to Maryville, south of Knoxville and the Holston River and afterwards to the north side, and by the latter move interposing between Knoxville and Cumberland Gap—his sudden change of base being accelerated by the appearance of our cavalry scouting towards the city to cover our left flank during the march from Bull's Gap.

From the 17th his [Wheeler's] report shows that "the next six days were spent in closely besieging this portion of the line (the north side of Knoxville) and engaging the enemy with both artillery and small-arms."[14] A few days afterwards he was defeated by our troops in an attack upon Kingston in the southeast, and relieved from command, which thereafter devolved upon General William T. Martin, who now confronted us with a division, somewhat reduced, but still superior in numbers to my own cavalry and field artillery.

The security of Cumberland Gap being still "the first consideration," I did not dare to risk it by a pitched battle with Martin, but I resolved to threaten him constantly for the double purpose of drawing him off from the siege, and to enable Burnside to forage for subsistence on the other side of the Holston.

On November 21st [at] 10 P.M., I telegraphed to General Halleck:

... Several scouting parties still out towards Knoxville, the latest news was at eleven (11) yesterday morning when firing was still heard by my advanced scout. The firing sounded as if five (5) miles below Knoxville. But the large rebel force remained above; perhaps the rebels were trying to draw Burnside out of his works. I am too distant to help Burnside but would have marched down from Bean's Station had not his orders been to make sure of Cumberland Gap.[15]

13. Willcox to Halleck, ibid., pp. 206–7.
14. *Report of Maj. Gen. Joseph Wheeler, C.S. Army, Commanding Cavalry Corps*, Knoxville Campaign, *OR*, vol. 31, pt. 1, p. 542.
15. Willcox to Halleck, ibid., p. 213. OBW's copy, quoted here, differs slightly from that printed in the *OR*.

On the 22d, General Grant telegraphed me: "At this distance it is impossible for me to direct positively what you are to do. Much will have to be left to your discretion with the full belief that you can tell best what is to be done in the present emergency. . . ."[16]

Before receipt of this dispatch, I had wired Halleck as follows: "I do not hear from Grant. Will you decide whether I shall run the risk of sacrificing all my cavalry by a demonstration below Clinch river in an attempt to relieve Burnside? If so I am ready. Please answer to night. . . ."[17]

After midnight I received the following stunning message:

Chattanooga, [November 23] 11:30 A.M.[18]
Gen'l Willcox:

Your dispatch of yesterday to General Halleck has just been reported to me. If you had shown half the willingness to sacrifice yourself and command at the start [as] you do in your dispatch you might have rendered Burnside material aid, now I judge you have got so far to the rear you can do nothing for him. Act upon the instructions you have and your own discretion and if you can do anything to relieve Burnside do it. It is not expected that you will try to sacrifice your command but that you will take proper risks.

U. S. Grant
Maj. Gen.

To which I replied: "Your reproof is unjust, as you shall see when I show you Burnside's instruction,"[19] as he soon afterwards fully acknowledged, particularly when he learned of my scheme for helping Burnside, and its good results. Now in regard to this hasty rebuff, it must be borne in mind that General Grant was already more or less worried and anxious over his

16. This dispatch from Grant to Willcox, dated Chattanooga, November 22, 10:35 A.M., does not appear in the OR. The copy quoted here was found among the Willcox papers. The remainder of the dispatch is as follows: "I have great hope that Burnside will be able to hold out and we reoccupy the whole [of] East Tennessee. In that case you should fall back no faster than forced to nor no further. Can your cavalry & mounted infantry get from where you are to Abingdon and so threaten the salt works to draw Williams back[?] Can you not easily & speedily get supplies to where you are[?]" It was obviously not OBW's intention to quote the entire dispatch in his memoirs.

17. Willcox to Halleck, November 22, 1863, 8 P.M., OR, vol. 31, pt. 3, p. 226.

18. OBW's copy of this dispatch is misdated November 22. See ibid., p. 233.

19. Paraphrased from Willcox to Grant, November 24, 1863, 10 A.M., ibid., p. 239. Original begins, "Your dispatches of 22d and 23d received. The first is unjust, as I will show you by my orders from Burnside."

impending battle with Bragg at Chattanooga; that he ignored, for the moment, Burnside's repeated orders for me to "hold the gap at all hazards"; and [that] he did not know that nearly all of my available command had been constantly, and was still actually, working towards Knoxville, thereby calling off the whole of the enemy's besieging force from the north side of Knoxville; nor in his haste did he take into view either General Williams' reported movements on the Kentucky side, nor a still more important report of the enemy's threatened movement towards the Abingdon salt works. Next came the following [from Grant]:

Chattanooga 11.30 A.M. [November] 23d
General O. B. Willcox
Your dispatch just received. Leave force enough in Cumberland Gap to hold it, and if you cannot move to Abingdon and Saltville with your cavalry and mounted infantry, fall back until you can supply yourself. We want to hold all the territory possible to be prepared to advance and retake that already abandoned.[20]

While making preparations for the move, and some further correspondence connected therewith, I received word from Burnside to place my "infantry within striking distance of Cumberland Gap and send your cavalry to harass the rear and left of the enemy in front of this place" (where they were pressing a second line of works.)[21] This message put me in a quandary. I transmitted it to General Grant and asked him to decide and no answer came. But Halleck suggested that Abingdon was too remote, and the Clinch having fallen, I put my columns again in motion towards Knoxville, keeping a brigade of infantry and some artillery at Tazewell.

The fact was that I had all along a scheme of my own which soon ripened into a handsome success. I have often wondered how that little blunder of the great strategist [Grant] got "mixed" in his dispatches, particularly as General Averell[22] was in the neighborhood of Abingdon and within easy reach. But General Grant had a thousand other things in view, all of which culminated within twenty-four hours by his crowning victory at [Chattanooga], giving him command of all our armies and enabling him to start Sherman's Corps at once towards Knoxville.[23]

20. Grant to Willcox, ibid., p. 232.
21. Burnside to Willcox, November 23. This dispatch, found in the OBW papers, was never published in the OR.
22. Brig. Gen. William W. Averell (26th, USMA 1855), then commanding in West Virginia.
23. Federal forces around Chattanooga defeated Bragg's besieging army in battles at Orchard Knob, Missionary Ridge, and Lookout Mountain on November 23–25, 1863, forcing

In the meantime it must not be thought that my cavalry operations had been limited to simple scouting for observation. No, there was many a skirmish and much done to draw off the besieger's pressure on the north side, enabling Burnside to concentrate his forces at Fort Sanders, where Longstreet finally made his chief [assault] at dawn on November 29.

A word as to the siege. The works were skilfully designed and thrown up by Capt. O. M. Poe of the engineers.[24] Fort Sanders, on the west side, was named after the gallant raider who had penetrated even into Georgia unscathed, but had lost his life in the early operations of the siege. The fort was commanded by Sam Benjamin, as we all loved to call "the Lieutenant."[25] The [Confederate] column of assault, three brigades, after a most gallant defense on the outside by General Ferrero, penetrated into the ditch, and, under an enfilading fire, assaulted the parapet, where Benjamin directed things in person, directing his Parrott guns and coolly lighting hand grenades with his cigar, so sensibly adding to the destructive work at close quarters. About 300 men and three stand of colors were taken in, and the enemy's killed and wounded amounted to 500. Our loss was about 26.

There are no accounts of the work going on along the rest of the lines, but you may be sure that so skillful a general as Longstreet did not fail to keep up the pressure, and that Martin's cavalry could effect little more than [to] stand off my people in his rear. Otherwise the siege continued to go on for some days, and the time had now come for me to "show my hand."

[I gave] directions to my cavalry to do all they could, [and, if] pressed by the enemy, to fall back slowly and [draw them] on to the Clinch River [at] Walker's Ford, where our forces would unite. The enemy, under [Brig. Gen. F. C.] Armstrong, with [Col. Thomas] Harrison's and [Col. George G.] Dibrell's brigades and a battery, were in the fight of December 2. They

---

Bragg to abandon the siege and retreat into northern Georgia. As a result of his continued success, Grant was appointed general in chief the following March. On November 28 Grant ordered Sherman to lead a relief force to Knoxville.

24. Capt. Orlando M. Poe had been colonel of the 2d Michigan and had led a brigade at Second Bull Run and Fredericksburg. Although appointed brigadier general of volunteers prior to Fredericksburg, his appointment was never confirmed by the senate, and in early March his commission in the volunteers expired, at which he reverted back to his regular Army rank of captain. At Knoxville Poe was chief engineer of the Twenty-third Corps. Later commissioned brevet brigadier general in the regular service, Poe rendered valuable service to Sherman during the Atlanta campaign and the March to the Sea.

25. Col. William P. Sanders had been killed on November 19 in cavalry skirmishing near Campbell's Station; Lt. Samuel Benjamin commanded Battery E, 2d U.S. Artillery. A devoted and skillful officer, Benjamin never rose above the rank of lieutenant, though he clearly deserved to.

endeavored to gain Graham's rear by a flank movement through one of the side gaps near the river, but were severely punished. They made several bold charges in the main road, over which my battery was posted, and they suffered accordingly, at least 100 killed, and we captured some 200 prisoners. On the whole it was a pretty little repulse. Colonel Dibrell was wounded and his adjutant general killed. . . . I have since learned through Judge S, who had commanded one of the Indiana cavalry regiments in the fight, that this repulse decided Longstreet to haul off at once, without awaiting the approach of Sherman, who was known to be on the way from Chattanooga to raise the siege.[26]

General John G. Foster[27] had come down from Cincinnati to command the department, and was waiting at Cumberland Gap for an escort to Knoxville, which our recent success enabled me to furnish, and both he and General Grant himself afterwards, when we met, were quite complimentary, the latter especially for "biding my time and resisting outside pressure." On his own part he explained his willingness to risk the loss of my command and the temporary loss of Cumberland Gap, in order, by our threatening movements, to keep Longstreet from turning back to rejoin Bragg during the pending campaign of Chattanooga.

And now, very quickly, I had another success to report to Foster, viz., the 16th Illinois, with 250 men, had defeated Col. [Campbell] Slemp's command at Jonesville, 350 strong, killing and wounding a large number and capturing 26 prisoners and 100 stand of arms.[28] My scouts also learned or heard that General Martin was wounded in the fight of December 2, and Longstreet, in his report of the siege, says that Wheeler, about the time of these events, wrote him that Bragg had ordered his cavalry to be returned. So that, on the whole, between Sherman's advance from Chattanooga, the failure to capture Cumberland Gap, and the . . . approaching departure of Wheeler's cavalry, Longstreet, as he wrote, "determined to abandon the siege and to draw off in the direction of Virginia, with an idea that we might find an opportunity to strike that column of the enemy's forces reported to be advancing from Cumberland Gap,"—viz., a portion of Foster's 23d Corps. "Our trains," he says, "were put in motion on the 3d," and his re-

26. Sherman reached Knoxville on December 6; Longstreet, aware of the imminent arrival of Federal reinforcements, began withdrawing from the city on the night of December 4.

27. Maj. Gen. John G. Foster (4th, USMA 1846). In May 1864 he was assigned to command the Department of the South, where he cooperated with Sherman in the siege of Savannah, Georgia. On February 18, 1865, Foster's troops would seize Charleston, South Carolina.

28. Slemp commanded the 64th Virginia Cavalry, of Col. H. L. Giltner's brigade, Ransom's cavalry division.

treat began, covered by General Martin, with his own and [Maj. Gen. Robert] Ransom's cavalry.[29]

On the 14th, General Foster reported that he had arrived at Knoxville and relieved General Burnside on the 11th, and that Parke, with his own and [Maj. Gen. Gordon] Granger's corps,[30] was following up Longstreet, which goes to prove that Longstreet was retreating, but slowly, and perhaps waiting "to strike the column coming from the direction of Cumberland Gap," and pay off the Clinch River affair.

Reinforced by a portion of Foster's corps . . . the column coming from the Gap under my command, moving by forced marches, reached the main body under Parke and Granger in front of Morristown, where Longstreet had turned and boldly stood. Longstreet knew Parke to be a cautious general and he knew Granger still better, for he "had probably played poker with him." And sure enough, after a reconnaissance in force (Granger's bluff perhaps), our two generals concluded that the enemy was too strongly entrenched and the chances were too slim, wherefore they retreated on Knoxville, followed up, but not pressed very hard, by the enemy. Being in command of the rear guard, I had occasion to know that [the Confederates] were not anxious to bring on a general engagement. In fact, my division, weakened by the absence of part of its cavalry, was quite sufficient to withstand their daily attacks. The last one was a skirmish on the outskirts of Knoxville, where I received a bullet on the breast—which would have been fatal but for the thick cape of my soldier's overcoat—thanks to the Lord of Hosts.

Soon afterwards I returned with my miscellaneous command to Tazewell, where in January 1864 I had the pleasure of spending a night with General Grant. He had been to Knoxville and with his staff took up his quarters in my tents, and it was there and then that I discovered his real greatness—I may say his genius.

LETTERS: SEPTEMBER 16–DECEMBER 14, 1863

Lexington, Ky.
September 16/'63
My dearest Mollie,
Enclosed you will find some of the photographs, also a letter from the 12th Mich. battery in regard to a pitcher. I have answered it and requested

29. See "Report of Lt. Gen. James Longstreet," *OR*, vol. 31, pt. 1, p. 462; the Twenty-third Corps, part of Foster's command, was actually commanded at this point by Brig. Gen. Mahlon D. Manson.

30. Granger (35th, USMA 1845), commanding the Fourth Corps.

Capt. Robertson to leave it with Gen'l Love. It does me good to see how glad the Lexingtonians are to see me. It is hard to get away—a hop for us to-night, and Judge Kincaid wants to give us a party to-morrow night, but I must get on as far as Camp Nelson to-morrow. Direct your letters [to] Camp Nelson *via* Lexington, Ky., care [of] Capt. E. T. Hall, A.Q.M., who will forward them from there. Much love to Lu, Elon, Ali & Grace and their dear Grandma.

> Thine,
> O.B.W.

Camp Nelson, Ky.
September 20/'63
My darling Wife,
This is Sunday evening, not much like the Sunday evenings at home. I have been full of business all day, superintending the outfit of a large command of troops, wagon trains, etc., for a long march.

The prisoners from Cumberland Gap passed here to-day on their way north. Gen'l Burnside paroled Gen. Frazer & his staff & they went by alone, much to the disgust of the Union people who consider how differently our own captured people are treated by the Confederates.[31] The other officers & the men were under guard. I hope to hear from you & Eben before I leave here, which I cannot do till after the middle of the week from present appearances.

Gen. Parke passed on yesterday. The mess have an excellent cook; he was head waiter at the Bates House, & is named Alexis—colored. Much love to Mother & all the children. I will write you again & send my pay accounts for September.

> Thine,
> O.B.W.

Camp Nelson, Ky.
24 September/'63
My dearest Mollie,
I shall be off early in the morning. I feel disappointed that no letter from you has yet reached this far, but presume you did not know how to direct your letters. You had better direct to me, Gen'l Burnside's army, care of Capt. E. T. Hall, Quarter Master, Camp Nelson, Kentucky. I hope you are all perfectly well & happy, Father returned, Elon a little man & doing

---

31. Frazer was not paroled but was in fact imprisoned at Fort Warren, in Boston harbor, where he remained for the remainder of the war.

well in his studies, Grandma satisfied with his progress, Lulu continuing to improve, Ali as sweet as ever, Grace growing strong & handsome, & you, my darling, as perfect as ever. I do not feel very buoyant, but am quite well & cheerful.

The Chattanooga reverse will turn out less than is feared, I trust, but as attention had been so long attracted to that quarter & it was so well known that a part of Lee's army had been sent to Bragg, I am surprised that Rosecrans was not strongly reinforced. I can only attribute the oversight to a lack of common sagacity, for so poor a judge as I have anticipated an overwhelming attack on Rosecrans. But I do not pretend to say who is to blame.

Robert received to-day a long letter from Abby, full of good wishes for both of us, Rob & me. I hope you will write Abby. Tell her I do not want to write William until I have something to write worth saying, for I know how much interest both he & Abby take in my career.

It is probably God's will that I should have been kept in a subordinate position so long & all for the best. The less am I disposed to murmur because we have been otherwise so highly blessed. If Mother has not returned from Chicago, I beg you to write her. If she has, you will see her often, & add to her happiness as much as you can.

Since my arrival here I have staid [*sic*] at Maj. Hawley's house & been hospitably entertained. It is one of the spots I want to bring you to see one of these days. I hope you will write Mira occasionally. I fear her hold on life will not be very long.

There are many darkies laboring at this depot. I can hear them singing this morning. They all confidently expect their freedom. Do not neglect your pen, as there is comfort & happiness for me on the end of it. Love to Father, Mother, & the little sweet ones.

Thine ever,
O. B.W.

Barboursville, Ky.
September 30/'63
My dearest Mollie,

To-day our road lay through a primitive neighborhood, where the people raise a scant subsistence on their hill sides. The young men are all "gone for a soldier," & none left but the women, children & old men. I saw this morning several sugar grinding or rather molasses grinding mills, worked by women & children & white-haired sires. Tell Elon I saw a little white-headed girl just his age driving the horse that turned the mill grinding sugar cane, & [her] mother told me the little girl worked so all day every day out in the sun. These poor people have been stripped of their scanty subsistence by the troops of both armies. This is the southern part of Kentucky, & to-morrow we cross the Cumberland River & shall be within fourteen miles of the famous gap.

I hear to-day by the telegraph that Burnside's resignation is accepted & that fighting Joe succeeds. Can this be true? I have nothing to say, but you know my feelings & opinions.

I have had very good luck with my raw troops & immense trains over the mountain roads. Of course I have to be very strict. My soldiers do not straggle so much as the Army of the Potomac. They have committed depre-dations for which I have had the people compensated. The 12th Michigan battery gives as much trouble as ever. Yesterday I issued orders for the guard to shoot any soldier committing depredations. The people here are all Union & shall receive every protection I can give them.

My staff are all well & work hard on the march. I have two new compan-ions, a little terrier puppy [Gyp] and a big black dog, which are both great pets with all. I hope you are quite well. Of course Father has returned well & in good spirits & cheers up Mother's drooping pinions. Did you receive the September pay accounts from Camp Nelson? Will try to write you again from Cumberland Gap.

Good night, kiss all the little sweet hearts & sweet lips around your pre-cious little motherly heart.

Thine,
O. B.W.

Cumberland Gap, Ky.
October 4/'63
My darling Wife,
Your letter of 23d ult. reached me through Capt. Hall yesterday. You cannot imagine the pleasure it gave me. I reached the Gap yesterday, though my advance got up before. The scenery from Barboursville here is grand & beautiful.

I have written several letters along the road which go by slow coach mail & may be later than this, for which Capt. Rowally of Gen'l Sturgis' staff is waiting. He will go through to Cincinnati post haste.

I do not know what further route I march, but probably not direct to Knoxville. I talked with Burnside over the wires last evening & he spoke of two proposed points, both eastward & towards the Virginia & Tenn. R.R., & we are now waiting for information.

I will write you again before marching, though I may not have so swift a messenger. Your letter gave unspeakable pleasure. Write often. Love to all. Glad to hear of Father's improving appearance & health.

Thine ever,
O.B.W.

Cumberland Gap, Ky.
October 4/'63
My dear Eb,

I was delighted on arrival here yesterday to be overtaken by a mail containing your letter of 21st ult. Of course you know from my Camp Nelson letter that I was detained there fitting out troops, & have been marching them along ever since the 24th. Had pleasant weather except a rain storm between Barboursville & Cumberland Ford, which made the road fearful.

How often I wish you were along. You would enjoy the scenery so much, especially as we got on to the Cumberland River, which wound along the road at the base of [a] magnificent range of hills, overhung in many places with cliffs of the most appended sort.

Reached here yesterday & shall lay over to-day. Which way we march from here is not yet determined, but we do not go into quarters anywhere but expect to go against the enemy, probably southeastward, against Bristol, or eastward, against Jonesville, where the rebels are supposed to be in some force. My Hoosiers are the wildest, roughest fellows, but I am getting them in some discipline. They are tractable. The officers are not much above the men, & there is little subordination among them. My body guard started out on a little scout last night, which may determine our next movements. Love to all, especially Mother.

Thine ever,
O.B.W.

Morristown, Tenn.
October 8/'63
My darling little Mother,

I reached here this morning. It is on the Richmond & Tenn. R.R., forty miles east of Knoxville. The cars are running. I expect to march to Bull's Gap to-morrow; some of the 9th Corps are there. What my command will be I don't yet know. The corps are scattered everywhere.

Had a terribly severe march yesterday. Forded two rivers & marched over Clinch Mts., the worst I ever saw. It is sickening to behold the ravages committed by the rebels in this country. Many houses are empty, many burnt, many families who were well off are left without a morsel to eat.

But it is a picturesque country. Within two days I have crossed several ranges of mountains. Cumberland Gap is grand. The hills on either side rise over two thousand feet & the Gap is visible far off. My last march of two days usually takes four. Nobody sees any newspapers here. You had better enclose stamps in your letters. All are well, including my horses Burnside & Kearney—another fine bay.

I suppose we shall go against the enemy in a few days, but you will probably hear the result before this reaches you. I am rather under the impression they will fall back. It is forty miles from Cumberland Gap here, & twelve from here to Bull's Gap. The enemy are at Greeneville & Jonesboro. Love to all. Kiss my little darlings & may God preserve us all to be together.

Thine,
O.B.W.

Greeneville, E. Tenn.
October 17/'63
My darling Wife,
We have moved Head quarters into town & laid here while Shackelford, with his cavalry, have been driving the rebels out of E. Tennessee. Burnside has gone to Knoxville with his staff. Before going he offered me either the 9th Corps with the speedy probability of Parke's superceding me again, or the District. I told him I preferred my division of the old corps to any District command. He is quite unwell & says he means to resign peremptorily, in which event the corps will fall to Parke.

I am waiting for Shackelford to finish his operations before going to Knoxville. The staff are comfortably quartered in a large new house belonging to a rebel officer named Arnold, while I am in a huge mansion belonging to the Widow Williams, with extensive grounds—the chief house of the town.

The W. is quite an extraordinary woman, looks a good deal like Mother & is very clever, very proud, very benevolent & a good Episcopalian. She was quite stiff with me at first, but we are now on very good terms. She has two sons in the rebel service & her sympathies are probably with them, though she pretends to be neutral & "for the Constitution." Her third son is a Union man & a farmer with twenty negroes, which exempts him from the rebel conscription. It may console Mother to know that the servants here are the bane of life. Mrs. Williams is as unhappy with them as you are at home.

Mr. Williams' farm three miles from here is called the College Farm, from the site of the old Greeneville College, where many of the great men of the south in the last generation were educated. William C. Preston & others. There is scarcely a trace of it left now, except the mansion of the president, Dr. Coffin, who was a New England Calvinist of great energy & eccentricity. The old house is but a ghost's walk now, held up mainly by its huge chimney stacks, which rise through the center of the building, & the foundations of which in the cellar are about twelve feet square. The Episcopal church stands in Mrs. W's garden, but the pulpit is vacant, for which I am sorry as to-morrow is Sunday.

Greeneville is also interesting as being the residence of Gov. Andy Johnson. His taste must be like Eben's for willows, which he has planted on top of a high hill where he says he wants to be buried. I wish I had wings that I might fly to you daily & talk with you. Great love to Father & Mother & kisses for the children. How is Grace?

Thine,
O. B. W.

Greeneville, E. Tenn.
October 19/'63
My dearest wife,

Mr. Patterson leaves here day after tomorrow for Lexington & will carry this letter probably more expeditiously than the mail. I have as yet received no letters through Capt. Hall of Camp Nelson, except one from you & one from Eb at Cumberland Gap.

Nothing new has transpired since my last. I am still domesticated at Mrs. Williams, enjoying a beneficial rest & recovery from some slight ailments due to camp exposures. Expected to start for Knoxville to-day, but am still waiting orders. If I were to remain here, I should project a raid into North Carolina, where there are thousands ready to join our standard.
[Continued Oct. 21]

Still here chafing with impatience for active service while the good weather lasts. In a few weeks the period for active operations will be over. The dangerous point is at the other end of our line, towards Chattanooga. I believe there has been some fighting at Loudon to-day. I have heard of the change of departments & relief of Rosecrans by [Maj. Gen. George H.] Thomas. I don't know how Burnside will like to be commanded by Grant, but think he will not object to it, especially for the short time he will probably remain.

I hope you will find time to write me at least twice a week. A mail came yesterday bringing letters for all but me. It was a cruel disappointment. I fear Capt. Hall has sent my letters by some slow train. You had better direct at once to Knoxville. Tell Caro it would be charity to write to me. There is a report of a riot in Indiana. I feared there would be difficulty as soon as my delicate but firm fingers should be withdrawn from the throat of the Hoosier Copperhead.

Give my love to all. Ask Miss Campbell how the Aid Society prospers. Did anyone speak for them at the fair? I wish Father would write. Does he drive out much? I am ignorant of affairs on the Potomac. Kiss my little darlings & mother for

> Thine,
> with ceaseless love,
> O.B.W.

Greeneville, E. Tenn.
October 25/'63
My darling wife,

I was rejoiced yesterday (Sunday too!) by the receipt of your letter of Oct. 6, after so long an interval. I am very sorry to hear your eyes have troubled you again & beg you to select a less dazzling seat at the next one of Madame Centeman's concerts. Remember me always to the dear madame, in whose prosperity & happiness I feel so much interest.

I am glad Mollie's photograph is to be added to our little collection of beautiful faces of the times, hers among the most beautiful & queenly. I am glad Mr. Lightner strikes Mother & yourself so favorably. I hope to make & enjoy so valuable an acquaintance. Long life to Peter, whose good star lights up dear old St. Paul's again. . . .

Your good accounts of Elon's schooling "pleases me much," as old Major Scott used to say. Tell him that nothing makes Papa more happy, way off here in Tennessee, than to hear that he is doing well at his school. Glad Lulu continues to gain strength, hope her trip to Peoria will be beneficial, but think Grandma had better have made the visit without encumbrance.

I am glad she has taken up her fine brush again, & will send you some leaves &c from Mrs. Williams' garden, which the old lady has just been gathering with kind regard for you. Her place must be beautiful in the spring; even now there are roses, violets & some pinks in bloom. Among the rarities I send you from her is a green rose, some crape myrtle leaves (not of the flower) & some twigs of box transplanted from Mt. Vernon. I think you would like her. She is one of those it would be pleasant to visit after the war. She treats me with great kindness & distinction. The staff take their meals here, but have quarters in another building.

We have had much wet & dreary weather lately, no sign of Indian summer yet. Luckily the troops have not had to march, for some of them are barefoot. I hope to hear from you oftener; your letters are more essential to my life than meat & drink. If eyes or anything else prevent your writing, have Father or Mother take the pen—do not let so long an interval occur again, as you "love, honor & obey" with a million kisses.

Thine,
O. B. W.

Greeneville, E. Tenn.
November 1/'63
[To Marie]
As beautiful a day my darling wife as you ever saw, as bright & balmy as any warm spring affords in any clime. But this is a changeable clime, it is always April—my natal month—but I am not changeable, am I, love?

Yours of 11th October is received enclosing Maynard's Chinese epistle, refreshing for its naivete. Your own epistle seemed a little low spirited. I fear you are too much of a hermit. I hope you go out often & see people— particularly bright, young people.

I have been very much taken with Mrs. Williams' description of the Moravian schools for children. She received her education at Salem, N.C., in one of them. She says there is one also at Bethlehem, Pennsylvania. Will you inquire about it? It would be just the place for Lu, & after a while for Elon, just what they need, the most perfect system, every hour of the day with the purest morals & gentlest disciples—& probably less expensive than any. Mrs. W. was just ten when she entered. There were five hundred scholars from everywhere, too. Don't be frightened, but inquire all about the Bethlehem affair. I should feel perfectly safe with the two children at such a place as Mrs. W. describes.

[Continued November 4]
I have just finished the foregoing with much self-complacence & jumped into bed when a telegram from Burnside arrived, saying Grant had ordered him to relieve Boyle & put a "discreet & capable" officer in charge of Kentucky, that he had asked Grant not to insist upon it, but if he did, I would have to go to Louisville & take command. I remonstrated against such a disposition of me & have been waiting to hear the result, but so far have not

heard. Such a change would extinguish my faint hopes of promotion in the field, and the only consolation in it would be that you could visit me. Burnside says I am the only officer that can fill the place, which is very likely. I shall not be surprised if I had to go. If I do, you may hear of the change from the papers, even before this letter reaches home. Good night. Let us not murmur at anything, but trust that all will be best.

> Thine,
> O.B.W.

Bulls Gap, Tenn.
Nov. 11/'63
My dearest wife,

I write you a line by the train on telegraph paper. You will think I am getting to be quite a fast man! I am well & roughing it extensively. I will try to write you to-day. Fell back here on Saturday from Greeneville without accident, by order of Gen'l Burnside, after Garrard's defeat at Rogersville. The nights are cold, but days pleasant & wood plenty. Love & kisses to all.

> Thine ever,
> O.B.W.

Bulls Gap, Tenn.
November 11/'63
My darling wife,

We had a severe night march coming down here from Greeneville. My friend Mrs. Williams parted with emotion. I hope we will move up & re-occupy before very long. The appointment to Kentucky in Boyle's place is countermanded, & I expect to remain. Still have command of the Left Wing, but without permanent assignment to any corps or division—all right. My present position is more distinct & larger & more important than anything I could expect. Burnside telegraphs me I shall have "a more *agreeable* command" soon, but I like this well enough, & am blessed in expecting [nothing] these days.

Keep your precious self in all calmness & trust in the assurance of all being well. Do not worry about me no matter how seldom you hear of or from me. The telegraph wires are frequently down & the mails irregular. We are looking for good news from Chattanooga, but know nothing certain. Rumors are current that Bragg has fallen back. If so, it will assist us here materially, of course.

I wrote you a brief note this morning. Have received your letters regularly up to 23d October. [Lt. Samuel] Benjamin & [Lt. Col. Orville]

Babcock[32] both take the greatest interest in me & write their sentiments freely. Benjamin sighs for the Army of the Potomac. Am much obliged for Caro's interesting letter. Will write William soon; have very little time at present. The roads & weather continue good, but we expect rough times soon in both respects. With love inexpressible to you & kisses for children & Father & Mother.

Thine,
O.B.W.

Cumberland Gap, Ky.
November 24/'63
My dearest Wife,

You must have wondered at not hearing from me for so many days during this exciting period. But night & day I have been in the midst of overwhelming cares & anxieties of every sort, without sleep or rest & knowing that you must hear by the newspapers of the daily movements; telegraphic communication not being cut off, I have not felt uneasy on this score. I told Brackett to write you one day, but, hoping to write myself, put him off.

I have been & am well. My greatest trial has been in thinking all the time that people at home must be expecting me to march to the relief of Burnside when I have not sufficient force to do it, & when his orders were clear & positive to fall back here & hold this gap, which he deemed of more importance than anything else I could do.

He has been holding out heroically & I hope the attempt made upon him will fail. Some person got through from there to-day, & rumors are heard that Longstreet has fallen back twelve miles below Knoxville. I should not wonder if the suspense continued some days yet. Firing has been heard by my scouts every day. All the accounts I have heard represent our army in good position & good spirits.

I was blessed with a letter from you on arriving here; it bore the date [of] the 10th [November]. The little darlings are well & this is a comfort. You do not seem in your usual calm good spirits but write a very spicy letter for all that! The universal carnival of gaiety & extravagance is absurd & vulgar—& I do not wonder the sight shocks you. I have written Abbie quite a lengthy letter (for me) but actually been too busy even to mail it, though I will this time, & hope it will not be "cut off" at last.

32. Babcock was then inspector general of the Ninth Corps. He would later join Grant's staff.

If we live long hereafter, the events of the last few weeks will be a fund for the fireside. Except a few skirmishes between cavalry outposts, I have not yet fought any battles, but performed a series of maneuvers which have accomplished their objects. God bless & keep you & my little ones & love to Father & both Mothers, Eb & Louise.

Thine,
O.B.W.

Cumberland Gap, Ky.
November 28/'63
My dearest wife,
Just a line to tell you I am very well, as Capt. Hinckey is going to Detroit. I expect Gen'l Foster up here every day. The weather is cruel on the rivers & roads & seems to war against our doing anything. I think Burnside will hold out long enough & that all will come out well. Love to all & do not feel uneasy.

Thine,
O.B.W.

Cumberland Gap, Ky.
November 29/'63
My dearest Wife,
Still in the midst of anxious fears & hopes for Knoxville & Burnside, hopes rather prevailing, as now I know Grant's troops are moving up to his relief—But will they be in time? I expect Gen'l Foster here to-morrow evening. This will relieve me of a huge load of responsibility.

Meantime, how are you, my darling? After a rain storm the weather has turned severely cold & frozen up the roads & the dreadful mud, but the men & the horses & mules suffer both with the cold & short rations. Falmouth was nothing to it. The men have been sometimes two & three days without bread, & a few scanty ears of corn without hay have to do for the horses. But if we can hold on & crush Longstreet, the reward will be ample. Write me often, if only a few lines at a time. Love to all.

Thine ever,
O.B.W.

[Letter continued later.]
Greeneville, E. Tenn.
In command left wing army.
December 1/'63
We have just passed through a big scare. We heard the rebels were largely reinforced & coming down upon us with a rush from western Virginia.

Gen'l Shackelford fell back to Greeneville with his cavalry division & one of my brigades that was at Jonesville, with orders from Gen. Burnside to report to me, but by the time he got here we found it was a false alarm & I ordered him back. My command now is largely increased, being in fact the left wing of Burnside's army. But everything is uncertain; the troops are constantly changing position to suit circumstances. All we can do is let Providence work it out, and I am confident He will work it out in our favor. I frequently think I have been a little overlooked by the Earthly powers, but if the Heavenly are on my side, who can be against me? My old lady friend, Mrs. W., has just presented me with a bible—the Devil I suppose having abstracted my own from my trunk—& I fear you will think I have preached a sermon from it. I had just received orders from Burnside to hold the Hoosiers ready to move down to the 9th Corps when the scare took place, & here we Hoosiers are yet!

Thine with love to all & kisses for *les enfans*,

O.B.W.

Near Walker's Ford
Clinch River, Tenn.
December 4/'63
My dearest Wife,

We are encamped on the Tazewell & Knoxville road on the north side of Clinch River. Have been roughing it for some days (with good health & spirits & some military success, for which the Lord be thanked). Gen'l Foster reached the Gap on the 30th. I had every preparation made for a move in the direction of Knoxville. One brigade of my cavalry was across Clinch River at Maynardsville, part of the infantry at Tazewell, & part at the Gap. We moved more infantry down to Tazewell on the 1st, & established head quarters there for the night.

Next morning, Dec. 2, I moved down here with the infantry at different points, one brigade & battery marching towards the ford. Meantime the cavalry had been falling back slowly before a heavy force of Wheeler & Jones' cavalry, which were confident of gobbling my cavalry brigade entire. But they kept up their camp fires at Maynardsville & got down to within three miles of the ford, where Col. Graham commenced making a stand in the mountains, where they contested the ground inch by inch with the rebels three times their number, until [Col. G. W.] Jackson's brigade[33] of my

33. Jackson's brigade consisted of the 116th and 118th Indiana and 2d North Carolina (Union) infantry regiments, and the 21st Ohio Battery.

infantry reached the ford, put artillery in position, crossed two regiments at the ford and we repulsed the rebels at from a half mile to a mile from the ford. Graham's ammunition being exhausted, he withdrew under Jackson's cover, in perfect order. The rebels drew back one & a half miles & before midnight commenced retreating towards Knoxville. Next morning my cavalry began to recross, & followed the retreating column, picking up some prisoners.

Col. Bowman is with me [acting as] chief of staff temporarily, his regiment being in Knoxville. All the staff are well. Tell Mrs. Williams that Richards is hearty & well & doing me efficient service, & Brackett is valuable as ever. If our blessings show by contrast, I have been blessed above my fellows, as no death has come to our dear ones, while Maj. Lyon has lost his only child, Brackett his father & Capt. Patton, who commands my escort, has lost his wife.

Gen'l. Foster seems friendly & cordial. I like his style altogether. It is flattering to me that with all the contradictory orders & suggestions I have had from Burnside, Halleck & Grant, with reference to the use of my overall forces, Foster has pursued the very plans I had already in train. I have exchanged several communications with Burnside since the siege began & telegraphed Mrs. B.

Sherman & Granger ought to be within striking distance of Longstreet to-day or to-morrow. Longstreet seems to look like making a fight with them, but as Sherman is [on] one side of the river & Granger on the other, & Longstreet is only strong enough to fight one, I think he will probably be compelled to retreat. (I hope so.) If I have done no other good, I think I have compelled Longstreet to keep all his cavalry on this side [of] the river, leaving the other open for Burnside to get forage & supplies. If all continues to go well, I shall soon be able to relieve you of all anxiety, & if I do not, you will remember that God directs all for the best. Love & kisses to all.

Thine,
O.B.W.

Tazewell, Tenn.
December 7/'63
My dearest Wife,
After the affair at Walker's Ford, I came back here—am very well. This morning I am starting down again on the Morristown road towards Bean's Station. I have sent some infantry near there in hopes of cutting off a force of rebel cavalry now fighting with our cavalry. Notwithstanding all the rumors, we did not have positive intelligence of Longstreet's situation till

yesterday, though he began the movement in the middle of the week & has been going very leisurely. I telegraphed Mrs. Burnside last night that I had no doubt the siege of Knoxville was raised.

Give my love to all & write the people in Chicago & Washington whenever you hear from me, so they will not feel anxious.

Thine as ever,
O.B.W.

Tazewell, Tenn.
December 9/'63
My dearest Wife,

Maj. Lyon leaves to-day for his home, going on leave. Gen'l. Foster started for Knoxville this morning with all his staff. My division of cavalry has gone also in pursuit of Longstreet, and with lots of work before me, I am at present quiescent.

A huge lot of things looms up in the future if Foster carries out his plans. One thing he has avowed to do, he will have *money*, & pay the people for their flour & corn; we have been robbing them worse than the rebels. We are well into the winter, but so far there has been no snow. The last week has afforded splendid weather, but rain & mud are the ruling deities of the season.

How are my little pets? You must not think I have not had time to think of them. You & they are *never* absent from my thoughts. The first & last idea always is how will Marie & the children be affected. I hold my life & fame but in trust for you & them. How is Mother this winter—and Father? Three such cultivated people as you three could make the time pass lightly & delightfully if each one would "come out of his shell" a little more. Pardon the hint. . . .

Your last letter was about the 15th. This is a long time back, but I hope the mails will soon bring me something.

Maj. Lyon is waiting. A thousand kisses.

Thine,
O.B.W.

Tazewell, Tenn.
Dec. 11th, 1863
My dear——

Have you a good map of Tennessee? If not you had better get one.

You will see what a critical position I occupied when I commenced my retreat from Bulls Gap (102 miles above Morristown) towards Cumberland Gap. You will see that I had two large rivers, Holston & Clinch, to cross, & nothing but mountain ranges all the way.

The enemy were just above Rogersville on one side and at Knoxville on the other. They had a nearer road to Cumberland Gap, with cross roads leading into my route. I had two brigades of cavalry with which to cover the movement of my infantry, and an immense train of wagons and artillery.

I began by sending scouting parties towards the enemy, threw both brigades of cavalry across the Holston, one above (east of) Rogersville, the other to Bean's Station and toward Knoxville, at the same time sending scouting parties up towards the Gap to seize the cross roads. One of these parties, under Capt. Hammond, 65th Indiana, with forty men, suddenly came on a whole regiment of rebels encamped at Mulberry Gap, near Powell River, surprised them, charged in & scattered them and routed the whole regiment.

Meantime, I halted half a day at Russellville with the infantry, and nearly two days at Bean's Station, reopening communication with Burnside, who still insisted upon my making Cumberland Gap secure. Scouted down to within five miles of Knoxville & finally got everything, without loss, to the Gap & Tazewell. The enemy did not strike Bean's Station until two days after I had left it.

But now my troubles were just begun. Starvation stared us in the face! I found no bread for my men at the Gap. The rains had made the rivers and roads impassable, so that no supplies could be got from Kentucky.

What is to be done? I telegraph Grant and Halleck for orders, and offer to attempt to fight my way through to Knoxville, if they said so. But one suggests this, another that, and both say "use your own discretion and help Burnside all you can." Then the Clinch River becomes impassable. Grant says fall back on your line of supplies and try and send your cavalry to Abingdon, Va. & the salt works. But two-thirds of the horses had lost their shoes. I had begun to cross my infantry over Cumberland Mountain, towards Kentucky, when I discover there are mills on Powell's River. I find there were also horses on the road from Camp Nelson. I seize the mills and grind wheat (some of the regiments 36 hours without bread), hurry up the horses; Clinch River falls. I send a brigade of cavalry across it again, a regiment towards Jonesville, another toward Jacksboro. I send a brigade of infantry back to Tazewell. My cavalry I spread over the country for forage. And after holding on by the skin of my teeth for ten days and overcoming the worst and getting all ready to harass the rebels' rear, up comes Foster and reaps all the harvest.

My Jonesboro expedition whips the enemy there. My Jacksboro expedition drives off the rebels, who had just come up to steal some thousands of hogs stopt on their way to Knoxville, and we secure the property. Moreover, on this road communication is opened with Byers at Kingston and then with Granger.

My cavalry across the Clinch attracts from Knoxville the whole of the enemy's cavalry force, five thousand, under Major Gen'l Martin, before whom ours fall back to the infantry supports at Walker's Ford, where we give them a handsome repulse, & pursue them at daylight [the next] morning.

This [is] an epitome of my Tennessee Campaign: between three forces, viz. 9,000 rebels on the east, Longstreet on the west, and starvation all around me. If I ever won the sword it was here. But no newspaper reporters were around.

You must know I never had over 5,000 effectives, with all the trains of the left wing of the army to draw off, Tennessee recruits to save without arms, & thousands of . . . refugees thronging the road, many with their families and household furniture. But nothing was lost. Good night.

Thine ever,
O.B.W.

Tazewell, Tenn.
December 13/'63
My dearest Wife,

This is Sunday, one of the milestones which I always notice on my way, particularly away from home, and glad am I always if quiet is permitted me to wrap myself in a little atmosphere of home memories. Indescribably sweet are the recollections which cluster round the rosy hours spent with you during so many years—so many & yet so precious that they seem few; & the uncertainties of the future & the separation of the present are so tantalizing when we look back upon the little Heaven of the Past. But I hope we are not thrust out of our Garden of Eden, nevermore to return. I hope the good days will come again, all the better for the suffering we have endured. . . .

And even now the consciousness that I have so dear an angel at home with the little cherubs, makes me happy & rich & not cast down. If we can only patiently endure & survive the necessary evils of the war & be together again, its almost the highest earthly blessing I can crave, & I believe we will do it. I never despair of the future, & never want you to. How glad I would be to be at home even a short time. I think I could cheer you all up.

I think the best thing to be done at present is to send you some money! I have not realized until I came to look for the collect of the day, how near we are to Christmas. I will make arrangements for your reeling funds if it has to be done by telegraph. Meantime, if you are in want of money to carry out any of your wishes or plans for Xmas, do not hesitate to borrow of Father.

I have this moment received a dispatch from Gen'l Foster, now at Knoxville, who says that he & Gen'l Parke will visit me in a few days to confer with my command. When Foster left here he expressed the greatest satisfaction with all my late military operations, culminating in the repulse of the enemy at Walker's Ford, Clinch River, & said he should continue me in command of the Left Wing & give me a largely increased force of cavalry. He spoke of placing Gen'l Cox in command of Kentucky. But just now I heard that it was said at Knoxville that I was to go to Kentucky. The old story. Burnside has got it in his head that nobody will do for Kentucky but me, & probably advises Foster accordingly. Parke wants to keep me out of the 9th Corps, & the three have probably settled it. At any rate I shall know in a few days. Boyle is to be relieved anyhow; that is a fixed fact, & if Foster asks me to take the place, I shall do it, as it would not be well to remain here with the influences against me, when I could go to Louisville with everything in my favor. But I think Cox is a better man for the place. One thing I am determined on. If I remain in the field, I will have a command according to my rank, or resign.

Maj. Walker, paymaster, has been here some time & afforded us much amusement with his fat laugh. I will make arrangements through him to have money sent you this week.

[Continued December 14.]

Just received a note from Foster offering me command of 23d Army Corps & the district east of Cumberland Gap. This is an agreeable surprise & comes on the eve of your birth day. I have sent you a Christmas & birth day present of $200....

> Good night,
> Thine ever,
> O.B.W.

Capt. Poe will take this & mail it.

Tazewell, Tenn.
Dec. 19/'63
Dear Love,

I enclose a letter to Mother by Major Walker. The major also takes my pay account for November & will send you a check for the amount $292....

Have not heard from Gen'l Foster since I wrote you last. Longstreet turned about that time & has been pushing our advance back toward Knoxville, isolating me again.[34] Meantime Gen'l Cox is on his way to the field, & as he ranks me who knows but he will get [the] 23d [Corps]. But don't trouble yourself about these things. If things turn out that way, perhaps I will apply for a leave.

Merry Christmas & Happy New Year to Father, Mother & dear little children.

Thine,
O. B.W.

Maynardsville, Tenn.
Dec. 30/'63
My dearest Mollie,

I am here still & particularly forlorn as the mail facilities, never very great, are less than ever.

Affairs are quiet on the Holston, which is now the Rappahannock of this field. Grant is expected at Knoxville in a few days when it is expected that many things now in the fog will be cleared up—among others the question of who is to go to Kentucky & the commands arranged.

In several of your letters you express the desire that I should get a leave of absence & pay a visit home. Things have not been situated so that the application would be proper, but if they do settle down so as to promise a lull in military operations, I will make the effort. My heart never yearned so much for home & for you as it has this whole dreary, disagreeable, unsatisfactory winter, which I know has proved as unpleasant to you as it has to me, & a visit home would do us good, & make up for many a lonely hour.

To-morrow morning I shall send both to Knoxville & to Tazewell for the mail & hope to have letters from home. I have had little or nothing to do for the last few days & time has hung heavily, no books to read except the trash in a country farm house. Col. Bowman has left for his regiment, & so his society is lost. He proved excellent company, & I miss him very much.

Robert wants to go home on leave before Lizzie sails. Don't know whether he will succeed, but think so.

Gen'l Foster has not yet heard from the sec'y of war. The Gen'l injured his wounded leg by a fall with [his] horse the other day. Good night. Kisses to all.

Thine,
O. B.W.

34. Longstreet had withdrawn from Knoxville, moving up to Rogersville, resting and refitting until the night of December 13, when he marched back to Bean's Station. There, on December 14, he struck the van of Parke's pursuing troops, under Shackelford, whose troops barely escaped capture.

§ NINETEEN

Remembrances of U. S. Grant

[*Unhappy with the inactivity of his command posted on the Clinch River guarding the Cumberland Gap, Willcox requested to be returned to duty with the Ninth Corps, then pursuing Longstreet's forces northeast of Knoxville. Accordingly, Willcox was relieved at Tazewell on January 15, 1864. Two days later he rejoined the Ninth Corps at Strawberry Plains, Tennessee, where he assumed temporary command, Maj. Gen. John Parke then being in overall command of all Union forces then pursuing Longstreet.*

As Parke began to fall back upon Knoxville from Dandridge, Willcox, with the Ninth Corps, was left behind as a rear guard, with orders to hold the enemy in check at Strawberry Plains. On January 21, having burned the bridge over the Holston, Willcox posted his artillery, managing to hold the enemy's cavalry and artillery at the fords until midnight, when the Union troops were withdrawn.

On the following day the Confederates took up the pursuit, coming upon Willcox's rear some five miles above Knoxville, near the Armstrong house. Willcox, with the Ninth Corps and a division of the Twenty-third Corps, managed to drive off the pursuing Rebels with little trouble.

On January 26, Parke resumed command of the Ninth Corps, while Willcox assumed temporary command of the Second Division. Encamped in the vicinity of Knoxville, the Ninth Corps and other Union troops pursuing Longstreet now fell under the control of General Foster, until February 9, when Maj. Gen.

John M. Schofield[1] relieved Foster as commander of the department. Skirmishing continued around Knoxville until March 16, when the Ninth Corps was relieved and ordered to Annapolis, Maryland. Refitted and reorganized, the corps, now some twenty-five thousand strong, was once again placed under Burnside, for service with the Army of the Potomac. Willcox, meanwhile, returned to the command of his old First Division. However, as he later wrote, "for some reason which I do not now remember, when the corps was reorganized, the First Division became temporarily the Third. This occurred during my absence from Annapolis, & it was as the Third Division that we crossed the Rapidan on the 5th of May & engaged in the bloody campaign of the Wilderness."]

LETTERS: JANUARY 1–17, 1864

Maynardsville, Tenn.
January 1, 1864
My dear little Wife,

Yesterday it rained all day. It was with difficulty [that] the camp fires of the men could be kept up. In the night it poured harder than ever, but suddenly the wind rose & killed the rain; it began to freeze, & to-day is the coldest of the season. The ink in my inkstand is hard frozen, reminding me of school days. This is certainly a trying field on the troops; it is rain, mud, frost [and] wind all the time in the "Switzerland of America." I am in a farm house colder than in a barn. The staff are in tents in the yard. Food & forage are both scarce. But all are cheerful.

I wonder how you are & what you are doing. Do you receive to-day? I hope you & Mother are nicely arranged & glorified with your best smiles, with house open & table well spread. But I almost fear the actual picture presents a closed mansion & a basket outside. If I were home I would throw open my window & door & drive out all the bats! I wish you would let Caro & me keep house for you one winter—you'd all live ten years longer for it. Tell Caro I congratulate her on the distinguished success of her little state dinner....

I wish I could relieve myself by a good talk with you & Father. Some days I feel dreadfully despondent & blue & it requires a great effort to keep from sinking into a state of confirmed disgust. I believe, however, that Providence humbles me for my own good, by disappointments which I could not bear if not supported by a superior power, & received as Christian trials intended

1. Schofield (7th, USMA 1853) replaced Foster in command of the Department and Army of the Ohio on February 9, 1864, as Foster had been injured in a fall from his horse.

for correction & improvement. But the worst of it is I don't know that I improve any under it.

Cox! Is he not my evil genius? He carried off all the *eclat* at South Mountain, & just as I was ordered the other day to the command of the 23rd Corps & thought I was to be fairly shed of the "Babes,"[2] Cox looms upon the horizon & claims the command by rank & gets it, & here the Babes & I are with one another still, waiting for something else to turn up. Grant must have got to Knoxville yesterday morning, as guns were heard in that quarter, supposed to be a salute, & I hope the uncertainty will soon be cleared up.

Perhaps I am too ambitious & should be satisfied with the command of the Left Wing. On the whole, I am able to bear these crosses and intend to rise superior to them all, doing my whole duty for the poor, distracted country, one half of which is in mourning & ashes, while the maniac other half are dancing in the gilded trappings they have snatched from the burning ruins of our once glorious temple.

And what are my trials or yours, compared with the wretched inhabitants of East Tennessee—ravaged, ruined & driven from their homes. On the whole I come back to the philosophy of my youth: "Sweet obscurity" is the best lot—while I am probably the last man to be contented in sweet obscurity. There is no lot or station in life that hath not its bitter train of attendant circumstances, & I dare say that if I should resign from the army, as sometimes tempted, a thousand minor troubles would harass any position to which I might descend.

From this gloomy picture of the common fate of humanity [illegible word] us & turn & look at more satisfactory objects. You are spared to me, my children are not snatched away from me. Our love is a mine of happiness which I would exchange for no other temporal advantage—would you?

The greatest burden to me is separation from you & your loneliness— which for my sake & for your own I beg you to bear cheerfully & without repining over any or all the disappointments that happen, & I will try to do the same for your sake.

I will keep this open till to-night, when I look for a mail.

2d January

The mail did not come in. Happy New Years. Love to all. Kiss Lu, Elon, Ali & Grace.

Thine,
O.B.W.

---

2. OBW's term for his raw Indiana troops.

Knoxville, Tenn.

January 12/'64

My dearest Wife,

I have been spending a day or two here very pleasantly. I found Gen'ls Granger, Parke, Wood,[3] Carter & others at Foster's headquarters, where I have been staying. A district called the District of the Clinch was assigned to me, & I came down to see about it, as it left me, under another name, the same command & troops I had before, & I was anxious to get back to the 9th Corps.

It seems that Gen'l Foster was under the impression I belonged to the 23rd Corps, & Foster said he thought he was doing a good thing by me in giving me a separate command. He promptly consented to relieve me, & I go back to Tazewell now, to turn over the Babes & then go to Blains Cross Roads, to report to Gen'l Parke for duty with the 9th Corps. Shall probably command it when P does not himself.

A few days before I left Maynardsville, Gen'l Grant & staff passed along & stayed over night with me. We smoked incessantly, as his wont is, till one o'clock at night, & it nearly killed me. I slept little after it & he not a wink! How he stands it I can't imagine.

Last night there was a gathering of generals at the house of a Union citizen of Knoxville, Col. Temple, where there were warm-hearted Union girls & some dancing, which I must confess I enjoyed hugely, having been on the outskirts of the world, hanging on so long by the eye brows.

I am interrupted—adieu—Kisses to the children & love to Father & Mother.

Thine,

O.B.W.

Head-Quarters 9th Corps

Strawberry Plains, Tenn.

January 17/'64

My dearest Wife,

I joined the 9th yesterday at this point, a vast plain of mud with the Holston winding through. All seem glad to have me return. Find Col. Bowman down from an injury recd by fall of his horse. Col. Babcock well & hearty. Am settling my head quarters to-day; shall pay a visit to Dandridge to-morrow & return next day. Love to all.

Thine,

O.B.W.

3. Probably Brig. Gen. Thomas J. Wood (5th, USMA 1845).

I never shall forget one night that I spent with Grant.[4] It was in the midst of the war [early January 1864], the battle of Chattanooga had been fought, [and] the siege of Knoxville was raised. . . . My quarters were scanty and we occupied a room together. During the early part of the evening the general was engaged with his a.a.g. over some important correspondence with his different field commanders. Grant wrote or dictated the more important letters, some of which were read in my hearing, and I was struck by the ease, conciseness and clearness of his composition. Every sentence was simple and pithy; there was little repetition, no indecision, nothing to correct. Few men can equal him in putting orders or reports concerning complicated movements into intelligible English.

Business over, the weary a.a.g. retired to bed, but Grant showed no signs of fatigue, and sat up with me long after the witching hour, smoking and talking over old times, and discussing the progress of the war, the character of men, and, to a certain extent, the future movements of the several armies. I had known him casually for many years, but never till now had I enjoyed so good an opportunity to judge of his intellectual caliber. His conversation flowed on placidly, a broad, strong, and full stream, from topic to topic, evincing such a keen but comprehensive judgment of men and measures, generals and generalship, statesmen and statesmanship, as few would give him credit for at that day. His perception of character, as tested in some cases by my own familiar acquaintance, was wonderful. He appeared to read men like an open book (at a glance), or by some one action, or some slight manifestation beyond the ordinary ken. Hence his "lucky" choice of generals.

The next thing that impressed me, and that which is least known of him, was the peculiar quality of his mental operations in complicated affairs, viz., a power to generalize, and to select and fasten his mind upon the prominent points, to the exclusion of enveloping details. His mind having once seized the right thread of any tissue of facts, he held to it with an inflexible grasp that was not to be shaken off by any power under the sun; there that fact stood, as plain to him as a mountain peak, lifting its head above the whole range; it was as simple to him, and in the course of his conversation it seemed almost as simple to you as the alphabet—so simple indeed that you were not half inclined to give the man credit for his sagacity.

Most men would have strained themselves in the process of arriving at the culminating points of their reasoning, whereas, to Grant's mind, the culmi-

4. The following monograph on U. S. Grant was originally published in the *Lynchburg Virginian*, November 10, 1868.

nations themselves were so apparent that there was no labor. These mighty plans that he talks over in such a plain, unassuming, unconscious way, seem like the most ordinary combinations of an ordinary mind. You do not realize their greatness until afterward, and then you begin to do justice to the man that does himself so little justice in his manner of speech. His thoughts are not the least clogged with the process itself through which a problem is solved. His insight cuts like a sword through each gordian knot, and there lies the result, divested of all mystery—the very pith and marrow of the matter in hand.

This power of dealing only with the preponderating facts, and of losing sight of all the cumbersome array which commonly weighs down weaker souls, is the law of Grant's mind. Call it abstraction, generalization, concentration, or what you will, it is the highest law of intellect, such as Caesar and Napoleon displayed in government, Newton and Laplace in science, and Goethe in art. Great truths are always clear to great minds. But Grant is a master-workman rather than a thinker. He disregards abstract rules and formularies, and advances straight from a survey of the field to the right conclusion as to the work to be done. He scarcely seems to know whether he has violated principles laid down in the books, but unconsciously carries out new principles, and his deeds speak for him. In every emergency the question with Grant is, what is the best thing to be done? and that, with him, is the only thing; that he always seems to discover at the right time and in the right place. It is a gift; not the gift of inspiration, but the intuition of prodigious common sense, genius bounded by utility.

I had good opportunities afterward, in the course of the war, to observe the strong leader as he knit together the links which throttled the rebellion. Always intent on essential objects, which he had for the most part long held in view, and which the public itself now began to discern, never embarrassed by troublesome details, he crushed the Confederacy by taxing the supreme resources of the country, and directing the blows of his generals, stroke after stroke, to the two or three main issues on which alone success depended. The rebellion collapsed so suddenly that the world was astonished. The idea of "luck" was dispelled, and the people began to estimate the greatness of the central figure which now loomed up above the heads of all our other chieftains.

It is because few persons have opportunities to see Grant in his proper element, at work, overmastering events, and because he makes such a commonplace show in his ordinary intercourse with people, that the elementary strength of his character was not visible to the world. Especially is he different in conversation with strangers on subjects which one might naturally expect would draw him out. But it is a rare thing for him to be drawn out. He does not talk for effect. He knows nothing but utility. Most men converse well in the line of their own art—they dote on the weapons of their skill; but, to Grant, his own art is no art—it is all common sense; and such is his dislike of every kind of display, that he would sooner pass, with the Welsh philosopher, for an idiot in a crowd, than for the best talker in America.

Human greatness can be measured by the magnitude of the difficulties that are overcome. In this case, other great soldiers being the judges, the difficulties were so great that Grant alone, of [all] the chieftains in the field, was able to overcome them. There were men of talent and genius around him, but only in Grant appeared that combination of mind and heart which was absolutely necessary to success in the late colossal struggle. I doubt whether there can be found one of his lieutenants who will not frankly admit that, in some particular quality, Grant excelled him, and that such a quality was essential to success. Many of his characteristics are well known, but they can be best grouped by comparing him with his best historical likeness, namely, Wellington.[5]

Wellington was not a genius, but the quintessence of common sense. He was cold, and inspired no enthusiasm in his troops; without personal ostentation, but with such perfect sincerity of character as forbade display or egotism; cool, cautious, daring, and indefatigable; of a mind so equally balanced that prosperity could not elate nor adversity depress him; undazzled by victory, undismayed by defeat, rugged in honesty, stanch in patriotism, concise in utterance, he was as intensely English as Grant is intensely American; he was the rock against which French enthusiasm dashed itself into froth, as Grant was the tower against which Southern chivalry tilted itself into splinters.

Yet [Wellington] was more a man of privilege than Grant. He worshipped his order and was a Tory, while Grant worships his country and believes in the common right of man. [Wellington] could, like Grant, endure everything, but could not, like Grant, dare everything. In this respect Wellington resembled Sherman; he feared no danger that he could see, while Grant fears no danger whether he can see it or not. Like Grant, the Iron Duke was strong in his clear heart. He could grasp the greatest events; howbeit he remembered the smallest details, and thus embarrassed himself in cases where Grant would have been free. Grant seizes the mightiest events, and leaves

5. Arthur Wellesley, First Duke of Wellington (1769–1852). For another comparison of Grant and Wellington, see John Keegan, *The Mask of Command* (New York: Viking, 1987).

the details to men of detail, judging and knowing his man by an intuitive sagacity equaled only by Napoleon.

No one but Wellington has been equal to Grant in simplicity, uprightness and massiveness of character; or so free from selfishness, jealousy, vanity, passion, meanness and irresolution. Nothing ever distorted the vision of either man; neither possessed the imaginative faculty; both were generous, but Grant is magnanimous, while neither Wellington nor Grant has been so much indebted to fortune as to the practical force of his own intellect.

In civil affairs it was to the wisdom, moderation and patriotism of Wellington that England looked to save her from revolution, as America now looks to Grant for a similar salvation.

The statesman, warrior—moderate, resolute,
    Whole in himself, a common good,
The man of largest influence,
    Yet freest from ambition's crime:
Our greatest, yet with least pretence—
    Great in council and great in war,
Foremost captain of his time;
    Rich in saving common sense,
And, as the greatest only are,
    In his simplicity sublime![6]

LETTERS: FEBRUARY 14–MARCH 16, 1864

Head-Quarters, 2d Division
Ninth Army Corps
Near Knoxville, Tenn.
February 14, 1864

This, my darling Marie, is the Sunday before Ash Wednesday, as I have ascertained by searching the Prayer Book. I think I would like to spend Lent at home & be there Easter. But there is no probability of any thing while the war lasts.

I was blessed with two letters from you last week; the last was January 27. I wrote you the other day by Gen'l Sturgis, & expected to write more while spending the hours on a bore of a court-martial. But I have not found it practicable. Nevertheless I have thought of you.

6. From Tennyson's "Ode on the Death of Dorothy Wellington." The third and fourth lines actually read "Mourn for the man of amplest influence / yet clearest of ambitious crime."

The newspaper correspondents have created a great state of uneasiness about the safety of Knoxville, which has never been felt here. For the sake of telegraphing or writing something important to their papers, they frequently make mountains out of molehills, as they did of the recent change in the position of the troops, which, as they could not understand, they imagined to be a retrograde movement, & picking up street rumors in Knoxville, they made a panic out of it for home consumption. I would like to hang a dozen of them for the anxiety they cause among the families of the troops. Knoxville is stronger than ever it was & better supplied. You must distrust every sensation[al] telegram you see.

I did not send my horse to Kentucky. Both of them are in good condition. I have seen Gen'l Schofield twice. He looks a little like Eben Ward. Gen'l Stoneman is here, commanding [the] 23rd Corps, & Cox is relieved & waiting orders.

Elon's praying [to] God to save the barn is an indication for which we cannot be too grateful. The good seed is sown early by his careful Mother. I hope Lu will carry out her intention of writing me a letter. You must not yield too much to the exactions of Miss Grace, or she will make a shadow of you. I hope Father & Mother will enjoy themselves in New York. Love & kisses to all the children. Write me often.

Thine,
O.B.W.

Head-Quarters, 2nd Division
9th Army Corps
Mossy Creek, Tenn.
March 4, 1864

I have just received your nice long letter of Feb. 21, my darling wife, & it gives me great pleasure. You wondered where I was. I am always where I am thinking of a certain pretty one who stole my heart long ago & retains possession of the trifle to this day, having strung around it a joyous set of pearls in the shape of four little children and one in Heaven.[7] You draw a cozy picture of the fire side library which my heart aches to visit, but I have a calm trust that I shall be spared yet to return.

We left Knoxville about the 26th, marched to Strawberry Plains, crossed on the pontoon boats & marched up to Morristown, ascertained that Longstreet had not yet left Greeneville, & fell back to this place, which is about thirty (30) miles above Knoxville. What will be the next move I do not yet

7. Referring to OBW's daughter, Caro Willcox, who died in infancy prior to January 1860.

Brig. Gen. O. B. Willcox in 1864. *USAMHI.*

know, but the inevitable papers will probably announce it with the usual embellishments before this reaches you.

We have had two or three days of drenching rain & have every reason to expect more throughout the month, as March is usually a wet month in these latitudes. I had hoped to see Greeneville again, & perhaps we may yet renew the forward movement. I believe our operations were partially suspended by orders from below. If the rains continue, I do not see that we can accomplish much, as the roads become awful until April.

My little division does very well for its size & will begin to fill up soon with the veteran returning regiments. I should be perfectly satisfied if I had some of the Michigan troops of my old division; those I have now are New Hampshire, Massachusetts, Maryland and Indiana boys.

Health continues good. Robert is temporarily with Gen'l Ferrero. My present adjutant gen'l, Capt. [Henry R.] Mighels, is the proper adjutant gen'l of the division. He was with Gen'l Sturgis when he was in command, &

is far from a congenial or even suitable person. But all I have to do is wait & changes bring themselves around.

Capt. Tompkins left for home the other day & promised to see you. I hope you will send me pictures of yourselves & some nice pickles—particularly Grace's picture. How I have got the pictures & pickles "mixed"! By the way, I have just received a letter from Mrs. Gen'l McClellan, asking for a photograph & autograph for a collection for the Sanitary Fair. Will you send her one of Runyon's best, & get a lot to send me. I have a number of applications. Write her a nice letter; little Mac certainly was very friendly to me. His injudicious friends have placed him in a false light before the country. With her letter came *two* from you of January 10th & December 28th, the much-longed-for Xmas letter. Let me read it.

I have read them both & nice letters they are, worthy of my own wife. I am glad Xmas passed off so happily & [I] should have enjoyed seeing you come out for church in your new bonnet, muff, veil, &c, the pride of my eyes. The children's presents were very nice. . . .

All the staff thank you for your kind remembrance & good wishes & send respects. I will send you some of their photographs. Glad you remembered Mira, Mrs. Dana & all. Have not yet received Lulu's letter. Love to each little darling & kisses for thee.

Thine,
O.B.W.

Morristown [East Tennessee]
March 14 [1864]
The troops are lying here quiet, except those engaged in reconnaissances. There is an occasional excitement in the camps by the enemy's cavalry dashing up to the picket lines here & there. It does not look at present as if anything extraordinary is to be accomplished here just now. We have not heard from Burnside concerning the movements of the 9th Corps since his conference with Grant at Washington. I am looking for the news from Washington with considerable interest, not to say anxiety, to see how the spring campaigns are going to open & who is to command the Army of the Potomac.[8]

O! Tempora, O Mores!

---

8. Grant had been called to Washington and commissioned lieutenant general on March 9, 1864. The following day he was appointed general in chief of all the Union armies. Though Grant would make his headquarters with the Army of the Potomac, Maj. Gen. George G. Meade retained his post at the head of that army.

March is March in Tennessee my dearest Marie; such violent winds & rains & cold & sun. All our heads & stomachs are upset completely. I am just emerging from a bilious disagreement, caused by the weather & a long march the other day, with the sun in a fit of force just after its chill. March is the aguc & fever month of the old luminary. To-day he is as cold as November, or as one of Mrs. John A. Welles' smiles.

I have not been sick, but headachey for a few days, but feel quite well to-day. I am very glad to hear that Mother [has] gone to Washington, & Father with her. The latter will be disgusted, of course, by the set there, but Mother will not see it, & will find enough to entertain her quite a while. I hope she will see Mrs. Ricketts & the Gillises. . . .

I think you had better take the children to New England this summer. It will do you all infinite good. I am very much pleased with the idea of it. I also received a copy of—speech for the Industrial school. Did he dress in cap & bells or Negro uniform[?] What fools people are making of themselves at home now a days. I am glad my little wife is so true & honest; it gives me one earthly pole star of faith in this ridiculous age. Love & kisses to Lu, Elon, Ali & Grace.

Thine,
O.B.W.

Morristown, East Tennessee
March 16, 1864
Your letter of March 6, enclosing others from Mother, Caro & Father was received yesterday, my darling Molly. The luxury of hearing from you within ten days is [as] inexpressibly charming as it is unusual.

I am glad Father accompanied the Vice Regent to the seat of government. It was just as it should be. And I am still more gratified with the account of Mother's peregrinations, all so satisfactory & pleasant. In fact, were it otherwise, I should have been both surprised & indignant. After all, it depends very much upon ourselves & the impression we have made by our reputation & that we make by our manners, & in both respects our Mother never need have cause to lament a want of attention wherever she goes. Her keen capacity for enjoyment will always do the rest for her. I think it is a pity she can find no adequate inducement *at home* for her to exert her powers to gladden society around her & make herself more glad in it. But the moss will gather around the most sparkling stone if it will not condescend to roll.

It is possible after all that I may see you soon. The order came last night for the corps to assemble at Annapolis. How many days . . . von Schofield may detain us here I cannot tell, as I am equally in the dark as to the precise object of this last move to Morristown. It is intended that we shall proceed via Chattanooga.

The very thought of revisiting home kept me awake nearly all night. To look into your eyes, to fold you in my arms, to embrace all the little ones & thus gratify the longings of a heart that only finds rest on earth beneath the shadows & sunshine of home, will relieve my longing, aching heart for a time. I feel most of the time as an actor must feel in a prolonged drama on the stage, every power continually strained for extraordinary efforts, coupled with a higher responsibility & real dangers, instead of mimic. And I never forget your great cares & loneliness, your torturing suspense & painful apprehensions, your household labors & motherly trials, with no husband's bosom on which to lay your aching head.

But you have borne it nobly & stand above all the world in my grateful heart. Without the feeling of confidence & security I feel in *you*, life would not be worth the struggle; but with you, nothing can prostrate me, & life is sweet indeed. But I fear you think I am running too far out of the usual course of prosy matrimony. Caro says married people ought not to be too much in love.

Well, I have no other news, only that this is one of the coldest & most freezing days of winter, after a burst of sunshine. Love to all.

Thine,
O.B.W.

TWENTY

The Wilderness to Cold Harbor

[By the end of 1863, it was painfully clear to President Lincoln, as it was to the rest of the Northern people, that the war in the east had been going wretchedly for the Union. The Army of the Potomac, the nation's number-one fighting force, had been defeated in every major campaign it had undertaken, with the exceptions of Antietam and Gettysburg, two victories that had been gained by fighting on the strategic defensive, repulsing Robert E. Lee's two invasions of the North.

In the west, however, things had been going quite differently, for there the war was being won. The Confederates had been pushed from western Kentucky into the far reaches of Mississippi, and from Tennessee into Georgia. Also, of course, following the fall of Vicksburg in July, the great Mississippi River itself had been reopened for navigation. One man, more than any other, had been responsible for these victories in the west: Ulysses S. Grant. On March 9, 1864, in a little ceremony at the White House, he was appointed general in chief of the Union armies, with the rank of lieutenant general.

Making his headquarters with the Army of the Potomac (now under the command of Maj. Gen. George G. Meade), Grant would personally oversee the implementation of the spring campaign in the east, and for the first time during the war Ulysses S. Grant and Robert E. Lee, the men who would emerge as the two supreme military figures of the war, would face one another in battle.

On May 4, 1864, the Army of the Potomac began crossing the Rapidan River, entering a region of bramble and second-growth timber known, appropriately, as

the Wilderness. The resulting two-day Battle of the Wilderness (May 5–6, 1864)
would be one of the most desperately fought engagements of the war, resulting in
a tactical standstill.

Grant withdrew from the Wilderness on the night of May 7, but much to
the surprise of nearly every officer and enlisted man in the army, he did not fall
back to lick his wounds, as the army's previous commanders most surely would
have done. He elected, instead, to move south. In that moment the war for the
Union had taken a new turn, and from that time until the surrender of
Lee's army at Appomattox Court House the following April, the Army of the
Potomac and the Army of Northern Virginia would be in close and bloody
contact.

As a result of the almost constant fighting, Orlando Willcox would have little
time for writing in his journal, or even for writing letters home, at least during
the initial phases of the campaign. Fatigued by the constant strain of
campaigning, he would often rely on his young staff officers to write home
for him. Those letters are included here with his own postbellum writings on the
campaign that would bring an end to the war.]

FROM THE [crossing of the] Rapidan, May 4, to Petersburg, June 15, was
almost a continuous struggle with disadvantages. It was an irregular campaign, undertaken contrary to accepted strategic laws. At first sight it would
look as if not the shortest or the best route to Richmond was selected, but
about the worst. And yet, after . . . weighing all the circumstances, Meade's
army, as it stood, could not well have been picked up and carried round
either to the Peninsula or to the James, leaving the Virginia Central and
Richmond and Fredericksburg railways in the hands of the enemy.

A left-flank march parallel to the sea from the Rappahannock down,
gave the best basis of supply and transportation and a movable fighting basis
for the scheme that Grant had in view, and enabled him to carry on the
campaign by a series of crab-like approaches to Richmond, even though
partially repulsed at one or more points. He judged, moreover, that the time
had come for the Army of the Potomac to fling away the scabbard and fight
to the bitter end; that mere fencing skill would no longer avail, but hard
knocks; that the army could live where Lee's could; that now he had come to
stay, and that one or both of the antagonists must be "chawed up," in which
case Sherman would have a walk-over.[1] And with his superior numbers
and resources, he was willing to force the fight. . . . "We must save our

1. In the original, OBW later repeats his observation that "one or both of the antagonists
must be 'chawed up,'" attributing it directly to Grant: "As he said to me, 'if Lee and I chaw each
other up, Sherman will have a walk-over.'"

men all we can but not save Lee a jot. Our blood comes from the skin, his flows from the heart."

McClellan, [Grant's] . . . only rival in the history of that army, had passed through the books—books which all the professionals knew, Lee with the rest of them. Great soldiers of this sort had transmitted their species from one generation to another. All had succeeded up to a certain point. Besides this, McClellan was magnetic and wore a charm over his breast which led men to dance and fence and fight as long as he waved his truncheon. The name of this truncheon was his magnetism. As long as he had the advantage and abundance of means, he was successful by skillful use thereof.

Grant had gone out from this school. He was most familiar with simpler schemes and his was the genius of common sense. The first element of his strategy was hard knocks. But not all of it. Every move was carefully planned on lines that promised the best results by the use of superior resources, combined with [an] intuitive sense that saw the end from the beginning, knew where, as well as when to strike, and to keep on striking. . . . "If we are badly off with all our resources, Lee must be worse off and suffer worst," he said.

His detractors said the campaign of the Wilderness and Spotsylvania Court House was a useless slaughter and showed [that] the chief [was] apparently cruel, [or] at any rate, indifferent to blood. Was he capable of becoming terrible? In the popular mind, a phrase saved him: "I will fight it out on this line if it takes all summer." This key note of the late campaign thrilled all chords in the popular heart, and ran through the ranks of his men. Whatever happens, we will not go back. McDowell, McClellan, Burnside, Hooker, had all gone back under mishap. Here was a Marshal Forward. [Grant] was at once desperate and sanguine, serious and cool. His survey covered not only the present field, but the whole field, the whole country; and the fates, which are at once cruel and certain, stood by him. He believed that Lee fought against the stars. . . .

He had but one passion, to overcome obstacles. Ill fortune, the persecutions of time, and a secret enemy fighting in his breast—these all had rendered him insensitive of expedients, perhaps reckless, but always daring. As long as the obstacle lived, his resources multiplied. His brain was never befogged by the intermediate welter of surroundings. He always saw the sky, and the mountains to be climbed. From the beginning, he had thrown away the scabbard, and if he had no other talisman, it was to overcome the giant that guarded Castle Dangerous by main force, never heeding that he might himself be thrown. . . . You may pound, you may flay, you may grind such a man to powder, but every particle of his dust is grit, inscribed "never surrender."

To give the enemy no rest, to find the weak point in his lines, to push him to the wall, not to let go the clutch, was the best chance of success, in fact the surest road. It was not a question of relative skill on which Lee prided himself with his faculty of divination and with his superior knowledge of the country, roads and rivers . . . but a question of possibilities and exhaustion. On Northern soil it was otherwise; there both McClellan at South Mountain and Meade at Gettysburg had baffled and beaten this *preux chevalier*, whom aristocrats in England still hold up to *their* world as the great genius of our American War. . . .

The friends of McClellan also have drawn the contrast between that general's cautious preparation and care for the lives of his men and the recklessness of Grant in [the] Chickahominy neighborhood. But even such comparisons are unnecessary and odious and rebound to the discredit of all concerned. For with all [of] McClellan's acknowledged skill and masterly movements on the Chickahominy, he did not ultimately succeed for the want of certain other qualities which crowned Grant's career. . . .[2]

It must be confessed that, aside from the strong McClellan passion in the Army of the Potomac, Grant, in taking supervision over [that army], virtually superseding George Meade, labored under some disadvantages in opinion of many West Point men. For instance, General Upton[3] says "McClellan was a more highly educated soldier and full of inspiration. T'was thought that Grant had nearly forgotten his education; he had for a long time labored under a cloud" before the war, and his great success in the Valley Campaigns of the Mississippi were attributed to luck. And even now he was charged with relying on "brute force." But his genius was that of common sense. In his report he said:

> From the first, I was firm in the conviction that no peace could be
> had that would be stable and conducive to the happiness of the people,

2. The foregoing introduction to this chapter was taken from a rough introduction by OBW for a proposed chapter on Cold Harbor, never finished. The introduction, however, seems more appropriate here.

3. Emory Upton (8th, USMA 1861) made his mark as a brigade and division commander in the Sixth Corps. At Spotsylvania Court House on May 10, 1864, he won his brigadier's star by an innovative column attack that pierced the Confederate lines. Author of *Infantry Tactics* (1867) and *Military Policy of the United States* (published posthumously, 1904). Upton, suffering from violent headaches, committed suicide at his post at the San Francisco, California, Presidio on March 15, 1881.

both North and South, until the military power of the rebellion was entirely broken. I therefore determined, first, to use the greatest number of troops practicable against the armed force of the enemy, preventing him from using the same force at different seasons against first one and then another of our armies, and the possibility of repose for refitting and producing necessary supplies for carrying on resistance; second, to hammer continually against the armed force of the enemy and his resources, until by mere attrition, if in no other way, there should be nothing left to him but ... submission. ... [4]

In pursuance of this policy of hammering with superior numbers, General Grant ordered the 9th Corps over from Tennessee to Virginia, adding by so much to the strength of the Army of the Potomac, which had so far been no more than equal to Lee's army. But with his usual kind consideration, he saved Burnside the mortification of reporting for duty to General Meade, whom he had formerly commanded, and Grant took personal supervision over both their armies.

The movement of the Army of the Potomac's long trains across the Rapidan revealed to General Lee the direction of our route, and he was rapidly concentrating and posting his own troops to confront Meade in the Wilderness of Spotsylvania County, but a few miles from the Rapidan. This stream, which is a branch of the Rappahannock, was crossed by Meade's army with little or no opposition, beginning at midnight of May 3, 1864, just before the 9th Corps' arrival at Bealton, Brandy Station and Manassas Junction, and Meade established his headquarters near Wilderness Tavern. [5]

At 1:15 [P.M.] of the 4th, General Grant telegraphed Burnside from Germanna Ford to move by forced marches to that crossing of the Rapidan, which accordingly we made, one of them forty miles long—and crossed the Rapidan by the night of the 5th and morning of the 6th. Thence Burnside was started off promptly with General Willcox's, General Potter's and General Stevenson's divisions, Stevenson being in command temporarily of my old division. ...

‹I never can forget the Wilderness and Spotsylvania Campaigns. The fighting reminded me of stories of Indian fighting in the northwest, when

4. Report of Lt. Gen. U. S. Grant, July 22, 1865, *OR*, vol. 36, pt. 1, pp. 12–13.
5. Upon crossing the Rapidan on May 4, Meade established his headquarters with those of Grant at a farmhouse atop the bluff on the south bank of the Rapidan, overlooking Germanna Ford. He did not move his headquarters to the vicinity of Wilderness Tavern until May 5.

the tribes were large and it was mostly in the native forest. The skirmishing for position was like bushwhacking from tree to tree.›⁶

We were just in position on the front line, between Hancock and Warren, both already engaged, with Grant's orders to Burnside to hold Stevenson in reserve near the Tavern, subject to Hancock's call for support, [and] to "pitch in" with the other two divisions at five next morning, and participate in the general engagement.⁷

The first shots came from the enemy on our right and left front, a little before five [A.M.], and punctually at five, two corps under Generals Warren and Sedgwick began the attack on the right. The two vigorous assaults were made against the enemy's entrenched line on Orange Court House Road, and were both repelled with severe losses, as was also Warren's attack on Ewell's right, nearer by.

Hancock's attack was less vigorous and somewhat handicapped by Grant's warning to look out for Longstreet, reported by some prisoners to be marching towards our left. After an hour's interval, the battle was renewed, Warren and Sedgwick being ordered to "press the attack." Severe fighting followed throughout the woods and heavy thickets—intersected by only the Plank and other more narrow and winding roads. The losses were heavy on both sides. . . .

Returning for a while to Hancock: About 8 A.M. Stevenson's division had reported to him at the intersection of the Brock and Plank roads, and subsequently, at nine o'clock, Hancock received a dispatch from Grant that aide-de-camp Comstock had been sent to point out to General Burnside where to attack, but this attack did not begin until 2 o'clock.

At 8:30 [A.M.] three of Hancock's divisions and part of Stevenson's had been "furiously engaged." The firing had scarcely become warm when Hancock was informed that his left, under [Brig. Gen. Francis C.] Barlow, was seriously threatened, and so he had to send a brigade under Getty, with [Col. Daniel] Leasure's brigade of Stevenson's division, to support Barlow on this ill-omened report of Longstreet's arrival, which, as I have said,

6. OBW wrote two drafts of his account of the Battle of the Wilderness. The basis for this chapter is taken from a draft originally enitled "Grant in the Saddle: The Battle of the Wilderness." The second draft, untitled, is briefer and rather incomplete; excerpts from that draft are contained here within single angle brackets ‹ ›.

7. OBW's memory fails him here. The Ninth Corps remained bivouacked along the Germanna Ford Road, north of Sedgwick's Sixth Corps on the extreme right flank until early on May 6. Willcox's and Potter's divisions did not reach their assigned position on the Chewning Farm heights, between Hancock and Warren, until 8:00 A.M., three hours after the fighting began.

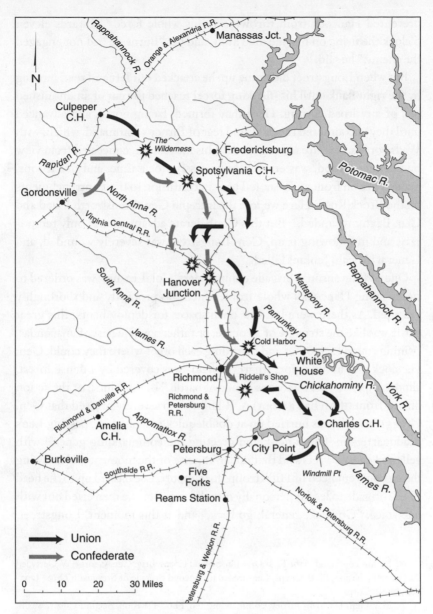

Grant's overland campaign, May–June 1864.

prevented Hancock from throwing in his whole force.[8] Towards eleven o'clock the firing on his line died away, and yet "Burnside had not engaged the enemy," he said.

But when Longstreet did come up, he attacked our left and rear, moving by the right flank until his [flanking force] reached the cut of an unfinished bed of a railroad cutting. Here they formed, facing north, and advanced until they encountered the flank and rear of Birney's command, which, with Wadsworth's, was already engaged.[9] This movement, concealed from view by the dense wood, was eminently successful for a time, and our troops, under a fire on front and rear, fell back in confusion to their entrenchments on the Brock Road. Here we lost the intrepid Gen. Wadsworth killed and Gen. Baxter wounded.[10] But this Confederate advantage was only temporary, and in following it up, Gen. Longstreet was severely wounded, and General [Micah] Jenkins killed.

One of [Stevenson's] brigade commanders, Col. Leasure, was ordered to sweep along Hancock's whole front, which was promptly and thoroughly executed. As there were but few open spaces for deployments, this great battle was like the struggle of a couple, or rather a whole nest of anacondas, twining round each other and throttling each other where they could. Gen. Hancock says in his report [that] the field "was covered by a dense forest, almost impenetrable by troops in line of battle." In the course of the action on our front (if we had a front) A. P. Hill was so severely pressed that Gen. Gregg's brigade was hurried up at doublequick to assist him, passing Lee's headquarters in Tapp's field, and greeting the commanding general with yells and cheers.[11] It is said that under impulse of the moment and knowing the most urgent need of Hill's troops for support, Lee dashed up to the head of the brigade to lead it personally into the fray. But the men cried out with one voice, "Go back, general, go back," and at this moment, Longstreet,

8. Barlow commanded the First Division, Second Corps; Brig. Gen. George W. Getty led the Second Division, Sixth Corps; Leasure led the Second Brigade of Stevenson's First Division, Ninth Corps.

9. Maj. Gen. David B. Birney, commanding the Third Division, Second Corps, was in direct command of Hancock's troops south of the Orange Plank Road. His troops received the brunt of Longstreet's flank attack; Brig. Gen. James S. Wadsworth, commanding the Fourth Division, Fifth Corps, was in direct command of Hancock's forces north of the Plank Road.

10. Wadsworth was mortally wounded on May 6, dying two days later; Brig. Gen. Henry Baxter led the Second Brigade, Second Division, Fifth Corps.

11. See "Report of Maj. Gen. Winfield S. Hancock," *OR*, vol. 36, pt. 1, p. 325. Brig. Gen. John Gregg, C.S.A., led the famed Texas Brigade of Maj. Gen. Charles W. Field's Division, Longstreet's First Corps. Gregg was wounded in the attack.

coming upon the ground, Lee was constrained to yield to their demand and turn to other duties.

Early in the morning, at half past six, General Hancock, not hearing any fire from Burnside's direction, had sent [a] request to Meade "that Burnside may go in as soon as possible. As General Birney reports, we about hold our own against Longstreet, and many regiments are tired and shattered."[12] But reiterated orders to General Burnside to push forward and attack did not bring about his expected cooperation, and I am sorry to add that, according to General Humphreys, as late as 11:45 [A.M.], General Rawlins, Grant's chief of staff, had to write him, "Push in with all vigor so as to drive the enemy from General Hancock's front and get in on the Orange and Fredericksburg plank road at the earliest possible moment. Hancock has been expecting you for the last three hours. . . ."[13]

In Burnside's defense it must be remembered that the movements of the enemy could not be observed until the lines were almost in collision—as Hancock writes. He might well have added that as supports were out of sight, he could not tell whether they were not also hotly engaged when called for and most needed. This may account in part for Burnside's "repeated failures" to move out.

[Burnside's] two available divisions were Willcox's and Potter's—the former composed entirely, says Humphreys, "of raw troops, inexperienced in every way." It must be remembered that I had not yet recovered command of my old division, temporarily commanded by Stevenson. . . .

«[We] followed the 2nd Division [Potter's] up Plank Road to Parker Store Road. [I] Detached Hartranft's Brigade to support the 2nd Division, and remained in position across Parker Store Road, with the 2nd Brigade (Christ's) and a section of [Capt. Jacob] Roemer's artillery.[14]

The 2nd Brigade was shelled by a battery of the enemy, on a ridge across Wilderness Run, and skirmished with the enemy on the right and front until 2 P.M., when it was withdrawn, by General Burnside's orders, to support Hartranft's brigade.

The 2nd Division having engaged the enemy in heavy force between the 5th and 2nd Corps, Hartranft advanced his brigade on the right of the 2nd Division, charged the enemy's works, which the 8th Michigan broke through, capturing some prisoners temporarily, but this advantage was lost

12. T. Lyman [for Hancock] to Meade, 6:30 A.M. May 6, 1864, *OR*, vol. 36, pt. 2, p. 440.
13. Rawlins to Burnside, May 6, 11:45 A.M., *ibid.*, p. 461.
14. Roemer commanded the 34th New York Battery.

by the 2nd Division falling back before the enemy. Still, with his ranks somewhat broken, Hartranft held his main line until I came up with Christ's brigade, when the enemy was completely checked.»[15]

‹At about 5 P.M. I was ordered to attack at 6, General Hancock being ordered to attack at the same time; but the enemy [attacked] him first. My lines were formed rapidly and pitched in about 5½ o'clock. We drove in the enemy's skirmishers, broke through their main line [of] entrenchments, which we held with their dead and wounded in our hands, but they stole through the woods and outflanked us, while the fire from their works was so galling on the right that Hartranft's further advance was checked. But we halted and held the ground up to the enemy's teeth until night, when [the] contumacious Southerners sullenly drew off, leaving the field in our hands and enabling us to open communication with the 2d Corps, which in fact was the main object of the movement. But our losses were considerable, my own division suffered nearly five hundred killed and wounded.›

This was the only part I had took or could even see of the tremendous struggle in the Wilderness. In all other engagements so far, the lines had been more or less under view of the generals, who could see where breaks occurred or advantages could be gained, and where to send the reinforcements; but here our fighting had to be carried on as [if] it were in the dark. Even the roar of cannon gave uncertain indications, and critical moments passed before knowledge could be obtained. Still, Longstreet and Lee's personal presence, as it were, in the thick of the fight, and Hancock's own superb bearing and magnetic influence, made up partially for the lack of vision on the respective sides. Moreover, the Confederates stood on their own soil, [of which they were] already more or less familiar, [and of] which we were densely ignorant, except as to the general direction of the railroads laid down in the maps. But if the battle [had] not [been] an "accident," as some hold, a different line of march from the Rapidan, according to military critics, might have brought the fighting into more open ground—and that would have been a decided advantage for our side.

Going again into particulars, the thickets took fire in many places, and 200 of our wounded were said to have perished in the flames. Such is War. The total loss of killed, wounded and missing was about equal on either side, and equal gallantry had been exhibited.[16] The enemy was not routed, but they were pretty well "hammered" in the woods; and on the outside, their

15. The foregoing, contained within the double angle brackets « », is excerpted from OBW's report.

16. Union losses for May 5–7, 1864, were 17,666. Confederate losses, for which there is no accurate record, have been estimated at between 7,500 to 11,000.

cavalry . . . were handsomely beaten by Sheridan, [Brig. Gen. George A.] Custer and [Col. Thomas C.] Devin; and on our moving out towards Spotsylvania on the 7th, Sheridan, with Gregg's and Merritt's divisions, attacked Jeb Stuart's and Fitzhugh Lee's whole mounted force and drove them to their barricades and rifle pits, which were then charged and captured.[17] So that on the whole, our army was in good spirits for the coming battle of Spotsylvania.

SPOTSYLVANIA COURT HOUSE

On the evening of the 8th we found ourselves near Perry's House, two miles from Chancellorsville, with but a confused idea of the geography of that or any other country—our maps were so poor, & we had just gotten ourselves so tangled up in the woods & the crossroad with the troops of other corps—& somewhat with the Johnny Rebs, & on the day of the 8th we had marched as the rear guard of the Army of the Potomac, protecting the field hospitals & standing off the enemy's cavalry. . . .[18]

At Chancellorsville we passed on by the other divisions of the corps. At 4 o'clock on the morning of the 9th we started, under orders from corps headquarters, for a point called, on my map, "Gate," at the crossing of the Spotsylvania & Fredericksburg road over Ny River. We had no orders what to do after getting there, but it was probably intended that we should hold the crossing, & the general movement of the army was in a southerly direction from Todd's Tavern.[19]

As I have just intimated, the topography of the country was very little known to us, & the maps that we had were the worst ever known. Even the

17. Maj. Gen. Phil Sheridan was then in command of the Cavalry Corps, Army of the Potomac; Brig. Gen. Wesley Merritt (22d, USMA 1860) commanded the First Division, Cavalry Corps; Maj. Gen. Fitzhugh Lee, C.S.A., nephew of Robert E. Lee, led a cavalry division of Stuart's Cavalry Corps.

18. The basis of this portion of the chapter is an account written by OBW in 1887 entitled "Engagement at Ny River."

19. The Fifth Corps, followed by the Second Corps, followed the Brock Road south, passing Todd's Tavern, toward Spotsylvania Court House. The Sixth Corps, followed by the Ninth, first moved east to Chancellorsville, where the two corps turned right onto the Plank Road, moving southeast to the junction with the Catharpin Road, near Alrich's. There the Sixth Corps turned off, following the Catharpin Road and Piney Branch Church Road nearly due south. The Ninth Crops, however, continued moving southeast, following the Plank Road and a network of other roads past the Alsop farm, to the Fredericksburg Road. Turning right on that road, Willcox moved his division southwest to the Ny River, on the far left of the army.

Confederates complained of a want of knowledge of the country, & both Grant and Lee got their geography mixed—or at least some of their subordinates did. On General Humphreys' map in his *Virginia Campaigns of 1864–5*, Gates house[20] is made to do duty at least a mile northeast from the crossing of the Ny, & no name is given to the crossing. We were much nearer Spotsylvania Court House than anybody supposed—if not nearer than any other division of the Army of the Potomac.

We found the enemy's pickets a mile before we reached the river, & chasing them rapidly, we were fortunate enough to gain possession of the bridge which spanned the little stream. Col. Christ's brigade was pushed across, with the 60th Ohio, Lt. Col. McElroy, deployed as skirmishers, and the rather high banks on the opposite shore were seized while Roemer's & [Capt. Adelbert B.] Twitchell's[21] batteries found a good supporting position on the hither side, their left resting near one of the Beverly houses. But they had to fire over our men.

From the commanding artillery position I could see some houses a short distance, perhaps a mile, in front of us, ambulance wagons, artillery and troops in motion, some marching across our front, and a considerable body halted, forming to attack us. They planted a field battery and rushed upon us, first [with] a brigade of dismounted cavalry, and then an infantry line, supposed to be one of Longstreet's brigades—our usual opponent during the war—with supports.

Meantime, however, we got Hartranft's brigade across; the hot and repeated attacks of the enemy were handsomely repulsed, though not without some breaks in our own line, leaving their wounded and fifty other prisoners in our hands. The affair lasted until about noon, when the Confederates withdrew behind a narrow strip of woods towards Spotsylvania Court House. Burnside sent up the First Division to me, unaccompanied by orders as to any further movements. One brigade of my division was moved up to the support of our front line, but the fighting was pretty much over—probably in consequence of the appearance of these supports.

Our casualties were one hundred-sixty-seven killed and wounded, and twenty-one missing, from the time we had started. The 17th Michigan, Col. [Constant] Luce, greatly distinguished itself, as did the 20th Michigan, under Lt. Col. B. M. Cutcheon, the 79th New York Highlanders, under Col. David Morrison, who was wounded, and the 60th Ohio, under Lt. Col. [James N.] McElroy; not to mention further the 50th Pennsylvania,

20. Appears simply as "Gate" on Humphreys's map. It was not a house but probably a toll gate.
21. Twitchell commanded the 7th Maine Artillery.

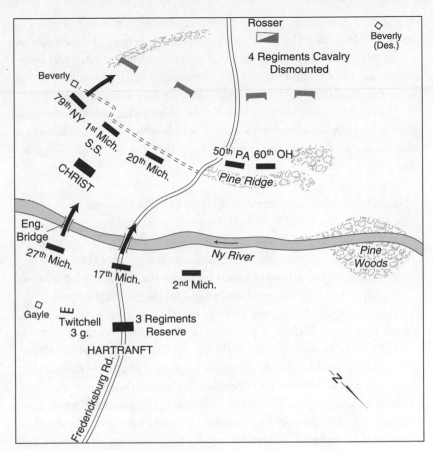

Ny River, Spotsylvania Court House, Virginia, May 9, 1864.

Lt. Col. [Edward] Overton and Capt. Schucuck, and the brave old Col. Ben Christ, who commanded the 2nd Brigade, on which the heaviest of the fighting fell. But the troops and officers all fought splendidly.

I received no formal brigade report until the following October, when Col. Cutcheon was commanding the brigade and he sent in the report. In his report he calls the house on the south side of the river the "Gales House," and there was another Gales house—spelled "Gayles" . . . further round to the south, where General Upton had his fight, and some claim for his troops the locality which we gained and held so near the Court House.[22]

22. There is a great deal of confusion concerning the Gales and Gayles houses, and the two Beverly houses, chiefly because of the poor maps at the time. OBW had his headquarters at the Gayles house ("Gales" on his map), south of the Fredericksburg Road and about one-half mile from the crossing on the north side of the Ny River. OBW observed much of the fighting from

Humphreys' map shows Upton's position correctly, but does not give . . . ours at all. His book is the most correct and reliable history of the campaign in Virginia that I know of. Before that gallant soldier's death, I had some correspondence with him in reference to omissions and mistakes, and at this place in particular—which he frankly acknowledged and promised to correct in a further edition of his book. But the able soldier and conscientious historian did not live to revise his work.[23] For my own part, I never felt more pride in any battle or of any troops than of those of Ny River, Virginia, May 9, 1864.

Next day, the 10th, the gallant Brig. Gen. Stevenson, commanding [the] 1st Division, was killed by a sharpshooter. On the afternoon of the same day, General Burnside came up, together with the 2nd Division, and a demonstration was made by the corps towards the Court House.

On the 11th, the division crossed back with the corps, but before daylight next morning, recrossed the Ny and fought the enemy again.

[On the] 12th of May, the division marched in reserve to the corps, until about —— o'clock. I was ordered up to attack on the left of the 1st Division. As my left—the 2nd Brigade, Col. [William] Humphrey, 2nd Michigan, now commanding the brigade, was already skirmishing with the enemy, I moved up in echelon, Hartranft's brigade on the right, and in advance. [I] found General [Thomas L.] Crittenden,[24] commanding [the] 1st Division, had refused his left, and I moved up Hartranft in line with his right. [I] posted Twitchell's battery on my right front, and Roemer's battery in rear of Humphrey's brigade, and reported to General Burnside that I expected an attempt of the enemy to attack and turn my left—now the extreme left of the Army of the Potomac.

---

the roof of this house. The farm referred to by Byron Cutcheon in his report as on the south side of the river appears on OBW's map as "Gales Jr.," but was actually one of the Beverly houses.

When the Sixth Corps moved to the left on the morning of May 14, Upton's brigade was posted near another "Gayles House," this one near the Massaponax Church Road, one-half mile south of the Ny. Upton was later driven off by Confederate cavalry and infantry.

23. The revisions made by Humphreys for his book *The Virginia Campaigns of 1864 and 1865* (New York: Charles Scribner's Sons, 1883), together with related correspondence between Humphreys and OBW, can be found in the Willcox collection. The editor was unable to find Humphreys's corrections of the portion of his book relating to Willcox's fight at Ny River, though there are lengthy corrections relating to OBW's fight in the Wilderness, before Petersburg, June 17, at the Battle of the Crater, on the Weldon Railroad, and at Reams' Station.

24. Crittenden assumed command of the First Division following the death of Stevenson.

The order was reiterated for me to attack in front and in line with Crittenden, and was obeyed as promptly as Humphrey's brigade could be moved up, but I took the precaution to advise Lt. [Samuel N.] Benjamin, chief of artillery, to mass artillery in rear of my left, which he promptly did, bringing up two additional batteries.

I had no sooner advanced my troops in two lines, when [the enemy] met my attack in the woods on my right front, and brought up a field battery to an opening opposite my left center, and fired solid shot and canister on the troops and batteries. The latter replied vigorously, particularly Roemer, and the troops partly changed front by my orders, and advanced handsomely along the whole line, until two columns of a brigade each charged upon the left batteries. A section of [Capt. Joseph W. B.] Wright's battery had its cannoneers shot down, and for a time was *hors de combat*. At one time the enemy was within ten paces, but the 2d Michigan, supporting this battery, re-manned the guns and with the aid of the canister of the other batteries, repulsed the charge splendidly. The brave Capt. [James] Farrand, commanding [the] 2nd Michigan, was killed. Barber's rebel brigade was completely scattered, and its commander, Col. Barber,[25] with some eighty others, [was] captured.

But in the woods, my front line suffered severely in killed, wounded and prisoners, the latter being swept off by the retreating enemy. Much confusion prevailed here, the captors of one moment being prisoner the next. The second line of both brigades, with little less loss in killed and wounded, pushed ahead, and held their ground in the woods with obstinate pluck, until their ammunition was exhausted, when, with fixed bayonets, they still held on until ordered to withdraw to the edge of the woods, where their ammunition was replenished, and a line of breastworks were hastily thrown up.

On the whole, my advance was checked, but the grand attempt of the enemy to capture our batteries and turn our left [had] decidedly failed, and with much greater loss to them than that which they inflicted on me.

The enemy next moved a strong skirmish line around my left and rear, which compelled me to detach two regiments to protect this flank, and connect with and support [Col. Elisha G.] Marshall's Provisional Brigade of new troops, which held the Fredericksburg and Spotsylvania road, and this last manoeuvre of the enemy effected nothing. Casualties of the day: killed and wounded: 768; missing: 292.

25. Referring to Col. William M. Barbour, 37th North Carolina.

From the 12th to the 19th, the division was not engaged in chief in the further operations at Spotsylvania, but my batteries rendered good service, and on several occasions silenced the guns of the enemy, firing on me and other troops of the army. On the 19th I moved by the Beverly and Burnt houses, and took a position on the left of Ricketts' division, 6th Corps.[26]

On May 21st, [my division] started for Guinea's Station, but was detained till night fall in support of the 6th Corps, which was attacked in moving out. Marched all night via Smith's Mill and Alsops. 22nd, marched to Bethel Church. 23rd, marched to Ox Ford on North Anna River, and relieved Mott's division, 2nd Corps.

24th, made a demonstration to cross the ford, silenced the enemy's artillery commanding the crossing, and advanced skirmishers to an island near the ford, with my troops and Robinson's brigade of [the] 1st Division ready to charge across, but the enemy was entrenched fully, and the order to charge was countermanded by General Burnside, as the sacrifice of life would have been undoubtedly too great for the result to be obtained, other parts of the army having crossed above and below, without serious opposition.

The rest of the operations on the North Anna were confined to demonstrations of the infantry and co-operating use of artillery, in support of other troops. Losses on the North Anna: killed and wounded: 40; missing: 8.[27]

COLD HARBOR

On the 27th of May, 1864, Sheridan seized a crossing of the Pamunkey River at Hanover Town, 15 miles from Richmond, Virginia, and built a bridge over which Meade crossed parts of the Army of the Potomac that day and the next. The rest of the army crossed four miles above. In anticipation of this move, Grant had ordered a transfer of base, and supplies now came up by steamer to White House [Landing], the head of navigation on the Pamunkey. To oppose this move, Gen. Lee quickly marched his army down towards Mechanicsville, and while Meade was securing roads from the Pamunkey to Richmond upon which to advance, Lee was endeavoring to cover these roads.

26. Brig. Gen. James B. Ricketts, with whom OBW had been imprisoned after their capture at Bull Run, was now in command of the Third Division, Sixth Corps.

27. The above excerpt (indented) is taken from the original draft of OBW's official report.

There are many roads from the Pamunkey to Richmond, and they all communicate with each other by small cross roads. There is a direct road from Hanover Town, seventeen miles to Richmond, passing through Hawes' Shop, four miles from Hanover Town, and through Pole Green Church on the Totopotomoy, a creek of barbaric name emptying into the Pamunkey. This road also passes through Huntley's Corners and Shady Grove Church; a road also runs from Huntley's Corners to Richmond by way of Mechanicsville, that comes all the way from White House by way of Old Church. From Old Church runs another road to Richmond by way of Cold Harbor. Other roads lead from New Castle Ferry and other points on the lower Pamunkey to Richmond, and that one from New Castle Ferry goes through Bethesda Church and Mechanicsville, on its way to the Confederate Capital. It may be as well to remember something of these routes, so important in the Cold Harbor Campaign to both sides.

On the morning of the 28th, Sheridan made a demonstration towards Richmond on the Hanover Town road, and discovered the enemy's cavalry entrenched about a mile beyond Hawes' Shop, had a hot contest lasting until late in morning, when Custer's brigade and Gregg's division carried some entrenchments and drove back the enemy.

In the meantime, Lee remained at Ashland, a station on the Richmond and Fredericksburg Railway, 14 miles north of Richmond, and from which roads radiate in all directions, and posted his troops in position: [Maj. Gen. Jubal A.] Early, with his right resting on Beaver Dam Creek, which empties into the Chickahominy near Mechanicsville, his left on the Totopotomoy near Pole Green Church, and about four miles from Hawes' Shop. Longstreet's corps, commanded by [Maj. Gen. Richard H.] Anderson, came up on the right of Early, crossing the road from White House and Bethesda Church to Mechanicsville and Richmond. [Brig. Gen. John C.] Breckinridge's command and Hill's corps extended from Early's left to the vicinity of Atlee's Station.[28]

On the morning of the 29th, Meade reconnoitered from the front of his lines, occupied by the 6th, 2nd and 5th Corps. [Maj. Gen. Horatio G.] Wright moved toward Hanover Court House;[29] Hancock, on the road from Hawes' Shop to Atlee's and toward Richmond, and Warren on the Shady Grove Road, while Sheridan, with [Brig. Gen. Alfred T. A.] Torbert's and

28. Early was then temporarily in command of the ailing Lt. Gen. Richard S. Ewell's Second Corps; Breckinridge had recently joined Lee's army, having brought his two brigades over from the Shenandoah Valley.

29. Wright had assumed command of the Sixth Corps upon the death of Maj. Gen. John Sedgwick, killed by a sharpshooter on May 9 at Spotsylvania Court House.

[Brig. Gen. David McM.] Gregg's divisions,[30] on the left of Meade's army, watched the roads to Mechanicsville, Cold Harbor and White House; and the 9th Corps was held in reserve, between the 5th and 2nd Corps. The enemy was found well entrenched in its position just described.

Next morning the infantry was ordered to move up close to the enemy's works: Wright to move at daylight and endeavor to place his corps across their left flank. Hancock put up batteries in his front and silenced the enemy's artillery fire, but the swamp and tangle of Crump's Creek, which lay in front of Wright, delayed the 6th Corps until too late in the afternoon to effect anything. Warren moved along the Shady Grove Road, the enemy's skirmishers falling back until they entered thickly wooded, swampy ground, formed by several affluents of the Totopotomoy, which here crossed the road in a ravine. On the opposite side of this swampy ravine was Huntley's Corners, occupied by Early, well entrenched. Neither nature nor art invited an attack here.

But Early did not rest behind his works, but moving down the Mechanicsville and Old Church pike, threw himself across Warren's left at Bethesda Church, near which there was some pretty fighting until night. On the whole, the Confederates were worsted, abandoned this part of the field, and moved back at night, on and covering the pike.

Meantime, Anderson, with Longstreet's corps, had moved into Early's position at Huntley's Corners. Hancock had essayed to relieve Warren, but found no assailable point beyond a line of rifle pits carried by Barlow, over obstacles that would have stopped a less energetic commander. Burnside, with sharp skirmishing on Hancock's left, had crossed to Totopotomoy and rested at night with his right on that euphonious stream. And Sheridan, looking to the extreme left for the enemy's cavalry, found it in position on the road from Old Church to Cold Harbor, attacked it with Torbert's division, and drove it to Cold Harbor, Torbert taking up a position within 1½ miles of that spot. [Brig. Gen. James H.] Wilson's cavalry division[31] was over on the other flank of the army at Crump's Creek, destroying the two railroad bridges across the South Anna.

Thus, on the night of the 30th, Meade and Sheridan together occupied a line extending from Crump's Creek nearly to Cold Harbor, across the swampy and tangled folds of the Totopotomoy and Matadequin branches,

---

30. Torbert (21st, USMA 1855) and Gregg (8th, USMA 1855) commanded the First and Second Divisions, respectively, of Sheridan's Cavalry Corps.

31. Wilson (6th, USMA 1860) commanded the Third Division, Cavalry Corps.

behind which Lee's army was admirably entrenched, with some natural advantages for a dash on Meade's right flank and rear, and for a crushing fall on (if he had known it) Baldy Smith, now landing at White House with reinforcements from Butler.[32] But Lee did not know of their coming, and Sheridan sent down a brigade which returned next day, reporting the road all clear.

Meade continued all day of the 31st threatening and feeling the enemy, but found no assailable point, and so Grant determined to try on Cold Harbor, with a view to throw Lee across the Chickahominy, and thus open the direct road to Richmond from that point.

Cold Harbor was [in] every way important. It was on our line of extension to the left, and nearly all the roads from the lower Pamunkey, the James, and the Chickahominy, intersected here, on their way to Richmond. Moreover, it was the last hopeful ground north of the ill-fated Chickahominy; and the next step was across the James and around by Petersburg. It [Cold Harbor] stood only six miles [from] the main fortifications round Richmond, and 12 miles from the city. There was nothing of it, besides Fitzhugh Lee's light entrenchment, but a tavern covered by a wide-spreading catalpa—a place for rest and shelter without fire, like its ancestors in Old England. The main road ran thence through New Cold Harbor and Gaines' Mill, the scene of McClellan's fight [two years] before, and only a mile or two away toward Richmond.

Lee appreciated the tactical value of the point no less than Grant and Meade. He sent a brigade of infantry (Clingman's of Hoke's division)[33] to reinforce Fitzhugh Lee, about dusk on the 31st, before which Sheridan withdrew his cavalry until ordered by Meade to hold the place at all hazards, when he returned in the night, modified the breastworks, and held on for the arrival of the 6th Corps. Gen. Wright was ordered to move that night and make every effort to get there by daylight. His night march, hot and dusty, plodded over "fifteen miles, through a strange country covered with an intricate network of narrow, ill-defined roads."[34] In the morning Hoke had withdrawn his brigade to the right, and Kershaw moved down with two

32. Maj. Gen. William F. "Baldy" Smith, commanding the Eighteenth Corps of Maj. Gen. Benjamin Butler's Army of the James, had moved up from Bermuda Hundred, where Butler's forces were bottled up on the James River. Smith brought with him some sixteen thousand men belonging to his own corps and Maj. Gen. Quincy A. Gillmore's Tenth Corps.

33. Brig. Gen. T. L. Clingman led a brigade of North Carolinians in Maj. Gen. Robert Hoke's division, which had recently joined Lee with some four thousand men.

34. This quote is from Humphreys, *The Virginia Campaign*, 172.

brigades, attacked twice, was repulsed by Sheridan, and finally withdrew at the appearance of Wright.

May 27, broke camp at Ox Ford and marched for the Pamunkey, crossed on the 29th near Hanover Town at 1 A.M., and on [the] same morning went into position near Hawes' Shop, on [the] left of 2nd Corps. Sent out reconnaissance same day under Col. Humphrey, to feel for the enemy on the left, and in connection with 2nd Corps.

30th
Crossed the Totopotomoy Creek and entrenched in face of the enemy, on the left of the 2nd Division, 9th Corps, and right of Griffin's division, 5th Corps.

May 31st
Advanced my whole line, skirmishing with the enemy, to within 200 yards of their main line of entrenchments.

June 1st
Extended my left to Shady Grove Road. Towards dusk an attack was made on the 5th Corps and 1st Division, 9th Corps, immediately on my left. The latter had their right across the road, and at this point were driven in, exposing my 2nd Brigade's left, which I threw back slightly, and which held its own, supported by a regiment of Hartranft's brigade until the 1st Division troops were rallied, and line re-established. My troops behaved with the utmost coolness and gallantry under circumstances so trying.

On June 2nd [we] marched to Bethesda Church with [the] 1st and 2nd Divisions. The enemy pressed down the road taken by the 1st Division, but was held in check by the 20th Michigan of Christ's brigade, until the 1st Division formed to resist an attack which followed very heavily, the enemy capturing an old line of works, hastily occupied by the 1st Division. No other troops of mine but the 20th Michigan were engaged in the affair.

June 3rd
I was ordered to attack the enemy in a line of works lost by a portion of the 1st Division the night before. Moved out at 6 in the morning, Har-

Brig. Gen. O. B. Willcox with some of his staff at Cold Harbor, Virginia, June 1864. *OBW Collection*.

tranft forming his brigade in two lines and taking the advance, supported by Christ's brigade. Hartranft dashed forward handsomely, gained this line of works, pushed ahead, and drove the enemy to a second line of entrenchments, advanced to within two hundred yards of this line, and found it flanked by an enfilading fire of the artillery, which had played upon us as we advanced. Here we halted, and I ordered up two pieces each of Roemer's and Twitchell's batteries, one being three-inch rifled, the other light [twelve-pounders].

After this successful advance, General Potter, 2nd Division, 9th Corps, moved forward in gallant style on my right, and General Griffin, of the 5th Corps, in like handsome manner, on my left. The enemy's musketry fire was so close and sharp, that it became necessary to throw up cover for my guns before they could be put in position to silence the enemy's artillery.

Being now called upon by General Burnside as to the practicability of carrying the works before me, I consulted with Major St. Clair Morton, chief engineer of the corps, and my two brigade commanders, Hartranft and Christ, and decided I would succeed, provided my artillery could be first got into position. This Roemer reported would be done by one o'clock. I reported accordingly, and General Burnside ordered the attack. Every effort was now made; details of infantry assisted the battery men of both batteries, but the workmen were shot down every moment, and at 2½ P.M. only two guns were got into position—when Gen. Burnside ordered the attack to be made.

It was still necessary to move Hartranft's brigade, under a severe fire, to the right, where the line approached nearest to the enemy, under cover of the woods, and at 3 P.M. the skirmishers, 27th Michigan, Col. [Dorus M.] Fox, began to advance, when an order was received forbidding the attack, and it was abandoned. At dusk Christ's brigade relieved Hartranft, who had suffered considerably, and who retired to the rear in reserve. An intermitting fire was kept up on [the] enemy, and he retired during the night. Next morning, when I examined his lines, there was every sign of the severe loss we had inflicted upon him, dead battery horses, numerous graves, &c. Loss at Bethesda Church: killed and wounded: 262; missing: 1.

On June 4th, . . . [we] moved to the Woodie House, Cold Harbor, and relieved a portion of Birney's troops, 2nd Corps. Afterwards relieved a brigade of [the] 18th Corps, built redoubt Fletcher, and advanced our line by boyau and parallels, towards [the] enemy's works, until June 12th.[35]

MISCELLANEOUS LETTERS: MAY 7–JUNE 1, 1864

[Letter from Col. Orville E. Babcock, aide de camp
to Lt. Gen. U. S. Grant, to Marie Willcox]
Wilderness [Virginia]
May 7, 1864
Madam——
Gen'l is well. Was engaged yesterday—Capt. Hutchins was wounded but not seriously—a flesh wound.[36] I would send to Gen'l so that he

35. The above indented account is excerpted from OBW's report.
36. Hutchins was wounded in the right leg. He would carry the bullet for six years, enduring numerous painful operations, before the bullet was finally removed.

could write—but it is too late. He will write soon as he can. Love to the little lady.

Very truly,
O. E. Babcock

[Letter from mother of L. C. Brackett to Marie Willcox]
Boston, Massachusetts
May 21, 1864
Dear Mrs. Willcox

You will pardon my thus addressing you, but I claim all as *dear* who are dear to my darling Boy, and I believe he would not hesitate a moment to lay down his life for your noble husband, or those belonging to him.

I this morning received a few lines from my son, written on the 11th inst., saying he was safe, and his "beloved Gen'l" was also safe and well, and wishing me to telegraph you to this effect, but the letter has been so long on the way that I thought it probable you had heard from your husband ere this, therefore thought it unwise to send by telegraph.

My son wished me to send you my address, thinking, perhaps, that in case of extremity he might send a message through the kindness of his commander to you, and through your kindness to his mother.

I need not mention to you the agony and fearful suspense of the past two weeks. I am confident you know it all, even to a greater degree (if that can be possible) than myself. May God grant that our dear ones return safely to us! But should He otherwise order it, may He grant us grace to endure.

My Boy is my earthly treasure, the only child God has given me, and I dare not think of myself left here without him. It is only one year since I buried the husband of my youth, the father of my child; since then my cry has been, morning & evening to my Heavenly Father, to spare my Child.

I would gladly say a consoling word to you, but hardly know how; this much I will say, however, that the praise of your noble husband is on every lip, and I not only trust that he will be spared to see the salvation of his country consummated, but that he will receive the reward justly due his devotion to that country.

I will not weary you longer, but hoping that you and your dear children are in good health, I am with much esteem,

Yours in suffering,
Mrs. Mary V. Brackett
81 Chambers St.
Boston, Mass.

[Letter from Capt. W. V. Richards to Marie Willcox]
Headquarters, 3d Div., 9th Army Corps
Near Spotsylvania Court House [Virginia]
May 20th/'64
Mrs. Gen'l O. B. Willcox
Detroit, Mich.
Dear Madam,

At the request of the Gen'l and my own desire, I continue a transcript of my diary for you since I last wrote you.

We were in camp in the position gained by the Gen'l's command on the 9th, and by the corps on the 12th, until the 17th, when orders came to make a night march on to the right flank of the enemy; this order however was countermanded shortly afterwards, and an order came to assault the enemy's works in the morning at 4 A.M. As the Gen'l held the only ground fit for artillery, he was ordered to hold his ground, open with artillery, and watch his opportunity to make a dash upon the enemy in our front.

As we conducted this fire on the 18th with great success, the enemy were particularly venomous toward us, and at one time directed all their fire on the General's Headquarters, which were with one of the batteries. Not much was gained during the day except to find out the force of the enemy. The loss of the corps was about two hundred this day, only four or five wounded in our division.

At night, the order given and countermanded the night before was again issued, and we start[ed] at 3.30 A.M. of the 19th. The General's command took position on the immediate left of Gen'l Ricketts' division, and our Headquarters are now together; there was very little fighting yesterday in our front, but on our right Ewell's Corps made an attack on the flank; they were handsomely repulsed by a portion of the 5th Corps, Gen'l Warren commanding, with a loss of many killed & wounded and about one thousand prisoners.

Today, the 20th, every thing has been unusually quiet. We made a reconnaissance and found the enemy in force and strongly entrenched in our front. We are strongly entrenched ourselves in our present position, ready to receive any attack, awaiting orders to advance or any thing else. All are very well and in good spirits, trusting in the God of battles for a final victory.

With respect, I remain
Your obed. servt.
W. V. Richards
a.a.a. gen'l

[Letter from Capt. W. V. Richards to Marie Willcox]
Headquarters, 3rd Div., 9th Army Corps
Near Hanover Town [Virginia]
June 1st, 1864
Mrs. Gen'l O. B. Willcox, Detroit

Since my last we have made some more of those grand flank movements peculiar to our new Commanding General, and by a succession of which we now find ourselves within about twelve (12) miles of Richmond, our much desired prize.

During this time we have had all the grandeur of warfare, with comparatively little of its horrors. On the 23rd of May, after a most wearing and fatiguing march of two days and one night with but four hours rest, we took up our position on the front line on North Anna river. To gain the opposite shore was the desideratum, but our position from the nature of the ground would not permit, although the rest of the army crossed almost without a struggle. We had however a very fine position for artillery, and the Gen'l amused himself with skirmishing heavily with his infantry and playing with [i.e., firing] twenty-four (24) pieces of artillery.

On the 24th, early in the morning—this commenced about ten—our wounded began to tell the tale of some work, but sagacity soon discovered the unpracticability of the work and our loss in numbers was slight.

At twelve o'clock, however, a terrible blow came upon us, our family. An orderly rode up and told us that our noble associate and brother, Lieut. [Nelson] Fletcher, had fallen, pierced through the heart by the bullet of a sharp shooter. We had known this gallant young man a long time; during the campaign in Tennessee he was connected with the Headquarters of the 9th Corps in the Engineers Dept. and none could be more beloved. Poor fellow, *we* feel his loss, but from his virtues, his many qualities, his true worth none can doubt; his change is for the best. The world has lost a bright, promising example; we a true brother, a gallant officer; his bereaved family a noble son.

We had some hard fighting on the North Anna but found the enemy in an impregnable position. Consequently, on the 27th, we moved again and by severe marches slipped by the enemy's right flank once more, and on the 29th took up position on the south side of the Pamunkey River. We are constantly under fire, but it is simply skirmishing for development's sake. Our base is now the White House on the Pamunkey. We cannot make many more flank movements for there is no room. We look for hard fighting now and the slowest twelve miles' march ever made.

The General and staff are all very well and in our rustic homes quite happy. All send their kindest regards.

Respectfully yours,
W. V. Richards
a.a.a. Gen'l

This portfolio was drawn by Pvt. Andrew McCallum, 109th New York Artillery. McCallum apparently served as an orderly to Willcox, as he appears in the staff photo on page 573, just under the bower. The portfolio is a part of the OBW Collection. The sketches are published here for the first time.

Roemer's battery at rest, Cold Harbor, Virginia, June 8, 1864. Captain Roemer is undoubtedly one of the officers talking in the foreground. The other artillerymen are enjoying a break, resting and writing letters. Note also the infantry marching past on the right of the sketch, heading for the front lines, which are just past the woodline on the left.

Redoubt Fletcher, Cold Harbor, Virginia, from the west, Brig. Gen. Willcox's division, June 10, 1864.

(Opposite top) Redoubt Fletcher, interior view, showing Roemer's battery at work, June 11, 1864. The artillerists in the center of the sketch are feverishly working the pieces, while Captain Roemer, standing atop the works on the upper right, observes the effects of the battery's fire. The men in the lower right-hand corner are cutting fuses, while the men running through the covered way in the lower center are carrying the rounds to the guns. An incoming round of spherical case has the second man diving for cover. Note, too, the battery's infantry supports (right of sketch) observing the action.

(Opposite bottom) The Ninth Army Corps in camp near the James River, Wilcox Landing, Virginia, June 16, 1864. Willcox and his staff are in the foreground.

Reserve Battery at work
June 18 1864
Redoubt Fort Hatcher

No 6

(*Top*) Although this sketch is titled "Fight of the 5th and 9th Corps before Petersburg, June 20, 1864," the artist may have inadvertently misdated the drawing, as no fighting involving those two corps took place on June 20. It is more likely that the sketch shows fighting on the Weldon Railroad on August 20, 1864, in which the Fifth and Ninth Corps fought side by side.

(*Bottom*) Roemer's battery shelling Petersburg, June 20, 1864.

Twitchell's battery in position before Petersburg, supported by the 109th New York Volunteers, June 25, 1864.

(*Top*) Position of the Ninth Corps before Petersburg, June 30, 1864. Roemer's and Twitchell's batteries are in the foreground.

(*Bottom*) View of the Rebel works in front of Petersburg, from the lines of the Fifth Corps during a cessation of hostilities, July 1864.

(*Top*) Headquarters, Third Division, Ninth Corps, July 20, 1864. (This is the same headquarters shown in photos on pages 560 and 573.)

(*Bottom*) Charge of the Third Division, Ninth Corps, on the Rebel fort (Battle of the Crater),

July 30, 1864.
The Friend House, near Petersburg, headquarters of OBW, December 5, 1864. Willcox is playing with his dog, Gyp, in the right foreground.

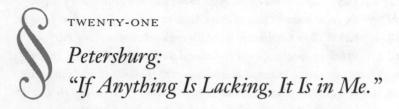

TWENTY-ONE

Petersburg:
"If Anything Is Lacking, It Is in Me."

*[Cold Harbor had been an experience the Army of the Potomac would never
forget. At its outset, after nearly a month of constant marching and fighting, the
weary Union soldiers had at last found themselves at the gates of Richmond, where
the Confederates were solidly entrenched. With Lee's army depleted in strength,
with its back to the Confederate capital, Grant believed that one more attack
might well bring about an end to the Army of Northern Virginia and bring as
well the long-awaited fall of Richmond. That effort, however, failed miserably,
culminating in the bloody, head-on assault of June 3, 1864, where some seven
thousand Federal soldiers fell in just one hour's time. Though Willcox and the
Ninth Corps had been spared the worst of that nightmare, the bitter aftertaste of
the disaster remained in the mouth of every soldier in the army.*

*Yet if the Army of the Potomac had been bloodied, it had not been beaten,
precisely because this man Grant refused to recognize defeat. In spite of the
disaster that had just befallen his army, Grant elected to head south once again.
What then transpired has since been termed one of the greatest achievements in
military history. On June 12, under cover of darkness and in the face of an
aggressive foe, Grant and Meade withdrew their army of over a hundred
thousand men from the trenches near Cold Harbor and headed south, stealthily
slipping their troops across the James River in an attempt to capture the vital rail
center of Petersburg, Virginia, twenty miles south of Richmond. For the next four*

days Robert E. Lee had no clear idea where the Federal army had gone. With the bulk of the Confederate troops still guarding Richmond, the lightly defended city of Petersburg—the "back door to Richmond"—was Grant's for the taking. With Petersburg in Federal hands, Richmond would soon follow.

Union troops began massing outside Petersburg's nearly empty fortifications, but valuable time was lost, and the window of opportunity began to close. With only three thousand Confederates defending the works, one solid, head-on attack by the gathering blue host would have captured the city. Yet the initial assault on June 15 was only a half-hearted effort, by an army that had grown wary of such attacks, and the great moment slipped away. General assaults followed on June 17 and 18 (in which Willcox's division was heavily engaged), but nothing was gained. Lee, at last aware that Grant had crossed the James, had already begun shifting troops southward, enabling him to thwart the Federal attacks. And so the armies, blue and gray, began to dig, and the investment of Petersburg, the last great campaign of the eastern theater, began. For the Army of Northern Virginia, it was now "a mere question of time."]

THE SPARRING and fighting around Petersburg were the most exciting work we had during the siege. Grant kept us prodding and grinding away at Lee incessantly. Before the dead were cold at Cold Harbor, [Grant] began the preliminary attacks that, by better management, should have given us the city. . . .

June 12th

In the night marched for James River and Tunstall's Station. Crossed the Chickahominy on 13th at Jones' Bridge, and the James on 15th near Wilcox Landing, and came up on the left of 2nd Corps in front of Petersburg on the afternoon of the 16th. On the night of the 16th, one brigade (Hartranft's) was ordered to the support of Barlow's division, 2nd Corps, and Christ's brigade held the extreme left.

June 17th, before Petersburg

On the morning of the 17th, Hartranft reported back, and I was ordered to attack the enemy on their works on the right of the Avery house, and in front of Shands' house. At the latter point there was a good position for a battery, which I requested to place there, but time would not allow.

My two brigades were formed, partly in the ravine in front of Shands', and partly on the crest beyond. Maj. Gen. Burnside indicated the point of attack on the enemy's breastworks in an open field. Fixing this required point caused a little delay by the necessary movement of troops in the tangled ravine, farther to the right than that at first indicated by Gen. Parke, chief of staff. Major J. St. Clair Morton, chief engineer of the corps, accompanied the commander of my leading brigade (Gen. Hartranft), and verified the point, compass in hand, after Hartranft's line was formed on the edge of the field. The direction indicated was so unfortunate that, as soon as my lines started from the brow of the ravine, they were swept by an enfilading fire of canister from a rebel battery, nearly opposite Shands' house. Our artillery did nothing at the critical moment.

My troops advanced at a double-quick, unsupported in any manner whatever. A cloud of blinding dust was raised by the enemy's artillery missiles. Hartranft's left struck the enemy's pits, but melted away in a moment. But eighteen out of ninety-five survived in the ranks of the left companies of the left regiment, and out of 1,890 men, which composed his lines, but 1,050 came out, and a few afterward through the 2nd Corps works on my right. Among the killed was the gallant Morton.

Hartranft's line having thus melted out of sight, Col. Christ halted, and held his brigade, lying down, about half way from the ravine to the enemy's works. This position the brave troops of Christ's brigade continued to hold until night, when they performed important service.

In the evening, with guns in position at the Shands house, the 1st Division moved over the same ground, but taking a better direction, with [Brig. Gen. Samuel] Crawford's division, 5th Corps, on their left.[1] Gen. Burnside's orders were that Gen. Potter, commanding 2nd Division, should go in after the 1st and my division follow the 2nd, but as at the time Gen. Ledlie,[2] commanding the 1st Division, commenced his attack, I thought Potter's troops could not be brought up in time, I ordered Christ's brigade to support Gen. Ledlie at once. Col. Christ threw forward his supports rapidly on both flanks of Ledlie's line, sharing the front attack, and capturing a stand of colors and 100 men of the 35th North Carolina Regiment, in the breast-works of the enemy. This consoling moment of victory was saddened by the loss of Capt. [Levant C.] Rhines, commanding 1st Michigan S.S. [Sharpshooters], who fell at the enemy's works amid the very cheers of his men, who had carried the point. The gallant Col. Christ was also wounded on the field. Hartranft's brigade was

1. Crawford then had command of the Second Division, Fifth Corps.
2. Brig. Gen. James H. Ledlie assumed command of the First Division following the departure of Crittenden, who resigned his command following the North Anna action.

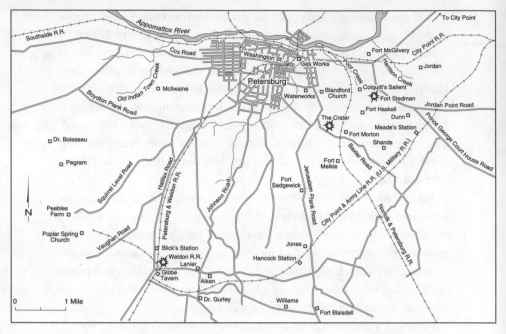

The vicinity of Petersburg, Virginia.

moved to supporting distance of Christ, but by Gen. Burnside's order was not sent forward.

June 18, at 4.30 A.M. I was ordered to move forward again and attack. A party of skirmishers was sent out in advance to feel for the enemy, and reported that the latter had fallen back, and with skirmishers deployed I moved on, Hartranft's brigade in front, across the fields and into the woods, toward the Taylor house.

In the woods we encountered the enemy's skirmishers, and a brisk shelling from their batteries across the Norfolk R.R. We drove back their skirmishers steadily out of the woods, and into the cut of the Norfolk R.R., which formed a deep cover. On coming to the edge of the open field near the Taylor house, we found that the enemy had built a strong line of entrenchments beyond the railway cut and a winding ravine, through which ran a small creek, whose banks, immediately in my front, were steep and covered with wood and thicket.

Here, then, were two lines of obstacles interposed between me and the enemy's works. Moreover, the advance to the railroad was over an open field exposed to fire. The enemy's line was about 800 yards from the Taylor house, running along the foot of Cemetery Hill, turning our right towards the Hare house, and crossing the railway at a point where a gun in position swept the railroad cutting for some distance. I brought up Roemer's battery and put part of it in position to command this gun, and part to reply to a battery which fired from the left and front.

Gen. Crawford's division, 5th Corps, had advanced through the woods in connection with me, and on my left, and Potter's 2nd Division, 9th Corps, now came up to support me. I ordered Hartranft to carry the railroad cut, which he did in good style. Crawford's troops did the same on our left.

After this, Gen. Barlow's division, 2nd Corps, came up on my right, and I proposed to Crawford and Barlow to make a general attack on the works at 12. Crawford acceded, but Barlow replied that he had no orders to attack. I considered a vigorous attack on Barlow's front essential to my success, as I was exposed to a heavy enfilading fire from the works that there curved around my right. The enemy's sharpshooters were picking off my men in the cut every moment, notwithstanding the traverses we threw up.

At 3 P.M. a general attack was ordered by the Maj. Gen. commanding the army, and Hartranft began to move his command again, with [Col. John I.] Curtin's brigade, of Potter's division, on his right, and Col. [William C.] Raulston, 24th N.Y. Dismounted Cavalry (now commanding Christ's brigade), supporting. The railway bank was quite high, and so steep that holes had to be dug in the side of it for the men to plant their feet, and as soon as a man showed his head he came under fire. This, of course, led to vexatious labor and delay, in order to prepare the line to climb the bank simultaneously. On the extreme left, where the bank was lower, the movement began at once, and here the troops got as far as the ravine, driving out the enemy at the same time with the 5th Corps troops.

Every preparation being made, under a galling fire, at 5.30 the whole of the division and part of Curtin's brigade made a determined advance. The whole ground from the railroad to the ravine was carried, officers and men falling at every step. The ravine was crossed, the crest beyond gained, and, under the fire of a heavy line of battle, my heroic troops fought their way up to within 125 yards of the enemy's entrenchments and held their ground. There was not over 1,000 uninjured left in the ranks to entrench themselves when night came on. The 2nd Brigade changed its commanders three times on the field: Col. Raulston, 24th N.Y. Dismounted Cavalry, and Lt. Col. [George W.] Travers, 46th N.Y., successively commanding this brigade, were shot down at their posts. Losses for the two days: killed and wounded: 1,102; missing: 129.

In the course of the night, my troops were relieved by the 2nd Division, and bivouacked in the woods.

June 20th

I relieved a division of the 2nd Corps, and on the 23rd relieved Crawford's division, 5th Corps, and remained in the trenches from that time till, and after, July 30th. Casualties in the trenches from June 19th to July 30th: killed and wounded, 339. I entered upon this campaign with about 6,000 men, of which one regiment, the 79th N.Y., left me on the Ny River, to be mustered out, and three—the 37th and 38th Wisconsin, and 24th N.Y. Dismounted Cavalry—joined me prior to the 18th of June.

The division lost [in action] 3,930, but very few of whom were taken prisoner. As a division it has done its duty quietly, but bravely and faithfully; never broke before an enemy; never lost a regiment or a gun, although its guns were always fighting near the main line; and never was saved from defeat by any other troops, although it has repeatedly saved others. The officers and men have done their duty; if anything is lacking, it is in me, whose name sheds so little splendor on their noble deeds.[3]

As soon as the works were sufficiently dug and strengthened to admit of their being held by small garrisons, whole divisions and corps were marched out, to extort new ground for the engineers, to seize the roads, and to threaten the enemy at points for strategic purposes.

While Lee kept up the scare in Washington, Grant fixed his gaze on Richmond, to defend which he finally compelled Lee to strip Early, thereby leaving that fat and doughty warrior to the tender mercies of Sheridan.[4]

‹Shortly previous to that ghastly spectacle, the Mine affair, two corps, the 2nd and 6th, left the end of our works at Fort Sedgwick, known to the rebels as Fort Hell, in the first expedition to take in the Weldon Railway. A. P. Hill, ever on the alert, met them half way, and slipping in between the two columns, marching without touch connection, struck one or two divisions in flank, and sent most of the 2nd Corps back to the Jerusalem Plank road, until next day, when they came up in line with the 6th, and extended our entrenchments to within one mile and a half of the railway; when the

3. The above indented passage is an extract from OBW's report. Losses given as 3,930 are from Wilderness through the Crater.

4. Lee detached Early on June 11, 1864, to combat Hunter in the Shenandoah Valley and threaten Washington. Early's battles with Sheridan would come later.

6th Corps [was] suddenly ordered off to meet Early at Washington, further movements were suspended to await the results of the Mine affair.>[5]

Before Petersburg, Va.
July 17/'64
My dear Mollie,

Another Sunday has rolled around & we still have not captured Petersburg, but I have a letter from you dated the 11th enclosing one from Mother, & the mail also brought something suspicious in a yellow envelope, which I opened & found, in a neat little white envelope, a nice letter from a young lady to her Papa, & lo & behold it was from *Lillebolero* to me! I was quite surprised at so good & well written a letter from one who is so young.

18th

This was interrupted last evening by the announcement from headquarters that they anticipated on our lines, about where I am & in Warren's front, an attack from Longstreet. Accordingly, everything was made ready, & from three o'clock till daylight this a.m., we fully expected the ball to open. But whether the information was false or whether the rebels changed their mind, they did not attempt anything.

The children seem to have had a good time on the 4th. Eben wrote me an account of the boys' celebration at the farm, in which I have no doubt Elon bore his full share. But I don't exactly like his going out to ride, even though it be on a mule, which is quite scriptural, *on Sunday*. I was pleased with his firmness in refusing to stay over night at Whitewood, being contrary to his instructions, & his Uncle admired him for it too. I dare predict he will turn out a good boy, having so much truthfulness & conscientiousness.

I cannot express to you my appreciation of your wise management of the little flock. It is a great thing for me to be free from all anxiety on the score of their training during my long absence. They seem a little backward in book learning, compared with prodigies, but their health is being confirmed & their education can be pushed as they grow older.

Lulu's perseverance in the music line seems so laughable to me when I remember her abortive efforts to catch a tune, but she must have an extra-

5. The Sixth Corps was dispatched to Washington on July 9 to block Early's raid on Washington. The troops entered the capital just as Early's troops appeared before the city's fortifications on July 11, and just in time to prevent the Confederates from entering the city. OBW wrote two versions of this chapter, both originally titled "Attacks around Petersburg." The excerpt here within single angle brackets < > is from the second version.

ordinary vein lurking somewhere in her little noodle, & I have no doubt she will be a musician, as we always do best in what we like best.

Your last letter is so full of accounts of the children that I enjoyed it highly. Dear little old woman, I wish I were with you to share the cares & pleasures, but Providence seems to have ordered a different arrangement, & it is no doubt for the best. . . .

I enjoyed Mother's Brattleboro letter. How light & smooth is her pen. You would not think there was any age or rheumatism in her fingers. Surely she must be enjoying herself & I hope Caro will get through the summer smoothly. If I were not so dull I would write the little snowdrop.

It is seldom I am in the mood for writing. My whole division has been on the line a month & my anxieties are without let up, & I am pretty much always *thinking*. The only relief I get is in dullness & sleeping over such rusty novels as the news boys bring into camp. But I have enjoyed one or two of Dickens.

I see that Halleck has translated & published Jomini's *Life of Napoleon*. If it is to be had in Detroit I wish [you] would send it by Capt. Johnstone. I received a very nice appreciation letter from him this evening, which I have a mind to enclose. Brave fellow, I hope you have seen him & Mrs. J.; he is an excellent man & so valuable. I miss him very much. Tell him I was glad to hear from him & hope his wound is doing as well, as his wife is happy.

Gracious! it is actually trying to rain. We have been nearly two months without it. There, it has stopped already. Provoking! . . .

I see you have taken to Grosse Point summer seats. There seems to be quite a colony rising there, & wish I could invest, although the hot period is too brief to make it worth while, even if the dollars allowed.

Have not seen much of Babcock lately. He has not been well & sent word he would not be up to see me till it rained. It is almost stifling to travel up from City Point through the dust.

Speaking of Mrs. [Alexia] Russell in your letter, I had a chance to take her brother David (who is in the 8th Regulars) on my staff some time since. I thought it might please Judge Campbell, but knew so little of the young man (except the blood) I did not think it worth while. He appears well & stands well & looks less foppish than he did at home.

Have you received the pictures I sent by Adams Express?—photographs of various generals & staff officers, quite a handsome collection. I sent some time since some of McCallum's pencillings to *Harper's Weekly* to see if they would fetch anything for his benefit, with directions that if *Harper* did not take them, he was to mail them to you. McC. is a private & draws better than Henry used to.

I see you are gradually reconciling yourself to my not being promoted major general. Burnside says that Meade is a warm friend & that Grant spoke of me in the highest terms lately. I also hear from various sources that my reputation has increased considerably in the North. Well, fortune is a queer mistress. Zack [Chandler] & Jacob [Howard] are her favorites you know, & I don't feel like *pushing*.

One advantage in being *dull* is that I don't chafe under this disappointment, but bear it like a philosopher, & I dare say I have more than I deserve anyhow. If I had a vixen of a wife & four deformed or maimed or frightful children, I have no doubt I should, by way of compensation, be a Field Marshal!

Robert returned the other day, in good spirits & determined to stay, although his wound is not quite healed. Everybody seemed glad to see him. I was very glad too. . . .

I hope Lulu will enjoy her trip to Chicago. How well I remember my visit there when about of her age! I staid a year & went to school in a log hut with the Indian boys & soldiers' children. . . .

The mess is flourishing. Dr. O'C is caterer, & the new cook, Allen, is an old Kalamazoo House cook—cake & custard for supper, think of it!

The Rebs still keep up their fire on part of my line, Hartranft's brigade, but let Humphrey's brigade alone. The great Washington scare rather amused us here, but I hope the rascals will not escape with all their plunder.

Hoping you are well & bear up tolerably under this cruel separation & with love to all

Your devoted husband,
O. B. Willcox

THE CRATER

[The "Crater," or "Mine Affair," has long been one of the most fascinating aspects of the Petersburg campaign, and with good reason. Initially a remarkable feat of engineering skill and military foresight, the Petersburg mine ended as a failure and the loss of a rare opportunity to capture the "Cockade City," the Confederate capital, and perhaps deal a fatal blow to the Army of Northern Virginia.

On June 25, 1864, the men of the 48th Pennsylvania, most of whom were coal miners in civilian life, began digging a mine that would measure some 510 feet in length from the Federal trenches to a point beneath the Confederate works, with two lateral galleries running some seventy-five feet along the length of the Rebel fortifications. The digging went on, undetected by the enemy, for nearly a month. When it was completed on July 23, four tons of powder, 320 kegs in all, was packed into the galleries, and a fuse was devised to run back to the mouth of the shaft.

Brig. Gen. Edward Ferrero's division of black troops had been trained to spearhead the assault upon the explosion of the mine, but on July 29, the day before the attack, Grant and Meade ordered Burnside to direct one of his white divisions to lead the attack. The two Federal commanders, like so many others in the Union army, had a low regard for the ability of black troops in battle and did not want them placed in such a responsible position. Moreover, they did not want to be accused of using black troops as cannon fodder, especially if the attack failed. The three remaining division commanders, Willcox, Ledlie, and Potter, drew straws for the assignment, the lot falling on Ledlie. It was a poor choice, and a poor way to choose troops to lead an attack. Ledlie was the worst division commander in the Army of the Potomac. When the attack was made, he (and supposedly Ferrero as well) would be found behind the lines drinking rum in a bombproof, while their unguided troops were being slaughtered in the crater.

When the mine was finally detonated in the early hours of July 30, the resulting explosion created one of the most awesome spectacles of the war, hurling a great cloud of smoke, earth, men, materiel, and debris high into the air, leaving a crater some 170 feet long and from sixty to eighty feet deep in the middle of the Confederate lines. A wide gap had been opened in the Rebel works, the defenders in that sector having been blown to bits, grievously wounded, or simply stunned into immobility.

The resulting Union attack, however, quickly degenerated into a mob, as the men of the leading division plunged directly into the crater instead of forming around it. There the troops milled about, without direction, inspecting the damage and pulling out Confederates who had been buried alive. Time passed, and Confederate reinforcements began to arrive. As the supporting Union troops advanced, they became entangled with Ledlie's troops and were thus unable to form properly into line of battle. Confederate artillery barked into action, ripping into the huddled troops as Rebel infantry pelted the blue mass with musketry. Thus an attack that had begun with so much promise ended in a nightmare of lost lives and lost promise. It produced 3,798 Union casualties (mostly captured), while the Confederates lost a relatively slim 1,500. Grant called the Mine Affair "the saddest affair I have witnessed in this war," adding that "such an opportunity for carrying fortifications I have never seen and do not expect again to have."[6]

6. Bruce Catton, *Grant Takes Command* (Little, Brown: Boston, 1969), p. 325.

Headquarters Third Division, Ninth Army Corps,
Before Petersburg, Va., August 6, 1864.

Colonel:

I have the honor to report that on the 30th ultimo Hartranft's brigade was promptly formed close in rear of the left of Ledlie's division, and ready to move forward at 3.30 A.M. Humphrey's brigade occupied part of the second line of our rifle-pits and the covered way leading to Hartranft's brigade, and was ready at the same hour.

The mine exploded at 4.45 A.M. As soon as the explosion, and the First Division advanced, Hartranft's advance passed through our front line of pits in column of battalions (at 5 A.M.), and three regiments occupied the left of the exploded work on the left of the First Division, their ranks considerably broken by the irregularity of the ground. The First Division, halting in the crater, soon closed up the way so that two regiments of Hartranft's brigade remained on the rear slope of the rebel work, and two regiments halted in rear of our works, waiting for space to move up. The distance between the two lines was about 140 yards.

In obedience to instructions from General Burnside I ordered General Hartranft forward without waiting for the First Division, with instructions to gain Cemetery Hill if possible. This was about 5.15 A.M. Meantime the enemy had recovered from their surprise, and now concentrated so heavy a fire upon the point that our troops, in seeking temporary shelter, became still more mixed with each other and with the First Division, lost their ranks and much of their regimental organization, in spite of the efforts of many of the officers, and every new regiment that marched into the breach only increased the huddle and confusion, and interfered the more with the officers in reforming for another advance. I did not, therefore, push the remaining two regiments of this brigade into the crater, but reported to General Burnside that no more troops could assault at this breach to advantage, and recommended attack on the right and left of it.

I sent repeated and peremptory orders to General Hartranft to advance, but he reported it impossible. I ordered him to send at least a regiment to the left and within the enemy's lines, clean out the rebels on that flank as far as possible, and then advance. I am sure that both he with his staff and the regimental commanders did all in their power to obey these orders. The Twenty-seventh Michigan Volunteers started toward the left, but its commanding officer, Lieutenant-Colonel Wright, was shot, and the enemy, while protected by their traverses, had so long a line of fire

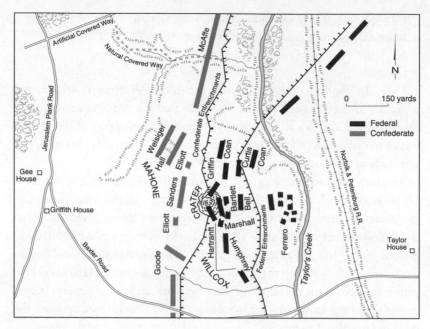

The Battle of the Crater, July 30, 1864.

from their pits, that the Twenty-seventh was unable to make any headway, notwithstanding that General Hartranft succeeded in disintering one of the rebel guns in the work and firing it down this flank in aid of the movement.

About 7 or 8 o'clock the colored division moved into and on the right of the crater, and I sent orders to Hartranft to follow up and support them, if they succeeded in advancing. At the same time I pushed forward Humphrey's brigade in a front attack against the rebel rifle-pits on the left of the crater. The Second, Twentieth, and First Michigan Regiments went in line, and with no great loss carried the pits the length of their line, capturing some 40 prisoners, but the Forty-sixth New York broke, and in their disgraceful retreat threw two remaining regiments of the Second Brigade into temporary disorder and separated them from the line of battle.

Meantime Hartranft got out another gun, and was able to use it on his right flank, when an assault was made upon that side and upon the negro troops, who now occupied it, without advancing toward Cemetery Hill. This assault on the crater was repulsed with much loss to the rebels, the troops of my division that were with Hartranft springing to the edge of the crater and firing until the enemy were driven back and sought the shelter of their rifle-pits.

The two guns spoken of were manned by men of this division and of the Fourteenth [New York] Heavy Artillery, under the guidance of Sergt. W. Stanley, Company D of that regiment, who behaved with great skill, coolness, and bravery, but unfortunately was killed during the day. Another assault was afterward attempted on the rear of the work and was again repulsed. The enemy brought field artillery into position on several points along the Jerusalem plank road and Cemetery Hill, and a barn to the left of the hill. Their mortar batteries also got the range of the crater, and the shells fell with destructive precision among our troops, so closely packed together. Nevertheless, General Hartranft reported that he had some of his troops in better shape, and thought they could hold the position if ammunition could be supplied. I had already brought ammunition up to within 200 yards of the crater, and immediately sent 10,000 rounds by men of the Fifty-first Pennsylvania, part of whom were shot in the attempt.

The enemy now had full sweep of the ground between the crater and our rifle-pits, and at my request Col. Guy V. Henry, commanding a brigade in the Eighteenth Corps, and General Ferrero, with detachments of colored troops, began three covered ways toward the crater, from which also the men began to work from their side toward us.

Affairs were in this condition when I was summoned, with the other division commanders, to corps headquarters about 12.30 P.M. During my absence the work was evacuated under orders of the brigade commanders inside, sent to them from the major-general commanding. At the time of the evacuation the enemy made a third assault with a column of re-enforcements from General Hill's corps. This assault was virtually repulsed by the fire of our artillery, particularly Roemer's (Thirty-fourth New York) and Mayo's (Third Maine) batteries, and by the men remaining in the crater whom the order to withdraw did not reach. The rebel column, marching down the hill over open ground, was so shattered by our fire that it broke to one side, and the other fell back, rallied, and finally swayed off to the left of the crater into their rifle-pits, and advanced again under cover, when the most of our troops had left the work.

In this last affair the division lost some of its bravest men, who staid fighting it out to the last. Eight regiments were engaged, two regiments held in reserve, and the three that failed through the cowardice of the Forty-sixth New York to reach the rebel breast-works, were employed partly as provost guard and partly in manning our breast-works on the right and left of the crater to keep down the fire of the enemy from their pits during the evacuation of the rebel work. After dark this division relieved that part of the Eighteenth Corps that had occupied its front during the action.

The losses of this division, amounting to 40 commissioned officers and 666 men, only 258 of whom were missing, have already been reported. We captured about 100 rebel prisoners.

I have the honor to be, very respectfully,

O. B. Willcox

Brigadier-General, Commanding.[7]

I do not propose at this late day to enter upon the details of these assaults, but rather propose to treat of the engagements . . . for the purpose of correcting some misapprehensions and false statements that have crept into print.

It is always painful to point out the serious faults of other people, and it requires some magnanimity to acknowledge our own. General Grant frankly acknowledges his share of responsibility for the failure of the Mine affair, while lesser officers and inferior critics heap all the blame on Burnside and his troops without stint. There was a class of writers during the war that hung around camps and in rear of battle fields like jackals seeking for moral plunder. Some such obscure scavengers start up every now and then since the war, in the newspapers and magazines, and attempt to make mince meat of the 9th Corps over the yawning crater in front of Petersburg.

Now, in the first place let us be frank, and while ignoring those who have attempted unduly to stigmatize the 9th Corps, let us acknowledge that there was bad management all around the Mine affair. Not for the reasons given generally by the heroes of the quill, but for military reasons, and moral as well, not given by the court of inquiry which was convened shortly after the affair.

We will not claim any justification for the worn out condition of the 9th Corps troops, so many weeks in the trenches under incessant fire, nor for the poor condition of the miscellaneous odds and ends of dismounted cavalry and bounty boys with which our thinned ranks had been partially filled up; but I claim that the sentiment of the Army of the Potomac officers generally was believed to be against the practicability, first of the tunnelling and exposing of the mine, and then of the practicability of the breach, as well as against the storming party being formed, even in part, of colored troops, and that these prejudices affected the [morale] of the troops, who did the best they could under the circumstances. Just let me say here that I have

7. Report of Brig. Gen. Orlando B. Willcox, *OR*, vol. 40, pt. 1, pp. 574–76.

since learned from General Ferrero that his colored troops had not only been highly trained, particularly for the assault, but that they were religiously and fanatically wrought up to a fever-heat of zeal for the work, believing that God himself had now given them a chance to prove the courage of their race and their gratitude for freedom. Therefore there was a misconception on the part of Generals Grant and Meade which lead those generals to change Burnside's plan on the very eve of its execution, in order to conciliate the views of the rest of the army.

We had now settled down to a regular siege of Petersburg with the whole army in front of us. It was thought that by breaking through at the mine we could reach Cemetery Hill and drive Lee out of Petersburg. Truly a large undertaking, yet in all the general arrangements Grant thought he had provided means to follow up the explosion of the mine, and he at least hoped for, if he did not believe in, a general success.

I believe the interference or substitution in Burnside's plan was one of the leading causes of the failure. We had all counted on the storming party being composed of the colored troops, the only troops of the 9th Corps not in the trenches, and the only troops trained and specially prepared in all instructions and details for occupying and issuing from the breach promptly; no one can deny to General Ferrero the highest order of tactical skill for drilling fresh troops.

General Grant says in his book that General Potter and myself "were the only division commanders Burnside had who were equal to the occasion."[8] But I must confess that I should have wanted more than one short summer night to have made the necessary preparations due to a sudden change of plan for one of the most difficult feats to perform in the art of war; one of a kind that had failed in front of Vicksburg, and such as had been known to fail over and over again in the Netherlands, in the Crimea, and at almost every siege in history where it happened to be tried. Assaults with mining and counter-mining are generally considered as a series of partial, though desperate, attempts in a siege, rather than counted on as finalities, and are limited to gaining or destroying some important part of the work. . . .

The abatis in our front was removed; there was really little left to move that night, certainly none that obstructed the passage of troops for a moment. It had nearly all been shot away. Every one of my brigade com-

8. U.S. Grant, *Personal Memoirs of Ulysses S. Grant*, (New York: Charles L. Webster, 1885), vol. 2, p. 313.

manders, the division officers of the day, and one of my personal aides saw that everything was sufficiently cleared in our front for the easy passage of troops, and so reported to me, with the remark that any further removal of the sticks and brush, particularly at night, would only excite the attention of the enemy pickets—who it was well known were on the look out for some sort of explosion and assault. Questions about "That 'ar mine" had been yelled out by the Rebs in the trenches for days before.

But there was not only insufficient time, particularly for a novice like General Ledlie, to make the necessary arrangements and to clear the way for a general assault, but the greatest fault of all was committed by the higher authorities not giving the necessary orders to the support, that is in detail, and to the troops of other corps on the right and left, thus leaving Ledlie to plan his own assault, and each other division and the corps commander to await the result of that assault; or as in the case of the division commanders of the 9th Corps, to pitch their troops pell mell into the crater after the storming party.

Whether right or wrong, my own impression of the vague orders given to me were that I was to follow *through the crater*, whereas, as we see it now, nothing could have been [more] absurd. Not even the whole of Ledlie's division, but only a small storming party, should have gone through the exploded crater. As it was, Hartranft's brigade of my division, following Ledlie, found itself so inextricably mixed up with the latter's troops, and so broken up in the crater, that he sent a swift message beseeching me not to put in another soul. I do not think the history of war shows a more fatal error than this attempt to plunge so many thousand men through such a bung hole.

The rest of our efforts that day . . . [were] to carry the rest of the works immediately to the left and right of the mine, which we did, and to penetrate beyond towards Cemetery Hill, which latter seemed to be the only thing thought of at the moment, and that only from the vicinity of the crater. A similar failure attended the attempt made by the Confederates at Fort Stedman, where even a larger force broke themselves all up in effecting a passage at that point, and then found themselves utterly unable to get farther.

Now I ask any candid man if it does not stand to reason that immediately on the explosion of the mine, the works on both sides of the mine should have been simultaneously assaulted? There were troops enough on hand to do it; why was it not attempted? Besides my own success on the left (which did not immediately follow, as might have been the case if the proper orders had been issued), General Potter also flung his troops over on the right and got some distance to the front, General Ord gained some part of the line, and Hancock's troops some, though [these movements all came too late].

Before Petersburg, Virginia
Aug 3rd/'64
My Dear Eb,

I enclose you the best accounts I have seen published in the papers. It is from the *Philadelphia Enquirer* of the 2nd. The other newspapers give little or nothing of the operations of my division, whereas we gained quite as much *credit* as any other troops, & did not *disgrace* ourselves at all, captured two-fifths of *all* the prisoners from the rebels, lost less prisoners ourselves, & had more killed & wounded than any other white division, made the only *successful* front attack on the unexploded part of the rebel works, dug out the two cannon & used them in the crater against the enemy, & drew off . . . our regiments in better order than any other division.

This is all *fact*.

Hitherto, the correspondent of the *N.Y. Herald* had been very friendly with my division, but lately he has been fearful of risking his precious body by coming up to the front where we are, & consequently he has little to say of us. He makes his stay at the 1st Division hospital in [the] rear, & you find he has most to say of them, while everybody knows that knows anything about the affair, that the 1st Division really behaved the worst.

The truth is that my division & Potter's behaved well, & Ledlie's division & the colored troops acted badly. You know I never would tell an untruth & this you may rely upon, & I tell you merely for the sake of the Michigan regiments that compose the bone & muscle of my division.

Of my individual part in the action I have nothing more to say than that I did all in my power, but that the mode & manner of the attack was not finally ordered as I expected & proposed. But it is too long a story to go into now.

I am satisfied that the rebel losses & our own are about even—in fact one of their officers admitted it to Brackett. We repulsed them twice, & my own battery (Roemer's) knocked them into *pie* a third time, while our troops were evacuating. We were not driven out at all, but evacuated under orders, simply because we could get no further & there was no use holding such an advanced point, isolated. Love to all

Yours Ever,
O.B.W.

[Capt. L. C. Brackett to Marie Willcox]
Head-Quarters, 3rd Div., 9th Army Corps
Before Petersburg, Va.
Aug. 4/1864
My dear Friend,

Your kind note with the 3rd Division (blue) tie enclosed I received with great pleasure.

A few days since I expected that by this time I would be promenading the streets of Petersburg with the tie to relieve my sun burnt appearance. But alas! a black cloud carried away my great expectations—and at the present time I am sufficiently blue to strut around in our old trenches—so the tie must remain new until something new and of importance transpires.

After the fight of the 30th, with me it was a question whether we would continue the siege or strike our tents and depart, leaving only graves and the ashes of our fires behind us—but it is the fourth of August and we are still here, and I dare say we will try Petersburg by "regular approaches."

We were all very much interested in the Mine, and a great many expected that the explosion of it would be the signal for the fall of Petersburg. On the eve of the 30th, every preparation was made to take advantage of the confusion that the explosion of the Mine would create among the rebels.

Half past three A.M. July 30th was the time set for the springing of the Mine. Three o'clock found Gen'l Willcox & staff at Roemer's Battery, anxiously waiting to see the Rebel Fort go up—staff officers roaming about looking at watches—in a mad hurry for the time to come, but growing hot and uncomfortable as the hour drew near—Four o'clock and no signs of the young earthquake.

Fifteen minutes of five, a rumbling sound and a cry, "There it goes."

And what a grand sight it was—like a fountain of earth with jets high up in the air—down near the ground it would fall over like a pond lily— clouds of dust would roll out from the Crater—Soon, very soon, the earth settled—The four (4) tons of powder had done its work—It had hurled about four hundred men and a number of guns—As soon as the earth had settled, our troops moved forward to the Crater—The enemy had opened from all their guns and we were under a heavy fire.

The General had moved his Head-Quarters to the front line of works, within seventy yards of the Crater. As soon as we had carried the first line to the right and left of the Crater, the blacks were ordered forward, but they only went as far as our advanced troops, for soon the cry was raised, "The Rebels are coming." What a lamentable sight to see the Negroes come back like a flock of black sheep. But what a grand sight it was to see our little band of white troops permit the colored troops to pass by—and then repulse the charge. I only counted four white men that returned with the blacks.

In regard to the colored troops I have nothing to say—In the hour of supreme trouble we are not apt to judge correctly—It was their first fight.

I saw an orderly that was next to the Gen'l shot—the General had his Head-Quarters in a warm place during the whole fight.

The Crater appeared like a large amphitheatre—it was about twenty-five (25) feet deep—Twice the rebels tried to take it, but they were repulsed each time—and we did not evacuate it till we received orders from the Lt. Gen'l commanding.

The Gen'l has not been in the best of spirits since the fight—but this morning he appears like himself again. He is in excellent health and sends his love to all. Give my love to the children and remember me kindly to Mr. & Mrs. Farnsworth.

From your sincere Friend,
L. C. Brackett

[W. V. Richards to Marie Willcox]
Near Petersburg, Va.
August 6th, 1864
My dear Mrs. Willcox,

I am much ashamed of myself for so long delaying to acknowledge your very kind note, written almost a month since, enclosing the beautiful souvenir of your regards. I had been waiting up to the 30th of July to wear that badge in our grand *entre* to Petersburg, but am sorry to announce that in our determined effort and in our elated hopes, we have been prostrated by sad disappointment. The happiness and assurance that rested on all of us scarce two weeks since at the prospect of the coming engagement, has settled down to gloomy despondency——

On the 30th we were up at two in the morning and soon repaired with the Gen'l to the scene of action—The explosion of the Mine, which was to be the signal of attack, was to have taken place at 3.30 A.M., but on account of the fuses going out, it did not explode till about 4.45 A.M., the fuses having been relit far up in the channel.

Gen'l Ledlie, commanding the 1st Division of this corps, was ordered to lead the assault. Gen'l Willcox, 3rd Division, to follow, and Gen'l Potter, in turn, to follow him with the 2nd Division.

OBW and staff at headquarters, Third Division, Ninth Corps, August 1864. *Seated, from left:* Capt. Robert A. Hutchins, assistant adjutant general; Capt. Henry Bowman, assistant quartermaster; Lt. Levi C. Brackett, aide de camp; OBW; and Capt William V. Richards, aide de camp. *Standing, from left:* Capt. Peter Heistand, assistant quartermaster; Surgeon Patrick O'Connell; Capt. David B. Cole, commissary; and Pvt. F. W. Knowles, 36th Mass., clerk. *USAMHI.*

Very shortly after the Mine was sprung, Ledlie [i.e., his division] dashed forward into the crater. Willcox took his place without delay, when, seeing Ledlie halted in the crater, he deployed his command to the left, taking considerable of the line and about one hundred and thirty prisoners. Potter also advanced in his turn and occupied the crater. Thus all of Ledlie's and Potter's command and about half of Willcox's were in this small space, of course greatly mixed up, so much so that when orders came to advance and take the opposite crest, the commands could not be got in hand.

The colored troops who were in a zigzag covered way were ordered up, and about 8.45 formed for assault. They formed very well and advanced with much spirit till they came under hot fire, when they ignominiously broke and ran in every direction.

About this time a furious assault was made on the white divisions still in advance, the weight of it coming on Willcox's division. This assaulting column was nearly annihilated by one of Gen'l Willcox's (Roemer's) batteries, the few that reached our line giving themselves up. Seeing the great disorder of the negro troops and the impossibility of getting them in hand for further action, the enemy formed again in heavy columns and assaulted.

Willcox's division, from its locality, had to take the blunt [*sic*] of this second charge also, but his brave troops stood well to their work and beat the enemy back. Perceiving two pieces of artillery partly buried in the mud, Gen'l Willcox's division dug them out and served them with murderous effect during this second charge; to this perhaps is due a large share of the success in repelling this attack and saving the commands of Willcox, Potter & Ledlie.

Soon after this the order came to withdraw to our former works, which was done just as the enemy were about making a third attack in vastly superior numbers, and accomplished under a most murderous fire. Thus ended one of the saddest days ever [in which] the 9th Corps were called upon to be the principal actors. We were shamefully repulsed. Petersburg was ours but we did not take proper advantage of our opportunity. The blame lays somewhere; it would not be proper for me to say where, even if I knew. Our division received much credit. Lt. Jones, acting division inspector on our staff, was captured. [Our] division lost 750, about forty (40) of whom were officers.

Please accept my sincere thanks for your very kind remembrance. To me it is a source of the utmost gratification to know that by any attention to duty with the commanding Gen'l for whom I have such deep affection, I should also merit the kind regards of his very estimable consort.

Very respectfully,
W. V. Richards

In great haste.

Near Petersburg, Va.

Aug. 8, '64

I thank you my darling wife for your letter of [the] 2nd inst., enclosing Lulu's letter from Chicago. She might write a better hand if she wrote more slowly. But this truth teach her by encouragement rather than fault finding. I hope she will learn a handsome free hand, as I think it is one of the best accomplishments & most prepossessing & charming. She must not be permitted to acquire, by carelessness & fast writing, a bad hand. It is just as easy to write well as not, & much harder to correct a poor hand once acquired— as I know from experience.

I think Lu promises to do very well in penmanship. As for ideas, she never can lack for them. I hope the atmosphere around her heart & head will always be kept as pure as possible and that her reading will be under your guidance.

Major [Claudius B.] Grant leaves here to-morrow on recruiting service & will take this, and I send also by him a model of the corps badge in clay from the mine whose explosion proved so disappointing on the 30th July. I have one in silver with a ribbon & very neat.

As I expected, the public wrath & clamor about the failure grows worse every day—judging from the papers. And gross falsehoods & unjust criticisms that are furnished in order to gratify the shameful public taste are worse than all. As the public is disappointed & mad, every contemptible scribbler attempts to invent if he cannot find something new to censure & somebody else to blame. It is so undignified & babyish to whine over every disaster in the war & expose our nakedness without shame to the eyes of the world.

And all this comes from the reports of a parcel of newspaper correspondents, who learn what is going on in front from what they hear about [in] the trains & hospitals in [the] rear—the birthplace of a thousand wild & silly rumors a day. There are many things which neither corps nor division commanders know or understand, which your newspaper correspondent communicates with all the gravity of any other owl or jackass. Besides this, the 9th Corps has been considered not an integral part of the old army of the Potomac, & there are not wanting those in the other corps that are glad to get a kick at the brave old dog now he is down.

Burnside is as confident as ever in his old theory of right prevailing in the end, & thinks that his good intentions & honest zeal in the service will finally put to flight all the slanders of his enemies. The effort which I made to reconcile him & Meade failed. There were too many points of ill feeling between them. M. has preferred charges against B.

The point which I tried to settle was this. On the 30th, Meade wrote a dispatch to Burnside, in which he begged to know what Burnside meant by saying "it was hard work for the troops to advance," and he wanted to know "the truth," i.e., he wanted Burnside to tell him frankly the true state of things, & if it was impossible to advance just to say so without hesitation. This is what Meade no doubt meant by "the truth." But Burnside thought that Meade meant to impute a want of veracity, & in his reply said "that if it were not insubordinate, he would say that the remark was unofficer-like & ungentlemanly."

Well, Meade explained his meaning to me, but as he did not particularly authorize me to communicate it to Burnside, he, B., would not withdraw the offensive remark, & it forms now one of the charges against him. I think he is very sorry that he did not take my advice & retract. I do not think I should have allowed the affair to rest, but I found there were so many grudges & charges on other points that the quarrel was bound to come.

I have no objection to you showing this letter to Father, the Bishop, or Judge Campbell, and Eben of course, but no one else. As to who is to blame for the failure it is hard to say; those who know the most about it are most reluctant to give an opinion.

I think, however, that (without imputing blame to anyone) if the *whole line* had been attacked, instead of only one *point* (the breach) & that immediately upon the explosion, we could have carried nearly the whole line, including at least three redoubts that were for a short time evacuated. But I think we should have had a bloody fight for Petersburg even after that.

We lost the benefits of the surprise by the 1st Division not pushing on at once after gaining the breach—which indeed did not cost a man on our side. Potter's division & mine followed up immediately, one [on] one side, the other on the other, as was our orders, but the golden moment was lost, the rebels recovered from the surprise & scare, & we were soon encircled by a sheet of fire of both musketry & artillery.

The stories you hear about the troops of [the] 9th Corps not coming up fast enough to support & not enough of them & all that, are wrong. The fact is, there were a great many troops in the breach or crater—too many; they crowded in upon each other until they got all mixed up, one regiment with another & one division with another, so that it was impossible to reform their ranks for a further advance. If the plan of the attack had been mine, I never should have let more than two or three regiments or a brigade go into the crater, but attacked vigorously on both sides, i.e., the line of rebel works in front of the 9th Corps, at least.

It is very fine to believe in days of final *eclaircisement* in this world, but I don't believe the whole truth ever will come out, & fear Burnside will have to bear his share of blame, notwithstanding his good intentions—unless another scapegoat of higher mark is found. Meade's enemies no doubt will avail themselves of such an opportunity. And humble division commanders like myself need not hope to escape. If my division would not advance, why did I not bring down a section of artillery & blow them out of the crater with grape & cannister—as a certain division commander of the old Army of the Potomac is reported to have said he would have done. That is the kind of talk we hear.

Well, a court of inquiry is in session & we shall soon have something tangible.[9] I hope a thorough examination will be made, & if any of us were at fault, let us bear the brunt like brave men who have tried their best. Meantime, the immaculate, patriotic, self-sacrificing, heroic public will eat their good dinners & make their cent per cent [*sic*] while they curse that infernal blunder & those blundering generals at Petersburg.

With the greatest of love to the children,

Thine Ever,
O. B. W.

[Near Petersburg, Virginia]
Aug. 14 [1864]
My darling Wife,
Burnside or Meade had to go & Meade stays so B. goes. He offered to offer his resignation for the 40-eleventh time & Grant said "no, take a leave for 20 days & I will perhaps give you a separate command."

Well, B. left last night, & again I am in command [of the Ninth Corps] temporarily, i.e. for a few days, only doing damage to me, you see.[10] But *n'importe*. I begin to think I had better step out altogether.

Thine in haste,
O. B. W.

9. The final opinion issued by the official court of inquiry found Willcox among those officers "answerable for want of success" in the mine affair. Specifically relating to Willcox, the court concluded that more "energy might have been exercised . . . to cause his troops to go forward." Grant later termed the episode "the saddest affair I have witnessed in this war. . . . Such opportunity for carrying fortifications I have never seen and do not expect to again have." Grant, however, placed no blame whatsoever on Willcox. The lack of success at the Crater, he believed, was "due to inefficiency on the part of the corps commander [Burnside] and the incompetency of the division commander who was sent to lead the assault [Ledlie]."

10. Following Burnside's dismissal, OBW assumed temporary command of the Ninth Corps but was soon replaced by John G. Parke. OBW then resumed command of the Third Division.

§

TWENTY-TWO

Gnawing into the Heart of the Confederacy

[As with any siege of a city, the key to capturing Petersburg lay in its lines of supply: chiefly the James River and the three railroads that led into it from the southeast, south, and west: respectively, the Norfolk & Petersburg, Weldon, and South Side railroads. With those avenues in Union hands, Petersburg would be starved into capitulation, and Lee's army would be forced either to withdraw or surrender. As the James River and the Norfolk & Petersburg Railroad had fallen under Union control early in the siege, Grant began to concentrate on capturing the Weldon and South Side railroads. Making the most of its greater manpower, the Army of the Potomac began to extend its lines to the left, stretching westward toward the vital arteries that supplied Petersburg and the Confederate army that protected it. Attacks were made north of the James, upon Richmond itself, but they were chiefly diversionary, designed to distract Lee's attention from the more important efforts to capture the railroads to the south.]

AFTER [the mine] event, the troops settled down awhile to regular work in the trenches and on the redoubts and return works, which were strengthened sufficiently to enable small garrisons to hold them with artillery and mortars. This set two-thirds of the army footloose, and allowed new outside operations, viz., to extend our lines and to threaten Richmond; for while our weak side at Petersburg was [the safety of] Washington, Lee's weak side was Richmond, and while Lee threatened Washington [with Early's force],

Grant kept his eyes on the James River side of Richmond. This not only prevented Lee from reinforcing Early, but soon made him bring back [Maj. Gen. Joseph B.] Kershaw's division,[1] which left Early at the mercy of Sheridan, as all the world knows.

Meantime, Butler lay at Bermuda Hundred, ready for a spring, confronted by strong works at Drewry's Bluff and Chaffin's Farm, [but] with entrenchments stretching unoccupied around Richmond, and outworks at Bailey's Creek or Deep Bottom. To these points Hancock was ordered over in August, in secrecy, hoping to find the enemy less prepared than when he had moved against them in July, when he had made a similar demonstration, but found them in full force.[2] But the enemy was found strongly entrenched in position, and this expedition met with little better success than the first. Field's Confederate division had remained at Deep Bottom, and [Maj. Gen. Cadmus M.] Wilcox's at Chaffin's Bluff, and these were reinforced in the nick of time by Mahone and W. H. F. Lee, all under Ewell.[3]

The enemy's works were carried above Fussell's Mill by Gen. [Alfred H.] Terry's division of the 10th Corps, under [Maj. Gen. David B.] Birney, and though [Brig. Gen. David McM.] Gregg, supported by [Brig. Gen. Nelson A.] Miles' brigade,[4] advanced fighting up the Charles City road to within seven miles of Richmond, yet the whole of the enemy's cavalry, supported by his infantry, flung back Gregg and Miles on our right, across Deep Creek, and retook the captured works. On the 18th the enemy attacked, but was repulsed, and Hancock held on, threatening until the 20th, by which time Warren, probably in consequence of this move, secured his lodgment on the Weldon Railway. The demonstration, therefore . . . was successful, though its generals had failed to open the gates of Richmond.

1. Kershaw's division (some 3,500 veterans) of Anderson's First Corps had been dispatched from Petersburg to assist Early in the Valley in mid-August. Pressure on the Petersburg front forced Lee to recall Kershaw on September 14. Kershaw returned to the Valley in late September, playing a major role in the Battle of Cedar Creek on October 19. On November 15, however, Kershaw finally left the Valley, leaving Early, whose army was all but finished, to the "mercy" of Sheridan.

2. On July 27, Hancock's Second Corps and two cavalry divisions under Sheridan moved north of the James in a diversionary move at Deep Bottom. The main assault, of course, would be on the works in front of Petersburg, south of the river, upon the explosion of the mine. Hancock made another attempt at Deep Bottom in mid-August, described here by OBW.

3. Major generals William Mahone and Cadmus Wilcox each commanded a division in A. P. Hill's Third Corps; Maj. Gen. William H. F. "Rooney" Lee, son of Robert E. Lee, led a division of Confederate horsemen. Ewell was then commanding the Department of Richmond.

4. Miles then led a brigade in the First Division, Second Corps. Miles, who began his Civil War career as a captain, rose to be commanding general of the U.S. Army from 1895–1903.

August 19/'64. Battle

Marched from Taylor House to the Yellow House. Humphrey's brigade was in the trenches & relieved under a heavy cannonade by troops of the 18th Corps about 2 A.M. Troops started at 3½ A.M. per orders. Reported to Warren at 7 A.M., who ordered the division to rest in an open field on the right & rear. My front covered by a line of pickets. The troops bivouacked in two lines, Hartranft's brigade in front.

At 4 P.M. a brisk fire opened in front of our left. Ordered the division under arms. In a few moments received despatch from Gen. Warren that a large force of enemy was seen coming down on Ayres.[6] Ordered Hartranft to oblique to the left & move to support of Ayres. He sent me word the enemy was attacking the division in front of him & I ordered him to go in where the fire was heaviest. He advanced at once & engaged the enemy who had broken Crawford's division & checked them.

Gen. Warren sent word that he thought the heaviest attack would be on the left, & directed me to move my force over there. This order was transmitted through Lt. Col. [Henry C.] Bankhead.[7] At the same time I was directed to assume command of [Brig. Gen. Julius] White's divi-

5. The Weldon Railroad was an important supply line for Lee's army, linking both Petersburg and Richmond with Weldon, North Carolina. The engagement described here, usually referred to as the Battle of Globe Tavern, took place on the left of the main Union line under the direction (on the Federal side) of Maj. Gen. G. K. Warren. Warren began his reconnaissance in force with his own Fifth Corps and a brigade of cavalry; on August 19th he was reinforced by the Ninth Corps divisions of White, Willcox, and Potter. Opposing the initial Federal movement was Heth's division of Hill's Third Corps and a brigade of cavalry; Heth was later reinforced by Mahone's division of Hill's corps, including some artillery and W.H.F. Lee's cavalry division. The fighting, August 19–21, cost the Union troops some 4,455 casualties out of 20,289 engaged, while the Confederates lost about 1,600 out of 14,000 engaged. Despite stout Rebel resistance, the Federals managed to keep their grip on Globe Tavern and the railroad, severing an important Confederate lifeline.

OBW wrote an article entitled "Actions on the Weldon Railroad" for the *Century Magazine* and originally intended to use that article in his memoirs, but the editor has not included it here. It is readily available in the often-reprinted Robert Johnson Underwood and Clarence C. Buel, eds., *Battles and Leaders of the Civil War*, vol. 4, pp. 568–73.

6. Brig. Gen. Romeyn B. Ayres then had command of the Second Division, Fifth Corps. Heth's division was the "large force" that "was seen coming down on Ayres." It was sad and all too typical that, as OBW later recalled, "Ayres, Griffin and myself were members of the same graduating class at the Military Academy, West Point, and so were two of our opponents on this field, A. P. Hill and Heth." OBW, "Actions on the Weldon Railroad," *Battles and Leaders*, vol. 4, p. 570.

7. Bankhead was inspector general of the Fifth Corps.

sion,[8] which I ordered to look well to their right flank, & I moved first Humphrey up to the left of the position lately held by Crawford, and Hartranft next to Humphrey, who opened fire. Ayres' division advancing, I ordered Humphrey to attack & recapture the works on the right of A., which he did in gallant style, taking one stand of (47th Va.) colors, 6 officers & 48 men prisoners.

The enemy threatening on the right, [Lt. Col. Joseph H.] Barnes'[9] brigade of White's division was sent to the extreme right, & as Crawford had partly rallied, his troops were moved into the woods on Humphrey's right, & Hartranft placed in the gap left by Barnes, with orders to advance & recapture the works in his front, which he succeeded in doing, after some delay owing to the thick growth of underbrush, early in the evening. Humphrey rested in the works on the right of Ayres, & Hartranft on the right of Crawford, connecting with White. Loss, 180.

August 20

The division was drawn out of the rifle pits to the open field where they first bivouacked on the morning of the 19th, leaving 300 skirmishers on the line between Ayres & White.

[August] 21. Battle

At 4 A.M. Hartranft's brigade was put on Ayres' line, 5th Corps, & constructed a line of entrenchments, connecting two batteries, across the Weldon R.R. At 9 A.M. the enemy attacked before this work was completed & were repulsed, chiefly by artillery. Humphrey's brigade was moved over to Griffin, 5th Corps, but sent back. Skirmishers were driven in. Loss, 157, chiefly on the skirmish line.

August 21–25

Picketing and road-building.

[August] 25

Started at 3½ P.M. with orders to march to [the] intersection of plank road & road to Reams' Station at Shay's Tavern, & there communicate & report to Gen. Hancock at Reams' Station. Twitchell's & [Lt. Alfred B.] Losee's[10] batteries reported to me en route.

8. White then commanded the First Division, Ninth Corps, having relieved Brig. Gen. James Ledlie following the Battle of the Crater.

9. Barnes led the Second Brigade, First Division, Ninth Corps.

10. Losee commanded the 19th New York Battery.

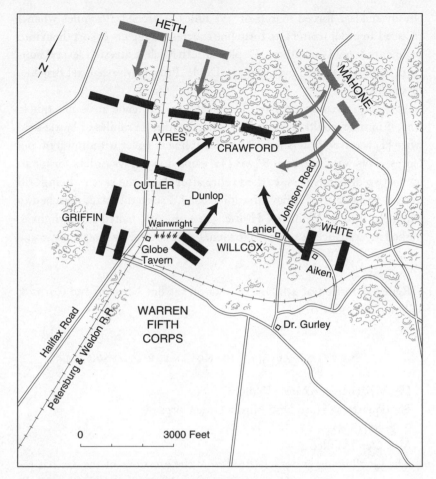

The Battle of the Weldon Railroad, August 19, 1864.

On plank road [I] received an order from Hancock to come on rapidly with my division & one battery, as he was engaged. This was at 5 P.M.[11] I had

11. Reams Station was an embarrassing setback for Hancock's once-stolid Second Corps. While engaged in tearing up the Weldon Railroad the divisions of Nelson A. Miles and John Gibbon were suddenly attacked by A. P. Hill's beefed-up corps. Hancock quickly found himself in dire straits and sent urgently to Willcox for help. The editor has found the original of Hancock's dispatch to OBW among the latter's papers. The note, in Hancock's hand, was scratched hastily in pencil. Dated Reams Station, August 25, 1864, 4:30 P.M., it reads as follows:

Gen. Wilcox [*sic*]
Cmdg. Division Ninth Corps,
For security here, I wish you would move your Division with perhaps a battery of artillery & no wagons, to this point, rapidly. Look out for both flanks when you arrive near me, if you hear any firing in the neighborhood.

W. S. Hancock M.G.C.

already made a forced march of 5½ miles. Marched 2½ miles when I received an order from H. to form line & arrest stragglers & sort them into regiments & hold them there. Deployed 20th Mich & arrested several hundred, who were turned over to Capt. Doyle, Provost Marshal, 1st Brigade, to organize.

At 6¼ received orders from H. to send up a brigade at double quick, who, if in time, could save the day. Arrived within 1½ miles of battle field when [I] received orders from H. to form line to cover withdrawal of 2nd Corps. This was done & at 8 [P.M.] H. came down, gave orders for me to let his two divisions pass, & then retire after them, the cavalry being still in rear. ½ hour after Miles' division passed, I started back & marched to within ½ mile of Williams' House. 3½ A.M. 26th, halted till daylight & pushed my way back & reported to Gen. Parke at Greeley House at 7 A.M.

[August] 27
Relieved portion of 4th Div. & went on the line between 2nd Corps & White's Div., 9th Corps.

LETTERS: AUGUST 20–NOVEMBER 27, 1864

[W. V. Richards to Marie Willcox]
Headquarters, Third Div., Ninth Army Corps
Aug. 20 [1864]
Mrs. Gen'l Willcox,

The Gen'l being extremely tired from the exertions of the day has requested me to write you. Here we are, drowned in mud on the Weldon R. R. The Fifth Corps, Maj. Gen'l Warren, commanding, came down and cut the road the day before yesterday. Yesterday morning at 3 A.M. we started from our entrenchments before Petersburg to reinforce Warren. It rained nearly all day.

We arrived at 7 A.M. and laid in the wet till 4.30 P.M., when we were startled with the rattle of musketry, and soon after, the announcement that the enemy had broken in on the line of the 5th Corps. We had scarcely got our troops in line of battle when we found that the enemy had completely turned the right flank of Warren, & capturing about one thousand prisoners, with Brig. Gen'l Hays,[12] all seemed lost to the eyes of many; but the old story was soon to be told again.

12. Brig. Gen. Joseph Hayes led the First Brigade, Second Division, Fifth Corps.

Gen'l Willcox moved up one of his brigades to the right of the broken line and drove the heavy column of the advancing enemy back in confusion; then, moving his 2nd Brigade, the Michigan brigade as it is called by many, to the left, he formed to secure that lost by Gen'l Ayres' division— Under a heavy fire the Gen'l brought this brigade up, when, stopping to get a good start, they took off their hats, gave three times three for Willcox, then with their trusty weapons in their hand, they dashed in and were the first troops to recapture and enter the works of the lost line. I have seen many of the troops of this gallant brigade fight before, but never have I seen more enthusiasm exhibited by them.

We covered ourselves with glory and wiped off for the whole Corps any stain of the 30th. Our division captured about two hundred prisoners and one stand of colors. Our loss was very light considering the work we did. Three terrible assaults were made by the enemy to drive us out of the re-taken works without success; their casualties were enormous.

The Gen'l received a letter from you today and will try to answer tomorrow. All are well but extremely tired and uncomfortable.

With respect,
W. V. Richards

Headquarters, Third Div., Ninth Army Corps
Aikens House [Near Petersburg]
Aug. 27, 1864
My darling Wife,

This house is about a mile & a half east of Blick's House, or the Yellow House, as latter is called in the papers. My division had a little share in Warren's fight of the 21st. Hartranft's brigade built & held a line of works in Ayres' lines & helped the artillery to resist a charge, & my skirmishers were engaged. But the artillery did about all the fighting, & slaughtered the rebels badly.

On the 25th I was ordered to take my division to a point on Hancock's line of communications, got there, & was sent for by him to come up to Reams' Station. Got up part way when he sent me word to stop & reorganize his stragglers, which were coming back to the rear in great numbers during the action. While engaged in this work [I] received another message from him to hurry up one, or, if possible, two brigades to the field, as he had lost part of his works & wanted a fresh brigade to recapture them. Double-quicked it for about 2 miles, when he sent me word to take position to cover his withdrawal, which I did accordingly, & returned up the Jerusalem Plank Road between 1 o'clock & daylight, acting as rear guard for the 2d Corps.

Had I been ordered down from where I was near the Yellow House direct along the R. R. to Reams' Station, 5 miles, I should have got to Hancock in time for him to have secured a victory. As it was, the route taken was ten or eleven miles, & then too late to do any good.

Meade says Hancock did not call for reinforcements, but he sent me to guard his line of communications. It would have been grand if I had gone the other way & repeated the success of saving a corps as I did Warren's on the 19th, or at least helped to do very materially.[13]

I don't like my present lines as the troops are lying in such swampy ground that I fear there will be much sickness if they stay long. I think [it] very likely, however, that I shall be called out again as soon as there is a row anyplace.

My own Headquarters are at a very nice place, around a house on dry ground with shade & a fine well. Cold pure water is rare in these parts, & this is the first I have had for a long time.

Maj. Bowman has named his little daughter Clara Louise, the latter for you. Tell Ali I have two little coons that drink their milk from a bottle through a bit of rag. Love to all the children. Send this letter to Eb.

Thine Ever,
O.B.W.

Head Quarters, Ninth Army Corps
Near Petersburg, Va.
Weldon R. R.
Sept. 4, 1864
My dear little Lulie,

Your nice letter is received, and gives me a great deal of pleasure. I am happy to hear that you have spent so pleasant a vacation. I am getting very impatient to see you and hope to do so before long. I want to see Elon, Ali and Grace very much indeed; it is hard to live away from you all so many days & months at a time. But if I live to see the war end, we will all be together again & have good times.

13. OBW later recalled Hancock's remark that "'had our troops behaved as they used to I could have beaten Hill,' he said to me. 'But some were new, and all were worn out with labor. Or had your force been sent down the railroad to attack the enemy's flank we would have whipped him; or a small reserve about 6 o'clock would have accomplished the same object.' These points were also mentioned in his report. He requested me to draw up my division as a rearguard and let his troops pass by after dark. I never had seen him in better form. It was more like abdication than defeat." Hancock's losses at Reams' Station were 2,742, most of whom were captured. Confederates suffered only some 720, mostly killed and wounded. OBW, "Actions on the Weldon Railroad," *Battles and Leaders*, vol. 4, p. 573.

Cockfight at OBW's headquarters, August 1864. Those identified are *(from left):* Capt. R. A. Hutchins, Capt. Peter Heistand, Lt. D. Holway (in straw hat), "George" (holding rooster), Gen. Willcox, "John" (with rooster), Capt. W. V. Richards, Capt. Henry Bowman (seated in straw hat and vest), Lt. Levi Brackett (seated on ground in front of Bowman), Patrick O'Connell, Pvt. F. W. Knowles (standing with hand on O'Connell's chair). Also, standing under the bower, just left of Captain Richards, is the sketch artist, Pvt. Andrew McCallum. *USAMHI.*

Do you not miss Grandma? When is she to be home? I suppose you are now at school again. What are you studying? How does Elon get on with his books? I hope nothing will happen to Ny and am glad he has a collar.

I have a very pretty camp which I wish you & Elon might see. It is along the crest of a little hill, and in the edge of a wood, with the tents in rows, just as when Mama visited me at Falmouth.

Major Bowman has made me a nice camp chair and a pretty round table that folds up & packs very conveniently. Dr. O'Connell and Lt. Brackett inquire after you very often. They both seem to like you a good deal.

Good bye my sweet little daughter. Kiss Mama, Elon, Ali & Grace and never forget to pray for

Your affectionate papa,
O.B.W.

Late in September, Ord, from the Bermuda [Hundred] front, and Birney, from the Petersburg front, commanding, respectively, the 18th and 10th Corps, leaving sufficient forces in their entrenchments, crossed the James by night.[14] Ord crossed at Aikens, two miles below Dutch Gap, to the Varina road, and Birney crossed at Deep Bottom, followed by Kautz, with his cavalry division.[15] The only troops known to be in the works on the north side of the James besides the heavy artillery and a couple of brigades of the local defense, were the three brigades of Field and one of Johnson's.[16] Both of our columns were safely across by daylight, moving on their designated routes and driving the enemy's skirmishers and advance before them.

Ord [was] steering up the Varina and New Market roads for Forts Harrison and Gilmer, the possession of which . . . would give us Chaffin's Bluff. Reinforcements were seen entering Fort Harrison, against which Stannard's division went in quick time, and Burnham's brigade, running through a severe fire of musketry and artillery, topped the hill and captured the fort with its two guns and garrison.[17] Stannard also captured the adjoining entrenchments, with six more guns. Burnham was killed in the assault, and both succeeding brigade commanders were wounded, and during the day Gen. Ord himself was severely wounded, leaving the command of his corps to [Brig. Gen. Charles A.] Heckman.[18] Heckman soon after attacked Fort Gilmer with his own division, but was repulsed with heavy loss.

Meantime, Birney had advanced up the New Market road towards Richmond, and captured the rebel picket line of entrenchments running northeast from Fort Harrison across to the Darby road on our right. Kautz advanced on the latter road abreast with Birney. Terry's division was sent to support him. The Confederate main line, now commanded by Ewell, ran about 3/4 of a mile in rear of the captured picket line. Field came into Fort Gilmer with Law's brigade.

14. Maj. Gen. Edward O. C. Ord (17th, USMA 1839). OBW here refers to the Union attacks on Fort Gilmer and Fort Harrison on the outskirts of Richmond, September 29–30, 1864.

15. Brig. Gen. August V. Kautz commanded the cavalry division of the Army of the James.

16. By late September only two Confederate brigades remained in the Richmond works north of the James: Brig. Gen. John Gregg's Texas brigade, under Col. Frederick Bass, and Benning's Georgia brigade, under Col. Dudley M. Dubose, both of Field's division. These were aided by Brig. Gen. Martin W. Gary's veteran cavalry brigade, numerous artillery units, and two inexperienced battalions from Richmond.

17. Brig. Gen. George J. Stannard led the First Division, Eighteenth Corps; Brig. Gen. Hiram Burnham commanded Stannard's Second Brigade.

18. Heckman commanded the Second Division, Eighteenth Corps.

Communication was established between our columns, and Grant, coming into Fort Harrison, informed Birney of Ord's success, and directed him to push forward in conjunction. The attack extended from Fort Gilmer, on our right, to the New Market road, on our left. Birney made the attack on Fort Gilmer with Ames' division and a colored brigade.[19] It was a brave and resolute attack, but it failed, although [Ames' division], struggling under fire over three ravines, got close to the works, and the leading colored troops reached the ditch and strove to climb the parapet over each other's shoulders.

Lee came over during the day, and during the night ten brigades were concentrated for the recapture of Fort Harrison. Next day, Longstreet's corps made the attack. The enemy's three bloody repulses by Stannard made up for some of our own losses. Stannard lost an arm, but our other losses were slight compared with those of Lee, which never could be replaced.[20]

Every move we now made gnawed into the very heart of the Confederacy, and the most skeptical officers, such as Upton, began to appreciate Grant's corrosive policy. The capture of Atlanta at this time also revived the whole country beyond danger of our ever recognizing the Confederacy.

Leaving [Maj. Gen. Godfrey] Weitzel[21] to hold [Fort] Harrison, Grant returned to our camp and started us off for Peebles Farm. This was at the junction of two roads coming into Petersburg from the southwest, where the enemy were constructing a redoubt and connecting it with their Petersburg works. This new line ran parallel to our works on the Weldon road. Their main line had been extended to Hatcher's Run, crossing the Boydton Plank [road] and Southside Railroad.

Our expedition [on September 30] consisted of [the Fifth and Ninth Corps under] Warren and Parke, with two divisions each, and Gregg's cavalry, all under Meade himself. Petersburg was now defended by Hill, with his own corps, [Maj. Gen. Bushrod] Johnson's division, and two divisions and Dearing's brigade of cavalry, under [Maj. Gen. Wade] Hampton.[22]

19. Brig. Gen. Robert S. Foster commanded Birney's Second Division, formerly commanded by Brig. Gen. Adelbert Ames; Brig. Gen. William Birney commanded the brigade of black troops.

20. Federal losses for the two days fighting before Richmond were roughly 2,272 killed, wounded, and missing. The Confederates lost an estimated two thousand.

21. Weitzel now commanded the Eighteenth Corps in place of Ord, away on medical leave.

22. Johnson commanded a division in the Department of North Carolina and Southern Virginia, under Gen. P.G.T. Beauregard; Col. Joel Griffin now commanded the brigade of Brig. Gen. James Dearing. Hampton assumed command of the Cavalry Corps of the Army of Northern Virginia following the death of J.E.B. Stuart, mortally wounded at Yellow Tavern on May 12, 1864.

Parke followed Warren. Gregg covered the roads on our left. Warren captured the entrenchments at Peeble's Farm. Parke advanced through the farm on Warren's left, toward the Boydton road entrenchments, Potter's division leading, supported by my command. We were met in the woods by Heth and Wilcox's Confederate divisions, who attacked so vigorously (outflanked us on the right where we expected Griffin to be) that, with their superior knowledge of the woods, Potter's division, and one of my brigades, were driven back. The rest of my division held firmly, and Parke was enabled to form a new line, which, with Griffin now on our right, stopt the enemy. But we lost heavily in killed and wounded and prisoners, who fell, for the most part, into Hampton's hands in the woods. We always seemed to grope blindly in these woods, giving the enemy obvious advantages, and as usual we missed a connection with Griffin (before the engagement). Mott's division coming up next day [October 1], Parke advanced, and, under artillery and musketry, established a line of entrenchments opposite those of the enemy, which were duly extended back to those on the Weldon road.

Kautz's cavalry division was not molested on the Darby road, where we left him on September 29th, until October 7th, when this threatening apparition, rising so near Richmond, was attacked by Field, with Anderson's and Bratton's brigades of infantry, and with Gary's cavalry, that swung round his rear. Kautz skilfully succeeded in getting across to the New Market [road], under shelter of the 10th Corps, with little loss, excepting his six guns to Gary (72 killed and wounded and 202 prisoners).

Field . . . attacked the right of the 10th Corps, which had moved out to assist Kautz, [but] was repulsed, leaving Gen. Gregg, of the Texas Brigade . . . killed, and fell back discomfited to his entrenchments. These movements and counter movements were the life of both armies during those dismal times.

Poplar Springs Rd.
[Near Petersburg]
Oct. 18, '64
My dearest Marie,
I presume your last week's letter must have miscarried. It is the only time I have not heard from you every week while I have been in the field & I take it for granted you wrote. . . . Maj. Bowman has had a handsome liquor case made, which I sent to Gen'l Meade to-day. He was out & I have no reply yet.

Chimney building has become fashionable in camp. Have not yet one in my tent, as I am having the tent enlarged one breadth of canvas. We have been expecting the 6th & 19th Corps down here from Sheridan's army, but it looks now as if Early would occupy them a while longer in the valley. I have taken to playing chess with Col. [Frederick W.] Swift.[23] Ferrero is on a short leave & Hartranft is commanding the Colored Division for the time.

Now I have given you all the news, how are you, is your health better? This is the burden of my thoughts, day & night. Yesterday Corey got a letter from his father, Dr. Whiting, who said he called, but the Chancellor said you were not very well & had retired. This was on the 10th. I am almost certain Father would write if you could not, but this silence is saddening. I can scarcely think of anything else. I fear, my dear child, you need me more than ever. You need nursing with relief from all care, & diversion of mind & rest of body.

I shall be glad to hear of Mother's return home & hope she will bring a good stock of health & spirits. It seems sometimes as if I must break away & fly back to you. You [last] saw me so cheerful—ah, it is not so when I am away.... So large a part of my existence is in you that ... without you, life is small indeed.

[October] 19th

I enclose a photograph of Gen'l Hartranft's little boy, just of Elon's age, nine this month. It is for Elon.

My tent is back & up with a nice fire place. Gen'l Meade sent me a nice note of thanks for the present this morning. Much love to Father, who I trust is well. Write me exactly how you are & write often if not more than a line. Did Lu receive my letter? Kiss her & Elon ... and Grace, who I trust is as bright as ever. I send this without waiting for the mail, which I hope will be as generous to-night.

Thine only,
O.B.W.

Poplar Springs Road
[Near Petersburg]
Oct 23 [1864]

Another week my dearest Marie without any letter from you. It seems strange that I should not have heard from you but once in four weeks. I cannot account for it at all, so different from your style, so unlike my devoted wife. It would be foolish to feign carelessness or disguise my astonishment,

23. Lt. Col. Swift, 17th Michigan, captured at Spotsylvania Court House, returned to his regiment on August 3, 1864, when he was placed on OBW's staff. He was promoted colonel of the 17th Michigan on December 4, 1864, following the resignation of Col. Constant Luce. Swift was awarded the Medal of Honor in 1897 for rallying his regiment at Lenoir Station, Tennessee, November 16, 1863.

or to deny that all sorts of surmises rise against reason & invade my very dreams. That there is any cause in *me* that an angel could find for coldness on your part I would indignantly deny, and the idea of coldness or indifference after such a life of love & devotion & almost unmixed happiness, seems so strange that I cannot entertain it. The mails cannot miscarry every week, and four or five days of confinement in bed is not sufficient reason. There must be something to account for it, & to be compelled to balance pros & cons is perfectly horrid.

And yet frankness compels me to say that I am surprized, annoyed & hurt at your not writing me. I would not have passed through the last fortnight for worlds. I would sooner die than doubt you, & as each mail arrives bringing a new disappointment, it falls on my heart as if a hammer struck it, causing a sharp pain that has no relief because there is no way of accounting for the cause.

Night before last I dreamed that we had a dreadful quarrel & that I met Caro & even she passed me coldly by, & yet it seemed that what we quarreled about was more than I could even imagine in my dreams. And now I write this not to question your love, but, true lover like, to show you how much you are in my thoughts & how silence puts me to suffering & almost drives me wild.

But enough—a few days will, I trust, solve the apparent mystery in some very simple manner, & I shall be happy again if you are only well.

To-day I reviewed [Brig. Gen. Napoleon B.] McLaughlen's brigade.[24] It was a beautiful sunshiny morning, & the troops & even the horses seemed to feel in fine spirits. [My horse] Kearney was full of life, but under perfect management with one hand. Tuesday I shall review Hartranft's [brigade], & Thursday [Col. Byron] Cutcheon's,[25] which is Humphrey's old brigade. The latter is mustered out, & Friday or Saturday I will give Parke a review of the whole division—weather & war permitting.

We are again breathing an atmosphere of dust. Since the first of the month there has been no rain & all the teams & artillery have pulverized the plain so that it seems afoam with dust. The weather is cool & bright. It seems a pity to be lying idle now, when our marches are so often made in rain & mud.

I am excessively annoyed about my reports of the campaign. I have reported all since & including the mine affair, but having no brigade reports of

24. McLaughlen, formerly commanding the 57th Massachusetts, had commanded the Third Brigade, First Division, since September 1864.

25. Cutcheon was then in command of the Second Brigade, First Division, Ninth Corps.

the Wilderness & Spottsylvania, I have not made mine & fear I shall be too late. There was no time till after our arrival before Petersburg, & then, from the 17th of June to the 19th August, the division was under such a constant fire that the regimental commanders could scarcely write to their homes, much less make out their reports. Then so many of them have been killed & even the brigade commanders changed so frequently, that it is difficult to get at it. Christ & Humphrey have promised to make out theirs at home & send them on, but I fear it will be too late to go into Meade's report of the campaign—the most extraordinary known in all history—so people say.

[Continued]
24th
Parke says we shall probably make a move this week. It will be a very serious one beyond doubt. The provoking mail again brought disappointment. I really begin to fear you are very ill & Father is afraid of alarming me. This would be wrong, as suspense is doubly painful with silence. That you may be ill is my only serious fear; the rest is only the gloomy coloring of a heart where love sits jealous mistress, &, like a tyrant, starts at every shadow.

If you are indeed abed, my letters should only bear soothing & healing, instead of fault finding. And were I by your side to whisper the beatings of my heart, I would pour into your ear such words of love, confidence & peace, that even disease would lift its pressure from your brow, & the light of happiness illuminate the gloom of a sick chamber. Time, that has added new ties & increased your attractions, has but strengthened & expanded my own love.

And so with kisses & prayers & with love to Father & the children, I remain

Only Thine,
O.B.W.

[Julia Willcox McNair to OBW]
Georgetown, D.C.
Oct. 26th/'64
My Dearest Brother,
I have just returned from Mrs. Ricketts, where I called to enquire after the health of the General.[26] As Mrs. Ricketts entered the room, she handed me your letter to read. She expressed great pleasure at the reception of it,

---

26. James B. Ricketts had been wounded while commanding the Sixth Corps at the Battle of Cedar Creek, October 19, 1864. He returned to duty just two days before Lee's surrender.

and asked me to write you all the particulars of the General's wound, his present condition, &c, and when she is more calm, she will write you.

The poor General's life I fear hangs by a mere thread. He was wounded by a minnie [*sic*] ball, which entered his chest in front of the shoulder blade, and came out the back under or near the arm. None of the ribs were broken, but some of them were flattened. The great cause for apprehension lies in the fact that a nerve is injured. Quite near the wound lies a little bunch of nerves, and the great fear is that in course of time, as these nerves slough off, they will open an artery, which of course will cause danger. Mrs. R. says the wound will have to be reopened, and the artery taken up, which will be a very *delicate* operation. But the operation has been performed before, and I suppose therein consists the hope that it may be accomplished again.

The Gen'l has the best of care and counsel; he has many army surgeons, and also the navy surgeon general, who sent to enquire while we were there. The surgeons are with him constantly and watch him every moment. He is under the influence of morphine most of the time, and therefore insensible. He takes great care himself, and also others about him, to keep him perfectly calm, as the least excitement would produce the *feared result*.

They both are fully aware of his critical situation. Mrs. R. says he is in excellent condition; he was strong and well when wounded. To show how carefully they have to avoid excitement, Mrs. R. went into the room to him this morning, saying, "It was too bad Gen'l Custer was promoted to a major generalship and he was so young, and came out as aide to McClellan, and they hadn't promoted *him* [Gen. Ricketts]." He looked at her, and said, "I may be promoted from a bed of death."[27] She remarked that even that expression hurt him.

Julia [the younger] was perfectly indignant last eve when she read of Custer's promotion instead of yours. I suppose you would like to know how the Gen'l was wounded. The 18th and 10th Corps fell back upon the 6th, where the Gen'l was in command; he rode to the front with his staff and raised his arm to rally his men, when they sent up shouts and cheers for Pap Ricketts (a name the men have given him for his kindness to them). As he raised his arm the ball did its work. Mrs. R. went directly to Martinsburg, [W. Va.], but the Gen'l had left four hours before; he was advised by his surgeons to leave at

27. George A. Custer, commanding the Third Division, Cavalry Corps, Army of the Potomac, then serving under Sheridan in the Valley, had had a major role at Cedar Creek. He was brevetted major general of volunteers to date from October 19, 1864. Ricketts had not yet received his promotion to the same grade, but when he did it would be postdated to August 1, 1864, so that he would rank Custer.

that stage of his wound or he would be obliged to remain fourteen days, after which time the danger will be passed.

The very day the Gen'l was wounded, Julia and I were a long time with Mrs. R., and had a most delightful call. She was speaking of her spirits and said she never worried or borrowed trouble. She never felt troubled with regard to her husband. She then told us that Gen'l Wright[28] had sent a message to her, begging her to write her husband not to expose himself so unnecessarily. She returned answer that she believed a cannon ball would find her husband in the rear as easily as a bullet would in the front, and she would rather have her husband shot leading his men in the front of battle. Was it not singular the next day we heard of his being wounded[?]

She told us of a conversation she had with [Zachariah] Chandler. He asked her if there was any thing he could do for her. She replied, no, there was nothing she wished him to do for her, but she had one request to make of him, which was to help his own state. He wished to know what she meant. She replied, there is Gen'l Willcox, who has fought nobly for his country ever since the war began, and why did he not promote him, that he deserved promotion. Chandler asked if she was a friend of Willcox's and she replied she was. I think she is truly a noble, kind woman. Sister Mary saw her to day for the first time, and it brought to mind the old prison scenes with you and made her feel very sadly. She sends much love and says she shall write in a few days.

We all enjoyed your letter very much, and appreciated your kindness for writing so soon after the battle. I do hope you will continue to do so, as you cannot comprehend the relief we feel when we have betidings that all is well with you. How much your staff has suffered. You cannot have many left of the original staff. How sad the death of poor young Lt. Fisher. In the photograph he looks very bright and smart. You have heard, I suppose, of the capture of Capt. Gilliss; he has just been promoted. The family must be suffering intensely, for to be taken prisoner now is only another term for murder by inches. How long have our noble braves got to endure this torture from those *fiends* in human form[?]

But I will now introduce a *sweeter* subject. Yesterday Julia sent you a quantity of ginger snaps. She sent them by William Hudson, a former servant of

---

28. Due to the absence of Maj. Gen. Philip H. Sheridan, Maj. Gen. Horatio Wright commanded Union troops in the opening actions at Cedar Creek. Though slightly wounded, Wright managed to regroup the shaken Union forces following Early's attack, but it was Sheridan, just returning to his command, who rallied them to victory.

Gen'l Greene,[29] who was bound for the 9th Corps. Julia sent a letter in the box. I hope you will receive said sweets. We are all well. My health is improving. Julia sends a great deal of love, and Dave also. Little Marie [Lulu] sends you a sweet kiss and says tell you she is at home. She speaks of you often. Good night. Write soon to your devoted sister,

Julia

Give our united regards to Lt. Brackett and thank him kindly for his letter, which proved a great relief and comfort.

J.

The next [movement] was the Hatcher's Run [Burgess' Mill] affair [on October 27, 1864]. This was planned on a considerable scale (embracing nearly 30,000 men) under Hancock, Parke and Warren. The main object was to turn and, if possible, surprise and capture the right of the enemy's works, resting on Hatcher's Run, and get on the Southside Railway. It was known that those works were held weakly, and sometimes not at all. Parke, with my division and Potter's, undertook to surprise the enemy, but [they] saw us coming in time to man these works. Warren came up to our support, and neither thought it wise to attack, and so set us to work entrenching, while Crawford crossed at Armstrong's Mill and moved up the creek around the enemy's flank.

Hancock swung round still further to the left, skirmishing on his way towards the Southside Railroad, halting at Burgess' Mill at the junction of the road leading to the [right?] and feeling out for Crawford, who should be on his right. But the Confederates, under Heth, had managed to hold Crawford in check, and Mahone crossed the run above him and managed to get in on Hancock's right and rear, while they planted some guns at the junction of the roads in his front, where [Brig. Gen. Thomas W.] Egan's[30] 2nd Corps division was deployed. Egan had already stormed the bridge and captured a gun, and would have soon opened his way to the railroad, when Mahone appeared [and] attacked his rear.

Without waiting for orders, Egan faced about and soon swept Mahone out of sight, with losses of men and colors. But Hampton was pressing Gregg very hard with the whole of his cavalry down to the left and rear, and Crawford could not, or did not, move up on his right, and so Hancock reluctantly halted. General Heth tells me [that] had Crawford but known

29. Probably Brig. Gen. George S. Greene (2d, USMA 1823).
30. Egan commanded the Second Division, Second Corps. He was brevetted major general for his actions at Burgess' Mill, October 27, 1864.

what a mere handful was in his front and brushed them aside and moved either to Hancock's support or turned in rear of the enemy's works where he was, the day would not only have been won, but Petersburg evacuated or surrendered.

As it was, and as neither ammunition, now exhausted, nor reinforcements could be got up to Hancock that night, owing to the drenched condition of the roads, he was obliged to fall back next day. Thus, some 30,000 of our men were baffled by the rain and the woods and by an insignificant but desperate force, skillfully handled, a picture at which we may ever blush!

In cooperation with the enterprise, Butler was ordered to make a dash on his front from Bermuda Hundred. That gallant officer sent Weitzel with the 10th Corps. His plan was to skirmish along the front of the Confederate line from the New Market to the Charles City road, and thereby screen a more serious attack on the works across the Williamsburg and New Bridge roads, supposed to be only picketed.[31] The plan was a daring one; but Longstreet was on hand and saw through the design, and [he] trotted Field's division into the Williamsburg works just as Weitzel attacked them. The attack was consequently a failure, enlivened for a moment by [Col. John] Holman's brigade,[32] which crossed the York Railroad and captured a salient with two guns. But the gallant brigade was finally driven back.

Poplar Springs Rd.
[Near Petersburg]
Oct. 29/'64

Our reconnaissance in force has just come in, dearest Marie, without disaster to my division, at least. The main force of the enemy was thrown upon Hancock's corps, & he told me this morning that he repulsed all three attacks but his ammunition gave out. I fear there will be a great row in the country, which will cast votes against the administration, as probably there were great expectations concerning the move.

For my part, I did not expect anything decisive, & thought it inopportune, but I do not pretend to understand the object of it further than that Meade hoped to surprize the enemy & catch them before their works were completed. In our own immediate front, 9th Corps & 5th Corps, we found strong works & well manned, & as their videttes gave the alarm as soon as we left our lines, they were all prepared for us.

31. Referring to the Battle of the Williamsburg Road, also fought October 27, 1864. Longstreet had just returned to duty after a throat wound received in the Wilderness.

32. Holman commanded an all-black brigade, the First Brigade, Third Division, Eighteenth Corps.

On my way back to camp with my division to-day, I was met by the mail carrier with a letter from you & one from Eb. Yours was a long & delightful one of the 22nd inst., bringing such solace to my heart as you only could afford, after feeling so anxious about you so long. Not the least of my anxieties was in *one respect* in which you informed me agreeably.

Now I hope you will woo health until you win her back again to your frail, overtaxed body, & the color again to your fair, pale cheeks. I am glad to hear Ellen was so devoted during your illness & hope you will remember me to her very kindly. I hope to see your new Scotch lassie one of these days. I hope Porter's place may be well supplied, & then, with the addition of a good cook, you will all be set up for the winter.

I write you a little while out of the saddle & am too much fatigued for a long letter. But I will send you a long kiss instead. Our tents are down at City Point & it will take a few days to get things on a comfortable footing again. I made my headquarters last night in the rain at a house abandoned so quick before my advance that a part of the breakfast was on the table, & everything scattered round in confusion. Some soldiers had got in & made havoc, but I saved most of the little household, [a] thousand & one things, & left it to-day comparatively uninjured. But it was touching to see such a sight. Glad to hear so fully of the children. Write often as you can.

Thine,

O.B.W.

Before Petersburg

Nov. 3/'64

My dear Lulie,

I have received your agreeable letter. You forgot to date it, but on the whole I am pleased to see that your handwriting is constantly improving.

I am glad to hear that you have missed no lessons & hope you will secure the prize. It gives me pleasure, too, to learn that you think you are improving, though ever so slowly, in music. I was delighted to see Grandma's handwriting on the back of the letter, showing that she was once [more] the head ornament of the dear old home that I love so much.

You ask whether we have the bright autumn leaves here. Yes, but they are perhaps not so brilliant as they are at the North. I always admired them.

Then Elon has a new dog. I wonder if he is as funny as Gyp. Gyp is already getting watchful at night. He sits on his hind legs, runs after a chip-[munk] & cracks chestnuts like a squirrel. He is covered all over with black curly hair. I hope your Mama & Grandma will combine their taste & select for you a pretty, *young looking* & bright bonnet. Of course I want it comfortable, but tell them & beg them to have it becoming.

I fear that our fine weather has left camp, for yesterday an old fashioned, steady, slow rain set in, & to-day the air is so loaded with vapor that a bird flying through makes the rain fall. Write very soon again to

Your affectionate Father,
O. B. Willcox

[The following is appended to the above letter.]

My dearest Madonna,

I am quite gratified with Lulie's progress. We shall soon get to be famous correspondents. I wish I had the talents of Burr to make her my Theodosia.[33]

Dr. O'Connell left yesterday to report to Gen'l Dix. I gave him a letter to Frank. The night before he left, my old staff made the sword presentation. Col. Coale was the spokesman, & I entertained them with oyster soup. The sword is very tasteful, with heavy gilt scabbard, sash, field glass, belt & ivory handled pistol. They insist on my wearing it for common use, & so I have sent my old sword to New York to Frank, together with a sword captured at Spotsylvania on May 12, of Col. Barber, who commanded a [Confederate] brigade.

[It would appear that the following is a continuation of the above letter.]

William seems as anxious as ever that I should be promoted, & is going at it again. Even here he made inquiries very busily & found that the Mich. regiments were all for it, & he proposes to have them ask for it, & on that basis make another effort. You may be right about the brevet, but it has not come yet, & if it does, I think it will be no stumbling block to the other. At any rate, [that] I am the pearl of your heart & the sunshine of your eyes is the balm of consolation at all times. . . .

I am sorry to hear that anybody in St. Paul's is annoying Mr. Lightner,[34] & that he takes notice of it from the chancel. Have you shown the Lightners any attentions? I wish you would. Caro has sent me the *Schonberg-Cotta Family;* have not read it yet.[35] Policemen in Detroit! Ye muses! The

33. Referring to Aaron Burr (1756–1836), third vice president of the United States (1801–1805) and to his devoted daughter Theodosia (1783–1813), who was lost at sea on her way to meet her father in Europe.
34. Rev. Milton C. Lightner, rector of St. Paul's Episcopal Church in Detroit since October 1863.
35. Elizabeth Rundle Charles, *Chronicles of the Schonberg-Cotta Family* (New York, 1863).

millennium must be at hand. Congratulate Lucius McKnight on his happy wedding for me. I hope they will settle down into a quiet life.

Gen'l Burnside was here the other day on a flying visit & returned to meet Grant at Washington.[36] He says he means to apologize to Meade as soon as he is assigned to a command. I think he regrets not doing it when I advised. They met at City Point without speaking. Senator Wilson[37] is here to-night. I have not seen him, but may to-morrow. Maj. Bowman has been ordered to Baltimore, & left yesterday.

We are under (confidential) orders to be ready to move, probably to take advantage of Lee if he sends any of his army against Sherman. Our force is too small for a besieging army.

I don't think I'd make any great preparations for Christmas presents beyond the household this year. You do not say how Mother found the children. Was she pleased, or otherwise? Love to her & to all.

Thine,

O.B.W.

Poplar Springs Road
[Near Petersburg]
Nov. 14 [1864]
I have received your letter of the 6th, my darling Marie, & am happy to hear that your health continues to improve. I received & answered dear little Lu's letter, & hope to hear from her soon again. I am seized again with the Moravian fever for both her & Elon. If you see any one that knows about the Institution at Bethlehem, I would make inquiries.

I saw Gen. Meade to-day & enquired about the brevets. He says they are still in his hands. Mine dates from Oct. 21, but he is holding it back, together with several others, to have it dated back so as to preserve the present relative rank of the generals breveted, & is corresponding with the Secretary of War on the subject. He did not say when he thought it would be settled, but I suppose it will be [as] soon as the clerks, &c, have returned from the election. He had just called at my headquarters, but I met him on the road home. The announcements that you see in the papers are, for the most part, pre-

36. Concerned about receiving his pay without performing any duty, Burnside wished to discuss the matter with Grant and had received permission from the general in chief to visit his headquarters in early November. Shortly after his arrival at Petersburg, however, Burnside learned that Grant had just departed to meet his wife in New Jersey; Burnside set out to overtake him. Eventually Burnside did meet with both Grant and Lincoln in Washington, offering to resign his commission. Lincoln, however, apparently thought Burnside had been wronged by the court of inquiry, and convinced him to remain in service.

37. Sen. Henry Wilson (R., Mass.)

mature. If it is all managed as Meade has recommended, I shall be senior brevet M[ajor] G[eneral] in both this army & Sheridan's, by virtue of my present seniority as brigadier.

Dr. O'Connell has gone to Hart's Island, recruiting rendezvous [in] New York Harbor. He felt it necessary to leave the field in order to brush up his professional reading. I have Dr. [Michael K.] Hogan in his place. I am also to lose Maj. Bowman, who has been ordered to Baltimore. Robert is expected back this week, & William Blodgett with him. He, Brackett [and] Richards are all that are left of my old stand-bys. . . .

Have you received one hundred-fifty-dollars from Maj. Richards through Dana? sent last week by mail. . . . We will get the mortgage cleared off before long, my love.

I must tell you how much I am pleased with the shirts. They are just the thing. I was sad & homesick yesterday, & longing to be with you. Love to all.

Thine,
O.B.W.

Before Petersburg
November 27/'64
Tattoo

The week has passed away with more variety than usual, my dear own wife. In the fore part of the week, heavy rain, then came severe cold, which turned on Thanksgiving morn into as bright & beautiful a day as I ever saw. We all combined our messes & sat down, twelve in number, to dinner, with the bill of fare gotten up by Brackett, a copy of which he sends you enclosed.

The soldiers' dinners did not arrive till next day, when an abundance of turkey, fruit, pickles, & various other goodies made all "feel gay" in camp. Capt. Richards leaves in the morning to see his mother & will return in a fortnight. I send by him my report, & those of the brigade commanders of the campaign as far as to the 30th of July, which perhaps Father or Mother will kindly read to you. I am having the reports of subsequent operations copied also to send home. I send also a domestic, or camp picture, painted by a soldier named Keller, quite a youth. I never knew or saw him until he brought the picture to me. He caught the likeness from seeing me occasionally on horseback. He is a recruit of the 50th Pa.[38]

Last night we had quite a shock in camp. Jimmy, a negro boy who has followed Rob Hutchins a year, suddenly fell dead. He came to Rob at Greenville, Tenn., & was a nice little fellow about fourteen. Lungs found

38. This artwork is not among OBW's surviving effects.

all decayed. Corey Whiting is now a 2nd lieutenant, & with his regiment. Brackett is promoted captain.

I am greatly delighted to hear that Elon has taken to the tree of learning. I hope he will keep clear of the *birch*. It is funny that he has commenced his career of fascination by captivating the grim Bacon[39]—the hereditary terror of Detroit boys. And Lulu my darling has won the prize. Indeed I am getting to be quite proud of both of them. Hope Lulu will soon regain her strength.

I suppose you know that Mrs. Ricketts has lost her only child, a very bright little girl of Elon's age. Received a nice letter from William Blodgett, filled with expressions of enjoyment of his late visit to camp. . . . Wish you could see the grounds in front of my headquarters, ornamented with stars, shields, monograms, corps emblems, etc. It would take Mother's fancy. Has she taken down the hedge? Love to all.

Yours Only,
O.B.W.

---

39. Washington A. Bacon, or "Old Bacon," as he was known to his students, had been instructor of a boy's school at Detroit since OBW's boyhood and was now teaching Elon. Bacon lived in the house formerly occupied by U. S. Grant.

TWENTY-THREE

Journals & Letters

DECEMBER 4, 1864 – MARCH 21, 1865

[As the investment of Petersburg continued and the year 1864 drew to a close, Grant and Meade continued to probe to their left with the long arm of the Army of the Potomac in an effort to cut the South Side Railroad, the last vital lifeline supplying Petersburg. Petersburg, together with the army protecting it, was slowly being strangled to death. Lee's army, weakened by dwindling rations and supplies and the onset of winter, was beginning to fall apart, as is apparent from the detailed list of Confederate deserters who were now stumbling into Willcox's lines on a daily basis. Although the Union troops were well supplied and most were certain of victory, the war was wearing them down as well, and Orlando Willcox was by no means immune to its effects.

The sustained combat and the terrible losses suffered by the Army of the Potomac from the crossing of the Rapidan to Petersburg were beginning to take their toll on Willcox. Added to this was the great burden of command. As senior division commander in the Ninth Corps, Willcox frequently alternated between command of his division and command of the corps (which he assumed whenever Parke was absent), a practice that would continue to the end of the war. The effects of all of this, combined with an intense longing for his family, are evident in his letters home during this period.]

[The Battle of Burgess' Mill was] followed in December by Warren's "Applejack Raid,"[1] with the 5th [Corps] and [Brig. Gen. Gershom] Mott's

1. Warren's "Applejack Raid" began December 7, 1864, when his command (22,000 infantry and 4,200 cavalry) set out to destroy the Weldon Railroad between Stony Creek and

589

division of the [2nd] Corps, and Gregg's stout cavalry, destroying the Weldon road and some other things, no doubt, to Hicksford, some forty miles out from Petersburg, this time eluding Hill and returning unscathed; and by Gregg's march upon the Boydton Plank in February. Gregg's object was to break up that wagon route of supply, now used from Hicksford to the city. To support Gregg, Warren went beyond Hatcher's Run, on the Vaughn road, and [Maj. Gen. Andrew A.] Humphreys, with Mott's and [Brig. Gen. Thomas A.] Smyth's divisions,[2] to Armstrong's Mill, and as far as the run, close up to the enemy's entrenchments. Humphreys' orders were to hold these points and to communicate with Warren on the one hand, four miles off, and with Miles at the end of our own entrenchments, about the same distance back.[3]

Lee concentrated Hill's and [Maj. Gen. John B.] Gordon's corps[4] on Humphreys, fortunately without success, while Gregg was doing his work. The work did not amount to much, as there was little or no hauling on the plank [road], and Gregg joined Warren in a reconnaissance next day along the Vaughn and Dabney's Mill roads, towards Five Forks, during which both were heavily attacked by Pegram, Evans[5] and Mahone, and driven back slightly; but finally the enemy was checked, and Warren resumed his reconnaissance next day, without encountering great opposition. The knowledge gained of the enemy's country became useful in the crowning work of the following spring, which terminated at Appomattox.

Meantime, however, the situation of Lee had become so intolerable that something had to be done to escape from Grant's clutches. With this view, the attack on Fort Stedman was devised—a temporary success, ending in a most disastrous failure, which reduced his scanty numbers just as they were most needed. Hitherto, the enterprises or aggressive movements around Petersburg had been from our side. But the ill [side] of Lee's genius was that he nearly always failed when he took the offensive. This our aristocratic cousins

---

Hicksford. In six days they destroyed seventeen miles of track, dealing another critical blow to Lee's already crippled supply line.

2. Humphreys, heretofore Meade's chief of staff, had assumed command of the Second Corps in November after the departure of Hancock, whose old Gettysburg wound prohibited further duty in the field; Smyth then had command of the Second Division, Second Corps.

3. The battle described here is Hatcher's Run, February 5–7, 1865. The Federals lost 1,539 men, while the Confederates suffered some one thousand casualties.

4. Gordon then had command of the Second Corps, Army of Northern Virginia.

5. Brig. Gen. John Pegram and Brig. Gen. Clement Evans commanded divisions in Gordon's Second Corps. Pegram, who had recently married, was killed on February 6 in the fighting at Hatcher's Run.

across the ocean will please notice, *vide* the Antietam and Gettysburg Campaigns, when they seek to set him above Grant, Sherman and Sheridan.

Before Petersburg
Dec. 4 [1864]

I received your letter of 27th ult., my darling wife, in due season. I am rejoiced at the improvement of Elon & Lulu at school, & will answer Lulu's letter. The approach of Christmas does not seem to fill you with "merry" thoughts this year, but I dare say it will be as pleasant as usual with the little folks, without the usual amount of gewgaws to which they are well enough accustomed to spare the omissions, & I hope you will not make it too much a season of labor. When we are in poor strength, trifles seem to magnify in importance. I must confess that I have not been in the best of spirits myself lately, without any particular reason for it worth mentioning.

This week the 9th Corps moved back to their old line near Petersburg, & the 2nd Corps took our place on the Poplar Springs Road. My own division holds on the Appomattox & along the front of Cemetery Hill. My headquarters are beautifully situated on a hill overlooking the river & the town at what is called Friend's House—a large, square Virginia mansion, with porches, trees, etc.

This a.m. I rode down the river three miles, visiting the picket line &c, at the end of which I could plainly see gunboats at Port Walthal & Butler's line at Bermuda Hundred. The ride is enjoyable. The country on both sides of the river must have been very rich & productive at an early day, but tobacco crops long since exhausted most of the soil, & besides the present waste fields, you see forests of 2nd-growth trees, pine & oak, in every direction. The sites on the river banks are noble & elevated. The country will be rejuvenated when the war & slavery are gone & form the seats of a better population & agriculture.

My troops are now more immediately in the presence of the enemy. There was much & constant picket firing the first day or two, but we are settling down on better terms. Yesterday my loss was only three wounded. Yesterday, an hour before dusk, our artillery had a magnificent duel with that of the enemy. Their principal battery near me is called the Chesterfield battery, across the river. Our practice seemed to have the advantage. Deserters say Gen'l Gracie was killed by one of our shells in the affair. He was a rebel major at Bull Run, & came to see Ricketts when we were lying wounded at the Lewis House & brought us a bowl of goose broth, which in our weak & starved condition we considered delicious. He was a northern man &

a West Pointer, but married his wife in Mobile—was not very strong above the shoulders.

Sorry to hear that Bethlehem does not keep up its reputation, as in case you migrate next summer to New England for the warm season it would be a good place for our two eldest, if well kept; in fact, I was in hopes it would prove a happy & a most improving place for their early years as a sort of home & school combined, & relieve you of much care during my own absence. Do you not deem the matter worthy of a little more inquiry? I want to see your shoulders lightened, my little woman, while you are equally anxious to see the weight of "another star" added to mine. Did you wade through my report, sent by Richards? I will send the others by the first opportunity.

From Lulu's account, the house must have been put in good order again for the winter. I am glad of it. Nothing pleases me more than a cheerful & comfortable picture of the old home. May it prove a pleasant picture for the children to remember after they grow up—I think it will.

I am indebted to Caro for a pleasant letter & to William [Blodgett] for a box of fine old whiskey. I should like to make Caro a present [for] Christmas. Do you know of any little thing she would like? I say little because my green backs are uncommonly short waisted at present, mess bills unpaid, etc. You must be practicing great economy—poor thing. I often wonder at your marrying in "a marching regiment." Model of your sex in every particular, may Heaven reward you for the clouds of earth.

Speaking of clouds, we have been blessed with fine weather, otherwise my troops would have had a hard time as the wood has been exhausted near the line; the quarters are bad—little more than holes in the ground, so that if we had been visited either with rain or severe cold, they would have suffered greatly.

Besides, the rain, which fell just before we moved, washed away the earthworks a good deal, so that our labors have been so far required on them. A few more days of fine weather will set us all right & then ho! for another change. I hear the 6th Corps is arriving at City Point, which of course has its meaning.[6]

Love to all. Why does not Father honor me with his pen? And surely Mother's fingers have not forgot their cunning. Good night.

Thine only,
O.B.W.

6. The Sixth Corps was just returning from its duty under Sheridan in the Shenandoah Valley, where it had manhandled Early's Confederate troops and laid waste to the "breadbasket" of the Confederacy. The return of the Sixth Corps of course, gave Grant more maneuverability and greater striking power when the main campaigns resumed in the spring.

[Maj. Gen. A. E. Burnside to O. B. Willcox]
Providence [Rhode Island]
Dec. 4, 1864
My dear Willcox——

I am just finishing up my report of the late campaigns, but lack the list of killed, wounded and missing in your division. . . . If possible will you please send it——

My interview with Grant and the President resulted in my remaining in service, at their request, but I was not informed of any duty upon which I am to be placed;—I suppose it is all right—at all events, I will hope so.

It was not at all agreeable to have to leave so early when I was visiting the corps last month, as I hoped to stay for two or three days at least—I look forward with great pleasure just now to the great results that we all hope will follow Sherman's movements.[7] It will be grand when we can all feel justified in leaving the service, and taking to more peaceful pursuits at home—but we should all content ourselves to do the work that is before us, no matter in what sphere, until this war is over——

Since the election we have nothing to do except watch the movements of the army—Public opinion is now in a very healthy state, and a few successes will make it enthusiastically loyal——

Please remember me most kindly to all your staff—Mrs. Burnside joins me in kind regards to Mrs. Willcox and yourself——

Sincerely your friend,
Burnside

Before Petersburg
Dec. 8 [1864]
My dear Father,

You will be gratified to learn that my brevet [to] m[ajor] g[eneral] has been corrected and duly received, to date from August 1st,[8] and that the service of my division has been recognized by eighteen officers in it being breveted, one m[ajor] g[eneral], three b[rigadier] g[eneral]s, my brigade commanders, & fourteen others, including Rob & Richards, who are brevet majors, & Brackett, who is brevet captain.

One of my brigades, [Lt. Col. Gilbert P.] Robinson's,[9] started out to-night. It is snowing & cold. I suppose ere this reaches you, you will hear of

7. Sherman's army, which had commenced on its famed "march to the sea" in mid-November, was nearing the city of Savannah, Georgia.

8. OBW was brevetted major general of volunteers for "distinguished and gallant services in the several actions since crossing the Rapidan."

9. Robinson now led the Third Brigade, First Division, Ninth Corps.

movements of this army. I am in charge of the 9th Corps line of entrenchments around Petersburg some five miles (confidential) & three miles further on the Appomattox. God grant us success. No particular news from Sherman, which is, I think, a good sign. Love to all.

Thine,
O.B.W.

Before Petersburg
Dec. 11 [1864]

I was happy yesterday on receipt of yours of the 4th, my dearest wife, to find all well at home. We have had a gloomy storm, beginning night before last with hail, & throwing a crust of frozen snow over the earth, which has partially melted with some rain, leaving the earth in pools of deep snow, water & slush. The trenches are bad enough, but when not actually on post, the men find warmth & shelter in their various covers, while the troops who are *out*—five of my regiments which have been moving about in all the snow & wet—suffer extremely, making me feel quite sad.

I am, moreover, a little furious about it, because, owing to the fact that "somebody blundered," the poor fellows were kept up unnecessarily one whole night, exposed to the whole wrath of the storm when they might just as well have enjoyed the cover of their shelter tents. In fact, they did not start until twenty hours afterwards. They have gone down to meet Warren. I sent Col. Robinson in command of them, & at his urgent request I let Brackett go along; poor, dear boy, I would not have anything happen to him for the world. I suppose they will not have far to march & the storm is over now.

The combination of wet & cold is about the greatest of soldier exposures. The marching will be worse than the fighting. Other troops of the 9th Corps have gone out—all under Potter.[10] Warren cannot have done all that was hoped, because of the storm. It may seem queer that every move of this army is accompanied by a storm or rain. But it is very easy to explain, & as easy to avoid. We generally go *after a spell of fine weather,* & just about the time one might naturally look for a change. This time the move, of course, is made by way of cooperating with Sherman, & the time could not be selected with reference to favorable weather. But generally I would make a start just *after bad weather.* Excuse this long digression. . . .

Have you ever received a copy of "Portrait Gallery of the War," sent you by William some time ago? He has recently sent me a copy. The likenesses

10. Potter's Division had been ordered to support Warren in the "Applejack Raid," which Meade believed to be in trouble.

are both elegant & correct. There are some slight mistakes in the sketch of me, which I will perhaps someday write the Compiler to correct, & if we settle down in winter quarters, I propose to draw up one correct account of my military services, if I am not too indolent.

I suppose you will send me *Frederick II* by [way of] Major Richards, if you have it—if not, don't purchase it—unless it be to complete the set. What mean you by Gen. "Morell's cards"—is he getting married?[11]

When Jim Biddle congratulates himself that he is not marching with Sherman—probably Sherman may congratulate *himself* too! Why is it that gentlemen's sons in this country must be either noodles or scamps? It is almost a source of satisfaction with me to think that Elon will not have riches to help him down. If anything under Heaven can save him, it will be the religious training he gets from his mother, & the fact that he will early be thrown upon his own resources.

Caro writes me very amusingly about the naming of her boy. It seems that she wants to give him my name, but Frank is going very slowly & cautiously about [it] & has got as far as "Jared"—which Caro thinks is pretty quick work for him, & is taking a calm survey as to proceeding further. Her letters are very nice & amusing. Abbie [Blodgett] pretends to be jealous of my writing Caro more than her. But between ourselves, I like Caro the best & I don't think madame [Blodgett] treated Mother as she ought last spring in N.Y. But don't whisper a word of this, because William is really my best friend & it would cut him deeply.

But naturally Caro has the first claim; & Mother, ought she not to thank the stars that she has a real brother for Caro, without bringing one up— which would have worried her life out? Yes, I love Caro like a brother, & should be proud to have the boy named for me because it is *her* boy.

I wrote Father all about the brevets. What a pity old Christ & Col. Humphrey have been mustered out! Both were brevetted brigadier general. I hope that your health & strength are perfectly restored. I see that the fears of a raid from Canada are periodically revived.[12] No doubt there are desperadoes enough that would like it, but not if there is danger in it—they are a set of fugitive cowards, who keep away from the field. Much love to Father & Mother.

Thine Ever,
O.B.W.

11. Gen. George W. Morell (1st, USMA 1835) had led a Fifth Corps division on the Peninsula.

12. Threats of a Confederate raid from Canada surfaced periodically during the war. On October 19, Bennett H. Young and some twenty-five Rebel sympathizers descended on St. Albans,

Before Petersburg
Dec. 11 [1864]
Sunday night
My dear Daughter,

I was very glad to receive your *nice letter*, and congratulate you on getting the prize at school. I am glad Ida received one also. I have been too busy to answer your letter before this, and shall be most happy to hear from you again very soon. The wedding must have been quite pretty & I dare say the bride & bridesmaids looked lovely.

Soon after I wrote you my pretty little owl flew away. I was not sorry, although it seemed to become attached, or at least accustomed, to me, & formed a poetic ornament to my tent. But it pined for freedom & I had to force it to eat.

Gyp remains as funny & bright as ever. If the officers don't spoil him [by] playing with him, I think he will be a nice little fellow worth taking home. He is a perfect little beauty with long and silken black hair like feathers on his head, & his tail is like a plume. At night he takes his place at the foot of the bed & keeps my feet warm after the fire in the tent goes down.

It is a very cold night & the wind [is] blowing a gale. Capt. Brackett has just come in from his expedition which has returned after a dreadful march, but without meeting the enemy. The men literally waded through the snow & water some forty-five miles, going & coming. Shall we not all "feel gay when Johnny comes marching *home*." I shall clasp you all in my arms & dance around the house, something like a wild Indian, I dare say.

Give lots of love for me to Elon & Ali & kiss Grace a score of times. Remember me to Ida Haigh & the Briodies. Hoping you will write me soon, I remain

> Your affectionate Father,
> O. B. Willcox

Vermont, robbing two banks of some two hundred thousand dollars. When the townsfolk began to resist, the raiders slipped back over the border, where Young and a dozen others were arrested. On November 2, 1864, Secretary of State William Seward informed the mayor of New York of a rumored plot by Confederate agents in Canada to burn the city on election day. The attempt was made on November 25, when Confederate agents set fire to at least ten hotels and P. T. Barnum's museum; none of the fires, however, caused much damage. The hoped-for assistance by Copperheads in New York never materialized, and the plot failed.

Before Petersburg
Dec. 25 [1864]
My dear Wife,

This will be handed you by Lieut. Holway,[13] one of my faithful aides, who leaves on a visit to his family at Adrian for twenty days. Please let him see the children, & if he stays in town pay him all attentions. I write you more fully by him.

Thine,
O.B.W.

Before Petersburg
Christmas night

Your letter came this morning, my dearest Marie, the choicest Christmas gift for me & very charmingly written, as all your letters are when you are well. I am very glad that you are so well; it is a relief from a long hanging gloom over me, & now I trust you may not relapse but grow younger, prettier & cheerfuller, in spite of Time & "this Cruel War"—which I think is coming to its close pretty fast.

Lieut. Holway will take this as well as a note of introduction. He is a nice, brave, modest young officer & been on my staff as engineer officer during most of the campaign—now aide de camp.

The day has been mild & bright. I visited the lines & called on my brigade commanders, also on Gen'l Hartranft, now commanding the new Third Division. His wife came down yesterday & brought him a surprize Christmas dinner. Called on Gen'l Parke & ate my dinner with Brackett alone; dined on oyster soup & roast pig—the first abomination of the sort I have tasted since I was starved on fresh pork in Tennessee all last winter. I expected Kent down, but was disappointed. Speaking of creature comforts, the *pickles* are perfectly delicious; if you knew how Brackett & I enjoyed them, you would feel somewhat repaid for your pains.

This eve I received a letter from Col. [Elisha G.] Marshall,[14] one of the colonels of the old First Division, & a second cousin, in which he says that Mrs. Marshall wishes to exchange pictures with you, & as you "rank" her, you are expected to make the first advance. Therefore please send her yours

13. D. N. Holway, 17th Michigan Infantry.
14. Marshall commanded the Second Brigade, First Division, Ninth Corps, in the attack on the Crater.

& write her a note, address Mrs. Col. E. G. Marshall, Rochester, N.Y. They have a little daughter—the product, by the way, of a runaway match. The colonel was captured in the attack on the crater, & just returned from the South feeling very bitter. He says none of his West Point graduate classmates in Dixie paid him any attention. Since my promotion the requests for autographs begin to pour in.

Then you actually got out to the Carpenters' party! I congratulate you & society too. Present my compliments to master E. F. Willcox, & tell him I think his specimen of handwriting is very good for a young gentleman of his years. I am delighted with his progress [in] every way. He certainly has made a great stride in grasping an abstract principle & making it a rule of action for himself—"where there is a will there is a way." I suppose Bacon thinks where there is a road there is a way. Hurrah for Bacon.

Elon's letter has not yet arrived. And how much would I not give to hear little Ali repeat the "Night Before Christmas." I hope she will remember it until I come home. I suppose, of course, your next will give me all the little details of Christmas. Last night I could scarcely sleep for thinking of it.

I have sent my copy of the Portrait Gallery to Eben by Holway. You know how sorry I am that I could not send you & Caro something, & Mother's both, & the children, all go neglected by me this year, but it cannot be helped. Love & prayers & airy kisses are all I can send you. To Heaven I raise my Christmas & New Year's thanks that all our children are so well.

Poor General Sherman has lately lost a young child—the second since the war began.[15] What are laurels when laid on the grave of those who are dearer than the earth & all its praises. I am thankful to say that I am perfectly well, not a sign of diseaze of any sort, and—don't laugh—not a bad habit worse than my usual moderate indulgence in smoking over my troubles, & in liquids as at home.

And yet in this most changeful & hazardous life one leads in the field, one is never free from a sober sense of the uncertainty & consequent vanity of life. You, my life, my love, my all, & our idolized children have been mercifully preserved & are all that the proudest husband & father could wish. Your bosom is my refuge against all disappointments, & your love my consolation. If you were as deeply sensible of this consolation & are in as good health & strength as one could wish, you would no doubt feel yourself

---

15. Sherman's oldest son, nine-year-old William Ewing "Willy" Sherman, died in the fall of 1863; another child, baby Charles Sherman, died December 4, 1864.

a little above the "jelly fish" you so wittily compare your inanimate life (dyspepsia) to.

To conclude this sermon on the close of the year, I wish you a most Happy New Year, & the same to Father, Mother & *les enfans*. . . .

Thine only,
O.B.W.

Before Petersburg
January 10 [1865]
See, my dearest Marie, what a nice paper I have got to write billets down on to you. All I need is a good pen & plenty of wit to write the most attractive letters.

It rained all night & it promises to rain all day, washing away my poor men's bomb proofs & filling the trenches with mud knee deep, a heavy summer rain storm with thunder.

Interrupted by four rebel deserters brought in. They say the people in Richmond are all down on Jeff Davis. "Why," I said, "I thought he was considered a second Washington." "Oh, that's played out," was the reply.

I am glad you liked the appearance of Holway. Whiting is leaving the duties of an officer with his regiment. Richards is judge advocate of the division. His mother professes great affection, admiration, etc., for me. What a happy time the children must have had on Christmas with all their presents exactly to their liking, & so many of them. I am dying to see the dear little things—in fact, I have been half homesick for some time. Everybody is going, & unless we have a move, I think I might have twenty days—which would give me about a fortnight at home with you. *What would be the best time for me to come?*

Meade has been telegraphed for, but I think it is on account of the removal of Butler—which has at last taken place. I shall go back to my division to-night or in the morning.[16]

Col. [Charles G.] Loring[17] returned from Baltimore last night. He could get no funds from the paymaster. I shall try Washington next, & see if they have any money there; if so, you will receive $100. Excuse this dull letter. I enclose a photograph of Gyp, whom I have recovered.

Thine always with love,
O.B.W.

16. OBW had been commanding the Ninth Corps since December 29, as Parke was then in temporary command of the army, owing to the absence of Meade, away on leave. OBW resumed command of his division on January 12, 1865.

17. Lieutenant Colonel Loring was a former aide of Burnside.

Before Petersburg
January 16 [1865]
My dearest Marie,

Your nice letter of [January] 8th is received with great pleasure & entire satisfaction, except some signs of low spirits due to your great confinement indoors & probably want of strength. If all suits, I think I shall start for home week after next. But you will please write as usual as it is not certain. There are no signs of a move now, but Sherman's movements may bring one on here, or in Richmond—which is the same thing. I have not much faith in the peace rumors so far as Richmond & Jeff Davis are concerned, but if the rebel states themselves once begin it, something may be effected.

I returned to my division headquarters last week. The long & dreadful storm is over, & we are having exquisite weather. But the roads are broken up till May.

I enclose you a letter from Dr. O'Connell's father. Is it not handsomely & feelingly worded? The shoulder straps were also beautiful & will grace the next new coat! I have also received a very fine letter from Caro, which I will answer as soon as a fit of inspiration seizes me. It is a pleasure to keep up "the romance of the heart" with her, & I admire her exceedingly. I am so glad that Elon takes such pleasure in his school. I will answer his good little letter very soon.

Col. [Constant] Luce was guilty of a bit of impertinence in speaking of me as he did to you. It's all nonsense about my not going out & officers not knowing me. I hope my proud little wife does not allow every fool to make pie of me in that style. The fact is that I compelled this Luce to quit the service for neglecting his duties at my headquarters & for drinking & playing cards with enlisted men in his tent. A pretty fellow to tell falsehoods, or even truths, to annoy my wife! He is now in the old Capitol Prison [in] Washington for fraud & disloyalty, & Col. Swift commands the 17th.[18]

The dog mania has got hold of my staff again & we have curs of every degree at headquarters. I expect to do that military sketch for you this week. My kind love to Father & Mother. I may get off next week. Kiss the children & take twenty sweet ones for yourself.

Thine,
O.B.W.

18. Colonel Luce, 17th Michigan, had commanded the regiment since March 21, 1863. Despite his arrest, Luce was granted an honorable discharge on December 4, 1864.

[Maj. Gen. A. E. Burnside to O. B. Willcox]
Providence [Rhode Island]
Jan. 16/65
My dear Orlando——

I laid your letter out to answer last week, but was suddenly called off to New York, to get some particulars attending the death of my wife's only brother, and his two daughters. They were lost in the Steamer *Melville*. Of course my time has been much taken up, so that I have not been able to do anything with reports—It is likely that I will take up the Tennessee report next week, certainly the week after! As soon as it is written I will urge my resignation. The list of casualties in [the] last campaign I will not need now, as they will be at Hd. Qrs. A[rmy] P[otomac].

Please give my love to all the corps near your hd. qrs., in fact any of my friends you may see—With kindest regards to Mrs. Willcox when you write, I remain

Your sincere friend,
A. E. Burnside

JOURNAL

January 18—Wednesday
Two deserters came in this a.m. from 59th Alabama and two from the 59th Va.

January 19—Thursday
One deserter, 45th Ala.

January 20—Friday
One deserter, 41 Ala.
One [deserter] 23rd Geo.

January 21—Saturday
2 deserters from 45th Ala.
1 59th [Ala.]
1 13th Va. Cav.
Report Wilmington [North Carolina] in our possession.

January 22—Sunday
Heavy Rain. Applied for 20 days leave of absence.
1 deserter from 59th Ala.
1 " " 43rd "

1 " " 59th Va.
1 " " 49th N.C.
4

Before Petersburg
January 22nd [1865]
Sunday night
My darling Marie,

I was made happy last night by receiving your most agreeable letter of [the] 16th enclosing Elon's. I had just written that promising lad. This morning I sent up an application for twenty days leave. I think the chances are it will be granted & I may get off about the middle of the week, for we have had another drenching rain & mud has resumed its ancient sway over the Old Dominion, forbidding any movements for some time to come. Still, George Meade may take a less ab-original view of it & refuse the application. Don't really expect me until you receive a telegraph of my probable arrival, & when you do, please send the carriage to the depot, as I had such a bother getting up last time. I will write Eben as soon as it is decided.

Thine with love,
O.B.W.

JOURNAL

January 23—Monday
Rain. Heavy artillery firing on the James.
2 deserters from 24th N.C.
2 " " 59th Ala.
2 " " 41st "

January 24—Tuesday
Moved over to corps hd. qrs. 7 deserters came in. *Ala.*, *N.C.* & *Va.*

The firing last night due to attempt of rebel gun boats from Richmond to run the river. One blown up, one disabled, two aground.[19] Attempt made by enemy pickets across the James equally unsuccessful. Recd. my leave of absence.

---

19. On January 23, eleven Confederate vessels attempted to pass obstructions in the James and head downriver to attack the Union squadron below Richmond. The attempt failed.

January 26—Thursday

Eleven rebel deserters, Ala. & N.C. reg'ts. Weather cold since the heavy rain.

January 27—Friday

4 reb. deserters from 24th S.C., 1 from 49th N.C. Quite cold. The deserters report great exposure & suffering in their trenches.

January 28—Saturday

Two deserters. Had arrangements for leaving to-morrow, but requested by Gen'l Parke to wait.

January 29—Sunday

Heavy art'y firing between Battery 5 [illegible name] & Goose Neck. Lt. Col. Hatch, Asst. Com[missioner] of exchanges, appeared with flag of truce near the Crater & asked passage thro' my lines for A. H. Stephens (rebel Vice Pres.), R. M. T. Hunter & W. J. Campbell as peace com[missioners] en route to Washington. Telegraphed to Gen. Parke at army hd. qrs., who referred the question to higher authority.[20]

Appomattox [River] frozen across near Battery 5. Weather still very cold. Mails delayed.

Headquarters, 9th Corps

Sunday, January 29 [1865]

To-night, my darling Marie, I expected to be leaping the waves on my way to Baltimore, but as I wrote you last night, the powers that be (Parke) being zero & afraid of its shadow, vetoed it. It may all turn out for the best. I try to philosophize myself into believing as usual, but a little natural wrath is my present humor. Meade, having granted the leave, I don't think P. need have interfered. Or if he thought so, why wait till the last day to tell me, after I had made my arrangement for going?

However, I feel partly compensated by the interest of to-day, for Stephens, Hunter & Campbell have been seeking to come in through my lines on their way to Washington to talk of peace. A flag of truce appeared at the old crater, which was met, & Lt. Col. Hatch, Assistant Commissioner of Exchanges for the rebels, came forward & said that the above named

20. The Peace Commission, appointed by Davis, consisted of Alexander H. Stephens, R. M. T. Hunter of Virginia, and John A. Campbell (OBW misidentifies him as W. J. Campbell), a former U.S. Supreme Court justice.

gentlemen wished to come through by virtue of an arrangement or promise on the part of Gen. Grant. I had no knowledge of such arrangement & had to refer it to Parke, who—as Grant is away—is probably communicating with Washington on the subject to-night. To-morrow, sometime, I suppose I shall see the three doves with olive branches in their mouths, & God grant that peace may ensue—though I must confess I fear the talk will amount to nothing quite yet.

Your letters are very interesting & need no apology for dullness. One who fills her sphere so fully & ornaments it so handsomely as you do, needs not the prattle of silly court ladies to set her off. If anyone ask for your monument in this world, point to your children, or even to your husband, to whom you have always been a true wife & wise counsellor. Talk me no more nonsense of your despondency & dullness. I owe everything to you. I want to see you, & mean to, if Grant will let me on his return. . . . Love & kisses to all.

Thine only,
O.B.W.

Write as usual.

JOURNAL

January 30—Monday

Corporal & two men from 59th Alabama came in.

Notified Col. Hatch that a message would meet Messrs. S., H. & C. from the President.

Weather moderated very little.

January 31—Tuesday

Peace Commissioners came through my lines; met by Lt. Col. Babcock of Grant's staff, Lydig & Brackett, at 5 P.M. took cars for City Point. Gen. Grant took responsibility of admitting them without waiting for President's message—a course which I proposed to Parke but without approval.

Five deserters, 3 from S.C. regiments.

Weather fine. Orders to be ready to move. Sick ordered to City Point— kept waiting at depot from 12 till morning.

February 1—Wednesday

Gen. Meade returned to army hd. qrs., Parke to 9th Corps & I to my division. Weather beautiful. Orders of yesterday based on some move in enemy's lines—return of Mahone's div.

February 2—Thursday
Weather beautiful.

February 3—Friday
Weather beautiful.

February 4—Saturday
Weather beautiful & warm. Visited City Point. Saw Gen. & Mrs. Grant.

February 5—Sunday
Movement of Gregg, Warren & Humphreys on Boydston Plank Rd. Gregg captured 18 wagons & 50 prisoners, including a colonel. Humphreys repulsed an attack. Weather fine. Hartranft's division moved down towards evening & reported to Humphreys.

February 6—Monday
I waited [for] orders with one brigade of my division & two of the 2nd, but was not ordered out. Warren carried the works at Hatcher's Run & advanced some ways when he came in contact with the rebels in force.
One deserter, 26th Va., a squalid, half-famished wretch.

February 7—Tuesday
Rain & sleet. Three deserters from N.C. regiments.

February 8—Wednesday
Thaw & roads soft. Froze at night.
Two deserters from 35th N.C. They report that Cook's brigade of Heth's Div. refused to charge yesterday.[21] Also that an abortive effort was lately made to get the N.C. brigade to pass war resolutions.

February 9—Thursday
Bright & cold. 1 deserter from 26th Va.

February 11—Saturday
Two deserters from 41st N.C.
Hartranft's div. returned last night from the left. Weather fine.

21. Brig. Gen. John R. Cooke, C.S.A., son of Union gen. Philip St. George Cooke and brother-in-law of J. E. B. Stuart. Cooke, one of the finest brigadiers in the Army of Northern Virginia, was wounded seven times during the war.

February 12—Sunday

One deserter, 49th N.C. Says that from 3 to 5 hundred men of his (Johnson's) division quit the army last week, together with their arms—Alabama & S.C. men.

Weather fine. . . . Furious cold wind & severe frost at night.

Before Petersburg
February 12 [1865]

I am very glad, dearest Marie, that you did not omit the weekly letter the second time—altho' I can easily pardon the first omission. I received it last night with great pleasure, a good little letter in good spirits—all, perhaps, from ventilating that care-filled head at the Rose of Castile opera, with Corporal Elon for a trusty escort—all of which was the most gratifying fact in your history for some time—you go out so little.

Here I am yet, you perceive. At the time Col. Ely[22] left, I thought I would bring the leave question to a crisis the last of the week, when lo! comes a letter from Eben at New York, saying he would soon be at Georgetown, expecting a pass to visit me at the front. Such a visit, of course, I would not forego for worlds. It will give both of us great pleasure, & I *hope*, do not *expect*, to get off with him. At any rate will try, unless there is another move on foot.

I am champing at the rein which holds me back from home, where I need so much to refresh my weary spirit before going into the spring campaign. I am especially impatient because spring is advancing, & so is Sherman, two events which will set the Army of the Potomac in motion, & I want to get back in time. Might have been off long ago & not missed anything or been missed, as my division is in the trenches & was not called out in the late affair [Hatcher's Run], during which I held one brigade *ready* and should have taken it with [the] other two brigades of [the] 2nd Division as my temporary command in case we were called for.

The affair in itself, as a whole, was neither a success nor a failure. As a demonstration, however, it answered the purpose, which probably was to threaten Lee & keep him from sending any troops south. I am inclined to believe there is a move going on in the direction of Wilmington, as Col. Babcock has gone down there with despatches from Ulysses.[23]

---

22. Lt. Col. Ralph Ely, 8th Michigan Infantry.

23. Maj. Gen. John M. Schofield, recently placed in command of the Department of North Carolina, was marshalling his forces at Fort Fisher preparatory to an attack on Wilmington. Federal troops entered the town on February 22 without opposition, as Bragg had withdrawn his troops before daylight.

Lee's army is certainly suffering for rations, as deserters tell me every day. There is no doubt that Sherman has cut the R.R. between Branchville & Augusta. He must soon be in rear of Charleston.[24] If that falls, I hope the jail at least will be destroyed—or filled with rebel officers as malefactors confined as we were. When the turn of Richmond comes, I hope Libby will be kept for the especial delectation of Jeff Davis.

The rebel authorities are pretending to make much capital over the peace fiasco—but they are "pumping thunder" to little purpose—provided the draft brings us plenty of good men.[25]

Why is Father so silent, has he nothing to write to me of the stirring events of the day? What does he do? I have just written Caro a Valentine letter—not in verse, but prose. I would be especially delighted if she could hook on to my arm in New York & trot off to Detroit to see you all, & have so signified to her—to little purpose, I fear. I suppose it was a little hasty to order the clothes, but I thought I was sure of going & knew you did not want to see me in top boots & blanket. There is no use paying the bill till we see whether they fit.

Brackett received a letter from Miss Alice Green of Annapolis last night; she wishes you reminded of a promise to send her a photograph. I hope you have complied with the like request made by Mrs. Col. Marshall. Send to Gurney for more if necessary. Little Alice seems to like Brackett, but he is a gay Lothario. She lost a betrothed lover in the wars. Whiting has got back. I have assigned him to Col. Cutcheon's 2nd brigade staff for the present.

Did you receive $100 & the flags by Col. Ely? I want the names of the battles embroidered on the flags by some patriotic young lady, & will give you the list. I hope Father, Mother & the children are all well. I enjoy Lu & Elon's letters beyond words. My love & kisses to all. I hope you make raids on Whitewood often & see the forlorn people. I will write Mother soon. *Au revoir*, with more love than Lake Erie can float.

O.B.W.

---

24. Sherman was nearing Columbia, South Carolina, which fell February 17.

25. President Lincoln conferred with the Confederate peace commissioners aboard the *River Queen* in Hampton Roads on February 3, 1865. Little came of the meeting, as Lincoln, who refused to recognize the Confederacy as a separate nation, made it clear that no peace could be considered that did not result in the dismantling of the Confederate government and of its armed forces, and its complete submission to national authority.

February 13—Monday
   Cold & bright.

February 14—Tuesday
Two deserters, 49th N.C. They report that Sherman has [torn up] 20 miles of R.R. between Augusta & Branchville, S.C.
   Capt. Robinson, Col. Cutcheon's staff, was killed by a sharpshooter to-day.

February 15—Wednesday
6 deserters from 49th N.C. 1 from 59th Va.

February 16—Thursday
4 deserters from 41st Ala.
4 " " 25th N.C.

February 18—Saturday
Weather mild, roads very soft & bad.
2 deserters, 46th Va., 1 60th Ala., 1 25th N.C.

February 19—Sunday
Telegraphed Mrs. W. to meet me in N.Y.

February 20—Monday
Started on 15 days leave of absence.

February 21—Tuesday
Arrived in Washington; found Eben at the McNairs.

February 22—Wednesday
Left for New York by evening train.

February 23—Thursday
Arrived in New York. Mrs. W. arrived also this morning. Stayed with the Harrisons.

March 5—Sunday
Left N.Y. for the front by evening Baltimore train.

March 6—Monday
Took steamer *Louisiana* for Fortress Monroe.

March 7—Tuesday
Arrived at div. hd. qrs. with Brackett & Lt. Triples, 96th N.Y.

Coleman's Eutaw House
Baltimore, Maryland
March [5 or 6], 1865
My dear Elon,

I received your letter in New York, but my time was so constantly occupied there that I could not answer it. But being delayed here a few hours on the way back to camp, I take advantage of my first leizure to write to you and to send you one of my photographs. I believe Lulu has one already.

My dear boy, you do not know how sorry I have been not to see you during this leave of absence from the army, but I dared not go so far as Detroit, for fear there might be an army movement & I unable to return in time to be with my division. Next fall, however, I hope to see you & perhaps stay at home, as the war cannot last much longer.

Write to me very often. Give my love to Grandma & Grandpa & kiss Ali and Grace.

Your affectionate papa,
O. B. Willcox

JOURNAL

March 8—Wednesday
Rain. 6 deserters.

March 11—Saturday
Recd. letter from Mrs. U. S. Terrill, Oswego, concerning her son, Lt. Fred Terrill, 184th N.Y., Army of the James, Harrison's Landing. Wrote to Ord. . . .

March 13—Monday
A. C. McGraw & Geo. Kirby of Detroit arrived at my hd. qrs. on a visit.

March 14—Tuesday
Last night Ransom's N.C. Brigade was relieved by a brigade of Gordon's Div., in my front.

Before Petersburg
March 18/65
My dear Father,

This morning I saddled up my horse, & taking Brackett & Holway, made a trip to City Point, where I saw & had a long, frank & friendly talk with him (Grant). First, he said the report of the Com. on the Conduct of the War . . . was misprinted in one respect, viz., where he is made to blame all the division commanders for not accompanying their troops in the assault. He only spoke of one division commander, Gen. Ledlie.

Second, he thought now, & always thought, that if my division had been the one to make the assault on the springing of the mine, it would have succeeded.

Third, he promised to write a letter to me, saying that, being on the ground during the attack, he had the same confidence in me as he ever had (notwithstanding the report of the Court of Inquiry) and as he had when he recommended me for promotion as major general. This he promised to do *of his own accord*, after I had told him how unjustly the Court had treated me, & read to him the finding against me—which, by the way, he said he never had even read before. He wanted to see the testimony & proceedings, which I will send him to-morrow.

I have prepared a very severe protest to launch against the Court, but if the Lt. Gen'l's letter is all he promises, it will be unnecessary to raise the tomahawk. I will keep you posted. Love to all.

Thine ever,
O.B.W.

P. S.

What do you think—it appears from the proceedings that one of the members of the Court, Gen'l Ayres, was sworn as a witness before the Court, and his *opinions* of the causes of the disaster [were] taken as evidence! Don't that beat the French Committee of Public Safety!

I have received a petition to the Sec. of War, signed by the governor & all his cabinet & all the legislature for my promotion as m[ajor] g[eneral]. What shall I do with it? If you think I had better send it to Washington, you had better send me the one Marie has, signed by the 9th Corps. Suppose you write to Beaman on the subject.

Private
Before Petersburg
March 19 [1865]
My darling Marie,

I wrote Father yesterday [concerning] the result of my visit to headquarters, but you will want to know more of the particulars. When I arrived at City Point the Gen'l [Grant] was not at home, but aboard a steamer giving his testimony before a naval court.

Gen'l Rawlings [John A. Rawlins] told me the Gen'l would return soon & I waited in the adjt. general's office, hearing the news that had come in from Sherman & Sheridan[26] until lunch was announced, & I went into the mess hall with Maj. [Adam] Badeau—private secretary [to Grant], & Brackett went in with Col. [Theodore S.] Bowers. A large number of others also took seats.

Finally Gen'l Grant came with Mrs. Grant. I arose & bowed to Mrs. G. The Gen'l announced my name to her, but did not bow nor speak to me himself, which I thought very queer—He sat down & seemed fatigued, but this did not seem to me sufficient to account for his silence.

They sat nearly opposite & a few seats above me. In a few minutes Mrs. Grant asked me if I had not been absent on leave, to which I replied with great formality, "Yes, madam, but I returned some days ago." Grant then entered into some conversation, but said not a word nor gave even a look to me, & I now began to feel that his neglect was studied; my heart began to throb & I scarcely tasted any more lunch. In fact, I thought of rising & leaving the table. Fortunately I held on a few moments longer, when he spoke up with his usual cordiality: "Well, Willcox, how did the races come off yesterday?" To which I replied that "I did not attend them, but I understood that the gray horse beat, & an officer was hurt." Someone else said the officer was killed, rejoined Grant, & the conversation became free & animated at once.

Lunch over, I walked over to quarters with the madam, & told her you sent her your kind regards & was very much pleased to hear that *she* remembered so many things & people at Detroit. The Gen'l walked on the other side of her, & they both invited me into the hut where they live. So in I walked & had a very pleasant chat with them, Mrs. G. getting out the famous gold medal & showing it to me, casket & all, in detail.[27] The Gen'l handed me a cigar, & I felt quite easy.

After chatting a while, I asked him if I could see him privately a few minutes; he said yes, took his hat, & we went out & had a long talk. Mrs. G. inquired very particularly after you & sent you her "love," with a good deal of heartiness. You can imagine whether or not I rode home with a light heart

26. Sherman was moving on Goldsborough, North Carolina, and fought the Battle of Bentonville on March 19, where his forces repulsed three Confederate attacks. Fighting continued on March 20 and concluded on March 21 when Johnston's troops withdrew, ending the last serious effort to impede Sherman's march. Sheridan, whose cavalry had been out wrecking the James River Canal and the Virginia Central Railroad, was moving to rejoin the Army of the Potomac for the final campaign against Lee.

27. Referring to the gold medal Grant had received from Congress for his victories at Vicksburg and Chattanooga.

after so auspicious an interview & satisfactory results. The six miles to my headquarters seemed scarcely three.

I sent Brackett down with the reports to-day. He has not yet returned. Eben writes me that Mother is rather feeble, which I am very sorry to hear. I hope you will make it convenient to dine out & see her often.

We have been having some magnificent weather, making us all wish we were at home. I took a look at two of my regiments this morning. They appear tolerably well, but I am anxious to get my division out of the trenches a week or two before the campaign begins. But I fear it can not be done. Parke is too shy of Meade to urge it.

Write me all about home & the children. I enclose a page from the March number of the *United Service Magazine*. With love & a thousand kisses to the children.

Ever thine,
O.B.W.

JOURNAL

March 21—Tuesday
   Gordon's Corps on my front.
   Walker's, Evans' & Grimes' Divisions.
   Walker's Div. has} Hoffman's Brig., Va.
                 Lewis' N.C. Brigade: 6th, 21st, 54th, 57th
                 Johnson's Brig., N.C.
   Evans' Div. has}   Stafford's Brig., La.: 1st, 2nd, 8th, 9th, 10th, 14th, and
                 5th, [and] 6th, 7th consolidated.
                 Terry's Va. Brig.: 4th, 5th, 10th, 22nd, 42nd, 48th.
                 Baker's Geo. Brig.: 12th Bat., 13th, 26th, 31st, 38th,
                 60th, 61st.

§

TWENTY-FOUR

Fort Stedman

[By the spring of 1865, time had nearly run out for the city of Petersburg and for the Army of Northern Virginia. Confederate supplies were nearly exhausted and the works thinly manned, as desertions continued on a daily basis. The strength of the Federal forces, meanwhile, not only remained constant, but following Maj. Gen. Phil Sheridan's March 2 victory over Maj. Gen. Jubal Early in the Shenandoah, more troops were on the way to the Petersburg front. Realizing this, Lee had determined to gamble everything on one last, desperate attack.

The plan called for Maj. Gen. John B. Gordon, using the three divisions of his Second Corps and elements from the First and Third Corps, to drive a wedge through the Union lines, seizing a number of forts and batteries in the process. If successful, Grant might be compelled to shorten his lines, allowing at least a portion of Lee's army to escape to North Carolina, where it could join forces with the army of of Gen. Joseph E. Johnston.

Fort Stedman was, like so many other of Lee's endeavors, a bold gamble; in spite of its initial success, it ended in miserable failure. The attack, which came in the predawn hours of March 25, fell directly upon the troops of Orlando Willcox's First Division, taking them completely by surprise. The Union line was broken, and Fort Stedman and three supporting batteries were quickly captured.

In spite of the initial surprise of the attack and breach in the lines, Willcox and his men reacted swiftly. The men of his division, aided by a portion of John Hartranft's division, quickly reformed and launched a counterattack that sealed off the Rebel infiltration, forcing the enemy back toward the Union trenches. With the arrival of the remainder of Hartranft's division the Confederates quickly found themselves pinned down by a wall of musketry and a merciless barrage of artillery in comparison to which, one veteran claimed, the cannonading at Gettysburg seemed to pale into insignificance. Unable to advance or retreat, they could do nothing but surrender or die. In the end, four thousand Confederates were either killed, wounded, or captured, a blow that would prove mortal for the Army of Northern Virginia. Union casualties amounted to about 1,500 in killed and wounded. Fort Stedman was the last serious assault Lee's army would ever make as an effective fighting force; the end was just days away.

Never had Orlando Willcox or the men of his division performed better service than that day in front of Fort Stedman. Yet the battle was hardly over before Hartranft himself tried to rob the First Division and its commander of their just honors, claiming the bulk of the credit for himself and the men of his command. The attempt began that very day, before the smoke had settled, when Hartranft took it upon himself to visit the Federal high command, where he knew Lincoln himself was in attendance. Giving the Union brass a detailed account of the fighting—his version of it, at least—Hartranft received a round of backslaps and congratulations and was promoted to major general on the spot—all of this while Willcox himself was yet at the front, assaying the damage to his lines, interrogating Confederate prisoners, and otherwise seeing to his duties as division commander.

Willcox's chapter is not so much a detailed account of the fighting (for which the reader may wish to refer to Willcox's official report on the battle, found in Appendix B) as an attempt on behalf of the officers of the First Division to obtain justice in the eyes of history, and the credit they had so dearly earned in the Battle of Fort Stedman.]

THE FORT Stedman affair . . . took place on the 25th of March 1865. It was an attempt of the enemy similar to our Mine affair, without the mine that is, a grand effort to break through the lines and strike a vital blow beyond. The main objective was Meade's Station and City Point and our depots, while our objective [in the Mine affair] had been Cemetery Hill and the railroad connections; and, like our Mine affair, the first step was successful.

Fort Stedman was finally stormed before daylight by General Gordon with some ten or twelve thousand Confederates. Though not surprised, it was, together with Battery no. X on the right and Batteries XI and XII on the left, captured. Most of the Army of the Potomac had swung around to the left to operate against the Danville and Lynchburg railroads, leaving but a ragged and weak garrison to hold the besieging works.[1] My division held the works from the Appomattox to Fort Morton, a distance of more than two miles with our much reduced numbers.

The covering force on which we relied for support in case of emergency was Hartranft's division, now the Third [Division], and my own orders to my troops of the First Division were given, that, if any point were broken on the line, the troops and artillery on the right and left were not only to hold their own but to attack the enemy on their flanks until Hartranft's should come up. I think this was well understood and bravely acted upon by the men in and out of our enclosed works on either side of Fort Stedman, it being well known that any point might be carried by the enemy if attacked in force. The main object was not to let him hold onto or break through our lines afterwards.

Both divisions did their work bravely and thoroughly, and the credit may be fairly shared without detracting from the praise of either division, and both General Hartranft and myself were handsomely complimented by the corps commander, General Parke, for the work accomplished by the bravery of our troops in common. And yet, in documents written and published since the war, a studied effort has been made to give all the credit to Hartranft's division. It is true that the unity of the First Division was badly broken up, both by the temporary cut of our center and loss of one fort, and that the Third Division was intact and free to move up solidly; but it is equally true that, as soon as the enemy moved on the works to the right and left of the fort, he was repulsed by the troops of this division, aided by [Brig. Gen. John C.] Tidball's[2] and Roemer's artillery, whose aid also Hartranft ignores, and that my troops in reserve moved up, alongside of and mingled with Hartranft's in the final attack against the fort itself. The 17th Michigan and the 100th Pennsylvania were deployed as skirmishers. The retreat of part of the enemy was most effectually cut off by my troops, who moved out to the front from inside our works for the purpose. Of the 1,494 prisoners [taken], 1,005 were captured by this division, partly in the repulses from and recapture of the side works, and partly by those who moved up with Hartranft's troops, and finally by others who sallied out between the retreating enemy and our own works, as before mentioned.

General McLaughlen's brigade of this division recaptured Battery XI in the bayonet charge, though he himself rode into Fort Stedman and was

1. OBW is mistaken here, as the final movement against Lee did not begin until four days later.
2. Tidball (11th, USMA 1848) was artillery commander of the Ninth Corps.

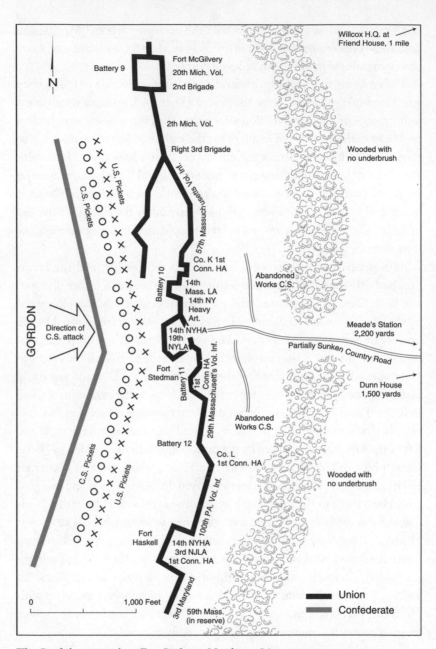

The Confederate attack on Fort Stedman, March 25, 1865.

captured there before he knew that the enemy had taken it. This gave ground to the false report that his brigade had been broken up. The first Union colors was planted in the recaptured fort by Sergeant [Charles] Oliver of the 100th Pennsylvania regiment of this division, who also captured a stand of rebel colors at the same time and place.[3] My report of the engagement shows that the 17th Michigan, on the extreme right, dashed forward and gained the trenches and captured some prisoners on that side, while the 100th Pennsylvania, under Major [Norman J.] Maxwell, and 3rd Maryland, under Captain [Joseph F.] Carter, captured many other prisoners, including one whole regiment with its colors in the general advance.[4]

Besides a large quota [of prisoners] which thus fell to our share, nearly all the captured colors fell into our hands. Yet Hartranft has had the hardihood to assert, since the war, in an article published in the *Philadelphia Press*, that "The prisoners were mostly passed through the lines to the rear, to be picked up and claimed by other commands, and all but one of the captured flags were claimed and taken from the soldiers by unknown officers." This is a story good enough for election purposes—but hardly worthy of a fellow officer and high commander in the corps to which we all belonged.[5]

Another story likewise has passed into Pennsylvania history, as I have lately learned, namely that our tents were hurriedly struck and packed to the rear in wagons. This was impossible as to the troops in or near the lines, and could only be true as to the tents of the provost guard and staff around the Friend House, my headquarters, a not unlikely precaution; but it so happened that the provost guard was the little but brave 17th Michigan, fighting,

3. Sergeant Oliver was later awarded the Medal of Honor for this action.
4. See OBW's report in Appendix B, p. 691. Capt. Carter also received the Medal of Honor for gallantry at Fort Stedman.
5. This passage, quoted from the *Philadelphia Press*, is identical to one in Hartranft's article for *Century Magazine*, "The Recapture of Fort Stedman," *Battles and Leaders of the Civil War*, vol. 4, p. 589. Hartranft also stated in his report on Fort Stedman, dated April 14, 1865, *OR*, vol. 46, pt. 1, p. 348, that

from the reports of my subordinate commanders as well as from my own observation, at least 1,500 of the prisoners, and all the battle-flags captured, were taken by and passed to the rear through the lines of my division, but were afterward collected by other troops, while but about 770 prisoners and one battle-flag were credited to my command. The officers and men were so eager to regain the lost ground, and regimental commanders so desirous to maintain their several organizations . . . that little or no attention was paid to the trophies of this brilliant victory.

Hartranft wrote a number of postwar articles concerning Fort Stedman, the most widely read being in *Battles and Leaders*. Also included in the Willcox papers is a copy of Hartranft's article (also titled "The Recapture of Fort Stedman," but altogether different from the *Century* piece) published in the veterans paper *Grand Army Scout and Soldiers Mail*, Philadelphia, Pennsylvania, March 27, 1886, with annotations by Joseph Carter, Third Maryland Battalion.

as we have seen, on the very front line, and actually recaptured the trenches lost by the 57th Massachusetts. It is vain for Hartranft to claim that any of the 9th Corps officers were unknown by him or his troops; many of them had been officers of his own former brigade when he was in our division.

All this unhappy, unseemly squabble might have been saved if our friend and former associate had either sent his report to corps headquarters through myself, or had made his claims in time to put their accuracy to the proof while yet we were all together enjoying a common triumph, over equal efforts and glorious results. The general made no such complaints to me, but in claiming afterward for himself and his division the whole credit, he was confronted by the two-fold discrepancy, that we had captured most of the prisoners and all the colors but one, which he had to account for in some way or other.

There are two phases of the Stedman affair to be considered in connection with the award of credit. It must be remembered that our division recaptured all the side works before Hartranft came up, and pressed the enemy against Stedman, and by one fierce flank fire prevented him from issuing in any sort of shape beyond, when there was but a small part of Hartranft's division in their front, and thus it may be said to both divisions belong the credit of checking the enemy in the first instance.

Another phase of the engagement was that by which the enemy was finally driven out of Fort Stedman. In this Hartranft and his division took the leading part, but it was effected with the hearty support and active cooperation of the troops of the First Division, both on the skirmish and main lines, and again on the flanks. And in the capture of prisoners, the troops of my division took a leading part from the circumstances of their being favorably situated to secure prisoners, part of our men being in advance of Hartranft's, and part pressing in simultaneously on the sides, and a third part sallying out from our works on the right and left, as the rebels broke to the rear as soon as they saw Hartranft's line advancing.

JOURNAL

March 25—Saturday

This morning at 4¼, Fort Stedman [was] attacked by enemy & carried. My men rallied on the right & left & opposed their advance down the flanks. I ordered the 200th & 209th Pa., of Hartranft's division, to oppose them in front. Hartranft's whole division came up. We repulsed them at Fort Hascall & Battery X, & finally recaptured Stedman & almost 1,800 prisoners. My division took 1005 prisoners, seven colors & one recaptured that they took from us at first.

Before Petersburg
March 26, '65
My dear Eb,

I wrote Marie last night on the affair of yesterday, but she may not have been home to show you the letters. It was just such an affair as that of 30th July, except that the rebels did not blow up any of our works, but made their breach by assault. Our artillery played on them from every direction, just as their artillery played on us at the Crater. Our infantry attacked them, right, left, & rear, just as theirs did on us.

But the result was, so far as I was concerned, more glorious in this case than it was disastrous in that, because besides those killed & wounded, my division captured 953 officers & men & 8 flags—which was more than my loss at the Crater in killed, wounded & missing. At the close of the action, Gen. Parke, in a despatch from corps headquarters, congratulated me & Gen. Hartranft & our "gallant men" on the "signal repulse" of the enemy. The total loss of the enemy in prisoners was some 1,800, & altogether must have been 3,000.[6] The affair on the left, in front of the 2nd Corps, was not, as I understand, so satisfactory.[7]

On 30th July we held the enemy's works some 8 or 9 hours, whereas yesterday they held Fort Stedman only two or, at most, three hours. The attack began about 4 o'clock on the pickets, & our firing ceased about 8. The 2nd, 17th & 20th Michigan, 100th Pa. & some other regiments fought well. The Michigan regiments captured about 400 prisoners. Love to Mother, Louise & the young people.

Yours Ever,
O. B. W.

[Following the war, a number of former Ninth Corps officers began to question much of General Hartranft's postwar writings about Fort Stedman and so

6. Confederate losses at Fort Stedman were never officially reported, but have been estimated at 2,681.

7. Believing that Lee may have weakened his lines elsewhere in order to launch the massive assault on Stedman, generals Humphreys and Wright made attacks on the Confederate lines on their respective fronts but were only able to seize the entrenched picket lines. The Second Corps lost 690 men in all categories in its attack, capturing 358 officers and men. The Sixth Corps lost about four hundred across the board, capturing 547 Southerners. The capture of the Rebel entrenchments was particularly valuable to Wright, as it facilitated his breakthrough of the Confederate lines on the morning of April 2. Humphreys, *The Virginia Campaign*, p. 321.

brought to General Willcox's attention numerous discrepancies between Hartranft's statements and their own recollections of the event. Willcox himself then began to write other officers who had fought at Stedman, soliciting their recollections. What follows is an exchange of correspondence between General Willcox and several of those officers. They offer a rare and revealing firsthand glimpse of the battle, providing a perspective of the event that has never been closely examined. As part of Willcox's personal papers, they are published here for the first time.]

[Joseph F. Carter to OBW]
Dorsey's, Howard Co., Maryland
May 17, 1885
Genl. O. B. Willcox
Dear Sir,

I desire to acknowledge the receipt of your kind letter of the 13th inst., containing a summary of your history and service, which will be of great assistance to Senator Gorman[8] and will enable him to urge it on the ground that your service in a Maryland command during the Mexican War gives you some claims to recognition at the hands of a Maryland senator. I shall forward it to him immediately, and urge that he make your case a matter of state interest.[9] You can rest assured that I intend to press the matter upon the Fort Stedman affair in order to have justice done to our Division through you, its old commander, and I am really glad that the summary has been prepared in order to make out a good case.

I always thought that Genl. Meade failed to recognize us in the General Orders issued, which was not very complementary to our Division, and reflected upon us somewhat as being careless and allowing a surprise. The truth is there was no surprise, as the Pickets informed me that they allowed the Enemy to come in with their guns, as had been the custom with deserters, in obedience to orders from Genl. Grant, that the Rebel deserters should receive pay for their guns. When the Enemy advanced, they said, "don't shoot Yanks, we are coming in." This induced them not to fire, and they were allowed to enter the picket pits, when they demanded the surrender of our men and proceeded to clear the picket line. So there was no surprise, but obedience to orders from Genl. Grant.

8. Arthur Pue Gorman served as a U.S. senator from Maryland from 1881 to 1899 and from 1903 until his death in 1906.
9. OBW served temporarily under Lloyd Tilghman upon his arrival at Vera Cruz. Tilghman was from Maryland. OBW was seeking aid from members of Congress in procuring regular promotion to brigadier general.

I have no acknowledgment of my services on that occasion except a Brevet commission as major, which simply states "for gallantry at Fort Stedman," and Col. Robinson did not recommend me for that. He was much incensed to hear of it after he had refused to recommend me, owing to his jealous disposition. He wished to wear all the honors. I would never ask him for any letter, as I knew that his feelings toward me were not of a kindly character, and he considered my Brevet as a reflection upon himself, as he should have commanded the Brigade after the capture of Genl. McLaughlen and the wounding of Col. Pentecost, of the 100th Penna. I believe that I gave all the orders to other Regiments [of the 3rd Brig.] that were given upon that occasion, and I think I can safely say that I virtually commanded the Brigade, along with the 211th Regt. Penna., of the 3rd Division.

I would like something in the shape of a letter from you, my old Division commander, setting forth my services that day, so that I can show it to Senator Gorman as proof that Maryland soldiers failed to receive any recognition at the hands of Penna. commanders, such as Meade and Hancock; for our Brigade of the 1st Division recaptured the works that Longstreet took from the 2nd Corps at the Wilderness on the 6th May, which Hancock told us on the field after he rode up, that we had "saved the day," but in his report claimed the credit for the 2nd Corps, having on two [previous] occasions performed works for which Penna. got the credit. I think the time has arrived to have justice done, and I am glad Major Brackett introduced that resolution, as it gives me the chance that I have so long waited for, to puncture some of the frauds who are wearing the laurels belonging to others.

In order to enable you to write me a short summary of services, I will make a statement as to my claims, and then give you a brief account of the part the [3rd] Brigade took in the Fort Stedman fight, with reference to that battle. I claim that when we were cut off by the Enemy from your headquarters, that after the capture of Genl. McLaughlen and wounding of Col. Pentecost, that I virtually commanded the Brigade. That I checked the advance of the Enemy upon Fort Haskell before the arrival of the 211th Regt. Penna., whom I ordered to charge the Enemy, but they refused; that I afterward drove the assaulting columns of the Enemy from before Haskell and relieved that fort. That we charged the Enemy and occupied the batteries between Haskell and Stedman, and then recaptured Fort Stedman before the 3rd Division started to advance. I was the first to enter Fort Stedman, followed by the 100th Penna. Regt. of our Brigade. That after securing its surrender, I ordered my men to follow, and we proceeded out to the right, to restore the line between Stedman & Fort McGilvery, and while engaged in that work I intercepted the retreat of the column that had advanced to attack

Roemer's battery on the ridge where your headquarters were located. That having become separated from my men, who were engaged in taking the Enemy prisoners, I intercepted the retreat of a Rebel Regiment, which had taken up a position in the road leading into Petersburg, and caused them to surrender, thus securing their colors. This statement I have made in brief, knowing you were in a splendid position to watch the battle and observe the movements of the whole Division.

In explanation of the above, I desire to say that on the morning of the 25th, I was in the camp of the 100th Penna., seeking information for Col. Robinson, when, happening to look to the rear, I observed the Enemy advancing from the rear and upon the flank of the 100th Regt. This I observed to the Adjt. of that Regt., who did not know what to do in the emergency, and asked me for orders (as Col. Pentecost was on the right, where he was mortally wounded) & told him to form his men perpendicular to the works and try to check the advance of the Enemy upon Fort Haskell, which was not prepared for an attack in the rear, and try to hold the Enemy until I could run down to our camp and bring up the 3rd Md. The Adjt. did so, and thus enabled Capt. [George] Brennan, of [the] 14th New York [Heavy Artillery], to get a brass gun in position to rake the Enemy. I informed Capt. Brennan of the Enemy's advance and urged him to close the fort.

I then proceeded down to the 3rd Regiment, gave orders to my own company to fall in and be ready to move, reported to Col. Robinson and showed him the column of the Enemy, and proposed that I should be allowed to deploy my company as skirmishers and advance to the support of the 100th Penna. He consented to my proposition, and that was the last order that I received from him, as he fell back with the other companies of the Regiment to a covered way on the left of our position, that ran at right angles from the main line. They occupied that position during the battle.

After deploying my men at right angles from the main line, I made this remark after the 100th Regt. had retired and left the fort undefended, as the gun had not been placed in position facing to the rear: "Men, the only thing that can save us is a good hearty cheer." This the boys gave with a will, which they knew how to do. I noticed the effect upon the Confederate column, that they seemed to hesitate, and I remarked, "we are all right; let us give another cheer and go forward to the edge of the wood," which was done in gallant style. I never saw men behave better.

We were joined by the 100th Penna. Veterans, who rallied upon my skirmish line. Then the gun opened upon the Rebels and I extended my skirmish line beyond Brigade headquarters, which I found deserted. This enabled me to fire upon the Enemy upon the rear and flank, which served to demoralize him, along with grape and canister from the fort. While engaged in this work, the 211th Regt. of Penna. approached, over which I assumed command, as I have previously explained.

While so engaged the men (100th Regt.) of the fort tried to make a sortie, but were driven back, and not until I advanced my old company on the left of the line did they dare to venture out, as we had driven the Confederate column from the rear, which no doubt you saw from headquarters.

After relieving the fort and engaging the Enemy in the camp of the 100th Penna. at close quarters, Lt. Col. Maxwell and myself proposed to advance on Fort Stedman, and signalled to the 211th Regt. Penna. to cease firing and join in the charge. They were so stupid that we were compelled to charge through their fire into the batteries. If they had ceased firing and joined us, we would have captured a great many more prisoners, and they would have been entitled to a share of the honors of that battle.

After the 100th Penna. & 3rd [Maryland] Regiment had recaptured the batteries and caused the surrender of the prisoners, whom we ordered to throw down their guns and get to the rear, as we did not have the men to spare to send to the rear with them, knowing that they would seek a safe place themselves after being disarmed, I started first toward Stedman, while Col. Maxwell followed. I entered by the gateway, and Col. Maxwell by the breastworks. When I went into the place, it was being raked by one of the hottest fires from our batteries in the rear. Leaving Col. Maxwell in possession, I then ordered the 3rd to follow, when we moved out towards the right. I met a great many Rebels moving towards Stedman by the covered ways leading from the rear. These surrendered, and my men marched them to the rear.

Thinking that my men were following me, I followed the covered way and came upon a Rebel Regiment drawn up in a deep cut of the road leading into Petersburg. Thinking my men were at hand, I went up to the edge of the bank in their rear, and, addressing the colonel or commanding officer, ordered him to surrender. He wanted to know who I was and where my men were. I told him that I was a Yank and turned to show him my men, when, to my surprise, I found that I was alone. Not coming to go back to Libby, where I had been a prisoner, the thought flashed across my mind, "this is a tight place, but I am going to cheek it." So I told him that we had recaptured Fort Stedman and that they could not get back to their lines.

And while engaged in this conversation, there was a staff officer of ours [who] rode out from Fort Stedman to signal to our batteries to cease firing into the fort, as it was occupied by our men. Happening to see him upon the top of the hill making the signal, I pointed to him as proof of my assertion. This seemed to convince him (Rebel officer), for he ordered his men to cease firing and asked me for orders. I ordered them to throw down their guns and march by the right flank, which they did until they came to an open place, where they were exposed to the fire of some (our) troops in the front. He then said that they could not cross that place or leave their cover while our men continued to fire, and wanted to know what to do. I told them to remain quiet and our men would come up and take them prisoners.

I tried to get our troops in front to cease firing, but they would not. I then left my exposed position, as I was alone, exposed as a target to our fire, and took a position in the cut of the road and engaged in conversation with the officer, for whom I expressed my sympathy . . . saying that I had been a prisoner myself last winter.

While talking with him I was thinking that I would like to capture some Rebel general as a trophy, when, looking up, I saw a Rebel lieutenant with the colors of the Regiment, along with 6 men as color guard, standing upon the bank where I had stood. I determined to take it as a trophy, so I jumped up and started towards them, picking up a gun that was loaded and the hammer raised.

I went up to the lieutenant and demanded the colors. He wanted to know who I was (not having shoulder straps, but wearing bars upon my collar, he did not take me for a Yankee). I told him that I was a Yank and that we had recaptured Fort Stedman and he could not escape. He, with an oath, refused to surrender the colors. I pointed my gun at him and was about to pull the trigger, when the color guard all pointed their guns at me, and I found that the game was up. He then ordered me to surrender the gun, and when he got possession he became very much excited and pointed it at me, and with an oath threatened to blow my brains out. Then I knew that I must not weaken in the least, but face the music, so I told him it was no use to kill me, that he and all his men would be butchered, that we had recaptured the fort and that he could not get back. He said he did not believe it, but it had the effect of quieting him.

It appeared afterwards that he was not present when the conversation took place between the Rebel officer and myself, and had not seen our staff officer in the distance, which arose from the fact that the color sergeant had been killed and he stopped to get the colors and bring them off the field. The officer in command, who had previously surrendered to me, came up, and the lieutenant asked him why they retreated, and he said it was

Col. Gracey's orders.[10] I then discovered that it was one of the Stonewall Brigade Regiments.

I then concluded that they were not very much demoralized, but seemed to be waiting orders. The commander did not know what to do, and the lieutenant said he would go back to see what was to be done and would bring orders to him. So that was the arrangement. He started to the rear with the color guard and ordered me to follow as a prisoner. I did not hurry, and edged off towards the covered way, intending to give them a run for it, which the guard in the rear discovered and threatened to shoot me if I did try it; so I *made haste slowly*, hoping that the spherical case [shot] that was sweeping across the open space between the road and our works would wound some of them, or me, as I preferred death almost to going back to Libby.

While moving along towards our works, I discovered some of the 100th Penna. moving along the works and crossing our path. I said to the lieutenant, "what do you think of that, there are our men." He seemed to be demoralized at the sight, and I said to him "you might as well give it up." He said "I surrender." Then I demanded that he should drop the gun, and said, "give me that rag you have got," meaning his colors, which he handed me.

We were now exposed to the fire from our batteries and musketry in the rear, being the only persons that presented a target for their fire. Having got the colors, I tried to signal to our men to cease firing at the Rebels in the cut of the road, and to come up and take them. Not having anything white to signal with, I began waving the Rebel colors. The more I did so, the hotter became our fire. I was at a loss what to do, so the thought struck me to throw down and trample upon it, which I did, and waving my sword, called to our men to advance and take the Rebels prisoners. . . .

Our men ceased firing to some extent, but the Rebels who held their main line, who had been watching the performance, instantly opened fire along their whole line when they saw me trample their flag in the dust. We were compelled to go towards them some 100 yds. before we got under cover of our works, which we did in safety.

I thus took the colors, lieutenant and guard, and caused the surrender of the whole Regiment, which I would have marched to the rear if our men would have stopped firing. When I reached Fort Stedman, I met Genl. Hartranft, just riding up in rear of the fort, which had been [in] our possession for at least half an hour.

10. The editor has not been able to further indentify Colonel Gracey.

This is a detailed statement of the part that our Brigade took in that affair, of which I was a witness, and I have made it in full, so as to verify my claim as to the virtual command of the Brigade. I would like it to keep as my military record for my children to refer to, and I want . . . Senator Gorman to see it, as proof of my claim that Maryland troops did their duty and got little credit for it. You can address it to him or me, setting forth your views as to the conduct of Maryland troops that served under you, as the 2nd Maryland Regiment was in the 2nd Division, and of course was under you when you were in command of the 9th Corps.

General, there are two little items that I would like you to include in the letter if addressed to me, if you can recall them: the fact that I had command of 160 picked men on the morning of April 2nd when the assault was made upon Petersburg. It consisted of 40 men from each Regiment in the Brigade. I took command of it after the commanding officers of the 100th Penna., 57th & 59th Regiments Mass., had refused to do so at Brigade headquarters, to Col. Robinson, who then ordered me to do so, and instructed me to carry the main line of the Enemy, and, if that was not possible, then their picket line anyhow.

We formed in rear of our picket line, but the Enemy discovered our numbers, and one of the Rebels called out to us, "say, Yank, why don't you bring over them 160 men and charge these works." This [was] before 4 o'clock, when we were ordered to charge. They then opened upon us all along the line, and my men would not advance beyond the picket line, and I so reported to Col. Robinson.

The next day, when we went into Petersburg, Col. Clarke, Adjt. Genl. of [the] Brigade, said to me in that city, "Well, Carter, your charge did do some good, as you kept 16,000 men waiting here to receive you." I suppose they had been informed by deserters or spies of the rumor in our Brigade camp, that the 5th Corps was going to charge Cemetery Hill, for I have since heard that it was a deserter from our Brigade that gave them the number of 160 in my command. I suppose they were keeping the 16,000 men waiting for the 5th Corps attack and were somewhat disgusted to think that we only had 160 men. Of course, if they had that large [a] body of men at Cemetery Hill, it weakened the rest of their lines and made easy work for the 6th Corps to break through on the morning of the 2nd.

On the morning of the 3rd, I was the officer that brought back the intelligence that we were in possession of the Enemy's works, which I reported at Brigade headquarters. There was one of your staff officers waiting there for the information, which I gave, having assisted Col. Robinson in advancing the Brigade pickets into the Enemy's line of defence before 3 o'clock in the morning. These two items I would like you to include with the Fort Stedman items. . . .

General, I simply desire such a letter to treasure up, so as to show my friends, and not be compelled to lay claims to the performance of deeds which have to rest upon my own statements, so please excuse this lengthy epistle, as I would not have presumed to perpetrate such a lengthy document. But feeling that it is but a plain statement of the truth, and that it might refresh your memory, I have taken this liberty with my old commander, hoping you will pardon me, with the promise that I will never do so any more, and glad of the opportunity of helping you to the promotion you justly deserve. I am very Respectfully Yours,

Joseph F. Carter

Pittsburgh, Pa.

July 21, 1889

Dear Sir & Comrade,

A few years ago I wrote to you in reference to the account given by Genl. Hartranft of the engagement at Fort Stedman. I got a reply from you, and I understood from the reply that you intended to reply to Genl. H. I see by the last vol. of "Century War Articles" that Genl. H. still adheres to his former declarations. Have you read his latest? You will notice that I am quoted as having been in the region of Bat. XII when H's ferocious charge was made.[11] In this charge Genl. H. claims he captured 1900 prisoners!! I think you should give your version of this engagement, for it is a reflection on your (& our) Div.

Very truly, &c
J. H. Stevenson
Late 1st Lt., Co. "K" 100th Pa. Vols.

[John C. Tidball to OBW]

South Bethlehem, Pa.

April 30, 1890

My Dear General,

You probably remember very well the 25th of March 1865, when, early in the morning, the rebel general Gordon broke into Fort Stedman on the Petersburg front. Fort Stedman was, I think, part of your line, and you probably have at hand full accounts of the whole affair, from which you can tell

11. Referring to Hartranft's article "The Recapture of Fort Stedman," vol. 4, *Battles and Leaders*. For the reference to Stevenson, see note, p. 589 of that work.

me how far to the left your line extended. Potter's division came next to yours on the line, and Hartranft's was in reserve, in a camp in rear of Potter. What, or whose brigade occupied Fort Stedman? Can you give me the regiments composing it? What regiments were to the right of Stedman, as far as Battery No. 9, and to the left of Stedman as far as Fort Haskell?

These two points—Battery No. 9 and Fort Haskell—about 1,000 yards apart, were the extreme limits of our line involved in the attack and repulse of the enemy. After getting possession of Stedman, the enemy moved to the right and left, but were checked at the two points mentioned. I have a complete list of the artillery on this part of the line, and a full report of its operations.

History is somewhat mixed in the account of this Fort Stedman affair. So careful a man as General Humphreys states—I have not his work at hand to quote verbatim—that the enemy, after gaining possession of Stedman, were, when repulsed, moving on the City Point road and telegraph, *and searching in vain for three forts in rear of Stedman which they had been ordered to take, and which in reality did not exist.*[12]

The fact is there were not only three, but several other such forts, constituting an interior line for some distance in rear of the Stedman front, and then, turning to the left, near the Jerusalem Plank Road, made a return line facing to the rear. This rear part was a shortening of the longer line extending on to Hatcher's Run, and was constructed in anticipation of any operation requiring the chief strength of the Army of the Potomac elsewhere, and which short line could be held by a smaller force holding the immediate front of Petersburg and ensuring the safety of City Point.

One of the forts just referred to was Fort Friend, about 1,000 yards directly in rear of Stedman, and near your headquarters. This fort (Friend) was occupied on the morning of the attack by Capt. [Edward J.] Jones' 11th Mass. Battery, and in rear of it was encamped a Penna. regiment, intended also for its defence. Can you give me the number of this regiment?

As soon as Captain Jones could distinguish, in the early dawn, what was going on, he opened fire upon the enemy in and about Stedman. A line of the enemy's skirmishers moved towards the point of the hill upon which Fort

12. Humphreys, *The Virginia Campaigns of 1864 and 1865*, pp. 317–18. Humphreys wrote: "[Gordon's] storming party was followed by three columns, which were to push through the gap made by the capture of Fort Stedman and seize three forts on the high ground that commanded Fort Stedman, and the lines on the right and left of it. These forts were supposed to be open at the gorge. But, in point of fact, there were no such forts. The redoubts that had a commanding fire upon Fort Stedman and the lines and open batteries on its right and left, were on the main line. In front of them was the line of intrenchments erected by our troops on the 18th of June, which probably led to the misapprehension of General Gordon."

Friend was situated. This line he met with canister, and checked until the Penna. regiment just referred to moved out and drove it back into Stedman.

The artillery fire across the narrow strip between Fort Stedman and the line of the enemy's works was so severe that the enemy were deterred from attempting to cross it, and were thus huddled up in Stedman, making no resistance. By this time Hartranft's division had come up, and moving forward took possession of Stedman with about 1,200 prisoners. Some 800 had come in before Hartranft's division arrived. Aside from moving forward and re-occupying Stedman in this manner, I did not observe that Hartranft's division had any part in the affair. Am I correct in this?

Very soon after the affair was over, President Lincoln, who was at that time at City Point, came up to Meade's Station (overlooking Stedman) and seeing Hartranft there, immediately dubbed him a major general, and from this circumstance, no doubt, it has gone into history that Hartranft's division did all the work. Genl. Humphreys was in command of the 2nd Corps, far to the left, and of his own knowledge knew nothing of the attack upon Stedman, or of Fort Friend, or the other forts.

Sheridan, in his memoirs, copies from Humphreys, and Hay & Nicolay copies from both. I have been asked by the Mass. Historical Society for some data, in order to make the historical correction, but I want to be assured of what I thought at the time were the facts of the case.

I believe General Lee never explained why he made this attack upon our lines. Gordon claims that the idea was original with him, but fails to give any sensible reason for it, or what object he had in view in case of success.

Please let me hear from you at your earliest convenience.

Yours truly,
Jno. C. Tidball
U.S. Army

[OBW to John C. Tidball.]
Governor's Office
U.S. Soldiers' Home
Washington, D.C.
May 6, 1890
Dear General,
In answer to your letter of 30th ult., I put my replies *seriation* [sic].

1st. Fort Stedman was part of my line, and I have full accounts of the whole affair. Enclosed is a copy of my official report, written 9 days after the affair, and copy of my order of congratulations to the troops and of General Parke's dispatch; also [a] sketch of the line.

2nd. My line extended on the left to the Norfolk Railroad, including Fort Morton; to the right it extended to the Appomattox, including Fort McGilvery—over 2 miles in all of works and trenches. Hartranft's division of 6 regiments was held as a reserve in several camps behind both my own and Potter's division, which was on my left.

3rd. To the right of Stedman, as far as Battery IX, the trenches were occupied [left to right] by the 14th N.Y. Heavy Artillery, the 57th Mass. and 2nd Michigan. To the left of Stedman, as far as Fort Haskell, the trenches were occupied as follows, viz.: Battery XI, 29th Mass; Battery XII, up to Haskell, the 100th Pa. Colonel McLaughlen, [57th] Mass., commanded the brigade. The [59th] Mass. in reserve.[13]

The points successively attacked were long a subject of dispute. But from all accounts, I am satisfied that an attempt was made to surprise Fort Stedman and Haskell simultaneously; after the front attack on Haskell failed and the enemy had got into Stedman (thro Battery XI) they made two flank attacks on Haskell and one on Battery No. IX, all of which were repulsed by my own troops, unaided, except by the artillery in the works, and your batteries on the hill in rear near Friend's house, which soon made it too hot for the enemy to advance or retreat.

In this condition of things Hartranft's regiments began to come up, and those of the 29th Mass., 14th N.Y., 3rd Maryland battalion and 100th Pa., who had been driven from the works, took the offensive on the flanks, while the 17th Michigan, 2nd Maryland, 57th Mass., and part of the 100th Pa., joined Hartranft's skirmish line in his succession [of] forward movements.

The first regiment of Hartranft's division to come up was the 200th Pa. This is probably the regiment you inquire about as encamped near Fort Friend. According to General Hartranft's *Century* article, this regiment had

13. In the original, OBW misstates McLaughlen as being from the "27th" Mass; he also states that the "57th" Massachusetts was in reserve. The latter mistake is understandable: he was undoubtedly referring to his map of the lines (among his papers) dated January 12, 1865, at which time the 57th was in reserve, with the 59th occupying the trenches to the right of Battery X. However, on March 12 the 57th relieved the 59th in the trenches. See Warren Wilkinson, *Mother, May You Never See the Sights I Have Seen: The Fifty-Seventh Massachusetts Veteran Volunteers in the Last Year of the Civil War* (New York: Harper and Row, 1990), p. 325. It is also interesting to note the comment of John C. Hardy, former captain in the 2d Michigan, who wrote in a letter to OBW dated November 18, 1898, "Ours was the 2d brigade, Commanded by Col. Ely. Gen'l McLoughlin's Brigade was in the Fort and to the rear and left of it. One of his Regiments, the 57th Massachusetts that had been between our Regiment and Fort Steadman (on Hare's hill) had been taken out on account of the low character of the ground and had been moved to higher ground in rear of the fort so that only the pickets of the 3d Maryland in front were the only ones between the left of our regiment and Fort Steadman."

the heaviest of his fighting of the day, viz., two preliminary attacks which were both unsuccessful and resulted in the regiment retreating to the shelter of some of our old works in rear of Stedman until the general advance. Most of the time, viz., from 4½ to 7½ o'clock, Hartranft was quite active, first moving forward with 200th Pa. in connection with my headquarters regiment, the 17th Michigan, which I sent to him with my aide, Captain Brackett, to assist him, and then posting regiments and forming lines as his regiments successively arrived, connecting with my own troops outside the works, and, by direction of corps headquarters, establishing a line covering the road to Meade's Station.

The only advance made by the enemy from Stedman to our rear that I know of was the skirmish line you mention, viz., towards the point of the hill upon which Fort Friend was situated and before any of Hartranft's troops came up and which was handsomely repulsed by your artillery on the hill.

I leave you to judge why the enemy's main body could get no further or form at all for any aggressive purpose, and what a helpless situation it was in, even to resist an attack in force. In fact, after the failure on Battery No. IX, and last flank attack on Haskell, my people assumed the aggressive and some captures were effected. Battery XII was retaken by [the] 100th Pa., 2nd Maryland, 57th Mass., and 14th N.Y. One whole regiment surrendered to Captain Carter between the lines, and the works which had been captured from the 59th Mass. were recaptured by the 17th Michigan before the reoccupation of Fort Stedman or in the general advance.

The final and general advance took place at 7½ o'clock, under orders from corps headquarters. General Hartranft calls it an "assault," but as you intimate, aside from moving forward and re-occupying Stedman, he had comparatively little fighting to do. But if an assault, it so happened that my own troops led the same on both flanks, as they captured the majority of the prisoners and nearly all the colors, and were the first to enter Fort Stedman. The fighting was about over.

Now as to the object of the enemy's movement on this point, Major Carter since the war has corresponded with Col. [Charles] Marshall, who was General Lee's secretary. I enclose a letter from Major Carter which certainly gives a more plausible theory than any other, viz., that Lee's object was to get off by the Cox road. I can give you further particulars if you wish.

Please return to me all the accompanying papers after you are done with them, and I should feel greatly obliged for a copy of your article on the Stedman affair, and value it most highly.

I had some correspondence with General Humphrey, who, had he lived to publish a revised edition of his book, would have set things right.

Very truly yours,

O. B. Willcox

You will find Hartranft's article, & one by Geo. H. Kilmer,[14] in Vol. IV, *Battles & Leaders of the Civil War*, Century Papers.

[John C. Tidball to OBW]
South Bethlehem, Pa.
May 22, 1890
My Dear General Wilcox [*sic*]:

Many, very many thanks for the trouble that you have taken to inform me upon matters connected with the Fort Stedman affair; and I herewith return your report of that battle, the map of that part of the line, and Major Carter's letter. I send you a copy of my report of the part taken by the artillery in the battle. You will see that your report and mine tally in unison, and together make a complete history of the fighting done.

From time to time I have seen accounts of this battle in which all the credit of re-capturing Stedman was given to Hartranft's division, a thing that did not at all agree with my recollection of the matter.

It very seldom occurs that troops, losing temporarily such a position, regain it, against vastly superior odds, with so little assistance from others, as did your division—or part of it—on this occasion. The regiments of Hartranft's division deserve great credit for their promptness in hastening up and placing themselves in positions to do all that might be required of them, either in re-capturing the works or in preventing the enemy from pushing forward to do further mischief, as it seems was his intention. But in reality, these regiments had almost no fighting to do—excepting always the 200th Pa., which certainly did good work, and brave.

Your troops, and your troops alone—in this I include the artillery on the line—effectually checked the further progress of the enemy at Battery No. IX and at Fort Haskell, and then forced him back to take refuge in Fort Stedman. This was practically the end of the fighting along the line.

In the meanwhile, a body of the enemy advanced from Stedman towards Fort Friend, in which was stationed Captain Jones, with his 11th Mass. Battery, and near by the 200th Regiment Pa., as a support. Jones met this body of the enemy with canister as they neared the brook at the slope of the hill

14. See George Kilmer, "Gordon's Attack at Fort Stedman," *Battles and Leaders*, vol. 4, p. 579. Kilmer served with Company I, 14th New York Heavy Artillery.

upon which Fort Friend was situated. This canister fire checked the enemy and held them until the 200th came up, and by a vigorous attack, prevented them from further progress. This regiment made two other attacks upon this body, and finally succeeded in causing them to withdraw to the shelter of Fort Stedman.

The enemy having thus been corralled in Stedman were prevented from escaping to his own lines by the artillery and infantry fire that crossed and swept the ground between the Union and Confederate lines at this point. While in Fort Stedman they were pelted from every direction by about thirty pieces of artillery. Under these circumstances they were but too glad to surrender as prisoners; and at this juncture Hartranft's line marched up and secured such of the prisoners as had not already fallen into the hands of your men. This is about as I saw and understood the business at the time, and my readings since have not changed my mind.

The whole affair, from beginning to end, was most singular—singular in its inception by the Confederates; singular that after getting possession of a half mile or so of our line they failed to push forward and gain possession of Fort Friend, Battery No. IV, and the ridge in front of Meade's Station. These two works, together with Fort Avery, were no doubt the three forts referred to by Jeff Davis and General Gordon as being the chief objective points of attack after breaking our line at Stedman.

Fort Avery was in rear of that part of our line held by Potter's division, and in the same line with Fort Friend and Battery No. IV. Like these, it was a regularly constructed inclosed work, mounting at that time four 4½ siege rifles, which commanded with their fire that part of our line from Fort Haskell to Fort Rice. Battery No. IV was armed with three 30 pdr. Parrotts, commanding all that part of the line from the Appomattox to Battery No. IX. Fort Friend, being near your headquarters, you know was a strong little work.

These were important works, judiciously located and armed as a provision against any break that the enemy might make in our line—such as did occur at Stedman. At the time of their construction, their object was not fully comprehended by the soldiers who had to do the labor, and who, grumbling, ridiculed the idea of building forts in rear of the main line.

Knowing all this, I was surprised to see in last November's number of the *Century*, in Hay and Nicolay's *Lincoln*, the statement that these forts did not in reality exist, and that Lee did not know what he was about when he projected their capture. I wrote to Hay & Nicolay, pointing out the error, and they replied that as they were not writing a purely military history, they had copied the idea from General Humphreys and from General Sheridan.

Humphreys, the most careful and conscientious of men, was at that time far to the left, commanding the 2nd Corps, and probably did not know of the construction and existence of these works; Sheridan was probably never there, and most likely copied from Humphreys; and thus the error is being passed along down the line of history.

Had the enemy, after gaining possession of Fort Stedman, pushed forward and captured these forts and established himself on the ridge in front of Meade's Station, he doubtlessly would have effected his object in withdrawing our troops from the left, thus opening to him a way of withdrawing by the Cox road and the Southside R.R. to join Johnston.

The whole plan and execution of the attack was admirable up to the point when the rebels got possession of our works, and here it petered out in such an absurd fiasco as to cause the wonderment as to why Lee made such a movement. The enemy had ample knowledge of the ground and knew the importance of the ridge commanding the line of communication to the left of our line, and had everything organized to establish himself on this ridge, but failed at the most critical moment to carry out his plans.

There was certainly some reason for this failure, for his attack had been desperate and determined, showing that he was hell bent on further mischief. I think the chief, if not the only reason for this, was that, in getting into our works, his organization was entirely broken up, and under the heavy fire of artillery then concentrated upon this point, he could not effect re-organization and form to make more than the rather feeble advances that were attempted. In no instance did he reach, with even skirmishers, beyond 300 yards in rear of our line.

Fort Stedman, with Battery No. X on its right, and Nos. XI and XII, on the left, were, to all intents and purposes, one work. For ten months it had been growing up under the close and searching fire of the enemy, and had become a labyrinth of bomb-proofs, traverses, gopher holes, huts, and all in every imaginable manner of irregularity. Even those who knew the place well could not find their way about in the dark. Getting over and into this labyrinth broke entirely the enemy's formation, and before they could reform for a forward movement, such a pelting fire of artillery was brought to bear upon them as to cause them to seek shelter in the bomb-proofs, behind traverses, or wherever else they could find cover.[15] From all accounts

15. An article in the *Petersburg Express* described the Union artillery fire as a "rain of iron, before which the experiences of Malvern Hill and Gettysburg are said by veterans to pale almost to insignificance. It was painfully distinct in this city, where our very dwellings were shaken to their foundations." Noah Andre Trudeau, *The Last Citadel: Petersburg, Virginia, June 1864–April 1865* (Boston: Little, Brown, 1991), p. 347.

they were very solicitous about their prisoners, each one of whom it seems required four or five of their men to escort to their lines. From this and from other causes, their numbers very rapidly melted away.

You will remember that about Meade's Station there was a great collection of hospitals, sutlers and Christian Commission establishments, together with the camps where were kept the horses and spare men of the batteries in position on the line. Upon the first alarm all these people from these various establishments rushed to the crest of the ridge to see what was up. In the craziness of the morning these people looked to the rebels in Fort Stedman like a formidable line of battle, which no doubt they took it to be; and reality was given to this delusion when guns from the artillery camps opened upon them. At the same time, Hartranft's regiments were making their appearance, and I have no doubt the enemy thought the country swarming with troops, and therefore lost heart in the business in which they were engaged.

Having thus lost their opportunity by not pushing forward at once, their whole attention was now given to escaping back as speedily as possible to their own lines. In this the principal officers seem to have left early, and the company officers busied themselves in poking their men out from hiding places and trying to force them back into their own lines; but the artillery, as well as musketry fire, sweeping the ground between the lines, deterred the men from making the attempt. This accounts for so large a number of prisoners falling into our hands when the place was re-occupied, and this was the condition of affairs within the fort, as described by Union prisoners who were there all the time and were recaptured with the fort.

General Parke's camp and mine were adjoining each other. At the first alarm we were aroused by the sentinel who was instructed to that effect. Soon we heard the rebel yell, and then we knew that something serious had happened. A few moments thereafter, I received a hastily scribbled note from the battery commander in Fort Stedman, informing me that the work had been assaulted and captured. At each place where there was mounted artillery I had them keep a mounted orderly ready for just such occasions as this, and the note came by one of these orderlies. The officer who wrote the note was captured, and I never knew how he managed to get the orderly out.

General Parke, in communicating with Meade's headquarters, discovered that Meade was absent at City Point, with which place telegraphic communication was broken (the enemy had taken the precaution beforehand to have the wires cut). Parke, being senior general next to Meade, was notified that his presence was required at army headquarters. Before starting, he, however, sent instructions to his division commanders to recapture the works at all hazards. He ordered up [Brig. Gen. Frank] Wheaton's division of the [6th] Corps, then in reserve some three or four miles distant.[16] Wheaton, together with four batteries which I had sent to Gen. Wainwright for, came up promptly, but just in time to be too late for the fray. In the absence of Parke, you were the senior commander in the Ninth Corps.

An abnormal condition of the atmosphere that morning prevented the cannonading being heard at City Point, and it was not until the battle was over that Gens. Grant and Meade knew what had occurred. They soon afterwards came up on a train, accompanied by Mr. Lincoln, and from the crest of Meade's Station viewed the scene of the morning's work. The President, meeting General Hartranft, and supposing him to have done it all, dubbed him then and there a major general.

Hartranft became a politician with the highest aspirations, and his services on this occasion were magnified by his party friends, to the eclipsing of all others. His troops, too, all from Pennsylvania, shared in the glory given to their commander; and thus the story grew until it came to be believed there were no other people around that morning but Hartranft and his Pennsylvanians.

I think, under the circumstances, I will come in and claim the chief honors for the artillery—nothing personal for myself, but for the arm. The artillery has had but little in this way, for it mattered not how much they did, the other branches—the cavalry and infantry—being more numerous, always gobbled up the glory part. I think this a good opportunity to step forward and settle all doubts as to who were the heroes of Fort Stedman, by saying that we artillerymen were the men.

Very truly yours,
Jno. C. Tidball
U.S. Army

Before Petersburg
March 28 [1865]
My dearest Marie,

I received your nice letter of last week from New York in due season. Am glad you staid over & hope you had a comfortable ride home in the cars. I like the Framingham plan. The expenses are not too great. I think it will be sickly in Detroit this coming spring & summer on account of rise of all the waters, & you had better be away.

16. Wheaton then commanded the First Division, Sixth Corps.

To-morrow the grand move will begin. I am sorry we are to be left in the trenches, but it may turn out for the best, & we may go out at some critical moment & win new laurels.

Great satisfaction is felt over the success of the 25th inst. No blame seems to be attached to the division, but great praise for its courage after the lines were broken, [and] for its tenacity in holding on & fighting on both sides of Fort Stedman. Some of my command, 3rd Maryland & 100th Pa., were first in the fort, & the colors of the 100th Pa. were the first planted on the ramparts. There is some dissatisfaction on the part of Hartranft's division over our capturing all the flags but one. But no contestants have appeared from that division to claim any of the captured flags. I had a full examination of my men who made the captures, with witnesses, & am satisfied that we are fully entitled to the credit. I have written William [Blodgett] to-night. Am very busy, must be up at 4 in the morning. God bless you, both of the Mothers, & all the children.

With love undying,
O. B.W.

JOURNAL

March 29—Wednesday
Tremendous artillery attack by the enemy at 10½ P.M., lasting till 12.30. Loss on our side 51 killed, wounded & missing. Army movements on the left began this A.M.

March 30—Thursday
Division commanders met Gen. Parke at the Avery House [at] 2 P.M. Attack by Hartranft's division decided upon to-morrow morning at daylight, if anything. My line to advance skirmish line & feel the enemy as soon as Hartranft succeeds, & if I find [a] weak point, take it.

TWENTY-FIVE

The Final Assaults: "The Army of Northern Virginia Is No More"

THE MONTH of April 1865 still found the old First Division of the 9th Corps manning the lines on the southeast of Petersburg. They extended from Fort McGilvery and the Appomattox on the right, to Fort Willcox and the Norfolk Railroad on the left. Both sides exhibited a good deal of sensitiveness, conscious of mutual weakness. On the 29th of March the enemy had a false alarm, and thinking themselves about to be attacked by us, opened all their artillery like a storm of thunder and lightning.

On the 31st of March and the 1st of April, we made our preparations in earnest for the capture of their works, but the order did not come and nothing was done but demonstrations for effect, to attract attention from outside operations over on the extreme left.[1]

On the 2nd of April, Hartranft attacked Fort Sedgwick, near our own left, with his division and a brigade [from each] of the other divisions from the Ninth Corps, while we were ordered to make a "vigorous demonstration" on our front. Sending Harriman's brigade on to Hartranft, well equipped with tools and ammunition, that brigade performed its work handsomely, as

---

1. On March 29, Sheridan moved out with the Union cavalry, supported by the Second and Fifth corps, to turn Lee's right and force him out of his entrenchments. Lee dispatched major generals George Pickett and Fitzhugh Lee to meet him. Though pressed hard by the Confederates at Dinwiddie Court House on March 31, Sheridan defeated Pickett at the Battle of Five Forks on April 1. The Federal army now had Petersburg nearly encircled and was within striking distance of the South Side Railroad, Petersburg's last functioning supply line.

usual, and received its due mead of praise, while, with the two other brigades, we occupied the enemy and prevented his reinforcing or otherwise assisting Fort Sedgwick in its last extremity. The enemy was also forced to busy [him]self in strengthening his lines opposite us up to midnight of April 2nd, when there were signs of his weakening, and both Colonel Ely, commanding the [2nd] Brigade, and Colonel [James] Bintliff, commanding the [3rd] Brigade,[2] sent in their reports that they believed the enemy was withdrawing on their front. The good news was received with due caution, but transmitted to corps and army headquarters, and General Benham,[3] with a force of cavalry, was ordered up from City Point to report to me for further orders in connection with the advance into Petersburg.

We started from our lines at two o'clock on the morning of the 3rd, and soon carried the works. Colonel Bintliff was ordered to move on to Cemetery Hill, the key point so long contended for, while Colonel Ralph Ely marched his own brigade and a section of [the] St. Louis Battery[4] straight for the city; at 4:30 A.M. on April 3rd, two Michigan flags were seen waving over Petersburg: that of the [1st] Michigan Sharpshooters was run up first over the court house; the other, that of the 2nd Michigan Volunteers, waving over the custom house.

Pursuant to orders, troops were sent out to ascertain which roads the enemy had taken, and to take up prisoners, while my officers and guard of the 17th Michigan, etc., took measures to prevent the troops of our own and other commands, soon seen rushing in on our left, from doing violence to the citizens and their houses and property.

The Confederate troops had set fire to the bridges, but negroes of the city manned the fire engines and helped to put out the flames. The mayor made formal surrender of the city to me. General Grant soon appeared in person to congratulate us, but made a short stay, only stopping to inquire which way the rebels went. One tobacco store only was plundered in the place, that having fallen after long resistance to the siege, and not duly surrendered to military authority after all, might have been given up to the soldiers; but we had nobler aims than plunder.

Our two thousand prisoners were captured about the works and in the vicinity, and seven battle flags, together with $20,000 worth of stores, the meager amount of the latter showing how the Confederates were reduced

2. Bintliff had just assumed command of the Third Brigade, First Division, as he ranked Colonel Robinson.

3. Brig. Gen. Henry W. Benham (1st, USMA 1837), commanding the Engineer Brigade.

4. Referring to Battery C / I, 5th U. S. Artillery, of the Reserve Artillery, commanded by Lt. (brevet captain) Valentine H. Stone.

for means; in fact, as to this, many respectable families seemed not only ragged but well-nigh starved. The scenes which greeted President Lincoln when he arrived in the afternoon beggar description. The colored population turned out in mass, and seemed quite ready to fall down and worship him.

<After the fall of Petersburg, the 9th Corps occupied the Southside Railroad below Burkesville, and after Lee's surrender it was ordered to Washington, where Gen. Willcox was assigned to the command of the District of Washington. His division gained there a high character for good conduct, and was the last to be mustered out of service of all the Army of the Potomac. . . .

On his division being mustered out, Willcox was ordered to report for duty to Gen. Ord in the Department of the Ohio, and was assigned to the command of the District of Michigan. Honorably mustered out January 15, 1866.

In the course of the war Willcox captured over 3,000 prisoners and seventeen flags, was hit four times, and had four horses shot under him.>[5]

JOURNAL

April 1—Saturday
News of Sheridan's success on the left. Meade orders enemy threatened with artillery &c thro' the night to keep him from moving troops. My skirmishers with axe parties make demonstrations along the whole line. Rifle pits captured at 2 or 3 points.

April 2—Sunday
Harriman massed in front of Fort Mahone at 4 A.M. 2nd & 3rd Brigades opened their demonstrations along the whole line from the Appomattox to Battery XIII at 4.
Harriman, Hartranft & Griffin[6] attack at 5 & carry the works.
Ely's 2nd Brigade—his demonstration captured the enemy's works near the Appomattox & held them for a time.

5. The above, contained within the single angle brackets < >, is from OBW's "Military Memoirs, April 20, 1864 to August 7, 1865," a brief account of his final service in the Civil War. Though a firsthand account, it was written in the third person.
6. Brig. Gen. Simon G. Griffin, formerly commanding the Second Brigade, Second Division, Ninth Corps, assumed command of the division following the wounding of Potter on April 2.

April 3—Monday

At 2 A.M. got up & ordered horses & coffee, Ely & Bintliff having reported enemy evacuating Petersburg. Ordered them to push in at once. Ely's brigade got in first & raised 1st Mich [Sharpshooters] . . . flag on the court house at 4.45. My division ordered to stop at Petersburg & guard the R.R.

Warren came up at night in command from City Pt. to Petersburg.

LETTERS: APRIL 3–4, 1865

Petersburg
April 3 [1865]
My dearest Marie,

I received your Detroit letter to-night with the recommendation for major general enclosed, & was very, very glad to hear a noise from home after the terrible turmoil of battle & sound of musketry & shriek of bursting shells of the last few days battles.

On the night of the 29th, about midnight, the enemy opened an awful cannonading on my line [as] I have ever known. The sight was one immense display of fire works, lighting up miles; the feeling was not so grand. I feared momentarily a rebel charge of infantry—particularly when the artillery lulled away. But they tried a dash or two which was easily repulsed.

Things continued in a feverish state [with] constant expectations of a move, up nights & no rest till the 2nd, yesterday, Sunday, when the ball opened in earnest, or rather it was begun on Saturday night on my lines, continued till morning, when the grand battle found its thunder & in we went. Two of my brigades made a *demonstration* which deceived the enemy. But Harriman's brigade partook in the essential charge with Hartranft's division & Griffin's brigade of Potter's division, & did gloriously.

My troops never behaved more magnificently. Even the *demonstration* of part of the division like to have resulted in our getting into Petersburg, & if I had had more strength at the point, we should have done it. But it did all that was intended, drawing off the enemy from the real point of attack, so that there the enemy was weak & the works were captured.

I was the first to discover that the enemy were retiring at 2 o'clock in the morning, & at daylight Ely's brigade was in Petersburg in command of the town. Such a sight, such enthusiasm you never saw. But the result was having got my division in so early [that] it was left here, & the rest of the corps has gone with the army, & here I am with my division, high cockolorom of the Cockade City—which I dislike exceedingly. Warren is in general command along the railway line. Love to all; will write Mother.

Thine,
O.B.W.

Petersburg
April 4 [1865]
My darling Marie

My troops, Ely's brigade, were the first to break into the town as I wrote you. I am glad to say that I am relieved from the bore of governing the city any longer, being ordered to Sutherland's Station on the Petersburg & Danville [South Side] R.R. to guard the road up to the army. We shall soon be with the army.

It is gratifying to state that my troops here have preserved public order so well that I have been waited on by the mayor of the city, to request that my troops might remain, & four petitions have been presented for the same object. To-night you cannot hear the least noise. It is more quiet & more safe here for everybody to-night than it is at Detroit. I am delighted, however, with the order to move forward.

Show this to Eb, whom I wrote this morning, & he will show you his letter. We have 2,000 prisoners, many flags, lots of artillery, much tobacco & some cotton—to say nothing of cars & locomotives & many thousand $ worth of public stores captured by my command. Kisses to the children. I received a fine letter from Burnside to-day. With love untold,

O.B.W.

JOURNAL

April 5—Wednesday

Ferrero's division of Hartsuff's command relieve my division at Petersburg, & I am ordered up to Sutherland's [Station] & beyond to guard the South Side R.R. Troops start at 1 P.M.

Sent 7 flags to City Pt., captured by my troops at Petersburg. No. of prisoners captured by me: 1,500—by others, 500 to this date. Pieces of artillery, about 15.

April 7—Friday
[My line] Extended up to Wellsville.

April 8—Saturday

Extended Harriman's brigade to Blacks & Whites. [Congressman Elihu B.] Washburne of Ill. spent the night with me. Also Gen. Mott wounded.

April 9—Sunday

Appointed Col. Swift provost marshal. Sent Capt. Manning[7] & detachment of cavalry to scout as far as Jones' Bridge on Nottoway River.

Rearranged lines: 2nd Brigade from Sutherland's to Ford's. . . . 3rd Brigade from Ford's to 1 mile above Wilson's. 1st [Brigade] to Blacks & Whites.

8 gen's & 8,000 prisoners arrive.

April 10—Monday

Ordered works sufficient for 200 men & two guns to be thrown up at Ford's, Wilson's, & Blacks & Whites Stations.

Lt. Gen. Ewell, Maj. Gens. [Joseph B.] Kershaw, [George Washington Custis] Lee, Gen. Hunter [Eppa Hunton] & other generals arrived as prisoners of war (7,000) last night at Wilson's Station.[8]

[Gen. Willcox received official word of Lee's surrender on April 10. The original telegraphic dispatch is preserved among his papers:]

U.S. MILITARY TELEGRAPH

April 10, 1865
  By Telegraph from Hd. Qrs. A[rmies] of U.S.
  To Gen. Wilcox [*sic*]
  Following Recd, Hd. Qrs. Armies of U. S. Appomattox C. H. April 9th.
  Col. Loring,
  Gen. Lee this afternoon surrendered his entire army to Lieut. Gen. Grant, officers and privates to retain private horses, arms & baggage. Officers & men to be permitted to return to their homes, but not be disturbed by the U.S. authorities as long as they observe the laws where they

---

7. Captain Manning, 2d Pennsylvania Cavalry.
8. These general officers had been captured at the Battle of Sayler's Creek, April 6. George Washington Custis Lee was the eldest son of Robert E. Lee.

reside. All public property to be turned over to ordnance & quarter master depts. Remnant of Lee's army surrendered is about thirty thousand (30000).

April 10th, surrender is completed this morning, munitions of war &c turned over to the U.S. and Gen. Grant leaves for City Point at 11 o'clock this morning. The army of northern Va is no more.

Schmechorn,
a. gen.

JOURNAL

April 11—Tuesday

Sent for Gen. Ewell, who spent the night with me. The prisoners all passed down this a.m. at 8 o'clock.

LETTER, APRIL 11, 1865

Wilson's Station, South Side R.R.
April 11
My dearest Marie,

The 9th Corps is still guarding the railroad communications. Yesterday we got the news of the surrender of Lee's army the day before at Appomattox Court House. Gens. Ewell, Custis Lee, & 7,000 prisoners passed down this morning. Ewell spent last night with me. He is very indignant at Jeff. Davis & the Confederate Congress & throws all the blame on them. I think U. S. Grant had something to do with the matter![9]

I am quartering in a house & have had a very severe cold—the usual consequence. Ewell has a wooden leg & only one spur. My provost marshal [Col. Swift] asked him for the spur & he gave it [to] him. But I immediately caused it to be returned.

I suppose Sherman is moving, but there must be a peace soon by military convention or otherwise.[10]

9. Ewell's fellow prisoner, Eppa Hunton, wrote that Ewell was "thoroughly whipped and seemed to be dreadfully demoralized." Douglas Southall Freeman, *Lee's Lieutenants: A Study in Command* (New York: Charles Scribner's Sons, 1944), p. 707.

10. Sherman was just then advancing on Goldsborough, North Carolina, and after slight skirmishing entered Smithfield, where he learned of Lee's surrender. Sherman met Johnston on April 17 at the Bennett House near Durham Station, where they discussed terms, but Johnston's surrender was not accepted until April 26.

I would write Father if I knew where to address him. Write me as soon as he arrives. I do not wish to seem negligent of him. I received a very nice letter from him in New York, also from Caro & Frank. William has not written me in answer to my letter after Stedman.

Love to Mother & kisses to all the little folks.

Ever Thine,
O. B. W.

JOURNAL

April [12]—Wednesday

A band of Negro marauders & horse thieves broken up by Capt. Manning, 2nd Pa. Cavalry, on Nottoway River.

April 14—Friday

Last night Manning sent out a sergeant & detachment of cavalry against the negro band, again plundering the neighborhood. They came upon their camp, found sentinels before the captain & lieutenant's quarters & three wagon loads of plunder. All were armed. Our men charged in, killed 3, wounded 4, & captured 10, but the captain escaped.

Moved my Headquarters to Capt. Hobbes' house, near Wilson's Station.

April 15—Saturday

Last night the captain of the negro band was brought in, but he got away from my provost guard. Gen. Bushrod Johnson, C.S.A., took tea with me.

[It is interesting to note that there is no mention at all in Gen. Willcox's diary of the assassination of President Lincoln. There is, however, carefully preserved among his papers, his copy of the circular telegraphic dispatch, which follows:]

U.S. MILITARY TELEGRAPH

April 16, 1865
By Telegraph from Washington
To Maj. Gen'ls Meade & Sheridan
The president died at 7.22 yesterday morning. J. Wilkes Booth was the assassin of the president. Secretary Seward passed a bad night, but is much

better this morning and probably out of danger. His son Frederick will not live, although he still lingers with wonderfull tenacity.

Tho. T. Eckert[11]

April 20—Thursday

Corps relieved & ordered to Washington. Started my division, leaving 1 regiment in place of each brigade, to guard the railway till [the] 5th Corps should arrive. Moved my headquarters down to 3 miles from Petersburg.

April 21—Friday

Arrived at City Point. 2nd Brigade all got in & on board. Gen. Parke arrived in the evening.

April 22—Saturday

Started for Washington with headquarters staff at 10 A.M. Gen. Gregg on board.

April 23—Sunday

Arrived in Washington at 8 A.M. Found Augur,[12] Rucker, etc. put up at Ebbitt House. Augur wishes me to take command of District of Washington. Division landing at Alexandria.

April 24—Monday

Remain in Washington, staying with Col. Kent at Dyer's mess.

LETTERS: APRIL 26–MAY 7, 1865

Washington
April 26
My darling Marie,

Yesterday I moved down to Alexandria & got established in the most beautiful headquarters, on a high hill in a beautiful house & grounds,

11. Frederick Seward did recover; Thomas T. Eckert was chief of military telegraphs, headquartered in Washington. He was appointed assistant secretary of war in July 1866 and later served as president of Western Union.

12. Maj. Gen. Christopher C. Augur was then commanding the Twenty-second Corps and the Department of Washington. Augur had grown up in Michigan and had received his appointment to West Point from that state. It is likely he and OBW had known each other before the war.

but at dusk received a telegram from Gen. Augur to come up here & see him. I arrived at 12½ & found him & Parke together. The first intention was to bring me over here without my division, but that made me look solemn & Parke consented to let the division come too. It will march over to-day, & my headquarters (District of Washington) will be in town.

The commutation of quarters, &c, will increase my pay enough to warrant your coming on with the children, & so make room for Caro & her little birdies. So you may commence your preparations at once, & I will find a healthy house in Georgetown or somewhere out of town.

I enclose a draft for $250. Love to all. Write me what time it will take you to get ready. Bring Ellen.

Thine Ever,
O.B.W.

George is with me & a very nice little trained boy besides. If agreeable to you, arrangements can be made to occupy Julia's house. What do you think of that? It suits me exactly.

[Julia McNair to Marie Willcox]
Georgetown, D.C.
April 31, [*sic*] 1865
Dearest Marie,

We are now in the enjoyment of the society of our dear warrior brother. I was asking him last eve if it could be true, that our eyes did not deceive us, and that it was he who was again in our midst, safe and unharmed. His division passed our house last week on their way to Tennally town. I never knew a happier day. We, with other friends, stood in the parlor window and waved our handkerchiefs and clapped our hands at the demolished flags, until the last teamster was out of sight. I often thought of you and contrasted this day with the one we passed together, seeing these same men (and many more who will never return) go to the last . . . battles of the war. How sad, sad, our hearts were then; but now, oh how light and happy. Our loved one has returned; one country for which *he* has fought and bled is restored, and I trust he may live many years to receive and enjoy the grateful acknowledgments of his country. We are all now absorbed in the hope of seeing brother and his precious family once more united and spending at least a few months together. . . .

Your loving sister,
Julia

Maj. Gen. O. B. Willcox near the end of the war. *USAMHI.*

Washington

May 7

My darling Marie,

I have just finished a long letter to Father on the question of "Lord, what wilt thou have me to do?" It is too bad to be troubling him, but while I shall do all in my power myself, his aid & counsel will be of great benefit.

I cannot tell you how badly I feel to think that our separation is still prolonged, especially after I had such hopes of having you here at once, a hope which was dispelled by the rapid crumbling of the rebellion & consequent prospect of the army being disbanded. You would have enjoyed being here & it would have been of life-long benefit to Elon & Lu to see the great generals, encampments, &c. It will be like Paris after the Crimean War, and I hope Father at least will come.

I must confess that it is only a question of two or three hundred dollars, but, just at this crisis, even that amount is important, as I have got nothing ahead. I telegraphed William to cut down my insurance to the peace premium on the 1st of May, but the insurance people refused, & there went $50 more than was necessary. It was too provoking just at this time.

But never mind it all, darling, the war is over & we have many bright days in store for us yet. You must not let the disappointment vex you—for it has its compensations. As for me, May has lost its brightness, but fortunately I am kept too busy in the day to brood over it, although the evenings are heavy & gloomy enough.

I made an engagement the other evening to call on Mrs. Joe Taylor, Gen. Meigs' daughter, but owing to a misunderstanding of the hour, did not go. Will make the call next week. Joe himself remembers you. Richards is just going over to New York for ten days to see Rob. I have written Rob & everybody in New York, but was too busy to write Mrs. Hutchins such a letter as I would like.

I hope Caro will honor me often—she is my chief war correspondent & writes with so much spirit that one of her letters is always equal to a pint bottle of the best champaign. Tell her I never needed her cheer so much as now, for I think that, of all solitudes, a great city where you miss the one you want with you is the dreariest solitude.

You may expect to see me in dog days, when we will all adjourn to Lake St. Clair to cool ourselves. Kiss all the children. Tell them I never missed them so much.

Ever Thine,
O.B.W.

Write twice a week.

Special Orders No. 57
Headquarters Dist. of Washington
July 25, 1865
Officers and Men of the 1st Division, 9th Army Corps:

The time has come when we must all separate and go to our welcome homes. The ties of comradeship—the bloody brotherhood into which we have been baptised for our Country's sake, will survive the change. The story of the old Division, various Regiments of which have left the bones of their dead to whiten battle-fields in seven different States, will form part of your individual life hereafter——

To the officers and men of the Division, my own thanks are due for their cheerful cooperation with me in the performance of mutual duties, and for the gallantry, self denial, devotion and good conduct they have always shown in the Service of the Country whenever acting under my Command. Your achievements will brighten many a page of impartial history.

Let us cherish the associations of the past four years; let us keep alive the patriotic fires which have burned so brightly under cloud and sunshine. The red Shield of the Division shines with full lustre and reflects a glory upon all who have fought under it.

Your families and fellow Citizens will welcome your return in peace and victory; you will carry about you in civil life a sense of your own worth, and self respect will characterize those who have done so well and deserved so well by their Country. Keep high the standard of your honor; preserve your honesty and integrity, and the worthy returned Soldier will purify the atmosphere of home, State and Country, by his own simple and steadfast purity of Character.

Wishing you every success and prosperity in life, your General bids you a sad but proud farewell.

O. B. Willcox
Brevet Major General, U. S. Vols.

Official,
Robert A. Hutchins
A. A. G.

The Boys in Blue
Twas at the Bull Run races,
  Arose the dreadful cry,

"The country is in danger!"
    To arms, to arms they fly;
Torn from their wives & sweethearts,
    They hurry to the front,
And seize the sword & musket
    To dare the battle's brunt.

Down in the dark Peninsula
    They lay their sunny youth,
And at Antietam stand like men,
    And conqueror's forsooth.
They cross the southern marshes,
    Four years of fierce campaign,
Fighting on quarter rations,
    Marching in sun & rain.

Long poised in doubt the struggle,
    Despair crept o'er the land,
Still undismayed in battle,
    The unconquerable band;
Or bound in Libby prison,
    Or wounded on the field,
Or starved to death at Anderson,
    Our comrades never yield.

Above the clouds with Hooker,
    Lost in the woods with Grant——
Those "seven days in the Wilderness"
    Shall make Valhalla chant!
Down thundering from the mountains,
    Down to Atlanta's plain,
On to the sea with Sherman,
    Our boys come home again!

And with them Peace comes smiling,
    Thank God the danger's o'er!
How sweet the martial music
    that marches by the door!
Where now the gallant fellows
    Who saved the Nation's life?

Bless God, the land is safe, you know,
 After this bloody strife.

Gone to their homes, that Army,
 In wars no more to roam:
But where's the last detachment
 That knows no wealth nor home?
Still following the banner,
 Those boys in blue remain,
Still at their posts, good soldiers,
 Last of the shining train.

And some their scars in Mexico,
 And Florida were won——
Names that at the Great Muster Day
 Shall come forth like the sun.
Aye, tear their fading laurels,
 Their swords be drawn no more,
Consign their age to Penney,
 Their battle days are o'er![13]

*[On July 4, 1866, in a moving ceremony on the Campus Martius at Detroit,
the faded, bullet-torn colors of the various Michigan regiments were formally
presented to Governor Henry Crapo. Gathered there together were the veterans of
those regiments, many of them as battle-scarred as their banners, listening as one
of their own, Bvt. Maj. Gen. Orlando B. Willcox, addressed them:]*

"I have seen the finger of providence through the thick smoke of battle,
and now that the dark curtain is lifted, and the sun of victory breaks
through in meridian splendor, I have more confidence than ever in our destiny. We have tried to do our duty, and we have done no more than that duty
which every citizen owes to a free and fraternal government."[14]

13. "The Boys in Blue" was written by O. B. Willcox in 1869, "On hearing that a large number of the officers of the Army were to be mustered out."

14. Quoted in "Michigan, My Michigan," by Roger L. Rosentreter, *Michigan History Magazine* (May–June 1998): p. 27.

§ CONCLUSION

The Postwar Years

"DURING THE War of the Rebellion I think I might have done some things better—& other things worse, as in the rest of my life," Willcox wrote in his journal, long after the war. "My 1st mistake was incurring hostility of a Senator [Jacob M. Howard] in *Shoepac Recollections*. This prevented my *confirmation* as Maj. Gen'l from Antietam & subsequent battles. But my chief fault is neglect of opportunities, social &c."[1]

It was an honest statement from an honest man. Orlando Willcox had little, if any, political influence to exercise during the war, each of his promotions being earned by his seniority and merit alone. Yet if politics was not the cause of Willcox's advancement, neither did it bring about a downfall. For as Willcox himself was well aware, many other general officers, fully as capable as himself, had survived shot and shell only to succumb to the political and professional backbiting that was so prevalent during the war: generals Fitz John Porter and Gouverneur Warren to name but two such victims.

After a brief stint commanding troops outside Washington following Lincoln's assassination, Willcox was ordered to report to his home in Detroit in August 1865. There he commanded the District of Michigan until he was finally mustered out of the volunteer service on January 15, 1866.

Once again, Willcox endeavored to make the adjustment back to private life, anxious to become reacquainted with the family he had been away from

1. From OBW's journal entitled "Military Memories."

for so long. For the next six months he worked in Detroit, practicing law with brother Eben and serving as the district assessor of internal revenue.

Although he no longer played an active public role in shaping the course of his country, Willcox was nonetheless concerned with the progress of Reconstruction and the growing rift between President Andrew Johnson and Congress. Johnson believed (as had Lincoln) that Reconstruction policy was a matter for the president to determine, rather than Congress, and began implementing his policy shortly after assuming office. Congress was then in recess and would not assemble again until December; as the president refused to call a special session, the members of the legislature had, for the moment, little recourse but to monitor events as they unfolded.

Johnson's chief aim was to reunite the states of the Union in the quickest manner possible. He initially hoped to punish the planter class, which had led the South to secession, while at the same time elevating the small farmers to power, but Johnson's lack of resolution and of political acumen caused this plan to fail. The president would eventually pardon all but the foremost Confederate leaders, and many men who had led their states to disunion would lead them again after the war.

Recognizing the Unionist state governments of Virginia, Louisiana, Arkansas, and Tennessee, which Lincoln himself had authorized before his death, Johnson set forth a policy for reestablishing the seven remaining ex-Confederate states. Appointing provisional governors, the president directed them to organize elections for conventions to form new state constitutions. Only those men who had been eligible to vote under the state laws of 1860 and who had previously received amnesty from the president were allowed to vote in the election or serve in the conventions. All that was required of the conventions was that they ratify the Thirteenth Amendment (passed in March 1865, freeing *all* slaves), nullify secession, and repudiate all Confederate debts. Beyond these provisions, the new states could be reestablished essentially as they had existed before the war.

When Congress reconvened in regular session in December 1865, the new governments were functioning in nearly every Southern state. Regular governors had been elected, and new members had been elected to Congress. Johnson declared Reconstruction over and requested Congress to seat its new Southern members.

Democrats were generally pleased with Johnson's Reconstruction program, but the Republicans, who had control of Congress, had grave reservations, and the Radical members of that party were, in a word, infuriated. It seemed to many that everything the Union had achieved during the war had been cast to the four winds. Men like former Confederate vice president

Alexander Stephens had been elected to Congress. Moreover, and in spite of the ratification of the Thirteenth Amendment, Black Codes in the Southern states had virtually reestablished slavery in all but name: under these laws blacks could not travel without a permit; they could not serve on juries; nor could they testify against whites in court. If they could not show proof of employment, they were subject to arrest for vagrancy and to being hired out to the highest bidder until such time as they could pay a fine and court costs. Once hired, blacks were required to stay with an employer for the remainder of the year. In many cases, they were not permitted to use public facilities with whites, an anticipation of the "Jim Crow" laws of a later generation.

Unfortunately, Johnson's refusal to compromise on any point of his Reconstruction policy not only invited the bitter retribution of the Radicals but alienated the moderate Republicans as well, eventually forcing them into the Radicals' camp and ending all hope for congressional backing of his plan.[2]

Nevertheless, most War Democrats, and some moderate Republicans, stood behind the president. Among them were many men who had fought for the Union cause, and who, now that the war was over and the Union preserved, were eager for the healing process to begin. Orlando Willcox was one such individual. He had come to detest the Southern aristocracy, but he was equally opposed to the Radical policy for Reconstruction. Regarding the issue of restoring the Union as "the most serious . . . political movement that has taken place since the formation of the Constitution of the United States," Willcox was determined to do all he could to ensure the survival of the president's plan.

As a result, in the summer of 1866, for the first and only time in his life, Orlando Willcox took an active interest in the political affairs of his state. With the regular midterm congressional elections coming in the fall, many Democrats and conservative Republicans sought to assert their support for the president and his policies by uniting in the new National Union Party.

Serving as president of the Michigan chapter of that party, which met at Detroit on August 9, 1866, to appoint delegates for the national convention to be held at Philadelphia five days later, Willcox stated his views of Reconstruction: "Sixteen months ago the war was brought to a close, and it was proclaimed to the world that this Union was one, that the States which

---

2. For a good one-volume study on this period, see Kenneth M. Stampp, *The Era of Reconstruction, 1865–1877* (New York: Alfred A. Knopf, 1966). Of related interest, see Hans L. Trefousse, *Andrew Johnson: A Biography* (New York: W. W. Norton, 1989).

attempted to go out of the Union, had not been permitted to go out, but on the contrary were still component parts of this Union." Although "the Government has the right and it is their imperative duty to quell insurrections and overcome all rebellious combinations," he stated, "yet the body politic of a State survives under the common Constitution, and still remains a component part of the Union."

Further, Willcox believed, it was the president's duty, as commander in chief, to determine when the rebellion had been suppressed and to declare it ended. "And when peace ensues, that the President should act so far at least as to remove all military restrictions on the force of the people to assemble and rehabilitate their State Governments in a republican form guaranteed under the Constitution." Finally, Willcox, speaking for the body assembled, announced "that we approve of the restoration policy of Andrew Johnson, and that the Southern States, which were not admitted to be out of the Union in time of war, are now that the rebellion is suppressed, as rightfully and should be as effectually in the Union as they were before the madness of their people attempted to carry them out."[3]

In the end, of course, Johnson's plan was defeated, and, in February 1868 the president himself was impeached for "high crimes and misdemeanors in office." Though Johnson was not convicted of any of the flimsy charges brought against him, the impeachment signaled the end of his program and brought forth the reign of the Radicals, who would dictate Reconstruction policy until 1877.

Willcox, however, did not enjoy his brief tenure in the political arena, and he eventually came to despise politics. Moreover, his role in the National Union Party earned him the further enmity of Radical Republican Sen. Jacob M. Howard, who dedicated himself to blocking Willcox's confirmation as a brigadier general in the regular army, chiefly because of Willcox's obvious parody of him in the character "O. H. P. Hustings, M.C." in *Shoepac Recollections*. Willcox's brother-in-law, David McNair, met with Howard in Washington the following February regarding the proposed promotion; McNair afterward reported to Willcox "that your prospects look *dark*." Sen. Howard had recounted to McNair

> what he had already said to Genl Grant and what he would say to you should he meet you—that he could not vote for your confirmation. I told him that I hoped this conclusion was not a final one, and asked him if he was aware of your sentiments and position. He replied, "I have seen a

3. Quoted in the *Detroit Free Press*, Aug. 10, 1866, OBW Scrapbook, OBW Collection.

letter from him to Chandler, and think I understand Genl Willcox." He then reviewed your political course from the time of your appt. at West Point, naming his instrumentality in obtaining it. Stated how much the Republicans have done for you and how continuously you have exerted an influence in opposition to the party. That your course last summer [the National Union Party convention] was particularly offensive, &c &c, and wound up by saying—that he regretted the course you have forced upon him. But that there was no help for it.[4]

Attempting to regain Howard's support, Willcox explained his position in a letter to the senator: "That last summer, when in civil life & not expecting to re-enter the service but imbued with a soldier's feeling of magnanimity towards conquered foes, I favored conciliatory measures, but that time & observation have taught me my mistake, & that now military measures are necessary in the South until those rebellious people completely acquiesce in the terms imposed by Congress for restoration."[5]

Willcox's attempts to ameliorate his relationship with Howard, however, went for naught; Howard became perhaps the only serious political enemy Willcox ever had, and perhaps the only man he ever truly hated. Willcox vented his anger by penning the following humorous diatribe against Howard in a journal entry for 1868. It may well be the most complete character study of Howard ever written (one-sided as it certainly is), but it is as revealing about the author as about his subject:

"HONEST JAKE"

H is a politician. The characteristics of politicians are dissimulation & falsehood, coupled with studied geniality (or cunning excentricity) of manners. H is no exception to the rule. But there is in him an excess of frankness, a guffaw of bonhomie, so to speak, that captivates & deceives the stranger. You would say without knowing him well, "there is a man of open & generous nature, incapable of deceit, dishonesty or meanness." And yet the man is base & coarse, unscrupulous, bold, & devoid of principle, full of low cunning & trickery, false to all men & the gods, mean in the smallest as in the greatest affairs, & dishonest to the very verge of larceny.

Among his other ways of covering his true character, he assumes a lofty radicalism that scorns to bend to time or circumstances, or to any ques-

4. Letter of David McNair to OBW, Feb. 20, 1867, OBW Collection.
5. Draft of letter of OBW to Jacob Howard, Feb. 22, 1867.

tion of expediency or policy. One can respect enthusiasm based upon principle or any lofty sentiment; but H's radicalism is an artful shield to his hipocrisy, & his enthusiasm is but the exuberant display of his baser passions. He believes in nothing, he trusts nobody, his heart is as cold as his soul is skeptical & his conscience callous.

The absence of every generous quality lets in suspicion. He is as suspicious as a coward can be & snuffs danger afar. He believed that President Johnson meditated a *coup d'etat* against Congress as early as the fall of 1865, & apprehended personal violence, even then. Again, in 1867, though Breckenridge was actually in Europe & Davis in Mississippi, he wrote a letter to the *Washington Chronicle* exposing a pretended meeting & plot by those men & others *in Canada*, to renew the war of rebellion.

Of course a cowardly & suspicious soul is cruel. The most degraded of the Caezars [*sic*] never was more cruel to a victim or less magnanimous to a foe than is H. Of a large & liberal surface, nature, under the hide of a lion, has given this animal the crafty brain of a fox & the rapacious bowels of a wolf.

H is an orator. He speaks with power when he gets up steam, & uses good anglo saxon words. But as he does not love truth for its own sake, & has none of the vehemence of the heart, his eloquence never convinces. The judge on the bench never trusts to his statement of the law, & the jury in the box never believes his facts. With all his excessive display of candor, frankness & honesty, he sheds distrust around him like an atmosphere. The unconscious exhalations of his soul are [as] offensive to the purity of honor as the insensible perspiration of certain animals taints the air.

Of course such a character is useful in a party. If an odious member of the party is to be whitewashed, or bolstered up, or an opponent to be attacked on the record, H can do it with an air of respectability. In his hands it does not seem to be the dirty work it really is, & scruples of honor or of delicacy, that make other men shrink from such a job, being unknown to his coarser nature, will never deter him from the office of jackal to his party or, if needs be, to his client. Hence he seldom bungles. A sly bribe, offered in half drollery, he knows how to insinuate, & the forgery of a word or two into, or out of, an important despatch he will execute so adroitly that it would appear as if he had detected somebody else in the crime & succeeded in convicting him of it on the spot.

Such a man never forgives an injury, fancied or real. Circumstances may conspire to make him pass over an offence, or the pressure of his party may compel him to make it up for the nonce. But after the settlement of a quarrel there is nothing of the pleasant fervor of forgiveness & peace. If you have put the knife in his hand, he will stab you in the back before the words of friendship have died upon his lips.

From the style of the man's conversation & manner you would look for a whole souled man, but he is far from it. I doubt whether he ever performed an act of kindness with his whole soul. He is incapable of conferring a favor heartily, unless it is largely for his own interest, or gracefully, except for his own adornment. There is ever some reserve. If he promises to do a thing he will do it by substituting some word or act for the true thing, so that, if necessary to his schemes, he can slip out of the promise, & yet make a plausible show of defence for his perfidy.

Beneath this sod with "honest" Howard
There lies a statesman, rogue, & coward.[6]

Just as Willcox grew to dislike and distrust all things political, the few brief months he spent as a civilian following the war convinced him that he was something of a fifth wheel in the civilian world. Even after four trying years of war and twenty years in the regular Army, Willcox still could not adjust to private life. It was merely a confirmation of a fact that he had first discovered during those four painful years he had spent in mufti immediately preceding the Civil War.

So it was that Willcox determined to reenter the service. Because his rank of major general during the war had been only a *brevet*, the close of the conflict saw him revert back to his regular commission as a colonel.Consequently, on July 28, 1866, he was assigned to command the 29th U.S. Infantry, an appointment commensurate with his regular rank.

In spite of his opposition to military occupation of the South, Willcox became military commander of the subdistrict of Lynchburg, Virginia. In that capacity and as colonel of the 29th U.S. Infantry, Willcox served in Lynchburg from November 1866 until March 1869. It was not an assignment he relished. Included within the subdistrict were numerous neighboring towns, including Lexington, home of the Virginia Military Institute and Washington College. As that town was filled with Southern boys, as well as boys from Northern states, it was marked early as an area of potential unrest. Indeed, the chief problem of the subdistrict involved confrontations between the Southern residents of the district and Northerners who were either visiting or had relocated to the area. (Surprisingly, there appear to have been few disputes between Southerners and the newly freed blacks of the region.)

6. OBW's *Second Journal*, under entry for Jan. 20, 1868.

One dispute arose in May 1867 involving H. Rives Pollard, former editor of the *Richmond Examiner,* regarding a lecture he proposed to deliver at the Lynchburg Masonic Hall, entitled "The Chivalry of the South, as Illustrated in the Late War." Pollard's proposed speech was little more than a venomous attack on northerners and a glorification of the Confederacy and the southern way of life. A handbill announced the event:

> Gen. Sherman's absurd definition "war is cruelty." No! War, *honourable* war, is beautiful—What it has done for the glory and interest of history—The strange satisfaction with which Southern soldiers sought wounds and lost limbs in the early periods of the late war . . .—How scarred and mutilated bodies were idolized by the women of the South . . .—Justification of the code of honour: the duello *not* "a relick of barbarism". . .—The revival of the tournament in the South—The sneer of Yankee scholars—How they show their ignorance of its history and signification . . .—How some Southern men now court the clatter and dirt of the Yankee civilization. . . .

Learning of the forthcoming speech from Bvt. Col. George Buell of the 29th Infantry, and believing it "calculated to foment a sectional spirit of strife and enmity within the nation" as well as being "incendiary and hurtful to the public peace," Willcox directed Col. Buell to notify the mayor of Lynchburg that "no such lecture will be allowed." As all "citizens seem to be engaged in their peaceful avocations, working to restore prosperity and to invite emigration and capital . . . to bring back the state to those relations which have been suspended by the late rebellion and subsequent events," it was Willcox's hope that the mayor would "see the obvious necessity" of forbidding "the introduction at this time of elements which disturb the public mind and injure the people. A free discussion of political issues is allowable, but a lecture setting at defiance both public morals and the laws of Virginia and violating the patriotic sentiment of the country cannot be regarded as a right."[7]

Pollard would later recall that after receiving the order prohibiting him from delivering the speech he personally called upon Genenal Willcox, in company with the mayor, to assure him that "there was *nothing incendiary or inflammatory* in the lecture; that it was purely an *historical* subject, and requested him to revoke the order of prohibition. He refused. I reminded him that the greatest latitude of speech had been tolerated recently in Virginia,

7. Program for Pollard's proposed lecture, OBW Collection; *Special Orders No. 3*, Lynchburg, Virginia, May 2, 1867, OBW Collection.

and asked in common justice, that I might not be restrained from delivering an address on a subject *in no way connected with the political issues of the day*. He still refused."[8]

Willcox's decision prohibiting Pollard's speech was made in light of relations that then existed between local white citizens and recently arrived northerners (including soldiers). Just two months earlier, Joseph Bailey, of Co. A, 29th Infantry, had been taken to the Lynchburg police station for public drunkenness. There, lying on the floor "perfectly unable to move," Bailey was assailed by "a citizin [*sic*] of notoriously bad character," who "stood over him & for some time continued to stamp his boot in his face & about his head & chest, inflicting wounds of no ordinary character."[9] The Bailey incident was typical of numerous other confrontations that had become all too familiar in Lynchburg.

The most serious affair to confront Willcox occurred at Lexington between a transplanted Northerner named E. C. Johnston and some town boys, including a number of students of Washington College. The "Johnston affair" would also bring Willcox into contact, perhaps for the first time, with Robert E. Lee, then president of the college. Johnston, a former Union soldier, had come to Lexington in the fall of 1865 as an agent of the American Missionary Association, which had been created to establish schools for freedmen. Johnston, however, eventually resigned from that position, and by the winter of 1868 was operating a store in town. His former association with blacks, however, had made him immensely unpopular with many whites.

According to Johnston's initial complaint, as expressed to the mayor of Lexington, J. M. Ruff, on February 5, 1868, Johnston had gone skating the previous day on the North River, directly above town where a dam had been built that when frozen over made for fine skating. Noticing he was being shunned by other skaters, Johnston had decided to move about a mile downriver, where he thought he would be alone. Turning a bend, he came suddenly face to face with a crowd of young boys, who immediately began to accost him. Johnston stated that "without the least provocation on my part I was set upon by not less than fifty or seventy-five young men, nearly all of them students of Washington College, [and] a few citizens of the town, who gathered around me soon after I went on the ice." The boys then set upon Johnston and began to hoot at him, "just as the rebels used to yell when making a charge in the army."

8. Lynchburg *News*, May 3, 1867.
9. Letter of W. D. Jamison, acting assistant surgeon, U.S.A., to OBW, Feb. 6, 1867.

Then, according to Johnston, the crowd turned violent, and "they struck me with their fists, and threw clubs of wood, pieces of ice, snow balls at me. Some of the missiles striking and bruising me severely, they also tripped and knocked me down several times." Asking why he was being attacked, the southern boys replied: "Because you are a D——d Yankee and have no business here. . . . You have ten days to leave Lexington and if you are not gone in that time we will *tar* & feather you and if you dare to say any thing about the affair we will take you out of your store at night and kill you."[10]

Johnston then went home, but a number of the boys showed up at his store at about eleven o'clock that night "and beat upon the doors and window shutters breaking the glass inside and calling to me 'Come out here, you D——d yankee son of a B——h we want to kill you.'"[11]

The following morning, Johnston filed a complaint with the mayor, but the mayor told Johnston there was little he could do. Johnston then decided to report the affair to the military and went to see Brig. Gen. Douglas Frazer, assistant military commissioner for the subdistrict. General Frazer reported the matter to Willcox on February 6, endorsing it as "correct":

I have only to add that the students five in number who assaulted his door . . . took complete possession of the main street of the town for several hours and carried openly deadly weapons which they several times discharged and which were seen in their hands by several passers-by: made use of the most obscene language in front of several residences and by their uproar induced all citizens out at that hour to leave the main street and get home by bye-paths.[12]

Frazer had paid a visit to Mayor Ruff to enquire why nothing had been done to stop the incident. The mayor "owned to me that it could not be stopped; that the civil power was completely powerless in the matter, and that there was absolutely no safety for life or limb as concerned these students in Lexington." Frazer continued in his report to Willcox:

It certainly seems to me that there will never be peace and quietness here till the college is closed, or U.S. troops enough are sent here to be able to cope with them. As it is a perfect reign of terror after dark each night and no one *dare* stop these students in their outrages. No information can be

10. E. C. Johnston to Gen. John M. Schofield, Feb. 5, 1868, copy in OBW Collection.
11. Ibid.
12. Brig. Gen. Douglas Frazer to OBW, Feb. 6, 1868, OBW Collection.

obtained to bring them to justice and it would be highly impolitic and even dangerous for Mr. *Johnson* [*sic*] to do so, if he were able, unless protected by U.S. troops. No night has passed for the last fortnight without the discharge of pistols in the main or neighboring streets.[13]

It was at this point that Willcox determined to go to Lexington and investigate matters for himself. He spoke with Johnston and also with various other witnesses to the affair, and also with Mayor Ruff, whom he found to be "lacking in energy and determination . . . but well disposed." In the course of these interviews Willcox found that Johnston had been holding back some information regarding the skating incident: Johnston had taken to wearing a pistol for protection and in the middle of the fray had seized one young hurler of epithets (a youth of about twelve years) and threatened to shoot him. The boy's older brother and some other young men had closed in on Johnston, who immediately let the boy loose and made his escape.[14] This revelation, of course, put a slightly different spin on matters, though it did not by any means exonerate the college students. It was at this point that Willcox went to see Robert E. Lee.

Up to now Lee had apparently heard little of the skating incident, except perhaps that a northerner had pulled a gun on a little boy and been driven from the ice. Willcox, however, acquainted Lee with the full particulars and gave him the names of three Washington College students who were allegedly involved. Lee, much embarrassed, expressed his deep regrets to Willcox and promised to investigate the matter. In the end the three suspected students were called into Lee's office, an event that must surely have been painful for Lee and a cause of deep regret and embarrassment to the students. One student was asked to withdraw from the college, and Lee wrote the parents of another, asking them to remove their son from the school. The third student requested permission to leave, which was granted.[15]

In spite of the measures taken by Willcox and Lee, Johnston seems to have met with continued harassment from a number of Lexington youths, who had offered to give him a "callithumps" if he did not leave town. Johnston himself, who was preparing to leave town for Covington anyway, was angered at Willcox's refusal to take extreme measures and so determined to strike back at Willcox, Lee, and Washington College.

13. Ibid.
14. Douglas Southall Freeman, *R. E. Lee* (New York: Scribner's, 1962), vol. 4, p. 347. The Johnston affair is covered in chapter XX of that work, pp. 344–69.
15. Ibid., pp. 347–48.

It so happened that winter that Washington College was launching a financial campaign among prominent Northerners. One of its most hearty spokesmen was the Rev. Henry Ward Beecher, who pled the college's case, asking for donations in the spirit of national reunification and healing, and to promote the cause of education. Many Northerners, however, particularly former abolitionists, were skeptical, and editorials to that effect began to appear in *The New York Independent*. One typical editorial, referring to Robert E. Lee, bluntly stated, "We do not think that a man who broke his solemn oath of allegiance to the United States, who imbrued his hands in the blood of tens of thousands of his country's noblest men, for the purpose of perpetuating human slavery, and who was largely responsible for the cruelties of Libby, Salisbury and Andersonville, is fitted to be a teacher of young men."[16]

When these articles were reprinted in the Lexington papers, Johnston and his friends determined to show prospective contributors "what really went on at Gen. Lee's college." One open letter appearing in the *Independent*, written anonymously by "A Resident of Lexington," attempted "to show the philanthropists of the North the animus of the institution to which they are contributing. The professors are, without a single exception, thoroughly rebel in sentiment, and act accordingly. . . ." The letter gave a detailed but partisan account of the Johnston affair as an example of the rampant spirit of rebellion in Lexington.[17]

The above letter and articles published in the *Independent* describing other instances of mistreatment of Northerners residing in Lexington of course hinted strongly that Willcox had been too lenient, if not outright negligent, in the Johnston affair, and in his conduct as subdistrict commander. This sparked a reply from one of Willcox's staff officers, Captain Lacey, who wrote an open letter giving a true account of the affair, published under the name "L" in the *New York Tribune*, and later in *The Independent*:

> This correction will, I trust, be sufficient to exonerate General Lee, but for whom and the cause of education, so essential to the welfare of the South, I should not notice the letter and article referred to. As to the slur which was sought to be cast upon General Willcox in the letter "for consulting with Lee and other notable rebels," instead of making military arrests, his duty and orders first required him to confer with and demand redress at the hands of the town and college authorities; and, as all was

16. Ibid., p. 351.
17. Ibid., p. 353.

done that could be properly demanded, no military interference was called for. . . . I can assure you that General Willcox is not the man to slight his duty, or refuse redress and protection when required; and, in this case, where the offenders were promptly punished by General Lee, and where the attack on the part of the boys was invited by Johnston's threat of shooting a little boy, and the presentation of pistol, he does not, certainly, deserve censure for not further prosecuting it. No further complaints have been received from Lexington which is as quiet as any college town in the United States.[18]

Ultimately, Lacey's letter largely relieved the doubts of many northern philanthropists, and Washington College received numerous donations; nevertheless, the college determined to end its northern canvass.

Willcox's management of affairs in postwar Virginia was commendable, especially considering that he had spent four years fighting Southern troops, and thirteen months in Southern prisons, where he was often the subject of ridicule and abuse. That experience had given Willcox a distaste for Southern "chivalry," which he had once termed "the scum of creation." In a speech given in Detroit upon his return from prison, Willcox had bitterly described his view of the Southern people and those who had led them to war:

I will tell you how, in a great measure, they have brought about the bitterness of feeling towards the North. It has been caused by the politicians, by the newspapers and by their influential men. The people of the South have been educated with the idea that the North was endeavoring to root out slavery in the first place, and in the next place to seize their plantations. The Southern uneducated man of small intelligence has an idea that a live Yankee is something with horns and a tail [laughter]—some monstrosity. When we were moving down from Richmond to Charleston a good many people came out to see what sort of men we were, whether we were made in the same way as Southern men, and as white men [laughter].

As a general thing, the people of the South are not a reading or reflecting people. Very few of them read anything but their local papers, and many of them cannot read or write at all. From being under a burning sun, their temper is more inflammable than ours, and their prejudices are easily aroused. The great mass of the Southern people to-day

18. Ibid., pp. 355–56.

hate the Yankees worse than the Frenchman ever hated the Englishman, or than any race ever hated any other race. This has been brought about by those few designing men, who have been operating for the last quarter of a century.[19]

Willcox's disgust for the Southern elite did not end with the war. That he continued to hold a certain class of Virginia gentlemen in disdain is reflected in a journal entry for January 24, 1868, titled "Lynchburg, Va. Reconstruction":

[Charles W.] Button, editor of the *Virginian*, out in a leader this morning denouncing certain Congressmen for inconsistency, & threatens no more polite attentions to such "Jonathan Sleeks" when they come South in future. Last month, during the 1st recess of Congress, Gov. Blair, Mr. Driggs, & Judge Ferry came down & paid me a flying visit. I invited a few gentlemen to call on them & had them at my house in the evening. Mr. Button was one of the guests. In his article he quotes conversation that took place, thus violating the usages of gentlemen. But what importance he attaches to the condescension of a Virginian who deigns to call on or show any politeness to a stranger! *The vulgar arrogance & narrow minded conceit of these people can only be equalled within the walls of a harem where the eunachs regard all Christian gentlemen as Nazarene dogs, or in a Hottentot village where the greasy black dandy struts before a broken bit of looking glass.*[20] [Editor's italics.]

In an entry of the same date, Willcox added, "Speaking of Virginia vanity, one evening Gen. Buell & I were at a supper party in this city last summer. One of the guests who sat next to the Gen'l was expatiating largely on the superiority of Virginians over all Creation, & said 'you can tell a Virginian, sir, whenever you meet him.' 'Yes,' replied the Gen'l, 'he is always sure to tell you of it.' "[21]

In addition to Willcox's prevailing attitude toward so-called "gentlemen" was the fact that he and his family by no means escaped the venom of southern natives. Just four days prior to the dinner with the southern editor, Willcox noted that on January 19 his ten-year-old son Elon had "stopped going to Sunday school, because the boys have made it too unpleasant

19. *New York Herald*, Aug. 30, 1862.
20. OBW's *Second Journal*, entry for Jan. 24, 1868.
21. Ibid.

for him as a 'Yankee.' "[22] In addition to Elon's treatment at Sunday school there was the fact that Marie Willcox had involved herself with the local Freedmen's Bureau, assisting "the poor colored people" in whatever way she could.

Considering Willcox's wartime experience, the contempt in which he held many southerners, and the treatment of his family and others in Lexington, he might well have been expected to rule his military subdistrict with an iron fist. The fact that he did not do so, that he gave the local populace every consideration when charges were leveled against them by transplanted northerners, speaks to his sense of fairness and justice. This is further illustrated by the profound respect and admiration he maintained for his former enemies, including Lee himself. Though Willcox never recorded his observations of his meeting with the general, the esteem in which he regarded Lee is evident in one of his postwar scrapbooks, which contains an engraving of Lee in uniform and a copy of his farewell address. In addition, Willcox continued to correspond with numerous other former adversaries, and while stationed in Lynchburg he had tea with generals Longstreet, Heth, and others.

One other notable event that occurred while General Willcox and his family were in Lynchburg outweighed even the Johnston affair and his interview with General Lee. On August 19, 1867, a second son (fifth child) entered the Willcox household, christened Orlando Blodgett Willcox.

Willcox remained in command at Lynchburg until March 1869, when, as he notes in his journal, "consolidation & reduction of the Army transferred me to the Colonelcy of the 12th Infantry." Assuming command of that regiment in Washington, D.C., on March 24, 1869, Willcox received orders to proceed with his unit to Angel Island, in San Francisco Bay. It was a remarkable journey, in that it took just twenty-four days, due to the near-completion of the Union Pacific Railway. Willcox recalled that the regiment "had rail all the way except some 45 miles in Utah (from Corinne) over which the Pacific R.R. was not completed. This gap we marched over. Camped out with my family. These were the first troops that traveled across the continent by rail. The next were the 21st Inf., under my friend Gen'l Stoneman. We came via Chicago & Omaha. The western 200 miles of the Union Pacific R.R. had been built during the previous winter on frozen ground, & here our journey was perilous—ran off the track some eight times."[23]

22. Ibid., entry of Jan. 19, 1868.
23. Ibid., undated entry, p. 169.

The posting to Angel Island was, without question, a plum assignment. The warm weather, the gentle breeze off the bay, and the scenery of the rolling countryside provided an ideal setting in which to raise a family. There, on March 10, 1870, a third son was born to the Willcoxes, baptized Charles McAllister Willcox, after Orlando's old West Point classmate, Julian McAllister.

Things progressed smoothly for the Willcox family at Angel Island until the spring of 1872, when Marie grew ill. The nature of her affliction is uncertain. In June she went east via Panama, hoping to regain her health by visiting her sister Caro and her parents in New York. Marie returned in October, but "not much benefitted in health." Willcox himself, meanwhile, was ordered to Arizona on court-martial duty, noting that "but for the anxiety concerning Marie, I should have greatly enjoyed the Arizona trip."[24]

By January 1873 Marie was beginning to fail, and Willcox, desperate for a posting closer to Michigan, wrote General of the Army William T. Sherman for assistance. Perhaps, Willcox wrote, another officer would exchange posts with him. Or, was there a chance that his command could be ordered east? What Willcox truly hoped for was a command in Michigan, which would put Marie close to her parents. Sherman responded in a letter dated January 17, 1873:

> I do not think there is the remotest chance of your Regiment the 12th being ordered East this year— I don't know why it is, but it is so, the officers of Infantry want the Lake Posts—If called on to make any change then I should give those posts to the 22nd, which have been on the Upper Missouri over 7 years. Hazen[25] who is at Fort Buford on the Upper Missouri would change with you quick, but your post is really the most desirable one I know of, at all events. I know that Hazen thinks so—whilst his at Fort Buford is of the worst. Fort Buford is inaccessible 4 months of the year, & the thermometer at 40° below zero.[26]

In other words, Sherman was telling Willcox to be happy with his posting: it could be worse, much worse. Sherman added, however, "I am sorry your wife is unwell, but in serious sober earnest I advise you for her sake as well as your own, not to [request] such a change which surely would be for

24. Ibid., entries under "1872" and "1872–3."
25. William B. Hazen (28th, USMA 1855).
26. Sherman to OBW, Jan. 17, 1873, OBW Collection.

the worse. I am always glad to do an act of personal favor, but must endeavor to be just & fair."[27]

By the spring of that year any thought of moving Marie back east was out of the question. "My angelic Wife gradually grew worse until the latter part of March, when I moved her to 'Hayward's,' just out of Alameda, for a change of air. But it was too late; she expired April 15, 1873 at 11½ o'clock A.M.—too good for this life."[28] Leaving Lulu (now nineteen years old) behind to look after the other children and accompanied by his son, Elon, Willcox started east with Marie's remains, arriving at Detroit on April 25. "Every preparation having been made for it, the funeral took place at once, services at St. Paul's Church (church of our baptisms & marriage & where both our Fathers had been vestrymen) & she was buried at Elmwood Cemetery." Bishop McCoskrey performed the service.[29]

After visiting with friends and family at New Rochelle, Washington, and Boston, Orlando took Elon to West Point, where he had secured an appointment as a member of the class of 1878. It must have been difficult for Elon to part with his family and enter the austere environment of the military academy so soon after the death of his mother. Yet there were old friends at the Point to look after the young plebe, chiefly Professor Church, Orlando's old mathematics instructor, who proved to be a lifelong friend even if as a teacher most cadets found him "dry as dust." Leaving Elon on June 5, Willcox "visited Detroit again, Jackson (the Withingtons) & Chicago & returned to Angel Island [on the] 23rd of the month."[30]

In August 1873, Willcox was temporarily reassigned to the east, detailed as superintendent of the general recruiting service in New York City. He left via rail on the 19th of the month, sending Lulu—who had cheerfully taken on the duties of a mother to her siblings—by sea with the children. The reassignment was a blessing, as it put Willcox close to West Point, which he frequently visited to inquire into his son's progress. He remained on duty in New York until October 1, at which time he returned to his command at Angel Island.[31]

On February 6, 1878, Willcox was assigned to command the Department of Arizona, headquartered at Whipple Barracks, Prescott, where his regiment was ordered to relieve the 8th Infantry, under August V. Kautz. It would prove to be the most difficult assignment of Willcox's career. Arizona

27. Ibid.
28. OBW's *Second Journal*, entry under "1872–3."
29. Ibid.
30. Ibid., entry for "1873."
31. Ibid.

in the late 1870s was already a powder keg of tension between white settlers and native Apaches, and the fuse had been lit. At the time Willcox assumed command, the Indians on the San Carlos Reservation were close to starving. Farming on the reservation proved unsuccessful, and government rations, which would have improved the situation immeasurably, never reached adequate levels.

Conditions at the San Carlos Agency were due in large measure to a succession of corrupt agents, specifically the contract profiteering and theft that occurred under their administration. Moreover, as all Indian agencies fell under the jurisdiction of the civilian Commissioner of Indian Affairs rather than under military control, the department commander's hands were tied unless violence should erupt. By that time the agents were only too happy to call on the Army for assistance, and the military was forced to fight a war it had been denied any hand in preventing. Willcox grasped the problem instantly: "After depriving the Indian of his lands and proper means of subsistence, at what point in his subsequent career of starvation, misery, and desperation shall you regard him as a public enemy? For it is only at some such point that the military can come in without being regarded as an intruder."[32]

As the noted western historian Robert M. Utley has so aptly stated, "Conditions at San Carlos would have severely tried the most docile and obedient Indians. The Apaches were neither docile nor obedient." General George Crook, who succeeded Willcox as department commander, referred to the Apaches as the "tigers of the human race," noting that they "resented anything like an attempt to regulate their conduct, or in any way to interfere with their mode of life"—and controlling the Indians was, of course, what the reservations were all about. And as Utley has further observed, "It may well be doubted that even an ideal reservation could have contained a people so warlike and so contemptuous of restraint."[33]

An infusion of white settlers into the department exacerbated the problem. Between 1880 and 1882 the population of Arizona doubled, from some forty thousand to eighty thousand settlers. In his first annual report, Willcox wrote that "as the railroads advance through this Department, the whites and Indians will be brought more and more in contact, and the machinery of the civil law does not seem applicable to the mixed society which ensues, something therefore needs to be done." The answer to the problem,

32. Robert M. Utley, *Frontier Regulars: The United States Army and the Indian, 1866–1891* (New York: Macmillan, 1973), pp. 397–98.
33. Ibid., p. 371.

as Willcox saw it, was to "civilize" the Apaches. As one who had admired the American Indian from his first association with them in his native Michigan, Willcox sought a peaceful approach to the problem. Nevertheless, Willcox's solution reveals both his naiveté and also the prejudice toward and ignorance of the Indians that was common even among the most well-meaning of white Americans at the time:

> If the moral and intellectual forces at work in the Indian Department, could be brought to bear on the question of preparing for these transformations going on all over the western territory, it might save wars and wasteful and inhuman sacrifices, and convert our heathen children into civilized societies. . . . But if something is not done to guide their industries, to give their children schooling, to teach them the first principles of town and county government, it will be found that contact with American institutions will soon make them seven-fold nearer the children of hell, than if they had never seen "a white man and a brother."[34]

Of all the Apache bands residing at San Carlos, none were more independent or more warlike than the Chiricahuas and the Warm Springs people, and among them was one who would emerge as the preeminent war leader, one of the most cunning guerrilla fighters of all time—Geronimo.

The first serious trouble began with the White Mountain Apaches in the summer of 1881. Many of this tribe, who lived in the forested mountains on the northern part of the San Carlos Reservation, had fallen under the spell of a medicine man named Nakaidoklini, who preached of a day when the Apache dead would be raised and the white race destroyed—a doctrine much like the one prophesied by the Ghost Dance religion, which would sweep through the Plains tribes some eight years later.

Col. Eugene Carr, commanding at nearby Fort Apache, did not view Nakaidoklini as particularly dangerous, but the agent at San Carlos, J. C. Tiffany, saw the Apache medicine man and his prophesies as imminent threats to the white settlers of the region, and he wanted Nakaidoklini arrested. In this case, Willcox was inclined to agree with the Indian agent, and in August 1881 he ordered Colonel Carr to bring the shaman in. Marching out of Fort Apache on August 29 with two troops of the 6th Cavalry (eighty-five men) and twenty-three White Mountain scouts, Carr headed for Nakaidoklini's village on Cibicu Creek, thirty miles northwest of the

---

34. *Annual Report of Bvt. Maj. Gen. O. B. Willcox, 12th U.S. Infantry, Commanding Department of Arizona, 1878–79* (Prescott, Ariz.: Whipple Barracks, 1879), pp. 3–4.

fort. Entering the Indian village the next day, Carr confronted Nakaidok-lini. Although the medicine man surrendered peacefully enough, his followers were clearly agitated. Trouble with the Apaches was clearly brewing, and the fact became obvious when a hundred or so warriors, "stripped for fight" and wearing only "breach-clout and cartridges," appeared on the flanks of the cavalry column as it headed back down the valley for Fort Apache.

Eugene A. Carr was an 1850 graduate of West Point who in 1894 would be awarded the Medal of Honor for the Battle of Pea Ridge and had already established a reputation as an Indian fighter in the army; certainly, he must have realized that an ambush was in the making. Indeed, that possibility should have been obvious at the outset of the march, when his own White Mountain scouts, affected by Nakaidoklini's preaching, attempted to lead the column down a trail that was favorable for an Apache ambuscade. When Carr chose the safer, more direct path, the scouts became angry.

As the troopers went into bivouac the night of August 30, Carr failed to take even the most rudimentary precautions. The horses were unsaddled, and the men were settling down for the night when the Apaches attacked, firing into the camp. The scouts immediately mutinied. A captain and six troopers were cut down by the first volley. Nakaidoklini himself (who had been warned that he would be the first to die should his followers attack) was shot by a bugler as he tried to crawl to safety; a sergeant with an ax finished him off. A band of warriors made a rush at the horses, attempting to drive them off. The encampment was now the scene of utter chaos, and Carr and his men were suddenly faced with annihilation. Somehow, in the midst of this melee Carr managed to throw a skirmish line together, forcing the Apaches back across the creek until, under cover of darkness, the troopers were able to withdraw. Carr's negligence had cost the command a captain and four men killed and another four wounded, two of whom later died.

Reaching Fort Apache the next day, Carr found his post facing an imminent attack. Telegraph lines to the fort had been cut, so that Carr could neither signal for help nor report the incident at Cibicu. The Indians attacked the next day, wounding one officer and shooting Carr's horse from under him. It was rare for Apaches to attack a fort directly, and the fact that they did so testifies to the intensity of their anger over the killing of the medicine man. The Indians were soon driven off, however, and there for the time being the matter ended.[35]

35. Utley, *Frontier Regulars*, pp. 371–74.

Initial reports of the Cibicu affair stunned the nation. Carr was first reported to have been killed and his entire command slaughtered, just as Custer and his men had been five years earlier. More accurate accounts from Arizona confirmed that Carr and most of his men were in fact still alive, but the Cibicu affair was to have profound repercussions. Relations between Carr and Willcox, cool to begin with, grew frigid. Willcox preferred charges against Carr for mismanaging the battle. Although Carr had known that his scouts were under Nakaidoklini's spell, and had clearly been guilty of ignoring signs of an imminent attack and of taking no precautions, a court of inquiry found him not guilty, except of certain errors of judgment in the disposition of his forces.

Meanwhile, the five mutinous scouts were court-martialed for their role at Cibicu. Three were hanged, and two others were sentenced to life in prison at Alcatraz Island—which, for an Apache, was a fate worse than death.[36]

The Cibicu affair, however, proved to be the spark that ignited the powder keg that was the Apache Nation. On the night of September 30, 1881, seventy-four Chiricahuas, under chiefs Juh, Nachez, and Geronimo, fearing an imminent attack by soldiers, set out for Mexico. With several hastily assembled troops of cavalry, as well as infantry and scouts, Willcox personally led the attempt to intercept the Indians before they could reach Mexico. On October 2, 1881, the soldiers overtook the Chiricahuas near Cedar Springs, at the foot of the Graham Mountains. Willcox, riding well ahead of his troopers, later recalled:

> I was the first man on the spot & found the burning remains of a couple of wagons of Samaniego's train, with the bloody corpses of my poor friend Samaniego & a couple of his Mexican teamsters, about half a mile from the adobe house at the springs. [His men overtook the Indians] before dark, chased them up, up into the crags & fought them till nine o'clock that night. In this fight a number of our men were killed & still more wounded. The Indians concealed their dead, & carried off their wounded in the darkness of the night with relays of ponies, by which means they usually travel—leaving, however, 18 dead horses & mules among the rocks, besides other signs of bloody losses. They were hotly pursued next day by *all* the cavalry, & again, struck both by this force & a squadron from New Mexico sent by rail at my request, who struck them in the Dragoon Mountains just across the railroad, & at Cochise's strong

36. Ibid., p. 373.

hold, scattered them & their plunder, & kept up a running fight with them through the mountains to the Mexican border, which, at that time, we were forbidden to cross.[37]

Escaping into the Sierra Madre, the Chiricahua band joined Nana and his Apache forces. There the Indians holed up until the following spring, when they launched a series of raids along the Arizona/New Mexico border, killing between thirty and fifty whites. U.S. forces of the 4th Cavalry under Lt. Col. George Forsyth pursued the Apaches all the way into Mexico, where Forsyth finally halted the chase.

In July 1882, trouble with the White Mountain Apaches once again erupted, when Natiotish, leading a small band of warriors who had refused to surrender after Cibicu, ambushed several policemen at the San Carlos agency, killing four of them. The warriors then proceeded to raid along a line northwest of the agency, pursued now by fourteen troops of cavalry. Seven miles north of General Springs, on the "Crook Trail" between Fort Apache and Verde, Natiotish prepared to ambush his pursuers. Concealing his warriors along the top of a narrow canyon known as Big Dry Wash, the Apache chief lay in wait for Capt. Adna R. Chaffee's troop of the 6th Cavalry, which the Indians far outnumbered. Chaffee's veteran guide, however, detected the trap; soon, reinforced by units of the 6th and 3rd Cavalry, the captain dispatched troopers to strike the Apaches in flank and rear. Chaffee's twin force hit the Apaches hard, taking them completely by surprise. Few of the warriors escaped. Wrote Willcox in his yearly report,

This, I think, has broken up the band of outlaws under Nan-tia-tish [sic] most effectually. My troops marched from four different points, hundreds of miles apart, and came together in time to render mutual assistance in actual battle; all were up within twenty-four hours. The scene of the engagement was of the wildest description, in a great wash forming a deep canyon with steep banks, two or more hundred feet high with rocky side canyons, through which the remnants of the hostiles escaped at night, leaving most of their dead on the ground; fourteen found on the field, and two more, including Nan-tia-tish himself, afterwards reported by Major Evans. Of course there were many wounded. They lost every thing they had, and scattered back to the mountains of the reservation, sick, sore, naked and on foot, a merciful hail storm, which fell like snow,

37. Ibid., p. 375; Letter of OBW, marked "unsent," to unspecified New York newspaper, 1885, OBW Collection.

washing out their tracks. This winds up the only considerable element of revolt left on the reservation.[38]

Big Dry Wash was the last Indian battle directed by General Willcox, and his last major role as commander of the Department of Arizona. Significantly, that action also marked the end of Apache hostilities in Arizona itself, though the bands of Warm Spring and Chiricahuas in Mexico would be a constant threat until the surrender of Geronimo.

Willcox's direction of affairs in Arizona has been criticized by several prominent western historians, chiefly for his role in the Cibicu affair, beginning with his insistence on the arrest of the medicine man Nakaidoklini. Yet he was commanding under difficult circumstances. He had a genuine compassion for the Native Americans in his charge but was unable to intervene in their favor, as their treatment on the reservations was out of his jurisdiction. Only when their mistreatment and abuse by corrupt agents finally caused them to break out of the reservations could he become involved, and then it was as a soldier in pursuit of a hostile enemy. His order to arrest Nakaidoklini, which came at the request of Agent Tiffany, was an attempt to nip a potential problem in the bud, before it spread across the territory and caused a widespread outbreak of Apache uprisings.

In 1885, responding to a newspaper editorial criticizing the army's management of Indian affairs in the southwest, Willcox wrote in defense of his service in Arizona. The letter, never sent, is published here for the first time:

Your issue of the 2d inst. contained surprising charges against military management in Arizona, that did gross injustice to myself & my troops—not to mention to Genl. Crook, who can speak for himself.

I must confess to hearty sympathy with the sufferers in New Mex[ico] & Arizona, & can afford to put up with legitimate criticism & bear my share of the responsibility. But you must remember that the men who howl the loudest against the military are among those who create or foment troubles, who live on & cheat or want to live on & cheat the Indian & the government: disgruntled officials, discharged employees, contractors & their crew, sutlers, gamblers & shang-abangers generally.

I have been most of the time in service for nearly forty years, was in the Seminole war & know something of the Comanche & Sioux wars, & can testify that neither of them compared in difficulty with the pursuit

38. *Annual Report of Bvt. Maj. Gen. O. B. Willcox, Commanding the Department of Arizona, for the Year 1881–82*, p. 13.

of the Apaches over thorny & jagged & rocky mountains & cañons & terrible deserts—hot, alkaline, foodless & waterless—with or without our heavy American horses. Nor was there ever any thing like the constant misrepresentation & indiscriminate abuse that has been showered upon officers & soldiers alike by the harpies that prey upon the public in Arizona.

The author of the article in your valued paper is not one of this sort, yet he has either been misled by false reports, strained through the foul medium referred to—or else has been wilfully false—which I am loath to believe. . . . Certainly he does not give credit to my troops for the good service they rendered in Arizona during my administration from the spring of 1878 to the fall of 1882, under cover of which two lines of railroad were peacefully laid across the Territory, & the Tombstone & other wide & rich mining districts were as peacefully developed. During three years of this time, the Apache hostiles were not only driven out of the Territory whenever they attempted to enter, by the 6th Cavalry & 8th & 12th Infantry soldiers, constantly scouting, but aid was constantly given to Genl. [Edward] Hatch against Victorio, Nana & the Apaches in New Mexico, & to Mexicans across the line.

Therefore I must deny the sweeping charges of inefficiency brought against the troops. In 1879 I had Juh & Geronimo brought into the San Carlos Reservation from the Sierra Madre country, now so famous, by the management & the skill of good men well known in the Territory. And there Juh & Geronimo might have peacefully dwelt to this day, but for irritating causes at the agencies, where there were jealousies of the military, unjust discriminations against these wards of the military, illegal attempts to appropriate the Indians interests in coal land, refusal to furnish [the Indians with] tools for irrigation & seed for cultivation & other outrages . . . for part of which Agent Tiffany was indicted at Tucson.

The immediate occasion of their [Juh's & Geronimo's] long brooded outbreak certainly grew out of my orders, which were to arrest certain other Indians mixed up with them, who had been implicated in the Cibicu affair, & the fear that they themselves would have their arms taken away from them. . . .

Having the Cibicu prisoners on my hands at Camp Thomas & two troops of 1st Cavalry under Major Sanford to guard them, I started with them across the track of the Chiricahuas, which we struck at Cedar Springs, between Camp Thomas & Fort Grant. . . .

I need not mention the disadvantages under which troops labor on coming up after a long chase, with exhausted horses & empty bellies, coming up with these mountain Arabs in their strong holds, or flying with their relays of tough ponies. Their wives, so far from being an encumbrance, are often a help both in flight & fight, if not packed off with the children & plunder by a different route to the place of rendezvous, while the troops follow the main trail of the warriors.

In justice to my troops, as well as myself, I may as well add a remark which will no doubt surprise both your correspondent & hundreds of others who think they know all about Arizona affairs, & that is this: there never was a hostile movement of Apaches or other Indians in Arizona from the spring of 1878 to the fall of 1882 that was not overtaken effectively within a few days thereafter, & the murderers punished, the best we knew how, & with all the means we had to employ. The longest delay was after the Cibicu massacre, which delay was caused partly by the overflown [*sic*] rivers, White & Gila, & the necessity of giving time to the peaceful Indians to come in before operating within the wide limits of the great San Carlos Reservation. But even then the result was all the more complete for the hostiles were so completely hemmed in that their main body was captured, & if I could have had my way, they would all have been hung or shot for murder & treacherous violation of the laws of war, or banished from Arizona forever.

But your correspondent only mentions that Dandy Jim & one other Indian were executed. He does not mention the bloody pursuit of Loco's band by Mackenzie's troops & my own under Forsyth & Tupper, nor the final destruction of the Cibicu outlaws at the Big Dry Wash.[39]

Apart from his dealing with the Apaches, Willcox had a host of other duties to perform as department commander, including entertaining dignitaries. One of the first to visit him was the new territorial governor of Arizona, John C. Frémont, whom he entertained in October 1878. General Sherman had written to Willcox on August 1, "warning" him of the forthcoming visit of the governor and his wife and asking the general to pay them special attention: "Mrs. Frémont is a strong character the daughter of Mr. [Senator Thomas Hart] Benton, and it is well to keep on her fair weather side." As for the new governor himself, Sherman added, "Frémont has been up & down in life, and I wonder at his accepting this office, but I believe necessity compels, and he expects to find opportunity to speculate in mining stock." The commanding general went on to warn Willcox to stay out of

39. Letter of OBW, marked "unsent," to unspecified New York newspaper, 1885, OBW Collection.

such transactions but to otherwise give the Frémonts "such facilities of commissary items, and transportation, as you can consistently with the interest of the military service."[40] The Frémonts thereafter were frequent guests at Whipple Barracks.

President Rutherford B. Hayes, accompanied by General Sherman, paid a visit to the territory, and to General Willcox, in the fall of 1880, becoming the first president to cross the continental divide. Sherman called on Willcox during his grand tour of U.S. outposts in the summer of 1882.

Fortunately for General Willcox, Lulu, now a young lady in her late twenties, was there to act as hostess for the honored guests, as well as at many other social occasions. By all accounts, she became a favorite with all the officers of her father's command. Willcox was also blessed to have his son Elon assigned to him as aide-de-camp.

The general, however, was not to remain a bachelor for the rest of his life. In October 1881 he took Julia Elizabeth (McReynolds) Wyeth, a forty-year-old widow from Detroit, to be his second wife. Although Willcox had intended to be married at Chicago, the recent Apache outbreak forced him to change plans, and the couple were married in Tucson.

In September 1882, Willcox was relieved as commander of the Department of Arizona by George Crook, who would further enhance his reputation as an Indian fighter by finally corralling Geronimo, forcing that intrepid warrior to surrender at last. Willcox and his 12th Infantry, meanwhile, reported to the Department of the Platte, from where they were soon transferred to a posting at Madison Barracks, New York, at Sackett's Harbor on Lake Ontario.

Upon his departure from Arizona, the territorial papers lauded their former commander, noting the difficulties that he had had to endure. The comments of the Arizona (Tucson) *Star* were typical:

> When he assumed the command there were about ten or fifteen thousand people (other than Indians) in the Territory. That number has been increased by immigration to perhaps fifty or sixty thousand. . . . This population is scattered over an area of country as large as all the New England States together. It is situated in many instances in little detached isolated communities, especially exposed to the attacks of predatory savages, on account of the difficulties of intercommunication by reason of few and poor roads. . . . Never since Gen. Willcox assumed command of the department has he had an adequate force at his disposal to cope with the

40. Sherman to OBW, Aug. 1, 1878, OBW Collection.

difficulties surrounding his position. In several instances his force has been reduced in the face of his urgent appeals and protests. That he has not been able to extend to all parts of the Territory the protection and safety he would have wished, is as much a source of regret to him as it can be to anybody else. . . . But I venture to say when the history of his administration in Arizona shall be written, it will be found that he has done as any other man could under the same disadvantageous circumstances. . . .[41]

Another local paper concurred with the above, stating that the Indian outbreaks "were suppressed as promptly and ably as though General Sherman, Sheridan, Grant or any other great commander had been right here on the ground to have given orders in person."[42]

In addition to his swift reaction to various Indian outbreaks, 576 miles of railroad track were laid in the territory during Willcox's administration, and the rich mining area of southeastern Arizona was developed. Indeed, the citizens of Arizona, who had to contend with the threat of Indian attacks on a daily basis, were pleased enough with Willcox's administration of the territory to name the little town of Willcox, in the southeastern portion of the territory, after the general—not as a parting salutation, but while he was yet in command.[43]

The peaceful posting at Madison Barracks, New York, proved to be a blessing for Willcox and his regiment after four strenuous and stressful years in Arizona. The new post also offered more of the comforts and amenities conducive to raising a family than did the far west, and it was there, on April 13, 1884, that Julian McAllister Willcox, the only child of Orlando and Julia, was born.

It was also about this time that the general began to contemplate seriously writing his memoirs, beginning with an account of the capture of Alexandria. He read with much interest the memoirs of others, particularly those of McClellan and Grant, as well as many of the early histories of the war. He was most intrigued by Andrew Humphreys's *Virginia Campaigns of 1864 and 1865*, and he began a correspondence with the author, particularly concerning the role of his division in the final campaigns. Willcox pointed out errors in the work and recommended additions and corrections for a new edition. The revisions were made by Humphreys before his death but were never included in later editions of the book.

41. Undated newspaper clipping, OBW scrapbook, OBW Collection.
42. Ibid.
43. *Annual Report of OBW, 1881–82*, p. 16. The town of Willcox, Arizona, was a station on the Southern Pacific Railroad. It is still in existence today.

Poring over his journals, letters, and dispatches, as well as the reports, dispatches, and battle accounts of others, Willcox took copious notes but did not actually begin serious work on his book until 1901. Frank Hosford, the manager of the Washington bureau of the *Detroit Free Press*, read the early drafts and published a few in his paper but offered little in the way of advice. Nor did he provide sufficient encouragement for the general to complete the work. Willcox wrote sporadically; after 1905 the onset of illness and the effects of old age began to take their toll, and work stopped altogether. The early chapters were perhaps as complete as he could have hoped to make them, but the later chapters certainly could have used further honing.

The proximity of Madison Barracks to New York City also allowed Willcox to visit many of his old classmates and comrades in arms who now lived in the city. He often visited Winfield Hancock at his Governor's Island home, and in February 1886 served as a pallbearer at his funeral.

Indeed, by the mid 1880s many of the soldiers Willcox had served with during his nearly forty years in the Army had already passed away, their obituaries carefully pasted into his scrapbook: Charles Griffin died in September 1867, Meade in November 1872, Burnside in September 1881, Andrew Humphreys in December 1883, Mansfield Lovell in June 1884, Grant in July 1885, McClellan in October 1885, and James B. Ricketts in September 1887.

The death that affected Willcox most during this period, however, was that of his old West Point roommate and lifelong friend Julian McAllister, for whom he had named two of his sons. McAllister, now senior colonel of ordnance in the U.S. Army, had served in California during the Civil War; while his service was therefore not as remarkable as that of many of his classmates, he had remained in the service until his death in January 1887 from kidney disease. Another classmate, General William W. Burns, wrote Willcox of Julian's death and the funeral service that followed, which Willcox was unable to attend. "We buried him grandly at the alma mater," wrote Burns, "the hills echoing to the grand funeral march. . . . The sappers fired the three volleys as one man, and the bugle taps brought the tears to all eyes. . . . 'One by one the roses fall,' '*Nous nous souvenons.*'" Of McAllister Willcox wrote, "I loved him like a Brother."[44]

On October 13, 1886, Willcox, then the senior colonel in the U.S. Army, at last received his long-awaited regular appointment as brigadier general. Along with the promotion came a new posting, this time to Fort Leavenworth, Kansas, where he assumed command of the Department of the Mis-

44. William W. Burns to OBW, Jan. 10, 1887.

souri, embracing not only that state but Illinois, Kansas, Colorado, New Mexico, Utah, and the Indian Territory (now Oklahoma). The assignment was to be a brief one, however, as the general was required, by law, to retire on his sixty-fourth birthday, April 23, 1887.

Returning east to Washington, where he bought a home on R Street-Northwest, Willcox accepted a position as superintendent of the Army and Navy Bureau of the Mutual Life Insurance Company, which he held for nearly a year and a half. On February 28, 1889, he was named superintendent of the U.S. Soldiers' Home in Washington, D.C., replacing Henry J. Hunt, the former superintendent, who had died two weeks earlier. A more agreeable or personally rewarding job Willcox could not have hoped for.

The superintendency of the Soldiers' Home was an ideal post, vied for by many retired officers. Situated on five hundred acres of high, rolling ground, "all beautifully laid out, and covered with handsome groves of oak trees," the facility consisted of nearly twenty buildings, including a library, infirmary, officers' quarters, and others. It has been said that the home was the most beautiful spot in Washington, and many of residents of the capital spent their Sundays strolling and picknicking on the grounds. President Lincoln, hoping to escape the heat, stench, and pressures of Washington, spent as much of the summer as he could at the Soldiers' Home, and it was there that he had entertained General Willcox upon the latter's release from prison in August 1862.

Established by Congress in the early 1850s as the result of repeated requests from General Winfield Scott, the U.S. Soldiers' Home was, at the time of Willcox's administration, the only place of retirement for soldiers of the regular Army, though six other facilities then existed for disabled volunteer soldiers. At the time General Willcox assumed the direction of the home, some five hundred veterans were living there. One newspaper article on the institution during the 1890s reported that "the inmates of the Soldiers' Home lead an easy but spiritless life. . . . Suicides are occasional." However, the article concluded, all of the soldiers "are more happy and comfortable than they could be elsewhere, and a large proportion of them take very kindly to the life."[45]

Willcox certainly enjoyed his nearly three and a half years administering the home. Its proximity to the capital allowed him and his family to enjoy an active social life, and the general and his wife were frequent guests at the White House. The general was also active in countless veterans' organizations that had been organized since the war, including the Society of the

45. Unnamed, undated newspaper clipping, OBW Scrapbook.

Army of the Potomac, the Grand Army of the Republic, the Veterans of the Ninth Army Corps, the Military Order of Foreign Wars, and the Aztec Club, all of which were constantly requesting him to speak. He also became active in the Michigan State Association, dedicated to preserving and studying the history of his native state.

In 1889, Willcox was stunned by the sudden death of his daughter, Marie Louise, "Lulu," in the Canary Islands, where she had gone with her husband, Lt. Stephen C. Mills (USMA 1877) of the 12th Infantry. Suffering from tuberculosis for many years, Lulu had sought relief by traveling to Africa, Gibraltar, and the Canaries, only to succumb to the disease on December 14. Described as one who cared more for the welfare of others than she did for her own, Lulu had stepped in to fill her mother's place upon the latter's untimely death, helping to raise her young siblings. Adored by all who came to know her, she was to be sorely missed.

Willcox resigned from the Soldiers' Home in the spring of 1892 "for personal reasons" that he did not detail. The chief reason, however, seems to have been a desire to travel while his health lasted. It was time to fulfill a lifelong wish to see Europe.

Sailing for the continent in the early spring of 1893 with Julia and nine-year-old Julian, Willcox spent over a year making the grand tour, visiting France, Switzerland, Belgium, and nearly all of Great Britain.[46]

On March 2, 1895, Orlando Willcox was awarded one of the greatest honors of his life, the Congressional Medal of Honor, for his action at the Battle of Bull Run on July 21, 1861, "where he voluntarily led repeated charges until wounded and taken prisoner."

Unbeknownst to Willcox, two former soldiers of his command, James O'Donnell and William H. Withington, both of Jackson, Michigan, had launched a campaign to secure a medal for their former commander. Their original application had been presented in late 1894; in it Withington had cited Willcox's "quick and thorough organization of the first regiment from Michigan and the conspicuous part Gen'l Willcox took in the Battle of Bull Run," his wounding, capture and imprisonment. The application was denied. As Assistant Secretary of War Joseph A. Doe noted in his reply of December 28, 1894, "the Congressional Medal of Honor is not awarded for general gallantry and good conduct, however faithful and meritorious it may have been but only for most *distinguished gallantry in action*." Medals were not given for wounds or imprisonment, as these were but the common expe-

46. OBW journals for 1893 and 1894, OBW Collection.

rience of many soldiers. Doe explained that "further evidence is necessary as to some specific act whereby this brave and gallant officer most distinguished himself on the field of battle, in order to bring this case within the true meaning of the law in reference to medals of honor."

Indeed, it was a rare thing for officers of higher rank to receive the much-coveted medal at all, as they were usually in the rear directing the movements of their troops, rather than in the front lines where the bullets were flying. With Willcox, however, such was not the case. Withington and O'Donnell now took a different tack. In a renewed application, O'Donnell explained:

As brigade commander his duty was to direct the movements of the regiments composing it, not to personally command or lead any one of them. As is well-known our troops were new to service, green as soldiers, and needed conspicuous examples and elan to bring them to face the deadly fire. By reference to the report of Major Bidwell commanding the Michigan Volunteers on that day . . . July 21, 1861, it will be plainly seen that Gen. Willcox at a critical moment, in which confusion resulted and part of the regiment had fallen back, personally led the regiment to the charge upon the enemies' batteries, placing himself at its front and center, and with a wave of his cap and by his personal exposure inspired the regiment to do its work. He did the same with a fraction of the Fire Zouaves on that same day, and he personally recaptured a battery (Ricketts) from the hands of the enemy. . . . On the last charge he had not a single staff officer with him. His staff officers are now all dead or could testify to the above.[47]

This was more than enough evidence for the War Department, and the medal was issued without further delay. It came as a great surprise to the general, and it remains a source of pride to his family to this day.

At his eightieth birthday, in 1903, Willcox remained in fairly good health, though his hearing was beginning to fail. He still enjoyed the Washington social scene, however, frequently attending dinners and receptions at dignitaries' homes as well as at the White House. He visited old comrades, including many ex-Confederates, such as Cadmus Wilcox and Henry Heth, and from time to time he worked on his memoirs.

47. Michigan Civil War Centennial Observance Commission, *A Study in Valor: Michigan Medal of Honor Winners in the Civil War* (Lansing: State of Michigan, 1966), pp. 57–60.

During the last few years General Willcox had taken to spending the summers at the Columbia Hotel in Cobourg, Ontario, Canada, becoming immensely popular with nearly everyone in the little lakeside community. By 1905, however, his health was such that he required the constant services of an attendant, making travel difficult. It was then that he moved permanently to Cobourg, though of course retaining his U.S. citizenship.

In early May 1907, the general contracted an acute case of bronchitis. On Friday, May 10, 1907, the long and adventurous life of Orlando Bolivar Willcox at last came to an end. The following Monday, Canadian officers of the community "turned out en masse" to honor a brother soldier. Although Willcox had fought under a different flag, they were determined to give him a military farewell. The coffin, draped with both the Stars and Stripes and the Union Jack, was conveyed under military escort to the railway station, where it was received for the United States by Brig. Gen. B. J. D. Irwin. The coffin, accompanied by Julia and Orlando Blodgett Willcox, was then carried by rail to Washington, D.C., for interment at Arlington Cemetery.

The group arrived at the Pennsylvania Station in Washington at 9:45 A.M. on May 14 and was met by a troop of cavalry, a battery, and band from Fort Myer. The somber procession then made its way over the river and up the hill to Arlington, where services were held. Few prominent Civil War military figures were present. Brig. Gen. Rufus Saxton, West Point Class of 1849, was there as an honorary pallbearer, but most of the prominent officers Willcox had served with were already dead. Many of the enlisted men and junior officers who had served under him were in attendance, however, as well as representatives of the numerous veterans' organizations to which he had belonged.[48]

Orlando Bolivar Willcox rests today in grave 18, section 1, at Arlington National Cemetery, just a short distance behind Arlington House, the antebellum home of Robert E. Lee. No resting place could have been more fitting. In row upon row they lie, Orlando and many of the men who served alongside him, in a final bivouac, forever guarding the capital of the Union they had defended in time of civil war. Here it may at last be said that all is quiet along the Potomac.

The life of Orlando Willcox makes up but a single thread in the tapestry of our nation's history. But it is a significant thread, tightly woven, intertwined

48. Article, "Death of General Willcox," *Cobourg World*, May 17, 1907; Certificate of Registration of Death, OBW Collection; obituary of OBW, *Washington Post*, May 15, 1907; burial certificate for OBW, issued by the quartermaster general, U.S. War Department, May 15, 1907, OBW Collection.

with the threads of other prominent individuals, and without it the fabric would be all the weaker.

In the ninety years and more since his death, the name of Orlando Willcox has slipped into comparative obscurity; there it would have remained had he never made the effort to record his life in his journals, letters, and memoirs, and had his family not sought to preserve them. Through his writing we come to know him, not simply as a figure from our past, but as a man. He has shared his innermost thoughts and fears with us. We have been with him on the plain at West Point and on the road to Mexico City. We have hunted buffalo with him on the plains and have marched with him through mob-filled streets of Boston. We have faced the storm of battle with him when he was wounded and captured at Bull Run, and we have spent thirteen months in prison with him as well. We have heard the din of battle again at South Mountain and Antietam and a host of other fields, and we have dined with President Lincoln and seen the face of a man who bore the burdens of a nation trying to rip itself apart.

Through his memoirs and private journals, Orlando Willcox has revealed himself in a most intimate and human way, and we at last are able to recognize the forgotten valor of a man and an age long past.

In a larger, sense, however, in having read the memoirs of Orlando Willcox we have not only come to know him as a person but have learned something about ourselves as Americans—and we emerge all the richer for it.

Good-bye, general. It has been a pleasure to have met you.

Appendix A

NOTES AND JOURNAL OF CAPT. IRA C. ABBOTT RELATING TO THE FIRST
BATTLE OF BULL RUN, WITH COMMENTS BY ORLANDO B. WILLCOX

July 20. Remained at Centerville all day, during which [I] recd. orders from Genl. Heintzelman (Comdg. Div.) for an advance early next morning (1 o'c). About 10 A.M. Maj. Bidwell sent for me & proposed that in view of the fight expected next day we make up our differences, to which I agreed, & with a cordial shake of the hand we parted for the night, & from that time I had no better friend in the regt.

21st. Battle of Bull Run. At one o'clock A.M. [the] regt. [was] in line & ready to move. There was a delay until about sun rise, when we heard artillery in the distance, when our march began for Sudley Ford. Immediately after crossing Cub Run we turned to the right, & our line of march was thro timber most of the way. (Mem. It was very hot & exhausting. OBW). Sudley Springs Ford is about 12 miles from Centerville. It was reached about 11½ o'clock. The day was very hot, & [there] being no water from Cub Run to Sudley Springs, our men were nearly famished with thirst. On reaching [the] ford, canteens were filled & we fell back on the bluff for dinner.

From this point we could plainly see the movement of troops & explosion of shells in the air & hear the crash of arms. At 2 o'clock our regt. was ordered to the front to support Arnold's Battery & immediately advanced, crossing Bull Run (Sudley Springs) up the road to Sudley Springs Church, filed to the left into a field & took up a position at the right of the battery, lying down upon the ground. (Mem. Capt. Richard Arnold's Battery, 2d Arty., was attached to my brigade. A. himself was a captain in the 5th Arty. His officers were Lieuts. Barringer & Throckmorton. OBW.)

This position was maintained for about ½ hour, when we were ordered to advance. Accordingly [we] moved to the right across a ravine on to an open field. Marching by [the] flank & filing to the left along the ravine, we came in range of rebel batteries. The 1st man who fell was Color Sergt——, struck by a shell which severed his head from his body.

The regt. was thrown into column by platoons to avoid as much as possible the deadly effect of the battery upon our line. While marching (viz. to support the 11th Fire Zouaves. OBW) in this order a shell passed along in front of my first platoon, the effect of which was to throw every man in the front rank to the ground & sent me spinning about 10 feet. None however were hurt.

We were soon in front of rebel infantry & the order of march was changed back to the flank & threw in line of battle facing the enemy, There was a ravine between us & we moved forward to the bottom along a fence when we were ordered to commence firing. After a few rounds, an order was given by the major then in command to retreat or fall back. This order was communicated to all of the companies so that those on the left, B, G, K, held the ground, while 7 companies went to the rear following the major. (Mem. Capt. Ives says verbally that the right wing was commanded by Capt. Lum, acting lt. col., & the left wing by Capt. Withington, actg. major. Lt. Col. Comstock was absent on recruiting service. OBW.) This was owing, as Col. Willcox says in his report, to a mistake (I meant a "blunder" by the major. OBW). When the 7 companies fell back, Capt. Graves of Co. K discovered the move & came to me & says, "Abbott, for God's sake, what shall we do? The regt. is all going to Hell." I replied, "Captain, hold your men in position, we must retake that Battery" (Ricketts'). There being no field officer present with the three companies, I stepped to my 1st Lieut., [John M.] Casey, & directed him to take command of the co., & I being the senior officer with the 3 companies, I assumed command.

The battery was Ricketts', which was at our left & in front about 10 rods across the ravine, & being captured by rebel infantry. I ordered (mistake, I think, but Abbott probably recd. my order & then gave the command, following after me. OBW) an advance, & the enemy was routed by the charge, & for the time being the guns were in our possession.

In this charge I recd. a slight wound, my 1st Lieut. Casey was killed, & others of my little command were left on the field. Col. Willcox, while in command of his brigade, saw the condition of his regt., rode forward (rode *back*, OBW) faced the retiring companies to the front, & came to our relief. As soon as possible a line of battle was formed & the regt. moved forward (OBW in front of it. See reports of Maj. Bidwell & Col. Hobart Ward, Vol. II, *Reb Records*, also letter from War Dept. forwarding my Medal of Honor, made up from the records on file. OBW), driving the enemy from the field. As we arrived at the top of the ridge, behind which the enemy had retired, the stars & stripes were displayed at our left & in front & the cry was raised that we were firing upon our own men. That was a mistake, as it was only a decoy. As the facts were communicated to the col., he ordered a change of front forward on the 10th co., by the command, "Left Wheel!" When this order was about ½ executed, a fire from a piece of woods on our right upon us, the col's horse was killed (shot in the breast, looking towards the front, not to the right. OBW) & himself wounded (by the fire in *front*, OBW) . . . & seeing that himself & regt. must all fall into the hands of the rebels, ordered it to break & save themselves any way possible (don't remember such order, OBW).

As I turned to go to [the] rear I saw a man standing alone with the colors. I went to him & asked him what he was doing there. [He] Said, "not able to go any further." I took the flag & his musket & bade him follow, & taking a double quick I immediately gave orders to my company, "every man for himself & report to the Stone Church" (Sudley's). Accordingly the regt. went to pieces. I went to the rear over the ground upon which we had advanced, taking the colors with me. I passed several of my dead comrades & some wounded ones, to whom I rendered all the assistance I could. We had gone but a short distance when we heard the sound of horses' tramps; looking back [I] saw two cavalrymen on the gallop. We stopped, raised our muskets; they discharged their carbines & rode back.

On arriving near [the] church I met several of my company, one a Sergt. H. H. Powers, to whom I gave the colors, & halting, I formed them as they came up, what 1st Mich. men there were, [including] hundreds of troops coming off the field in a state of demoralization, & rallied [them] on the 1st Mich. colors. In ½ hour there must have been in line 1,000 men made up of several states of the North. Remaining in this position about an hour, about 150 1st Mich. had joined our colors.

The major came up & ordered our regt. into line & as soon as line was formed we moved toward Centerville. The route [was] filled with stragglers, & many places [were] blockaded by broken down wagons & ambulances. On reaching Cub Run, where the Centerville & Manassas Pike crosses, we found enemy had posted a battery about a mile back on the pike & on a ridge from which they commanded Cub Run bridge. Here the retreating forces were exposed to the deadly shells & solid shot as they were hurled from that position at this bridge; a section of Arty 2 guns (probably of Arnold's Battery, OBW) came up, & as the 1st gun went on bridge, the fore wheel struck against something & stopped the team. The rider jumped from his saddle, cut the traces & left the gun. A few cool heads now ran the gun over the bridge & let the other pass over. (See Arnold's report, Series 1, vol. 2, *Rebel. Record*, p. 416, which differs from this acct. He says the bridge had broken down & he had to spike two of his guns. But the gun helped over by Col. Abbott may have been one of the two saved. OBW) Maj. Bidwell dismounted. Here I noticed a 32 lb. Parrot gun dismounted & lying in a ditch, just across the bridge. Everything was confusion & disorder.

Our regt., or part of it, reached Centerville about 8 P.M. & went into camp on the ground we had left in the morning. Here we expected to remain over night. But about 10 o'c., when all was still except noise of moving wagon trains & arty., I recd. an order from the major to take command of the regt. & march direct to Washington. Accordingly I directed [the] adjt. to notify company officers to that effect, have the regt. formed, & prepare for a move at once. I requested the major to send me a horse, but was informed "none to spare." Placing myself at [the] head of regt. on foot, about 150 strong, [we] moved off.

The night [was] very dark & roads filled with men & teams, impossible to keep my men together. On arrival at the road leading toward Alexandria *via* Cloud's Mill, I halted & decided to go to Alexandria instead of Washington, in order to save, if possible, our sick left there, & camp & garrison equipage, under Capt. Clarkson on the 16th inst.

July 22. As soon as I had collected 40 men (4 A.M.) I moved on towards the mill. Arrived there about 6 o'c., immediately ordered all the sick who were unable to walk placed in wagons with knapsacks & guns, & taking what I could of regimental property, started for Alexandria. The men who were able to walk went on foot. I pushed on to the city to make arrangements for my sick & wounded, having with me about

40 men but no comd. officers. On arrival at Ft. Ellsworth was halted by a strong guard & directed to go into the fort. I left my men, went up to Genl. Runyon's quarters, stated circumstances & asked [for a] permit to take my men to the city. He gave me a pass for all my men with me & all who might come & I left a sergt. there to direct the men to City Hotel. I proceeded to the city, made arrangements for the sick & wounded at Washington St. Hospital, & then went to provost marshal for quarters for [the] men. He directed me to take 1st vacant building that would answer. Taking with me Sergt. Pomeroy, Co. B, [I] went down King St., & at corner (probably corner K & Washington) observed a large 3 story brick [building], with doors & shutters all closed & a man pacing up & down the side walk. Crossing over to him I asked if that was vacant. [He] replied, "Yes." I asked who had charge of it. [He] said he wished to know what I wanted it for. Told him qrs. for troops. He said it could not be had. I walked to the door, he following. I asked him to open it. He said he had no key. I then directed the sergt. to open it with his musket, which was done at once, by jamming off the lock. I sent a man back to the hotel & fort with instructions to send the men to quarters. Made requisition for rations for 200 men for 1 day, & by 12 o'c. I had 150 men without one commissioned officer, as all had gone to Washington.

Spent the p.m. getting in the regimental property from the mill, providing for the sick in quarters, & the wants of the men in general, & at 6 o'clock had dress parade, the companies in command of sergeants, Sergt. Pomeroy acting as sergt. major. The men were coming in constantly, & by midnight I had 250 men with 200 muskets.

23d. At 10 A.M. recd. an order from Maj. B. (presumably at Washington, OBW) to report forthwith with regt. at Washington. Capt. Clarkson made his appearance with his 1st Lieut. I went to Provost Marshal with my orders, who informed me that troops were allowed to leave city only on orders of Genl. Mansfield, then in Washington. Telegraphed copy of my orders for his endorsement, waiting until 2 P.M. & no answer. I sent Lt. Merethew up to Genl. M. Lt. returned about 5 with approval & at 5½ we took up line of march. Arriving at Long Bridge just after sundown, [we] met Messrs. Lincoln & Seward. As they rode past I brot [the] regt. to present arms, when they stopped, & Mr. Lincoln beckoned me to the carriage & gave me a warm & cordial grasp. He inquired what regt. it was, & in being told it was Col. Willcox's First Mich. Inf., he asked if that was all there was left. I informed him the col. was killed or a prisoner & that our loss could not at that time be estimated. The tears ran down his furrowed cheeks as he again took my hand & said good bye. The men gave three cheers for Abraham Lincoln.

We reached our quarters about 9 P.M., the same occupied on arrival, May 19. Here I found Maj. B., Capts. Roberts, Roth, Whittlesey, Hubbard & Clarkson (who came up in advance). Graves & Lum were wounded, Butterworth killed (not killed at once, had leg shot off, died in hospital, OBW). Capt. Withington & Lt. Parks (Co. H) prisoners.

24th. At roll call next morning I found my Co. loss 16 out of 44 taken into action, of whom Lt. Casey [was] killed (rest absent, wounded or missing).

Appendix B

Head Quarters 1st Division 9th Army Corps[1]
April 2nd, 1865
Colonel:

At ¼ past 4 o'clock on the morning of the 25th [March], the enemy attacked the entrenchments held by the 3rd Brigade of this division. The brigade picket officer, Capt. Burch, 3rd Md., reports that he visited the picket line at 4 o'clock of that a.m. and saw that the men were on the alert. After visiting the line, he returned to his headquarters in front of Fort Stedman and Battery No. 11. He states that in a few minutes after his return, a man on the lookout gave notice that the enemy were approaching. At the same time, the men on the post fired their pieces. One column moved toward the right of Battery No. 10; a second column moved towards a point between Fort Stedman and Battery No. 11; a third column moved direct towards Stedman. These columns were preceded by a strong storming party which broke through the pickets, clubbing their muskets, and made [an] opening in the abatis.

The trench guards made sufficient resistance to arouse the garrisons of the enclosed works in the immediate neighborhood, but the column which struck to the right of Battery No. 10 quickly succeeded in breaking through and effecting an entrance to that Battery, which is entirely open in the rear. This success gave them at once a great advantage over Fort Stedman, as the ground just in rear of Battery 10 is on a level with the parapet of the fort.

---

1. OBW's report, and others relating to Fort Stedman, can been found in *OR*, vol. 46, pt. 1; OBW's report is on pp. 322–25 of that volume.

The fort had also a comparatively small line of infantry parapet; particularly was this the case in front, which was cut up with embrasures for artillery. The garrison of the fort consisted of a detachment of the 14th N.Y. Heavy Artillery, under Major [George M.] Randall, and made quite a spirited resistance, but were finally over powered and most of them captured. The commanding officer of the brigade, Bvt. Brig. Gen. N. B. McLaughlen, had reached Battery No. 11 from his headquarters before this, and given some directions about the disposition of the troops on the left flank.

The guns and even the mortars in both Stedman and Battery No. 11 were used against the enemy. Detachments of the 1st Conn. Heavy Artillery, at the mortars, behaved very handsomely. General McLaughlen was captured near the gorge of the fort, but whether after the enemy had got into, or while they were attacking, is unknown. Captain Swords, ordnance officer on my staff and division staff officer of the day, also reached Fort Stedman, from these headquarters, before it was fully in the enemy's possession, and was captured at the fort.

The right [Confederate] column, with the aid of troops from Stedman, now succeeded in gaining Battery No. 11. Their left column turned down the works to their left, towards Battery No. 9, taking the 57th Mass., in the trenches, in the flank and rear, capturing a part of them. The remainder retired to the rear, reassembled, and afterwards did good work as skirmishers with General Hartranft's troops. The 2nd Mich. fought the enemy on this flank from their bomb-proofs and traverses, in the most spirited manner, until they were drawn in by order of their brigade commander, Bvt. Col. Ralph Ely, to Battery No. 9, which, though small, is an enclosed work.

In pursuance of my orders, Col. Ely deployed, perpendicular to and to the rear of his entrenchments, a portion of the 1st Mich. S.S. as skirmishers, promptly taking them from the right of our line for this purpose. I also directed him to press the enemy on his left as much as possible. Finding themselves opposed in this direction, the enemy halted for more of their troops to come up.

The enemy's skirmishers now came down the hill directly to the rear of Stedman, and moved towards my headquarters, the Friend House, the Dunn House Battery, and in the direction of Meade's Station, and for a time rendered my communication with the 3rd Brigade long and circuitous. Meantime, I had ordered out the 17th Michigan, acting as engineer regiment at my headquarters, and sent word to the commanding officers of the 200th and 209th Penn., encamped between Meade's Station and [the] Dunn House Battery, to move, respectively, one to the Friend House, the other in front of the Dunn House Battery. These regiments promptly appeared.

Brig. Gen. Hartranft, commanding the 3rd Division, now came up in person, and I requested him to move his available force direct upon the fort. He promptly and gallantly took command of the two regiments already out, without waiting for the rest of his command. I ordered the 17th Michigan to deploy as skirmishers on his right. This regiment, with only one hundred (100) men in its ranks, under command of Major Mathews, moved forward at the same time with General Hartranft's line, capturing most of the enemy's skirmishers in their front, about twenty-five (25) in number, and, including the right, connected with the skirmishers of Ely's brigade.

While Hartranft was operating in rear of Stedman, the enemy's force, which had moved towards Battery No. 9 and halted, was reinforced by Ransom's Brigade,[2] and opened an attack upon that battery. This attack was handsomely repulsed by my skirmishers and troops of the 2nd Brigade in Battery 9, assisted by the artillery, particularly one piece of Roemer's Battery, under Major Roemer himself. The enemy attempted to retreat back to his own entrenchments, when they were charged by detachments of the 2nd Michigan, who captured some prisoners. Troops of the 20th and 2nd Mich. also threw themselves into the picket line of the 2nd Brigade, and poured such a fire on the flanks of the retreating enemy, that over three hundred (300) threw down their arms and surrendered themselves on the spot.

On our left, the enemy proceeded through the trenches, driving before them the 29th Mass., a small regiment, which made the best resistance it could, over its traverses and works, being attacked in front, flank and rear. From Battery No. 11 they [the enemy] proceeded towards Battery No. 12, in the same manner, killing, wounding and capturing a part of the 100th Penn. In this attack, Colonel [Joseph H.] Pentecost, commanding 100th Penn., was mortally wounded. A part of this regiment was deployed as skirmishers in the rear, and a part went into Fort Haskell. Bvt. Col. Robinson took a part of the 3rd Md. from a portion of his line on the left of Haskell, and deployed it on the left of the skirmish line of the 100th Penn. Soon afterwards, by my directions, Colonel Robinson assumed command of the 3rd Brigade.

I would here state that last winter, when it was thought that the enemy were mining towards Stedman, I gave directions to the brigade commanders that, in the event of the line being broken at Stedman or any other point, they should immediately take out troops where they could best be spared from their respective front, and attack the flanks of the enemy, and by no means to abandon their works. This order was handsomely carried out by the brigade and regimental commanders on this occasion, and led to the most beneficial results.

In pursuance to this order, Col. [Samuel] Harriman, commanding [the] 1st Brigade of this division and posted on the left of the 3rd Brigade, ordered up the 109th New York and 37th Wis. Vols., to report to Gen. McLaughlen, but as Gen. McLaughlen could not be found, these two regiments were formed in line in rear of the skirmishers already mentioned, and entrenched themselves to resist the large force moving down the rear of the line towards Haskell. The enemy was now confronted on this flank by the troops in Fort Haskell, and the skirmishers of the 100th Penn. and 3rd Md. The enemy made three (3) advances upon Fort Haskell, all of which were gloriously repulsed.

Meantime, several ineffectual attempts were made by General Hartranft, with a portion of his division, to regain Fort Stedman by an advance on the rear of that work, but very soon after the repulse of the enemy at Fort Haskell, the 2nd Brigade of Hartranft's division came up and formed on his left, the left of this brigade stretching towards Fort Haskell. On the appearance of this new line, the enemy, already repulsed on both flanks and considerably demoralized by the fire of our well-served artillery, were seen breaking away in small detachments from Stedman back to their own lines.

2. Brig. Gen. Matt W. Ransom, elder brother of Confederate Brig. Gen. Robert Ransom, Jr., led a brigade of Maj. Gen. Bushrod Johnson's division.

This was quickly perceived by our troops on all sides. Major Maxwell, 100th Penn, with the skirmishers of his regiment under Captains [John L.] Johnson and Book, and those of the 3rd Md. under Captain Carter, immediately started along the trenches towards Stedman, capturing a large number of prisoners in the bomb-proofs, from Battery No. 12 to Battery No. 10. The first Union colors on the recaptured fort were planted there by Sergt. Oliver, 100th Penn. Vols., who captured a stand of rebel colors at the same point and at the same time with his own hands. Hartranft's line advanced rapidly, enveloping the rear of the works. The 17th Mich., on the extreme right, dashed forward and gained the trenches lately occupied by the 57th Mass., but now held by the enemy, capturing prisoners on that side.

The retreat of the enemy was soon cut off by the troops of this division gaining the rear of the main body along the parapet of the works, and a large number of prisoners and some colors were captured by the troops of both divisions. One thousand and five (1005) prisoners, besides some of the wounded, fell into the hands of my own command, also seven (7) of the enemy's colors, together with one of our own flag staffs, recaptured.

It was found, on regaining our works, that the enemy, while they held possession of them, were not able to carry off or effect any damage on our artillery, which they temporarily held and partially used against Battery No. 9 and Fort Haskell; they carried one Coehorn mortar over the parapet, but it was regained, and not the least damage was inflicted upon any of the gun carriages. No colors or guns were lost by us.

The following are the names of the captors of [the] enemy's colors in this division: Captain John L. Johnson, Co. B, 100th Penn. Vet. Vols; Captain Jos. F. Carter, 3rd Md. Battln. Vet. Vols.; Sgt. Major Chas. H. Pinkham, 57th Mass. Vols.; Color Sgt. Charles Oliver, Co. M, 100th Penn. Vet. Vols.; Corporal M. D. Dewire, Co. A, 100th Penn., captured a rebel staff and recaptured one of ours; Private John B. Chambers, Co. F, 100th Penn. Vet. Vols.; Private Pat McCran, Co. C, 3rd Md. Battln. Vet. Vols.; Private James K. Brady, 14th New York Heavy Artillery.

The following is a tabular statement of casualties, the nominal list having already been forwarded:

O Officers
M Men (enlisted)
A Aggregate

Command	Killed		Wounded		Missing		Total		
	O	M	O	M	O	M	O	M	A
First Brigade	—	—	—	—	—	—	—	—	—
Second Brigade	—	4	3	23	—	19	3	46	49
Third Brigade	1	32	15	120	17	413	33	565	598
Total	1	36	18	143	17	432	36	611	647

I also forward herewith the reports of the commanders of the 2nd and 3rd Brigades, and respectfully call attention to the recommendations for gallantry therein contained.

Of my own staff, all of whom were active throughout the engagement, I would honorably mention Capt. L. C. Brackett, 57th Mass. Vols., for gallantry in assisting in the charge of the 3rd Division, and Bvt. Maj. William Richards, U. S. Vols., [for] carrying orders and gaining information under heavy fire. I am,

Very respectfully,

O. B. Willcox

Bvt. Maj. Gen., Commanding

Lt. Col. P. M. Lydig,

Asst. Adjt. General, 9th Army Corps.

This work is primarily based on the unpublished papers of Orlando Bolivar Willcox. At the time of writing, those papers remain in private hands. However, numerous other sources, including books, articles, essays, and public documents, have been consulted in preparing this edition. While many of those works are obscure volumes, long out of print, many others are easily accessible to the reader through bookstores or public libraries.

The purpose of this essay is not to cite every source consulted in editing *Forgotten Valor*; it is rather to refer the reader to important, easily accessible sources relating to Orlando Willcox's life and career, with particular emphasis on his military service.

The best published source (though long out of print) for life in Detroit at the time of OBW's youth is Gen. Friend Palmer's *Early Days in Detroit* (Detroit: Hunt & June, 1906). Palmer, a friend of OBW, recounts much of the town's history, recalling many of its citizens, both prominent and obscure, including some episodes involving OBW himself.

John G. Waugh's *The Class of 1846* (New York: Warner Books, 1994) is by far the finest source on West Point at the time OBW (Class of 1847) attended. An indispensable reference work is *Reminiscences of West Point in the Olden Time, and Register of Graduates of the United States Military Academy to September 1st, 1886* (Saginaw, Mich., 1886), listing the graduates of each class, beginning with the first in 1802, with graduates listed in order of standing. The editor had the privilege of working from OBW's personal copy.

John S. D. Eisenhower's *So Far from God: The U.S. War with Mexico, 1846–1848* (New York: Random House, 1989) remains the best one-volume treatment of the conflict that prepared so many officers for the Civil War. For army life on the plains in the 1850s, the editor found Robert N. Utley's *Frontiersmen in Blue: The United States Army and the Indian, 1848–1865* (Lincoln: University of Nebraska Press, 1981) to be very informative.

For the Anthony Burns riot I found Virginia Hamilton's *Anthony Burns: The Defeat and Triumph of a Fugitive Slave* (New York: Knopf Books, 1989), a book for young adults, surprisingly helpful, as so little has been published on that event.

As for the Civil War, a number of important reference works are invaluable to any researcher of the conflict. Foremost, of course, is *The War of the Rebellion: A Compilation of the Official Records of the Union and Confederate Armies*, 128 vols. (Washington, D.C.: U.S. Government Printing Office, 1880–1901). Familiarly referred to as the *Official Records* or simply the *OR*, the work contains campaign and battle reports and dispatches from officers on both sides. General officers in the U.S. Army who had served during the war were given advance copies of the published records on request.

OBW referred to these often while preparing his manuscript, as well as to his own reports and dispatches, many of which were never published in the series.

Patricia Faust, ed., *Historical Times Illustrated Encyclopedia of the Civil War* (New York: Harper & Row, 1986) was a handy reference as well, as it contains biographical sketches of most of the major and many of the minor figures of the war, as well as entries for campaigns, battles, ordnance, etc. E. B. Long's *The Civil War Day by Day: An Almanac, 1861–1865* (Garden City, N.Y.: Doubleday, 1971) is indispensable. And of course the classic edition of Robert U. Johnson and Clarence C. Buel, eds. *Battles and Leaders of the Civil War,* 4 vols. (New York: Century, 1884–1889) was an important source. The work is a collection of firsthand accounts by the leading participants in the Civil War, a priceless and underappreciated treasure for the Civil War scholar. Volume 4 contains an article by OBW, "Actions on the Weldon Railroad" (pp. 568–73).

Regarding published memoirs of leading Civil War generals, OBW constantly referred to George B. McClellan's *McClellan's Own Story* (New York: Charles L. Webster, 1886) and Ulysses S. Grant, *Personal Memoirs of Ulysses S. Grant,* 2 vols. (New York: Charles L. Webster, 1885) while writing his own story. Horace Porter's *Campaigning with Grant* (Bloomington: Indiana University Press, reprint 1961) is arguably the finest memoir of a staff officer to come out of the war. Porter, who served on Grant's staff, provides a rare, intensely observant, and up-close glimpse of Grant and his campaigns, from Chattanooga to Appomattox. Also of import are Gen. James Longstreet, *From Manassas to Appomattox* (Bloomington: Indiana University Press, reprint, 1960), and William T. Sherman, *Memoirs of Gen. W. T. Sherman* (New York: Charles L. Webster, 1891).

For biographies, the reader would do well to consult Douglas Southall Freeman, *R. E. Lee,* 4 vols. (New York: Charles Scribner's Sons, 1934–1935). For readers serious about studying Lee, however, I would strongly recommend Alan T. Nolan, *Lee Considered: General Robert E. Lee and Civil War History* (Chapel Hill: University of North Carolina Press, 1991), which provides balance to Freeman's fine but understandably biased work. Also by Freeman, *Lee's Lieutenants: A Study in Command,* 3 vols. (New York: Charles Scribner's Sons, 1942–1944) offers excellent insight in the Army of Northern Virginia and its officers. William S. McFeely's Pulitzer Prize–winning *Grant: A Biography* (New York: W. W. Norton, 1981) is highly recommended, and Stephen W. Sears, *George B. McClellan: The Young Napoleon* (New York: Ticknor & Fields, 1988), is the best appraisal of "Little Mac" to date. Also of import by Sears is *The Civil War Papers of George B. McClellan* (New York: Ticknor & Fields, 1989). William Marvel's *Burnside* (Chapel Hill: University of North Carolina Press, 1991) proved a valuable source, particularly for the campaigns in east Tennessee.

Particularly valuable in identifying the many obscure officers mentioned by OBW in his memoirs was Thomas H. S. Hamersly, ed., *Complete Regular Army Register of the United States: For One Hundred Years, 1779–1879* (Washington, D.C., 1881).

Those researching Michigan regiments in the Civil War are fortunate to have at their disposal George H Turner, comp., *Record of Service of Michigan Volunteers in the Civil War, 1861–1865,* 46 vols. (Kalamazoo: Ihling Bros. & Everard Stationers, 1903). The first volume is devoted to *The First Michigan Infantry,* containing a complete roster and brief sketch of service for the officers and enlisted men of the regiment. A good single-volume work is Jonathan Robertson, comp., *Michigan in the War* (Lansing, Mich.: W. S. George, 1882), containing capsule histories of the state's various regiments. The Michigan Civil War Cenennial Observance Commission's *A Study in Valor: Michigan Medal of Honor Winners in the Civil War* (Ann Arbor: Publications Committee, 1966) offers thumbnail sketches of the state's Medal of Honor winners, including several members of OBW's 1st Michigan Infantry. The story regarding Willcox's Medal of Honor is told on pp. 58–59.

For the Battle of Manassas, William C. Davis's *Battle at Bull Run* (Baton Rouge: Louisiana State University Press, 1977) remains a popular favorite. For a description of the prisons in which OBW was incarcerated, and of many others, see Lonnie R. Speer, *Portals to Hell* (Mechanicsburg, Pa.: Stackpole Books, 1997). For the Battle of South Mountain, see John Michael Priest, *Before Antietam: The Battle of South Mountain* (New York: Oxford University Press, 1997). Stephen Sears, *Landscape Turned Red: The Battle of Antietam* (New Haven: Ticknor & Fields, 1983) is still the definitive source on that battle; also of interest is Francis W. Palfrey, *The Antietam and Fredericksburg* (New York: Charles Scribner's Sons, 1882), to which OBW referred in writing on both battles.

A modern study of the Battle of Fredericksburg is desperately needed, but the editor found Edward J. Stackpole's *Drama on the Rappahannock: The Fredericksburg Campaign* (Harrisburg, Pa.: Military Service Publishing, 1957) to be helpful.

Morgan's Ohio raid and the Knoxville campaign are both covered in William Marvel's previously cited biography *Burnside*. Dee Alexander Brown's *Morgan's Raiders* (New York: Smithmark, 1994) is an informative source as well. Longstreet's *From Manassas to Appomattox* is also a good source for the Knoxville campaign, from the Confederate point of view.

For Grant's campaign of 1864–1865, the reader might want to begin with Robert Garth Scott, *Into the Wilderness with the Army of the Potomac* (Bloomington: Indiana University Press, 1992). William D. Matter, *If It Takes All Summer: The Battle of Spotsylvania Court House* (Chapel Hill: University of North Carolina Press, 1988), is also helpful. OBW himself frequently referred to Andrew Humphreys, *The Virginia Campaign of 1864 and 1865* (New York: Charles Scribner's Sons, 1883). Noah Andre Trudeau's *Bloody Roads South: The Wilderness to Cold Harbor, May–June 1864* (Boston: Little, Brown, 1989) and *The Last Citadel: Petersburg, Virginia, June 1864–April 1865* (Boston: Little, Brown, 1991) are noteworthy, the latter work being the finest book yet written on Petersburg.

The editor relied heavily on volume four of Freeman's *R. E. Lee* for events that occurred during OBW's reign as military commander of the subdistrict of Lynchburg, Virginia. Kenneth M. Stampp, *The Era of Reconstruction, 1865–1877* (New York: Alfred A. Knopf, 1966) and Eric Foner, *Reconstruction: America's Unfinished Revolution, 1863–1877* (New York: HarperCollins, 1989), are two excellent studies on that crucial period of American history.

Finally, for the period that OBW commanded the Department of Arizona, the editor would recommend Robert M. Utley, *Frontier Regulars: The United States Army and the Indian, 1866–1891* (New York: Macmillan, 1973).

Those interested in more obscure sources consulted in editing this work should refer to the chapter notes.

§ INDEX

698

Baltimore: as hotbed of secession, 251–52, 257; secured by Union troops, 259

Bankhead, Henry C., 567

Banks, Nathaniel P., 398

Barbour, William M. (CSA), 521, 585

Barlow, Francis C., xiv, xix, xx, 512, 524, 542, 545

Barnes, Joseph H., 568

Barney, Dr. (CSA), 308

Barradas, Isidro, 96–97

Bartlett, William H. C., 58

Bartow, Francis S., 290

Baxter, Henry, wounded, 514

Beall, Benjamin L. (1st Dragoons), 141, 150; OBW's description of, 137–38

Beaman, Fernando, 417, 610

Beardsley, Sergeant (1st Mich.), 284

Beaubien, J. B., 25

Beaufait, Capt. Louis, 124, 125

Beauregard, P. G. T., 290, 297, 301

Bee, Barnard E., 60, 290

Beecher, Henry Ward: campaigns for donations to Washington College, 664; description of, 319; quoted, 318–19

Beltzhoover, Daniel M., 52, 87

Benham, Henry W., 639

Benjamin, Judah P., 314

Benjamin, Samuel N. (Battery E, 2d U. S. Arty.), 381, 402, 473, 521

Bennet, Maj. Stephen, 93

Bennett, Benjamin G. (1st Mich.), 251

Benton, Thomas Hart, 47, 98, 677

Berard, Claude (West Point instructor), 59, 88, 121

Bermuda Hundred, 566

Bertrand, Henri Gratien, 74

Biddle, James (71st Ind.), 429, 430, 431

Bidwell, Alonzo F. (1st Mich.), 249; at Bull Run, 294, 683, 687, 688, 689, 690

Big Dry Wash, Battle of, 674, 677; OBW's report of, 674–75

Bingham, Thomas (2d Dragoons), 162

Bintliff, James, 639, 641

Birney, David B., commands Tenth Corps, at Second Deep Bottom, 566; at Fort Harrison, 574–75; division of, at Wilderness, 514, 515

Black, Henry M., 87

Black Codes, 655

Black Hawk (Chief of the Sacs), 27, 29

Black Hawk War, 22, 27–31

Black troops, at Battle of the Crater, 550, 552, 554, 555, 557, 558–59, 560, 561; in assault on Fort Gilmer, 575

Blackburn's Ford, engagement at, 288

Blair, Austin (Mich. gov.): 3, 239, 244, 250, 398, 666; calls for volunteers, 246; reluctant to designate 1st Mich. for three years service, 274, 275, 288; on Israel B. Richardson, 250; quoted, 242

Blair, Francis P., 43

Blake, Cyrus (grandfather of Marie Willcox), 345, 350

Blake, Louise, 400

Blodgett, Abigail (wife of William T.), 477, 595

Blodgett, William T., 283, 339, 342, 344, 366, 367, 417, 477, 587; campaigns for OBW's promotion to major general, 415, 416; OBW's affection for, 595; visits OBW in camp, 588

Blue Springs, Tenn., engagement at, 464–65

Boag, Lt. (CSA), 313, kindness toward Union prisoners, 311, 315, 316

Bolio, Franklin (1st Mich.), 337, 338

Bomford, James V., 327

Bonham, Milledge L., 260; report quoted, 266

Book, Capt. (100th Pa.), 694

Booth, John Wilkes, 645

Booth, Junius Brutus, 60

Boston, OBW stationed at, 194–202

Bowers, Theodore S., 611

Bowlegs, Billy (William Cruikshanks, Seminole chief), 205, 207, 208, 211

Bowman, Henry, (a.q.m. to OBW), 371, 488, 493, 572, 573, 576, 586, 587; injured, 497; OBW's opinion of, 375; as prisoner of war, 314, 321, 327

Boyle, Jeremiah T., 431, 432, 484, 492

Brackett, A. G. (2d U.S. Cav.), 254n. 12

Brackett, Levi C. (a.d.c. to OBW), 368, 372, 375, 400, 402, 414, 415, 460, 485, 582; accompanies OBW to Indiana, 426; affection for "Lulu" Willcox, 573; on "Applejack Raid," 594, 596; at Battle of the Crater, 557, 558–59; Christmas dinner with OBW, 597; death of father, 488; escorts Marie Willcox to Washington, 407; at Fort Stedman, 621, 631, 695; at Grant's headquarters, 609, 611, 612; as ladies' man, 455, 607; letter to Marie Willcox concerning the Battle

in Knoxville Campaign, 445, 462, 468, 472, 476, 478, 480, 485, 486, 488; relieved from command of, 475
—at Fredericksburg: council of war, 391; on Franklin's failure to carry out orders at, 389–90; and lost pontoon bridges, 383–84; orders to OBW at, 385; plan of assault at, 383; plans for second assault at, 404; pressured to make assault at, 404; reliance on Franklin at, 387–91
Burnside, Mrs. Ambrose E., brother's family drowns, 601
Burnside's (Rohrbach) Bridge, Antietam battlefield, xxii, 359
Butler, Benjamin F., at Baltimore, 259; at Bermuda Hundred, 566, 583; commands Army of the James, 525; at New Orleans, 319; relieved of command, 599
Butler, Gen. William O., 115
Butterfield, Daniel, 262, 387, 416
Butterworth, Ebenezer B. (1st Mich.), 243, 244n. 16, 249, 268; in First Bull Run campaign, 284, 287; death of, 303n. 21; mortally wounded, 302, 690; writes to OBW, 303
Button, Charles W., 666

Cadillac, Antoine De La Mothe, 246
Cadwallader, George S., 112
Calhoun, Sen. John C., OBW describes, 46
Call, Richard K., 206
Caloosahatchee River, OBW's description of, 216
Camp Morton, Ind., 432, 445, 455
Camp Nelson, Ky., 424, 462, 476
Campau, Joseph, 15
Campbell, David, 548
Campbell, John A., 603, 604
Campbell's Station, Tenn., engagement at, 468
Carr, Eugene, 671, 672–73
Carrington, Henry B., intoxicated, 439–40; OBW's estimation of, 428; political pawn of Governor Morton, 427–28
Carter, Joseph F. (3rd Md.): in capture of Petersburg, 626; at Fort Stedman, 617, 620–27, 631, 632, 694
Carter, Samuel P., 447, 451, 452, 497; action at Blue Springs, Tenn., 464–65;

commands provisional division, Ninth Corps, 426
Casey, John M. (1st Mich.), 688, 690
Cass, Lewis: 3, 120, 242, 243, 350; OBW's opinion of, 121; reviews 1st Mich., 250; supports raising of Michigan troops, 241
Castle Pinckney, 308, 309; OBW incarcerated at, 311, 312, 333
Caw Indians, 144, 164; OBW encounters, 142
Center, John P. (6th U.S. Inf.), 223, 224
Cerro Gordo, Battle of, 104, 107, 115
Chaffee, Adna R. (6th U.S. Cav.), 674
Chambers, John B. (100th Pa.), 694
Chambloss, Capt. (quartermaster), 380, 384
Chandler, Sen. Zachariah, 4, 239, 261, 274, 276, 281, 350, 549, 657; accompanies 1st Mich. to front, 254; Fanny Ricketts requests assistance in OBW's promotion, 581; OBW requests assistance in gaining promotion, 413, 414; to raise regiment, 344; supports raising of Michigan troops, 241; visits Army of Potomac after Fredericksburg, 406;
Chantilly, Battle of, 351
Chapultepec, Battle of, 91, 107
Charleston, S.C., city jail: condition of, 310–11; OBW incarcerated at, 309–13;
Charleston S.C., fire in, 317
Chattanooga, Tenn., Battle of, 472
Chicago: cholera epidemic at, 29–30; early history, 22–32; OBW's first visit to, 31–32
Childs, George W., 347
Christ, Benjamin C., 351, 515, 579; brigade of, at Cold Harbor, 526–28; at Ny River, 518, 519; at Petersburg, 542–43; at Wilderness, 515; mustered out of service, 595; wounded, 543–44
Church, Albert Ensign (West Point instructor), 59, 669
Churubusco, Battle of, 91, 107
Cibicu Creek Affair: 671–73, 676
Cicotte, Francois, 243, 246
Clark, Joseph C. (Battery E, 4th U.S. Arty.), 360
Clarke, Annie L.: as character witness for OBW in court-martial, 62; OBW's relationship with, 49, 88
Clarke, Johnny, 49

Clarke, Matthew St. Clair, 49

Clarke, Newman S., 139

Clarkson, Isaac L. (1st Mich.), 243, 244n. 16, 249, 277, 689, 690

Clay, Mrs. Henry, 451

Clay, Henry: OBW describes, 46, 239; mentioned, 451

Clay, William (boyhood friend of OBW), 20

Clinch, Duncan L., 206

Clinch River, engagement at. *See* Walker's Ford

Clingman, T. L. (CSA), 525

Clitz, Henry B., 18n. 10, 51, 60

Cluke, R. S. (CSA), 422

Coale, John H. (commisary officer), 375, 378, 393, 394, 398, 403, 585

Cochise (Apache chief), 674

Cochrane, John, 392

Cocke, Philip St. George, 259, 260

Coffin, John N., 354

Cold Harbor, attack of June 3, 527–28, 541; strategic importance of, 525; Federals approach, 522; Federal casualties at, 541; Federal withdrawal from, 541

Cole, Ed, 124, 128

Cole, Eliza, 126

Cole, Porter, 49, 72, 78; resigns from West Point, 76, 77

Columbia Prison (S.C.), condition of, 317; OBW incarcerated at, 317–20, 335–36

Commanche Indians, 155

Committee on the Conduct of the War, 347

Comstock, Loren L. (1st Mich.), 249; considers resigning, 275

Confederacy, possibility of foreign recognition of, 318

Conger, James L., 171

Connecticut regiments: 1st Heavy Artillery, 692; 8th Infantry, 384

Contreras, Battle of, 91, 100, 107

Cook, Asa M. (8th Battery, Mass. Lt. Arty.), 354, 360, 402

Cooke, John R. (CSA), brigade refuses to charge, 605

Corcoran, Michael, 320, 325, 347, 446; dines with Lincoln, 348n. 2; as hostage for privateers, 313–14; at Libby Prison, 322; at Ligon Tobacco Factory prison, 320; OBW's opinion of, 322, 337; as

prisoner of war, 308, 310; released from prison, 327

Couch, Darius N., 395, 412; and Anthony Burns riot, 200; commands Second Corps, 381, 385, 387

Cox, Jacob D., 493; commands Twenty-third Corps, 496, 502; to command Dept. of Kentucky, 492; in Maryland campaign, 353, 359–60, 361, 363, 365; to leave for western Virginia, 369

Cox, Thomas (1st Ky.), 314

Coyota (Chief of the Arapahoes), 149, 158

Crater, Battle of the, 549–64; Burnside blamed for, 554; casualties at, 550; compared to Fort Stedman, 556; court of inquiry regarding, 555, 564; OBW on failures of, 554–57, 563; OBW on use of black troops at, 554, 555, 557; OBW's letters regarding, 557, 561–64; OBW's report on, 551–54; public repercusions of, 562

Crawford, Samuel W., at Burgess' Mill, 582–83; Division of, at Petersburg, June 17 and 18 assault, 543, 545; at Weldon R.R., 567, 568; wounded, 364

Creek Indians, 205

Crittenden, John J., 175, 424

Crittenden, Thomas L., 520, 543n. 2

Crocker, Charles, 18

Crook, George, on the Apache Indian, 670; brigade of, 359, 360; commands Dept. of Arizona, 670, 678

Crosby, Pierce (capt., U.S.N.), 419

Cruikshanks, William. *See* Bowlegs, Billy

Cullum, George W., 383

Cumberland Gap, 462, 478; description of terrain, 479–80; engagement at, 476; falls to Union forces, 467; OBW's defense of, 467–75; strategic importance of, 467

Curtin, John I. (brigade), 545

Curtis, Joseph B. (4th R.I.), 387

Cushing, Caleb: OBW describes, 47; in Mexican War, 101

Cushman, Charlotte, 193

Custer, George A.: brevetted major general, 580; cavalry brigade, 517, 523

Cutcheon, Byron M. (20th Mich.): brigade of, 578; at Ny River, 518, 519

Cutts, Adele (Mrs. Stephen A. Douglas), 91–92

Cutts, James Madison, 91, 390

Dade Massacre, 205

Dade, Francis L., 205

Dana, James J.; 368–69, 374, 376, 379–80, 394, 397–98, 401, 403, 407, 409: OBW wishes to acquire as quartermaster, 375, 377, 394, 399

Dana, Napoleon J. T., wounded, 364

Dana, Richard Henry, 194

Darby, Dr. (CSA), 298, 299

Dashiel, Rev. T. G., 321

Davis, George (husband of Mira Willcox), death of, 238

Davis, Jefferson, 4, 607; as U.S. secretary of war, 196, 200, 201; Confederate president, 315, 316; Confederate soldiers' disdain for, 599

Davis, Mira Willcox (sister of OBW), 189; OBW fears for life of, 477; OBW visits, 170; visits OBW at Fort Ontario, 190; widowed, 238

de Janon, Patrice (West Point instructor), 59

de Mowbray, Elizabeth Abbott (OBW's great-granddaughter), and Willcox papers, xiv–xx

de Mowbray, Stuart (OBW's great-great-grandson), xvi–xvii, xx

De Russy, John, 56

Dearborn, O. M. (a.d.c. to OBW), 401

DeCourcy, John F., 467

Deep Bottom, 566

Delafield, Richard (West Point superintendent), 57, 76

Deland, Charles V. (1st Mich. S.S.), 432

Dempsey, Lt. (69th N.Y.), 325

Denny, St. Clair, 120

DeRussy, Gustavus A., 402

Deshon, George, 54

Detroit, 17; celebration welcoming OBW home from prison, 3, 346, 349–50, 352; cholera epidemic at, 29; Hull's surrender of, 13n. 3, 124–26; OBW's boyhood at, 11, 32–40; OBW moves to after Seminole war, 233, 234; OBW returns to after Civil War, 653; OBW visits after Mexican War, 119–28

Devin, Thomas C. (cavalry brigade), 517

Dewire, M. D. (100th Pa.), 694

Dibrell, George G. (CSA), 473, 474

Dickenson, George (Battery E, 4th U.S. Arty.), 385, 387

Dix, Dorothea, 280

Dix, John A., 418, 566; OBW's estimation of, 419

Dodge, Rev. G. W. (11th N.Y.), 311, 320

Doe, Joseph A. (asst. Sec. of War), 682

Doubleday, Abner, 399

Douglas, Henry Kyd, xx

Douglas, Stephen A., 175, 239

Downey, John (11th N.Y.), 321

Duffield, D. Bethune, 189, 247

Duffield, Rev. Dr. George, 21, 33, 73, 80, 121, 122, 128, 247; advises OBW to attend West Point, 41, 173; quoted, 177–78

Duke, Basil: captured, 443; quoted, 436, 441

Dupont, Samuel F., 313

duSable, Jean Baptiste Point (early black settler of Chicago), 26

D'Utassy, F. G., 287n. 3

Dutton, William, 63

Dyer, Alexander B., 646

Early, Jubal A. (CSA): Corps of, 523, 524, 546, 547; in Valley Campaign, 565–66, 577

East Tennessee: hardship of inhabitants in, 465–66, 478, 479–80, 496; campaign in, object of Federal troops, 467; OBW's achievements and role in, 462, 488. See also Knoxville

Eckert, Thomas T., 646

Eddy, Rev. H. (2d Conn.), 311, 320; whipped by prison guards, 321

Edie, John R. (ADC to OBW), 280, 282

Edmands, B. F., 197

Egan, Thomas W., division of, 582

Eighteenth Corps, at Cedar Creek, 580; at Cold Harbor, 525

Elderkin, James D. (1st Mich.), 249, 252

Ellis, C. M., 195

Ellsworth, E. Elmer (11th N.Y.), xviii, 253, 260–61, 268, 271, 293; character of, 270–71; death and funeral of, xxv, 3, 263, 264–65, 269–72; impetuosity of, 263, 271

Ely, Alfred, 318

Ely, Ralph, 606, 607, 639, 641, 642, 692

Evans, Clement A. (CSA), division of, 590, 612

Evans, Nathan G. (2d Dragoons, CSA), and buffalo hunt, 145; at Bull Run, 290; escorts wagon train to Santa Fe, 162; at Fort Leavenworth, 137, 138, 139; in march across Kansas plains, 142, 144,

Evans, Nathan G. (*cont.*)
148, 150, 157, 159, 161; visits to OBW, 298, 317
Ewell, Richard S. (1st Dragoons, CSA): captured, 643; Corps of, 512, 530, 566; demoralized, 644; on Kansas plains, 162

Fairbanks, John D. (1st Mich.), 249
Fairchild, Harrison S. (89th N.Y.), 384
Farnham, Noah L. (11th N.Y.), 263, 268; commands 11th N.Y. after Ellsworth's death, 266; reports Ellsworth's death, 269
Farnsworth, Caroline. *See* Harrison, Caroline "Caro" Farnsworth
Farnsworth, Elon (father-in-law of OBW), 15n. 6, 124, 127, 170, 374, 400, 607, attempts to gain OBW's release from prison, 338; campaigns for OBW's promotion, 412, 413; OBW asks for daughter's hand, 187; OBW requests assistance in gaining promotion, 381, 401; visits OBW at Fort Ontario, 190, 192; visit to Washington, 505
Farnsworth, Hannah Blake (Mrs. Elon Farnsworth): 15n. 6, 124, 400; and Mt. Vernon Ladies' Assoc., 168; OBW writes to, 278–79, 479–80; visits N.Y. and Washington, 446, 448, 505; visits OBW and Marie at Fort Ontario, 190–91
Farrand, James (2d Mich.), 521
Favish, Captain (69th N.Y.), 325
Fenton, William M., 367, 368, 394
Ferrero, Edward, 395, 503, 577, 642; brigade of, at Fredericksburg, 385; Burnside attempts to relieve from command, 392; commands division, at Battle of the Crater, 550, 553, 555; commands division, in defense of Knoxville, 473; in engagement at Blue Springs, Tenn., 465
Field, Charles W. (2d Dragoons, CSA), 129; division of, 566, 574, 576, 583
Field, James, 193
Fifth Corps, in "Applejack Raid," 589–90; at Burgess' Mill, 583; at Petersburg, June 18 assault, 545; at Spotsylvania Court House, 530; at Weldon R. R., 567, 570
Fillmore, President Millard, 171; visits Mt. Vernon, 175, 176
Fish, Hamilton, 328, 329

Fish, Ross A. (32d N.Y.), 320
Fitch, Rev. Chauncey M. (teacher of OBW), 18
Five Forks, Battle of, 638n. 1
Fletcher, Nelson, 531
Floyd, John B., 241, 242
Follett, Martin P., 342
Forrest, Nathan Bedford, 421
Forsyth, George (6th U.S. Cav.), 674, 677
Forsyth, Maj. Robert A., 36, 120
Fort Apache, 671, 672
Fort Center: OBW's march to, 222; OBW stationed at, 221, 222–23, 227–30
Fort Dearborn (Chicago), 26
Fort Deynaud: low morale of troops at, 220; OBW's march to, 209–11; OBW stationed at, 209;
Fort Donelson, 320
Fort Gilmer, Union assault on, 574–75
Fort Harrison, Union assault on, 574–75
Fort Henry, 320
Fort Independence, OBW stationed at, 192
Fort Leavenworth: OBW commands Dept. of the Missouri at, 681; OBW describes post at, 137; OBW ordered to (1850), 134; OBW returns to after march across Kansas, 165
Fort Myers, OBW arrives at, 208–9
Fort Ontario: OBW stationed at, 167, 186–92; Marie Willcox arrives at, 189
Fort Sanders (Knoxville), 473
Fort Sodom, OBW builds, 159
Fort Stedman, Battle of, 6–7, 590, 613–37; Gen. Hartranft claims chief credit for, 614, 615, 618, 627; losses at, 614, 615, 618, 619; OBW's report of, 691–95
Fort Sumter, Federal bombardment of, 458
Fort Washington, OBW stationed at, 167
Foster, John G., 486, 487, 489, 495, 497; arrives at Knoxville, 475; assumes command, Dept. of the Ohio, 474; commends OBW in East Tennessee, 492; injured, 493; OBW's estimation of, 488; offers OBW command of Twenty-third Corps, 492
Foster, Robert S., 575n. 19
Foster, William S. (4th U.S. Inf.), 224
Fox, Dorus M. (27th Mich.), 528
Fox's Gap. *See* South Mountain, Battle of
Franklin, William B., 49; in Bull Run campaign, brigade of, 284, 287, 288, 289; at Fredericksburg, 385, 387–91; Burnside relieves from duty, 392;

Griswold, Capt. John, 13
Griswold, Dr. (38th N.Y.), 316;
Gyp (dog), 584, 596, 599

Habitants (French settlers of Detroit), 15
Hale, Capt., 93, 95
Hall, E. T. (quartermaster), 476, 478, 481
Hall, Nathan Kelsey, 175
Halleck, Henry W., 348, 349, 351, 403,
    444, 470, 488, 490; Burnside requests
    dismissal of, 392; concerns for the safety
    of Washington, 358; distrust of Pope,
    348; as historian, 548; places McClellan
    in command of Washington defenses,
    357–58; visits Burnside as Warrenton,
    383
Hallett, Benjamin F., 194
Hammond, Captain (65th Ind.), 490
Hampton, Wade (CSA) 293, 298; at
    Burgess' Mill, 582; commands
    Confederate Cavalry Corps, 575n. 22;
    at Peebles Farm, 575–76
Hamtramck, John F., 242
Hancock, Gen. Winfield S. (Second
    Corps commander), xviii, 402, 408, 557;
    at Burgess' Mill, 582, 583; on character
    of battlefield, 514; in Cold Harbor
    campaign, 524; death of, 680; at Deep
    Bottom, 566; division of, at Fred-
    ericksburg, 385; favoritism toward
    Pennsylvania troops, 621; in Florida,
    209; importance of his presence on the
    field, 516; marries Almira Russell,
    130–31; at Reams Station, 568–70, 571,
    572; at the Wilderness, 512, 515
Hardie, James A., 388, 389–90
Harney, William S. 207, 208, 213, 214,
    218, 219, 227, 230; visits Fort Deynaud,
    221
Harriman, Samuel, brigade of, 638, 640,
    641, 643, 693
Harrison, Caroline "Caro" Farnsworth
    (sister-in-law of OBW), 15n. 6,
    188–89, 275, 276, 341, 410, 460, 495,
    585; illness of, 396, 399, 401; illness of
    daughter, 376, 414; Marie Willcox
    visits, 331, 342, 413, 668; marries Frank
    Harrison, 235; OBW dreams of, 578;
    OBW's affection for, 595, 600; as
    OBW's chief war correspondent, 649
Harrison, Frank, 330, 342, 344, 380, 396,
    595; marries Caro Farnsworth, 235;
    visits Fort Ontario, 190–91

Harrison, Maud (daughter of Caro
    Farnsworth Harrison), illness of, 376
Harrison, Thomas (CSA), 473
Harrison, William Henry, 242
Hartranft, Gen. John F., 605, 692, 693; at
    Cold Harbor, 526, 527, 528; commands
    black division, 577; commands 51st
    Penn. at Antietam, 359; commands
    reorganized Third Division, 597, 638,
    640, 641; at the Crater, 551, 552, 553; at
    Fort Stedman, 7, 614, 615, 617, 618, 625,
    627; at Ny River, 518; at Petersburg,
    June 17–18 assault, 542, 543, 544, 545;
    at Spotsylvania Court House, 520;
    at Weldon R. R., 567, 568, 571; at
    Wilderness, 515, 516; promoted major
    general, 614
Hartsuff, George L., 364, 425, 452;
    OBW's opinion of, 451
Hascall, Herbert A. (4th U.S. Arty.), 218,
    219, 222, 225
Hascall, Milo S., 427, 435; pursues J. H.
    Morgan, 440
Hatch, Edward, 676
Hatch, Lieutenant Colonel, 603, 604
Hatcher's Run, engagement at, 590, 605,
    606
Havens, Benny, 53
Hawes' Shop, cavalry engagement at, 523
Hawkins, Rush C. (brig.), 381, 384
Hay, John, 629, 633
Hayden, Henry A., 241
Hayes, Joseph, 570
Hayes, Rutherford B., 678
Hays, John C., 101
Hazen, William B., 668
Hazzard, George W. (4th U.S. Arty.), 170,
    172, 175
Heckman, Charles A., 574
Heintzelman, Samuel P., 3, 260, 261,
    276, 281, 289, *291*, *333*; in Bull Run
    campaign, 287, 288, 290, 292, 293,
    294, 687
Hendricks, Thomas A. (U.S. sen., Ind.),
    428
Hendrickson, Thomas, 120
Henry (OBW's horse), 275, 276, 282; shot,
    295
Henry (OBW's servant), 275, 282
Henry, Guy V., 553
Heth, Henry (1st Dragoons, CSA), xviii;
    at Burgess' Mill, 582–83; as cadet, 55,
    56, 85; friendship with OBW, 4, 667,

Lee, Robert E., 168, 546, 629; abilities as commander, 510; in Cold Harbor campaign, 522, 523, 525; commands Virginia troops, 259, 260, 266; at Fort Gilmer, 575; importance of presence on the field, 516; learns Federals have crossed James River, 542; and "Lee to the rear" incident, 514–15; in Maryland campaign, 351, 353; OBW's estimation of, 590–91; as president of Washington College, 661, 663, 664; in Second Bull Run campaign, 346; surrenders to Grant, 643–44; on Winfield Scott's staff, 106

Lee, S. P. (adm., U.S.N.), 419

Lee, W. H. F. "Rooney" (Cavalry Div. CSA), 566

Leoser, Charles M. (11th N.Y.), 287

Lewis House (Portici), 297, 298, 299, 301

Lewis, Dr. (2d Wisc.), 298, 300, 302; character of, 301; paroled, 306; in Richmond, 305

Lewis, William G. (CSA), brigade of, 612

Lexington, Ky., hospital fire at, 450–51; OBW transferred to, 421; officers' ball at, 424

Libby Prison, 321–22, 323; OBW incarcerated at, 321–25; OBW's treatment at, 336–37

Lightner, Rev. Milton C., 585

Ligon Tobacco Factory, OBW transferred to prison at, 320

Lincoln, Abraham, 270, 382, 383, 681; assassination of, 645–46; calls for troops, 2, 239, 241, 256; confers with Burnside, 586n. 36, 593; confers with Confederate peace commission, 607n. 25; and death of Ellsworth, 272; disapproves General Orders No. 8, 392; and 1st Mich., 252–53, 276, 288, 690; favors OBW's promotion to major general, 407; at Fort Stedman, 614, 629, 636; and McClellan, 364, 382; message to Congress, 403n. 41; nominates OBW for promotion to major general, 363; OBW dines with, 3, 347–48; OBW's description of, 348; on OBW's faithfulness, 370; OBW's esteem for, 393; and prisoner exchange, 328; and privateers, 315, 316; promotes Hartranft major general, 636; Reconstruction views of, 654; reviews Ninth Corps, 370; urges Burnside to act, 383; visits

Antietam battlefield, 369; visits Petersburg, 640

Lincoln, Mary Todd, 348

Lind, Jenny, 171

Little Cloud (Seminole chief), 205

Livermore, Edward St. Loe, xvi

Long, Richard H., 57

Long Bridge, Federal crossing of, 260–62, 263

Longfellow, Henry Wadsworth, OBW meets, 192–93

Longstreet, James (CSA), xviii, 380, 667; at Fredericksburg, 383; importance of his presence on the field, 516; in Knoxville Campaign, 468, 470, 473, 474, 485, 486, 488–89, 492, 493n. 34, 502; OBW pursues, 494; at Wilderness, 512, 514; and Williamsburg Road engagement, 583; wounded, 514

Loomis, Gustavus (4th U.S. Arty.), 214, 227

Loring, Charles G., 599

Losee, Alfred B. (19th N.Y. Bat.), 568

Louisiana regiments: 1st Battalion (La. Tigers), 294

Love, John, 133, 435, 438, 458, 461, 476; visits Detroit, 454–55, 456–57

Love, Mrs. John, 131

Lovell, Mansfield (4th Arty., CSA), 165, 170, 327; death of, 680; en route to Fort Leavenworth, 135, 136; at Jefferson Barracks, 131, 133, 134; in march across Kansas, 138, 144, 148, 149, 150, 151, 158, 159–60, 161, 162; hunts buffalo with OBW, 139–40, 142, 146, 153–55, 163; marries Emilia Plympton, 130–31; in Mexican War, 99, 107, 108, 113, 117; OBW's affection for, 319;

Luce, Constant (17th Mich.), 518, 600

Lum, Charles M. (1st Mich.), 243, 244n. 16, 249, 688, 690

Lydig, Philip M., 390, 604

Lyman, Col. Theodore, xvii,

Lyon, G. Collins (division inspector), 426n. 11, 460, 489; death of child, 488

McAllister, Julian, 61, 86, 193; death of, 680; OBW's friendship with, 53–54, 668

McCall, George A., 348n. 2

McCallum, Andrew (sketch artist), 548, 573; sketches of, 533–40

McClaws, Lafayette, 353

McClellan, George B., xviii, 282, 350, 368, 376, 504, 525; as cadet, 55, 57; commands Washington defenses, 357; commends OBW, 364; contrasts with Grant, 510; death of, 680; forbids OBW's advance on Sharpsburg, 361; impatience with Burnside, 356–57, 363; Lincoln dissatisfield with, 364; in Mexican War, 106; OBW's opinion of, 55, 349, 394; personal magnetism, 509; on reassignment to command Army of Potomac, 358; recommends OBW's promotion to major general, 381, 401; relieved as commanding general, 394, 398; reorganizes Army of Potomac, 348–49; reviews Ninth Corps, 370; withdraws from Peninsula, 346; mentioned,

McClellan, Mrs. George B. (Ellen), 504

McClelland, Robert, 201, 350

McClure, Alexander K., 424

McCook, Daniel, death of, 442

McCook, Robert L., 442

McCoskrey, Bishop S. A., 120, 188, 250, 279, 669

McCown, John P. (4th U.S. Arty., CSA),188, 207, 221

McCran, Pat (3rd Md.), 694

McDowell, Irvin, xviii, 276, 280, 281, 395; in Bull Run campaign, 284, 286, 287, 288, 289; on capture of OBW, 333; council of war, 289; on OBW's gallantry, 342; promises OBW brigade, 279

McElroy, James N. (60th Ohio), 518

Mackenzie, Lewis (mayor of Alexandria, Va.), 267; surrenders town to OBW, 272–73

Mackenzie, Ranald, 677

Mackinac Island, Mich., 23

McKnight, Charles A. (a.d.c. to OBW) 372, 415, 426n. 11; joins OBW's staff, 402; OBW dismisses from staff, 455

McKnight, Lucius, 586

McKnight, Sheldon, 15

McLaughlen, Napoleon B., brigade of 578, 615, 617, 630, 693; captured, 621, 692

McNair, David A. (husband of Julia Willcox), 60, 656–57

McNair, Julia Ann Trumbull Willcox (sister of OBW), 42, 60, 128, 170, 402, 411, 412, 415; early visit to Chicago, 22,

24, 25, 28, 31; visits OBW at Fort Washington, 181–83; visits Rickettses, 579–81; writes to Marie Willcox at end of war, 647; writes to OBW, 579–82

McNair, Orry, 279

Macomb, Alexander, 45n. 9, 206

McQuade, Capt. (38th N.Y.), 302

Madison, Dolley, 44

Madison, James, 13, 44

Magilton, Albert L. (4th U.S. Arty.), 216

Magruder, John Bankhead, vists OBW in hospital, 306, 334

Mahan, Dennis Hart (West Point instructor), 58

Mahone, William (CSA), 566, 604; at Burgess' Mill, 582; at Hatcher's Run, 590,

Maine regiments: 3rd Artillery 553; 7th Artillery, 518

Manassas, Battle of. See Bull Run

Manning, Capt. (2d Pa. Cav.), 643, 645

Manning, John L. (S.C. gov.), 298

Mansfield, Joseph K. F., commands Dept. of Washington, 253, 257, 260–61, 269, 690; mortally wounded, 364

Marbury, Bettie, 183

Marbury, Fendall, 183

Marcy, Randolph B., 201

Marshall, Charles (CSA), 631

Marshall, Elisha G. 597–98; brigade of, 521

Marshall, Gen. Thomas, 107–8; 110, 111, 113, 114

Martin, John W. (3d Dragoons), 115

Martin, William T. (CSA), 473, 475, 491; relieves Gen. Wheeler at Knoxville, 470; wounded, 474

Maryland Federal regiments: 2d Infantry, 626, 630, 631; 3rd Infantry, 617, 622, 630, 637, 693, 694

Mason, Emily, 130, 171, 174, 176, 183, 184; as writer, 169

Mason, Maggy, 133

Mason, Mrs. Richard B., 131, 132

Mason, Richard B. (commanding at Jefferson Barracks), 130, 131; character of, 132; quoted, 132–33

Massachusetts regiments: 11th Artillery, 628, 632; 6th Infantry, 251, 257, 259; 8th Infantry, 257; 20th Infantry, xiii, xvii; 28th Infantry, 399; 29th Infantry, 630, 693; 35th Infantry, 380; 36th Infantry, 367, 371; 57th Infantry, 618,

New Orleans, Federal capture of, 319;
OBW passes through on way to
Mexico, 92–93
New York regiments: 34th Artillery, 518,
553; 24th Cavalry, 545, 546; 7th
Infantry, 257, 262; 11th Infantry (Fire
Zouaves), 2–3, 253, 261–74, 287, 289,
290, 293, 683; 12th Infantry (Militia),
262; 14th (Heavy Artillery), 553, 622,
630, 631, 692; 25th Infantry: 262;
38th Infantry, 282, 294; 39th Infantry
(Garibaldi Guards), 287n. 3; 46th Infantry, 367, 384, 545, 552, 553; 51st
Infantry, 359, 419; 69th Infantry, 310;
79th Infantry, 354, 367, 408, 518,
546; 89th Infantry, 384; 109th Infantry,
693
Newell, Robert H. *See* Kerr, Orpheus C.
Newton, Dr. (CSA), 304–5
Newton, John, 127, 389, 392
Nicolay, John, 629, 633
Nimmo, William A. (4th U.S. Arty.), 172,
185
Ninth Corps: at Antietam, xxii, 359–61,
363, 366–67; and Battle of the Crater,
554, 557, 562; crosses James River, 542;
detached from Army of the Potomac,
416n. 48; enters Petersburg, 7; First
Division, 349, 369; First Division
redesignated as Third Division, 495;
Lincoln reviews, 370; losses of, 391n. 21,
694; OBW assumes command of, 370,
497, 594; ordered to Washington, D.C.,
646; reorganization of, 495, 505; at
South Mountain, 353–59; rejoins
Army of the Potomac (1864), 511; at
Strawberry Plains, 494; transferred to
Kentucky, 6, 421; transferred to
Mississippi, 6, 426
—Third Division: at Cold Harbor, 527,
528; at the Crater, 554, 557, 561; at Fort
Stedman, 619, 694; at North Anna, 522;
in overland campaign, 546; at Peters-
burg, 543, 545, 546, 639, 642; at South
Mountain, 357, 365; at Spotsylvania,
521; at Weldon R. R., 568; at
Wilderness, 516
North Anna River: operations at, 522, 531;
OBW's losses at, 522
North Carolina regiments: 35th Infantry,
543; 37th Infantry, 521
North, Guilford, family of,
Ny River, Battle of, 517–20

O'Brien, John P. J., 207
O'Connell, Patrick (surgeon), 549, 573,
585, 586
O'Donnell, James (1st Mich.), 682–83
Ohio regiments: 7th Cavalry, 466n. 6;
21st Infantry 463n. 3; 60th Infantry,
518
Oliver, Charles (100th Pa.), 617, 694
O'Maher, Tim (West Point clerk), 49
O'Meara, Timothy (42d N.Y.), 326, 339
O'Neil, John, 441, 442
Ord, Edward O. C., 557, 574, 640
Osceola (Seminole chief), 204, 205–6;
Ould, Robert, 327
Overland campaign of 1864, Grant's
strategy in, 508–11
Overton, Edward (50th Pa.), 519
Owen, Col. J. V. D., 25

Palmer, Friend (boyhood friend of
OBW), 20
Palo Alto, Battle of, 90
Panic of 1857, OBW comments on,
235–36
Parke, John G., 395, 476, 497, 543, 570,
597, 637, 647; caution of, 475; to
command Ninth Corps, 480;
commands Ninth Corps, 463–64, 475,
494, 575–76, 582; congratulates OBW
and Hartranft for defense of Fort
Stedman, 615; desire to keep OBW out
of Ninth Corps, 492; and Fort
Stedman, 635–36; shy of Meade, 612;
supersedes OBW in command of
Ninth Corps, 6, 426; in temporary
command of Army of the Potomac,
603, 604
Parker, Francis H. (a.d.c. to OBW), 282,
285, 288
Parker, Theodore, 166, 195, 197, 199
Parks, Rev. Martin P. (West Point
chaplain), 54–55, 85
Patrick, Marsena, 397
Patten, George, 57, 87
Patterson, Robert, 99, 101, 104
Patton, John, 430, 488
Pawnee Indians, 144
Peace Commission: confers with Lincoln,
607n. 25; passes through OBW's lines,
603–4
Peachy, Dr. (CSA), cruelness toward
Union prisoners, 303–4
Peebles Farm, engagement at, 575–76

Sedgwick, John, xiii, 407, 408, 416, 450;
death of, 523 (n. 29); rumors he is to
command Ninth Corps, 394, 412; tents
with OBW, 414; at Wilderness, 512;
wounded, 364
Seminole war, origins of, 204–5
Seward, Augustus H., 57, 84
Seward, Frederick, 646
Seward, William H., 241, 318;
assassination attempt on, 645–46;
meets officers of 1st Mich., 253n. 9;
predicts "sixty-day war," 239, 240,
249
Shackelford, James M., in capture of
Cumberland Gap, 467; in Knoxville
Campaign, 480–81, 482–83, 487; in
Morgan Raid, 434n. 19, 443, 444
Sharpsburg, Battle of. See Antietam
Sharpsburg, Md. (town), xxi, xxii; Ninth
Corps advances on, 359–61
Sheldon, John P., 175
Shephard, Colonel (51st N.Y.), 419
Sheridan, Phillip H., xviii, 546, 629;
Cavalry Corps destroys Virginia
Central R.R., 611; at Cold Harbor, 522,
524, 525; at Five Forks, 638n. 1, 640; on
Fort Stedman, 633–34; at Hawes' Shop,
523; in Valley Campaign, 566, 577; at
Wilderness, 517
Sherman, Thomas W., 257, 313n. 8
Sherman, William T., xviii, 508, 594,
606, 607, 644; brigade of, 293;
comparison to Wellington, 500; death
of son, 598; on the Frémonts, 677; as
general of the army, 668; in Knoxville
Campaign, 472, 488; march to the sea,
593; in North Carolina, 611; replies to
OBW regarding Great Lakes post,
668–69; in Vicksburg Campaign, 410;
visits Arizona Territory, 678
Shillinglaw, Robert T. (a.d.c. to OBW),
334, 398, 400; OBW dismisses from
staff, 414
Shirer, William (CSA), 317, 319, 320
Shoepac Recollections, 201, 202, 653
Short Hair (Commanche chief), 158
Shurtleff, Giles W. (a.d.c. to OBW), 400,
415
Sibley, Ebeneezer Sproat, 120
Sibley, Henry H., 138, 254
Sickles, Daniel E., 389, 402
Sigel, Franz, 380
Simmonds, Seth J., 359–60

Sixth Corps: attack of March 25, 1865,
619; at Cedar Creek, 580; return from
Valley Campaign, 577, 592
Slemp, Col. Campbell (col., 64th Va.
Cav.), 474
Slocum, Dr. George D. (USN), 327
Smead, John R., 261
Smith, Cyrus (1st Mich.), 249
Smith, J. V. C., 198
Smith, James A., 465
Smith, Persifor F., 117
Smith, Richard S. (West Point instructor),
49
Smith, Walter W. (privateer), 314
Smith, William F.: Burnside attempts to
relieve from duty, 392; commands
Eighteenth Corps at Cold Harbor, 525;
commands Sixth Corps at Fredericks-
burg, 388–89; critical of Burnside, 392;
as temporary commander Ninth Corps,
416n. 48, 417, 419
Snelling, James G., 51
Soldiers' Home, 176, 681
South Carolina regiments, Hampton's
Legion, 293
South Mountain, Battle of, 4–5, 353–57,
365–66; Federal losses at, 357
Spaulding, Ira, 384
Spotsylvania Court House, Battle of,
520–22; Federal movement toward, 517;
OBW's losses at, 521
Sprague, Captain (7th Ohio), 317, 319
Sprague, Dr. Lawrence (4th U.S. Arty.),
167, 187, 189; death of, 191
Sprague, John T., 167, 206
Sprague, William (Rhode Island gov.), 167
Stanley, Sgt. W. (14th N.Y.H.A.), 553
Stannard, George J., 574, 575
Stanton, Edwin, 348n. 2; Burnside
requests dismissal of, 392; OBW's
disgust for, 412; controversy with Gov.
Oliver Morton, 426–27
Steely, Isaac, on charge of 17th Mich. at
South Mtn., 355n. 18, 356n. 21
Stephens, Alexander H. (vice president,
CSA), 603, 604, 655
Stephens, William I. (1st Mich.), 249
Stevens, Isaac, 351
Stevenson, J. H. (100th Pa.), letter urging
OBW to respond to Hartranft's claims
regarding Fort Stedman, 627
Stevenson, Thomas G.: at Battle of the
Wilderness, 511; killed, 520

Wheelock, Joseph H., 215

Whipple, Amiel W., 379, 401, 408; death of, 449–50

Whipple, Henry, 121

Whistler, Garland "Beau" (boyhood friend of OBW), 22–23

Whistler, Maj. William, 23, 127

White, Julius, division of, 567, 568, 570

Whiting, Corey, 588, 599, 607

Whitman, Dr. Marcus, 48

Whittlesey, Franklin W. (1st Mich.), 244, 249; at Bull Run, 295, 690

Wigfall, Louis T., 256

Wilcox, Cadmus (CSA), 683; division of, 566, 576

Wilcox, Maj. De Lafayette, 26, 28, 30

Wild Cat (Seminole chief), 204, 206

Wilderness, Battle of, 507–8, 511–12, 514–17; losses at, 516n. 16; topography of, 517–18

Wilkins, Ross, 247–48

Wilkins, William D., 189, 244, 252, 281

Willard, Sidney, 380, 381

Willcox Papers: condition of, xxiii; discovery of, xiii–xxiii; editorial problems, xxv–xxviii

Willcox, Almira Cora "Ali" (second daughter of OBW), 255n. 13, 397, 399, 410, 447, 448, 452, 572, 598; illness of, 280, 281, 330

Willcox, Almira Rood Powers (mother of OBW), 17, 140, 274; character of, 15–16, 180; illness of, 612; injured, 170, 171; letter to OBW, 179; marries Charles Willcox, 13, 14; marries John Powers, 14; OBW writes to, 403; relationship with OBW, 9, 179–80; as teacher, 14; visits OBW at Fort Ontario, 190; visits New York and Washington, 446, 448

Willcox, Capt. Joseph, 12

Willcox, Caroline (third daughter of OBW), birth of, 238

Willcox, Charles (brother of OBW), 15, 81, 178; marriage of, 189

Willcox, Charles (father of OBW), 11, 13, 14, 15; love for Indians, 205

Willcox, Charles McAllister (third son of OBW), birth of, 668

Willcox, Eben North (brother of OBW), 178, 186, 187, 189, 238, 280, 374, 414, 598, 606; as attorney, 15; character of, 185; law partnership with OBW, 234;

with OBW in Detroit after Mexican War, 121, 124, 126, 128; OBW writes to, 71–73, 76–80, 335–36, 479, 557, 619; travels to Washington after OBW wounded, 330; visits Mt. Vernon with OBW, 184–85; and war furor, 281

Willcox, Edward (distant uncle of OBW), 12

Willcox, Edward (uncle of OBW), 13

Willcox, Elon Farnsworth (first son of OBW), 276, 278, 397, 399, 400, 448, 452, 455, 547, 572; as aide-de-camp to OBW, 678; birth of, 202; character of, 344; first birthday, 219; illness of, 342, 344; mistreated by Southern boys, 666; OBW worries for safety of, 453; OBW writes to, 255; reaction on hearing OBW wounded, 332; religious devotion of, 502; schooling of, 476–77, 482, 588, 598, 600; enters West Point, 669

Willcox, Grace North (fourth daughter of OBW), birth of, 431, 454, 572

Willcox, Grace North (great-grandmother of OBW), 12

Willcox, John (grandfather of OBW), 12

Willcox, John (great-grandfather of OBW), 12

Willcox, John (great-great-grandfather of OBW), 12

Willcox, Julia McReynolds Wyeth (second wife of OBW), 684

Willcox, Julia Ann Trumbull. See McNair, Julia Ann Trumbull Willcox

Willcox, Julian McAllister (fourth son of OBW), 679

Willcox, Louise Cole (wife of Eben), 124, 128

Willcox, Marie Farnsworth (wife of OBW), 183, 201, 202, 274; death of, 669; distressed over OBW's absence from home, 407; and Freedmen's Bureau, 667; gives birth to Marie Louise, 190; illness of, 579, 584, 668–69; marries OBW, 186–87, 188; OBW concerned at not hearing from, 577–78, 579; OBW courts, 127, 128, 175, 177, 182; OBW engaged to, 170; OBW longs to marry, 184; OBW's early opinion of, 128; OBW's love for, 397, 506, 598; on state's refusal to strengthen existing regiments, 344; photo, 332; travels to Washington after OBW wounded, 330–31; urges OBW to seek promotion to brigadier general, 341–42; visits Antietam battlefield, 5, 371–74; visits OBW in camp, 407, 411; writes to OBW, 330–33, 341–43, 344–45

Willcox, Marie Louise "Lulu" (first daughter of OBW), 202, 276, 397, 399, 400, 420, 446, 448, 449, 455; affection for OBW, 332; assumes duties of later mother, 669; birth of, 190, 192; death of, 682; as hostess, 678; illness of, 453, 459, 460, 477; marries Stephen C. Mills, 682; musical abilities of, 547–48; OBW explains reasons for war to, 278; OBW on penmanship of, 561–62; OBW writes to, 255, 572–73, 596

Willcox, Mira (see Davis, Mira Willcox)

Willcox, Orlando Blodgett (second son of OBW), 667, 684

Willcox, Orlando Bolivar, *169, 347, 379, 503, 527, 560, 573, 648*; accepts colors of 1st Mich., 247; accuses government of waging "brainless war," 347n. 1; as acting chief of staff to Burnside, 415; affection for American Indians, 205, 671; and Anthony Burns riot, 194–202; at Antietam, 5, *359–61*, 362–64, 366–67; on the Apache wars, 675–77; as attorney, 2, 238, 654; on Battle of Big Dry Wash, 674–75; capture of Alexandria, 260–73; and Battle of the Crater, 551–59, 563; on becoming a minister, 41, 173; birth and childhood of, 1–2, 11, 32–40; on Catholicism, 122–24; on civilian life, 2, 236, 238, 659; character of, 329n. 33; at Coburg, Ontario, 684; in Cold Harbor campaign, 526–27; concerned for safety of Washington, 358; on condition of troops, 594, 599; considers resigning, 407; court-martialed, 62–66, 88–89; death of, 684; desires promotion to major general, 394, 401, 408, 409, 414, 549; directs troops in intercepting Morgan's Raid, 433–40; early love, 32; in East Tennessee (Knoxville) Campaign, 463–70, 491, 494; engaged, 170; on exchanging prisoners of war, 317; false reports of death, 332; farewell address to First Division, 650; at Fort Stedman, 6–7; at Fredericksburg, 406, 385; 391; 406; health fails, 684; homesick, 395–96, 397, 491, 493, 506,

599, 606; hunts buffalo, 145–46, 153–55, 162, 163; as insurance executive, 681; as IRS agent, 654; and Johnston Affair, 661–65; on knowledge of self, 39–40; lack of political influence, 653; and Lincoln, 3, 252–53, 347–48, 583; lost on plains, 153–55; love of literature, 14, 18, 20, 21; love of nature, 84; in march to Mexico City, 101–7; march across Kansas, 140–66; marries Julia Wyeth, 678; on McClellan's failure to pursue Lee after Antietam, 364; marries Marie Farnsworth, 186–87, 188; and Medal of Honor, 3, 682–83; and Morgan Raid, 6; and newspaper correspondents, 275, 501–2, 562; night with Grant, 475; no time to write reports, 578–79; as novelist and poet, xxv, 169, 201, 202, 233, 234, 650–52; at North Anna River, 531; at Ny River, 517–20; on modern warfare, 230–32; as orator, 86, 88; ordered to Fort Independence, 192, 201; ordered to Fort Leavenworth, 134; ordered to Texas, 201; on political dissension in the North, 453; on prosecuting the war, 3–4; as page in territorial legislature, 18; at Peebles Farm, 576; at Petersburg, 7, 542–48; political views, 239, 655–57; and "Potato Band," 19–20, 33; promotions of, 170, 3, 349, 593, 680–81; on Reconstruction, 655–56; relationship with mother, 9, 179–81; and religion, beliefs, 32, 34, 35–37, 60–61, 68–69, 233, 234, 239; and religion, struggles with, 85, 87, 89, 174, 177–78; requests Great Lakes post, 668; resigns commission, 233, 234; resolutions, 39, 70, 82–83, 238–39; retires from army, 681; self-deprecation, 32–33, 86; at South Mountain, 353–57; on Southerners, 3–4, 665–66; speeches of, 3–4, 652, 665–66; at Spotsylvania Court House, 517–22, 530; staff presents sword to, 585; story of short and long sweetening, 466; on stress of command, 548; studies law, 202, 233, 234; superintendent of Soldiers Home, 681; on thought, 38; urges state to prepare for war, 239–40; vices, 598; visits Chicago, 22–32; visits Europe, 682; visits Gen. Grant, 605, 609–12; visits Robert E. Lee, 663; visits Washington, (1843) 42–49, (1851)

Willcox, Orlando Bolivar (*cont.*)
182–83; voyage to Mexico, 95–96;
on women, 38–39; on the world, 69, 74,
75; worship services after Antietam,
367–68; at Weldon R. R., 567–69, 571;
at the Wilderness, 511–12, 514–17;
wounded, 295, 475, 688; writes
memoirs, 679–80
—Commands of: at Angel Island,
California, 667; assumes brigade
command, 279–80, 286; Dept. of
Arizona, 669–80; Dept. of Indiana and
Mich., ordered to Indianapolis, 426;
Dept. of Missouri, 680–81; District of
Central Kentucky, 6, 421–25, 446–52;
District of Michigan, 640, 653; 1st
Michigan, 2, 240–50; First Division,
Ninth Corps, 4, 346; Ninth Corps,
assumes command of, 374, 494; Second
Division, Ninth Corps, 503; subdistrict
of Lynchburg, Va., 659–67; 12th U.S.
Infantry, 667; 29th U.S. Infantry, 659
—Prisoner of war, 3–4; at Columbia, S.C.
prison, 317–20, 335–36; in Charleston
prisons, 308–17, 333; as hostage for
privateers, 313–14, 315–16; at Libby
Prison, 321–25, 336–37; at Ligon
Tobacco Factory, 320; released, 3,
327–28, 345; shipped to Richmond
hospital, 302; at Salisbury, N.C. prison,
325–27, 338–40, 343–44; treatment of,
301, 305–6, 309
See also Unites States Military Academy
Willcox, William H. (great-grandson of
OBW), xix
Willcoxson, John (ancestor of OBW), 12
Willcoxson, Joseph (distant uncle of
OBW), 12
Willcoxson, William (ancestor of OBW),
Williams, Eleazar, 30
Williams, Alpheus S., 243, 280, 281
Williams, Dr., 339
Williams, Hugh T., 438
Williams, John S. (CSA), 465n. 5
Williams, Seth, 400
Williams, Thomas (4th U.S. Arty., CSA),
207, 209, 211, 227; Gen. Harney critical
of, 221; OBW's dislike of, 213–14, 216,
220; subordinates' disgust with, 218
Wilmington, N.C., falls to Union forces,
606n. 23

Wilson, Eliza, 45–46
Wilson, Henry, 586
Wilson, James H. (Cavalry Div.), 524
Wilson, Mrs. Richard H., illness of,
219
Wilson, Richard H. (4th U.S. Arty.), 215,
illness of, 217, 219; sickness and death of
child, 211, 216, 217
Winder, John (CSA), 311, 320; OBW
requests interview with, 321; and
treatment of Union prisoners, 312
Wisconsin regiments: 37th Infantry, 546,
693; 38th Infantry, 546
Wisner, Moses (Mich. gov.), 239, 344
Withington, William H. (1st Mich.),
243, 247, 249, 301, 329n. 33, 334, 365,
368, 371, 688; assists OBW when
wounded, 295, 297, 298, 299; captured,
295, 689; commands 17th Mich. at
South Mtn., 354–55, 357; Marie
Willcox's affection for, 333; Medal of
Honor, 299n. 17; OBW's opinion
of, 277; prepares for visit from wife,
419; as prisoner of war, 302, 307;
quoted, 242; released from prison,
319; requests Medal of Honor for
OBW, 682–83
Wolford, Frank, 443
Wood, Alfred M., 348n. 2
Wood, Thomas J., 497
Wood, William H., 261, 288
Woodbridge, Mrs. William, 73
Woodbridge, William (sen., Mich.), 42,
44, 49, 119–20
Woodbury, Daniel P., 409
Woodruff, George A. (OBW's staff), 282;
OBW's opinion of, 280
Woodruff, W. E. (2d Ky.), 314, 320
Woods, Joseph J., 57
Woodward, Dr. C. Vann, xxvi
Worth, Gen. William J., in Black Hawk
War, 29; in Mexican War, 102, 114, 115;
in Seminole war, 206
Wright, Horatio G., commands Sixth
Corps, 523, 524, 525, 619n. 7
Wright, Joseph W. B. (14th Mass. Arty.),
521
Wright, Lt. Col. (27th Mich.), 551
Wyndham, Sir Percy, 327, 341

Yellow Bear (Arapaho chief), 151, 152